OXFORD PRIVATE INTERNATIONAL LAW SERIES

The 2019 Hague Judgments Convention

OXFORD PRIVATE INTERNATIONAL LAW SERIES

Series Editors: ANDREW DICKINSON & JONATHAN HARRIS KC
The aim of this series is to publish works of quality and originality in a number of important areas of private international law. The series is intended for both scholarly and practitioner readers.

ALSO IN THIS SERIES

Intellectual Property and Private International Law (Third Edition)
PAUL I C TORREMANS

Torts in UK Foreign Relations
UGLJEŠA GRUŠIĆ

Civil Jurisdiction and Judgements in Europe (Second Edition)
TREVOR HARTLEY

Private International Law in English Courts (Second Edition)
ADRIAN BRIGGS

Singapore Private International Law: Commercial Issues and Practice
ADELINE CHONG AND YIP MAN

European Private International Family Law: The Revised Brussels IIa Regulation
MICHAEL WILDERSPIN, MARIA ÁLVAREZ TORNÉ, AND GEORGINA GARRIGA SUAU

Asymmetric Jurisdiction Clauses
BROOKE MARSHALL

Employment Contracts in Private International Law (Second Edition)
LOUISE MERRETT

Choice of Law in International Commercial Contracts
DANIEL GIRSBERGER, THOMAS KADNER GRAZIANO, AND JAN L NEELS

International Negotiable Instruments
BENJAMIN GEVA AND SAGI PEARI

Private International Law Online: Internet Regulation and Civil Liability in the EU
TOBIAS LUTZI

The Anti-Suit Injunction (Second Edition)
THOMAS RAPHAEL KC

Sovereign Defaults before Domestic Courts
HAYK KUPELYANTS

Conflict of Laws and Arbitral Discretion: The Closest Connection Test
BENJAMIN HAYWARD

Human Rights and Private International Law
JAMES FAWCETT, MÁIRE NÍ SHÚILLEABHÁIN, AND SANGEETA SHAH

Choice-of-Court Agreements under the European and International Instruments
TREVOR HARTLEY

Freedom of Establishment and Private International Law for Corporations
PASCHALIS PASCHALIDIS

Substance and Procedure in Private International Law
RICHARD GARNETT

The Arrest of Ships in Private International Law
VERÓNICA RUIZ ABOU-NIGM

Intellectual Property and Private International Law (Second Edition)
JAMES J FAWCETT AND PAUL TORREMANS

Cross-Border Divorce Law: Brussels II *bis*
MÁIRE NÍ SHÚILLEABHÁIN

The Rome II Regulation: The Law Applicable to Non-Contractual Obligations
ANDREW DICKINSON

Cross-Border Consumer Contracts
JONATHAN HILL

Agreements on Jurisdiction and Choice of Law
ADRIAN BRIGGS

Civil Jurisdiction Rules of the EU and their Impact on Third States
THALIA KRUGER

Conflict of Laws Within the UK
KIRSTY J HOOD

Insolvency in Private International Law (Second Edition)
IAN F FLETCHER

The Transfer of Property in the Conflict of Laws: Choice of Law Rules in *Inter Vivos* Transfers of Property
JANEEN M CARRUTHERS

International Sale of Goods in the Conflict of Laws
JAMES J FAWCETT, JONATHAN HARRIS, AND MICHAEL BRIDGE

The 2019 Hague Judgments Convention

RONALD A. BRAND
Chancellor Mark A Nordenberg University Professor and Academic Director, Center for International Legal Education, University of Pittsburgh School of Law

MICHAEL S. COFFEE
Professorial Lecturer in Law, George Washington University Law School

PAUL HERRUP
Member of the Pennsylvania Bar

OXFORD
UNIVERSITY PRESS

OXFORD
UNIVERSITY PRESS

Great Clarendon Street, Oxford, OX2 6DP,
United Kingdom

Oxford University Press is a department of the University of Oxford.
It furthers the University's objective of excellence in research, scholarship,
and education by publishing worldwide. Oxford is a registered trade mark of
Oxford University Press in the UK and in certain other countries

First Edition published in 2023

Published in the United States of America by Oxford University Press
198 Madison Avenue, New York, NY 10016, United States of America

British Library Cataloguing in Publication Data
Data available

Library of Congress Control Number: 2023944924

ISBN 978–0–19–288983–6

DOI: 10.1093/law/9780192889836.001.0001

To Hans van Loon, who thought it could happen; to the memory of John Kim, who helped make it happen; and to Willy de Zoete and Laura Molenaar, without whom nothing would happen.

Series Editors' Preface

The Hague Convention of 2 July 2019 on the Recognition and Enforcement of Foreign Judgments in Civil or Commercial Matters ('the 2019 Judgments Convention') is an important and ambitious instrument for the mutual recognition and enforcement of judgments between the courts of Contracting States. It entered into force on 1 September 2023 between the EU Member States (other than Denmark) and Ukraine.

The vision for a global instrument on cross-border recognition and enforcement of judgments has long existed. As the authors note, TMC Asser proposed the idea of an international instrument in the nineteenth century. The Convention on the Recognition and Enforcement of Foreign Judgments in Civil and Commercial Matters was adopted in 1971, but without success. In 1996, the Hague Conference on Private International Law began work on a proposed convention on jurisdiction and the recognition and enforcement of judgments but it was not possible to establish the necessary consensus. That project led, in due course, to the conclusion of a convention of more limited scope, namely the Hague Convention of 30 June 2005 on Choice of Court Agreements ('the 2005 Choice of Court Convention'). That convention contains provisions on the recognition and enforcement of judgments where the courts of a Contracting State have taken jurisdiction pursuant to an exclusive jurisdiction clause falling with the Convention's ambit. Its successful conclusion fuelled ambitions for a more comprehensive instrument.

Of course, regional instruments of broader scope exist, such as Regulation (EU) No 1215/2012 on Jurisdiction and the Recognition and Enforcement of Judgments in Civil and Commercial Matters (Recast) ('the recast Brussels I Regulation'). Hitherto, however, there had been no global equivalent for court judgments to the United Nations Convention on the Recognition and Enforcement of Foreign Arbitral Awards 1958. This left a lacuna for an international instrument in the field, particularly for the benefit of those who trade, act, or move between borders and may not have included an exclusive jurisdiction or arbitration clause in a contractual agreement (or had access to legal advisers to draft such a clause), or whose claims in any event fall outside their ambit. The 2019 Judgments Convention offers a mechanism for mutual enforcement of court judgments in civil and commercial matters, including in respect of jurisdiction agreements falling outside the ambit of the 2005 Choice of Court Convention.

The 2019 Judgments Convention has taken on a particular significance as a potential means of re-establishing a broad regime for the mutual recognition and enforcement of judgments between courts in the United Kingdom and the European Union. After the recast Brussels I Regulation ceased to apply in, or to, the United Kingdom and its application to rejoin the Lugano Convention was unsuccessful, no regime for the mutual recognition and enforcement of judgments in civil and commercial matters falling outside the ambit of the 2005 Choice of Court Convention now exists within this sphere (save in transitional cases, and those where bilateral arrangements may have revived). The United Kingdom is currently considering its position on ratification of the 2019 Judgments Convention following a consultation issued by the Ministry of Justice in December 2022.

Although there are notable exclusions from its scope, the ambit of the 2019 Judgments Convention is nonetheless broad. It operates not by establishing harmonized rules of jurisdiction (eg as the recast Brussels I Regulation does), but by setting out detailed bases of recognition and enforcement and grounds for refusal to do so. The result is a Convention that, although it may give rise to various issues as to its interpretation and application, has the promise to develop into a truly global regime.

Against this background, this book provides a detailed, insightful, and lucid commentary on the 2019 Judgments Convention. The authors are highly respected and experienced in this field. Ronald Brand and Paul Herrup are co-authors of a leading work on the 2005 Choice of Court Convention; and Michael Coffee served as the head of the US delegation to the Diplomatic Session that adopted the 2019 Judgments Convention. The authors also provide an expert perspective on how the 2019 Judgments Convention might operate in the United States (which signed the Convention in 2022), in the event that it proceeds to ratify it.

This is a very timely and important work and, as editors of the *Private International Law Series*, we warmly congratulate the authors on its publication.

Professor Jonathan Harris KC (Hon.)
London
Professor Andrew Dickinson
Oxford
11 July 2023

Contents

Table of Cases

Table of Legislation

NATIONAL LEGISLATION

Brazil

Canada

France

Germany

Italy

Netherlands

Switzerland

United Kingdom

United States

1

A Basic Introduction to the 2019 Convention

Structure, Core, Context, and Choices

I. Introduction

The Convention on the Recognition and Enforcement of Foreign Judgments in Civil or Commercial Matters, done at The Hague, 2 July 2019 ('the Judgments Convention' or 'the Convention') provides rules governing the recognition and enforcement of judgments from a court of one Contracting State (the State of origin/court of origin) presented to a court of another Contracting State (the requested court/requested State). The Convention creates international obligations of unprecedented sweep and power: a judgment that falls within its scope may be eligible for recognition or enforcement in any and all Contracting States—or barred from recognition or enforcement in any and all Contracting States. On the other hand, the potential power of the Convention is constrained because very specific requirements must be satisfied for a judgment to be eligible for recognition or enforcement under the Convention. **1.01**

II. The Structure of the Convention

The Convention consists of a preamble and thirty-two articles arranged in four chapters, followed by a jurat clause stating that the official texts in the English and French languages are equally authentic. **1.02**

Chapter I of the Convention is entitled 'Scope and Definitions' and contains Articles 1–3. This chapter delineates the stuff of the Convention—the material on which the Convention rules will work. Articles 1 and 2 set out the substantive scope of application of the Convention: that the Convention applies to 'judgments' and describes the kinds of judgments to which it applies or does not apply. Article 3 provides definitions and elaboration of three terms used in the Convention. **1.03**

1.04 Chapter II, 'Recognition and Enforcement', which consists of Articles 4–15, contains the operational core of the Convention: a judgment given by a court of a Contracting State shall be recognized and enforced in other Contracting States in accordance with the provisions of Chapter II (art 4). As will be seen, Chapter II *regulates* recognition and enforcement of judgments within the scope of the Convention; it is mandatory, but its operation does not generally mandate actual recognition or enforcement of judgments within its scope. It provides criteria for eligibility of recognition and enforcement of judgments with certain features in Article 5, but these eligibility criteria are often narrow.

1.05 Article 6 creates an obligation that both provides for recognition and enforcement of judgments that ruled on rights in rem in immovable property given by a court of the State in which the property is located, and prohibits recognition or enforcement of all other judgments ruling on such rights, whether recognition or enforcement is sought under the Convention or under domestic law. Article 6 overrides other provisions.

1.06 Article 7 provides discretionary grounds for refusal of recognition or enforcement of judgments within the scope of the Convention. These grounds are, in some respects, broader than the grounds in the similar list in the 2005 Hague Convention on Choice of Court Agreements (COCA). As a consequence of this, and of the often narrow specificity of the criteria of eligibility for recognition and enforcement in Article 5 and the sweeping bar to recognition and enforcement in Article 6, any assertion that the fundamental object and purpose of the Judgments Convention is actual recognition and enforcement of judgments, as opposed to regulating recognition and enforcement of judgments within its scope, reads the text of the Convention with eyes wide shut.

1.07 Article 8 addresses the status of certain judgments that may contain content outside of the scope of the Convention, including 'preliminary questions'. Article 9 provides a severability rule. Article 10 addresses the treatment of damage awards. Article 11 brings 'judicial settlements' (transactions judiciaries) into the Convention for purposes of enforcement. Article 12 describes documents to be produced, while Article 13 addresses other points of procedure. Article 14 addresses costs of proceedings. Article 15 preserves the ability of Contracting States to recognize or enforce judgments under their national law, including their conflict of law rules, but then bars doing so with respect to judgments ruling on rights in rem in immovable property that are subject to Article 6.

1.08 Chapter III, the 'General Clauses' chapter of the Convention contains eight articles, Articles 16–23, that have potential for major impact on the outcome of specific requests for recognition or enforcement. These include transitional rules determining when Convention provisions will apply to recognition and enforcement of judgments based on the date from which the Convention has effect between the State of origin and the requested State (art 16). In Articles 17–19, the Convention authorizes certain declarations by States that will tailor the application of specific Convention rules under specific circumstances. These include declarations limiting recognition or enforcement of certain judgments that the requested State might not view as truly 'international' (art 17), and two declarations that are effectively small determinants of scope. These are declarations with respect to specific matters (art 18) and declarations with respect to judgments pertaining to the declaring State (art 19).

1.09 Article 20 provides a statement regarding the need to promote uniformity in the interpretation and application of the Convention, while Article 21 authorizes Hague Conference on Private International Law review of the operation of the Convention. Article 22 specifies rules for application of the Convention regarding 'non-unified legal systems' while Article 23 addresses the relationship between the Convention and other international instruments.

The final chapter of the Convention is Chapter IV, the 'Final Clauses', and consists of Articles 24–32. These articles address the mechanics of ratification, approval, acceptance, and the like; notification; who may be a party; and how treaty relations will be established between Contracting States. Article 24 is entitled 'Signature, ratification, acceptance, approval or accession'. Article 25 addresses declarations by Contracting States with respect to their non-unified legal systems. Article 26 addresses regional economic integration organizations as Contracting States, and Article 27 addresses the effects of the Convention on the member States of the regional economic integration organization. Article 28 deals with entry into force. 1.10

Article 29 is a pivotal provision describing how the Convention will or will not establish or otherwise affect the relations between specific Contracting States through a bilateralization mechanism. Article 30 provides for the mechanics of declarations. Article 31 addresses requirements for denunciation. Finally, Article 32 provides for notifications by the depositary. 1.11

III. The Core of the Convention

The Convention sets a framework and formulates rules that *regulate* recognition and enforcement of certain judgments—including the prohibition of recognition or enforcement—in limited and specified circumstances. This point bears repeating: the Convention regulates recognition and enforcement in certain instances; any examination of the actual provisions of the text refutes the proposition that the basic object and purpose of the Convention is to maximize actual recognition and enforcement of judgments generally. As will be discussed in Chapter 4, this proposition should not be used to drive the interpretation of the Convention. 1.12

The Convention is built upon three core functional provisions, each of which is subject to three general limitations and to significant conditions. 1.13

Article 4(1) is the first core functional provision, providing that judgments within the scope of the Convention shall be recognized or enforced in accordance with the provisions of Chapter II, and subject to other provisions of the Convention. While core, in a sense it is a truism: it requires Contracting States to act according to their agreement. 1.14

Article 5(1) is the second core functional provision, providing that a judgment becomes eligible for recognition or enforcement if it satisfies a criterion of eligibility listed in that provision. Article 5(1) provides a list of thirteen separate categories of eligibility for recognition or enforcement under the Convention. A fourteenth category is found in Article 6. Each independent criterion constitutes a cluster of highly specific and often complex properties that delineate approved connections between the State or court of origin and various combinations of persons, conduct, and various classifications of claims, and which may require examination of different sources of law to determine the content of each property in each cluster. 1.15

Article 6 provides the third core functional provision, providing that, for judgments ruling on rights in rem in immovable property, a court in a Contracting State shall recognize or enforce the judgment only if the property is situated in the State of origin. This 1.16

obligation that prohibits recognition or enforcement even under national law is the most powerful obligation in the Convention: unlike other articles, Article 6 explicitly overrides the possibility of recognition or enforcement under national law pursuant to Article 15. While other provisions create obligations *to* recognize and enforce, Article 6 also creates an obligation *not* to recognize and enforce a judgment (ie a prohibition against recognition and enforcement).

1.17 The first general limitation is that the request for recognition or enforcement be 'international' in the sense that a judgment subject to the Convention must be issued by a court of one Contracting State and presented to the courts of a different Contracting State. The Convention does not purport to—and cannot—take cognizance of the circulation of a judgment that either does not cross a national border, or that does not move between Contracting States.

1.18 The second general limitation derives from the restricted scope of the Convention. The Convention begins in Article 1(1) by stating that it applies to the recognition or enforcement of judgments in 'civil or commercial matters'. This is a somewhat inchoate classification, unknown in some legal systems and subject to significant variation in those legal regimes that refer to it. The Convention does not apply to any matter not 'civil or commercial' within the autonomous Convention meaning of those terms, but, as in other Hague Conventions, provides no definition of that phrase. Article 2 then provides that the Convention does not apply to 'matters' that are often broad categories that otherwise might be classified as 'civil or commercial' as that term is understood in the Convention. Furthermore, the declarations available in Articles 18 and 19 permit States effectively to remove from scope other specific matters and certain litigation involving specific declaring State interests.

1.19 The third general limitation consists of the discretionary grounds for refusal of recognition and enforcement, found primarily in Article 7, but also in the declaration provided in Article 17 relating to the 'international' nature of a judgment. These grounds, if satisfied, permit a State to refuse recognition or enforcement of a judgment to which the Convention otherwise applies and that meets a criterion of eligibility listed in Article 5 or Article 6.

1.20 Finally, an effective condition to recognition and enforcement under the Convention derives from the highly specific and complex features of each of the criteria of eligibility for recognition or enforcement. While the Convention has teeth, they are small.

IV. The Context of the Convention

A. Factual Context, Current and Future

1.21 The basic fact against which any transnational litigation Convention must be measured is the contemporary progress of developments in global communication, transportation, and technology, and the near certainty that these developments will accelerate in the future. This has resulted in a greater knowledge of opportunities across borders and a dramatic lowering of transaction costs to explore and engage in those opportunities. There now is an unprecedented—indeed, from the vantage point of a half-century past, unimaginable—ability of people, goods, ideas, electrons, and even microbes to move across borders, easily and cheaply, with attendant social, cultural, and economic connections, and the inevitably attendant disputes. The general availability and relatively low cost of means to move increases both movement and the range of people who can move or make movement. Far more people, even with limited means or capacities, will be able to participate in global flows than at any time in human history. We have lowered the entry cost of movement, yet the transaction costs of resolving disputes arising from those movements have not notably diminished. For many, current transaction costs of transnational litigation are a far more pervasive and serious barrier to access to justice than any other.

Not only is there a far greater number of persons engaged in global mobility, but the breadth, flexibility, and plasticity of the relationships—including new types of relationships—has proliferated. We are seeing the emergence of new types and variations in the commercial relationships falling within the Convention, from licensing and other arrangements in the area of intellectual property, to block-chain methods for carrying out commercial functions. **1.22**

Another critical fact accompanies this new form of the democratization of global movement. The number of countries with a significant connection, legal or factual, to a given transaction has also increased. For example, in the sale of goods, the stream of commerce can move from searching for opportunities to purchase each individual item or lot, storage, transportation to a marshalling site, stuffing the container, transportation of the container to a dock or further storage, loading and stowage on (at least one) ship, embarkation, transit (almost invariably with multiple stops as the cheapest option), final arrival at destination, debarkation of the container, storage of the container, movement of the container to be unstuffed, actual unstuffing, dispersal of the goods, marketing, sale, and distribution of monies received. As a matter of fact, there are multiple significant connections to a myriad of countries—likely with no lawyer in the chain because the costs of legal participation would reduce, if not eliminate, the benefit to the trader. **1.23**

B. Legal Context Related to Factual Developments

The Judgments Convention must be set in the specific context of global approaches to the recognition and enforcement of judgments, or similar instruments that determine legal rights and obligations. Currently, efforts at a global level to regulate the recognition and enforcement of judgments and similar instruments that determine legal rights and obligations occupy certain intervals on a broader spectrum of means of dispute resolution. **1.24**

At one end of the spectrum is private, international arbitration, with enforcement mechanisms provided by the United Nations Convention on the Recognition and Enforcement of Foreign Arbitral Awards ('New York Convention'). International commercial arbitration generally is considered to be best used to resolve disputes of sufficiently high value, acknowledging its higher costs to the disputants: it may not be a recommended method to resolve disputes involving less than US$50 million—and certainly not for disputes involving less than US$10 million. International arbitration may have even more restricted utility when money is not the main object of the proceedings. **1.25**

COCA provides mechanisms for recognition and enforcement of judgments within its scope. These are judgments from courts designated by the parties to exercise direct jurisdiction over the dispute. But the existence of an applicable choice of court agreement usually implies that lawyers have been involved in the initial transaction. This, in turn, usually **1.26** requires a transaction, series of transactions, or relationships of a certain size between persons who can afford to involve lawyers in such transactions—and who realize the importance and utility of doing so. While the transactions to which COCA is likely to apply may be smaller as a class than those that bring private international arbitration into play, they will be subject to certain value and size thresholds.

1.27 What then, is the place of the Judgments Convention on this spectrum of disputes leading to issues of recognition and enforcement? The New York Convention and COCA likely leave open a significant interval on the spectrum, namely the world of the numerous small entrepreneurs and other actors with whom this discussion began, who are finding opportunities and making movements created or permitted by new and inexpensive forms of communication and transportation, but not receiving guidance on the inclusion of choice of forum (court or arbitration) in their contracts. (At some point, of course, a small percentage of these small actors may become quite big, and will move to other intervals on the spectrum.) These transactions frequently occur with no prior legal advice, or other specialist, learned advice. The cost of legal advice might be prohibitive to the transaction or movement. If a dispute occurs, it will likely be handled on a low budget by generalist lawyers with only limited knowledge of the law in the area and without the financial support to spend substantial time on the case or to educate themselves. Most such disputes in most countries will be heard by generalist, first-instance judges whose task is to move dockets. Because of the financial realities, appeals should not be expected. There is one shot to resolve the dispute and resolve it well. Cases of this sort are likely to involve a substantial part of the traffic under the Judgments Convention and the people involved in such transactions are expected to be the ones who need a framework the most—and the people most likely to be overlooked in the treaty-making process and the discussions around it. (This is not to say that arbitration, dispute resolution under choice of court agreements, and general litigation constitute inherently exclusive and mutually impenetrable spheres of dispute resolution. They do not. Indeed, each mechanism may be improved in certain classes of circumstances by a limited recourse to other modes. However, in most cases—and certainly those of the small actors identified here—resolution of the dispute will be contained largely within one of these specific mechanisms.[1])

1.28 The spectrum of transactions that can lead to disputes requiring judgments that can be taken to courts in second countries for recognition and enforcement are not limited to contractual relationships. It may well be—and many of the Article 5(1) connecting factors indicate—that the Judgments Convention will most often provide the rules for recognition and enforcement of judgments in non-contractual matters. There are many relationships that do not lend themselves to anticipatory planning for dispute resolution. Common tort cases, which constitute a significant portion of transnational litigation, normally do not involve previous contractual relationships between the plaintiff and the defendant(s). The opportunity to plan for dispute resolution simply has not existed in all situations. Thus, the Judgments Convention provides the framework for those disputes where planning the forum for a dispute has not been possible, no matter what the value of the transaction or the

[1] One should also note efforts to give effect to mediated settlements, United Nations Convention on International Settlement Agreements Resulting from Mediation, done at New York, December 20, 2018 (Singapore Convention) and various efforts at on-line dispute settlement.

amount of the damages resulting from tortious or other relevant conduct that can create financial liability.

Another aspect of legal context flows from the new plasticity, flexibility, and breadth of real-world relations that have emerged and will continue to emerge. New types of relations—and new aspects of more familiar types of relationships—lead to a proliferation of possible claims and types of claims, many of which will not fit easily into familiar boxes. **1.29**

V. Choices Made in the Convention

The text of the Convention reflects a cascading series of choices made in the course of the negotiation of the Convention. The wisdom of these choices and the adequacy of the result will be discussed in our final chapter (and will be learned through the implementation of the Convention). **1.30**

The threshold choice is that this is an international convention. It is not a model law. It is not a set of principles, or other form of guidance. This is a convention in which Contracting States have agreed among themselves to act in certain ways as a matter of international obligation. This fundamental fact has two important implications. First, the Convention is an instrument of a governmental and sovereign nature, even if many of the situations it regulates involve private persons acting in their own interest, and the law involved might fall within an academic classification referred to as 'private international law' or 'conflict of laws'. There is an indelible and irreducible public core to the Convention. **1.31**

Second, the Convention consists of international obligations that Contracting States have taken upon themselves. The Convention should not be interpreted or applied in a way that creates obligations that States did not anticipate and to which they did not agree. This point will be taken up in more detail in a number of places in this book. **1.32**

A third critical choice is the topic of the Convention itself: this is a convention that regulates recognition and enforcement of judgments by courts. It follows a particular model for such conventions, which has operational features that further intensify and expand the proper public core of the enterprise. This choice, and the operational features that follow, create specific, significant results: **1.33**

(1) The first result of the choice of topic is that a 'judgment' is the culmination of an exercise of State power by a public institution of a State (its courts) pursuant to the laws of that State. Recognition or enforcement of that judgment is itself a legal exercise that requires the further exercise of State power by another State—including, potentially, the coercive power of the second State—by a public institution of the second State (its courts) pursuant to the laws of the second State. The process operates because States have determined that it should, subject to certain parameters. States do not turn their courts over for the sole convenience and at the beck and whim of private persons and interests by virtue of becoming Contracting States to the Convention.

(2) The second result of the choice of topic is that conventions such as this, providing for recognition and enforcement of judgments, themselves should be seen as one kind of a family of mutual legal assistance or cooperation conventions. They involve the institutions of one State giving assistance to, and cooperating with, institutions of another

State (directly or indirectly), based upon both self-interest of the States involved and beliefs regarding the proper role and obligations of States to each other in an international legal system consisting of juridically independent sovereigns in an increasingly interdependent world. Other examples of such conventions are conventions providing for coordination and assistance in service of process, reduction of legalization requirements, and gathering of evidence. Generally, these mutual legal assistance conventions fall within one of two models that might be referred to as the 'agency' model and the 'lock-and-key' model. The first, the 'agency' model, has the court or other institutions of the requested State acting as the 'agent' of the requesting State or its institution. The court of the requested State, as agent, is vested with the powers of the requesting institution under the laws of the requesting State, including the limitations on those powers. Under an 'agency' model, for example, a court in one State executing a request for evidence in connection with proceedings in a court in another State will be limited to gathering the types of evidence and to the methods of doing so of its principal under the law of the requesting State, or, at least in theory, applying requested methods or procedures not otherwise available under its own law if doing so is not incompatible with the law of the requested State. Furthermore, under an 'agency' model, a requested court would be obliged to enforce the remedies issued by the court of origin, even if those remedies were unknown, disfavoured, or even otherwise illegal in its own system. Whatever the virtues of the 'agency' model between countries with long and shared histories, similarities of outlook, and closely related legal systems, this model with its disruptive and intrusive effects within the legal system and judicial processes of the requested State is a poor candidate for a global convention seeking widespread acceptance.

1.34 Not surprisingly, as a result of the incompatibility of an agency model of treaty structure with the subject matter of the Convention, the Judgments Convention adopts a 'lock and key' model of legal assistance and cooperation. Generally, the Convention provides a key that unlocks the door of the legal system and legal institutions of the requested State to permit entry of an act of the State of origin—a judgment—which, upon entry, will be evaluated under the Convention, but subject to the streams of procedure and limitations on the power and authority of the institutions of the requested State. Ultimately, the court of the requested State will determine whether the foreign judgment presented to it can or cannot somehow be assimilated into the local legal system or given effect as if it had been issued by a court in the requested State.

1.35 A fourth critical choice in the Convention is that it touches upon only 'indirect' jurisdiction and eschews touching upon 'direct' jurisdiction in any fashion, except perhaps in Article 6. These are terms that are not used in the Convention itself, are not used in a number of legal systems, and, when used in connection with this Convention, can be misleading. But this is a core choice underlying the Convention.

1.36 For purposes of understanding the Convention, direct jurisdiction essentially is the classic jurisdiction to adjudicate, that is, the power and authority of a court to proceed to resolve a dispute presented to it. In the context of recognition and enforcement of judgments, direct jurisdiction attaches at two different points: the jurisdiction to adjudicate the claim in the court of origin, and the jurisdiction of the requested court to proceed to resolve the application for recognition or enforcement. The Convention does not contemplate that the requested court will examine in any way the bases of jurisdiction invoked by the court of origin to issue the judgment. Conversely, the Convention takes as a datum the jurisdictional rules of the requested State that require, permit, or bar a court in that State from proceeding to adjudicate a request for recognition or enforcement. Thus, if the law of the requested State requires the presence of persons or property in the State in order to adjudicate an application for recognition or enforcement, and the requirement is not met, nothing in the Convention requires the requested court to move forward in contravention of its own law.

Indirect jurisdiction in terms of the Convention refers to a process by which the requested court identifies and measures the connections of the judgment—or features related to it—with the State or court of origin to determine whether the criteria of recognition or enforcement under Articles 5 and 6 are satisfied. It goes not to the power and authority of a court to proceed to resolve a dispute, but to the outcome of such a resolution if the requested court is permitted by its own law to proceed. The indirect jurisdiction inquiry is an independent inquiry as to whether or how the judgment presented satisfies the separate criteria of eligibility for recognition or enforcement contained in Articles 5 and 6. As noted above, these articles present a list of separate categories of eligibility for recognition or enforcement under the Convention. Each independent category is a cluster of highly specific and often complex properties that delineate Convention-approved connections between the State or court of origin and various combinations of persons, conduct, and various classifications of claims. If, upon examination, the requested court determines that at least one provision of Article 5 or Article 6 is satisfied, the Convention requires the requested court to recognize or enforce the judgment, subject to the separate further grounds for refusal of recognition or enforcement found in Article 7. If the inquiry results in a determination that the judgment does not satisfy one of the identified criteria, this does not invalidate the judgment (which might still be recognized or enforced in accordance with Article 15), but instead removes a Convention-based obligation to recognize or enforce that judgment. **1.37**

The fifth and final choice we will discuss involves a road not taken. In a number of legal systems, recognition or enforcement of a foreign judgment is keyed to the basis of jurisdiction exercised in the court of origin. Jurisdiction is required or prohibited as provided by a lengthy list of highly specific jurisdictional bases or potential bases. An example of this approach is the system within the European Union (EU), codified in Regulation (EU) No 1215/2012 of the European Parliament and of the Council of 12 December 2012 on jurisdiction and the recognition and enforcement of judgments in civil and commercial matters (the Brussels I (Recast) Regulation). The Brussels I (Recast) Regulation divides the world of jurisdiction in many respects by sometimes conclusory classifications or categorizations of content, and then allocates direct jurisdiction for each such category based upon very specific features presented, which are interpreted and applied in a mechanical fashion. This approach will be referred to as 'Brussels boxes'.[2] It is familiar to many of the States involved in the negotiations at the Hague Conference on Private International Law. **1.38**

[2] An example of this approach is provided in Section 3 of the Brussels I (Recast) Regulation.

Jurisdiction in matters relating to insurance

Article 10

In matters relating to insurance, jurisdiction shall be determined by this Section, without prejudice to Article 6 and point 5 of Article 7.

Article 11

1. An insurer domiciled in a Member State may be sued:
   (a) in the courts of the Member State in which he is domiciled;

Yet, inflexible micro-categories, mechanically applied, will yield results in terms of efficiency of litigation and the realities of modern mobility that are directly at odds with the goals of this Convention to reduce the transaction costs of transnational litigation as an aspect of access to justice. For example, Article 5(1)(i) provides a criterion of eligibility if a 'judgment ruled against the defendant on a contractual obligation secured by a right

(b) in another Member State, in the case of actions brought by the policyholder, the insured or a beneficiary, in the courts for the place where the claimant is domiciled; or
(c) if he is a co-insurer, in the courts of a Member State in which proceedings are brought against the leading insurer.

2. An insurer who is not domiciled in a Member State but has a branch, agency or other establishment in one of the Member States shall, in disputes arising out of the operations of the branch, agency or establishment, be deemed to be domiciled in that Member State.

Article 12

In respect of liability insurance or insurance of immovable property, the insurer may in addition be sued in the courts for the place where the harmful event occurred. The same applies if movable and immovable property are covered by the same insurance policy and both are adversely affected by the same contingency.

Article 13

1. In respect of liability insurance, the insurer may also, if the law of the court permits it, be joined in proceedings which the injured party has brought against the insured.
2. Articles 10, 11 and 12 shall apply to actions brought by the injured party directly against the insurer, where such direct actions are permitted.
3. If the law governing such direct actions provides that the policyholder or the insured may be joined as a party to the action, the same court shall have jurisdiction over them.

Article 14

1. Without prejudice to Article 13(3), an insurer may bring proceedings only in the courts of the Member State in which the defendant is domiciled, irrespective of whether he is the policyholder, the insured or a beneficiary.
2. The provisions of this Section shall not affect the right to bring a counter-claim in the court in which, in accordance with this Section, the original claim is pending.

Article 15

The provisions of this Section may be departed from only by an agreement:

(1) which is entered into after the dispute has arisen;
(2) which allows the policyholder, the insured or a beneficiary to bring proceedings in courts other than those indicated in this Section;
(3) which is concluded between a policyholder and an insurer, both of whom are at the time of conclusion of the contract domiciled or habitually resident in the same Member State, and which has the effect of conferring jurisdiction on the courts of that Member State even if the harmful event were to occur abroad, provided that such an agreement is not contrary to the law of that Member State;
(4) which is concluded with a policyholder who is not domiciled in a Member State, except in so far as the insurance is compulsory or relates to immovable property in a Member State; or
(5) which relates to a contract of insurance in so far as it covers one or more of the risks set out in Article 16.

Article 16

The following are the risks referred to in point 5 of Article 15:

(1) any loss of or damage to:
  (a) seagoing ships, installations situated offshore or on the high seas, or aircraft, arising from perils which relate to their use for commercial purposes;
  (b) goods in transit other than passengers' baggage where the transit consists of or includes carriage by such ships or aircraft;
(2) any liability, other than for bodily injury to passengers or loss of or damage to their baggage:
  (a) arising out of the use or operation of ships, installations or aircraft as referred to in point 1(a) in so far as, in respect of the latter, the law of the Member State in which such aircraft are registered does not prohibit agreements on jurisdiction regarding insurance of such risks;
  (b) for loss or damage caused by goods in transit as described in point 1(b);
(3) any financial loss connected with the use or operation of ships, installations or aircraft as referred to in point 1(a), in particular loss of freight or charter-hire;
(4) any risk or interest connected with any of those referred to in points 1 to 3;
(5) notwithstanding points 1 to 4, all 'large risks' as defined in Directive 2009/138/EC of the European Parliament and of the Council of 25 November 2009 on the taking-up and pursuit of the business of Insurance and Reinsurance (Solvency II) ([14]).

in rem in immovable property located in the State of origin, if the contractual claim was brought together with a claim against the same defendant relating to that right *in rem*'. It was considered necessary to include this provision because, under Article 6, judgments ruling on rights in rem in immovable property are eligible for recognition or enforcement only if they are issued by a court in the State where the immoveable property is located. Absent the micro-provision in Article 5(1)(i) it might not be possible to recognize a judgment on a related contractual claim brought in that State in the absence of satisfaction of another criterion in Article 5(1); for example, the debtor was habitually resident in that State (art 5(1)(a)). Another potential example is a situation in which a transaction or series of transactions gives rise to tightly connected claims both in contract and in tort, but the place of performance of the contractual obligations involved is in one State and place of the act or omission directly causing the tort claims is in another State, and neither claim qualifies as a counter-claim (art 5(1)(g), (j), and (l)). In order for judgments ruling on the claims to be eligible for recognition and enforcement under the Convention, the Convention may require that each component of the case be decided by courts of different States.[3]

In many respects, the Convention looks backwards to nineteenth-century legal science to create a twentieth-century treaty for a twenty-first-century world. There was an alternative model available for a convention on recognition and enforcement of judgments that was not chosen, that would have avoided this rearview-mirror approach. Understanding that alternative model facilitates a better understanding of the model that was chosen. The alternative model begins with the very public nature of such a treaty, bases itself on the goals of mutual legal assistance treaties to foster appropriate cooperation among independent sovereigns in an interdependent world, and provides results that may better reflect the realities of global mobility. **1.39**

The first step of the alternative analysis begins with the traditional connecting factor employed in numerous instruments adopted by the Hague Conference on Private International Law to link persons to fora, namely the concept of habitual residence. Use of habitual residence as an initial definer of subsets of cases yields four basic subsets of cases subject to instruments of this type: **1.40**

(1) Non-resident plaintiff, non-resident defendant
(2) Non-resident plaintiff, resident defendant
(3) Resident plaintiff, non-resident defendant
(4) Resident plaintiff, resident defendant.

The second step of the analysis then gives more precision to the typology above, namely by identifying the judgment holder in each subset. This yields eight subsets, which are the cases to be considered under any instrument on international recognition and enforcement of the resulting judgment: **1.41**

(1) Non-resident plaintiff, non-resident defendant, judgment for plaintiff
(2) Non-resident plaintiff, non-resident defendant, judgment for defendant
(3) Non-resident plaintiff, resident defendant, judgment for plaintiff

[3] This is not a fanciful situation. See, eg, the Court of Justice of the European Union (CJEU), C-59/19, *Wickingerhof*.

(4) Non-resident plaintiff, resident defendant, judgment for defendant
(5) Resident plaintiff, non-resident defendant, judgment for plaintiff
(6) Resident plaintiff, non-resident defendant, judgment for defendant
(7) Resident plaintiff, resident defendant, judgment for plaintiff
(8) Resident plaintiff, resident defendant, judgment for defendant.

1.42 Having identified these eight subsets of cases which exhaust the situations to which an instrument would apply, there are two common-sense principles that should be generally acceptable in providing a framework of decision for recognition and enforcement by a court in one State of a judgment from another State. In essence, they reflect a basic respect that generally should come into play when an institution of one sovereign is asked to examine an act of another sovereign.

(1) A person who has chosen to present a claim to a court in one country, or to consent in certain specified ways to adjudication in that court, should not be heard to complain about the result in a court of another country; and
(2) A person who is habitually resident in one country should not be heard to complain about the actions of a court in that country to a court in another country.

1.43 These are general principles of common sense rooted in the existence of and need for cooperation of multiple, juridically co-equal sovereigns. While these principles can be expressed in ponderous terms of jurisdictional doctrine, that expression is not necessary to their operation and may hinder it.

1.44 An immediate point to note is that, generally, application of these two principles on their face resolve six of the eight aforementioned subsets of cases. The principle that a claimant cannot complain about the fate of his claim generally disposes of the subsets in which the claimant loses (points 2, 4, 6, and 8). The principle that a habitual resident of a country cannot complain in the court of another country about the action of his own forum generally disposes of the two subsets of cases in which judgment is against such a defendant (points 3 and 7).

1.45 Generally, the specific criteria of eligibility for recognition and enforcement in Article 5(1)(a)–(f) and Article 5(1)(l)–(m) can be generated by these two principles. However, recourse to the principles is much simpler (and easier to understand) than the elaborate specific criteria in the Convention.

1.46 This leaves only two subsets of cases not generally resolved on their face by our principles, namely the two cases involving judgments for plaintiffs against non-resident defendants (points 1 and 5) (and point 1 may be less of a concern because there is no reason to posit local favouritism in cases in which all the parties are non-residents of the forum). The gateway connecting factor rules of Article 5(1)(g)–(k), Article 5(3), and Article 6 are needed only for these two subsets.

1.47 In considering a solution to the problems posed by these two subsets, it may be useful to look to considerations of public international law and the functioning of a system of juridically equal States. In such a system, one State should not project its power beyond its borders into a global commons or in ways that affect the interests of other States unless there is a general consensus in treaty or custom that such an exercise of power is acceptable. National jurisdiction is an exercise of State power, and properly may be systematically constrained—or at least given no encouragement—by the international legal system if its exercise impinges on these systemic or particular national interests. Each State within the international system has a general interest that commonly accepted constraints not be violated by certain projections of national jurisdiction and a more specific interest (and even responsibility) that its citizens (and, perhaps, residents) not be subject to exercises of jurisdictional power by other States in ways not sanctioned by treaty or custom. Thus, there may be a legitimate role for additional rules rooted in public international law in the situation of judgments against defendants not resident in the State of origin.

Such rules, flowing from public international law constraints on the exercise of State power, would provide for recognition and enforcement of judgments in these two subsets up to the point that the original judgment violates generally accepted public international law concerns. There would be recognition and enforcement unless the underlying jurisdiction in the court of origin is 'exorbitant' in some public international law sense. This is precisely the other end of the stick from the current approach in a number of countries, which is to allow recognition or enforcement only if a particular mechanical connection to the State of origin is satisfied—an approach that is increasingly unsatisfactory in our modern world as multiple strong connections proliferate to a variety of States in any given transaction or act. An example of this approach would be a Convention rule that recognition and enforcement should be given unless the connection of the parties, and/or the conduct, to the forum was either non-existent or fell below an internationally acceptable standard, for example, a lack of a substantial connection. The Convention then would provide specificity and boundaries for determination by the requested court of when the connection with the State or court of origin fell below the general standard of a substantial connection (eg based upon the nationality of the plaintiff, the alleged presence of property of the defendant in the State of origin, or conduct unrelated to the claim). 1.48

VI. Resulting Tensions

The conditions of creation and the choices made in the Convention potentially create tensions between its parts and in its operation. These tensions largely result from areas of collision between the Convention and the realities of global mobility that it attempts to address. 1.49

An initial point of tension arises from the collision between the need to craft a text that will attract widespread ratification with the dynamics of our world of movement. If the text does not receive support, it is yet another in a long line of pieces of paper gathering dust in Chancery filing cabinets and electronically-filed records unlikely to receive much further attention. This consideration puts a premium on familiar features: States are more likely to ratify agreements that require little or no change in their current domestic legal arrangements and that march in step with prevailing local dogmas. Local arrangements and local dogma set the parameters of a global convention—and they are even now palpably inadequate to meet regional, let alone global, challenges. Conventions that must operate in a future global world are crafted with both eyes firmly fixed in the rearview mirror, rather than on the road ahead. Particularly in its recognition and enforcement aspects, the Convention deploys classifications and categories, and sets requirements of eligibility for recognition and enforcement, that may become unwieldy or even anachronistic in the light of the realities of modern trade and other movements. 1.50

1.51 A second, related point is that the Convention is a consensus product, and any given international legal obligation created by the Convention is one that States clearly agreed by consensus to impose upon themselves.[4] Interpretation cannot and should not extend the international legal obligations of the Convention to burdens States did not choose to shoulder. Yet, as will be seen, the Convention abounds in uncertain terms, terms without definition, or established Convention sense, to be given meaning from unspecified sources of law that may yield significant variation in results. It will be a challenge in these circumstances to restrict interpretation to those international obligations that the Contracting States may fairly be said to have assumed.

1.52 This point is related to another area of potential tension: whether the terms of the Convention should be given a static meaning that might be assigned to them at the time of drafting of the text, or a dynamic meaning to match evolution in the world. The former approach will protect Contracting States from surprise, but at the potential expense of increased divergence of the Convention from evolving realities and increased inadequacy. The latter will more closely maintain a consonance of the Convention with the realities of global movement, but will also risk imposing new and unconsented to obligations on the Contracting States.

1.53 Another aspect of potential tension arises from the likely conditions of implementation of the Convention. A major part of traffic under the Convention is expected to be disputes involving actors with limited resources and limited sophistication, with one appearance only before generalist judges with crowded dockets that largely consist of wholly domestic disputes. The Convention will serve these parties best, and remain within the confines of the legal obligations actually assumed by the Contracting States, by placing a premium on being simple and intelligible to the users who will benefit most from the Convention, and to the judges and lawyers faced with making it work properly. This requires, first and foremost, simple and powerful rules on the recognition and enforcement of judgments within an easily intelligible and manageable scope. Yet, as will be discussed in detail in the rest of this book, the text of the Convention in many respects deploys undefined terms and calls for extensive depecage that will require ranging between multiple sources of law.

1.54 In our interpretations, we try to maintain sensible balances, among the language of the text, the logical consequences of its terms, good sense, and ease of application—but the reading of the text itself ultimately controls. Our general appraisal of the strengths and weaknesses of the Convention will be presented in the final chapter.

[4] The consensus process and its significance are discussed in more detail in Chapter 4, particularly paragraphs 4.03 and 4.04.

2

Judgments Recognition in the Absence of the Judgments Convention

I. Introduction

The recognition and enforcement of judgments from the courts of other States involves the recognition of a sovereign judicial act of one State by the sovereign judicial system of another State. It demonstrates respect for the foreign legal system, and the foreign legal authority, from which the judgment originates. But the act of recognition of a foreign judgment is something more than simple comity in the sense of respect for the other legal system. It grants legal effect to the decision of the other legal system within the judicial system in which the judgment is received, thus giving effect to the foreign decision as a decision of the local judicial system. It can make the foreign court an instrument of the local judicial system for deciding disputes. This makes judgments recognition a rather significant element of any legal system. **2.01**

Despite the significance of judgments recognition in a domestic legal system, prior to the conclusion of the 2019 Hague Convention on the Recognition and Enforcement of Foreign Judgments in Civil or Commercial Matters, only a limited number of multilateral legal instruments existed that covered the law of cross-border judgments recognition. **2.02**

II. Multilateral Instruments on Judgments Recognition Preceding the Judgments Convention

The Hague Conference on Private International Law has a long history of efforts to adopt a successful convention on the recognition and enforcement of foreign judgments. TMC Asser had floated the idea of an international instrument in Paris in 1878,[1] prior even to his convening the first Hague Conference on private international law in 1893. **2.03**

[1] Arthur Eyffinger, 'Dreaming the Ideal, Living the Attainable: T.M.C. Asser [1838–1913] Founder of the Hague Tradition' (2011) 29 <https://www.asser.nl/media/1554/eyff_asser-100_book_lr.pdf>.

2.04 In 1963, a Special Commission of the Hague Conference on Private International Law prepared a Draft Convention on the recognition and the enforcement of foreign judgments in civil and commercial matters. This was followed with a Draft Convention of 26 April 1966 on the recognition and the enforcement of foreign judgments in civil and commercial matters. On 1 February 1971, the Hague Conference on Private International Law adopted the Convention on the Recognition and Enforcement of Foreign Judgments in Civil and Commercial Matters. While five States have ratified or acceded to the 1971 Convention (Albania, Cyprus, Kuwait, Netherlands, and Portugal), none have concluded the bilateral supplementary agreements required by the Convention to establish the obligation to recognize or enforce foreign judgments.[2]

2.05 One of the most significant developments in judgments recognition law has been the evolution of regional instruments. In Article 220 of the Treaty of Rome, creating the European Economic Community (EEC) in 1957, the original six Member States committed to 'enter into [further] negotiations with each other with a view to securing for the benefit of their nationals . . . the simplification of formalities governing the reciprocal recognition and enforcement of judgments of courts or tribunals and of arbitration awards'.[3] This commitment was met in 1968 with the conclusion of the Brussels Convention on jurisdiction and the recognition and enforcement of judgments in civil and commercial matters.[4] It was followed by the Lugano Convention, bringing in the Member States of the European Free Trade Association (EFTA) in 1988.[5] With the evolution of the European Community into the more federal structure of the European Union (EU), Articles 61 and 65 of the 1997 Treaty of Amsterdam,[6] provided for the adoption of 'measures in the field of judicial cooperation in civil matters',[7] including the recognition of judgments.[8] The resulting centralization of European private international law has included the promulgation of the Brussels I,[9] and Brussels I (Recast) Regulations on jurisdiction and the recognition and enforcement of judgments in civil and commercial matters,[10] as well as the revision of the Lugano Convention through exclusive EU competence.[11] This evolution has moved the EU instruments from the nature of international instruments to internal legal instruments of a federal State, regulating mainly the relationships among

[2] <https://www.hcch.net/en/instruments/conventions/status-table/?cid=78>.

[3] Treaty Establishing the European Community (TEC or 'European Community Treaty'), art 293 (ex art 220). The current version of the TEC can be found at OJ Eur Comm C 321E/37, 29 December 2006, <https://eur-lex.europa.eu/legal-content/EN/ALL/?uri=CELEX:12002E/TXT>. The provision is now art 293 TEC.

[4] European Convention on Jurisdiction and Enforcement of Judgments in Civil and Commercial Matters, done at Brussels, 27 September 1968, 41 OJ Eur Comm C 27/1, 26 January 1998 (consolidated and updated version of the 1968 Convention and the Protocol of 1971, following the 1996 accession of the Republic of Austria, the Republic of Finland and the Kingdom of Sweden) ('Brussels Convention').

[5] The Convention of Lugano on Jurisdiction and the Enforcement of Judgments in Civil and Commercial Matters [1988] OJ L319/9.

[6] Treaty of Amsterdam, signed on 2 October 1997, and entered into force on 1 May 1999, <https://www.europarl.europa.eu/about-parliament/en/in-the-past/the-parliament-and-the-treaties/treaty-of-amsterdam>.

[7] Art 61 (ex art 73i) TEC.

[8] Art 65 (ex art 73m) TEC.

[9] Council Regulation (EC) No 44/2001 of 22 December 2000 on jurisdiction and the recognition and enforcement of judgments in civil and commercial matters (Brussels I Regulation), OJ Eur Comm L 012/1, 16 January 2001.

[10] Regulation (EU) No 1215/2012 of the European Parliament and of the Council on jurisdiction and the recognition and enforcement of judgments in civil and commercial matters (Recast) (Brussels I (Recast) Regulation) [2012] OJ L 135/1, art 81, <https://eur-lex.europa.eu/ LexUriServ/LexUriServ.do?uri= OJ:L:2012:351:0001:0032:En:PDF>.

[11] Convention on jurisdiction and the recognition and enforcement of judgments in civil and commercial matters (Lugano Convention) [2007] OJ L 339/3. The exclusive competence of the EU to enter such treaties was confirmed by the Court of Justice of the European Union in Opinion 1/03, Request by the Council of the European Union for an Opinion pursuant to art 300(6) [2006] OJ C 101/1 ECR I-1145.

those internal States. The resulting EU legal framework for judgments recognition will be dealt with in more detail below.

In 1979, the Organization of American States adopted the Inter-American Convention on Extraterritorial Validity of Foreign Judgments and Arbitral Awards ('Montevideo Convention').[12] The Convention is in effect between Argentina, Bolivia, Brazil, Colombia, Ecuador, Mexico, Paraguay, Peru, Uruguay, and Venezuela.[13] Article 2 of the Montevideo Convention provides the operative rule, stating: **2.06**

> The foreign judgments, awards and decisions referred to in Article 1 shall have extraterritorial validity in the States Parties if they meet the following conditions:
> a. They fulfill all the formal requirements necessary for them to be deemed authentic in the State of origin;
> b. The judgment, award or decision and the documents attached thereto that are required under this Convention are duly translated into the official language of the State where they are to take effect;
> c. They are presented duly legalized in accordance with the law of the State in which they are to take effect;
> d. The judge or tribunal rendering the judgment is competent in the international sphere to try the matter and to pass judgment on it in accordance with the law of the State in which the judgment, award or decision is to take effect;
> e. The plaintiff has been summoned or subpoenaed in due legal form substantially equivalent to that accepted by the law of the State where the judgment, award or decision is to take effect;
> f. The parties had an opportunity to present their defense;
> g. They are final or, where appropriate, have the force of res judicata in the State in which they were rendered;
> h. They are not manifestly contrary to the principles and laws of the public policy (ordre public) of the State in which recognition or execution is sought.[14]

In the Gulf Region of the Middle East, two conventions have provisions dealing with the recognition of judgments. All Gulf Cooperation Council Members,[15] and numerous other States in the region, are party to the 1983 Riyadh Arab Agreement for Judicial Cooperation.[16] Article 25(b) of the Riyadh Agreement provides for the recognition of foreign judgments where: **2.07**

> 1) the foreign court was competent under the rules of jurisdiction in the requested country;
> 2) the requested country does not have exclusive jurisdiction over the subject matter; and
> 3) the judgment is final under the country of origin's law.[17]

[12] Inter-American Convention on Extraterritorial Validity of Foreign Judgments and Arbitral Awards (Montevideo Convention), done at Montevideo, Uruguay, 8 May 1979.

[13] <http://www.oas.org/juridico/english/sigs/b-41.html>.

[14] Art 2 Montevideo Convention.

[15] The Gulf Cooperation Council (GCC) was established in 1981. Its six Member States are Bahrain, Kuwait, Oman, Qatar, Saudi Arabia, and the United Arab Emirates (UAE).

[16] Riyadh Arab Agreement for Judicial Cooperation, 6 April 1983 (entered into force on 30 October 1985), reprinted in UAE Federal Decree 53/1999 ('Riyadh Convention').

[17] See Nicholas Bremer, 'Seeking Recognition and Enforcement of Foreign Court Judgments and Arbitral Awards in the GCC Countries' (2016–2017) 3 McGill J Dispute Resol 37, 40.

Article 30(1) then provides grounds for non-recognition if:

1) recognition would contradict the principles of Islamic law or the constitution and ordre public of the requested country;
2) the party against which the judgment is invoked was not duly summoned;
3) the laws of the requested country concerning legal representation of ineligible persons or persons of diminished eligibility were not taken into consideration;
4) the dispute is subject to a final judgement in the requested country, or in a third country, provided that the requested country has already recognized this judgement; or
5) the dispute is subject to a case currently being heard by the requested country's courts filed prior to the application for recognition.[18]

2.08 The 1996 Gulf Cooperation Council (GCC) Convention for the Execution of Judgments, Delegations and Judicial Notifications also provides for reciprocal recognition of judgments in GCC courts. Unlike the Riyadh Agreement, however, it does not provide a procedure for recognition.[19]

2.09 The Minsk Convention on Legal Aid and Legal Relations in Civil, Family and Criminal Matters was adopted on 22 January 1993 and is in force as between the following States: Armenia, Belarus, Kazakhstan, Kyrgyzstan, Moldova, Russian Federation, Turkmenistan, Tajikistan, Ukraine, and Uzbekistan. Articles 51–55 provide for the reciprocal recognition and enforcement of judgments in civil and family matters, as well as judgments for damages rendered in criminal proceedings.[20]

2.10 While not a treaty, the Model Law of the Commonwealth States also provides a regime for the recognition and enforcement of judgments. The Commonwealth is 'an association of 54 countries working towards shared goals of prosperity, democracy and peace', resulting from the British Commonwealth of nations.[21] In 2018, it published its Model Law on the Recognition and Enforcement of Foreign Judgments.[22] The text of the Model Law appears to have been designed to coordinate with the draft of the Hague Judgments Convention as it existed at that time, and prior to the 2019 Hague Diplomatic Session at which the Judgments Convention was adopted. Thus, its structure is much like that of the Convention.[23]

2.11 A number of post-colonial treaties provide for the reciprocal recognition and enforcement of judgments between the former colony and the colonizer. An example is the Agreement providing for the Reciprocal Recognition and Enforcement of Judicial Decisions and Authentic Acts in Civil Matters Between the Kingdom of the Netherlands and the Republic of Suriname, signed at The Hague, 27 August 1976,[24] which was extended

[18] ibid 41.

[19] ibid 40.

[20] Minsk Convention on Legal Aid and Legal Relations in Civil, Family and Criminal Matters done at Minsk, 22 January 1993.

[21] <https://thecommonwealth.org/our-work>.

[22] <https://thecommonwealth.org/sites/default/files/key_reform_pdfs/ D16227_1_GPD_ROL_Model_Law_Rec_Enf_Foreign_Judgements.pdf>.

[23] The Commonwealth website does not report how many Commonwealth States have enacted some form of the Model Law.

[24] <https://treaties.un.org/doc/Publication/UNTS/Volume%201135/volume-1135-I-17802-English.pdf>.

also to include Aruba, Curaçao, and Sint Maarten in 2015 and to Bonaire, Sint Eustatius, and Saba in 2021.

2.12 Apart from the 2019 Hague Judgments Convention, there is very little in the form of an existing, truly multilateral framework for the recognition and enforcement of foreign judgments. This makes national law on judgments recognition particularly important in the absence of wide ratification, acceptance, approval, or accession with respect to the 2019 Convention, and perhaps even with wide ratification as a result of Article 15 of the Convention.

III. The Potential Role of National Law under the Judgments Convention

2.13 At first glance, the text of the 2019 Convention appears to replace otherwise applicable national law for judgments originating in the courts of other Contracting States. One provision of the Convention, however, makes it possible that a Contracting State could continue to rely heavily on national law, even for judgments coming from other Contracting States. This makes national law important both in order to understand what the Convention might replace, and what might in fact be retained.

2.14 Article 15 of the Convention provides:

> Subject to Article 6, this Convention does not prevent the recognition or enforcement of judgments under national law.

The obvious purpose of this provision, aside from the reference to Article 6, is to make the Convention obligations to recognize and enforce foreign judgments a floor and not a ceiling. If the Convention conditions are met, a State 'shall' recognize and enforce the foreign judgment being considered.[25] What Article 15 does is to allow States to recognize judgments more liberally than is required under the Convention. While some may see the Convention as encouraging judgments recognition on a global basis, its real effect is to regulate that process. Thus, Article 15 allows a Contracting State to recognize and enforce a foreign judgment, even if the Convention rules would not require that result, both for judgments that are beyond the scope of the Convention and for judgments within the scope of the Convention but that involve connecting factors with the court of origin not included in the Article 5(1) list. As with other provisions of the Convention, national law remains important.

2.15 Article 15 thus makes it possible for a State to become a party to the Convention while retaining the ability to recognize and enforce foreign judgments under domestic law, particularly for judgments that may not circulate under the Convention. If that domestic law would result in the recognition and enforcement of all judgments that would be recognized and enforced under the Convention rules, in the manner contemplated by the Convention, but also allow other judgments to be recognized and enforced, then a Contacting State could implement the Convention internally by authorizing its courts to continue to apply

[25] Art 4(1). The Convention contains exceptions to this obligation.

national law. Doing so could have obvious advantages. It could avoid requiring dual systems of judgments recognition where the legal profession and judiciary are both familiar and comfortable with the existing national law. It could also reduce litigation costs and delays by avoiding what may be more complex (and uncertain) rules found in the Convention, which might in turn need to be reflected in separate provisions of national law. These benefits for inbound judgments could be accomplished while still gaining the advantages of recognition and enforcement in other Contracting States of outbound judgments from the courts of the State following this approach.[26]

IV. Pre-Convention National Law on Judgments Recognition

2.16 Whether a Contracting State relies heavily on existing national law through Article 15 of the Convention, or turns primarily to Article 5(1) and the Convention architecture that relies on that Article's list of criteria of eligibility as the gateway test for circulation of a judgment under the other Convention rules, national law on judgments recognition will remain important for judgments originating in States that are not Contracting States to the Convention as well as judgments from Contracting States for which the Convention does not establish an obligation for recognition or enforcement. Thus, it will continue to be necessary to have an understanding of national law, along with an understanding of the Convention rules.

A. The United States

2.17 As in most countries, in the United States,[27] the recognition of foreign judgments serves two primary functions. A party may seek to affirmatively enforce a foreign money judgment through access to local assets of the judgment debtor, or to have a court in the United States give preclusive effect to the judgment of a foreign court in order to prevent re-litigation of claims and issues in the United States. In either setting, the goal is to use the foreign judgment to prevent the need for extended and duplicative proceedings in courts in the United States.

2.18 The 1895 US Supreme Court decision in *Hilton v Guyot*,[28] provides the starting point for understanding current US law on judgments recognition. Today, however, many questions involving the recognition of foreign judgments are determined by applying US state law, found in statutes in some states and in the common law in other states.

[26] For a more detailed discussion of this possible issue in the implementation of the Convention, see Ronald A Brand, 'The Hague Judgments Convention in the United States: A "Game Changer" or a New Path to the Old Rules of the Game?' (2021) 82 U Pitt L Rev 847 (suggesting that such an approach could avoid transaction costs created by the complexities of the art 5(1) list of *indirect bases of jurisdiction*; avoid burden of proof uncertainties; and avoid the limitations that art 5(2) creates in countries that do not use private international law rules to play a substantive role in consumer or employee protection).

[27] For a more detailed explanation of US judgments recognition law, see Ronald A Brand, 'Federal Judicial Center International Litigation Guide: Recognition and Enforcement of Foreign Judgments' (2013) 74 U Pitt L Rev 491, <https://www.fjc.gov/content/recognition-and-enforcement-foreign-judgments-0>.

[28] 159 US 113 (1895).

1. Internal Judgments Recognition: Sister State Judgments

When the judgment in question is from another US state, or from a US federal court, the Full Faith and Credit clause found in Article IV of the US Constitution provides the rule for recognition. That clause provides that, 'Full Faith and Credit shall be given in each [s]tate to the public Acts, Records, and judicial Proceedings of every other [s]tate.' Thus: 2.19

> The concept of full faith and credit is central to our system of jurisprudence. Ours is a union of [s]tates, each having its own judicial system capable of adjudicating the rights and responsibilities of the parties brought before it. Given this structure, there is always a risk that two or more [s]tates will exercise their power over the same case or controversy, with the uncertainty, confusion, and delay that necessarily accompany relitigation of the same issue.... [I]n order to fulfill this constitutional mandate, 'the judgment of a [s]tate court should have the same credit, validity, and effect, in every other court of the United States, which it had in the [s]tate where it was pronounced.'[29]

Even though the language of the Full Faith and Credit clause states that each 'state' shall accord full faith and credit to the acts of each other 'state', the clause has been applied to encompass recognition within the entire state-federal judicial system.[30] Thus, a judgment rendered in any state or federal court in the United States is entitled to full recognition in any other state or federal court in the United States. 2.20

2. Foreign Judgments: Federal Common Law Roots

Judgments from foreign courts are not subject to the Full Faith and Credit clause in Article IV of the US Constitution. In his 1895 opinion in *Hilton v Guyot*,[31] Justice Gray began by focusing on comity, which he described as 'neither a matter of absolute obligation, on the one hand, nor a mere courtesy and good will, upon the other', but 'the recognition which one nation allows within its territory to the legislative, executive, or judicial acts of another nation'.[32] He found comity to require that: 2.21

> [W]here there has been opportunity for a full and fair trial abroad before a court of competent jurisdiction, conducting the trial upon regular proceedings, after due citation or voluntary appearance of the defendant, and under a system of jurisprudence likely to secure an impartial administration of justice between the citizens of its own country and those of other countries, and there is nothing to show either prejudice in the court, or in the system of laws under which it was sitting, or fraud in procuring the judgment, or any other special reason why the comity of this nation should not allow it full effect, the merits of the case should not, in an action brought in this country upon the judgment, be tried afresh.[33]

29 *Underwriters National Assurance Co v NC Guaranty Assn*, 455 US 691, 703–04 (1982).
30 See 28 USC § 1738.
31 159 US 113 (1895).
32 ibid 163–64.
33 ibid 202–03.

This did not, however, prevent denial of recognition upon the finding that a requirement of reciprocity found in general principles of international law prevented recognition.[34]

2.22 While in *Hilton* the Court applied a federal common law rule, the early decades of the twentieth century saw the development of state law, with both state and federal courts applying state law, including state common law.[35] As the question became one determined under state substantive law, courts continued to apply the comity analysis from *Hilton*, with most states abandoning the reciprocity requirement.[36] While the National Conference of Commissioners on Uniform State Laws ('Uniform Law Commission' or ULC) has promulgated two uniform acts, attempting to unify state law on the matter, the law in about one-third of the states remains the common law, so there is now a mix of common law and enactments of uniform acts. The Restatement (Fourth) Foreign Relations Law, created by the American Law Institute to recognize common principles, has recently adopted a position following the 2005 version of the ULC's uniform act, but including a rule of reciprocity.[37]

3. Foreign Judgments: State Statutes and the Retained Common Law

2.23 In 1962, the ULC adopted the Uniform Foreign Money-Judgments Recognition Act ('1962 Recognition Act'). The Act 'applies to any foreign judgment that is final and conclusive and enforceable where rendered even though an appeal therefrom is pending or it is subject to appeal',[38] making such a judgment 'conclusive between the parties to the extent that it grants or denies recovery of a sum of money'.[39] The Act then builds on the federal Full Faith and Credit clause, providing that, when no grounds are proven for non-recognition under section 4, the judgment is 'enforceable in the same manner as the judgment of a sister [s]tate which is entitled to full faith and credit'.[40] The 1962 Act remains the law in a number of states.

2.24 The ULC updated and revised the 1962 Recognition Act in 2005, adopting the Uniform Foreign-Country Money Judgments Recognition Act ('2005 Recognition Act'). The 2005 Recognition Act maintains the same basic approach as the 1962 Act, but adds several grounds for non-recognition and deals explicitly with matters such as the method for seeking recognition and burdens of proof.[41]

[34] ibid 210–28.

[35] *Erie RR v Tompkins*, 304 US 64 (1938). See *Johnston v Compagnie Generale Transatlantique*, 242 NY 381, 152 NE 121 (1926).

[36] See, eg, *Somportex Ltd v Phila Chewing Gum Corp*, 453 F.2d 435, 440 n.8 (3d Cir. 1971), *cert. denied*, 405 US 1017 (1972) (stating that the reciprocity element of the *Hilton* holding has 'received no more than desultory acknowledgment' as a 'condition precedent to the recognition of comity').

[37] Restatement (Fourth) Foreign Relations Law (2018) §§ 481–484.

[38] 1962 Recognition Act § 2.

[39] 1962 Recognition Act § 3.

[40] ibid.

[41] The 2005 Act provides: (1) that if recognition of a foreign judgment is sought as an original matter, the judgment creditor must file an action to obtain recognition (a party may also raise the issue of recognition in a counterclaim, cross-claim, or defense, seeking preclusive recognition), 2005 Recognition Act § 6; (2) that the party seeking recognition has the burden of proving that the judgment falls within the scope of the Act, and the party seeking non-recognition has the burden of proving any of the grounds available for non-recognition, 2005 Recognition Act § 3(c), 4(d); and (3) a statute of limitations prohibiting an action requesting recognition any time after the earlier to occur of the date on which the judgment is no longer enforceable in the country of origin or fifteen years from the time the judgment is effective in the country of origin. 2005 Recognition Act § 9.

Section 4 of the 2005 Recognition Act provides the core of the rules for recognition of a foreign judgment, listing both mandatory (§ 4(b)) and discretionary (§ 4(c)) grounds for non-recognition once the initial requirements (a final and conclusive money judgment) have been met: **2.25**

SECTION 4. Standards for Recognition of Foreign-Country Judgment.

(a) Except as otherwise provided in subsections (b) and (c), a court of this State shall recognize a foreign-country judgment to which this [act] applies.

(b) A court of this State may not recognize a foreign-country judgment if:

(1) the judgment was rendered under a judicial system that does not provide impartial tribunals or procedures compatible with the requirements of due process of law;

(2) the foreign court did not have personal jurisdiction over the defendant; or

(3) the foreign court did not have jurisdiction over the subject matter.

(c) A court of this State need not recognize a foreign-country judgment if:

(1) the defendant in the proceeding in the foreign court did not receive notice of the proceeding in sufficient time to enable the defendant to defend;

(2) the judgment was obtained by fraud that deprived the losing party of an adequate opportunity to present its case;

(3) the judgment or the [cause of action] [claim for relief] on which the judgment is based is repugnant to the public policy of this State or of the United States;

(4) the judgment conflicts with another final and conclusive judgment;

(5) the proceeding in the foreign court was contrary to an agreement between the parties under which the dispute in question was to be determined otherwise than by proceedings in that foreign court;

(6) in the case of jurisdiction based only on personal service, the foreign court was a seriously inconvenient forum for the trial of the action;

(7) the judgment was rendered in circumstances that raise substantial doubt about the integrity of the rendering court with respect to the judgment; or

(8) the specific proceeding in the foreign court leading to the judgment was not compatible with the requirements of due process of law.

(d) A party resisting recognition of a foreign-country judgment has the burden of establishing that a ground for nonrecognition stated in subsection (b) or (c) exists.

The last two grounds for non-recognition in section 4(c) were new to the 2005 Recognition Act and do not exist in the 1962 Recognition Act.

In March of 2022, the Uniform Law Commission listed twenty-eight states and the District of Columbia as having enacted the 2005 Recognition Act.[42] Ten states and the US Virgin Islands were listed as having enacted the 1962 Recognition Act without having replaced it with the 2005 Recognition Act.[43] This leaves twelve states and Puerto Rico as having retained common law rules for recognition and enforcement of foreign judgments. **2.26**

[42] https://www.uniformlaws.org/committees/community-home?CommunityKey = ae280c30–094a-4d8f-b722–8dcd614a8f3e.

[43] ibid.

2.27 The rules on recognition of a foreign judgment have developed state-by-state, but with substantial uniformity. That uniformity has been reflected in the Restatements of Foreign Relations Law prepared by the American Law Institute (ALI). In 2018, the Restatement (Fourth) Foreign Relations Law, updated some of the provisions of the Third Restatement, including those dealing with the recognition and enforcement of foreign judgments. Those provisions now read as follows:

§ 481. Recognition of Foreign Judgments

Except as provided in §§ 483–484 and § 489, a final, conclusive, and enforceable judgment of a court of a foreign State granting or denying recovery of a sum of money, or determining a legal controversy, is entitled to recognition by courts in the United States.

§ 482. Procedure to Obtain Recognition

A person seeking recognition of a foreign judgment must either initiate a civil proceeding for that purpose in a court of competent jurisdiction or properly raise the issue in an existing proceeding.

§ 483. Mandatory Grounds for Nonrecognition

A court in the United States will not recognize a judgment of a court of a foreign State if:

(a) the judgment was rendered under a judicial system that does not provide impartial tribunals or procedures compatible with fundamental principles of fairness;
(b) the court that rendered the judgment did not have personal jurisdiction or subject matter jurisdiction; or
(c) the judgment rested on a claim of defamation and the SPEECH Act forbids its recognition or enforcement.

§ 484. Discretionary Grounds for Nonrecognition

To the extent provided by applicable law, a court in the United States need not recognize a judgment of a court of a foreign State if:

(a) the party resisting recognition did not receive adequate notice of the proceeding in the foreign court in sufficient time to enable it to defend;
(b) the judgment was obtained by fraud that deprived the party resisting recognition of an adequate opportunity to present its case;
(c) the judgment or the claim on which the judgment is based is repugnant to the public policy of the State in which recognition is sought or of the United States;
(d) the judgment conflicts with another final and conclusive judgment;

(e) the proceeding in the foreign court was contrary to an agreement between the parties to commit resolution of the dispute in question exclusively to another forum;
(f) in cases in which the foreign court's jurisdiction rested only on personal service, the foreign court was a seriously inconvenient forum for resolution of the dispute;
(g) the judgment was rendered in circumstances that raise substantial doubt about the integrity of the rendering court with respect to the judgment;
(h) the specific proceeding in the foreign court leading to the judgment was not compatible with fundamental principles of fairness; or
(i) the courts of the State of origin would not recognize a comparable U.S. judgment.

The grounds for non-recognition found in §§ 483 and 484 now track, almost verbatim, those grounds found in the 2005 Recognition Act. Notably, however, § 484(i) inserts a reciprocity rule that was not found in the Third Restatement, effectively returning the law to that stated in 1895 by Justice Gray in *Hilton v Guyot*.[44] Whether each state that retains a common law approach to the matter includes a rule of reciprocity is, however, not dictated by the Restatement and is for the courts of that state to determine. Some state legislatures have added a reciprocity requirement (either mandatory or discretionary) when enacting the 1962 Recognition Act or the 2005 Recognition Act.[45]

B. The European Union

1. Internal Judgments Recognition: Judgments from EU Member States

In the European Union (EU), the Brussels I (Recast) Regulation provides the rules for recognition and enforcement of judgments across internal EU borders.[46] Article 36 of the Regulation provides that '[a] judgment given in a Member State shall be recognized in the other Member States without any special procedure being required'. This is tempered by Article 45, which provides that 'the recognition of a judgment shall be refused': 2.28

(a) if such recognition is manifestly contrary to public policy (ordre public) in the Member State addressed;
(b) where the judgment was given in default of appearance, if the defendant was not served with the document which instituted the proceedings or with an equivalent document in sufficient time and in such a way as to enable him to arrange for his defense, unless the defendant failed to commence proceedings to challenge the judgment when it was possible for him to do so;
(c) if the judgment is irreconcilable with a judgment given between the same parties in the Member State addressed;
(d) if the judgment is irreconcilable with an earlier judgment given in another Member State or in a third State involving the same cause of action and between the same parties,

[44] See nn 29–38, and accompanying text.
[45] See, eg, Ariz Rev Stat 12–3252(B)(2); Fla Stat § 55.605; Mass Gen Laws ch 235, § 23A.
[46] Brussels I (Recast) Regulation.

provided that the earlier judgment fulfils the conditions necessary for its recognition in the Member State addressed; or

(e) if the judgment conflicts with:
   (i) Sections 3, 4 or 5 of Chapter II where the policyholder, the insured, the beneficiary of the insurance contract, the injured party, the consumer or the employee was the defendant; or
   (ii) Section 6 of Chapter II.

Subparagraph (e), which was added in the 2012 Recast Regulation, is an explicit exception to the Article 45(3) rule that 'the jurisdiction of the court of origin may not be reviewed'.[47] It allows the recognizing court to revisit the originating court's application of the special rules on jurisdiction over insureds, consumers, and employees. The rationale for assuming that the originating court's application of these particular Brussels I jurisdictional rules is less trustworthy than its application of the other jurisdictional rules of the Regulation is not entirely clear.

2.29 Article 5(2) of the Regulation, by reference to Article 76(1), effectively provides that jurisdictional provisions in the Member States that go beyond those explicitly authorized in the Regulation 'shall not be applicable as against' persons domiciled in a Member State. By prohibiting the use of such 'exorbitant' bases of jurisdiction against a person domiciled in another Member State in the court of origin, the system in the Regulation requires no indirect review of jurisdiction by the court addressed for purposes of recognition and enforcement. Thus, 'the jurisdiction of the court of origin may not be reviewed',[48] any review of the substance of the original decision by the recognizing court is prohibited,[49] and the reviewing court is bound by the findings of fact in the originating court on which jurisdiction was based.[50]

2.30 While a person domiciled in an EU Member State may not be sued in the courts of other Member States where the only source of jurisdiction is one of the Article 5 'exorbitant' bases of jurisdiction, Article 6 allows a defendant not domiciled in a Member State to be subject to such grounds of jurisdiction. Thus, a judgment rendered against a defendant not domiciled in any Member State is enforceable in all Member States, even if rendered under jurisdictional grounds that all other Member States consider to be improper with respect to nationals of another Member State. Article 6(2) extends this result by making national exorbitant jurisdiction provisions available to any plaintiff domiciled in a Member State who asserts jurisdiction against a defendant not domiciled in a Member State.

2.31 The Regulation provides that '[a] judgment given in a Member State which is enforceable in that Member State shall be enforceable in the other Member States without any declaration of enforceability being required'.[51] Thus, the party against whom recognition and enforcement is sought must act to seek refusal of recognition of the judgment.[52]

2. Judgments from Non-Member States

2.32 The recognition and enforcement of judgments from courts outside the EU remains governed by national law and is not covered by the Brussels I (Recast) Regulation. The national

47 Art 45(3) (original art 35(3)) Brussels I (Recast) Regulation.
48 Art 45(3) Brussels I (Recast) Regulation.
49 Art 52 Brussels I (Recast) Regulation.
50 Art 45(2) Brussels I (Recast) Regulation.
51 Art 39 Brussels I (Recast) Regulation.
52 Art 45(1) Brussels I (Recast) Regulation.

laws of EU Member States provide at least three distinct approaches to the recognition and enforcement of foreign judgments. One approach is to require a treaty in order to allow recognition and enforcement. If no treaty exists, then a new local action is required, in which the foreign judgment may be presented as evidence, but not as binding on the decision of the local court. A second approach is to use the national rules of direct jurisdiction in the court addressed for purposes of recognition and enforcement, as rules of indirect jurisdiction in order to provide a gateway test of the judgment presented for recognition. A third approach is to have separate rules of direct and indirect jurisdiction, with the rules of indirect jurisdiction being more limited in scope and nature. These are the general approaches followed in other countries around the world as well, making the set of EU Member State approaches a useful example.

a. Recognition and Enforcement Limited to Judgments from Courts in Treaty States

The Netherlands provides an example of a system in which the Code ostensibly prevents direct recognition and enforcement of a foreign judgment, subject only to treaty exceptions. Article 431 of the Civil Procedure Code of the Netherlands (*Rv*), originally enacted in 1838, provides that: **2.33**

1. Except for what is Stated in articles 985–994 *Rv*, no decision rendered by foreign judges, nor authentic deeds issued abroad can be enforced within the Netherlands.
2. The matters can be dealt with and settled de novo by the Dutch judge.[53]

While this statute appears to preempt any direct use of a foreign judgment, the courts of the Netherlands, including the *Hoge Raad* (the Netherlands Supreme Court), have interpreted the provision to allow recognition of a foreign judgment when:

1) There is proper jurisdiction in the foreign proceedings—'The standard used here is the one of an internationally acceptable forum, of course a standard that does not imply that all the grounds on which a Dutch court assumes jurisdiction in similar cases will also be acceptable when the foreign court bases its jurisdiction on the same grounds (I.e. forum actoris).'[54]
2) The judgment does not infringe Dutch public policy—'This requirement includes a two-level test encompassing on one hand non-violation of core Dutch legal principles and, on the other, the impact such recognition or enforcement of a foreign judgment will have on the Dutch legal system.'[55]
3) The foreign court respected due process standards, 'such as service of process, fair hearing, reasoning of the judgments and the existing of appeal possibilities—essentially includes protection for basic procedural safeguards found at the core of the Dutch legal system.... [T]his condition may very well be introduced under the heading of public policy.'[56]

[53] Translation from Norel Rosner, *The Requirements for Execution of Foreign Money Judgments in the Netherlands Absent a Treaty*, <https://www.llrx.com/2003/01/features-the-requirements-for-execution-of-foreign-money-judgments-in-the-netherlands-absent-a-treaty/>.
[54] ibid. Note that this allows the type of jurisdiction gap discussed in Section IV.B.2.c.
[55] Rosner (n 53).
[56] ibid.

4) The foreign judgment is final and irrevocable in the country of origin—'in itself not a condition but rather a standard showing the point in time when recognition or enforcement takes effect in the Netherlands.'[57]
5) '[T]he foreign decision is not incompatible with a decision of the Dutch court between the same parties, or with a previous decision of a foreign court between the same parties in a dispute concerning the same subject matter and base on the same cause of action, provided that this earlier judgment is subject to recognition in the Netherlands.'[58]

Other EU Member States have similar Code provisions, with varying degrees of judicial liberalization of the rules over time.

b. Direct Jurisdiction Rules as Indirect Jurisdiction Tests

2.34 The use of direct jurisdiction rules to test the jurisdiction of the court of origin in an action for recognition and enforcement of the resulting judgment is the approach taken in the United States,[59] as well as in some EU Member States, including Germany and Italy. This is a mirror-image approach to judgments recognition, with the indirect bases of jurisdiction being the same as the direct bases of jurisdiction. Section 328(1)(1) of the German Code of Civil Procedure has included a requirement that the foreign court from which a judgment originates had 'jurisdiction under German law'.[60] In Italy, Article 64 of Law 218/1995 allows recognition of a foreign judgment when 'the authority rendering the judgement had jurisdiction pursuant to the criteria of jurisdiction in force under Italian law'.[61] Thus, so long as the case could have been brought in the recognizing State on similar jurisdictional facts, the court addressed will accept that jurisdiction was proper in the court of origin.

2.35 Legal systems using direct jurisdiction rules for indirect jurisdiction purposes in the recognition and enforcement of judgments, like the United States,[62] include other bases for non-recognition. Section 328(I) of the German Code of Civil Procedure provides a good example of this approach, with the following text:

I. Recognition of a judgment handed down by a foreign court shall be ruled out if:
   1. the courts of the State to which the foreign court belongs do not have jurisdiction according to German law;
   2. the defendant, who has not entered an appearance in the proceedings and who takes recourse to this fact, has not duly been served the document by which the proceedings were initiated, or not in such time to allow him to defend himself;
   3. the judgment is incompatible with a judgment delivered in Germany, or with an earlier judgment handed down abroad that is to be recognized, or if the proceedings on which such judgment is based are incompatible with proceedings that have become pending earlier in Germany;

57 ibid.
58 *Recognition and Enforcement of Foreign Judgments in the Netherlands*, <https://www.hg.org/legal-articles/recognition-and-enforcement-of-foreign-judgments-in-the-netherlands-54658>.
59 See nn 28–47 and accompanying text.
60 See I Philip Weems, *Enforcement of Money Judgments Abroad FRG-29* (looseleaf, 1993).
61 Art 64(1)(a) Law 218/1995, Italy.
62 See nn 28–47 and accompanying text.

4. the recognition of the judgment would lead to a result that is obviously incompatible with essential principles of German law, and in particular if the recognition is not compatible with fundamental rights;
5. reciprocity has not been granted.[63]

c. *Separate Direct and Indirect Jurisdiction Lists*

An example of a legal system with indirect jurisdiction bases that are more limited than direct jurisdiction bases comes from a State that is no longer a member of the EU. In the United Kingdom, Practice Direction 6B of Part 6 of the Civil Procedure Rules provides a court with discretion to order service outside the jurisdiction of the United Kingdom by listing numerous criteria of eligibility, each of which effectively states an acceptable basis of direct jurisdiction over a foreign defendant.[64] The comparable list for purposes of indirect jurisdiction when a judgment is brought from a foreign court for recognition and enforcement is much more limited. For this purpose, a UK court applies 'The Dicey Test', found in the most recent edition of Dicey, Morris, and Collins, *The Conflict of Laws*,[65] which provides only four grounds of indirect jurisdiction.[66] The resulting direct–indirect jurisdiction gap might be interpreted either as acknowledgement that the longer list of direct bases of jurisdiction found in Practice Direction 6B contains otherwise questionable bases of jurisdiction, or that there is a desire to discriminate against judgments from foreign courts.[67] **2.36**

V. National Law and the Convention

The three basic types of national law approaches to judgments recognition, demonstrated above in the law of individual EU Member States, make the choice of convention architecture in the 2019 Judgments Convention important. Simple reciprocity was rejected in that architecture by including the Article 5(1) list of *criteria of eligibility* that serve as the gateway to circulation of a judgment under the Convention. Also rejected was an approach that would rely on a mirror-image of direct jurisdictional bases in the receiving State. What **2.37**

[63] See <https://www.ilo.org/dyn/natlex/docs/ELECTRONIC/89715/103683/F-595450696/ZPO.pdf>.

[64] Part 6 of the Civil Procedure Rules 1998 of the Supreme Court of England and Wales (CPR), Practice Direction 6B. The list of jurisdictional grounds is tempered by para 6.37, which adds a *forum conveniens* element by granting the court discretion and limiting jurisdiction based on any of the grounds to those cases in which the court is 'satisfied that England and Wales is the proper place in which to bring the claim' <https://www.justice.gov.uk/courts/procedure-rules/civil/rules/part06/pd_part06b#2.1>.

[65] Dicey, Morris, and Collins, *The Conflict of Laws* (16th edn, Sweet & Maxwell 2022) Rule 47 (14R-058) ('Dicey, Morris, and Collins'). See, eg, *Rubin v Eurofinance SA* [2012] UKSC 46, at 7–10, in which Lord Collins, the General Editor of Dicey, Morris, and Collins, follows the 'Dicey Test', and traces its history.

[66] Dicey, Morris, and Collins (n 65) Rule 47. These four grounds are: (1) the judgment debtor was present in the forum State at the time the proceedings were instituted; (2) the judgment debtor was the claimant or counterclaimant in the foreign proceedings; (3) the judgment debtor submitted to jurisdiction voluntarily by appearing; and (4) the judgment debtor had consented to jurisdiction in advance. For further discussion of the *Dicey Rule*, see Ardavan Arzandeh, '"Gateways" within the Civil Procedure Rules and the Future of Service-out Jurisdiction in England' (2019) 15 J Priv Intl L 516.

[67] See Arzandeh (n 66) (suggesting that the direct jurisdiction gateways of Practice Direction 6B have become superfluous and should be abandoned); and Ardavan Arzandeh, 'Reformulating the Common Law Rules on the Recognition and Enforcement of Foreign Judgments' (2017) 39 Legal Studies 56 (recommending that the full list of gateway direct jurisdiction bases found in Practice Direction 6B should be applied for indirect jurisdiction purposes in testing foreign judgments for purposes of recognition and enforcement).

was chosen was an approach that allows States to continue to limit the recognition of foreign judgments by using a list of criteria of eligibility that may be more restrictive than those States use for purposes of direct jurisdiction. This necessarily made the Convention more complex, and thus means that national law remains important when considered in the context of Article 15 of the Convention, especially in States that use their full list of bases of direct jurisdiction as their list of bases of indirect jurisdiction.

3

The History of the Negotiations

I. The Jurisdiction and Judgments Project at the Hague Conference

The 2019 Judgments Convention is the second instrument resulting from a request submitted to the Hague Conference on Private International Law in 1992. Edwin Williamson, then Legal Adviser at the US Department of State, sent a letter at that time to the Secretary General of the Hague Conference proposing that the Conference take up the negotiation of a multilateral convention on the recognition and enforcement of judgments.[1] In October of that year, a Working Group of the Hague Conference on Private International Law 'unanimously recognized the desirability of attempting to negotiate multilaterally through the Hague Conference a convention on recognition and enforcement of judgments'.[2] In May 1993, the Seventeenth Session of the Hague Conference established a Special Commission, not to negotiate an instrument, but to study the matter further.[3] **3.01**

A June 1994 meeting of a Special Commission on the Question of the Recognition and Enforcement of Foreign Judgments in Civil and Commercial Matters determined that it would be 'advantageous to draw up a convention on jurisdiction, recognition and enforcement of foreign judgments in civil and commercial matters' and recommended that 'this question ... be included in the Agenda for the future work of the Conference at its Eighteenth Session'.[4] In June 1995, the Special Commission on General Affairs and Policy of the Conference recommended to the Eighteenth Session of the Hague Conference that the proposal for a judgments convention be included in the Conference's agenda for future **3.02**

[1] Letter of 5 May 1992 from Edwin D Williamson, Legal Adviser, US Department of State, to Georges Droz, Secretary General, The Hague Conference on Private International Law (5 May 1992) (distributed with Hague Conference document L.c. ON No 15 (92)), <https://2009-2017.state.gov/documents/organization/65973.pdf> accessed 1 July 2023.

[2] *Conclusions of the Working Group Meeting on enforcement of judgments*, 3, Hague Conference on Private International Law, Preliminary Doc No 19 of November 1992 for the attention of the Seventeenth Session.

[3] *Final Act of the Seventeenth Session 17*, Hague Conference on Private International Law (SDU Publishers 1993). At that time, the Hague Conference generally held a Plenary Session every four years. The work of the Conference, however, was accomplished primarily through Special Commissions of governmental experts who met between Plenary Sessions to prepare preliminary drafts of the conventions to be presented, discussed, and adopted at the Plenary Session of the Diplomatic Session.

[4] *Conclusions of the Special Commission of June 1994 on the Question of the Recognition and Enforcement of Foreign Judgments in Civil and Commercial Matters*, Hague Conference on Private International Law, Preliminary Doc No 1 (June 1994).

work.[5] The negotiation of such a convention was then included on the Agenda of the Hague Conference's Nineteenth Session as part of the Final Act of its Eighteenth Session, held in October of 1996.[6]

3.03 The process in the Eighteenth Session had begun with consideration of a report prepared by Professor Arthur von Mehren, and included with the original proposal in 1992, which suggested preparation of a 'mixed' convention.[7] Earlier Hague Conventions,[8] had been described as single (sometimes referred to as 'simple') conventions, with rules dealing only with questions of jurisdiction in an indirect manner, for purposes of review in a court asked to recognize or enforce a judgment from another country. At the time negotiations began in the 1990s, the existing model came from what was then the European Community: the Brussels and Lugano Conventions.[9] Those conventions are often referred to as 'double conventions', providing both rules of direct jurisdiction applicable in the court in which the case is first brought ('the court of origin'), as well as rules applicable in the court of another State asked to recognize or enforce the resulting judgment ('the court addressed'). This allows greater uniformity in both the statement of the rules of direct jurisdiction and in the resulting jurisprudence through which they are interpreted and applied, especially when there is a single court (as in the European Union (EU)) to provide that interpretation. This preempts the need for indirect consideration of the jurisdiction of the court of origin by the court requested to recognize or enforce a judgment, because the check on jurisdiction comes in the court of origin, under rules of jurisdiction agreed to by all Contracting States and subject to uniform interpretation by the Court of Justice of the European Union (CJEU). The Brussels Convention has evolved into EU internal legislation as the Brussels I (Recast) Regulation.[10]

3.04 The mixed convention model proposed by Professor von Mehren would have provided rules for both direct jurisdiction in the court of origin and the recognition and enforcement of judgments in the court later addressed, as is the case in a double convention. Unlike the Brussels and Lugano Conventions, however, those rules would be neither exhaustive nor

[5] *Conclusions of the Special Commission of June 1995 on General Affairs and Policy of the Conference*, Hague Conference on Private International Law, Preliminary Doc No 9, 31 (December 1995).

[6] *Final Act of the Eighteenth Session*, para B(1), *Hague Conference on Private International Law* (19 October 1996).

[7] Arthur T von Mehren, 'Recognition Convention Study: Final Report' (copy on file with authors).

[8] Convention of 1 February 1971 on the Recognition and Enforcement of Foreign Judgments in Civil and Commercial Matters, <https://www .hcch.net/en/instruments/conventions/full-text/?cid = 78>; Convention of 1 June 1970 on the Recognition of Divorces and Legal Separations, <https://www.hcch.net/en/instruments/conventions/specialised-sections/divorce>.

[9] The Brussels Convention was completed among the existing members of the European Economic Community (EEC) in 1968. European Convention on Jurisdiction and Enforcement of Judgments in Civil and Commercial Matters, done at Brussels, 27 September 1968, 41 OJ Eur Comm (C 27/1) (26 January 1998) (consolidated and updated version of the 1968 Convention and the Protocol of 1971, following the 1996 accession of the Republic of Austria, the Republic of Finland and the Kingdom of Sweden) ('Brussels Convention'). On 1 May 1999, the Amsterdam Treaty became effective for the European Union (EU) Member States, and competence for coordination of rules on jurisdiction and recognition of judgments now lies with the Community institutions, which have used that authority to replace the Brussels Convention with a Community Regulation. Council Reg (EC) No 44/2001 of 22 December 2000 on jurisdiction and the recognition and enforcement of judgments in civil and commercial matters, [2000] OJ L 12/1 ('Brussels I Regulation'). The Lugano Convention was agreed in 1989 between the members of the EEC and the members of the European Free Trade Association (EFTA). Convention on Jurisdiction and Enforcement of Judgments in Civil and Commercial Matters [1988] OJ L 319/9 ('Lugano Convention'), reproduced in (1989) 28 ILM 620.

[10] Reg (EU) No 1215/2012 of the European Parliament and of the Council of 12 December 2012 on jurisdiction and the recognition and enforcement of judgments in civil and commercial matters (recast) [2012] OJ L351/1 ('Brussels I Recast Regulation').

exclusive. A list of required bases of direct jurisdiction (which all Contracting States must apply internally) would be juxtaposed against a list of prohibited direct bases of jurisdiction (which no Contracting State could apply internally). Judgments founded on required bases of jurisdiction would be entitled to recognition and enforcement, and (because the control function would exist in the court of origin) there should be no judgments resulting from prohibited bases of jurisdiction.

Unlike the double convention approach, the jurisdictional lists in a mixed convention **3.05** would be neither exhaustive nor exclusive, and any jurisdictional basis not included on either of the required or prohibited lists would be permitted to exist outside the convention structure. A judgment in a case in which jurisdiction was founded on such a permitted (but not required) jurisdictional basis would not be entitled to recognition and enforcement under the convention, thus encouraging litigating parties to bring cases in courts that have jurisdiction on a required basis. A judgment based only on a permitted basis of jurisdiction would be subject to review in the court addressed for purposes of recognition or enforcement in the manner applicable under its domestic law, without any treaty obligation to recognize or enforce the judgment.

A Special Commission on the Question of Jurisdiction, and Recognition and Enforcement **3.06** of Foreign Judgments in Civil and Commercial Matters met in June 1997, in March 1998, in November 1998, in June 1999, and in October 1999, to consider a convention on international jurisdiction and the effects of foreign judgments in civil and commercial matters.[11] In November 1998 the first document containing draft language for convention provisions was issued by the Drafting Committee,[12] containing provisions addressing issues of convention scope, required bases of jurisdiction, provisional and protective matters, prohibited grounds of jurisdiction, *lis pendens*, declining jurisdiction (*forum non conveniens*), rules of recognition, legal aid, and damages. It was considered further during two weeks in June and one week in October 1999, at which time a Preliminary Draft Convention text was produced.[13]

While the original 1992 Working Group had recommended the negotiation of a mixed **3.07** convention,[14] the 1999 Preliminary Draft Convention text had the language of a double convention. Only in June of 1999 did the Special Commission vote specifically to pursue a mixed convention model,[15] but by then it was too late to make the major changes that would meet that goal. The draft language reflected that of earlier double conventions, particularly the Brussels Convention.

[11] *Preliminary Results of the Work of the Special commission concerning the Proposed Convention on International Jurisdiction and Foreign Judgments in Civil and Commercial Matters*, Hague Conference on Private International Law, Information Document (September 1997); see Catherine Kessedjian, *Synthesis of the Work of the Special Commission of March 1998 on International Jurisdiction and the Effects of Foreign Judgments in Civil and Commercial Matters*, Hague Conference on Private International Law, Preliminary Doc No 9 (July 1998).

[12] *Special Commission on International Jurisdiction and the Effects of Foreign Judgments in Civil and Commercial Matters*, Hague Conference on Private International Law, Working Doc No 144 (20 November 1998) ('Committee Draft').

[13] The text of the Preliminary Draft Convention is available at <http://www .hcch.net/e/conventions/draft36e. html>.

[14] *Conclusions of the Working Group Meeting on Enforcement of Judgments*, Hague Conference on Private International Law, Preliminary Doc No 19 of November 1992 for the attention of the Seventeenth Session.

[15] *Preliminary Draft Convention on Jurisdiction and the Effects of Judgments in Civil and Commercial Matters*, adopted provisionally by the Special Commission, Hague Conference on Private International Law, Special Commission on International Jurisdiction and the Effects of Foreign Judgments in Civil and Commercial Matters, Working Doc No 241 (18 June 1999).

3.08 Hague Conventions usually are finalized and adopted at a Diplomatic Session, after the Special Commission meetings have moved the text to near completion. For the Jurisdiction and Judgments Convention, the Diplomatic Session would have been expected to meet in autumn 2000. However, the problems with the 1999 Preliminary Draft Convention, which would have been the focus of the Diplomatic Session, were substantial. After a letter noting those problems from Jeffrey Kovar, Assistant Legal Adviser for Private International Law at the US Department of State, it was decided both to delay the Diplomatic Session, and to adjust the procedural rules under which the draft text would be considered. The Diplomatic Session was split into two parts. The first part, held in June 2001, applied a consensus process, rather than the standard majoritarian procedures, and resulted in a new text. This Interim Text looked much like the 1999 text, but with many more bracketed provisions, footnotes, and explanations of various positions.[16]

3.09 The June 2001 Interim Text continued to read more like a double convention than the mixed convention the Special Commission had decided to prepare. This was largely a result of the majority vote process carried out prior to June 2001. There was a clear numerical advantage in the negotiations held by European States, and ultimately by the EU (with individual delegations from the fifteen—and later twenty-five—EU Member States voting on specific articles during this process). There were also a number of other States involved who were eager to become Member States of the EU, and thus tended to follow the lead of the EU Member States. This contributed to the fact that the 1999 Preliminary Draft Convention and 2001 Interim Text language looked much like that of the Brussels and Lugano Conventions then in force between European countries. This was a problem especially for the United States, with text that created clear inconsistencies between the civil law-oriented Brussels system approach and a US jurisdictional system incorporating constitutional limitations that produce a very different focus in jurisdictional rules.[17]

II. The 2005 Choice of Court Convention

3.10 In response to the concerns about the 2001 Interim Text, on 24 April 2002, Commission I of the Nineteenth Session of the Hague Conference set up an informal Working Group to consider a convention based on the jurisdictional provisions on which broad agreement existed, beginning with jurisdiction based on agreement of the parties. The Working Group met three times, and in March 2003 produced a draft text of a choice of court convention.[18] That text was circulated among the Member States of the Hague Conference, upon a decision of the Special Commission on General Affairs and Policy of the Conference, held in April 2003. After one more Special Commission meeting was held in April of 2004, the

[16] Hague Conference on Private International Law, Commission II, Jurisdiction and Foreign Judgments in Civil and Commercial Matters, Summary of the Outcome of the Discussion in Commission II of the First Part of the Diplomatic Conference 6–20 June 2001, Interim Text, http://www.hcch.net/index_en.php?act=publications.details&pid= 3499&dtid = 35> ('Interim Text'). Bracketed text, in Hague Conference practice, indicates matters on which final agreement has not been reached.

[17] See, eg, Ronald A Brand, 'Due Process as a Limitation on Jurisdiction in U.S. Courts and a Limitation on the United States at the Hague Conference on Private International Law' (1999) 60 U Pitt L Rev 661.

[18] *Preliminary Result of the Work of the Informal Working Group on the Judgments Project*, Hague Conference on Private International Law, Prel. Doc. No. 8 of March 2003 (corrected) for the attention of the Special Commission of April 2003 on General Affairs and Policy of the Conference, http://www.hcch.net/index_en.php?act=publications .details&pid = 3506&dtid = 35.

Convention on Choice of Court Agreements was adopted at the Twentieth Session of the Hague Conference on Private International Law on 30 June 2005.[19] The Convention was then open for signature and ratification. The official Report on the Convention was issued in early May 2007.[20]

The Hague Convention on Choice of Court Agreements entered into force for Mexico and the EU (for twenty-seven of its (then) Member States—including the United Kingdom) on 1 October 2015;[21] for Singapore on 1 October 2016; for Montenegro on 1 August 2018; and for Denmark on 1 September 2018. Israel, the People's Republic of China, the Republic of North Macedonia, Ukraine, and the United States have signed, but have not ratified, the Convention.[22] **3.11**

The Choice of Court Convention contains three basic rules: Article 5 provides that a court chosen in an exclusive choice of court agreement shall have exclusive jurisdiction over a dispute; Article 6 provides that a court not chosen shall defer to the chosen court; and Article 8 provides that the courts of all Contracting States shall recognize and enforce judgments from a court chosen in an exclusive choice of court agreement, subject to an explicit list of bases for non-recognition found in Article 9.[23] Thus, the 2005 Convention is both a jurisdiction convention (limited to one basis of jurisdiction: consent to exclusive dispute settlement in the courts of one State) and a judgments convention (providing for circulation of judgments from cases based on exclusive choice of court agreements). **3.12**

III. The 2019 Judgments Convention: A Product of a Disjointed Process

In October 2011, the Council on General Affairs and Policy of the Hague Conference established an Experts' Group to consider the resumption of the Judgments Project.[24] There was a desire on the part of some delegations to return to the original project and again draft a convention that would deal with both direct jurisdiction and the recognition and enforcement of judgments. In 2012, the Council on General Affairs and Policy split these two objectives when it established a Working Group to prepare proposals for a judgments convention and **3.13**

[19] The 30 June, 2005, Final Act that included the Hague Convention on Choice of Court Agreements also included an amendment to the Statute of the Hague Conference on Private International Law, authorizing the inclusion of Regional International Economic Organizations (RIEOs) as Members, allowing the European Union to become a Member.

[20] Trevor Hartley & Masato Dogauchi, *Hague Conference on Private International Law Convention of 30 June 2005 on Choice of Court Agreements Explanatory Report*, http://www.hcch.net/upload/expl37e .pdf.

[21] On 31 January 2020, the United Kingdom notified the Depositary that 'the United Kingdom and the European Union have signed, ratified and approved a Withdrawal Agreement, which will enter into force on 1 February 2020 (the "Withdrawal Agreement"). The Withdrawal Agreement includes provisions for a transition period to start on the date the Withdrawal Agreement enters into force and end on 31 December 2020 (the "transition period"). In accordance with the Withdrawal Agreement, during the transition period, European Union law, including the Agreement, continued to be applicable to and in the United Kingdom.' See status table, <http://www.hcch.net/index_en .php?act = conventions.status&cid = 98>.

[22] For Convention status, see <https://www.hcch.net/en/instruments/ conventions/status-table/?cid = 98>.

[23] Convention of 30 June 2005 on Choice of Court Agreements, <https:// www.hcch.net/en/instruments/specialised-sections/choice-of-court>. For a more complete discussion of the Choice of Court Convention, see Ronald A Brand and Paul M Herrup, *The 2005 Hague Convention on Choice of Court Agreements: Commentary and Documents* (Cambridge University Press 2008).

[24] For references to the Hague Conference documents leading up to the conclusion of the Judgments Convention, see https://www.hcch.net/en/ publications-and-studies/details4/?pid = 6842&dtid = 61.

directed the Experts' Group to give further study to a separate jurisdiction convention. The Working Group completed a Proposed Draft Text of a judgments convention in 2016, and the Council on General Affairs and Policy established a Special Commission to move the text forward. The Experts' Group was instructed to move forward on a jurisdiction convention only after a judgments convention text had been concluded.[25]

3.14 Special Commission meetings for a judgments convention were held in June 2016, February 2017, November 2017, and May 2018. The Diplomatic Session concluded on 2 July 2019, with the adoption of the Convention on the Recognition and Enforcement of Foreign Judgments in Civil or Commercial Matters as its Final Text. The Convention entered into force on 1 September 2023 for the European Union (and its Member States) and Ukraine. As of that time, Costa Rica, Israel, Montenegro, North Macedonia, the Russian Federation, the United States, and Uruguay had signed but not ratified.

[25] ibid.

4

Interpretation

Approaches and Methods

I. Introduction

This book is primarily an exercise in interpretation. Most of it is an article-by-article, clause-by-clause, and sometimes word-by-word exposition and interpretation of the text of the Convention. In this chapter, we introduce the methods, approaches, and considerations that guided our interpretation of each of the specific provisions of the Convention. **4.01**

We begin, and try to end, with the words of the text of the Convention. Our approach focuses intensively and often exclusively on official text. Extra-textual sources and canons of interpretation generally are consulted or referenced only if the text itself does not provide an answer. We generally abstain from speculation as to rationales for inclusion or exclusion of particular provisions. The text of any provision could be supported by a variety of different rationales, not necessarily articulated in interventions at the Diplomatic Session that adopted the Convention, or in earlier Special Commission sessions that prepared a draft Convention for consideration by the Diplomatic Session. In that sense, our approach is rigorously positivist. No one interpretation of the object and purpose of the Convention can overcome the text itself. This is why we begin, and end, with analysis of the text. **4.02**

Our approach to interpretation is also rooted in the nature and process of approval of the Convention text. The text is the culmination of a consensus process that resulted in an instrument that, once in force, will impose legal obligations on Contracting States by way of a lock-and-key model of judicial cooperation. The interpretation of the Convention and of any of its parts must begin with the basic fact that this is a global convention created in a global forum intended to operate globally to open the door of one legal system to a public act (issuance of a judgment by a court) of another. This basic fact suggests that, ideally, interpretation should favour giving the terms in the Convention a meaning autonomous to **4.03** this Convention, unless the Convention is best read as pointing to a particular national law or general international law.

4.04 The consensus process that produced the Convention places special emphasis on the words in the provisions of the Convention; those words and nothing else were the subjects of consensus and thus create the obligations contained in the Convention. In some instances, text was included where no delegation objected to the inclusion. This does not suggest that all delegations supported the text or any particular policy underlying that text. Therefore, this reveals that, at most, delegations were willing to accept some treaty provisions in the spirit of compromise and in the hope that the process would result in a treaty to which no delegation would object. Accordingly, we are cautious about finding in the text either the imposition of an international legal obligation or the invasion of sovereign internal arrangements unless clearly stated by the consensus text.

II. Interpretive Challenges

4.05 We will return to the focus on the treaty text, but another set of issues first must be addressed. The Convention terms and rules present at least three interpretive challenges. The first challenge is to identify the source that will give meaning to the terms contained in the text, namely whether a given term requires an autonomous Convention meaning, has its meaning taken from some general international or comparative law referent, or should be given the meaning it has in the law of the State of judgment origin, or the law of the requested State for purposes of recognition and enforcement. The second challenge, regardless of the source, is how to interpret terms and to understand the force of provisions that may be ambiguous, vague, or even pragmatically nonsensical.

4.06 The first dimension to the third interpretive challenge is a lack of autonomous definitions of Convention terms. Of the critical concepts that determine the scope of the Convention, only 'judgment' is defined in the Convention (and that definition raises issues as well). Intensive definitions in Article 3 are limited to two explicitly defined terms (defendant and judgment), and a third (indirectly defined) term (habitual residence of non-natural persons). There is virtually no grist within the Convention for formation of extensive definitions. For example, the Convention does not provide a definition of the basic concept required for matters falling within its scope, namely 'civil or commercial matters'. The only real list of concepts identifies those matters to which the Convention does not apply in Article 2, which thus tells us what is not in the Convention. Yet the Convention may call for an autonomous meaning for these and other key concepts. In these circumstances, the approach we will follow towards definitions is an operational, functional, pragmatic approach. The meaning of a term will rest heavily on what the term does in the Convention, or in a particular rule, or what the term has done to it, as subject or object within the text. This requires careful examination of the various occurrences of a term in the text, both to discern similarities and differences, and to find a common-sense appreciation of how each term can best be put to use in its litigation context. Let us be quite clear: the field of reference for this exercise is the text of the Convention, leavened where appropriate with the text of the earlier Convention on Choice of Court Agreements (COCA). This is a general inquiry, not one trapped in the details of a particular case in litigation; it is not an invitation to courts to succumb to the temptation to torture the text when faced with 'exceptional' cases or 'bad' results.

A second dimension of this third interpretive challenge, one that illuminates some of the Convention's terms, is that the Convention is permeated with public power and public action: it begins with an exercise of public power by a public institution acting pursuant to public standards, a 'judgment', and ends with an exercise of public power by a public institution acting pursuant to public standards, a decision to 'recognize' or 'enforce' that judgment. We must ask not only what any given term does in the Convention, but also what the Convention purports to ask of the public bodies that do its work. A component of the development of the content of the terms will be the extent to which a proposed aspect of that term sits well with an exercise of public power, such as the propriety of bringing the legal system and its potentially coercive powers to bear on persons, and the costs to the public of a Contracting State in doing so. The Convention creates international law obligations for the States that become party to it, and its interpretation should take the nature of such obligations into account, including the possibility that a given interpretation may make States less willing to become party to the Convention. It must be stressed again, however, that this aspect of the inquiry is categorical, not case-by-case.[1] **4.07**

A third dimension to the pragmatic approach to the interpretation of terms within the Convention is the role the Convention can play as a type of mutual legal assistance treaty in a world of separate but increasingly interconnected sovereign States. We will find some guidance in interpretation by considering the features that best help a term function in this type of Convention. **4.08**

Often, we will be satisfied to present the logical possibilities available to interpret a term and some of the implications that must be weighed when choosing among those possibilities. Fire-walking over doctrinal pyres, almost always fuelled by the *a priori* metaphysical commitments of the arsonist, usually results not to light the eyes of the reader but to scorch the feet of the pedestrian.[2] **4.09**

III. Sources of Law in Interpreting the Convention Text

Even when the Convention employs language that runs in parallel with language from a given legal system, the use of the words in this Convention is not and should not be captive to existing concepts or use of terms in a particular municipal or regional system of law. The point is made explicit in Article 20, that '[i]n the interpretation of this Convention, regard shall be had to its international character and to the need to promote uniformity in its application'. **4.10**

There is no international court to determine the 'correct' application of Convention provisions. The Convention will be interpreted and applied by national courts in requested States in the context of particular cases. If those national courts take a parochial approach to the Convention, the benefits of the Convention in terms of uniformity, certainty, and **4.11**

[1] The use of 'public policy' as a way to resolve these issues on an inspection case-by-case and country-by-country has been rejected in the text of this and other Hague Conventions, see, eg, art 7(1)(c) and art 9(e) of COCA.

[2] We are content to follow John Locke, for whom 'it is ambition enough to be employed as an under-labourer in clearing the ground a little, and removing some of the rubbish that lies in the way to knowledge ....'. John Locke, *An Essay Concerning Human Understanding* (Paul Niddich ed, Clarendon Press 1975) 9–10.

efficiency will be lost. Loss of these benefits, in turn, might encourage parties not to use the Convention, but rather to find other mechanisms to deal with the additional risks and costs of trans-border commerce. The Convention will fail if it is used as an instrument to project one particular law or concepts drawn from one particular legal system. Success will require an exercise of self-discipline and a willingness on the part of courts to avoid confining their interpretive inquiry to the familiar.

4.12 Yet the proposition that Convention terms should be given an autonomous meaning unless the Convention points to another source of law is more easily said than done. Part of the problem is a product of the traditional reluctance of Hague Conventions in this area to define terms. As noted, while the Convention provides definitions in Article 3, it contains three items, one of which is not a definition (or is very narrow to the extent that it might be considered to be a definition), and two of which do not receive frequent usage in the text. Yet the Convention bursts with undefined terms that call for an autonomous Convention meaning, such as critical scope terms (eg 'civil or commercial' in art 1.1) or gateway terms with respect to recognition or enforcement (eg 'review of the merits' in art 4.2) that should not hold the operation of the Convention hostage to local law.

4.13 Our approach to this situation builds upon a number of considerations. At the outset, we must acknowledge that it will be difficult in many instances to craft a single, rigid Convention definition, particularly with respect to terms that have well-worn and entrenched local meanings and that are embedded in national legal systems. Realistically, the best that can emerge is not a rigid designator but a Convention 'sense' of a term: a field of application confined to a neighbourhood of meaning that might not be completely uniform from State to State, but will result in the set of decisions under the Convention constituting a tight cluster on a given topic. The key determinant should be not *a priori* metaphysics but actual results. Thus, at various points the Convention uses phrases such as 'arose out of' or 'based on' or 'related to' to express a connection between such things as conduct and a claim, or conduct and a judgment, or a claim and a judgment. Much may pivot on the meaning of such terms, but Contracting States should not expect to achieve an exact Convention definition for such terms in practice; the goal will be to get a shared sense that, when applied, gives reasonable results. To achieve that sense, we take a pragmatic and operational approach: what makes the best sense in terms of use and operation of the Convention provisions. This is a Convention designed to attract widespread ratification and use: a rigid designation that makes no sense in terms of the operation of the Convention, would undermine prospects for widespread acceptance of the Convention and should be avoided.

4.14 As noted, the Convention is festooned with scores of undefined terms. The ability of national courts to generate a precise uniform definition is limited (and ancillary methods, such as academic *a priori* expostulation, tend to obscure rather than enlighten). Nor can we do so. Nor, often, do we try. When we view a term as requiring an autonomous Convention sense, often this book tries to provide the criteria that courts should examine and the goals they should keep in mind in fashioning that sense, rather than offering *ex cathedra* our own stipulation, because our future world is quite likely to be surprisingly different from the past. In these circumstances, the appropriate role for a commentary may be to present the logically possible interpretations or permutations of a rule, and some of the considerations that might be brought to bear in making choices among them. In those situations, largely *a priori* pronouncements on an abstract basis as to the 'proper' reading of a text simply lends what authority the commentator may have to a position that rests on fragile empirical foundations. There simply are some things that counsel a certain modesty, and abstention from trying to bind our successors. They will have a far better basis in experience to draw conclusions.

The dynamism of global mobility raises another issue: whether the terms of the Convention require a static or a dynamic interpretation. Is the meaning of a term to be that at the time of adoption of the text, the time of ratification for each State, the time when each State accepts treaty relations with another, or at the time of the request for recognition or enforcement?[3] This question is illustrative of one of the inescapable problems in the Convention: the need to balance predictability with the flexibility necessary to make the Convention actually work and work well in a changing global environment. **4.15**

When the Convention deploys a term that, explicitly or pragmatically, cannot be given a Convention sense, alternative sources for interpretation are the law of the State of origin or the law of the requested State. But to suggest that one of these should bind the other in the interpretation of the treaty would be misleading. Nonetheless, local law remains a critical component of the application and interpretation of the Convention.[4] National law will govern the operation of the Convention at numerous points. This was a deliberate choice. The Convention cannot force dual interpretations of unitary national law—one interpretation for proceedings under the Convention and another interpretation for everything else. Nor can it force a singular interpretation of the Convention and the otherwise-applicable national law. Obviously, in implementing the Convention, it would be desirable for Contracting States to examine their laws to determine if specific modifications to accommodate the Convention are appropriate. However, there is no obligation under the Convention that they do so. **4.16**

Generally, we turn to the law of the State of origin if the term involves a specific step that a person takes in a legal process in that State. This situation often occurs in conjunction with a reference to a core scope or gateway term that, itself, should be given a Convention sense rather than being bound to the law of the State of origin. These situations call for a form of depecage. For example, a number of provisions refer to the 'time' at which 'proceedings' were 'instituted' or when a person became a 'party' to the proceedings in the court of origin. The Convention does not give a definition of what constitutes, for example, a 'proceeding', yet taking the definition of the term from either the law of the State of origin or the law of the requested State introduces significant uncertainty and potential unfairness in recognition or enforcement under the Convention. Thus, courts should strive to fashion a Convention sense of what constitutes a 'proceeding' under the Convention. As will be seen, our proposal is that anything counts as a 'proceeding' for this purpose if it is an action or activity in a court that is subject to general and neutral rules and can result in a 'judgment' within the meaning of Article 3.2 of the Convention. However, the 'time of institution' refers to a concrete step taken by a person in the legal system of the State of origin, and should be fixed according to the criteria provided in that law. **4.17**

That said, our general default inclination in the absence or unlikelihood of a Convention sense to a term is to look to the law of the requested State as source. It is the requested State that **4.18**

[3] Customary international law, as reflected in Art 31(3)(b) of the Vienna Convention of the Law of Treaties (VCLT), allows for subsequent practice in the application of a treaty to be taken into account in interpreting that treaty.

[4] However, choice of law clauses in choice of court agreements or in trust designations may come into play in, eg Art 5.1(k) and (m).

bears the burden of legal obligations created by the Convention. It is that State whose powers are being invoked, including, potentially, its coercive powers over persons and property. This also flows from the choice in the Convention to regulate indirect jurisdiction only. It is the duty and obligation of the requested court to measure and evaluate the relevant connection to the State of origin. How the law of the State of origin classifies connections—or whether it recognizes or gives significance to a particular connection—is not determinative. In any event, it is not reasonable to expect or demand that each Contracting State be acquainted with the internal law of dozens of other Contracting States that might be applicable at any given time to a myriad of situations that result in judgments to which the Convention might apply. Yet such a demand would put each Contracting State in a position of having to exercise its coercive power without having a good sense *ex ante* of when that power might be invoked or how it must be applied. This would constitute a significant deterrent to ratification.

4.19 However, national law, and especially the law of the requested State, does not apply without constraints, whether contained within the Convention or closely connected to it. Within the Convention, Article 20 requires that, '[i]n the interpretation of this Convention, regard shall be had to its international character and to the need to promote uniformity in its application'. Even when applying national law, courts have a Convention obligation to give regard to the international context of the Convention and the need to avoid disparate divisive results. Beyond the four corners of the Convention, international law and considerations of the international system may further constrain the operation of national law, especially of the requested State. At a general level, the international law of treaties may place independent limitations on the content of national law that might be applied, for example, if the particular national law content might lead to a result that contravenes other treaty terms. More specifically, some of the terms or references in the Convention are taken from other international instruments: courts in interpreting those terms should give due regard to the evolving jurisprudence regarding those terms in the other instruments. (An example is provided in art 2(1)(p), providing that the Convention shall not apply generally to 'antitrust (competition)' but permits application with respect to conduct uniformly considered to be illegal use of combinations or a monopoly position. The parameters of such hard-core cartel conduct lean heavily on work done by the Organization for Economic Cooperation and Development (OECD), and interpretation of the concept in this Convention properly should take account of evolution in international competition law, as expressed in influential international instruments such as those of the OECD while still looking to the words selected by the negotiators of this Convention.

4.20 Thus, the Convention navigates between the Scylla of an imposed uniformity and the Charybdis of respect for local values enshrined in national law and policy. Approaching either too closely would produce a document incapable of general acceptance. There is an inherent tension arising from the very structure of the Convention, which explicitly or implicitly uses national law as scaffolding around the central pillars of the Convention.

4.21 An additional, important source for interpretation requires mention, namely, the French language text of the Convention. The official languages of the Hague Conference are English and French. The text of the Convention in the two languages is equally authoritative. This commentary begins with and is based upon the English language version, but with consultation of the French language version.[5]

[5] In the process of drafting the French language text of the Convention, the Drafting Committee reported that it made some minor divergences from the French language text of COCA. This was done to achieve slight

IV. Extra-Textual Sources of Meaning and Aids to Interpretation

Even after the issues related to the proper source for interpretation of a term are resolved, there remains the inescapable challenge that many of the terms deployed in the Convention are ambiguous or vague. **4.22**

In approaching this challenge, it is important to underscore yet again that the text is a product of a consensus process. There was a consensus that the final text be adopted by the Diplomatic Session. There was a consensus on the form of words of each article of that final text. There was not necessarily a consensus on the import and proper interpretation of each word or clause in every article. The words chosen narrowed the possible interpretive differences, but did not and could not pretend to eliminate them. Ultimately, discrepancies regarding the proper interpretation of the Convention will be resolved by time and practice—precisely as should be the case. However, in that resolution, extra-textual sources will play a part. **4.23**

The interpretation of the Convention will be straightforward in many areas. In addition, there are issues for which a consensus existed on the meaning, and an extra-textual source was created deliberately to preserve and memorialize that consensus understanding. An example of such an understanding is matters for which, after extended discussion and debate, a consensus interpretation of a provision was read into the record of the Diplomatic Session by the chairman of the Drafting Committee.[6] **4.24**

There are other areas, however, where interpretation will require careful consideration of the weight the text will bear when viewed as a consensus document. Thus, on some matters, the text reflects a consensus that the content of the Convention would be given an autonomous meaning, but for which it was neither possible (nor necessarily desirable) in the Diplomatic Session to reduce that meaning to specific language. At the same time, certain textual provisions contain language for which there may have been no clear consensus on either their meaning or the proper method for providing meaning. In such situations, the 'meaning' of a provision cannot be imposed on the basis of a unilateral reading of the text. Thus, as noted above, the content of the Convention to some extent will be developed in subsequent national practice, rather than being frozen in place by the Diplomatic Session.[7] **4.25**

A comprehensive understanding of the Convention thus requires consideration both of the sources that justify a conclusion that there is a consensus regarding the meaning of a particular word in the Convention, and of sources which should be used with caution **4.26**

improvements in accuracy of expression and felicity of style. A colloquy on the floor of the Diplomatic Session established that these variations in the French language text were not intended to create divergences from the meaning of the cognate COCA provision. As a result, a variation in both the English and French language versions of the text of this Convention from the COCA text may signal a variation in meaning between the two instruments; a variation in the respective French language versions alone should be treated with great caution and should not necessarily be taken as a signal of variation in the two Conventions.

[6] For such an example, see Trevor Hartley and Masato Dogauchi, 'Hague Conference on Private International Law, Convention of 30 June 2005 on Choice of Court Agreements, Explanatory Report (2007) 205, setting out a very careful and explicit explanation of the Art 11 rule on damages. The COCA article was repeated word-for-word, and preserved, in the Judgments Convention, art 10.

[7] In addition to development through subsequent national practice, Art 21 provides a mechanism for review of the operation of the Convention by the Hague Conference.

in drawing a conclusion that a consensus exists on a given proposition. Nonetheless, in actual interpretation and application, courts should be wary of invitations to over-analyse: efforts of exegesis should not make the Convention more complicated than it needs to be. The following goes on to discuss the extra-textual sources that aid in interpretation.

A. The Preamble

4.27 The Preamble to the Convention was adopted as part of the consensus process, and may be consulted to assist in fixing the meaning of terms of the Convention, as well as illuminating the background and context for each of the provisions of the Convention. However, the substance of the preamble was not debated at the Diplomatic Session when the provisions were introduced. The Preamble states:

> The States Parties to the present Convention,
>
> Desiring to promote effective access to justice for all and to facilitate rule-based multilateral trade and investment, and mobility, through enhanced judicial co-operation,
>
> Believing that such co-operation can be enhanced through the creation of a uniform set of core rules on recognition and enforcement of foreign judgments in civil or commercial matters, to facilitate the effective recognition and enforcement of such judgments,
>
> Convinced that such enhanced judicial co-operation requires in particular an international legal regime that provides greater predictability and certainty in relation to the global circulation of foreign judgments, and that is complementary to the Convention of 30 June 2005 on Choice of Court Agreements,
>
> Have resolved to conclude this Convention and have agreed upon the following provisions—

4.28 The Preamble consists of three distinct statements. Each of these statements may provide some assistance in the proper interpretation of the terms of the Convention in particular cases.

> Desiring to promote effective access to justice for all and to facilitate rule-based multilateral trade and investment, and mobility, through enhanced judicial co-operation

4.29 The lead recital in the Preamble is clear, and stresses two points that are constant themes in this book. The primary objectives of the Convention are to promote equal access to justice for all; and to facilitate trade, investment, and mobility. This requires first and foremost, the creation of a structure that will lower the transaction costs of resolving disputes arising from global mobility, and that will support—and certainly not deter—global flows of people, goods, services, investment, ideas, and other forms of mobility. Transaction costs can be a significant—perhaps the most significant—barrier to access to justice as a real-world matter. The means chosen to accomplish these objectives is judicial cooperation (as opposed to, eg, harmonization of substantive law). At a minimum, national courts should be cognizant of the need to avoid applying the Convention in a manner which, if generalized, is likely to raise transaction costs of dispute resolution, or obstruct or thwart mobility across borders. At the same time, because the means employed in the Convention is judicial co-operation, any attempt to hinder the ability of national courts to perform the functions of interpretation and application delegated to them under the Convention runs counter to a primary object and purpose of the Convention.

Believing that such co-operation can be enhanced through the creation of a uniform set of core rules on recognition and enforcement of foreign judgments in civil or commercial matters, to facilitate the effective recognition and enforcement of such judgments,

The Convention gives to national courts a vehicle to achieve the objectives in the first recital, namely uniform rules on the recognition and enforcement of foreign judgments in civil or commercial matters. Thus national courts, in their application of the Convention, should consider the jurisprudence of courts of other Contracting States under the Convention. This obligation is serious, and must be treated seriously. However, the Convention itself does not and cannot create a rule that a court in one Contracting State will be bound by the interpretation of a provision reached by a court of another Contracting State or even by courts of multiple Contracting States. The strength and force of this preambular statement must be gauged by reference to Article 20 as well, which provides that '[i]n the interpretation of this Convention, regard shall be had to its international character and to the need to promote uniformity in its application'. The obligation is to give proper *regard* to the international character and the need to *promote* uniformity of the Convention. There is no 'first in time' rule for proper interpretation of the Convention. **4.30**

It is also important to bear in mind that uniformity is to come from a set of '*core* rules on recognition and enforcement of foreign judgments' (emphasis added). While the Convention regulates, it does not create a comprehensive regulatory code: it provides only core rules for regulation. The Convention leaves many matters to be decided by national law, and does not require uniformity in substantive law among Contracting States. As a matter of practical necessity, many provisions may call for an autonomous rule under the Convention, but the content of that rule must be developed in subsequent national practice. **4.31**

Convinced that such enhanced judicial co-operation requires in particular an international legal regime that provides greater predictability and certainty in relation to the global circulation of foreign judgments, and that is complementary to the Convention of 30 June 2005 on Choice of Court Agreements,

This third recital in the Preamble refers to the legal regime established by the Convention with the objective of enhanced judicial cooperation. This statement has two components. The first is the provision of '*greater*' predictability and certainty. The comparative is deliberate. Enhanced judicial cooperation to achieve the ends in the first recital does not genuflect at the altar of the false god of absolute certainty; the Convention aims to improve predictability (which precedes the reference to certainty, and would be unnecessary if the primary objective was certainty), that is, to make the world better in this respect than a world without the Convention. Second, the Convention is '*complementary*' to COCA. This point will be discussed in greater detail below; suffice it to say here that '*complementary to*' **4.32** should be taken in the sense of generally running parallel with, avoiding mutual interference, and enhancing the operation of both.[8]

B. Extra-Textual Sources of Consensus

4.33 In light of the lengthy and continuous negotiating history of the Convention, the number of participants in the negotiations, and the need to produce a text of manageable dimensions, there are points that may fairly be said to represent a consensus but that are not stated on the face of the Convention text. However, in establishing such points, it is critical to be mindful of the danger of over-reaching and thus trying to bind Contracting States to propositions to which they did not assent. Accordingly, while extra-textual sources may be used to demonstrate consensus, they can do so only if there is strong support in the record for consensus on a given point, and if the Convention text and good sense support the suggested proposition. There are two primary sources that may be considered in the effort to demonstrate a consensus proposition beyond the face of the text, the Explanatory Report and statements in the Plenary of the Diplomatic Session.

C. The Explanatory Report

4.34 The Explanatory Report ('Report') on the Convention provides analysis of the Convention beyond the agreed text.[9] The Report represents significant work by its authors, both during and after the negotiations. It evolved through several drafts submitted to national delegations for consideration and comment, and thus may be consulted as a source regarding the Convention text. However, it must be borne in mind that the consensus document is the Convention itself and not the Report, and that not all comments of the national delegations were accepted in creating the final Report. The Report cannot trump the face of the text, or considerations of logic, or of practical consequences (including effects of an interpretation on the prospects of widespread implementation). Nor may it require an interpretation that does not reflect the shared view of the Convention's negotiators.

D. Statements in the Plenary of the Diplomatic Session

4.35 Certain types of statements made in the plenary provide strong evidence of consensus. As noted above, a consensus statement read into the record by the chairman of the Drafting Committee on a provision that had been the subject of long and intense debate and negotiation bears great weight.[10] In addition, the minutes of the negotiations may be helpful.

[8] The parallel reference in the Preamble to COCA began with the phrase '[b]elieving that ...' rather than '[c]onvinced that ... '. We do not inquire how belief is transformed into conviction in the halls of the Hague Conference. There are other significant differences in the wording of this recitation in this Convention and that in the cognate COCA recitation. The significance of the differences will be discussed below.

[9] The Report is set out in full in the Appendix to this volume.

[10] The principal example of this is the statement on Art 11 of COCA regarding damages. See Hartley and Dogauchi (n 6) 205.

Reference to minutes must be tempered, however, by the understanding that they are merely a summary and do not provide a verbatim transcription of the negotiations. They also relate only to the interventions made. They do not necessarily reflect the views of other negotiators, who might have decided not to intervene for any number of reasons. While the minutes are thus useful as indicators, they are not an infallible record of the negotiations.

More fundamentally, interventions in the plenary in themselves do not establish a consensus understanding of language. They are at best indications, made at various points (and with the text in various stages of development) in the Diplomatic Session or Special Commission of what a specific delegate was willing to announce as their understanding of the meaning of a proposed text. Indication by intervention at various points in a negotiation process is a weak reed on which to lean, and cannot trump the final text. In such circumstances, citing various statements or documents that assert one interpretation does not establish that there was a consensus on that interpretation—only that there was support for it at a particular point in time by a specific intervenor framed against the background and in the context of a particular version of text—including the totality of the remainder of the articles—before them. **4.36**

Furthermore, the absence of a controverting statement in the plenary of the Diplomatic Session does not end the inquiry. There may be statements that were not controverted in the plenary but that nonetheless do not establish consensus. In part, this may be because they were not understood at the time as purporting to establish a consensus interpretation of the provision, as opposed, for example to a statement of national practice. A first step in evaluating a statement in the plenary is to determine what force can fairly be attributed to it. Even if it appears that an uncontroverted statement by an individual delegate, or even several delegations, in the plenary purports to establish a consensus interpretation, history and context are critical in evaluating the force to be accorded to those statements. It is worth noting that, by the time of the Diplomatic Session, many delegations had decided to limit their battles in the hope of achieving an agreed text. Their silence does not necessarily indicate that they agreed to any particular interpretation of particular text. **4.37**

For example, certain positions, or amplifications of positions, may not have been advanced in the plenary even though they had been raised with respect to identical text in the Special Commission or in the plenary of COCA. It is not advisable or fair to the Contracting States to infer from subsequent silence alone that these positions had been abandoned. The fact is that the Diplomatic Session moved rather quickly on some issues. There may have been situations where key personnel were not on the floor to reiterate earlier statements. Also, in the interest of getting to a final text, certain objections may not have been registered in the plenary in the belief that they had been preserved by being raised in the Special Commission, or in the COCA process, or in the first session of the 2001 Diplomatic Session, or in earlier phases of the original project and noted in the Nygh/Pocar Report that emanated from those earlier phases.[11] **4.38**

[11] *Report on the preliminary draft Convention on Jurisdiction and Foreign Judgments in Civil and Commercial Matters, drawn up by Peter Nygh and Fausto Pocar*, Hague Conference on Private International Law, Proceedings of the 20th Session, 14 to 30 June 2005, Tome II (Nygh/Pocar Report) 207–313 <https://assets.hcch.net/docs/49cdf8b6-b466-45d6-9aa9-17151f93a804.pdf>. The Report is a treasure trove of information, analysis, and insight in the areas it addresses, irrespective of the fate of the original project.

4.39 Another set of situations that warrant caution in finding consensus arise from provisions adopted by the Diplomatic Session that had not really been discussed in depth (if at all) in earlier Special Commissions. While views may have been expressed by individual delegates or Working Groups on the interpretation of certain aspects of those provisions, many delegations simply did not have time to take these points on board and to think them through in a thorough fashion, or did not want to interrupt progress through the agenda. Nonetheless, to the extent those provisions are clear in the text, no contextual analysis of the negotiations should be allowed to alter the application of the rules created.

4.40 History can be deceptive, and acquaintance with it warrants a certain wariness. That said, evidence *may* be found in two additional situations: when the proponent of a narrow, adopted text accepts a broadening on a particular point, such as with the 'privacy' provision in Article 2.1(l), or when the proponent of broad text accepts a narrow reading on that provision.

E. Extra-Textual Sources Outside the Diplomatic Session but Within the Judgments Project

4.41 While the discussion above addresses the issue of consensus based on statements made in the plenary of the Diplomatic Session, the possibility must also be examined of the existence of consensus in the absence of statements at the plenary. This is a matter of some difficulty, and must be addressed tentatively and with serious circumspection. This circumspection is particularly necessary because it was made clear throughout the process that led to the final text that all the work of all the Special Commissions, Working Groups, and other preparatory effort was simply preliminary. Attendance at all of these preliminary stages was by experts in their personal capacities. Experts participated in the Working Group and Special Commission meetings in their personal capacities, even when they were identified by the Member States of the Hague Conference. Accordingly, they did not necessarily speak on behalf of the Member States during those meetings. Experts attending earlier stages of the process had no mandate to bind their States. Past may have been prologue, but nothing was binding; the world began anew with the Diplomatic Session. Much was not said earlier on the understanding that the whole enterprise would be revisited at the Diplomatic Session, and because of the desire not to raise continuous obstructions on the road to that Diplomatic Session. All the preliminary work, including its documents, are rungs on Wittgenstein's Ladder, only to be kicked out from under when the highest rung is reached, the text adopted by the Diplomatic Session.

4.42 It may be useful to differentiate between two potential sets of sources. The first is identical text that was carried from the Special Commission and adopted in the Convention text. By and large, however, the existence of continuous text merely begs the interpretive question: a continuous consensus on a particular form of words does not establish a consensus on the meaning of those words, or establish that any such consensus itself was continuous from Special Commission (or Working Group) to final text—especially given the changing shape of various interim and usually incomplete drafts.

4.43 Second, there may be specific statements on the record in the Special Commission that may constitute evidence of a shared understanding of a provision. However, it must be borne in mind that the Special Commission was working from a preliminary and incomplete text, and a number of delegates noted that the acceptability of given provisions might depend on the content of other provisions not yet known. To be acceptable as evidence of consensus, and subject to the qualifications noted above regarding the limitations on the use of statements made in the plenary, statements made in the Special Commission and proffered as evidence of consensus on this basis should have been made by multiple experts on the record in the Special Commission, with respect to provisions whose text and context did not change between the time of utterance and the adoption of the final text, and with no contradiction. (A drafting change which left meaning unaltered does not count as a 'change' for this purpose.) Even if an utterance satisfies these three conditions, it remains weak evidence of consensus meaning.

F. The Convention on Choice of Court Agreements

The Convention was not created in a vacuum. Critically, it was crafted deliberately and explicitly to be 'complementary' to the 2005 Convention on Choice of Court Agreements (COCA). Many provisions of the Convention are identical to COCA provisions or are patterned upon them. Identical provisions should be interpreted identically, unless doing so would thwart objectives specific to this Convention. Generally, the starting point for drafting the Convention was COCA: variation in language reflects a conscious choice in this Convention resulting from a recognition that, while complementary, there is inevitable divergence in the content and objectives of the two instruments that required different language. This commentary will take some pains to discuss related COCA provisions in the article-by-article march through the text. Our discussion will include both points of similarity and also divergence between the two Conventions. Not surprisingly, where appropriate, the discussion here will bear a distinct resemblance to that in the earlier work on COCA, *The 2005 Hague Convention on Choice of Court Agreements* by Ronald A Brand and Paul H Herrup, two of the authors of this book. **4.44**

However, COCA can be a false friend on another count. It is absolutely correct to state that a fundamental object and purpose of COCA is to maximize actual recognition and enforcement of judgments issued by courts designated in exclusive choice of court agreements. It is simply impossible to make a similar statement about the object and purpose of this Convention. As has been noted, and will be repeated, the most powerful obligation in this Convention prohibits the recognition or enforcement of certain judgments, while the criteria of eligibility for recognition or enforcement are often complex and constrained. The difference in preambular recital marks this difference in fundamental policy: the third recitation in the Preamble to COCA refers to a 'legal regime that provides certainty and ensures the effectiveness', while the cognate preambular recital only refers to 'provid[ing] greater predictability and certainty'. This significant difference in policy puts a limit on the interpretive use of COCA for the terms of this Convention: insofar as a COCA-assisted interpretation of a given term or provision is based upon the policy of COCA to maximize recognition and enforcement, that interpretation cannot carry over into the terms of this Convention. Such a move is illicit bootstrapping. **4.45**

G. The Original Project

4.46 An even more delicate issue is the interpretive relationship between the final text of this Convention and work done up to and including the first session of the Diplomatic Session of the original project in 2001, which produced a 1999 Preliminary Draft Text (1999 Draft Text) and a 2001 Interim Text. First, in substance, scope, and structure, this Convention is very different from the 2001 Interim Text, which began by requiring or prohibiting bases of direct jurisdiction, then keying recognition and enforcement to the exercise of that direct jurisdiction. The Interim Text was riddled with brackets and footnotes. The only real consensus was an agreement that it should be passed forward in that condition to a planned second meeting of a Diplomatic Session, which never happened. We cannot posit some sort of transitive relationship that simply transfers an interpretive statement made about the 1999 Draft Text or the Interim Text to the adopted 2005 COCA text and thence to the text of this Convention. Second, the Nygh/Pocar Report is based upon a 1999 Draft Text which resulted from majority vote rather than reflecting a consensus process.

4.47 The fact that an earlier text was the result of a majority decision and not a true consensus text does not imply a lack of consensus on every proposition. It would be unwarranted and unfortunate to reject categorically the relevance and usefulness of the entirety of the earlier work. The question becomes whether criteria can be articulated that will respect the fundamental differences between the earlier work and this Convention, while finding an appropriate use for the earlier work.

4.48 Subject to all of the above caveats, and with even greater circumspection, we may consider as evidence of consensus a statement made in the Nygh/Pocar Report and not controverted in the plenary of the first meeting of the 2001 Diplomatic Session if two additional conditions are met. The first condition is the presence in the record of a continuous shared understanding of, and agreement to, a provision or a critical concept within a provision. Evidence of this continuous shared understanding and agreement may be found, for example, by the presence of the same terms in the 1999 Draft Text, the Nygh/Pocar Report, the 2001 Interim Text, COCA, and the current Convention text (always allowing for mere drafting adjustments). In light of the major changes in structure and substance of the project between 1999 and the present, this condition requires more than a mechanical search for identical words in a particular place. Due attention must be given to the intended context and operation of the provision or term within it. For example, if the Nygh/Pocar Report provides an interpretation of an article in the 1999 Draft Text, which interpretation is premised on the relation of that article to a different article or chapter of the 1999 Draft Text, and the article or chapter referred to has itself changed, it may be inappropriate to rely on the Nygh/Pocar Report (or the 2001 Interim text) as a basis for an assertion of consensus within COCA or within our Convention—even if the words remain the same. Another example is an article in the 2001 Interim Text that reappears in the 2005 text, but in a different chapter.

4.49 The second condition for evidence of a consensus would arise when the statement in the Nygh/Pocar Report was not controverted in the plenary of the first meeting of the 2001 Diplomatic Session, or subsequently in any session or text up to and including those related to the Judgments Project strictly construed.

A final word of caution is appropriate regarding the use of sources outside the Convention text or clear consensus statements at the plenary to establish consensus. While the Special Commissions and the Diplomatic Session were well-attended by members (and non-members) of the Hague Conference, there was not uniform attendance at each of these events, and attendance may not have been for the entire duration of the Special Commission or Diplomatic Session. A claim of a consensus based on sources outside the final Convention text or authoritative presentations in the plenary raises a possibility of surprise to States whose participation in the process was late or sporadic. Any claim of a consensus interpretation on this basis should have a content that is consistent with general private international law understandings of the law in the specific subject area. Obviously, to the extent the language of the Convention text is clear, a State may not dispute the meaning simply because it was not present when that provision was adopted. 4.50

5
Scope and Definitions (Articles 1–3)

I. General

Chapter I of the Convention is entitled, 'Scope and Definitions'. Articles 1 and 2 set out the substantive scope of application of the Convention, while Article 3 provides definitions and elaboration of three terms. 5.01

The basic structure of the scope provisions of the Convention begins in Article 1(1) with a scope of application to 'judgments in civil or commercial' matters. This basic criterion of scope is a threshold policy choice, which is reflected in a number of provisions of the text, with consequences that ripple throughout the entire instrument. Article 2 then proceeds to list matters to which the Convention does not apply, as well as to provide further clarifications and amplifications on scope. Article 3, *inter alia*, deploys a broad definition of the fundamental scope term 'judgment'. 5.02

The best understanding of the framework established in Chapter I comes from addressing its articles by linked content rather than by numerical order. Article 1 forms a logical unit with the supporting definition of 'judgment' in Article 3. Article 2 then qualifies the operation of that unit. This reflects a basic characteristic of the Convention text: it is a highly coordinated and inter-connected web. Very few articles can be discussed in isolation. 5.03

II. Article 1—The Key Concepts of Scope

Article 1
Scope

1. **This Convention shall apply to the recognition and enforcement of judgments in civil or commercial matters. It shall not extend in particular to revenue, customs or administrative matters.**
2. **This Convention shall apply to the recognition and enforcement in one Contracting State of a judgment given by a court of another Contracting State.**

A. Scope and Article 1(1)

Article 1
Scope

1. **This Convention shall apply to the recognition and enforcement of judgments in civil or commercial matters. It shall not extend in particular to revenue, customs or administrative matters.**

5.04 The first sentence of Article 1(1) specifies the concepts that, taken together, provide the scaffolding and overall framework for the substantive scope of operation of the Convention. The Convention shall apply to (1) 'judgments' (2) when questions are presented of their 'recognition and enforcement' (3) in 'matters' (4) that fall within a classification of 'civil or commercial'. The second sentence of Article 1(1) then provides some additional clarification of the concept of 'civil or commercial' by specifying, on a non-exhaustive basis, that certain matters (revenue, customs, or administrative), among others, are not within the scope of the Convention.

1. Judgments

5.05 This Convention applies to the recognition and enforcement of judgments; the stuff of the Convention is judgments, and it is natural that any discussion of the Convention begins with its concept of a judgment. Indeed, of the critical scope concept in Article 1(1), 'judgment' is the only one with a Convention definition. Article 3(1)(b) defines judgment:

> **'judgment' means any decision on the merits given by a court, whatever that decision may be called, including a decree or order, and a determination of costs or expenses by the court (including an officer of the court), provided that the determination relates to a decision on the merits which may be recognized or enforced under this Convention. An interim measure of protection is not a judgment.**[1]

[1] The definition is taken virtually verbatim from the 2005 Convention on Choice of Court Agreements (COCA), art 4(1), with a reference to 'that decision' in place of 'it' in COCA, to reduce a perceived ambiguity.

Article 3(1)(b) consists of two sentences. The first talks about what a 'judgment' is. At its most general, a judgment is a decision that may be recognized or enforced under this Convention. The second states something that is not a judgment for Convention purposes. **5.06**

The core components of the definition of a 'judgment' under the Convention are that it is a decision 'on the merits' given 'by a court'. Neither element is further defined, they have no international law referents, and both display significant variation in meaning among countries and legal systems. In light of this lack of specificity within the text of the Convention, our approach is to provide a reading of these core components that gives them a sense anchored in the text but that also takes account of the nature of the Convention as creating international legal obligations. **5.07**

a. *On the Merits*

For purposes of the general sense (as opposed to the strict definition) of 'judgment' in the Convention, it is our view that 'on the merits' should be taken as requiring the following elements: (1) a resolution of the fundamental dispute, or substantive aspects of that fundamental dispute, presented to a court, (2) based upon a pleading that presents averments of fact, whether or not the court makes independent findings of fact in its decision.[2] The reference to merits should be taken as a reference to the factual basis of the underlying dispute, and not the legal 'merits' of consequential or ancillary claims and proceedings, such as the determination of the law applicable to a particular question or whether a judgment qualifies for recognition or enforcement. **5.08**

A judgment includes 'any decision' on the merits. 'Any' is to be taken broadly. Thus, a default judgment is a 'judgment' for the purposes of the Convention. The important point is that a determination of legal rights or obligations has been made arising from an averment of a specific set of factual circumstances. This is true whether the judgment was entered by a formally-invested judge of the court or a lower officer, and whether entered by order or registration or embedded in a full-blown opinion. **5.09**

The reference to 'on the merits' in the definition of 'judgment' does not differentiate between judgments based upon the remedy ordered. An award of strictly compensatory damages, an award of non-monetary remedies, and a money award that goes beyond pure compensation are all included in the definition of 'judgment' for Convention purposes. However, there may be restrictions on the enforceability of certain remedies, whether as a matter of public policy under Article 7(1)(c) or the provision on damages in Article 10. **5.10**

Nor does the reference to 'on the merits' in constructing a sense of 'judgment' vary with the procedural mechanisms that may produce a decision on the merits. Judgments for Convention purposes include the classic individual claim as well as class actions and other claims brought through mechanisms of collective redress. **5.11**

Decisions that are interim or address preliminary issues are not judgments for purposes of the Convention. In part, this flows from a consideration of what is an appropriate international legal obligation to place on States other than the State of origin of the judgment: States should not be required to exercise their legal and coercive powers or undertake **5.12**

2 We note that the term 'decision on the merits' in art 3 is substantially different from the concept of 'review of the merits' found in art 4(2), which differs yet again from what might be involved when a defendant 'argued on the merits' as a criterion for eligibility for recognition or enforcement under art 5(1)(f).

the expense of dealing with a decision that is inherently temporary or transient.[3] The second sentence of Article 3(1)(b) removes any doubt that interim measures of protection are not judgments for the purposes of the Convention.[4] However, nothing in the Convention precludes a court from giving effect to such measures under its municipal law rather than as a matter of international legal obligation, or independently to order its own provisional measures to assist with proceedings in another court.[5]

5.13 The definition of 'judgment' does not explicitly address the question of finality in the sense that a decision on the merits may be beyond review by another court in the State of origin or possibly subject to re-examination in the court that rendered it. Aspects of finality, or the consequences of non-finality, appear in Articles 4(4) and 7(2). Because these provisions provide discretion allowing the requested State to postpone recognition or enforcement for non-final decisions, it would appear that the Convention would otherwise require their recognition and enforcement where a court does not rely on either of these provisions.

5.14 To satisfy the 'on the merits' requirement, the decision of ultimate resolution of the dispute should be based upon a determination of fact, even if the determination is drawn from the pleadings of one party in a default judgment, or derived from prior findings by a magistrate, hearing board, or the like. Thus, hypothetical judgments and advisory opinions are not judgments for Convention purposes. Procedural and evidentiary rulings are not judgments on the merits. Orders of garnishment, unless based upon factual findings, are not judgments.

5.15 A judgment to recognize or enforce a judgment likewise is not a decision on the underlying merits, and hence not a judgment under the Convention. This proposition follows both from the nature of the instrument as an international agreement and from considerations of other aspects of the text. First, if the rule were otherwise, serious issues of bootstrapping would arise. A court of a Contracting State could recognize a judgment on any basis in its national law and from any country whatsoever, and the Convention would obligate all other Contracting States to recognize and enforce that judgment of recognition and enforcement if it met Convention criteria. Courts subsequently asked to recognize and enforce a judgment of recognition would have no ability to validate whether the criteria of eligibility in Articles 5 and 6 were satisfied in the original proceedings. This is a potentially dramatic extension of international legal obligations of Contracting States under the Convention, and such an interpretation should not be espoused without very clear evidence that the States so intended. We are aware of no such evidence. Second, this interpretation would lead to a sharply asymmetric set of obligations to recognize and enforce—if there

[3] The content of an interim measure can be converted into a permanent judgment, but it is the permanent judgment that will be eligible for recognition or enforcement under the Convention. Likewise, a ruling on a preliminary question that is incorporated into a judgment will be eligible for recognition or enforcement under the Convention by virtue of that incorporation, unless the ruling is on a matter to which the Convention does not apply or is inconsistent with art 6 relating to rights in rem in immovable property. See art 8(1).

[4] The text of art 3(1)(b) maintains parallelism with the same provision in COCA. In our view, although the second sentence of art 3(1)(b) was drafted in a manner that excludes '[a]n interim measure of protection' rather than the more general 'interim measure' from the definition of a 'judgment', it makes little sense that the status of an interim order as within or without the Convention should pivot on the purported purpose of the order and the qualification is an invitation to litigation. Furthermore, orders of protection tend to be far more decisive in litigation than other interim orders; excluding them from scope while including other interim orders would be doubly puzzling.

[5] See discussion of art 15 of the Convention in Chapter 7. However, to the extent that the 'measure' is not considered to be a 'judgment' pursuant to the Convention, art 15 would not apply, with the result that the court may give effect to the measure without reference to art 15.

were any obligations at all. An obligation to recognize and enforce a judgment of recognition would apply to all civil or commercial judgments within the scope of the Convention, regardless of subject matter, and which satisfy a criterion in Article 5 or 6. Yet the criteria in those articles almost all involve a connection between conduct or property and a particular forum—which will often not be the case for a request to recognize and enforce in a third country a judgment of recognition or enforcement. The most likely candidate among the criteria in Articles 5 and 6 that might operate with respect to recognition and enforcement in third countries of a judgment of recognition or enforcement is Article 5(1)(a) (habitual residence of party against whom recognition or enforcement is sought)—and even its applicability is not clear. At most, then, an interpretation of 'on the merits' to include judgments in proceedings subsequent to the fact-based judgment in the court of origin would likely operate only as to persons habitually resident in the first court where recognition or enforcement is requested. As with the first point, we are aware of no evidence that indicates that any State contemplated this result—however desirable the authors may view it as a matter of policy.

Finally, it is worth noting that the Convention may not compel the requested court to recognize or enforce every feature contained in a document labelled 'judgment' and presented to it—for example, dictum. In such situations, it will be for the requested court to determine what in the document presented to it actually is a judgment on the merits for Convention purposes. **5.16**

b. By a Court

The term 'court' is not defined in the Convention, but should sweep broadly. The term 'court' is not dependent upon the taxonomy or terminology in national legal systems created to distinguish between tribunals with different subject matter jurisdiction. A 'court' can include tribunals designated as civil courts, civil and commercial courts, administrative courts, US District Courts, etc. Conversely, there may be tribunals that are not accorded the full trappings of other 'courts' within a national system, but that issue 'judgments' otherwise within the meaning of Article 3(1)(b). The critical inquiry is not the label but the nature and function of the tribunal.[6] **5.17**

A court must be a public institution, created as an institution with public authority, but which retains independence from other public authorities in reaching decisions. An arbitral tribunal is not a 'court' within Article 1(1). The entire structure of the Convention is directed at adjudicatory bodies established by States (see, eg, art 4(1) referring to 'a court of a Contracting State'). Moreover, should there be any question as to whether an arbitral tribunal is a court of a Contracting State, 'arbitration and related proceedings' are explicitly excluded from the scope of the Convention by Article 2(3). **5.18**

While a tribunal, in order to be a court, must be a public institution created by an institution with public authority, it is a fair question whether it must act only on the basis of **5.19**

[6] Thus, a body not capable of issuing decisions on the merits is not a court for Convention purposes, and its decisions are not judgments. (Even if it is a 'court' for domestic purposes, it will not issue a 'judgment' to which the Convention applies.) It should be noted that decisions of 'common courts'—in which several States may pool, delegate, or assign judicial functions—are not specifically addressed in the Convention. The status of their judgments under the Convention will be a topic of further development. A major concern in dealing with common courts is the assurance of reciprocity, ie that States employing common courts will have judicial institutions capable of recognizing and enforcing judgments from other Contracting States.

available and applicable rules of procedure in the administration of applicable law in order for its judgments to be eligible for recognition or enforcement under the Convention. Should a decision by a tribunal that is otherwise a court but acting in some ways in the fashion of an arbitral panel, for example, reaching an ultimate resolution of a dispute on the basis of a set of procedural rules devised by the parties or substantive law presented to the court by them, necessarily be a body whose decisions fall outside the scope of this Convention? Alternatively, should such a decision be treated as an arbitral award that falls within the New York Convention? Resolution of this issue will be a matter of future practice.

5.20 Another boundary question is the status of administrative or ad hoc bodies, or hearing boards and panels housed within or operating under the direction of a government ministry and administering the rules and regulations of that ministry. These bodies may make binding findings of fact, or their decisions may be given the force of law within their own legal systems. If these bodies are not independent, their decisions might not be treated as 'judgments' for purposes of the Convention. However, if, as may be the case, their decisions acquire the force of law in the absence of an appeal to a reviewing court, it would be undesirable to penalize the prevailing party on the basis of a choice by other parties not to appeal. Otherwise, a recalcitrant losing party could stymie recognition and enforcement of the decision simply by not pursuing available avenues.

5.21 Finally, Article 3(1)(b) clarifies that a judgment under the Convention may be a determination of costs or expenses of the proceedings, provided that the determination relates to a decision on the merits that may otherwise be recognized or enforced under the Convention. 'Relates to' is a broad term and should be given a generous sweep. However, if an order of costs or expenses does not relate to a decision on the merits, it is not a judgment for Convention purposes.[7] Furthermore, the cost determination that is treated as a judgment for purposes of the Convention may be made either by the court or by an officer of the court.

2. Recognition and Enforcement

5.22 Article 1.1 refers to 'recognition and enforcement of judgments' but there is no Convention definition of either 'recognition' or 'enforcement'. As will be discussed below, both terms must be given the meaning they have in the law of the requested State.

5.23 The reference is to 'recognition and enforcement' as a conjunction. In a provision defining a scope of application, this makes perfect sense: the Convention applies to both recognition and enforcement. However, the conjunction can create a certain amount of confusion. Recognition is a separate concept from enforcement. A judgment can be capable of being both recognized and enforced, barred from both recognition and enforcement,[8] recognized but not enforced,[9] or enforced but not recognized.[10] This is acknowledged in the text of the

[7] It should be noted that, insofar as a cost order is a judgment for purposes of the Convention, the discretionary grounds for refusal of recognition or enforcement contained in art 7 remain available.

[8] See art 6 prohibiting recognition or enforcement in situations involving rights *in rem* in immovable property.

[9] This may happen either because the nature of the judgment does not lend itself to enforcement, such as a negative declaratory judgment (although it may have collateral effects) or because the court requested determines not to enforce a judgment it has recognized. A judgment denying a claim may be recognized to prevent the same claim being asserted in the courts of a second State.

[10] This may be the case with judicial settlements, art 11.

definition of a 'judgment' in Article 3(1)(b), where the reference is to 'a decision ... which may be recognized or enforced'.

As noted above, the Convention provides no definition of either 'recognition' or 'enforcement'. Thus, on its face, the Convention does not address whether the definitions of these terms are to be taken from: **5.24**

(1) the law of the requested State; or
(2) the law of the State of origin; or
(3) traditional private international law doctrine (which in itself is not necessarily uniform among legal systems); or
(4) an autonomous Convention meaning, with that meaning to be built up in practice under the Convention.

Because this Convention functions to provide for a kind of national treatment in a requested State of a judgment coming from another Contracting State, we take the view that the terms should be given the meaning they have in the law of the requested State, which is the State that will provide the governing procedural law pursuant to Article 13(1) and the State whose courts are being asked to exercise its judicial, and potentially its coercive, powers. This solution eliminates the need for imposition of *a priori* metaphysical concepts, which likely will be ignored in practice by most courts in any event. **5.25**

Whatever test may ultimately prevail, 'recognition' and 'enforcement' constitute two distinct terms not only in common legal parlance but also in the Convention. We offer the following very broad observations to provide some additional guidance regarding concepts of 'recognition' and 'enforcement' as they occur in the Convention: **5.26**

> 'Recognition' in an intuitive, basic sense, involves the acceptance by the requested court of the determination of all or part of the rights and obligations of the parties made by the court of origin in a way that makes them eligible to be accorded some kind of legal effect in the requested State similar to effects accorded legal artefacts originating in that requested State. Depending on each legal system and the circumstances presented, such 'acceptance' may be non-discretionary or discretionary with the requested court.[11]
>
> 'Enforcement' in an intuitive, basic sense, is the process (or result) whereby the requested court sets in motion the mechanisms available to it, including the potentially coercive power of its State, to give effect to rights or obligations established by the judgment.

As noted above, it is possible to have recognition without enforcement. For example, a judgment by a court of origin that a defendant owes nothing to a plaintiff with respect to a particular claim is unlikely to raise an issue of enforcement, at least if a requested court is in a common law State. However, the determination in such a judgment that there is no **5.27**

[11] 'Recognition' as the act of moving rights and obligations between legal systems should not be confused with preclusion or estoppel, which may be a consequence of recognition. Quite often, preclusion pertains to a rule of decision in proceedings before the requested court, which may follow from recognition of the foreign judgment, or may be an independent result of choice of law rules. In the context of this Convention, one of the practical effects of recognition will be preclusion of further litigation of the judgment or those parts of it that have been recognized.

obligation by one person towards another certainly may be eligible for recognition. Similarly, a pure declaratory judgment may require no additional act or event for enforcement.

5.28 On the other hand, for the most part, it is difficult to have enforcement of a judgment without 'recognition' in some sense or other. The thing to be enforced by a State is a right or obligation, with attendant consequences, which, under the Convention, is fixed by a decision on the merits by a foreign court. This generally will involve giving the judgment or parts thereof some legal status in the State of the requested court before it will be given effect by an exercise of the coercive powers of the State. However, as will be discussed, judicial settlements in Article 11 generally will be capable of enforcement but not recognition. This will not, however, prevent a court of a Contracting State from recognizing the judicial settlement under national law, outside the Convention.

3. Civil or Commercial Matters

5.29 The phrase 'civil or commercial matters' in Article 1(1) is an autonomous concept, the content of which does not depend on national law or previous international instruments, regional or otherwise.[12] The use of the fundamental term 'matter' at various places in the text sheds little additional light on the meaning of the term.[13] The phrase 'civil or commercial matters' is not explicitly defined in the Convention. Nor is there a definition that is generally applicable from other sources. There is good reason for this absence. While there are bodies of law in some States applicable to 'civil or commercial' matters,[14] bodies of law in some States that treat 'civil' matters,[15] bodies of law that treat 'civil' matters separately and distinctly from 'commercial matters',[16] the definitions of these terms often are neither precise nor capable of being articulated in a coherent fashion that meets basic requirements of logical rigour, and are rooted in place and time in a way that makes their deployment difficult in a truly global convention that will be applied in many different legal systems. Over and above issues of logic, the purported extensions of the terms fail as a matter of empirical adequacy.

[12] We will treat the three words 'civil or commercial' as a single term. Traditionally, civil codes applied to a medley of legal relationships among persons generally, while commercial codes applied to business relations among business persons. For our purposes, this is largely a distinction without a difference. The discussion in this sub-section leans heavily on Ronald A Brand and Paul M Herrup, *The 2005 Hague Convention on Choice of Court Agreements* (CUP 2008) 47–49.

[13] There appears to be no identifiably consistent sense of the term 'matter' in the Convention. The inclusion of 'civil or commercial matters' is immediately followed by a statement that the Convention does not extend in particular to revenue, customs, or administrative matters. 'Revenue' and 'customs' matters turn on the particular activities of a specific actor (eg taxing efforts of a State) while 'administrative' has no international law definition and varies from domestic legal system to domestic legal system, but seems to involve a sense of the State or other public authority regulating behaviour of a person. Other appearances of the term 'matter' in the Convention provide little additional help. Art 8 speaks of a 'matter' referred to in art 6, which combines a reference to property of a particular type (immovable) and a categorization of a kind of right (*in rem*). The term appears in art 5(2) in 'matters relating to a consumer contract' and 'matters relating to the employee's contract of employment' which simply establishes that a matter can be something that can have a relationship to certain kinds of contracts.

The imprecision of the concept of 'matter' in the Convention should be noted in the context of the declaration system in Chapter III, specifically art 18 (declarations with respect to specific matters) as the term provides little by way of coherent restriction on the type of things that a State may make subject to such a declaration.

[14] See Brasil, Law No 10.406 of 10 January 2002 (Civil Code) that includes many provisions that previously had been treated separately in the Commercial Code.

[15] See, eg, the French Civil Code, the Swiss 'Code of Obligations' and the Italian Civil Code of 1942. See generally Rudolf B Schlesinger, Hans B Baade, Peter E Herzog, and Edward M Wise, *Comparative Law* (6th edn, Foundation Press 1998) 503.

[16] See, eg, the French Commercial Code, the German Civil Code, and the German Commercial Code.

There is no consensus as to whether the use of this or similar phrases in earlier Hague Conventions determines the meaning of 'civil or commercial matters' in this Convention.[17] 5.30

4. Revenue, Customs, or Administrative Matters

The second sentence of Article 1(1) identifies a number of matters that are outside the scope of the Convention, namely 'revenue, customs or administrative matters'—none of which is defined in the Convention, none of which has an international law referent, and none of which is invariable as a matter of comparative law. These three 'matters' are identified as matters to which the Convention does not apply 'in particular'. Thus, the three do not constitute an exhaustive list of matters outside the scope of the Convention; what else may not be subject to the Convention remains unspecified.[18] When a multilateral treaty is produced through a consensus process, however, it is sometimes just this type of ambiguity that can garner necessary agreement. 5.31

Despite this ambiguity, there are a number of statements that can be made to help give meaning to the autonomous phrase, 'civil or commercial matters' for purposes of this Convention. The Convention definition applies the Convention to both 'civil' matters and 'commercial' matters, even if a given system of law treats those subjects in separate bodies of law. It then states that the Convention 'shall not extend in particular to revenue, customs or administrative matters'. 5.32

Whatever their precise contours, 'revenue' matters, 'customs' matters, and 'administrative' matters all involve conduct by States or by political authorities. Some assistance in construing 'civil or commercial' may be gleaned by reference to things that States do that may be classified as 'civil or commercial' as opposed to things that they do that generally are viewed as something else. 5.33

We suggest that a feature of the term 'civil and commercial' for purposes of this Convention should be the generality of certain features. Specifically, when a person—including a State—acts in a way that that is generally available for any other person to act, when an alleged injury that is the subject of the claim is of the type that can be sustained by any other person, and if the relief requested is relief generally available to remedy the alleged injury in the circumstances of the case, the matter generally should be found to be 'civil or commercial'. For example, a dispute arising from a contract for construction of a sports stadium by a public authority, or for provision of tents and food for a State reception, should be viewed as a civil or commercial matter, whether the claim is brought by or against the public authority. Similarly, a matter should also be viewed as 'civil or commercial' under the Convention when a State agency acts on behalf of private persons to marshal private claims, usually under a *parens patriae* or similar theory, such as when a State agency seeks 5.34

[17] However, the term is beginning to reflect certain common understandings in the work stemming from the project originally proposed in 1992. While not definitive, the treatment of various aspects of this problem in the Nygh/Pocar Report (*Report on the preliminary draft Convention on Jurisdiction and Foreign Judgments in Civil and Commercial Matters, drawn up by Peter Nygh and Fausto Pocar*, Hague Conference on Private International Law, Proceedings of the 20th Session, 14 to 30 June 2005, Tome II (Nygh/Pocar Report) 207–313, para 41 <https://assets.hcch.net/docs/49cdf8b6-b466-45d6-9aa9-17151f93a804.pdf>) and the explanatory reports of this Convention and COCA contain useful material.

[18] We would suggest that other 'matters' beyond revenue, customs, and administrative that also are not civil or commercial under the Convention, nonetheless, should share some of the salient, common features that may be distinguished in each of the terms 'revenue' or 'customs' or 'administrative' matters. This will be discussed further below.

to recover compensatory damages for defrauded consumers or investors, or in mass environmental disasters.

5.35 On the other hand, at a minimum, 'civil or commercial matters' does *not* include matters governed by criminal law. There is general agreement in the national law of both civil code and common law countries on this point. However, a judgment within the scope of the Convention may be issued by a court of criminal jurisdiction, if it provides restitution for damage done by conduct that may be classified as criminal and that is adjudicated in a 'criminal' proceeding, but that has authority to make determinations of private, compensable injury. Examples of this are awards to injured individuals as *partie civile*, *Nebenkleger*, *acusador privado*, *enagos politikon*, or certain restitution orders issued by US courts in the course of criminal proceedings, but that may be enforced in subsequent civil proceedings by the injured person.

5.36 For purposes of this Convention, 'civil or commercial' should not include matters in which only a public authority (or its agent) can act because it is clothed in a sovereign capacity, such as collection of taxes and customs duties, which are explicitly excluded from the scope of the Convention in Article 1(1). It also should not include the conduct of a public authority acting as a sovereign regulator—even though these may be classified as 'civil' matters in many common law countries.[19]

5.37 Finally, careful attention should be paid to the case law and other developments on this point under the 2005 Convention on Choice of Court Agreements (COCA), a cognate convention that deploys the same standard.[20]

B. Article 1(2)—Limitation to Judgments from Other Contracting States

Article 1

Scope

2. This Convention shall apply to the recognition and enforcement in one Contracting State of a judgment given by a court of another Contracting State.

5.38 Article 1(2) specifies the geographic reach of the Convention. The Convention only applies to a judgment that crosses a border from one Contracting State to another, and then

[19] In light of the above, at least as a starting point for analysis, a claim might be considered 'civil or commercial' if a State would not be entitled under international law to immunity from jurisdiction to adjudicate were the claim brought against it in a foreign court, and, conversely, a claim should be classified as outside the realm of 'civil or commercial' if a State would be entitled to immunity if sued on the claim. While this will not provide either a complete identity with the scope of the Convention nor complete uniformity in application, there are sufficient commonalities of result in immunity law to make this a useful benchmark if not applied too rigidly.

[20] The text of COCA does not include the second sentence of art 1(1) of the Convention. However, the 1999 Preliminary Draft Text (a more comprehensive convention text) explicitly excluded from scope 'revenue, customs or administrative matters'. *Preliminary draft Convention on jurisdiction and the effects of judgments in civil and commercial matters*, adopted provisionally by the Special Commission, Hague Conference on Private International Law, Special Commission on International Jurisdiction and the Effects of Foreign Judgments in Civil and Commercial Matters, Working Document No 241 (18 June 1999), art 1(1). This provision was not carried forward into later drafts because it was stated that it was tautologous in that 'civil or commercial matters' could not include penal, revenue, customs, or administrative matters. See *Explanatory Report on the Convention on Choice of Court Agreements, drawn up by Trevor Hartley and Masato Dogauchi*, Proceedings of the Twentieth Session, 14 to 30 June 2005, Tome III (2010) <https://assets.hcch.net/docs/8e05df5e-e9fd-4097-a1ab-9b086038db30.pdf> (Hartley/Dogauchi Report) 785–863, fn 73. The proposition that this is tautologous in many legal systems is dubious. See, eg, *Re State of Norway's Application* [1990] 1 AC 723.

only to recognition and enforcement of such a judgment. If the judgment does not cross a border between Contracting States, or if the issue presented is not recognition or enforcement, the Convention does not apply.

But Article 1(1) also reminds us that, as with any judicial assistance treaty, the Convention is rooted in movement: the movement of a particular kind of legal object—a judgment—generated in one country and for which some action is sought in another country.[21] 5.39

The requirement that the movement of a judgment must be between Contracting States has several implications. First, the Convention does not apply to recognition or enforcement of judgments unless both the State of origin and the requested State are Contracting States between which the Convention has effect pursuant to Article 29.[22] The Convention creates no obligation of Contracting States to non-Contracting States. Second, the Convention does not apply to movement of judgments within a State, whether or not that State is a Contracting State, and regardless of whether the State is unitary or federal, or whether it has a unified or a non-unified legal system.[23] 5.40

Finally, Article 1(2) reiterates the point in Article 1(1) that the Convention applies to recognition and enforcement of judgments: other questions that may be related to judgments fall outside its scope.[24] 5.41

III. Article 2—Other Matters to Which the Convention Does Not Apply, and Related Topics

Article 2
Exclusions from scope

1. **This Convention shall not apply to the following matters—**
   (a) **the status and legal capacity of natural persons;**
   (b) **maintenance obligations;**
   (c) **other family law matters, including matrimonial property regimes and other rights or obligations arising out of marriage or similar relationships;**
   (d) **wills and succession;**
   (e) **insolvency, composition, resolution of financial institutions, and analogous matters;**

[21] COCA has a related scope requirement with respect to 'international cases' in art 1. Because COCA applies to both jurisdiction and to recognition and enforcement of judgments, it provides separate criteria of 'internationality' for each aspect.

[22] While the Convention applies to a judgment that moves between Contracting States for recognition or enforcement, art 17 permits a Contracting State to declare that its courts may refuse to recognize or enforce a judgment within the Convention in circumstances that the declaring State views as depriving the case of an international character, ie when the parties were resident in the requested State and the relationship of the parties and all other elements relevant to the dispute were connected only with the requested State.

[23] This point, implicit in art 1(2), is made quite explicit with respect to non-unified legal systems in art 22.

[24] As has been noted, if a judgment falls within the scope of the Convention, that means the rules of the Convention apply to its recognition and enforcement. It does not mean the judgment will be recognized or enforced under the Convention, merely that it is eligible for such treatment. To be recognized or enforced under the Convention, a judgment within its scope still must satisfy the criteria for recognition or enforcement in art 5, escape the bar to recognition or enforcement in art 6, and not be caught by the discretionary grounds for refusal in art 7.

(f) the carriage of passengers and goods;

(g) transboundary marine pollution, marine pollution in areas beyond national jurisdiction, ship-source marine pollution, limitation of liability for maritime claims, and general average;

(h) liability for nuclear damage;

(i) the validity, nullity, or dissolution of legal persons or associations of natural or legal persons, and the validity of decisions of their organs;

(j) the validity of entries in public registers;

(k) defamation;

(l) privacy;

(m) intellectual property;

(n) activities of armed forces, including the activities of their personnel in the exercise of their official duties;

(o) law enforcement activities, including the activities of law enforcement personnel in the exercise of their official duties;

(p) anti-trust (competition) matters, except where the judgment is based on conduct that constitutes an anti-competitive agreement or concerted practice among actual or potential competitors to fix prices, make rigged bids, establish output restrictions or quotas, or divide markets by allocating customers, suppliers, territories or lines of commerce, and where such conduct and its effect both occurred in the State of origin;

(q) sovereign debt restructuring through unilateral State measures.

2. A judgment is not excluded from the scope of this Convention where a matter to which this Convention does not apply arose merely as a preliminary question in the proceedings in which the judgment was given, and not as an object of the proceedings. In particular, the mere fact that such a matter arose by way of defence does not exclude a judgment from the Convention, if that matter was not an object of the proceedings.

3. This Convention shall not apply to arbitration and related proceedings.

4. A judgment is not excluded from the scope of this Convention by the mere fact that a State, including a government, a governmental agency or any person acting for a State, was a party to the proceedings.

5. Nothing in this Convention shall affect privileges and immunities of States or of international organizations, in respect of themselves and of their property.

5.42 Article 2 is entitled 'Exclusions from Scope'. The title is somewhat inaccurate because half of its paragraphs are not exclusions from scope. Article 2(2) establishes that a judgment otherwise within scope remains so if 'a matter to which this Convention does not apply arose merely as a preliminary question'. Article 2(4) clarifies that judgments involving States may be within scope. Article 2(5) does not address scope, but rather privileges and immunities of States and international organizations.

5.43 It is also somewhat misleading because Articles 2(1) and 2(3) are phrased not in terms of exclusions from scope, but as positive injunctions: '[t]his Convention shall not apply . . . '. This is not merely a quibble over word choice in the title. The use of the term 'exclusion' can easily slide to acquire the sense of 'exception' to some sort of general rule. The Convention contains no such general rule, and these are not exceptions from it. The matters to which the Convention does not apply stand on their own feet, *pari passu*, with matters to which the Convention applies.[25] No canon of interpretation attaches to the Convention that the matters to which the Convention does not extend are to be interpreted narrowly by virtue of being exceptions to a general rule. Each matter must be evaluated on its own terms, and, given the interpretation—including the interpretation of the scope of the specific term—that evaluation must be based upon the language of the text, must be appropriate to the place of the term in the text, and take into account the creation of international legal obligations for sovereign States.[26]

A. Article 2(1)—Excluded 'Matters'

Article 2

1. This Convention shall not apply to the following matters—

Article 2(1) contains a list of 'matters' to which the Convention does not apply. If a judgment involves a matter within Article 2(1), it is outside the scope of the Convention (unless the 'matter' arose as a preliminary question under Article 2(2)). The matters to which the Convention does not apply that are contained in Article 2(1) generally were viewed by many States as 'civil or commercial' matters for purposes of the Convention. Thus, the scope framework to this point is: the Convention applies to the recognition and enforcement of judgments in 'civil or commercial' matters—but not to all matters that might be classified as 'civil or commercial'. Things described as 'matters' that might be classified as 'civil or commercial' but to which the Convention does not apply appear in Article 2(1). **5.44**

Many of the matters to which the Convention does not apply by virtue of Article 2(1) are presented in very abbreviated fashion, for example 'maintenance obligations' or 'wills and succession'. While these are generally accepted categories of exclusions in the private international law of many States, and in regional treaties, and while they have common cores, they generally do not have accepted international law referents, nor are they necessarily identical in substance from State to State. A number of the terms in Article 2(1) were carried into this Convention from both COCA and the earlier, larger project. Their interpretation has not changed dramatically from those projects to this one.[27] There was a conscious effort in drafting this Convention to maintain as much parallelism in scope as possible with COCA, to better serve the objective of complementarity, as mentioned in the Preamble, and of consistency in function in subsequent application. Accordingly, for 'matters' that appear in both Article 2(1) of this Convention and in Article 2(2) of COCA, COCA itself, the Nygh/Pocar Report on the original project, and the Explanatory Report **5.45**

[25] As is true of revenue, customs, and administrative matters, as opposed to civil or commercial matters, referenced in art 1(1).

[26] COCA also titles its art 2 'Exclusions from Scope'. It appears that the title of art 2 was carried over from COCA to this Convention. It is worth noting that COCA applies to exclusive choice of court agreements—the exemplar of voluntary arrangements. As an intuitive matter, an inclination towards a broad scope of inclusion in a convention that pivots on consent seems to raise less potential unfairness than such a bias in a Convention whose core building blocks are not necessarily consensual.

[27] This stability and general comparative law usage for these more precise and limited terms is in contrast to the more difficult terms 'civil' or 'commercial'—or the distinction that in many ways underlies the classifications of 'civil' or 'commercial', namely a public law/private law dichotomy that does not exist as such in the legal systems of many States.

for the Judgments Convention contain useful discussion, bearing in mind that these are aids to interpretation of this Convention, and that explanatory reports are the views of their individual authors.[28]

5.46 Furthermore, a number of the matters to which the Convention does not apply by virtue of Article 2(1) are the subjects of other treaties or conventions. Notably, the Hague Conference itself has been quite active in the area of family law. Other conventions, particularly Hague Conventions that use these terms, may be consulted for guidance as to their interpretation here, even if their treatment of the terms is cursory. Of course, any such guidance is not conclusive for this particular text.

5.47 As noted earlier, the term 'matters' comes with no underlying unifying principle or sense in the collection. We will proceed to discuss each matter in Article 2(1) term-by-term rather than in any collective aspect.[29]

1. Article 2(1)(a)

Article 2

1. This Convention shall not apply to the following matters—
(a) the status and legal capacity of natural persons;

5.48 Article 2(1)(a) is the first of four scope terms dealing with matters that involve families, or the disposition of property in situations likely to be heavily laden with considerations relating to families and natural persons (status and legal capacity of natural persons, maintenance obligations, other family law matters, and wills and succession). While these articles must be interpreted as individual provisions, they also must be taken together as a block that reflects a general attitude that these matters stand outside the Convention.

5.49 On its face, Article 2(1)(a) provides that the Convention shall not apply to judgments regarding the status and legal capacity of natural persons. It only applies to natural persons. Accordingly, judgments regarding these questions involving non-natural persons are not captured by Article 2(1)(a)—although the frequency of occurrence of such judgments is not clear, and any such judgments may well be captured by other elements of Article 2(1). Article 2(1)(a) insulates from the scope of the Convention matters of status such as marriage, divorce, death, paternity, and adoption. It also insulates from the scope of the Convention matters relating to capacity, such as the ability of children or the mentally incapable to have legal consequences assigned to actions.[30]

[28] Accordingly, the discussion in this Commentary of relatively well-worn terms will be abbreviated and somewhat summary, with more focus on provisions in art 2(1) that were not in earlier texts or that may have changed in reference. These discussions draw heavily on Brand and Herrup (n 12).

[29] COCA contains an initial scope divergence from this Convention because COCA does not apply to choice of court agreements involving consumers or contracts of employment. Art 2(1) of COCA. In contrast, judgments in these areas fall within the scope of this Convention, but with limitations on the eligibility for recognition or enforcement of judgments. Art 5(2) of Judgments Convention.

[30] For a similar conclusion, see Convention of 2 July 2019 on the Recognition and Enforcement of Foreign Judgments in Civil or Commercial Matters, Text adopted by the Twenty-Second Session, Explanatory Report by Francisco Garcimartín & Geneviève Saumier (Explanatory Report) 57, para 45 <https://assets.hcch.net/docs/a1b0b0fc-95b1-4544-935b-b842534a120f.pdf>.

2. Article 2(1)(b)

Article 2

1. This Convention shall not apply to the following matters—

...

(b) maintenance obligations;

Article 2(1)(b) is identical to Article 2(2)(c) of COCA, and the scope of the two provisions should be interpreted identically. Maintenance obligations have been addressed in other Hague Conventions.[31] For much the same reasons as their treatment in COCA, there was a general agreement from an early stage of the negotiations that they should stand apart from this Convention. **5.50**

3. Article 2(1)(c)

Article 2

2. This Convention shall not apply to the following matters—

...

(c) other family law matters, including matrimonial property regimes and other rights or obligations arising out of marriage or similar relationships;

Article 2(1)(c), which takes 'other family law matters' out of scope, demonstrates the impropriety and inapplicability of any rule of 'narrow' interpretation of terms to which the Convention does not apply. Article 2(1)(c) sweeps broadly on its face and was intended to do so. It is identical to Article 2(2)(c) of COCA and should receive the same interpretation. In a sense, the two identical articles recognize that the generic category of 'family law' stands apart and is independent of these Conventions. This provision applies broadly to family matters, for which there are multiple conventions.[32] To remove grounds for dispute in interpretation of the breadth of the term, 'family law' for purposes of the Convention specifically encompasses matrimonial property regimes, that is, rights in property which persons may have by virtue of a marital relationship as established in the national law of Contracting States. Article 2(1)(c) also applies to 'other rights or obligations arising out of marriage or similar relationships'. This again sweeps broadly. The provision contains no limitation of its scope with respect to the rights or obligations involved. If rights or obligations arise out of marriage or a similar relationship, they are covered by Article 2(1)(c). The phrase 'similar relationships' is best interpreted as referring to relationships that are not strictly matrimonial, but which arise under national law as a result of relationships deemed similar to matrimony and that might include property regimes applicable to their dissolution. **5.51**

[31] See, eg, Convention of 2 October 1973 on the Recognition and Enforcement of Decisions Relating to Maintenance Obligations; Convention of 2 October 1973 on the Law Applicable to Maintenance Obligations; Convention of 23 November 2007 on the International Recovery of Child Support and Other Forms of Family Maintenance.

[32] See, eg, Convention of 29 May 1993 on Protection of Children and Co-operation in Respect of Intercountry Adoption; Convention of 19 October 1996 on Jurisdiction, Applicable Law, Recognition, Enforcement and Co-operation in respect of Parental Responsibility and Measures for the Protection of Children; as well as the Conventions identified in n 31.

5.52 This provision would exclude from the scope of the Convention any matter that is considered to be a 'family law matter'. For example, this provision would exclude from the scope of the Convention judgments establishing or modifying child custody.[33] While extremely broad, Article 2(1)(c) does not come into play simply because the parties to a dispute are also parties of a different sort to a marriage or similar relationship. The issue in dispute must be a family law matter, including matters arising out of or related to marriage or similar relationships. For example, a non-family law dispute over a commercial contract between husband and wife does not fall within Article 2(1)(c).

4. Article 2(1)(d)

Article 2

1. **This Convention shall not apply to the following matters—**

...

(d) wills and succession;

5.53 Article 2(1)(d) provides that the Convention does not touch matters involving disposition of property at or after death, whether the disposition is by voluntary act or by operation of law. It is identical to Article 2(2)(c) of COCA, and should be accorded the same broad interpretation. However, not all matters related in any fashion to the fate of property transferred at death fall within Article 2(1)(d). For example, it does not extend to disputes between trustees and beneficiaries of a testamentary trust, or between estate administrators and third parties.[34]

5. Article 2(1)(e)

Article 2

1. **This Convention shall not apply to the following matters—**

...

(e) insolvency, composition, and resolution of financial institutions, and analogous matters;

5.54 Article 2(1)(e) is largely identical to Article 2(2)(e) of COCA, but has been expanded to include 'resolution of financial institutions' (not explicitly referenced in the COCA provision). The two Conventions should be accorded the same broad interpretation, as the same objectives and concerns underlie this provision in both.

5.55 There has been a strong trend in international commercial law and policy to centralize insolvency and analogous proceedings in a single forum—usually the forum of domicile or residence of the insolvent person—and to restrict the practice of 'ring-fencing' whereby courts in various countries take jurisdiction over assets within the particular country and parcel the assets out according to local rules. The objective is to create a fair and uniform global result for all claimants in a global economy, not dependent on the quirks of local

[33] Recognition and enforcement of a child custody determination is addressed by the Convention of 19 October 1996 on Jurisdiction, Applicable Law, Recognition, Enforcement and Co-operation in respect of Parental Responsibility and Measures for the Protection of Children.

[34] We share the conclusions in this regard of the Explanatory Report (n 30) 58, para 48 and the Nygh/Pocar Report (n 17), para 37.

attachment law and local bankruptcy or insolvency procedure.[35] It was viewed as undesirable to have COCA intrude on this emerging regime, especially as the intrusion might result in fracturing litigation among various courts according to prior choice of court agreements.

This Convention follows suit. It would be particularly undesirable to create an international legal obligation in this Convention to recognize or enforce judgments coming from a court engaged in ring-fencing or the like, thus undercutting efforts to rationalize and to make the consequences of insolvency somewhat fairer on a global basis. (The same rationale applies to limitation of liability for maritime claims in Article 2(1)(g).) **5.56**

Article 2(1)(c) applies broadly to proceedings that attempt to find a fair distribution of limited assets in response to claims arising from the insolvency of a person. Thus, 'insolvency' applies to the bankruptcy both of natural and legal persons (however labelled as a matter of municipal law, for example 'liquidation' or 'winding-up' as opposed to personal bankruptcy). 'Composition' involves any set of procedures allowing agreements between a debtor and creditors for re-scheduling, moratoria, suspension, or discharge of debts. 'Resolution of financial institutions' provides a supplemental clarification of the COCA article, and re-affirms the broad coverage of Article 2(1)(e) by removing any interpretive question regarding the difference in scope for purposes of this Convention of the treatment of financial institutions as distinguished from other persons. The phrase 'analogous matters' is intended to catch a broad range of mechanisms and proceedings created under national law to assist an insolvent party in coping with the insolvency, including mechanisms that allow the continued operation of the insolvent while steps are taken to regain solvency.[36] **5.57**

Article 2(1)(e) does not pivot on the name of the tribunal assigned jurisdiction over such matters under the national law of a given Contracting State. **5.58**

While the core of Article 2(1)(e) should be clear enough, there may be issues concerning scope at the margins. It is not clear whether an issue falls within Article 2(1)(e) merely because it could be resolved in an insolvency proceeding (leaving aside the issue of preliminary question in Article 2(2)). Issues that intrinsically can be raised only in an insolvency proceeding, such as the priority of creditors, clearly are included in Article 2(1)(e). However, not all judgments *relating to* an ongoing insolvency proceeding necessarily fall within it. For example, if a person asserts a debt due from an insolvent by virtue of a contract, the Convention text provides no clear resolution of whether a judgment finding the existence (or non-existence) of the contractual obligation should be treated as a matter within Article 2(1)(e) or not. **5.59**

[35] For work on transnational insolvency generally, and which reflects trends towards a more internationally-coordinated approach, see, eg, UNCITRAL Model Law on Cross-Border Insolvency (1997) <https://uncitral.un.org/sites/uncitral.un.org/files/media-documents/uncitral/en/1997-model-law-insol-2013-guide-enactment-e.pdf>; UNCITRAL Model Law on Recognition and Enforcement of Insolvency-Related Judgments (2018) <https://uncitral.un.org/sites/uncitral.un.org/files/media-documents/uncitral/en/ml_recognition_gte_e.pdf>; UNCITRAL Model Law on Enterprise Group Insolvency (2019) <https://uncitral.un.org/sites/uncitral.un.org/files/media-documents/uncitral/en/19-11346_mloegi.pdf>.

[36] We reach the same conclusions generally as the Explanatory Report (n 30) 58–59, paras 49–50. See also the Nygh/Pocar Report (n 17) paras 38–39. Chapter 11 of the US Bankruptcy Code, Part II of the UK Insolvency Act 1986, and Canada's Companies' Creditors Arrangement Act (R.S.C., 1985, c. C-36) are examples of analogous matters.

6. Article 2(1)(f)

Article 2

1. This Convention shall not apply to the following matters—

...

(f) the carriage of passengers and goods;

5.60 Article 2(1)(f) is identical to Article 2(2)(f) of COCA and provides that neither Convention extends to the carriage of passengers and goods—by any means of transportation or combination of means. The carriage of passengers and goods is subject to pre-existing international regimes, either by way of multilateral arrangement[37] or in national law. As in other aspects of Article 2(1), the Convention intends to avoid intrusion on existing or potentially emerging international regimes. Cases construing the scope of treaty regimes or national law in this area are helpful sources of interpretation of the scope of both this article and its COCA complement.

7. Article 2(1)(g)

Article 2

1. This Convention shall not apply to the following matters—

...

(g) transboundary marine pollution, marine pollution in areas beyond national jurisdiction, ship-source marine pollution, limitation of liability for maritime claims, and general average;

5.61 Article 2(1)(g) provides that the Convention does not apply in five areas of maritime interest. Unlike the exclusion in Article 2(1)(f), and in Article 2(2)(f) of COCA applicable to carriage of passengers and goods, which applies regardless of the modality of carriage involved, the exclusion in Article 2(1)(g)—and its analogue Article 2(2)(g) of COCA—are soaked in a maritime context.

5.62 Article 2(1)(g) invites a narrow construction. Not only does it operate only on water—usually ocean water—rather than a broad field of anything under foot, under flight, or under keel, but the referents of its terms are quite specific, in contrast to the broad, generic terms employed in earlier provisions of Article 2(1). In addition, in many respects Article 2(1)(g) marks a deliberate narrowing, after intensive discussion, of its predecessor Article 2(2)(g) of COCA.[38] Specifically, the categorical reference in COCA to marine pollution has been reduced significantly, to encompass only pollution judgments arising from claims with certain territorial characteristics or emanating from one type of source. In addition, the application of Article 2(2)(g) of COCA to a generic category of 'emergency towage and salvage' has been stripped entirely from this Convention. As a result, this Convention applies to

[37] See, eg, the International Convention for the Unification of certain Rules of Law relating to Bills of Lading, signed at Brussels, 25 August 1924; the Protocol to amend the International Convention for the Unification of certain Rules of Law relating to Bills of Lading, signed at Brussels, 23 February 1968; and the Protocol to amend the International Convention for the Unification of certain Rules of Law relating to Bills of Lading as Modified by the Amending Protocol of February 23, 1968, signed at Brussels, 21 December 1979.

[38] Art 2(2)(g) of COCA applies to 'marine pollution, limitation of liability for maritime claims, general average, and emergency towage and salvage'.

significant categories of judgments arising from marine pollution, and emergency towage and salvage generally.

The first two limbs of Article 2(1)(g) establish territorial limitations on judgments arising from marine pollution that may be recognized or enforced under the Convention. 'Marine pollution' here refers both to pollution originating from a maritime entity, regardless of where the harm from the pollution is sustained, such as upon shorelines, and to pollution from land-based sources that cause harm to the marine environment. This reading is bolstered by the third limb of Article 2(1)(g) that refers to pollution from a particular source ('ship-source marine pollution') as the pollution to which the Convention does not apply, but makes no other limitation based upon source. Finally, the provision on its face applies to 'marine pollution' and does not reach pollution other than marine pollution (although Article 5(1)(j) (torts) may place other limitations on claims arising from non-marine pollution). **5.63**

The first limb of Article 2(1)(g) provides that the Convention shall not apply to 'transboundary marine pollution'. This text was introduced in a working document late in the Diplomatic Session,[39] and the wording may not have received the requisite polish. A literal reading of this provision suggests that, to avoid capture by Article 2(1)(g), the pollution involved must be contained entirely within the territorial boundaries of one country; the limb appears to shelter from the reach of the Convention any judgment arising from a pollution incident in which one particle of a pollutant moves across an international boundary, making operation of the Convention pivot not on the movement of judgments, but on the chance movement of particles with wind and tide. This seems an unlikely and harsh result. A less literal reading may be preferable here. The thrust of the idea was to restrict international legal obligations contained in the Convention in this area to judgments that adjudicated claims of domestic pollution, that is, those in which both the activity causing the pollution and its effects occurred in the territory of the forum. Insofar as the adjudication applies to aspects of a marine pollution event that are extraterritorial, the matter falls within the 'transboundary marine pollution' limb of Article 2(1)(g). Such a reading allows this limb of Article 2(1)(g) to work in tandem with Article 5(1)(j) of the Convention. **5.64**

As has been discussed in the Introduction, Article 5(1) provides eligibility criteria for recognition and enforcement under the Convention of judgments in various categories. Article 5(1)(j) applies to recognition and enforcement of judgments ruling on non-contractual obligations arising from damage to or loss of tangible property and requires that the act or omission directly causing the harm occurred in the State of origin, irrespective of where the harm occurred. Many pollution claims will likely be claims for damage to or loss of tangible property. The result of Article 5(1)(j) in conjunction with this suggested reading of the first limb of Article 2(1)(j) would permit circulation under the Convention of a judgment arising from maritime pollution if recognition or enforcement is sought for damages within the State of origin.[40] **5.65**

[39] See Working Document No 77.

[40] Such a reading would also parallel the reading of the territoriality clause in the exception to anti-trust (competition) in art 2(1)(p).

5.66 The second limb of Article 2(1)(g) provides that the Convention does not apply to marine pollution in areas beyond national jurisdiction. This language is carefully crafted, stating its rule in terms of 'national jurisdiction' rather than national territorial boundaries. It essentially means that the Convention does not apply to marine pollution on the high seas, but generally will apply to marine pollution in the territorial sea, contiguous zone, and exclusive economic zones—all of which are within national jurisdiction of one sort or another under the law of the sea.[41] This is also consistent with the approach taken in Article 5(1)(j); marine pollution originating in an area beyond national jurisdiction will not have occurred in the State of the forum, while pollution of the high seas themselves is best treated as a matter for other international instruments.

5.67 The third limb of Article 2(1)(g) provides that the Convention does not apply to 'ship-source marine pollution'. On its face, this limb of the exclusion does not apply to land-source pollution. The text does, however, raise the issue of what is a 'ship' and consequently a 'ship-source' for the purposes of Article 2(1)(g). On this point, we must recognize that we should navigate making full use of established landmarks. The classification of a vessel as a 'ship' in a particular context should pay due heed to the classification established (and evolving) under the law of the sea.

5.68 The justification for the fourth limb of Article 2(1)(g), limitation of liability for maritime claims, is similar in part to the justification for treatment of bankruptcy in Article 2(1)(e). There are long-established international conventions and legal regimes with respect to limitation of liability proceedings that have garnered wide support, and that result in a centralized, rational, and relatively efficient adjudication of claims to a limited pool of assets, rather than producing a helter-skelter race to the best forum for a particular litigant.[42] This Convention should not encourage the latter.

5.69 The fifth limb of Article 2(1)(g) is identical to the predecessor provision in COCA, Article 2(2)(g), and has been carried over into this Convention to maintain complementarity.

5.70 The 'emergency towage and salvage' limb of Article 2(2)(g) of COCA has been excluded from this Convention. During the negotiations, no serious justification for placing them outside either Convention was provided. As a matter of policy, there is generally a wish to encourage salvors and others who will preserve property from the perils of the sea—and it is almost tautologous that those perils will be greatest and the risks highest in an emergency. Recognition and enforcement across borders of judgments arising from these activities is fully consonant with international policy and eminent good sense, and is the rule of this Convention.

5.71 Finally, it is worth noting a point that is important in the maritime context: a judgment for a claim for indemnification by a judgment debtor against an insurer may be within the Convention's scope, even if the underlying insured event involves transboundary marine pollution or other limbs to which the Convention does not apply by virtue of Article 2(1)(g).

[41] See the structure of the United Nations Convention on the Law of the Sea (UNCLOS).

[42] See, eg, International Convention for the Unification of Certain Rules relating to the Limitation of the Liability of Owners of Seagoing Vessels, done at Brussels, 25 August 1924; International Convention relating to the Limitation of the Liability of Owners of Seagoing Ships, done at Brussels, 10 October 1957; Convention on Limitation of Liability for Maritime Claims, London, November 1976.

8. Article 2(1)(h)

Article 2

1. This Convention shall not apply to the following matters—

...

(h) liability for nuclear damage;

Article 2(1)(h) provides that the Convention shall not apply to 'liability for nuclear damage'. An identical provision is found in Article 2(2)(i) of COCA. **5.72**

Many States view matters of nuclear liability regimes as subject to strong, local public policy, often including comprehensive or near-comprehensive frameworks in national law that regulate matters such as jurisdiction and venue, limitation of liability, relationship to insurance, and sources of funding. Other States are parties to international conventions dealing with this subject matter area.[43] In light of the underlying concerns, both COCA and this Convention tread lightly in this area. **5.73**

These same concerns counsel a broad interpretation of Article 2(1)(h). However, the choice of words in this provision, if taken literally, may be in tension with the considerations underlying it. The provision applies to 'liability for nuclear damages'. This would suggest that judgments related to nuclear power are outside Article 2(1)(h) and otherwise within the scope of the Convention so long as they do not involve either liability or nuclear *damage* issues (strictly construed) and are otherwise civil or commercial. While this literal reading may be a reasonable result in an instrument that seeks to give effect to party choice, such as COCA, interpretation of the words may need to be adapted in light of the context and foundations of this Convention. **5.74**

9. Article 2(1)(i)

Article 2

1. This Convention shall not apply to the following matters—

...

(i) the validity, nullity, or dissolution of legal persons, and the validity of decisions of their organs;

Article 2(1)(i) is identical to Article 2(2)(m) of COCA and provides that the Convention shall not apply to the validity, nullity, or dissolution of legal persons, or to the validity of decisions of their organs. The provisions of the two Conventions were intended to be read and should be read in parallel. **5.75**

Article 2(1)(i) is restricted on its face to 'legal persons'. Under some systems of law, there may be a variety of entities, such as unregistered companies or certain types of associations or cooperative arrangements, which are not 'legal persons', but which may be parties to court cases. Entities that are not 'legal persons' under domestic law do not fall **5.76**

[43] See Hartley/Dogauchi Report (n 20) para 64, fn 92; Paris Convention on Third Party Liability in the Field of Nuclear Energy 1960; Convention Supplementary to the Paris Convention, 1963; Vienna Convention on Civil Liability for Nuclear Damage, signed 21 May 1963; Convention on Supplementary Compensation for Nuclear Damage, 1997; also Joint Protocol relating to the Application of the Vienna Convention and Paris Convention, 1988.

within Article 2(1)(i). The field of application of Article 2(1)(i) may be compared to the definition of residence in Article 4(3), which leaves no gaps, because legal person refers to 'an entity or person other than a natural person'. Here, the failure to include a possible class (non-natural persons that do not qualify as legal persons under local law) can be construed as intent to exclude that class from the provision. Thus, at least conceptually, the Convention will apply in such matters as the validity of decisions of an organ of a non-natural person which is not a legal person, but the Convention does not apply if the entity is a legal person.

5.77 Article 2(1)(i) is focused on matters internal to the structure and operation of the legal person. It does not apply to the consequences of decisions made by the legal person. The phrase 'the validity of decisions of their organs' includes nullity.

10. Article 2(1)(j)

Article 2

1. This Convention shall not apply to the following matters—

...

(j) the validity of entries in public registers;

5.78 Article 2(1)(j) is identical to Article 2(2)(p) of COCA, and should be given the same interpretation. In some legal systems this matter is not regarded as a civil or commercial matter and would fall outside the scope of the Convention for that reason alone.

5.79 Article 2(1)(j) extends only to entries in public registers and applies only to the validity (or nullity) of the entry. It does not extend to the legal effects that an entry will have. Nor does it apply to anything that is not an entry, or any register that is not a public register.

11. Article 2(1)(k)

Article 2

1. This Convention shall not apply to the following matters—

...

(k) defamation;

5.80 Article 2(6)1(k) and (l) provide that the Convention does not apply to the categories of defamation and privacy, respectively. The Convention does not enter the world of recognition or enforcement of judgments arising from what may be referred to as dignitary torts.[44] Neither 'defamation' nor 'privacy' have international law referents, and there is wide variation in the understanding of the concepts in domestic law around the world, including variations in burdens of proof, persuasion, and remedies. This variation is an important consideration for the scope of the Convention, and these are important subjects in national law: often they are the subject of constitutional provisions or mandatory local public policy. Article 2(1)(k) and (l) are categorical and should be interpreted as broadly applicable to the categories involved.

[44] This is a point also apparent in art 5(1)(j) (torts), which provides eligibility of a judgment for recognition or enforcement only if the judgment ruled on death, physical injury, or damage to or loss of tangible property.

Accordingly, it is our view that the general contours of an autonomous Convention sense of 'defamation' would include any published utterance that contains a proposition that is untrue of another person. The core of the concept is an utterance that contains a proposition. The utterance may be carried in any medium, and may take any original form (eg words, pictures). The proposition it conveys must make an untrue statement about another person, whether natural or non-natural, or, perhaps, put that person in a false light. Finally, the utterance must be published to third persons. For Convention purposes, nothing turns on whether the cause of action or claim is characterized in a given legal system as 'defamation' or 'libel' or 'slander' or the like. 5.81

12. Article 2(1)(l)

Article 2

1. **This Convention shall not apply to the following matters—**

...

(l) privacy;

Article 2(1)(l) provides that the Convention does not apply to 'privacy'. As with virtually all scope terms in the Convention, the Convention provides no definition. Nor is this an international law concept. As a point of comparative law, the legal concept of privacy varies dramatically among States, and is currently the subject of rapid change and evolution, including whether or not it is assigned constitutional dimensions (unlike defamation, with a longer history and which tends to be found in more stable form within each legal system). 5.82

While the Convention attempts no definition, as an operational matter in litigation, privacy claims tend to have as a central feature an unwelcome and uninvited intrusion into a sphere of life that is deemed 'private' or 'personal' by legal systems. Depending upon the legal system, publication may or may not be a necessary component of a privacy claim, but should be expected to play a part in consideration of remedies, including damages.[45] 5.83

As with other provisions in Article 2(1) that are formulated in terms of broad, natural categories, Article 2(1)(l) should be accorded a broad interpretation commensurate with its category. This interpretive stance is supported by the development of Article 2(1)(l). The original proposal was that the Convention not apply to 'privacy' except where the proceedings were brought for breach of contract between the parties.[46] This formulation created substantial risks of uncertainty in outcomes, inconsistent application of the Convention, difficult questions of the stance of local courts towards aspects of foreign public law, and frequent recourse to the public policy exception, all of which would complicate ratification discussions in some States. A number of questions arise. 5.84

[45] For purposes of the Convention, certain aspects of 'privacy', may be usefully contrasted with 'defamation'. First, defamation requires a publication, whereas privacy pivots on an intrusion into some sphere which is assigned protection by legal systems. Second, the proposition published in a defamation must be untrue or put a person in a false light, whereas privacy does not stand upon content of publication but upon the fact of intrusion. Finally, defamation may affect non-natural persons as well as natural persons, whereas, at least at present, privacy claims would appear to be restricted to natural persons (on the grounds that non-natural persons do not occupy a sphere of life that might be deemed 'private' or 'personal'—although views on this could shift).

[46] See Explanatory Report (n 30) 63, particularly fnn 64–66 for development of discussions in this area.

For example, does a statement of policy posted on a website in one country create contractual terms that may be deemed to be breached under the law of another country? Indeed, the answer to this question may vary with the laws of multiple jurisdictions from which the website may be accessed. May a court in one country in determining the existence or terms of a contract, imply terms into the contract, including terms not known in the laws of another country? Furthermore, given that much of the rapidly developing law in this area is statutory, or even constitutional, will mandatory terms of law be inserted into these contracts in one country with a subsequent legal obligation under this Convention to recognize and enforce these mandatory obligations in a resulting judgment? Significant strains on the public policy exception might include invocation of constitutional grounds of the State requested to bar recognition and enforcement. These and many more considerations would arise in ratification debates in each country and make the Convention less attractive to a number of countries. Accordingly, the Diplomatic Session adopted the categorical, broad exclusion in Article 2(1)(l).

5.85 Because Article 2(1)(l) addresses an area of great and growing importance, and due to the novelty of its occurrence in Hague Conventions, our discussion will go into some detail. In approaching its interpretation, Article 2(1)(l) provides a good case study of the potential interplay of the scope provisions in Chapter I of the Convention, the criteria for recognition and enforcement in Article 5, the discretionary grounds for refusal of recognition and enforcement in Article 7, and the declaration mechanism in Article 18. There are a number of possible approaches to a rule with respect to privacy, which are listed below. The choices made among these possibilities are relevant to interpretation of the final text.

(1) 'Privacy' as a category not within the Convention, but with one or more narrowly defined exceptions to that rule. This solution would bring certain things that might be considered 'privacy' within scope, but those included things would be specifically designated and still would need to satisfy an Article 5(1) eligibility factor for recognition or enforcement while not falling afoul of an Article 7 ground of discretionary refusal.
(2) 'Privacy' as a category not within the Convention, but with a definition of 'privacy' that limits the breadth of the term for purposes of the Convention. Depending upon the definition, this approach would then allow into scope certain matters not within the definition. As with alternate variant 1 above, a judgment on any such 'privacy'-related matters would still need to satisfy Article 5(1) and would remain subject to Article 7.
(3) No general rule that the Convention does not apply to 'privacy', but a listing of specific items that might be considered aspects of 'privacy' to which the Convention would not extend. Depending on the list, this could leave a very small range of residual items within scope, and each residual item would still need to satisfy Article 5(1) and remain subject to Article 7.
(4) No general rule that the Convention does not apply to 'privacy' but with a narrow, highly specific, and exclusive criterion for recognition or enforcement of 'privacy' judgments in Article 5(1) (preventing recognition and enforcement on any other grounds in Article 5(1)), or by providing a narrow definition of 'privacy' within that Article 5(1) sub-rule.

(5) No general rule that the Convention does not apply to 'privacy', but with a specific, non-exclusive criterion for recognition or enforcement of 'privacy' judgments in Article 5(1). Depending upon policy objectives, this might allow a broad field for recognition and enforcement, as it would also permit recognition and enforcement if any other sub-rule in Article 5(1) is satisfied.

(6) Silence, which would mean that 'privacy' matters are within the scope of the Convention, but any judgment in the area would still need to satisfy Article 5(1) and would remain subject to Article 7.

(7) Silence within both Article 2 and Article 5, allowing each State to declare out of an obligation to recognize or enforce privacy judgments (although this would create the issue of whether the declaration would be strictly reciprocal or *erga omnes*, effectively acting as a scope exclusion with respect to judgments that bear a connection to the declarant State specified in the declaration).

As can be seen, each of these logical possibilities would have brought some privacy judgments within the scope of the Convention; none of them was embraced. Accordingly, 'privacy' should be read broadly for purposes of the Convention.

However, there was one particular situation that was identified as best characterized as a contract matter rather than a privacy matter, namely when recognition or enforcement is sought of a judgment arising from an alleged breach of a contract that is generally available commercially and that provides for the protection of personal data, for example, the contract between the holder of personal data and a provider of services in relation to the use of such data.[47] **5.86**

13. Article 2(1)(m)

Article 2

1. **This Convention shall not apply to the following matters—**

...

(m) **intellectual property;**

Article 2(1)(m) provides that the Convention shall not apply to the category of 'intellectual property'. There is no Convention definition of 'intellectual property'. What is included in the term is subject to sharp debate and great variation (eg 'traditional knowledge').[48] **5.87**

[47] Diplomatic Session, Minutes No 8, paras 116–19. This understanding is framed to apply to generally available contracts offered in commercial marketplaces so as not to reach barter or other types of exchanges between private persons on an exclusive and informal basis.

[48] However, some guidance to the scope of the term may be found in a number of international agreements addressing intellectual property. For example, the Paris Convention for the Protection of Industrial Property, as revised at Stockholm in 1967 (the 'Paris Convention'), the Convention Establishing the World Intellectual Property Organization (WIPO) (as amended 28 September 1979), the Agreement on Trade-related Aspects of Intellectual Property Rights (TRIPS), the Berne Convention for the Protection of Literary and Artistic Works, the WIPO copyright treaties, and other existing and future international instruments under the auspices of WIPO. Specific subjects that, at a minimum, are included in the term are rights that protect patents, utility models, registered and unregistered designs, registered and unregistered trademarks, trade names, plant variety protection (also known as plant breeders' certificates), geographical indications, appellations of origin, copyright and related rights, rights seeking to prevent unfair competition (as understood with reference to art 10 bis of the Paris Convention), rights to protect undisclosed information (as understood with reference to art 39 TRIPS), trade secrets, databases, moral

Accordingly, some of the considerations that counsel broad interpretation of the concept of 'privacy' also operate with respect to 'intellectual property'.

5.88 This broad interpretive stance is reinforced by reference to the corresponding COCA provisions. Article 2(2)(n) and (o) of COCA provide that COCA does not apply to 'the validity of intellectual property rights other than copyright and related rights' (art 2(2)(n)), or to 'infringement of intellectual property rights other than copyright and related rights, except where infringement proceedings are brought for breach of a contract between the parties relating to such rights, or could have been brought for breach of that contract' (art 2(2)(o)). In the Judgments Convention, there is no differentiation between copyright and other intellectual property rights, no differentiation between validity and infringement, and no accommodation for breach of contract as opposed to other claims.

5.89 This broad reading is modulated somewhat by the position in the Diplomatic Session of two States centrally involved in the creation of this provision, the United States and China. They submitted a joint Working Document, observing that Article 2(1)(m) does not extend to all contractual disputes simply because there is an intellectual property aspect. A judgment falls within Article 2(1)(m) 'if the dispute is better characterized as an intellectual property matter instead of as a contractual matter. In characterizing such judgments, a substantive intellectual property law matter at issue necessarily indicates the matter is best deemed an intellectual property matter rather than a contractual matter.'[49] The Working Document gives examples: a licensing dispute over a standard essential patent (SEP) with a fair, reasonable, and non-discriminatory (FRAND) licensing commitment or a dispute involving a determination of ownership issues on the basis of substantive intellectual property law would fall within Article 2.1(m), while a contractual dispute on the sale of intellectual property or a security agreement on the basis of an intellectual property right might fall outside it if not raising substantive intellectual property law issues.

5.90 In addition, it should be noted that if intellectual property claims or defences were raised as a preliminary question under Article 2(2)—for example in a licensing dispute or breach of contract case—the proceedings are not thereby removed from the scope of the Convention. The 'object of the proceedings' was to adjudicate the issue of whether a licensing agreement, contract, or other agreement, had been breached. The asserted obligation of the defendant to the plaintiff arises from these legal instruments, not from an intellectual property regime.

5.91 There are a number of sound reasons for a broad interpretation of Article 2(1)(m). First, as noted above, in many respects intellectual property mirrors the problems in privacy, for example wide variation in understanding of the term, strong public policies sometimes reaching constitutional dimensions, sharp divergence in bases of liability, and available remedies.

5.92 Second, intellectual property law is a specialized area of great complexity. Work in the area calls for a joint venture with specialized bodies rather than being a project solely of generalists in private international law.[50]

rights, traditional knowledge, genetic resources, traditional cultural expressions, technological protection measures, and rights management information.

[49] 2019 Diplomatic Session, Working Document No 80.

[50] The Hague Conference on Private International Law has worked with the World Intellectual Property Organization on cross-cutting matters. An example of this collaboration is 'When Private International Law Meets Intellectual Property Law: A Guide for Judges' <https://assets.hcch.net/docs/679f66c5-b701-4318-a82a-129cefc64010.pdf>.

Third, much intellectual property litigation is as complex as the substantive law underlying it. It would be a daunting task for a court presented with a judgment—and often little more—for recognition and enforcement to disentangle parts of these judgments that might fall within the scope of the Convention and other parts that do not. **5.93**

Finally, it is worth putting intellectual property into a broader context of structural issues in private international law conventions. There was an inclination to bar or prohibit giving effect to a category known as 'foreign public law'.[51] Many legal systems, however, do not have a private law/public law dichotomy, or, if they do, it is not well developed, and, even if developed, the classification shows great variation. The result was that matters from technical requirements of service of process to virtually any issue involving the relationship between a State and an individual—regardless of the relationship involved—might fall afoul of the foreign public law exclusion. The categorical bar to giving effect to foreign public law has eroded, beginning with its absence in the Inter-American Convention on the Law Applicable to International Contracts, signed at Mexico City, 17 March 1994. However, to state that there should not be a categorical bar in private international law conventions to giving effect to foreign public law does not mean that COCA and the Judgments Convention can or should give effect to all matters that might be treated as foreign public law: certain specific areas may remain problematic. Intellectual property is such an example. An intellectual property right essentially is a State-endowed territorial monopoly with a private right of enforcement through litigation. To ask a foreign court to recognize or enforce a judgment requires it to give effect to the consequences of foreign monopolies granted by sovereign States. Anti-trust, involving State regulation of domestic markets, is another area that might be classified as foreign public law that could come into play in a private international law convention; it receives specific treatment in Article 2(1)(p).[52] **5.94**

14. Article 2(1)(n)

Article 2

1. **This Convention shall not apply to the following matters—**

...

   (n) **activities of armed forces, including the activities of their personnel in the exercise of their official duties;**

Article 2(1)(n) provides that the Convention shall not apply to activities of armed forces, including the activity of their personnel in the exercise of their official duties. It is the first of three scope provisions placing certain State activities outside the Convention, in addition to Article 2(1)(o) (law enforcement) and Article 2(1)(q) (sovereign debt restructuring). These scope provisions must be read in light of Article 2(4) and (5), which address the inclusion **5.95**

[51] See, eg, Dicey and Morris, *The Conflict of Laws* (15th edn, 2012) Rule 20 ('English Courts have no jurisdiction to entertain an action . . . for the enforcement, either directly or indirectly, of a penal, revenue, or other public law of a foreign State').

[52] Finally, it is difficult to negotiate international litigation treaties without acknowledging 'protective' jurisdictions found in many legal systems that create special rules to shield persons viewed as at a disadvantage in the marketplace, such as consumers and employees. While this Convention does not operate by way of jurisdictional protections, it does provide specific enhanced protections to these persons in art 5(2). Whether privacy will develop into an example of public law remains to be seen.

generally of judgments to which governments are parties while preserving privileges and immunities. Article 2(1)(n), (o), and (q) do not have parallels in COCA, in part because the building block of COCA is the consensual exclusive choice of court agreement, which poses fewer problems in these areas than does this Convention, which encompasses judgments arising in a large array of involuntary situations.

5.96 Article 2(1)(n) provides that the Convention does not extend to an entire category, in this case, 'activities of armed forces'. The article pivots on the identity of the actor—'armed forces'—and covers all activities of armed forces. It does not hinge on whether the activity would attract immunity in some legal system. The second clause, 'including the activity of their personnel', is not a limitation but a clarification that removes any doubt that Article 2(1)(n) applies to judgments arising from the activities both of the institution of armed forces and the individuals who act for that institution. The term 'personnel' encompasses anyone acting for an armed force, including civilian employees, and contractors, rather than restricting the ambit of Article 2(1)(n) to those with employment status as 'soldiers' or 'sailors'. However, an activity by an individual member of an armed force falls outside Article 2(1)(n) if the activity giving rise to the judgment was not in the exercise of the official duty of the individual.

5.97 Article 2(1)(n) and its counterpart Article 2(1)(o) reflect the critical importance to States of their sovereign interests in these areas, and were necessitated by a combination of factors. First, there remains some variation State to State and court to court on the content and circumstances of jurisdictional immunities in this area, including the circumstances in which the immunity of the State runs to its officials. Second, armed forces engage in some activities that may not attract jurisdictional immunities in international law, but usually fall within status of forces agreements or the like, that create exclusive dispute resolution mechanisms, including specific remedies and payment mechanisms. It would be undesirable for this Convention to provide a temptation to litigants or a justification for recognition or enforcement of judgments in these circumstances.[53] These concerns are heightened by the unprecedented power of this Convention: once a judgment issues, it may be presented for recognition or enforcement in every (or almost every) Contracting State, thus greatly multiplying the number of fora in which proceedings for recognition or enforcement can occur.

15. Article 2(1)(o)

Article 2

1. **This Convention shall not apply to the following matters—**

...

(o) **law enforcement activities, including the activities of law enforcement personnel in the exercise of their official duties;**

5.98 Article 2(1)(o) is the companion to Article 2(1)(n) and marches alongside it. The only structural difference is that Article 2(1)(o) refers to 'law enforcement activities' rather than 'activities of armed forces'. The difference in wording is deliberate and reflects that an

[53] Accordingly, art 2.1(n) is intended to insulate from the Convention, among other matters relating to armed forces, anything that falls within the scope of a status of forces or similar agreement, regardless of the result that otherwise might obtain under art 23 of this Convention (relationship with other international instruments).

'armed force' is more amenable to delimitation than is law enforcement or law enforcement agencies. Similarly, the reference to personnel is to 'law enforcement personnel' rather than to 'its' or 'their' personnel, which would have been parallel in structure to Article 2(1)(n). As a result, this provision can apply to individuals having law enforcement responsibility without regard to their affiliation to a particular entity or organization. These points further underscore that Article 2(1)(o) should be given a broad scope of interpretation. It applies to all law enforcement activities, including investigations, arrests, extraditions, prosecutions, requests for evidence and other mutual legal assistance, fines, forfeitures, incarceration, pardons, and releases.[54] It applies regardless of whether the activity would qualify for immunity in some legal system. It applies to anyone engaged in those activities; the use of the term 'personnel' avoids restricting those whose activities are covered by reference to a particular agency, type of institution, or personal employment status. The only limitation is that such personnel must act in the exercise of their official duties. Finally, as with the concern to protect the operational integrity of status of forces agreements in Article 2(1)(n), Article 2(1)(o) operates to protect the integrity of the complex panoply of law enforcement agreements that extend around the world; a dispute that arises out of activity connected to such an agreement is a dispute and judgment to which the Convention does not apply.[55]

16. Article 2(1)(p)

Article 2

1. **This Convention shall not apply to the following matters—**

...

(p) **anti-trust (competition) matters, except where the judgment is based on conduct that constitutes an anti-competitive agreement or concerted practice among actual or potential competitors to fix prices, make rigged bids, establish output restrictions or quotas, or divide markets by allocating customers, suppliers, territories or lines of commerce, and where such conduct and its effect both occurred in the State of origin;**

Article 2(1)(p) begins by providing that the Convention does not apply to 'anti-trust (competition) matters' as a category, then proceeds to identify exceptions to the general rule, and, finally, specifies that these exceptions are subject to satisfying territoriality requirements. Article 2(1)(p) contrasts with Article 2(2)(h) of COCA, which states that COCA does not apply to the entire category of 'anti-trust (competition) matters'. **5.99**

Article 2(1)(p) begins by stating that the Convention does not apply to the broad category of 'anti-trust (competition) matters'. The article is phrased as 'anti-trust (competition) matters' because anti-trust and competition law, as categories in various legal systems, are not identical concepts. **5.100**

[54] The law enforcement activity need not be classified as 'criminal' in some legal system, but might be regulatory enforcement by a regulator outside a *parens patriae* or similar role in which compensatory damages are sought for injured private persons. As such, this is likely to fall outside the field of 'civil or commercial' and be 'administrative' for purposes of the Convention.

[55] Accordingly, art 2(1)(o) is intended to insulate from the Convention, among other matters related to law enforcement, anything that falls within the scope of a mutual legal assistance treaty or similar agreement in law enforcement matters, regardless of the result that otherwise might obtain under art 23 of this Convention (relationship with other international instruments).

5.101 Anti-trust (competition) matters are viewed as matters of strong, local public policy—or even mandatory local public law—which should be free of a Convention obligation to recognize and enforce judgments reflecting foreign regulatory regimes. Consequently, at least at the start of the inquiry, anti-trust (competition) refers to the relevant body of national law of each Contracting State, and does not designate an autonomous Convention category. At least at first blush, if a judgment is in a matter that falls within the anti-trust or competition law of the requested State, the Convention does not apply to it.

5.102 Having begun in a familiar fashion for this Convention, Article 2(1)(p) then takes an unfamiliar turn—a turn that may become more trafficked if the regulatory regimes of individual States converge in some aspects. The Diplomatic Session concluded that while anti-trust (competition) is strongly rooted in domestic policy and shows significant variation in substance, procedural approaches, and remedies, certain objectives are generally shared and certain behaviours can be identified as hard-core cartel behaviour. Hard-core cartel (ie combinations or conspiracies involving more than one party) and monopoly (ie single-party exploitation of a dominant market position) behaviour is proscribed by most if not all States with anti-trust (competition) regimes. Article 2(1)(p) does not exclude from the scope of the Convention hard-core cartel behaviours. The language does leave hard-core monopoly behaviour excluded from the scope of the Convention.

5.103 In formulating the text, the Diplomatic Session examined the work of the Organization for Economic Co-operation and Development (OECD) in this area, particularly the Recommendation of the OECD Council Concerning Effective Action against Hard Core Cartels, adopted on 25 March 1998.[56] This Recommendation and its progeny should be consulted for useful and important guidance in the interpretation of Article 2.1(p). A delicate question may arise as to the effects on interpretation of Article 2(1)(p) as OECD recommendations evolve and develop in the future. Article 2(1)(p) presents a closed, exclusive, and exhaustive list; actions by the OECD or other bodies cannot in themselves amend the list. However, it may well be the case that the interpretation for Convention purposes of the behaviours on the excepted list may take into account evolving standards and interpretations to create an autonomous Convention approach.

5.104 The exception to Article 2(1)(p) may be analysed as consisting of three components: conduct, identities, and purpose. First, the conduct giving rise to the judgment must constitute an anti-competitive agreement or a concerted practice. No other conduct falls within the exception.[57] Second, the agreement or practice must be among actual or potential competitors, bearing in mind that there may be some delicate aspects to the determination of when persons are 'potential' competitors. Finally, the purpose of the conduct among these competitors must be to fix prices, make rigged bids, establish output restrictions or quotas, or divide markets by allocating customers, suppliers, territories, or lines of commerce. Other purposes, no matter how heinous, are beyond the reach of the exception contained in Article 2(1)(p).

5.105 Even if a judgment meets the criteria for hard-core cartel conduct within Article 2(1)(p), it must still satisfy two additional conditions for recognition and enforcement under

[56] The 1998 Recommendation has now been replaced by the Recommendation of the OECD Council concerning Effective Action against Hard Core Cartels, adopted on 2 July 2019.

[57] Thus, monopoly conduct in and of itself is not within the scope of the Convention unless it involves an agreement or concerted practice.

the Convention. One condition is contained in Article 2(1)(p) itself, namely a territorial condition, while the second results from the requirement that the judgment must satisfy a criterion for recognition and enforcement in Article 5(1). These two additional conditions place significant burdens on recognition and enforcement of anti-trust and competition law judgments, and will do much to restrict such recognition and enforcement to purely domestic violations, steering clear of difficult issues of extra-territorial regulatory reach.

The 'conduct' upon which the judgment 'is based' must have occurred in the State of origin, and its effects also must have occurred in that State. Accordingly, the requested court will be required to determine that a judgment presented to it for recognition or enforcement was 'based' upon an anti-competitive agreement or concerted practice—but there is no Convention criteria to fix the meaning of the notoriously slippery term 'based upon'.[58] Nor, in an era of transboundary electronic communication, will the determination of where the conduct occurred necessarily be easy. Finally, a judgment is outside Article 2(1)(p) to the extent that it takes into account effects beyond the State of origin, although a mixed territorial judgment may still be eligible for recognition or enforcement to the extent that it is limited to effects within the State of origin and that component of the judgment is severable under Article 9. **5.106**

Even if outside the scope of Article 2(1)(p), and, therefore, within the scope of the Convention, a judgment must still satisfy the criteria for recognition or enforcement in Article 5(1). Notably, Article 5(1)(j), which establishes criteria for recognition or enforcement of judgments ruling on non-contractual obligations, only applies to damage to or loss of tangible property, thus not including monetary or financial loss. **5.107**

Article 2(1)(p) operates without regard to the identity of the claimant. It encompasses claims brought by private individuals and claims brought by governmental authorities, provided those claims are otherwise civil or commercial within the meaning of the Convention. Thus, a judgment in favour of a government for compensatory damages for loss from a domestic cartel fixing prices on domestic government contracts such as for purchase of construction supplies may fall within the exception to the exclusion established by Article 2(1)(p), and, thus, within the scope of the Convention, but a regulatory enforcement action seeking conduct remedies and fines for injury to third parties likely would not. **5.108**

Under Article 2(2), if a claim under anti-trust (competition) law is raised as a preliminary question, for example in a licensing dispute or breach of contract case, the proceedings are not thereby removed from the scope of the Convention. The 'object of the proceedings' would be to adjudicate the issue of whether a licensing agreement, contract, or other agreement, has been breached. The asserted obligation of the defendant to the plaintiff arises from these private law instruments, not from the anti-trust regime. **5.109**

17. Article 2(1)(q)

Article 2

1. This Convention shall not apply to the following matters—

...

(q) sovereign debt restructuring through unilateral State measures.

[58] See analysis of art 4(2) in Chapter 6, for discussion of the review performed by the requested court.

5.110 Article 2(1)(q) is the third provision in Article 2(1) clarifying that the Convention does not apply to certain matters of significant sovereign State concern, sovereign debt restructuring through unilateral State measures.[59] As with its predecessors, Article 2(1)(q) reflects the uncertainty caused by variations in foreign State immunity doctrine coupled with the unprecedented power of this Convention to oblige recognition and enforcement to judgments in multiple States even when there are strong sovereign objections to the basis of the judgment. Absent the development of an *erga omnes* declaration system, reciprocal declarations do not provide protection against recognition and enforcement of questionable judgments in third or fourth States under the Convention. There is no parallel provision to Article 2(1)(q) in COCA, due to the consensual nature of entry into the scope of COCA. If a State wishes to execute a choice of court agreement to resolve sovereign debt restructuring controversies, both the State and its counterparts should enjoy the benefits of COCA.

5.111 The text of Article 2(1)(q) operates on a specific and qualified matter rather than a broad, general category. It requires three components, each of which plays a necessary and equal part, and that should not be treated as mere appended conditions of application: an activity, a specified mechanism for its achievement, and a causal connection. The activity is sovereign debt restructuring, the mechanism is unilateral State measures, and the restructuring must occur through those unilateral measures. Absent any one of these components, Article 2(1)(q) does not apply.

18. Provisions in COCA Without Parallel in This Convention

5.112 COCA contains a number of scope provisions in Article 2(2) that are not found in the cognate Article 2(1) of this Convention. In addition to consumers and contracts of employment in Article 2(2)(1) previously noted, these provisions are Article 2(2)(j) (claims for personal injury brought by or on behalf of natural persons), Article 2(2)(k) (tort or delict claims for damage to tangible property that do not arise from a contractual relationship), and Article 2(2)(l) (rights *in rem* in immovable property, and tenancies of immovable property). In some respects, these provisions accommodated certain exclusive jurisdictional bases found in a number of States, which might be disturbed by their operation within the scope of COCA, with its jurisdictional aspect. In part, some of the concerns in this area are addressed in this Convention by provisions other than scope provisions, specifically in Chapter II on recognition and enforcement. Thus, treatment of tort or delict in this Convention is through criteria for recognition and enforcement in Article 5(1)(j), while aspects of judgments arising from disputes involving real property are found in Article 5(3) and Article 6.

B. Article 2(2)—Preliminary Matters

2. A judgment is not excluded from the scope of the Convention where a matter to which this Convention does not apply arose merely as a preliminary question in the proceedings in which the judgment was given, and not as an object of the proceedings. In particular,

[59] See also art 2(1)(n) (activities of armed forces) and 2(1)(o) (law enforcement activities).

the mere fact that such a matter arose by way of defence does not exclude a judgment from the Convention, if that matter is not an object of the proceedings.

Article 2(2) is phrased in civil law system terms to state a situation in which a judgment is not excluded from the scope of the Convention.[60] It may at first appear strange on its face to the common law practitioner. When properly understood, however, it makes eminent sense in its context—and litigators in common law systems work with similar considerations on a daily basis, albeit with different terms and some procedural variations. **5.113**

An understanding of Article 2(2) may be assisted by reviewing briefly the general structure of the scope of the Convention. As an initial matter, the design of the Convention encompasses 'civil or commercial matters' within scope, while specifying certain items that fall outside that designation (revenue, customs, administrative matters). This initial scope is then modulated further by Article 2(1), which provides that the Convention does not apply to 'matters' that might be viewed as 'civil or commercial', and potentially further modified *de facto* via the declaration mechanism of Article 18 (allowing a State to declare that it will not apply the Convention to a particular 'matter'). **5.114**

Articles 2(1) and 18, however, raise the danger that a judgment may be taken out of the Convention because an issue that falls within them was raised in the proceedings in the court of origin. An example of this, although somewhat distorted for purposes of illustration, may be taken from patent litigation. A person apparently holding rights under a patent enters into a contract that licenses someone in another country to use the apparently patented process in exchange for payment of royalties, provided that the patent is valid. The licensor brings an action in a non-exclusive chosen court for breach of contract, seeking royalties allegedly owed under the licensing agreement. It would almost amount to professional malpractice for the defendant's counsel not to assert that the patent is invalid, and to seek a declaration to that effect. However, under Article 2(1)(m), the validity of a patent right is not within the scope of the Convention. Proceedings for recognition or enforcement of a judgment under the Convention could be brought to a halt by the presence of the intellectual property issue as a preliminary question in the original adjudication. **5.115**

The operation of the Convention should not be held captive to the vagaries or strategies of pleading. Article 2(2) is intended to avoid that result. It provides that adjudication may proceed in the requested court for recognition or enforcement of a judgment **5.116**

[60] Art 2(2) of the Judgments Convention runs parallel in many respects to art 2(3) COCA, which states:

> Notwithstanding paragraph 2, proceedings are not excluded from the scope of the Convention where a matter excluded under that paragraph arises merely as a preliminary question and not as an object of the proceedings. In particular, the mere fact that a matter excluded under paragraph 2 arises by way of defence does not exclude proceedings from this Convention, if that matter is not an object of the proceedings.

The major differences are the references to para 2 COCA, substitution of 'judgment' for 'proceedings' and a corresponding change of tense to the past tense in this Convention. Accordingly, the discussion here leans on Brand and Herrup (n 12) 71–73. The term 'preliminary question' was discussed in the original project as well, albeit under slightly different terminology, and an autonomous, unified conception of its use in Hague Conventions may be developing. Accordingly, useful guidance may be had from the explanatory reports accompanying this project and its predecessors. See Hartley/Dogauchi Report (n 20) paras 77 and 194. The terms 'incidental questions' and 'principal issue' are used in the Nygh/Pocar Report (n 17) para 177, which may be somewhat less alien to common law litigators than the terminology finally adopted.

pursuant to the Convention where a matter otherwise within Article 2(1) or an Article 18 declaration arises 'merely as a preliminary question ... and not as an object of the proceedings'.

5.117 Unfortunately, as noted, there is no established common law category of 'preliminary questions'. The Convention then juxtaposes that unknown concept against another concept not commonly used by common law lawyers—'an object of the proceedings'. The initial terminological problems aside, common law lawyers do have something operationally close to the concept embodied in Article 2(2). A preliminary question may be thought of as an issue that does not appear on the face of the complaint, but that must be determined in order for the Court to decide whether it can or cannot grant some or all of the relief requested. Another example may illustrate the nature of a preliminary question (although for other reasons this example may not actually arise under this Convention). Company A in one country enters into a contract (say a franchise or agency contract) with Company B, which is resident in another country. Company A brings a breach of contract action. It is asserted on the face of the complaint (or simply assumed) that the contract is valid. The court examining the complaint as received has no reason to doubt the validity of the contract, has no reason to know whether the validity of the contract will be called into question, and, if the validity is called into question, has no basis to forecast from the face of the complaint the grounds of the challenge to validity. However, once the question is raised, it must be resolved in order for a judgment to issue. Company B asserts that the contract is invalid because Company B (or its organs) could not validly decide to enter into a contract of the type at issue (eg a franchise or agency contract—both of which do have restrictions applied in some jurisdictions). See Article 2(1)(i). Nothing on the face of the complaint would lead a court to believe, *ex ante*, that it must determine whether, under the appropriate law, Company B could validly decide to enter into the type of contract involved. However, there can be no breach of contract without a valid contract, which would be a contract that Company B could validly enter. Hence, the validity of the decision of Company B (or the appropriate organ) to enter into the contract is a preliminary question which the court must decide in order to get to the ultimate issue of whether the plaintiff may have some or all of the relief sought in the complaint.

5.118 The second sentence of Article 2(2) acts both as an illustration (a matter can arise as a preliminary question by way of defence, and most likely will arise in that posture) and to make clear that preliminary questions are not limited to matters raised by way of defence. A preliminary question may arise, for example, by way of counterclaim.

5.119 This provision was particularly important in COCA in conjunction with subparagraphs (n) and (o) of Article 2(2), on intellectual property. In this Convention, it may come into play particularly in intellectual property matters under Article 2(1)(m) and anti-trust (competition) matters under Article 2(1)(p), as noted above, and, perhaps, with respect to privacy under Article 2(1)(l), depending upon the evolution of privacy law.

5.120 Finally, it is important to note that, while Article 2(2) keeps a matter within the scope of the Convention even if the court of origin ruled on a matter outside scope as a preliminary question, Article 8 acts in a somewhat complementary fashion to take out of the Convention recognition or enforcement of rulings on preliminary questions that resolve matters to which the Convention does not apply or matters referred to in Article 6, on which a ruling occurred by a court other than a court of the State in which the property is situated.

C. Article 2(3)—Arbitration and Related Proceedings

3. This Convention shall not apply to arbitration and related proceedings.

Article 2(3) provides that the Convention shall not apply to 'arbitration and related proceedings'. There is a functioning international regime governing arbitral proceedings, including the highly successful United Nations Convention on the Recognition and Enforcement of Foreign Arbitral Awards ('New York Convention').[61] Article 2(3) makes clear that the Convention does not disturb the existing arbitral regime. Article 2(3) refers to 'arbitration' as a category, and it should be construed broadly. In addition, the deployment of the phrase 'and related proceedings' demonstrates that the reach of Article 2(3) is expansive. Thus, any 'proceeding' related to an arbitration falls within Article 2(3) and outside the Convention, whether it be a proceeding for the appointment of arbitrators, a proceeding to resolve disputes over the validity of an arbitral clause, or a proceeding in which a court is asked to provide relief in aid of arbitration. **5.121**

Article 2(3) is identical to Article 2(4) of COCA. Indeed, 'arbitration' was segregated from scope from the earliest negotiations leading to the Convention, as demonstrated in Article 1(2)(g) of the 1999 Preliminary Draft, which is discussed in the Nygh/Pocar Report.[62] **5.122**

Finally, it should be noted that, while the terms 'arbitration and related proceedings' in Article 2.3 should be interpreted broadly, they are not so broad as to include other distinct forms of dispute resolution that do not involve a court, such as mediation.[63] Thus, related proceedings are not proceedings generically related to non-judicial dispute resolution, but proceedings related to a particular arbitration. **5.123**

D. Article 2(4)—States as Parties to Civil or Commercial Matters

4. A judgment is not excluded from the scope of this Convention by the mere fact that a State, including a government, a governmental agency or any person acting for a State, was a party to the proceedings.

Article 2(4) and (5) address issues arising when States and international organizations are parties to or affected by judgments within the scope of the Convention. They are virtually identical to Article 2(5) and (6) of COCA.[64] **5.124**

Article 2(4) serves to clarify the phrase 'civil or commercial matters' in Article 1(1) by emphasizing that a judgment otherwise within scope as involving a civil or commercial matter is not excluded from the scope of the Convention merely because a State was a party **5.125**

[61] United Nations Convention on the Recognition and Enforcement of Foreign Arbitral Awards, done at New York, 10 June 1958, 21 UST 2517, TIAS No 6997, 330 UNTS 38 ('New York Convention'), <https://uncitral.un.org/sites/uncitral.un.org/files/media-documents/uncitral/en/new-york-convention-e.pdf> (accessed 1 July 2023).

[62] Nygh/Pocar Report (n 17) at para 41.

[63] A judicial settlement under art 11 does involve a court.

[64] The differences are found in art 2(5) COCA, which refers to 'proceedings' rather than to 'a judgment' and a change of tense to reflect that, in the recognition and enforcement posture of this Convention, the relevant time for when a State is a party is the past time of the proceedings in the court of origin.

to the proceedings. The scope of the Convention generally does not pivot on the identity of the parties to a proceeding in a civil or commercial matter, except in proceedings arising from the activity of armed forces (art 2(1)(n)), law enforcement activities (art 2(1)(o)), or sovereign debt restructuring (art 2(1)(q)). If a matter is 'civil or commercial' if engaged in by a private person, it will remain 'civil or commercial' when engaged in by a State. Insofar as States do things that their private partners in commercial transactions also do, the benefits and burdens of the Convention are to be shared evenly.[65]

5.126 As noted above, some guidance in construing the concept of 'civil or commercial matters' for this purpose may be found in the restrictive theory of foreign State immunity. Under the restrictive theory, a State is not immune from the jurisdiction of a foreign court when the State engages in conduct of a commercial nature.[66] While the formulations vary, it is reasonable to take the position that the benefits and burdens of this Convention should apply in those circumstances in which a court would deny foreign State immunity under the restrictive theory.

5.127 For purposes of this provision of the Convention, 'State' is construed broadly, and includes—but is not limited to—a government, a governmental agency, or any person acting for a State. The 'including' reference in Article 2(4) is a reference of example rather than limitation. This broad usage reflects reality, because a 'State' as an abstract entity must act through institutions, and, ultimately, through natural persons. A consequence of the extension of the term 'State' as used in this provision is that a private person acting for a State may be clothed with public authority and may be found to act in a fashion that is 'civil or commercial' for purposes of the Convention. Again, the scope of the Convention generally does not pivot on the identity of the parties to the underlying litigation.

5.128 Finally, proceedings are not excluded from the scope of the Convention 'by the mere fact' that a State is a party to those proceedings. The phrase 'mere fact' was carefully chosen. There may be background provisions of public international law that come into play to effectively limit and constrain the scope of the Convention with respect to governmental litigation. For example, while it is clear that the Convention will apply to a dispute in a commercial matter between a State and a private person, it is not clear that an action brought by a State in its own courts against a foreign sovereign would be within the scope of the Convention. First, there is an arguable view that a State should not employ courts that it created to sue another juridically equal sovereign. Second, there is an argument that such State-to-State disputes, while they may arise from commercial transactions, have public law and diplomatic implications beyond the realm of 'civil or commercial matters' and should not be characterized as such.

5.129 Article 2(4) is phrased in terms of a 'State' while Article 2(5) refers both to States and to international organizations. There was no affirmative effort to exclude international organizations from the ambit of Article 2(4). Arguably, they should have the benefits and bear the burdens of the Convention in respect of their judgments. The absence of the term 'international organization' from Article 2(4) should not be taken as an intention by the Diplomatic Session to place a limitation on that article. To the contrary, this issue would

[65] The possibility of additional protections for States is provided by art 19, which makes a declaration available for judgments pertaining to States (discussed below).

[66] See, eg, the commercial activity exception to the US Foreign Sovereign Immunities Act, 28 USC § 1605(a)(2).

be resolved by Article 26(4) ('Any reference to a ... "State" in this Convention shall apply equally, where appropriate, to a Regional Economic Integration Origination'). It would appear to be appropriate to treat States and international organizations equally for the purposes of Article 2(4). The resolution of this issue will have to be developed in subsequent practice.

Article 2(4) was present in draft texts from very early in the negotiating process. Its predecessor is Article 1(3) of the 1999 Preliminary Draft, which is given a thorough discussion in the Nygh/Pocar Report.[67] Useful guidance also may be found in the explanatory reports produced in the course of this Convention and COCA. It is safe to say that a consensus is developing in recent Hague Conference instruments applicable to transnational litigation that prominent among the criteria for determining when State conduct is to be classified as civil or commercial are: **5.130**

(1) the conduct upon which the claim is based is conduct in which a private person can engage;
(2) the injury alleged is an injury which can be sustained by a private person; and
(3) the relief requested is of a type available to private persons seeking a remedy for the same injury as the result of the same conduct.[68]

E. Article 2(5)—States as Defendants/Privileges and Immunities

5. Nothing in this Convention shall affect privileges and immunities of States or of international organizations, in respect of themselves and of their property.

Concerns were expressed in early discussion on the original project and on COCA that the rule contained in Article 2(4) might be interpreted as having substantive effects, specifically by affecting claims to privileges or immunities that might be asserted under national or international law. Article 2(4) addresses only the governmental status of one of the parties for purposes of characterization of a matter as 'civil or commercial' and thus, on its face, does not deal with other public international law matters. Nonetheless, Article 2(5) was included to allay any residual concerns on this point. It is identical to Article 2(6) of COCA and should be interpreted in identical fashion. **5.131**

The Convention does not affect privileges and immunities of States, or of international organizations. This lack of effect operates regardless of the source of the privileges and immunities, whether customary international law, treaty, national legislation, or common law. The text provides no restrictions or limitations in any fashion of the 'non-effect' of the Convention in this area. If it is a privilege or immunity, and if it otherwise would apply without the Convention, it will apply despite the Convention. Further, even if a State has waived its immunity from, for example, jurisdiction to adjudicate, its immunities with respect to remedial measures, enforcement, and execution may remain unaffected. **5.132**

[67] Nygh/Pocar Report (n 17) paras 43–45.

[68] See Nygh/Pocar Report (n 17) para 43; Preliminary Doc No 4 of December 2016, para 40; Explanatory Report (n 30) para 83.

5.133 The term 'States' in Article 2(5) is to be given the same meaning as the use of the term in Article 2(4).

5.134 While the language of this provision was adjusted to better align the Convention with developments in immunity law, the gist of this provision was present early in the negotiations. It was contained in Article 1(4) of the 1999 Preliminary Draft Convention and is discussed in the Nygh/Pocar Report.[69]

IV. Article 3—Definitions

Article 3
Definitions

1. **In this Convention—**
   - (a) **'defendant' means a person against whom the claim or counterclaim was brought in the State of origin;**
   - (b) **'judgment' means any decision on the merits given by a court, whatever that decision may be called, including a decree or order, and a determination of costs or expenses of the proceedings by the court (including an officer of the court), provided that the determination relates to a decision on the merits which may be recognized or enforced under this Convention. An interim measure of protection is not a judgment.**
2. **An entity or person other than a natural person shall be considered to be habitually resident in the State –**
   - (a) **where it has its statutory seat;**
   - (b) **under the law of which it was incorporated or formed;**
   - (c) **where it has its central administration; or**
   - (d) **where it has its principal place of business.**

A. Article 3(1)(a)—'defendant'

1. **In this Convention—**
   - (a) **'defendant' means a person against whom the claim or counterclaim was brought in the State of origin;**

5.135 The term 'defendant' is specifically defined as a person against whom the claim or counterclaim was brought in the State of origin. The term occurs in Article 5(1)(d), (e), (f), (g), (i), and in Articles 7(1)(a) and 19(1). It is connected either with certain 'bases' or criteria for eligibility for recognition or enforcement under the Convention, with the discretionary ground for refusal of recognition or enforcement based upon notification to parties, or with an anti-discrimination limitation on declarations involving judgments pertaining to States. The definition distinguishes a 'defendant' from the 'person against whom recognition or enforcement is sought' found in Article 5(1)(a), (b), and (c). The differentiation in terminology may avoid confusion in application: the person against whom recognition or

[69] Nygh/Pocar Report (n 17) para 46.

enforcement is sought in the requested State in the circumstance of Article 5(1)(a)–(c) need not be and may not be the same as the person against whom the claim or counterclaim was brought in the State of origin, or, due to subrogation or the like, the same person against whom judgment ultimately was rendered.[70]

The term 'defendant' is constituted of a disjunct; it refers to either the person against whom the claim was brought in the State of origin, or the person against whom a counterclaim was brought in the State of origin. '[A] person' here means 'any person'—it is not restricted in number. Although not specifically referenced, the natural reading of the definition would extend to third-party claims in which an existing party to an action (usually a defendant to the original claim) seeks to join a third party. If the application to join is successful, the third-party defendant also becomes a 'defendant' within the meaning of the Convention. **5.136**

B. Article 3(1)(b)—'judgment'

1. In this Convention—

(b) 'judgment' means any decision on the merits given by a court, whatever that decision may be called, including a decree or order, and a determination of costs or expenses of the proceedings by the court (including an officer of the court), provided that the determination relates to a decision on the merits which may be recognized or enforced under this Convention. An interim measure of protection is not a judgment.

The term 'judgment' has been discussed extensively above, and the reader is referred to the relevant section on scope. **5.137**

C. Article 3(2)—Entities and Persons Other Than a Natural Person

2. An entity or person other than a natural person shall be considered to be habitually resident in the State—

(a) where it has its statutory seat;

(b) under the law of which it was incorporated or formed;

(c) where it has its central administration; or

(d) where it has its principal place of business.

Article 3(2) is not a definition, but instead a list of States in which a person other than a natural person is considered to be 'habitually resident' for purposes of the Convention, in particular under Article 5(1)(a) (criteria for determining eligibility for recognition or enforcement against a person habitually resident in the State of origin at the time they became party to the proceedings). It refers to an 'entity or person other than a natural person' to take into account the possibility that some non-natural persons may not be classified as 'legal persons' (such as corporations) within a given legal system. Article 3(2) is identical **5.138**

[70] There is no parallel or related definition in COCA.

to Article 4(2) of COCA, except that the COCA provision refers to 'resident' rather than 'habitually resident'. This change merely clarifies that transient residence does not qualify as residence for purposes of this definition. These criteria were also found in the original project. Guidance in construing them may be had from the relevant reports accompanying this and earlier phases of the work.[71]

5.139 Article 3(2) effectively multiplies the number of States of origin from which judgments will be eligible for recognition or enforcement against a non-natural person under Article 5(1)(a). It is a disjunct; each of its limbs operate independently and equally. None of them is subordinate to another. Assuming that more than one of these tests leads to a different country, such an entity or person may have multiple habitual residences under the Convention.[72]

5.140 '[S]tatutory seat' and the State under 'the laws of which [the entity] was incorporated or formed' refer to connections with a State generated by some sort of law, whether external or internal to the entity or person. Statutory seat is not a term of art in common law parlance, but for purposes of the Convention (and COCA) it should be taken as generally referring to a place designated by the internal constitution of the entity or person (such as by-laws or similar binding internal documents) as something akin to a registered office. This is in contrast to the State under whose law the entity or person 'was incorporated or formed', which derives from the public aspects of creation of the entity or person and by which it is bestowed with such legal capacities as it may have.[73]

5.141 The limbs of Article 3(2) referring to 'central administration' and 'principal place of business' are rooted more in fact. The 'central administration' of an entity or non-natural person is expected to be the place where policy and decisions are made that guide or govern the entity as a whole, as a unitary being. 'Principal place of business' is expected to be the place where the bulk of actual activity occurs.[74]

D. Other Definitional Elements in the Convention

5.142 At scattered points, definitions or quasi-definitions are provided in specific articles of the Convention. Thus, Article 5(1)(m) provides within it a definition of 'exclusive choice of court agreement' while Article 22(1) provides guidance on the use of terms in the context of non-unified legal systems. These are tentative steps on a path not generally taken in the Convention: more frequent use of definitions or explications of terms as they occur in individual articles in addition to an over-all definition section. Whether this path will be taken in future transnational litigation conventions remains to be seen.

[71] See Nygh/Pocar Report (n 17) paras 63–66; Hartley/Dogauchi Report (n 20) 120.

[72] The disjuncts in art 3(2) refer to 'its' or 'it' when listing places of habitual residence. They refer to the entity or person as a unitary being. The presence of branches or other local establishments do not create habitual residence for Convention purposes. Similarly, insofar as it has sensible meaning in this context, a State is habitually resident in its own territory.

[73] See the discussions in the Explanatory Report (n 30) 77, para 106; Hartley/Dogauchi Report (n 20) 54–55, paras 117–23 (very useful discussion); Nygh/Pocar Report (n 17) paras 63–64.

[74] The phrase 'principal place of business' also occurs in art 5.1(b) with respect to natural persons. For reasons discussed below, the proper interpretation of the term in art 5.1(b) may differ substantially from the use of the term here.

V. Other Provisions That May Affect Scope

Chapter III (general clauses) of the Convention contains articles that may affect substantive scope, and must ultimately be considered before all issues of scope are covered. Article 18 allows States to make declarations that remove specific matters from scope for the operation of the Convention in the declaring State. Article 19 allows States, by declaration, not to apply the Convention to judgments to which that State is a party. These declarations operate on a reciprocal basis, that is, the State making the declaration is not obligated to recognize or enforce a judgment within the scope of its declaration, but will not receive the benefits of the Convention with respect to judgments that originate from its own courts and that fall within the scope of the declaration. **5.143**

6
The Basic Recognition and Enforcement Obligation and Criteria for Eligibility (Articles 4–6)

I. Introduction

Chapter II, 'Recognition and Enforcement', contains the operational core of the Convention. **6.01**
Chapter II regulates recognition and enforcement of judgments within the scope of the Convention; its rules are mandatory, but their operation does not necessarily mandate actual recognition or enforcement of judgments within scope. Articles 4–6 provide the basic framework for judgment recognition and enforcement under the Convention and are discussed in this chapter of this book. Articles 7–15 then add additional rules layered on top of that framework and are discussed in Chapter 7.

Chapter II begins with Article 4, the first paragraph of which provides that a judg- **6.02**
ment given by a court of a Contracting State shall be recognized and enforced in other Contracting States in accordance with the provisions of Chapter II. Article 5 then provides criteria of eligibility for recognition and enforcement of judgments with certain features, but these criteria of eligibility are specific and often narrow. Article 6 then creates an obligation that overrides other provisions of the Convention, both requiring, on the one hand, and prohibiting, on the other, recognition or enforcement of certain judgments.

Article 7 then provides discretionary grounds for refusal of recognition or enforce- **6.03**
ment of judgments that are both within scope and meet the Article 5(1) eligibility criteria; these grounds in some respects are broader than the grounds in the similar list in the 2005 Convention on Choice of Court Agreements (COCA). As a consequence, any assertion that the fundamental object and purpose of the Convention is actual recognition and

enforcement of judgments (as opposed to regulating recognition and enforcement of judgments within its scope), is misleading.

6.04 Article 8 addresses the status of certain judgments that may contain content outside of the scope of the Convention, including 'preliminary questions'. Article 9 provides a severability rule. Article 10 addresses the handling of damage awards. Article 11 brings 'judicial settlements' (transactions judiciaries) into the Convention for purposes of enforcement. Article 12 describes documents to be produced when recognition or enforcement is sought, while Article 13 addresses other points of procedure. Article 14 addresses costs of proceedings. Article 15 preserves the ability of Contracting States to recognize or enforce judgments under their national law, including their conflict of laws rules, but then bars doing so with respect to judgments ruling on rights *in rem* in immovable property that are subject to Article 6.

II. Article 4—General Provisions

Article 4

General provisions

1. **A judgment given by a court of a Contracting State (State of origin) shall be recognised and enforced in another Contracting State (requested State) in accordance with the provisions of this Chapter. Recognition or enforcement may be refused only on the grounds specified in this Convention.**
2. **There shall be no review of the merits of the judgment in the requested State. There may only be such consideration as is necessary for the application of this Convention.**
3. **A judgment shall be recognised only if it has effect in the State of origin, and shall be enforced only if it is enforceable in the State of origin.**
4. **Recognition or enforcement may be postponed or refused if the judgment referred to under paragraph 3 is the subject of review in the State of origin or if the time limit for seeking ordinary review has not expired. A refusal does not prevent a subsequent application for recognition or enforcement of the judgment.**

A. Article 4(1)—The Basic Rule

Article 4

General Provisions

1. **A judgment given by a court of a Contracting State (State of origin) shall be recognised and enforced in another Contracting State (requested State) in accordance with the provisions of this Chapter. Recognition or enforcement may be refused only on the grounds specified in this Convention.**

6.05 Article 4(1) provides in its first sentence that a judgment issued by a court in one Contracting State shall be recognized and enforced in another Contracting State in accordance with the provisions of Chapter II. It then establishes in its second sentence that recognition or enforcement may be refused only on grounds specified in the

Convention—which acknowledges that recognition or enforcement may be refused on grounds outside Chapter II, such as on grounds provided by the declaration system in Chapter III.

The first sentence of Article 4(1) introduces two important designations that are used in other articles in Chapter II: the 'State of origin' is the State of the court that gave the judgment, and the 'requested State' is the State in which recognition or enforcement is sought. (The expressions 'court of origin' and 'requested court' are not used in the text of Article 4(1), but appear in other articles with these explicit designations.) 6.06

Article 4(1) is similar to Article 8(1) of COCA absent the necessary qualification in COCA that the judgment was given by a court designated in an exclusive choice of court agreement. However, in light of the significant differences in the structure, operation, and goals of the two conventions, there are limitations on the proper use of COCA as a guide to Article 4(1) of this Convention. 6.07

As has been noted earlier,[1] the Convention defines neither 'recognition' nor 'enforcement'. Both concepts refer to something that a requested court must do within its own legal system. In light of the lock-and-key model employed in the Convention, this counsels that the interpretation of both 'recognition' and 'enforcement' will be that given to the terms in the law of the requested State. However, this application of the law of the requested State should not be a free-form exercise. Article 20 requires that regard be paid to the international character of the Convention. The use of the terms in the decision-making of the courts of any Contracting State should fit comfortably within comparative law contours and a general Convention sense. Thus, within that Convention sense, 'recognition' generally should be seen as a determination by a requested court that a foreign judgment or part of one can be treated as having some legal status within the legal system of the requested State.[2] As stated in Chapter 5 of this book, 'enforcement' in an intuitive, basic sense, is the process (or result) whereby the requested court sets in motion the mechanisms available to it, including the potentially coercive power of its State, to give effect to rights or obligations established by the judgment. 6.08

Article 4(1) cannot operate unless a judgment is within the scope of the Convention. This is not stated on the face of the text, but any notion to the contrary would make surplusage of Chapter I of the Convention. The requested court has an obligation to make an independent determination that a judgment presented to it for recognition or enforcement satisfies the scope criteria of the Convention. That court must be able to determine for itself the existence and extent of the international obligations imposed by the Convention upon it—and upon those who might ultimately be subject to the coercive powers of the requested State. 6.09

The question of whether a judgment falls within Article 4(1) as a matter of the scope of the Convention is different from the questions of whether and when a judgment may be and is, in fact, recognized or enforced under other articles of the Convention. Notable in this respect are Articles 4(3) and 4(4), which tie recognition and enforcement in the requested 6.10

[1] See paras 5.22–5.28.

[2] This goes beyond, and involves a more powerful step, than merely providing preclusive effect, which might not involve conferring on the foreign judgment or decision any particular status as part of or incorporated into the legal system of the requested State.

State to the status of recognition or enforcement in the State of origin; Article 5, which lists the criteria for recognition or enforcement of particular judgments; Article 6, which prohibits recognition or enforcement in certain situations; Article 7, which provides discretionary grounds for refusal of recognition or enforcement; and the declarations available under Articles 17–19.

6.11 The judgment presented for recognition and enforcement must be from a court of a Contracting State other than the State of the requested court. This is a requirement of internationality although the term 'international cases' is not used in this Convention (unlike COCA). The Convention does not establish obligations concerning the movement of judgments within a State or between courts of a single State, nor questions of subject matter competence or proper venue and the like that might govern the particular court in a Contracting State to which a judgment should be presented for recognition or enforcement. These are entirely a matter of national law.[3]

6.12 Article 4(1) refers to recognition and enforcement of a judgment in a Contracting State other than the State of the court of origin. It places no limits on the number of Contracting States to which a judgment may be presented for recognition or enforcement under the Convention. Indeed, this is part and parcel of the unique and unprecedented power of this Convention. Every Contracting State is bound by Article 4(1), no matter the number of other fora in which recognition and enforcement are sought. Thus, if assets that might satisfy a judgment are spread among several States, recognition and enforcement may be sought in some or all of them. Just as Article 4 does not limit the number of Contracting States to which a judgment may be taken for recognition and enforcement, it also does not bar a court addressed from taking into account relief already received by the judgment creditor in other States.

6.13 It is the judgment of the court of origin that is entitled to recognition and enforcement. The appropriate parties to the original litigation and the parties designated in the judgment will be determined by the national law rules of subrogation, alter ego, succession, and the like of the law of the State of origin. The identity of parties to the judgment is not subject to review or modification by the requested court, although rules on alter ego analysis and the like of the law of the requested State may add persons who may be bound by, or who may benefit from, the judgment.

6.14 The second sentence of Article 4(1) provides that recognition or enforcement may be refused 'only on the grounds specified in this Convention'. The use of the word 'only' means that the grounds of refusal specified in the Convention are exhaustive. If a ground is not explicitly specified in the Convention, it is not to be found, and not to be had. In this sense, the Convention is asymmetrical. Recognition or enforcement may be refused only on a ground specified in the Convention, which effectively sets a floor below which recognition and enforcement cannot sink. However, nothing prevents enhanced recognition or enforcement over and above Convention criteria pursuant to national law under Article 15. Similarly, other than in Article 6, the Convention does not require a requested court to refuse recognition or enforcement even where the Convention permits it to do so.

[3] A limitation on the Convention obligation to recognize and enforce judgments in cases otherwise 'international' may result from a declaration under Art 17 of the Convention, discussed in Chapter 8.

B. Article 4(2)—No Review on the Merits

Article 4

General Provisions

2. **There shall be no review of the merits of the judgment in the requested State. There may only be such consideration as is necessary for application of this Convention.**

Article 4(2) sets some initial contours to the inquiries that the requested court may make into the judgment presented to it for recognition or enforcement. The first sentence of Article 4(2) marries a misnomer to a shibboleth, to the improvement of neither. The second sentence then provides the basis for a pragmatic, operational meaning for its predecessor. **6.15**

The first sentence of Article 4(2) prohibits 'review of the merits of the judgment' by the court of the requested State. The term 'review' as used here is misleading, and, at least as generally understood by judges and litigators in the common law world where it is a term of art, refers to a category of operation different from that contemplated in the Convention. Rather than a re-evaluation of either findings of fact, rulings of substantive law, or compliance with procedural requirements in the proceedings of a lower court by a higher court in a hierarchy of courts within one legal system, we are dealing here with limitations on an inquiry by a court of a Contracting State into a judgment issued by a court of different Contracting State.[4] 'Review' has no Convention definition, no referent in international law, and its meaning varies considerably from legal system to legal system. The key point here is that we are not dealing with a technical concept of 'review' drawn from a given legal system—particularly the legal system of the requested State—but the kinds of inquiry a court in the requested State may make when asked to exercise its public powers to recognize or enforce a foreign judgment under the Convention. **6.16**

The meaning of the phrase 'of the merits' fares no better in this context. It has no definition in this Convention or in international law and varies not only in comparative law but also may vary within a given legal system depending on the context in which it is used. For example, 'merits' might refer to (1) any issue that is not strictly jurisdictional; (2) any issue that is neither jurisdictional nor otherwise procedural (including choice of law); or (3) any substantive issue for which a finding of fact was made. Joining two such terms into one phrase does not noticeably add to clarity. **6.17**

To make matters worse, application of many provisions of the Convention actually requires inquiry into matters that may be classified as 'on the merits'. Several of the criteria for eligibility for recognition or enforcement in Article 5 rest on the relationship or connection between a person subject to aspects of the action, factual or legal, giving rise to the judgment and the State of origin. In applying the Convention, the requested court may be required to examine independently that relationship or connection. Simply to begin with the first criterion for eligibility for recognition or enforcement in Article 5(1)(a), the requested court may have to consider the habitual residence of a person, and do so at a particular time. Article 5(1)(b) may require a factual inquiry into the principle place of business of a **6.18**

[4] Art 4.4 then uses the terms 'review' and 'ordinary review' to describe processes that can only occur in the court of origin, which does not improve clarity.

natural person at a particular time. Article 5(1)(d) might require consideration of whether an entity is a branch, agency, or other establishment, and, possibly, its separate legal personality, again with reference to a particular time. Such need for consideration in application of the Convention can arise outside of Article 5, for example Article 6 (rights *in rem*, immovable property, situs); Article 7 (notification, fraud, etc); Article 8 (aspects of whether a question is preliminary); Article 10 (aspects of damage awards); and scope provisions, including declarations. It will not necessarily be clear on the face of a judgment whether the court of origin addressed such issues and how it might have done so. In any event, the requested court may have to engage in consideration of such points.

6.19 Indeed, the fundamental choice of the Convention to restrict its operation to indirect jurisdiction requires the requested court to inquire into and measure a number of points that might be classified as 'on the merits' but doing so is not a review: the court of origin need not have determined those points, and its determinations may well be irrelevant to the requested court in performance of its obligations under the Convention.

6.20 Fortunately, a pragmatic, functional approach to interpretation of the phrase 'review of the merits' may shed light on the operational requirements for the requested court of Article 4(2). The successful operation of the Convention requires that the Contracting States, and the persons who would employ the Convention, have great confidence that judgments to which it applies will be recognized and enforced—or not—with a relatively low level of transaction costs. The successful operation of the Convention thus requires that any inquiry by the requested court into the decision of the court of origin be limited and predictable. Nothing could be more antithetical to reaching this objective than redundant litigation, especially on matters of fact.[5]

6.21 Accordingly, the second sentence of Article 4(2) carries the operational import of the article. The inquiries by the requested court are limited only to 'such consideration' as may be 'necessary' for the application of the Convention. The second sentence holds the key to a proper interpretation of 'review of the merits': any inquiry by the requested court not 'necessary' for the application of the Convention should be considered 'review on the merits' for purposes of the first sentence of Article 4(1)—and should not occur. Article 4(2) should not and need not become a matter of metaphysical dispute.[6]

6.22 The term 'necessary' in Article 4(2) should be read as implicitly including within it 'and appropriate' to the application of the Convention. This will avoid additional litigation over whether 'necessary' carries with it a requirement of strict logical necessity, and, if so, what that entails in a particular case. While, in general, the term should be construed strictly to sharply limit re-litigation of matters decided in the court of origin, Article 4(2) does not completely eliminate the exercise of good sense in litigation situations (and, properly, would be ignored or negated by courts if it did). Moreover, it may be entirely appropriate for a requested court to examine the facts underlying the original judgment, as well as the analysis resulting in that judgment, when the requested

[5] By implication, Art 4(2) established beyond cavil that mere dislike or objection to the results of a judgment is not one of the 'grounds specified in this Convention' (Art 4(1)) for which recognition or enforcement may be refused.

[6] 'Review of the merits' by a requested court for recognition or enforcement will be different yet again from what might be involved if a defendant 'argued on the merits' as a criteria for eligibility for recognition or enforcement of a judgment under Art 5(1)(f).

court considers whether to apply some of the grounds for refusal or recognition or enforcement.

Finally, the first sentence of Article 4(2) refers to 'review of the merits of the judgment' while the second sentence simply refers to 'such consideration' as is necessary for application of the Convention. The referent of 'such consideration'—seemingly, putting aside consideration of anything unnecessary to the application of the Convention—appears far broader than the limitation of review to 'the judgment'. If this is so, while the requested court may not review the merits of the judgment, it is also barred from 'consideration' of anything not necessary to application of the Convention, whether contained in the judgment or not. This is in accord with lowering transaction costs. 6.23

In any event, the requested court should tread very lightly if a matter of fact has been determined, or its determination is necessarily entailed in the judgment presented for recognition or enforcement. 6.24

COCA contains a similar provision in Article 8(2).[7] Essentially, Article 4(1) in this Convention reverses the order of the clauses in Article 8(2) of COCA, and puts each clause into separate sentences, while jettisoning the third sentence of Article 8(2) (treatment of findings of fact except in default judgments). The rationale for the change in Article 4(2) was less a change of substance than a matter of style and rhetoric: the general rule (no review on the merits) should open the article, while its qualification should follow. Unfortunately, this rationale misses a critical feature of the COCA provision, whatever may be said about its drafting: the introductory clause ('[w]ithout prejudice . . .') actually carries at least equal operational weight to the 'no review on the merits' clause. It also should be noted that the proponents of the structural change from COCA had no such qualms in starting Article 15 with its qualification (subject to the provisions of art 6) as opposed to providing the focus on the main rule (the Convention does not disable recognition or enforcement under national law), thus re-affirming in a way that the paramount obligation of the Convention is to prohibit recognition and enforcement of certain judgments. 6.25

C. Article 4(3)—Effect in the State of Origin

Article 4

General Provisions

3. A judgment shall be recognised only if it has effect in the State of origin, and shall be enforced only if it is enforceable in the State of origin.

Paragraphs (3) and (4) of Article 4 exist in large part (but not exclusively) because the time at which a judgment will 'take effect' or is 'enforceable' varies with different legal 6.26

[7] According to art 8(2) of COCA:

Without prejudice to such review as is necessary for the application of the provisions of this Chapter, there shall be no review of the merits of the judgment given by the court of origin. The court addressed shall be bound by the findings of fact on which the court of origin based its jurisdiction, unless the judgment was given by default.

systems (as does the meaning of those terms). These paragraphs are virtually identical to paragraphs (3) and (4) of Article 8 of COCA, with the slight addition of a clarifying clause in Article 4(4).[8]

6.27 Article 4(3) creates a Convention standard for time and duration of recognition and enforcement, respectively. It ties time and duration of recognition and enforcement in the State of the court addressed to time and duration of the effect and enforceability of the judgment in the State of the court of origin. The rule is mandatory ('shall') under the Convention.

6.28 The first clause of Article 4(3) provides that a judgment shall be recognized only if it has effect in the State of origin. While an issue to be controlled by the law of the State of origin, it is our view that, as a general matter, having 'effect' in the State of origin means that the judgment constitutes a legally binding and operational determination of some or all of the rights or obligations of some or all of the parties to a litigation. Thus, a judgment rendered in the State of origin but that, under the law of the State of origin, does not take effect until certain conditions are met, may not be recognized by the requested court under the Convention. It may not be given legally binding and operational force in the requested State if it does not have those qualities in the State of origin. For example, in some situations, a judgment rendered by a court of first instance may not 'take effect' within that legal system until all appeals are exhausted, or until 'ordinary' appeals are exhausted.[9] In some systems, a 'judgment' within the meaning of Article 3(1) of the Convention rendered as to only some persons or claims in a case may not take effect until the entire case has been resolved.[10] In such instances, recognition in the requested court may not be had under the Convention before the judgment takes effect in the State of origin.

6.29 The second clause of Article 4(3) states that a judgment shall be enforced in the requested State only if it is enforceable in the State of origin. Thus, an injunction issued by the court of origin that, by its terms, will lapse after a specified period of time, will not be enforceable in the requested State after the time period of effectiveness has run in the State of the court of origin.

6.30 An issue that was not raised in discussion at the Diplomatic Session, is whether this Convention standard disables the operation of national law of the requested State on time and duration with respect to judgments within the meaning of Article 3(1). For example, it is conceivable that a national law rule might provide that once a foreign country judgment is ordered to be enforced, that enforcement is subject to national law, even if that judgment might subsequently be altered or annulled in the State of the court of origin. If so, and if time and duration are matters of the procedural law of the requested State, then Article 4(3) limits the operation of Article 13 in this respect.

[8] The discussion here draws heavily on Ronald A Brand and Paul M Herrup, *The 2005 Hague Convention on Choice of Court Agreements* (CUP 2008) 106–09.

[9] See, eg, Fed R Civ Pro 62(d) (allowing for a stay of execution of judgments during appeal).

[10] See, eg, Fed R Civ Pro 54(b) (allowing 'entry of a final judgment as to one or more but fewer than all of the claims or parties' in some circumstances).

D. Article 4(4)—Postponement or Refusal Pending Review

Article 4

General Provisions

4. **Recognition or enforcement may be postponed or refused if the judgment referred to in paragraph 3 is the subject of review in the State of origin or if the time limit for seeking ordinary review has not expired. A refusal does not prevent a subsequent application for recognition or enforcement of the judgment.**

Article 4(4) addresses situations converse to those covered in Article 4(3), such as where by the law of the State of the court of origin, a judgment, or partial judgment takes effect immediately upon issuance, or regardless of the disposition of the entire case. In such event, Article 4(4) allows the court addressed either to postpone or refuse recognition or enforcement in either of two situations: the judgment is subject to review in the State of the court of origin, or the time limit for seeking ordinary review has not expired. However, the scope of application of Article 4(4) is restricted to judgments referred to in Article 4(3). Accordingly, the postponement or refusal mechanism in Article 4(4) only applies to judgments that have effect or are enforceable (as the case may be) in the State of origin. This requirement essentially requires the requested court to apply the law of the State of origin to determinations of effect or enforceability as foundations for postponement or refusal of recognition or enforcement in the requested State. **6.31**

Article 4(4) allows a court addressed to await certain outcomes from courts in the State of origin before committing the judicial and national resources of the State addressed to recognition or enforcement of a judgment. It thus allows the requested court to assess certain aspects of what in some legal systems is classified as the 'finality' of the judgment presented to it. However, the term 'finality' (or the term 'conclusive') is not used in the Convention, for good reason. There is no Convention definition of either term, nor do they have international law referents. The meaning and effect of these terms vary sharply from legal system to legal system. Article 4(4) accordingly creates Convention criteria for postponement or refusal of recognition or enforcement, and restricts them in this context to situations in which the judgment is subject to review in the State of origin, or the time limit for seeking ordinary review has not expired. No other aspect of 'finality' in national law may trigger operation of Article 4(4). Accordingly, Article 4(4) restricts the operation of the national law of the requested State under Article 13(1). **6.32**

The authority granted by Article 4(4) is discretionary. In contrast to the mandatory nature of Article 4(3), Article 4(4) permits, but does not require, recognition or enforcement to be postponed or refused in certain conditions, whether under the Convention or under national law. **6.33**

Article 4(4) has two distinct temporal limbs. Recognition or enforcement under it may be postponed or refused under the first limb if the judgment actually is the subject of review in the State of origin. The term 'review' in this limb is unqualified and would appear to apply to any process classified as 'review' under the law of the State of origin. The second limb permits the requested court to stay its hand if the time limit for seeking 'ordinary review' has **6.34** not yet expired. This limb certainly applies to review that is available but has not yet been sought. It also would appear to apply to timely applications for leave to appeal, as required in some legal systems, even if review on appeal has not yet been granted. 'Ordinary review' is undefined in the Convention, but, by virtue of the anchor of Article 4(3), would appear to point the requested court to the law of the State of origin.

6.35 If the requested court issues an order of enforcement, and the judgment of the court of origin is modified, vacated, or reversed by further proceedings within its own legal system, any order of the requested court recognizing or enforcing the original judgment will have to be rescinded as a result of Article 4(3). In order to take this possibility into account, a requested court that is asked for enforcement during review or potential review in the State of origin may, within its discretion, require measures to protect the judgment debtor, as allowed under its national law.

6.36 If the operational effect of an order of enforcement is suspended in the State of origin due to appeal considerations, the requested court cannot issue enforcement measures under the Convention because these measures are blocked by Article 4(3) (the judgment is not enforceable in the State of origin). However, nothing in the Convention prevents the court addressed from ordering interim measures available under national law.

6.37 If the requested court chooses to refuse recognition or enforcement under Article 4(4), it does so without prejudice to a subsequent application for recognition or enforcement of the judgment. This appears to be a Convention rule that cannot be displaced by national law. If a requested court has limited authority under national law to issue a stay of proceedings, or otherwise chooses not to stay the proceedings, the court may dismiss the action for recognition or enforcement. However, the Convention effectively requires that any such dismissal be 'without prejudice' and thus subject to a subsequent application for recognition or enforcement. This ability to make a subsequent application is simply for renewed consideration for recognition or enforcement under the Convention. For actual recognition or enforcement, the judgment must still pass the tests of scope and the tests of the criteria of eligibility for recognition or enforcement in Articles 5 and 6, and would remain subject to the discretionary grounds for refusal in Article 7 as well as the effects of any declarations.

III. Article 5—Bases for Recognition and Enforcement

6.38 Article 5 addresses the 'bases' for recognition and enforcement under the Convention. 'Bases' as used in Article 5 is shorthand for the specific criteria that determine the eligibility of a judgment within the scope of the Convention for recognition and enforcement under it. We will refer to the 'bases' by using this longer but more accurate and descriptive formulation. (The more accurate formulation also encompasses art 6, which also prohibits recognition or enforcement of certain judgments.) It should be stressed that even if a judgment satisfies the criteria for eligibility in Article 5, recognition and enforcement may be refused pursuant to Article 7 (discretionary grounds of refusal) and must be in accordance with the declaration system.

6.39 Article 5 consists of three numbered paragraphs. Article 5(1) lists each of the criteria that, if anyone is satisfied, make a judgment eligible for recognition or enforcement under the Convention. Article 5(2) then limits the operation of four of these criteria in certain areas involving consumers and employment. Article 5(3) disables the rules of Article 5(1) with respect to judgments that rule on a residential lease of immovable property or on the registration of immovable property, and creates a specific criterion for recognition or enforcement based upon the situs of the property.

The criteria of eligibility contained in Articles 5 and 6 are exhaustive. If a judgment does not satisfy at least one of the criteria, it is not eligible for recognition or enforcement under the Convention. However, pursuant to Article 15, judgments other than those governed by Article 6 still may be recognized or enforced under national law. **6.40**

The burdens of proof, production, and persuasion in demonstrating that a judgment satisfies a sub-paragraph of Article 5 generally rest upon the person seeking recognition or enforcement. While not specifically addressed, this distribution of the burden may be inferred on a number of grounds. First, it is the person seeking recognition or enforcement that is invoking the judicial—and perhaps coercive—powers of the requested State. Second, this distribution of the burden generally is consistent with Article 12, which explicitly places burdens of production on the person seeking recognition or enforcement. Finally, the criteria of recognition or enforcement actually deployed in Article 5 are specific, detailed, and narrow. They can carry no presumption of recognizability or enforceability: the person seeking it should show it. However, due attention must be paid to the specifics of each sub-paragraph: the burden may shift on specific issues, such as with respect to the requirement in Article 5(1)(f) that a defendant's failure to contest jurisdiction while arguing on the merits would have been futile. **6.41**

A. Article 5(1)—Criteria of Eligibility for Recognition or Enforcement

Article 5

Bases for recognition and enforcement

1. **A judgment is eligible for recognition and enforcement if one of the following requirements is met—**

Article 5(1) consists of a list of thirteen individual criteria that create eligibility for recognition or enforcement of a judgment under the Convention. They are disjunctive criteria of equal weight: eligibility is established if any one criterion in Article 5(1) is satisfied, and none is subordinate to any other. However, satisfaction of a criterion must be established individually as to each person or defendant that might be subject to an order of recognition or enforcement, even if a judgment determines that liability is joint and several among a number of persons. The criteria do not operate in any way analogously to doctrines of, for example, pendent or supplemental jurisdiction. A person cannot be dragged into recognition or enforcement on the coattails of another—albeit this point is without prejudice to doctrines such as alter ego doctrines in the law of the requested State. The criteria must still be satisfied with respect to the person found to be an alter ego. **6.42**

While to be eligible for recognition or enforcement, a judgment must satisfy one of the criteria in Article 5(1), it need satisfy only one criterion. The set of judgments generated by one criterion may intersect with the set generated by another; for example, enforcement **6.43** might be sought against a person habitually resident in the State of origin art 5(1)(a)), who also was the person who brought the claim (art 5(1)(c)), and the judgment ruled on a contract obligation and was given by a court in the place of performance (art 5(1)(g)). One is enough.

6.44 Article 5(1) applies its criteria to four different types of objects, forming four distinct subsets. Each set does different work and the structure and language of the paragraphs was carefully drafted (after much discussion) in order to avoid particular problems that help define the four groups:[11]

> Paragraphs (a)–(c) apply to 'the person against whom recognition or enforcement is sought'.
> Paragraphs (d)–(f) apply to 'the defendant'.
> Paragraphs (g)–(k) apply to 'the judgment' and focus on the subject matter of the cause of action.
> Paragraphs (l)–(m) also apply to 'the judgment', but differ from (g)–(k) in that they perform particular functions not related to subject matter.

6.45 Accordingly, paragraphs (d)–(f) apply only when the action for recognition and enforcement directly involves the defendant in the original action. This allows the judgment to be raised both in an action to recognize or enforce the judgment against the original defendant, or an action by such defendant to recognize or enforce a judgment in their favour.

6.46 Paragraphs (d)–(f) are triggered by facts that relate only to the defendant in court of origin.

6.47 Paragraphs (g)–(k) comprise criteria based primarily upon a connection between the cause of action and the State of origin (ie subject matter), and do not begin, as do (a)–(f), with a relationship between a specified person and the State of origin.

6.48 Paragraphs (l) and (m) perform particular functions that result in a proper focus being on the judgment.

6.49 Paragraphs (a)–(c) are triggered by possibilities of recognition or enforcement that can involve persons other than the defendant in the court of origin, for example plaintiffs or third-party defendants. Unlike paragraphs (d)–(f), they do not apply logically only to the defendant in the court of origin. The important party is the person against whom recognition or enforcement is sought in the requested State.[12]

6.50 The court requested must measure a judgment presented to it for compliance with at least one of the criteria of eligibility for recognition or enforcement under the Convention. Such consideration is 'necessary for the application of the Convention' under Article 4(2) and cannot be classified as a prohibited 'review of the merits' under the Convention. However, there may be some issues in which the sense and operation of the Convention would indicate that the requested court should tread lightly, for example the question in Article 5(1)(a)

[11] These are not the exclusive characteristics that may be used to form subsets within art 5(1). Other bases for distinguishing subsets within art 5(1) are possible. We believe that this set of characteristics best accounts for the specific language used to describe the subject in each of the paragraphs of the article.

[12] Art 5(1) does not address internal rules of party succession to rights and liabilities in either the State of origin or in the requested State. In addition, rules on such questions as transfer, succession, subrogation, assignment, or the effect of mergers, acquisitions, or consolidations march to the beat of their own drum. In considering recognition or enforcement of a judgment, a requested court presented with such an issue, including questions of validity of party succession, will consult its own law, including its own private international law rules.

of whether a person was a 'party to the proceedings in the court of origin' ('party' having no Convention definition).

Nothing in Article 5—indeed, nothing in the Convention—calls upon the requested court to evaluate the adequacy, propriety, or justification of the decision by the court of origin to exercise jurisdiction to adjudicate the case (sometimes referred to as 'direct jurisdiction'). Such consideration is not 'necessary for the application of the Convention'. Accordingly, it is a consideration barred by Article 4(2), whether or not it falls within the rubric of 'review of the merits' under some national law. **6.51**

Our general approach to each paragraph in Article 5(1) is to provide first a quick sketch of its logical structure, including its terms and their logical relationships to each other. We then parse each operative term. Finally, we provide observations on the law that the requested court should apply in the determination of each term, although we might not adhere in uniform fashion to this order of presentation. In terms of applicable law, our general approach is to urge an autonomous Convention sense for key gateway terms, application of the law of the State of origin when a feature of a paragraph of Article 5(1) is keyed to a specific step in the proceedings in the court of origin or in a legal process in the State of origin (such as the time of institution of proceedings in art 5(1)(k) or who is a 'counterclaimant' in art 5(1)(l), or registration of immovable property in art 5(3)), and a pragmatic approach with an eye to litigation efficiency and a tilt towards the law of the requested State for the remainder, on the grounds that the State that is requested to exercise its coercive powers as a matter of international legal obligation should be able to exercise a significant check on the occasion for the exercise of those powers.[13] **6.52**

Finally, we provide some structural observations of a general character regarding the provisions of Article 5(1). Those provisions fall into two groups. Article 5(1)(a)–(f) and Article 5(1)(l)–(m) can be generated easily by the general international law and system considerations discussed in Chapter 1 concerning the choices made in the Convention. With Article 5(1)(g)–(k), the Convention enters the world of Brussels boxes, in which the focus is on what the 'judgment ruled on' (French '*porte sur*') rather than the relationship between an individual bound by the judgment and either the State or court of origin. Five of the thirteen paragraphs in Article 5(1) are of this type (art 5(1)(g)–(k)). **6.53**

There are important differences in logical structure and in functional origin between the two groups of paragraphs. The first group (art 5(1)(a)–(f) and 5(1)(l)–(m)), involve an active subject[14] whose actions create a relationship with a State or with a court of that State. In **6.54**

[13] However, there are limitations to the general approach. For example, if a key gateway term is unlikely to be amenable to development of a Convention sense (eg 'immovable property') or if reference to the law of the State of origin might allow that State unilaterally to create international law obligations on the requested State that the latter had not contemplated or to which it had not given consent ('rights in rem'), the general default position is for the requested court to interpret treaty terms under its own law, albeit bearing in mind the injunction of art 20 that, in the interpretation of the Convention, regard should be had to its international character and to the need to promote uniformity in its application. As a general rule, the gateway terms in Art 5(1)(g)–(k) will not lend themselves easily to autonomous global development; another factor to be considered in weighing the adequacy of criteria based upon Brussels boxes (jurisdictional rules included in the Brussels I (Recast) Regulation). Regulation (EU) No 1215/2012 of the European Parliament and of the Council of 12 December 2012 on jurisdiction and the recognition and enforcement of judgments in civil and commercial matters (the 'Brussels I (Recast) Regulation'). Insofar as the mantra of a number of participants in the Hague Conference process was the existence of a uniformity in comparative law understandings on certain matters, the application of its own law by the requested court should not have significant impact. The Convention will be a laboratory to empirically ascertain the accuracy of this view of the current horizons of comparative law.

[14] The 'person against whom recognition or enforcement is sought' (art 5(1)(a)–(c)), the defendant (art 5(1)(d)–(f)), or a person who makes a counterclaim art 5(1)(l) or enters into a choice of court agreement (art 5(1)(m)).

a world of co-existence of sovereign States in a legal and political international order that requires both limitations on the exercise of sovereignty as a matter of respect and accommodation for others, and enhanced cooperation and assistance to achieve common goals, a requested court should avoid as far as possible frustrating the operations or effectiveness of the court of origin and also take steps as far as possible to assist the foreign sovereign by opening its own legal system to the foreign judgment. The rules in the first group may be generated easily from some very basic and general principles that give life and structure to our international condition.

6.55 The logical structure of the second group, the Brussels boxes, is quite different and more complicated. Each involves an implied active subject (a court) with a particular location (the State of origin), which State in turn has a geographic attribute (it is the place where something exists, happens, or should have happened), and that a judgment of that court 'ruled on' (French '*porte sur*') a particular kind of obligation created under the law of the State of origin (a contractual obligation, a non-contractual obligation, a lease, a trust). Generally, these paragraphs require the requested court to determine what the judgment 'ruled on', classify the thing ruled on within some legal rubric based upon 'the nature of the claim', and if the rubric is one listed in a paragraph of Article 5(1), then determine whether the judgment otherwise satisfies the criteria that refers to that rubric. They are not consequences of basic, general, and relatively straight-forward rules generated by the nature of international law and the international system, but are parochial to specific legal systems and rooted in the history of those systems. As has been and will be discussed, whether they are well-adapted to the facts of twenty-first-century mobility remains to be seen.

1. Article 5(1)(a)—Habitual Residence of the Judgment Debtor

Article 5

Bases for recognition and enforcement

1. A judgment is eligible for recognition and enforcement if one of the following requirements is met—

(a) the person against whom recognition or enforcement is sought was habitually resident in the State of origin at the time that person became a party to the proceedings in the court of origin;

6.56 Article 5(1)(a), the habitual residence rule, consists of a number of terms that require examination. The logical structure of Article 5(1)(a) consists of an active subject (a person) with an attribute (party to proceedings in the court of origin), a specified relationship of the person to the State of origin (habitual residence), and a temporal condition (at the time that person became a party).

6.57 The 'person' against whom recognition or enforcement is sought may be either a natural or a non-natural person. However, any such person must have the legal capacity under the law of the requested State to have a judgment recognized or enforced against them. This is a different question from the legal capacity of a person to sue or be sued under the laws of the State of origin. Even if the court of origin made an explicit determination of the latter point, that determination would fall outside the scope of the Convention under Article 2(1)(a) for a natural person, and possibly under Article 2(1)(i) if a legal person or association. However, an ensuing judgment may nonetheless be subject to the Convention.

The person against whom recognition or enforcement is sought can be anyone bound by the judgment. It includes not only defendants to the original complaint, but plaintiffs and third-party defendants. It includes any person against whom recognition or enforcement is sought, without reference to or limitation by the number of such persons. **6.58**

That person must have been a 'party to the proceedings in the court of origin'. There is no Convention definition that determines when a person is a 'party' to proceedings, and this may vary from State to State. Because the referent in the term is to 'proceedings in the court of origin', the law of the State of origin should determine the question. Consistent with the pragmatic approach to interpretation adopted here, the court requested should proceed on the basis that a person subject to a judgment, in whatever capacity (plaintiff, defendant, etc) issued by a court of origin was a 'party' to the proceedings in that court. **6.59**

The essential attribute upon which eligibility of a judgment for recognition or enforcement under Article 5(1)(a) is based is 'habitual residence'. The Convention lists four places in which a non-natural person may be habitually resident (art 3(2), above). It does not provide any guidance for the determination of 'habitual residence' for natural persons; as a pivotal term of Article 5(1)(a), this lacuna should be filled with a consistent autonomous Convention interpretation rather than be left to the vagaries of the domestic law of the Contracting States. Hopefully, such a definition will take shape as practice develops under the Convention. At this point, *a priori* and abstract adventures in definition of this term are, in our view, misdirected: they are almost inevitably captive to parochial concepts of direct jurisdiction in national law, and cannot keep pace with the rapid development of global movement and mobility. **6.60**

However, a pragmatic approach to interpretation may guide courts and practitioners in shaping an autonomous Convention interpretation of 'habitual residence' for natural persons. First, this Convention enshrines a form of international judicial assistance among interdependent sovereigns. Courts must ask themselves the characteristics that might be assigned to the term 'habitual residence' of natural persons for purposes of recognition or enforcement of judgments that will best perform two general functions: a negative function of not frustrating or impeding the effectiveness of operation of a judgment of the court of origin with respect to a person related to it in a way that might be described as 'habitual residence', and a positive function of opening the door to the legal system of the requested State for judgments that apply to a person with that kind of relation to the State of origin. A person with the characteristics assigned to 'habitual residence' should have one of those fundamental relationships with the State of origin such that the person should not be heard to complain of the actions of its courts in the court of another State (this is distinct from other criteria of eligibility that involve a person having taken some action before the court of the State of origin or engaged in some activity in that State). In this light, a pragmatic Convention definition of 'habitual residence' might emanate from either or both of two poles: first, the physical presence of the natural person at some significant point in time or over some interval of time, and, second, the nature of the relationship of the person with the State of origin in terms of the person making general claims or under the general shelter of the legal system and society of the State of origin **6.61** (as opposed to claims or shelter on specific points). A limitation factor would also be appropriate: the proper State of origin should be one in which the person has either their primary presence or makes their primary claims for protection as a general matter. (There is nothing that, logically, would prevent a natural person from having more than one 'habitual residence' for purposes of the Convention, but this limitation gives appropriate weight to the need in a convention of this type not to promiscuously multiply possible States of origin.)

6.62 Although the term 'habitual residence' is used in multiple conventions adopted by the Hague Conference, the Diplomatic Session did not consider how the term was used in those other instruments. As a result, no inference may be made that the negotiators of this Convention intended to carry over any meaning from those other instruments.

6.63 Article 5(1)(a) carries a time requirement: the person against whom recognition or enforcement is sought must have been habitually resident in the State of origin at the time they became party to the proceedings in the court of origin. Because a person's habitual residence—however defined—might change over time (indeed, during the course of the litigation or even because of the litigation), the Convention designates a time for the operation of Article 5(1)(a) that loosely corresponds to the point in time that the court that issued the judgment was authorized to act upon that person. There is no Convention definition of the point in time when a person becomes party to a proceeding, and this point in time can vary from legal system to legal system, for example from the point that a request for authorization to serve is received to authorization for service, to notification in compliance with service rules, to confirmation of such notification, to first responsive appearance. As with the interpretation of the term 'party' under Article 5(1)(a), and for the same reasons, the best approach to interpretation of the time element is by reference to the law of the State of origin.

6.64 The point in time on the face of Article 5(1)(a) is when the person became a party to the proceedings in the court of origin. However, some latitude should be accorded this aspect of the term, with a pragmatic focus on the proceedings that gave rise to the judgment rather than purely on the identity strictly construed, of the court of origin. The Convention does not purport to regulate such matters as proper venue and transfer within the State of origin. Article 5(1)(a) should operate from the point in time when a person became party to the proceedings giving rise to the judgment, even if those proceedings were transferred from a court initially presented with a claim to a court that ultimately issued the judgment pursuant to internal rules of the State of origin.

2. Article 5(1)(b)—Principal Place of Business of a Natural Person

Article 5
Bases for recognition and enforcement

1. A judgment is eligible for recognition and enforcement if one of the following requirements is met—

…

(b) the natural person against whom recognition or enforcement is sought had their principal place of business in the State of origin at the time that person became a party to the proceedings in the court of origin and the claim on which the judgment is based arose out of the activities of that business;

Article 5(1)(b) provides for eligibility for recognition or enforcement of a judgment as to a natural person based upon their principal place of business. It comprises an active subject (a natural person), two attributes (a principal place of business and an activity of that business), a causal connection with two analytic components (the 'claim on which the judgment is based' and 'arose out of the activities'), a geographic condition (the principal place of business of the natural person was in the State of origin), and a temporal condition (the situs of that principal place of business at the time the person became a party to the proceedings in the court of the State of origin). 6.65

Article 5(1)(b) has as its subject 'natural persons'. In that respect, it differs from the other provisions in Article 5(1), whose logical operations apply to the entire category of persons without further distinction (although, in actual practice, aspects of the other paragraphs of art 5(1) may apply only to, eg, legal persons, such as art 5(1)(c) (branches)). The term 'person' and particularly 'natural person' is almost a logical primitive in the Convention. However little the term 'natural person' may be amenable to satisfactory definition, a court is likely to know one when it sees one. (The thornier questions tend to relate to capacity, as noted in art 5(1)(a).) 6.66

For Article 5(1)(b) to apply, the natural person must have a principal place of business and the judgment must be based upon the activities of that business. As a gateway term, 'principal place of business' should be accorded a general sense for use in this Convention. Consistent with the underlying attribute of the Convention that it enshrines a form of international judicial assistance among interdependent sovereigns, the requested court must be guided by the characteristics that might be assigned to the term 'principal place of business' of natural persons for purposes of recognition or enforcement of judgments that will best perform two general functions: a negative function of not frustrating or impeding the effectiveness of operation of a judgment of a court of origin with respect to a person who has what might be described as 'a principal place of business in that State', and a positive function of opening the door to the legal system of the requested State for judgments that apply to a person with that that kind of relation to the State of origin. 6.67

'Business' here should be read broadly and should include the exercise of professions. The reference to 'principal place of business', has a number of aspects. First there must be a 'place of business' of the natural person. The Convention does not establish what is encompassed by this, and it raises some boundary problems and issues of law applicable. For example, does the place of business of a natural person only apply when the natural person is an 'owner', or are other arrangements included in Article 5(1)(b) as well? Neither the Convention text nor the Explanatory Report addresses whether Article 5(1)(b) may apply to a defendant who is an employee of another entity. It may be that many cases against an employee will really be against the employer in a respondent-superior capacity, so will not raise Article 5(1)(b) questions. The issue will require development through interpretation and application of the Convention. 6.68

The term 'place of business' in Article 5(1)(b) is limited by the adjective 'principal'. In other words, the place of business that falls within Article 5(1)(b) must be the place either where more activity occurs quantitatively than in other places of business, or, perhaps, the place where the activities of most critical strategic importance occur. This is a factual matter, to be decided by the requested court in determining whether a judgment falls with Article 5(1)(b).[15] 6.69

[15] The use of the term 'principal place of business' in art 5(1)(b) may vary from the application of the term as a place of habitual residence for legal persons or associations in art 3(2). While the factual inquiries likely will be

6.70 The second attribute of Article 5(1)(b) that the claim on which the judgment is based 'arose out of the activities of that business' is an attribute of the claim rather than of the natural person.

6.71 As a preliminary note, there is an ambiguity in this part of Article 5(1)(b). It is unclear whether 'that business' should be construed as the business actually conducted at the principal place of business, or as any activity that the business conducts as a unified enterprise that might operate in multiple countries. The first interpretation would make Article 5(1)(b) run alongside Article 5(1)(d) ('activities of that branch, agency, or establishment'); the latter makes Article 5(1)(b) more like Article 5(1)(a) (principal place of business of a natural person functions as something akin to a criterion for habitual residence in art 5(1)(a)). Based upon the text, the latter interpretation is preferable and seems more appropriate. The text refers to 'the activities of that business' rather than to the 'activities of that business at its principal place of business' or the like. Placement is also telling: Article 5(1)(b) follows on the heels of Article 5(1)(a), but is separated from Article 5(1)(d) by the unrelated provision regarding the person bringing the claim in Article 5(1)(c). Furthermore, the former reading results in a decided anomaly. Under it, a judgment-holder reaps the benefits of Article 5(1)(b) if the claim on which the judgment is based arose out of activities only at the principal place of business, while the holder of a judgment based upon a claim in otherwise identical circumstances occurring at a secondary place of business is denied the benefit of the Convention.

6.72 '[A]ctivities of that business' is comprehensive, sweeping, and unqualified in Article 5(1)(b). It encompasses anything done by the business. Nothing is excluded. The limitation to the sweep of the term is found in the requirement of a causal connection between the judgment, the claim, and the activities.

6.73 Article 5(1)(b) requires the requested court to determine both the 'claim on which the judgment is based' and that the claim 'arose out of the activities' of that business. Rather than engage in metaphysical probing of what a 'claim' is, for purposes of Article 5 of this Convention, 'claim' should be treated pragmatically as the thing that the judgment of the court of origin actually ruled upon and that is at the core of the judgment presented to the requested court for recognition and enforcement under the Convention, not including dictum. The requested court will make its own determination as to what constitutes the 'claim on which the judgment was based' but should tread lightly, taking due account of any characterizations by the court of origin. Determination of the claim on which the judgment was based may require the requested court to obtain additional information in situations in which the judgment is cursory, conclusory, or parsimonious. Article 12(2) provides for some additional inquiry by the requested court.

6.74 Having determined the claim on which the judgment was based, the requested court must determine whether the claim 'arose out of' the activities of the business (French '*resultait de*'). This determination may present mixed questions of fact and of law. Insofar as the court of origin determined fact on this point, those determinations should be classified as 'merits' determinations under Article 4(2) and should be binding on the court addressed. The question of 'arose out of' presents a more complex inquiry, and, in part,

parallel with respect to the adjective 'principal' and involve application of the law of the requested State, the inquiry into 'place of business' may be more complex.

will pivot on underlying notions of causation under applicable law, for example a claim may arise from an activity if there is but-for causation somewhere in a causal chain, a direct one-step nexus of mechanical cause and effect, etc. (The French '*resultait de*' sheds little additional light.) As with the issue of what is included within the concept of 'place of business' in this article, and for the same reasons, significant problems arise with recourse to national law to determine the question. Ultimately, the use of certain causal connections in the Convention (eg 'arose out of' or 'based on' or 'related to') will be a matter of the law of the requested State. Courts and other persons charged with interpretation of the Convention should work towards a Convention sense to these causal connectives, giving regard to the international character of the Convention and the need to promote uniformity in its application under Article 20, in light of the experience gained in practice.[16]

The geographic and temporal conditions (principal place of business in the State of origin, and at the time the natural person became a party to the proceedings in the court of origin) employ language identical to the referents in Article 5(1)(a)—and that recur in Article 5(1)(d). These conditions should be uniformly applied in the three provisions, and have been discussed above. **6.75**

3. Article 5(1)(c)—Party Bringing the Claim

Article 5

Bases for recognition and enforcement

1. **A judgment is eligible for recognition and enforcement if one of the following requirements is met—**

...

(c) **the person against whom recognition or enforcement is sought is the person that brought the claim, other than a counterclaim, on which the judgment is based;**

Article 5(1)(c) provides that a judgment is eligible for recognition or enforcement if the person against whom recognition or enforcement is sought is the person that brought the claim. Article 5(1)(c) consists of an active subject (the person against whom recognition or enforcement is sought), an attribute of that subject (is the person who brought the claim), an attribute of the claim (it is the claim on which the judgment is based), and an exclusion (the claim cannot be a counterclaim). **6.76**

With the exception of the term 'counterclaim', the operative terms in Article 5(1)(c) have been encountered in earlier paragraphs of Article 5(1). The interpretation of those terms proffered above should be deployed in Article 5(1)(c) as well. **6.77**

[16] 'Arose out of' or 'arising out of' is a term that occurs in Arts 5(1)(b), 5(1)(d), 5(1)(j), and (5)(1)(l) and in each instance refers to a relationship between a claim and an activity underlying that claim. It should be noted that there is a built-in reciprocal effect to application of the law of the requested State in this and other instances. A requested State with a broad interpretation of, eg, 'arose out of' will recognize or enforce a broader swath of judgments than a State with a narrower reading of the term. Insofar as 'arose out of' also has direct jurisdiction referents, the narrower the direct jurisdiction that employs this causal connective, the broader will be the obligation to recognize or enforce.

6.78 However, for purposes of Article 5(1)(c), 'claim' does not include a 'counterclaim', which is the subject of specific treatment in Article 5(1)(l), and the interpretation of which will be addressed in the discussion of that paragraph. Thus, a judgment that falls within Article 5(1)(c) cannot also fall within Article 5(1)(l) and vice versa.

6.79 Article 5(1)(c) is one of five paragraphs in Article 5(1) that provide that eligibility for recognition or enforcement pivots on a voluntary action of a person in respect to a court proceeding, actual or potential. The others are Article 5(1)(e) (express consent), Article 5(1)(f) (argument on the merits), Article 5(1)(l) (counterclaims), and Article 5(1)(m) (choice of court agreement).[17] From the perspective of an international judicial assistance arrangement intended to further and improve cooperation among sovereign States in an interdependent world, it would be unseemly for a court in one State not to give effects to a judgment of a court in another State when the original proceedings were founded upon the kinds of conduct encompassed in these provisions. In addition, these are circumstances that clearly call for minimization of transaction costs connected with global mobility, in particular, litigation costs. However, because of the unique power of this Convention, that opens the doors of courts in all Contracting States to exercise the coercive power of their courts based upon a judgment issued by a court in any Contracting State, and because rules on 'consent' or participation can become traps for the unwary, the criteria for eligibility of a judgment for recognition or enforcement arising from this conduct are specific, detailed, and circumscribed. They cannot and should not be aggregated together to create a general rule on 'submission'—a word that is not found in the text of the Convention.

4. Article 5(1)(d)—Branch, Agency, or Establishment

Article 5
Bases for recognition and enforcement

1. **A judgment is eligible for recognition and enforcement if one of the following requirements is met—**

...

(d) **the defendant maintained a branch, agency, or other establishment without separate legal personality in the State of origin at the time that person became a party to the proceedings in the court of origin, and the claim on which the judgment is based arose out of the activities of that branch, agency, or establishment;**

6.80 Article 5(1)(d) provides criteria for eligibility for recognition or enforcement of a judgment against a defendant that maintained a branch, agency, or other establishment in the State of origin. It is the first of three sequential paragraphs that are introduced by the phrase 'the defendant' (art 5(1)(d)–(f)). The language in each of these three paragraphs resembles language in text from the original project. However, in the original project, this language was formulated in the context of direct bases of jurisdiction, and interpretations of the language in that context does not transplant well—if at all—to this Convention regulating recognition and enforcement of judgments.

[17] Insofar as a trust instrument is created by agreement and designates a court for determination of a dispute, art 5(1)(k) might join this list as well.

The eligibility criterion for recognition or enforcement in Article 5(1)(d) includes a subject (the defendant), two attributes (maintenance of a branch, agency, or other establishment without separate legal personality, and activities of that branch, agency, or establishment), a causal connection with two steps (the claim arose out of activities and the judgment was based on the claim), and geographic and temporal conditions (the branch, agency, or establishment was in the State of origin, and was so at the time that the person became a party to the proceedings). 6.81

The subject of Article 5(1)(d) is 'the defendant' as defined in Article 3(1)(a), namely a person against whom the claim or counterclaim was brought in the State of origin. This is narrower than the subject of Article 5(1)(a)–(c) (the 'person against whom recognition or enforcement is sought'). The pivotal attribute of Article 5(1)(d) (maintenance of a branch, etc) attaches to the defendant and to no other person.[18] 'Defendant' here can include both natural and non-natural persons, although it may not be likely that a natural person can maintain a 'branch' (as opposed to an agency, or another establishment, such as a professional office). 6.82

Article 5(1)(d) pivots on the attribute of the defendant of having 'maintained' a branch, agency, or other establishment without separate legal personality. 'Maintain' has no definition in the Convention, but to 'maintain' conveys a sense of deliberate effort to keep something in existence over time, and imports a dimension of permanence or stability to the establishment in question. The interpretation of the term should not be left to the vagaries of national law because doing so might create an asymmetry in actual recognition or enforcement. In creating an autonomous Convention definition, courts should exercise common sense in light of the factual situations presented—which will develop and evolve with shifts in transboundary mobility of persons, goods, and services and the modalities of serving various aspects of this dynamic mobility. Of course, regard should be had, as required by Article 20, to the international character of the Convention and the need to promote uniformity in its application. 6.83

The gateway to Article 5(1)(d) is a 'branch, agency, or other establishment without separate legal personality'. Several ambiguities immediately present themselves. First, it is unclear whether 'other establishment without separate legal personality' is a comprehensive residual term that sweeps into Article 5(1)(d) every establishment without separate legal personality that is involved in activities in the State of origin, or whether the focus of the core are branches and agencies, and, only after those, establishments that are somehow like branches and agencies in ways that go beyond lacking separate legal personality. The former reading appears preferable. It avoids difficult and often technical legal questions of what a 'branch' might be under the law of the State of origin or of the requested State, or what constitutes an 'agency'. Application of Article 5(1)(d) should not be held hostage to the technicalities of local corporation law or agency law. The broader reading allows courts to sidestep metaphysical disputation and focus on the true core concept of the provision, an action that establishes a permanent platform (as opposed to mere transient presence) in a given State for the conduct of activities of benefit or interest to the defendant—the second attribute contained in Article 5(1)(d). In terms of its focus on stable presence, Article 5(1)(d) 6.84

[18] This does not affect application of the alter ego rule or the like of the requested State when a requested court is presented with an application for recognition or enforcement.

runs alongside and shares the focus of Article 5(1)(a) (habitual residence) and Article 5(1)(c) (principal place of business).

6.85 The second ambiguity should be noted, but should make no difference in application of Article 5(1)(d), namely whether 'without separate legal personality' modifies only 'other establishment' or also includes 'branch' and 'agency'. The former interpretation would, by virtue of the sweep of the adjectival phrase, make a common attribute of the three nouns that they have no separate legal personality, while the latter would make a difference only if, in some legal system, branches or agencies could have separate legal personality. While we are not aware of any legal system that contemplates the latter, the possibility with its attendant complications and consequential increase in the transaction costs of litigation, is avoided by the first interpretation.

6.86 Article 5(1)(d) contains a causal connection, the claim on which the judgment was based must have arisen out of the activities of that branch, agency, or other establishment that the defendant maintained in the State of origin. As with Article 5(1)(b) (principal place of business), 'activities' is without qualification; the requirement is satisfied by anything done through the branch, agency, or other establishment. However, Article 5(1)(d) differs from and is narrower than Article 5(1)(b) on a critical point: the activities that satisfy this criterion must be activities of the branch, agency, or other establishment maintained by the defendant in the State of origin, in contrast to Article 5(1)(b), which is rooted in the location of a principal place of business but captures any activity of that business. The attribution ('arose out of') of an activity of a branch, etc, must be made independently by the requested court, but, in doing so, that court should be bound by any relevant findings of fact of the court of origin, as has been discussed with respect to Article 5(1)(b).

6.87 The geographic and temporal conditions of application (the branch, agency, or other establishment was in the State or origin, and was so at the time that the person became a party to the proceedings) are equivalent in substance to similar aspects of Article 5(1)(a) and (b). The reader is referred to the relevant discussion of those provisions.

5. Article 5(1)(e)—Express Consent

Article 5

Bases for recognition and enforcement

1. A judgment is eligible for recognition and enforcement if one of the following requirements is met—

...

(e) the defendant expressly consented to the jurisdiction of the court of origin in the course of the proceedings in which the judgment was given;

6.88 Article 5(1)(e) (express consent) provides that a judgment is eligible for recognition or enforcement if the defendant expressly consented to the jurisdiction in the court of origin in the course of the proceedings in which the judgment was given. It contains an active subject (the defendant), and action of that subject (expressing consent), two limitations on that action (the consent must be both express and to the jurisdiction of the court of origin), and a temporal relation (the consent must have been given in the course of the proceedings). It is one of five paragraphs in Article 5(1) that anchor eligibility of a judgment for recognition or enforcement in a voluntary action directed at the court of origin by a person allegedly bound by the judgment: Article 5(1)(c) (claimant); Article 5(1)(e) (express consent); Article 5(1)(f) (argue on the merits); Article 5(1)(l) (counterclaim); and Article 5(1)(m) (choice of court agreement).

The subject of Article 5(1)(e) is the 'defendant' as defined in Article 3(1)(a) as a person against whom a claim or counterclaim was brought in the court of origin. The 'defendant' is less inclusive than the subject of Article 5(1)(a)–(c), the person against whom recognition or enforcement is sought. **6.89**

As with the other paragraphs noted above that provide eligibility for recognition or enforcement based upon an action toward the court of origin, this provision identifies a heightened and readily-ascertainable form of acceptance of jurisdiction in the court of origin. In Article 5(1)(e), that acceptance is consent given expressly. **6.90**

'[E]xpressly' requires an explicit statement by the defendant of that acceptance. The statement must be made by the defendant, or someone authorized to make the expression on their behalf. A statement of consent made by someone who is not authorized by the defendant to make that class of statement does not meet the requirements of Article 5(1)(e).[19] **6.91**

Article 5(1)(e) does not specify either the particular form of an express consent, the medium in which the statement is made, or the forum in which the statement was given (eg in open court as opposed to in a letter between counsel). However, in judgments against consumers or employees, Article 5(2)(a) requires that the consent was addressed to the court orally or in writing. The requested court must make its own determination under its own law and giving regard to the international character of the Convention whether express consent was given in a way that satisfies Article 5(1)(e). The requested court does not inquire into the rules on consent as a basis for jurisdiction under the laws of the State of origin, or whether the court of origin got its own law right. **6.92**

Express consent must be given 'to the jurisdiction of the court of origin'. Express consent to matters other than the jurisdiction of the court to adjudicate the case does not fall within the criterion established by Article 5(1)(e), for example a briefing schedule on threshold legal issues, or an agreement that, if jurisdiction is found, certain assets will be designated to satisfy any judgment. The consent must be to the jurisdiction of the court of origin; a general reference to, for example, resolving disputes in courts is not sufficient.[20] **6.93**

The express consent must be given 'in the course of the proceedings'. Because this points to a step taken in the proceedings in the court of origin, the law of the State of origin generally should apply to determine the issue. Consent prior to the initiation of proceedings does not fall within the criterion of this paragraph (although it may fall within art 5(1)(m), choice of court agreements). **6.94**

[19] However, totem pole authorization is not precluded, ie an utterance of consent may qualify under art 5(1)(e) if made by a person appointed for that purpose by an agent with general powers given by the defendant to make such an appointment.

[20] The Convention, however, does not regulate internal rules of, eg, venue or transfer. Consent to the jurisdiction of a specific court in the State of origin that, subsequently in the proceeding, transfers the case by operation of internal law to another court in the State of origin should be deemed to satisfy this paragraph.

6. Article 5(1)(f)—Argument on Merits Without Objection to Jurisdiction

Article 5
Bases for recognition and enforcement

1. **A judgment is eligible for recognition and enforcement if one of the following requirements is met—**

...

(f) **the defendant argued on the merits before the court of origin without contesting jurisdiction within the timeframe provided in the law of the State of origin, unless it is evident that an objection to jurisdiction or to the exercise of jurisdiction would not have succeeded under that law;**

6.95 Article 5(1)(f) provides a carefully circumscribed criterion for eligibility of a judgment for recognition or enforcement with a core based upon the defendant's having 'argued on the merits' before the court of origin. It applies to a specific behaviour in the course of a court proceeding, and, even then, only under specific circumstances. It is not and should not be read as a broad criterion of 'submission'—a concept that varies substantially from legal system to legal system.

6.96 Article 5(1)(f) consists of an active subject (the defendant); a behaviour (argument on the merits); a limiting condition (without contesting jurisdiction); a situs (before the court of origin); a temporal condition (within the timeframe provided in the law of the State of origin); and a general qualification (unless it is evident that an objection to jurisdiction or to the exercise of jurisdiction would not succeed under the law of the State of origin).

6.97 The subject of Article 5(1)(f) is the 'defendant' as defined in Article 3(1)(a), as a person against whom a claim or counterclaim was brought in the court of origin. The 'defendant' is a more specific subject than the subject of Article 5(1)(a)–(c), the person against whom recognition or enforcement is sought.

6.98 The behaviour that is at the core of Article 5(1)(f) is argument on the merits by the defendant.[21] The argument must be by the defendant, or someone with authority to make the argument on their behalf. Arguments on the merits by other parties or other interested persons do not bind the particular defendant for purposes of recognition or enforcement under Article 5(1)(f).

6.99 Both 'argue' and 'on the merits' are nebulous terms. Neither is defined in the Convention, and neither has international law referents. Reliance on national law, whether that of the State of origin or the requested State, is perilous. 'Argue' is hardly a precise, technical term of art. As has been discussed, the referent of 'on the merits' varies significantly from legal system to legal system, and may vary significantly within legal systems, depending on the context.[22] In the circumstances of Article 5(1)(f), an untampered application of

[21] This phrase should be compared to a 'decision on the merits' by the court of origin (art 3(1)(b)) and 'review of the merits' by the requested court (art 4(2)). In these three articles, similar phrases are used to describe different persons doing different things for different purposes. There should be no ascription of meaning by rote application to these phrases.

[22] See the discussions in Chapter 5 of this book concerning 'judgment' and the discussion in this chapter concerning 'of the merits' in art 4(2).

national law will result in asymmetries in the benefits and obligations found under the Convention, increased recourse to the public policy basis for refusing to recognize or enforce a judgment (art 7(1)(c)), and higher transaction costs by virtue of the increase in litigation regarding the content of 'public policy' in each Contracting State. Once again, a pragmatic approach to interpretation may be helpful in shaping an autonomous Convention sense for this paragraph. Article 5(1)(f) reflects a delicate balance of general fairness. It stems from a sense that it is unfair to other litigants to be denied the benefits of the Convention, or for a defendant to elude its burdens, once a defendant has crossed a litigation Rubicon by staking out a position on the facts to which the other litigants must respond, usually involving additional time and expense for all.[23] On the other hand, it is unfair to a defendant to be exposed to the rigours of the Convention if their conduct is a forced crossing of a Rubicon. The requested court, acting as an instrument of cooperation in an inter-connected global legal system, should take both aspects of the situation into account. Operationally, in light of these considerations, 'argued' here suggests an adversarial posture, while the core of the concept of 'merits' in this context appears to require averments of fact, or adversarial challenges to averments of fact, presented to a court as a basis for decision.

Article 5(1)(f) places a limiting condition on the core requirement of argument on the **6.100** merits, namely, that, in doing so, the defendant did not contest jurisdiction. The effect of failure to contest jurisdiction is not qualified by considerations of the reasons that might justify such a choice. The defendant gets no safe haven if they failed to contest. On the other hand, having contested jurisdiction as required by Article 5(1)(f), the defendant qualifies for the shelter it provides. This entitlement to shelter is not affected by subsequent behaviour in the court of origin, whether the behaviour be, for example, a default or a full contestation of the facts and litigation to the hilt. This takes account of the feature of many legal systems that requires a defendant at first appearance to contest jurisdiction and make averment of fact simultaneously, or forfeit the ability to do so later. If the defendant contested jurisdiction, this criterion of eligibility for recognition or enforcement is disabled.

It is the defendant against whom recognition or enforcement is sought who must con- **6.101** test jurisdiction; a defendant cannot rely subsequently on the point that another party may have contested jurisdiction in the proceeding. The paragraph specifies that it is 'jurisdiction' that must be contested. At a minimum, this is jurisdiction of the court to adjudicate. Contesting other aspects of the claim does not suffice to bring a defendant within Article

[23] However, the general condition of application of art 5(1)(f), non-futility of an objection, applies to both jurisdiction and objections to jurisdiction, such as through *forum non conveniens*. The sense of the text is not entirely clear whether it requires a *forum non conveniens* motion to be filed within the time frame for filing an objection to jurisdiction; such a requirement makes little sense because often the basis for a *forum non conveniens* determination is not apparent until there is additional factual development after resolution of jurisdictional disputes. If a *forum non conveniens* motion is subject to the timeframe applicable to such applications in the law of the State of origin, the defendant might be given shelter under the general condition of application even after some discovery or other factual disclosures. On the other hand, if the interpretation is that *forum non conveniens* applications must be filed within the timeframe of jurisdictional applications, defendants as a matter of good practice will make premature forum non conveniens applications within that shorter timeframe to preserve their safe haven under art 5(1)(f), even if the application is subsequently found to lack foundation. Presumably, courts in this situation will take the *forum non conveniens* motions under advisement until their determination is ripe, then grant leave to amend before ruling on them.

5(1)(f). Article 5(1)(f) does not specify a modality or a form in which jurisdiction must be contested; whether a given form or a given medium of contestation satisfies the limitation will rest in the judgment of the requested court. Nor does Article 5(1)(f) specify who carries burdens of proof, production, or persuasion on these points: they likewise are left to the requested court under its own procedural system.

6.102 Article 5(1)(f) specifies a situs for a defendant's contestation, 'before the court of origin'. Contestation in other fora, whether it be other courts, administrative tribunals, or the court of public opinion, does not qualify. However, a contestation in an originating court which subsequently transfers the case to another court within the State of origin as a result of applicable venue or transfer rules will not deprive a defendant of the benefit of this shelter from the paragraph.

6.103 Article 5(1)(f) includes a temporal condition; the contestation must be made within the timeframe provided in the law of the State of origin. The presence of this condition reflects one side of the balance the paragraph seeks to achieve by disallowing any safe haven for a defendant who multiplied costs of other parties by making a late, delayed, or strategic contestation of jurisdiction. The law of the State of origin applies on this point.

6.104 Finally, Article 5(1)(f) contains a general qualification that applies to the entirety of the text preceding it, namely, the paragraph does not apply even if jurisdiction is not contested by the defendant if it is evident to the requested court that an objection to jurisdiction or to the exercise of jurisdiction would not succeed under the law of the State of origin. It would simply be unfair to all parties to multiply costs of adjudication by requiring the filing of futile motions in the court of origin in order to preserve a safe haven in the requested court.

6.105 However, a defendant seeking shelter within this condition shoulders a substantial burden. It must be 'evident' that an objection would not have succeeded. This seems to suggest a showing stronger than more probable than not. The wording of the text (an 'unless' clause as a general qualification to a stated rule) and the requirement that futility be 'evident' indicates that burdens of proof, persuasion, and production fall on the shoulders of the defendant appealing to this condition. Of course, the requested court will apply the law of the State of origin in making its determination of the futility of a properly filed jurisdictional objection.

6.106 The general qualification in Article 5(1)(f) is a disjunct: the objection may be either to 'jurisdiction' or to the 'exercise of jurisdiction'. The latter limb captures situations in which *forum non conveniens* is available, but in which the doctrine assumes the existence of jurisdiction and goes to the exercise of that jurisdiction.[24]

6.107 Article 5(2)(b) disables this paragraph if recognition or enforcement is sought against a consumer in matters relating to a consumer contract or against an employee in matters relating to the employee's contract of employment.

[24] As with the other criteria of eligibility contained in art 5(1), failure of a judgment to meet the criterion of art 5(1)(f) does not affect eligibility for recognition or enforcement under other paragraphs of art 5(1) or under national law. See Convention of 2 July 2019 on the Recognition and Enforcement of Foreign Judgments in Civil or Commercial Matters, Text adopted by the Twenty-Second Session, Explanatory Report by Francisco Garcimartín & Geneviève Saumier (Explanatory Report), paras 174, 178, and 179 <https://assets.hcch.net/docs/a1b0b0fc-95b1-4544-935b-b842534a120f.pdf> for hypothetical examples related to art 5(1)(f).

7. Article 5(1)(g)—Contractual Obligations

Article 5

Bases for recognition and enforcement

1. A judgment is eligible for recognition and enforcement if one of the following requirements is met—

...

(g) the judgment ruled on a contractual obligation and it was given by a court of the State in which performance of that obligation took place, or should have taken place, in accordance with

i. the agreement of the parties, or

ii. the law applicable to the contract, in the absence of an agreed place of performance, unless the activities of the defendant in relation to the transaction clearly did not constitute a purposeful and substantial connection to that State;

Article 5(1)(g) creates a criterion of eligibility for recognition or enforcement of judgments that rule on contractual obligations, provided that a number of additional attributes are satisfied. **6.108**

The implied active subject of Article 5(1)(g) is a 'court'[25] located in a State with a particular geographic attribute: it is the State in which performance of a contractual obligation 'took place, or should have taken place'. Accordingly, in evaluating a request for recognition or enforcement under Article 5(1)(g), the requested court must determine that an obligation exists, that it is contractual, what constitutes a 'performance' of the obligation, and the location in which performance took place or should have taken place. The requested court will make its own determination under its own law, including its conflict of law rules, of whether an obligation exists,[26] what it is, and whether it can be classified or categorized as 'contractual' (although the requested court should hesitate to contradict a court of origin decision on the existence of an obligation, as opposed to its categorization as contractual). If a contractual obligation is found, the requested court should first turn to the contract to determine what constitutes a performance of the obligation, but, if the contract does not resolve the question, then turn to its own law, including its conflict of laws rules. **6.109**

The relevant place of performance is the place of performance of the particular contractual obligation on which the judgment ruled. The contract might call for performance in multiple places, but the only place that matters for Article 5(1)(g) is that of the performance on which the judgment ruled.[27] The Convention itself provides that the place of performance is governed by the application of a mutually exclusive disjunct: the agreement of the **6.110**

[25] For the concept of 'court' in the Convention, see paras 5.17–5.21.

[26] A number of paragraphs in art 5 require a determination of whether an obligation exists. This is a consideration 'necessary for the application of this Convention' under art 4(2) that the requested court must make but, as we point out, in doing so, the requested court should take into account its own private international law rules and tread extremely lightly in light of the judgment presented to it from the court of origin.

[27] Of course, if a judgment ruled on multiple contractual obligations, each of them might have its own place of performance. In such situations, if a party is relying on art 5(1)(g), the requested court must proceed obligation by obligation. It should be noted that the location of the performance of an obligation not to act poses puzzles not resolved on the face of the text.

parties or, in the absence of an agreed place of performance, the law applicable to the contract. While these two potentially applicable sources are stipulated by the Convention, the requested court will determine the specific issues that follow in their train: whether there was an agreement of the parties on the place of performance (including such matters as consent to and the validity of the agreement); if so, the content of the agreement; if not, which law is applicable to the contract, and whether it identifies a place of performance for the obligation in question. If there is no agreement of the parties on the point, and if the law applicable to the contract does not supply an answer, the requested court is left to its own law, including conflict of laws rules.

6.111 Article 5(1)(g) requires the court of origin to have issued a judgment that 'ruled on' the contractual obligation. '[R]uled on' is an expansive and expandable term. It has no Convention definition, and no international law referent. The meaning of the phrase may vary significantly from State to State and circumstance to circumstance, from inclusion of dicta to a glancing reference to squarely resolving all issues in dispute. For reasons that have been identified generally and in other contexts, it is important that courts create a sense of the term for purposes of the Convention rather than acquiesce in the development of asymmetries of application and an increase of litigation costs. A pragmatic approach to the sense of 'ruled on' in Article 5(1)(g) would indicate the following points: (1) determination that a 'contractual' obligation exists or does not exist;[28] (2) if it does exist, the content of the obligation; (3) the persons obligated and the persons to whom the obligation runs; (4) what constitutes non-fulfilment of that obligation; and (5) whether an operative obligation has been fulfilled (hopefully, with some explanation for the conclusion).

6.112 A general qualification traverses the entire length of Article 5(1)(g); the paragraph applies 'unless the activities of the defendant in relation to the transaction clearly did not constitute a purposeful and substantial connection' to the State of origin. The wording of the text is that of a general limitation based upon a conclusion of insufficiency. 'Activities' is a general term, and should be construed broadly to include, as appropriate in the context, conduct from negotiation to preparation to performance. 'In relation to the transaction' should also be construed broadly: the reference is not to activities in relation to the specific contract obligation but to the 'transaction' as a whole in which a particular contract obligation might be embedded. The activities in relation to the transaction must be activities of the defendant, which might include employees, agents, subcontractors, and others within the reach of the term under the applicable law. However, the activities subject to the limitation with respect to a particular defendant do not include activities performed by other persons. The logical structure underlying the limitation provides a good example of the logical complexity of many of the criteria of eligibility for recognition or enforcement in Article 5. For the limitation to operate, it must be the case that the activities of the defendant in relation to the transaction and which connect the claim to the State of origin were both purposeful and substantial. The Convention does not specify what constitutes a

[28] A question arises as to whether art 5(1)(g) would apply to a judgment ruling that a contractual obligation does not exist. As the provision focuses on the State in which performance took place or should have taken place, combined with the focus on agreement of the parties or the law applicable to the contract, it would seem that the negotiators intended to limit the application of this provision to judgments that ruled only on the existence of an obligation.

'connection' for purposes of Article 5(1)(g), nor when that connection is not 'purposeful' or not 'substantial'—and these terms are not terms of technical art in the law of a number of States. Accordingly, they will have to be given an autonomous Convention meaning, but that should be done in consultations with the laws of States that employ such terms in this context. Finally, not only are the burdens of proof, production, and persuasion placed upon the defendant who seeks shelter under this limitation,[29] but that defendant must meet a heightened standard to elude the operation of the main body of Article 5(1)(g): the limitation only springs to life if the defendant clearly established that its activities in relation to the transaction did not constitute a purposeful and substantial connection to the State of performance.[30]

Article 5(2)(b) disables this paragraph if recognition or enforcement is sought against a consumer in matters relating to a consumer contract or against an employee in matters relating to the employee's contract of employment. **6.113**

8. Article 5(1)(h)—Leases of Immovable Property

Article 5

Bases for recognition and enforcement

1. **A judgment is eligible for recognition and enforcement if one of the following requirements is met—**

...

(h) the judgment ruled on a lease of immovable property (tenancy) and it was given by a court of the State in which the property is situated;

Article 5(1)(h) provides the criterion of eligibility for recognition or enforcement of a judgment that ruled on a lease of immovable property. The criterion is met if the court of origin was a court of the State in which the property is situated. **6.114**

The implied active subject of Article 5(1)(h) is a 'court'[31] located in a State with a particular geographic attribute: it is the State in which 'immovable property' is situated. Neither 'immovable' nor 'property' is defined in the Convention and may be subject to some variation State to State. The term appears in Article 5(1)(h), 5(1)(i), 5(3) and in Article 6, and should be given as consistent an interpretation as is possible in each instance. The law of the requested State, including its private international law rules, should provide the classification of whether a thing is 'property' and, if so, whether it is 'immovable'. **6.115**

Article 5(1)(h) requires the court of origin to have issued a judgment, as defined in Article 3(1)(b), that the judgment have 'ruled on' a 'lease', and that the lease be of immovable property. '[R]uled on' for purposes of Article 5(1)(h) should be interpreted broadly in terms of its scope of coverage, to include any dispute connected to a lease, from issues of its existence or non-existence to disputes over payment of rent to disputes **6.116**

[29] The burden of proof on the defendant is accentuated by the language of the limitation: it applies only if 'the activities of the defendant in relation to the transaction *clearly* did not constitute a purposeful *and* substantial connection to that State'. (Emphasis added.)

[30] Art 5(1)(g) may become particularly salient in contractual obligations to perform in cyber-space. It is not the only paragraph of art 5(1) that provides criteria explicitly for contractual obligations, see art 5(1)(i) (contractual obligation secured by right in rem in immovable property). Of course, art 5(1)(g) co-exists with rules on recognition or enforcement of choice of court agreements, whether under art 5(1)(m) or COCA.

[31] For the concept of 'court' in the Convention, see the discussion in paras 5.17–5.21.

over interpretation of the lease agreement, of rights of occupancy or eviction, of alleged failure to provide the property in the condition proffered. '[L]ease' (or 'tenancy' as used in some legal systems), is an unqualified term: it applies to any lease, regardless of its particularities or purpose (commercial, residential, personal, professional), although for the Convention, residential leases, are treated separately in Article 5(3). A pragmatic approach to the sense of 'ruled on' in Article 5(1)(h) would indicate the following points: (1) determination that a lease exists or does not exist; (2) if it exists, it applies or does not apply to something classified as immovable property; (3) if it does apply, the content of the obligation in dispute in the lease; (4) the persons obligated and the persons to whom the obligation runs; (5) what constitutes non-fulfilment of that obligation; and (6) whether an operative obligation has been fulfilled (hopefully, with some explanation for the conclusion).

6.117 As with 'immovable property', the requested court makes the determination of whether the legal arrangement upon which the court of origin ruled constitutes a lease, and whether it is a lease 'of' immovable property.[32] If the legal arrangement is not classified as a lease, or if the thing to which the legal arrangement applies is either not property or not immovable property, then Article 5(1)(h) does not apply to create eligibility of the judgment for recognition or enforcement under the Convention.[33]

9. Article 5(1)(i)—Contractual Obligations Secured by Rights In Rem in Immovable Property

Article 5

Bases for recognition and enforcement

1. **A judgment is eligible for recognition and enforcement if one of the following requirements is met—**

...

(i) **the judgment ruled against the defendant on a contractual obligation secured by a right in rem in immovable property located in the State of origin, if the contractual claim was brought together with a claim against the same defendant relating to that right in rem;**

6.118 Article 5(1)(i) is the tightest of the Brussels boxes among the criteria for eligibility for recognition or enforcement of a judgment in Article 5(1). The implied active subject of Article 5(1)(i) is a court, with a geographic attribute (in the State in which immovable property with certain additional attributes is located) that has taken an action resulting in the creation of a certain legal result (issued a judgment). The legal result in turn involves scrutiny of four attributes: it takes a certain action ('ruled against') a specified person (the defendant), but only if the ruling satisfies a content and characterization requirement (ruled on a contractual obligation), and then only if that contractual obligation has an additional

[32] While the requested court will apply its own law in making this determination, the general sense of a lease as used in the Convention is of a legal relationship providing a finite term of occupancy or use of immovable property. In some legal systems, rights in a lease may be regarded as property rights with an in rem aspect, while in others such rights may be viewed as contractual. This classification should not affect whether or not the criterion in art 5(1)(h) is satisfied in a given dispute.

[33] As with other paragraphs of art 5(1), the failure to satisfy the criterion in art 5(1)(h) does not prevent recognition or enforcement under other paragraphs of art 5(1), or under national law.

attribute ('secured' by a 'right in rem in immovable property'). Finally, the entire provision is subject to a general qualification of a procedural nature; the criterion for recognition and enforcement in Article 5(1)(i) fails unless the contractual obligation which was the thing ruled upon was 'brought together' with a claim, and that other claim has two additional attributes—it was brought against the defendant and relates back to the right *in rem* that secured the contractual obligation.

The concepts of 'court' and 'judgment' have been discussed above in relation to the scope of the Convention and the definition of 'judgment' in Article 3(1)(b). The term 'immovable property' has been discussed with reference to Article 5(1)(h), and as noted, is also employed in Article 5(3) and in Article 6. The requested court should have few difficulties ascertaining whether the property was located in the State of origin. **6.119**

Article 5(1)(i) is unique among the paragraphs of Article 5(1) in that, to meet its criteria for eligibility for recognition or enforcement, the judgment 'ruled against' a particular person, the defendant.[34] Whether a particular ruling is 'against' a person is not always clear and will be determined by the requested court. However, the analysis is whether the ruling was against a person on the contractual obligation at issue; it is not a broader and more difficult inquiry as to the 'prevailing party' in the litigation generally in the court of origin. 'Defendant' is defined in Article 3(1)(a) as the person against whom the claim or counterclaim was brought in the State of origin, and has been examined elsewhere in this book. 'Defendant' here specifies that the ruling on the contractual obligation must be against the particular defendant in the court of origin who is subject to proceedings for recognition or enforcement of the judgment. Rulings against other defendants or against persons not the defendant under the Convention definition do not qualify a judgment for eligibility for recognition or enforcement under this paragraph, although this does not disable the operation of the alter ego rules and the like in the requested State. **6.120**

The requested court will determine whether an obligation is contractual, as described in the discussion of Article 5(1)(g). It must also make its own determination of whether the contractual obligation was 'secured' and, if so, whether it was secured by a 'right in rem' in immovable property. **6.121**

'[R]ight in rem' has no Convention definition; it is a construct found in national legal systems, and may vary with each. It appears in this paragraph and in Article 6, in both instances anchored to the term 'immovable property' although 'immovable property' appears without reference to 'rights in rem' in Articles 5(1)(h) and 5(3). Consistent with the general obligation in the Convention for the requested court to determine whether a judgment qualifies for recognition or enforcement (or denial thereof) under the Convention, it is our view that whether or not a right is 'in rem' should be determined by the law of the requested State, including its private international law rules. Otherwise, a significant imbalance would arise in the international law obligations created by the Convention in the required exercise of the coercive powers of the requested State in favour of Contracting States that bestow a wide ambit to the concept of 'rights in rem' or to the kinds of immovable property to which they can apply, and could create **6.122**

[34] Arts 5(1)(g), 5(1)(h), 5(1)(j), and 5(1)(l) are phrased in terms of the judgment that 'ruled on' something, art 5(1)(k) requires that the judgment 'concerns' a specific set of legal conclusions, and art 5(1)(m) pivots on the identity of the court that issued the judgment.

a temptation to further unilateral expansion. In addition, the Convention text provides some constraints on permissible national law interpretations, and helps identify the ground on which national law should operate. The Convention refers to immovable property in four places: Article 5(1)(h), Article 5(1)(i), Article 5(3), and Article 6. In Article 5(1)(i) and Article 6, the reference is to a right *in rem*, and such a right is referred to as being 'in immovable property'. In Article 5(3), residential leases or registration is 'of immovable property'. The French-language text is helpful. The equivalent usage for 'rights in rem' in French is '*droits reels*'. The sense appears to be that a 'right in rem' somehow is *in* the property itself, it attaches to the property, and, from the French text, that it is a real property right, the core of which is ownership or possession of immovable property. In these situations, the Convention calls for application of mixed sources of law: the Convention provides a sense, for example, that a right of ownership in immovable property be considered a right *in rem*, but the precise attributes of 'ownership' will be provided by the law of the requested State.

6.123 Article 5(1)(i) is limited further by a threshold procedural requirement that has two attributes: the contractual claim was 'brought together with' a claim that, in turn, was against the same defendant and that related to that right *in rem*. The Convention does not define the term 'brought together with', nor does it require that the claim on the contractual obligation be filed simultaneously with the claim relating to the right *in rem* that secured the contractual obligation, nor does it even require that the court of origin has ruled on a claim relating to the right *in rem*. The only procedural requirement is that the two claims had been 'brought together'. While the requested court will have to make its own determination, it is our view that the best approach to the term 'brought together with' in Article 5(1)(i) is to treat it as a narrow procedural term to be construed in light of the procedural rules of the court of origin. This will require an investigation by the requested court into the arcana of foreign procedural law, but the concept seems bound to the operation of the original proceedings. (NB the rationale for inclusion of art 5(1)(i) provided in the Explanatory Report is a perfect example of the inadequacy of Brussels boxes in a global convention in a twenty-first-century world: it was included to catch a small class of related claims that, in some civil code systems, would have to be treated separately for jurisdiction purposes and some of which might otherwise not be qualified for recognition or enforcement under the Convention.)

6.124 The 'same defendant' for purposes of this paragraph means a defendant under Article 3(1)(a) and, specifically, a defendant who will be bound in the recognition and enforcement proceedings.

6.125 '[R]elating' in Article 5(1)(i) and 'concerns' in Article 5(1)(k) present related problems. They function as connectives: to tie a claim to a right (art 5(1)(i)), or the judgment to one or more listed and specific aspects of a trust (art 5(1)(k)). On the basis of English usage, these words indicate a looser connection than the sense of the term 'ruled on' that introduces the other Brussels boxes in Article 5(1)(g)–(l), and which seem to require that the judgment actually determine the existence and content of a legal right or obligation (although art 5(1)(i) is phrased in terms of 'ruled against the defendant'). If so, the difficult question arises of the different shades of meaning to be accorded these different terms in a global, multilateral Convention. Once again, we urge a pragmatic approach. The French-language text is consistent in its use of the verb '*porte sur*' (or '*portant*' in art 5(1)(i)), which is consistently translated in the other English paragraphs as 'ruled on'. Rather than spend time searching for different shades of meaning in 'ruled on' or 'relating to' or 'concerns', courts should follow the consistent path charted by the French-language version.[35]

10. Article 5(1)(j)—Tort Obligations

Article 5
Bases for recognition and enforcement

1. A judgment is eligible for recognition and enforcement if one of the following requirements is met—

...

(j) the judgment ruled on a non-contractual obligation arising from death, physical injury, damage to or loss of tangible property, and the act or omission directly causing such harm occurred in the State of origin, irrespective of where that harm occurred;

Article 5(1)(j) provides criteria of eligibility for recognition or enforcement under the Convention of several specified classes of 'non-contractual' obligations. While Article 5(1)(j) applies to a certain range of obligations that fall within classic types of tort or delict, the provision is precise and highly specific in its coverage. It is not a generalized 'tort' provision. **6.126**

Article 5(1)(j) has an implied active subject (a court), which has engaged in an activity that has produced a legal result (issued a judgment) with a primary attribute (the judgment ruled on a non-contractual obligation). The primary attribute is then limited by a disjunction and a conjunction operating in tandem. The disjunct has four limbs (the obligation arises from either death, or from physical injury, or from damage to tangible property or to loss of tangible property). Satisfaction of any limb of the disjunct moves the judgment further into the ambit of Article 5(1)(j). However, even if the disjunct is satisfied, the judgment must still satisfy a causal requirement framed as a conjunction (the direct cause of the harm occurred in the State of origin), which in turn consists of two limbs of a disjunction (the cause might be either an act or an omission). Finally, Article 5(1)(j) concludes with a clarifying clause (the location where the harm occurred has no effect on the operation of the paragraph). **6.127**

As a preliminary point, Article 5(1)(g) and Article 5(1)(j) work a complete partition of the universe of obligations. Any obligation is either contractual or non-contractual (without prejudice to the possibility of being characterized as both, or given other labels as well). Within the Brussels boxes in Article 5(1), if an obligation is determined to be contractual, a court or litigant should examine Article 5(1)(g), if non-contractual, Article 5(1)(j) is a starting point (although it may end quickly). While the judgment might satisfy other paragraphs of Article 5(1), due diligence requires attention to these paragraphs. As with other paragraphs in Article 5(1), the requested court has the responsibility to determine both the existence of an obligation on which the judgment ruled and to characterize the particular obligation as 'non-contractual' as a 'consideration ... necessary for the application of this **6.128**

[35] The 'Done at' clause of the Convention specifies that the Convention was concluded with texts in the English and French languages. The clause clarifies that the English—and French-language texts are 'equally authentic'. Therefore, the wording selected in the one of the texts might help clarify wording selected in the other.

Convention' under Article 4(2), but generally should defer heavily to the court of origin on the former question.

6.129 The concepts of 'court' and 'judgment' have been discussed above in relation to the scope of the Convention and the definition of 'judgment' in Article 3(1)(b). The reader is referred to the relevant sections above.

6.130 The ambit of Article 5(1)(j) narrows rapidly after its initial broad catchment of 'non-contractual obligations'. The non-contractual obligation must 'arise from' one of four specified types of injuries. Only these four types of injury fall within the ambit of Article 5(1)(j). This is an exhaustive list. Any one type of injury will do. Each occupies an equal status: there is no subordination in importance or effect of one to any other. However, in light of the wide variation in national law in this area, ranging from what constitutes an injury to acceptable methods of proof, to remedies, Article 5(1)(j) was framed narrowly with a focus on things that can sustain 'physical' or 'tangible' injuries—injuries to material objects or persons—and should be interpreted in that spirit.

6.131 The first two limbs of the disjunctive involve bodily injury: death or physical injury. Physical injury should be taken as a harmful impact on a corporeal body of a natural person. It does not include purely mental effects. The third and fourth limbs require that something happen to 'tangible' property. Tangibility is not defined, but the sense of use in the Convention is something that is property and is material. It thus excludes, for example, intellectual property rights (excluded from scope in art 2(1)(m)), defamation (excluded from scope in art 2(1)(k)), and claims for economic loss, none of which would constitute 'damage to or loss of tangible property'. As with 'death' and 'physical injury', the terms 'damage to' and 'loss of' seem to have a sense in the Convention of injury resulting from a physical impact or intrusion on tangible property. The two property terms differentiate between impacts that may leave some of the property intact and other impacts that result in complete destruction. 'Loss of tangible property' should not, however, encompass an inability to use tangible property, or to use it in the most profitable or preferred fashion, divorced from the injuries arising out of physical impact.

6.132 Article 5(1)(j) places no restriction on the identity of claimants; be they the person physically injured, the owner of the affected property, heirs, insurers or other subrogees, or the like. The paragraph does not address the issue of whether it encompasses claims for mental damages arising from and derivative of death or physical injury, or damage to or loss of tangible property. Nor does it address the issue, if such claims might fall within it, of the persons who might have 'standing' to present such claims: for example the person directly killed or injured, relatives, witnesses to the event, the owner of the damaged or lost property, persons who enjoyed its use. Given the very narrow tenor of Article 5(1)(j), a very cautious attitude should be adopted towards any attempt to expand its ambit.

6.133 The reach of Article 5(1)(j) is further narrowed by yoking its restrictive disjunctive to an additional necessary requirement which, in turn, contains both a territorial and a causal component: the act or omission *directly* causing the harm occurred in the State of origin. The requested court must identify an act or omission that caused the harm. While this is a consideration necessary for application of the Convention under Article 4(2) and thus for the requested court, the requested court should pay due deference to any findings or factual determinations of the court of origin.

6.134 Article 5(1)(j) refers to *the* act or omission directly causing the harm, which raises the issue of how the requested court should treat situations in which harm was caused by multiple acts or omissions, no single one of which was sufficient in itself to 'cause' the injury. While the requested court should treat as conclusive findings of fact of the court of origin, it should not be required to delve into causality doctrines of foreign law, and, subject to the comments in the following paragraph, should make its own determinations on the legal conclusion of causality. The same may be said for the often-vexed issue of determining the location of an act causing harm—especially when the harm results from a series of acts—and even more so with respect to the situs of an omission. To some extent, this may vary with the choice by the claimant specifying the harmful act or omission. If a judgment holds multiple persons liable for an injury within Article 5(1)(j), the requirements of the paragraph must be satisfied as to each person as to whom recognition or enforcement is sought.

Article 5(1)(j) is narrow in substantive scope and further restricted in geographic scope. This is reinforced by the requirement that the act or omission involved have 'directly' caused the harm. The use of the adverb 'directly' points the way to the development of a Convention sense of the causality requirement in Article 5(1)(j). It deliberately conveys the sense of a very tight nexus between an act or omission and a harm. 'Cause' should be construed under Article 5(1)(j) in light of this sense of tight connection: it requires something more than 'but-for' causation or a harm the materialization of which requires intervening and contingent acts or events subsequent to the act or omission identified in the judgment. **6.135**

Finally, Article 5(1)(j) concludes with a clause of clarification: the place where the harm occurred is irrelevant to the operation of this paragraph. The sole focus of the requested court is on the place where the act or omission directly causing the harm occurred, to the exclusion of all other territorial considerations. Consequently, judgments deciding claims for harm caused by acts or omissions outside the territory of the State of origin are not qualified for recognition and enforcement eligibility under this provision, even if the person claiming the harm subsequently is located in that State and asserts that the harms are continuing. 'Territory' here means just that: regulatory jurisdictions not part of the territory of the State of origin do not satisfy this criterion (otherwise, the international law obligations of requested States would be determined by unilateral regulatory assertions of other States). **6.136**

11. Article 5(1)(k)—Internal Trust Matters

Article 5

Bases for recognition and enforcement

1. **A judgment is eligible for recognition and enforcement if one of the following requirements is met—**

...

(k) the judgment concerns the validity, construction, effects, administration or variation of a trust created voluntarily and evidenced in writing, and—

(i) at the time the proceedings were instituted, the State of origin was designated in the trust instrument as a State in the courts of which disputes about such matters are to be determined; or

(ii) at the time the proceedings were instituted, the State of origin was expressly or impliedly designated in the trust instrument as the State in which the principal place of administration of the trust is situated.

This sub-paragraph only applies to judgments regarding internal aspects of a trust between persons who are or were within the trust relationship.

6.137 Article 5(1)(k) provides the criterion of eligibility for recognition or enforcement of judgments concerning certain aspects of trusts. Although a creature of the common law (but with some anticipations in the Roman law concept of *fideicommissum*), a significant level of international assets is controlled by trusts or trust-like entities. They are a feature of an evolving, global world.

6.138 The logical structure of Article 5(1)(k) is a proposition consisting of a conjunction, one of the limbs of which is phrased as a disjunct, with the entirety subject to a general limitation.

6.139 The implied active subject of Article 5(1)(k) is a court that has performed an action (issued a judgment), and the judgment will be eligible for recognition or enforcement under the Convention if that judgment both possesses certain attributes contained in the first limb of the conjunct and satisfies a territorial and temporal requirement set in the disjunct.

6.140 The concepts of 'court' and 'judgment' have been discussed above in relation to the scope of the Convention and the definition of 'judgment' in Article 3(1)(b). The reader is referred to the relevant sections above.

6.141 To satisfy the requirements of the initial branch of the conjunction, a judgment must 'concern' a 'trust'—and, more specifically, it must concern one of five aspects of a trust: its validity, construction, effects, administration, or variation.

6.142 'Trust' is not defined in the Convention. Whether or not a judgment concerns a 'trust' for purposes of Article 5(1)(k) will be determined by the requested court. We do not venture specifics, but make the following observations about the general contours of the sense of the term. The concept should reflect an autonomous sense for this Convention, bearing in mind the international character of the convention. Given that a trust is a common law concept, that autonomous sense should reflect the content it generally is assigned in common law systems (similar to the approach that will be urged with respect to a civil law concepts in the Convention, judicial settlements, in Article 11, which should be given a Convention sense that leans heavily on use in civil law systems). The sense given to 'trust' should be dynamic, in step with developments in the law and realities of transnational mobility, rather than petrified in time at the point of conclusion of the Convention.[36]

6.143 The judgment must 'concern' certain aspects of the trust. 'Concern' here functions to tie the judgment to one or more listed and specific aspects of a trust. It has been treated in the context of the term 'relating to' in Article 5(1)(i), which performs a connective function in that paragraph; the reader is referred to that discussion.

6.144 To satisfy the requirements of Article 5(1)(k), the requested court must find the existence of a trust and that the judgment for which recognition or enforcement is sought must 'concern' the validity, construction, effects, administration, or variation of that trust. These are considerations necessary for the application of the Convention under Article 4(2), but, once again, factual findings of the court of origin relevant to these determinations should

[36] Accordingly, we are wary of an approach to content that would create a straitjacket based upon previous draft treaties—including draft Hague Conventions—that were prepared with different objectives in the context of a different world, have never entered into force, and will never enter into force

be given great weight. It probably is too much to ask national courts to create autonomous Convention rules on what constitutes the 'validity' or the 'construction' or the 'effect' or the 'administration' or 'variation' of a given trust. The requested court should follow the law it determines applicable to the trust, or to these issues.

The first limb of the conjunction in Article 5(1)(k) contains two additional requirements **6.145** for a judgment to qualify for recognition or enforcement under it, which go to origin and evidence. The first is that the trust was created 'voluntarily' as opposed to, for example, imposition by courts. Constructive trusts, which are often a form of equitable relief, fall outside this paragraph. On the other hand, Article 5(1)(k) refers to trusts 'voluntarily' created without any restriction: trusts created by contract, other agreement, bequest, etc all qualify.[37] The final requirement of the first limb of the conjunction in Article 5(1)(k) is that the trust be 'evidenced in writing'. This is a formal requirement. It does not require a written trust instrument, but simply that the trust be evidenced in some writing.[38] The requested court will determine, under the law applicable to the trust, whether a proffered writing satisfies this requirement—but there must be a writing (compared to art 5(1)(m) that applies to choice of forum clauses, that might be concluded or documented in writing or by any other means of communication which renders information accessible).

The second part of the conjunction in the logical structure of Article 5(1)(k) is phrased **6.146** as a disjunct. The judgment must satisfy one of two possible requirements. The first limb gives effect to a form of choice of court clause; the State of origin was 'designated in the trust instrument as a State in the courts of which disputes about such matters are to be determined'. While the requested court will determine whether a designation exists in the trust instrument, it should be bound by facts found in the court of origin relevant to that determination, and apply the law of the trust to that question and to the question of the validity of the designation. The designation must be in the trust instrument; it cannot be in another instrument (although the Convention does not require that the 'trust instrument' necessarily be a unified, single document). Unlike the situation in the second limb of the disjunct, the designation cannot be implied (otherwise, the provision in the second limb would be unnecessary). The designation is of the State of origin as *a State* (emphasis supplied) in which matters may be litigated. The designation need not be exclusive. Any State among several that are designated will satisfy the requirement.

The second limb bears some resemblance to a 'habitual residence' requirement. The judg- **6.147** ment will be eligible for recognition or enforcement if the State of origin was 'expressly or impliedly designated in the trust instrument as the State in which the principal place of administration of the trust is situated'. Unlike the situation in the first limb of the disjunct, the requirement here is an exclusive designation: '*the State* as opposed to a State'. The designation must be in the trust instrument, but in this limb it may be either express or implied. The requested court will make the determination of the existence of a designation and of the principal place of administration of the trust, but should be bound by findings of fact

[37] While the Convention does not apply to wills or succession, a judgment concerning the listed attributes of a trust created by a will may still fall within art 5(1)(k); however, insofar as a judgment might rule on a matter to which the Convention does not apply, whether as a preliminary question or otherwise, that ruling is not eligible for recognition or enforcement under the Convention. The remainder of the judgment might still benefit from recognition or enforcement.

[38] It should be noted, however, that the leading clause of art 5(k) is conjoined with a disjunct, arts 5(1)(k)(i) and 5(1)(k)(ii), each of which explicitly refers to a 'trust instrument'.

of the court of origin relevant to these issues. It should apply the law of the trust on these questions and on the questions of what constitutes an implied designation and the validity of any designation.

6.148 Both limbs of the disjunct are constrained by the same temporal factor: the geographic situs of the designation must exist at 'the time the proceedings were instituted'. The Convention does not specify a point in time at which proceedings are instituted. Because this issue goes to procedural rules of the court of origin—and at a time when it might be unclear whether recognition or enforcement of any judgment might be required or desired—the issue should be determined under the rules of the court of origin. However, the point in time at which proceedings are instituted govern—amendments, changes, or modifications after institution of the proceedings have no effect on the operation of this paragraph.

6.149 Article 5(1)(k) in its entirety is subject to a general limitation: it only applies to judgments regarding 'internal aspects' of a trust 'between persons who are or were within the trust relationship'. This limitation poses three issues: what is 'an internal aspect' of a trust, who are persons 'within the trust relationship', and a temporal span that encompasses both past and present. The first two issues should be determined by the law applicable to the trust. It should be noted, however, that while Article 5(1)(k) is limited to 'internal aspects of a trust', its scope is restricted to judgments concerning the 'validity, construction, effects, administration or variation' of a trust. While it is conceivable that in some domestic law, 'internal aspects of a trust' may have a broader scope than the subsequent specified list, the actual list in Article 5(k) exhausts the field of application of this criterion of eligibility for recognition or enforcement. The second and third issues, that the judgment applies between 'persons who are or were within the trust relationship' extend this aspect of eligibility for recognition or enforcement both to persons currently within the trust relationship and to those who at one time were within that relationship but no longer hold such a position at the time that recognition or enforcement is sought.

12. Article 5(1)(l)—Judgment on a Counterclaim

Article 5
Bases for recognition and enforcement

1. A judgment is eligible for recognition and enforcement if one of the following requirements is met—

...

(l) the judgment ruled on a counterclaim—
(i) to the extent that it was in favour of the counterclaimant, provided that the counterclaim arose out of the same transaction or occurrence as the claim; or
(ii) to the extent that it was against the counterclaimant, unless the law of the State of origin required the counterclaim to be filed in order to avoid preclusion;

6.150 Article 5(1)(l) provides the criterion of eligibility for recognition or enforcement of judgments ruling on counterclaims. It partitions the universe of judgments ruling on counterclaims into two mutually exclusive and collectively exhaustive sets, based upon the effect of the ruling on the counterclaimant, and provides a separate criterion for eligibility for recognition or enforcement for judgments in each set.

Article 5(1)(l) consists of an implied active subject (a court) taking an action (issued a judgement) that included a ruling that affected a specified person (a counterclaimant), with a disjunctive then providing two sets with an attribute that leads to eligibility for recognition or enforcement. **6.151**

The concepts of 'court' and 'judgment' have been discussed above in relation to the scope of the Convention and the definition of 'judgment' in Article 3(1)(b). The reader is referred to the relevant sections above. **6.152**

The term 'counterclaim' is undefined in the Convention. Consistent with the general approach taken in this book, the classification generally should be drawn from the law of the State of origin because it refers to a step in a court proceeding taken in that State. However, as with all references to national law, the interpretation of the term should be constrained by the injunction in Article 20 to give regard to the international character of the Convention and considerations of uniformity when engaging in interpretation. **6.153**

The judgment must have 'ruled on' a counterclaim, and that ruling must be either in 'favour of' or 'against' the counterclaimant. These terms should be given a Convention sense, with regard to the international character of the Convention and uniformity under Article 20. The ruling must be on the counterclaim presented for recognition or enforcement, and that ruling must be either in favour of or against the counterclaimant. A judgment that disposes of a claim but does not squarely dispose of a counterclaim pressed in the court of origin does not fall within the scope of this paragraph. '[R]uled on' in this sense goes to a determination of the existence or not of a legal right or obligation. A judgment should be treated as in favour of a counterclaimant if it fixes a right of the counterclaimant or an obligation which runs to that counterclaimant. A judgment should be treated as against the counterclaimant if it denies the existence of the asserted right or obligation. Whether the judgment also includes a remedy does not figure into this part of the analysis. Article 5(1)(l) calls for a specific analysis of the fate of the counterclaim in the judgment; it does not turn on whether the 'prevailing party' overall in some sense was the counterclaimant. **6.154**

The 'counterclaimant' here should be treated as the person who brought the counterclaim in the proceedings that resulted in the judgment, albeit without prejudice to operation of succession, alter ego, or subrogation doctrines in the law of the requested State. This approach will maintain some parallelism with the concept of 'defendant' as defined in Article 3. A claim in proceedings other than those resulting in the judgment, whether against the person who was the plaintiff in the original action or in a related proceeding, is not a counterclaim for purposes of this paragraph. **6.155**

The first disjunct of Article 5(1)(l) provides that a judgment ruling on a counterclaim is eligible for recognition or enforcement if it ruled in favour of the counterclaimant, provided that the counterclaim arose out of the same transaction or occurrence as the claim. 'Transaction or occurrence' gives a wide scope to the underlying basis that supports the counterclaim. There is no specification of or limitation on the kind of transaction or occurrence that qualifies a judgment for recognition or enforcement under Article 5(1)(l)(i). The subordinate 'arose out of' clause should not be treated as providing an independent Convention definition of a counterclaim, but as setting an additional Convention condition of eligibility for recognition or enforcement on things that are classified as counterclaims **6.156** under the law of the State of origin. The requested court will make its own determination whether the counterclaim arose out of 'the same' transaction or occurrence as the claim. As in its other occurrences in Article 5(1), 'arose out of' should be given a Convention sense as described above.

6.157 The second disjunct of Article 5(1)(l) provides that a judgment ruling against the counterclaimant is eligible for recognition or enforcement unless the law of the State of origin required the counterclaim to be filed in order to avoid preclusion. Unlike Article 5(1)(l)(i), there is no limitation in this paragraph putting conditions on the relationship of the counterclaim to the original claim. It is sufficient that the counterclaimant chose to press it. The limiting condition goes to the voluntary nature, or lack thereof, of the action of pressing the counterclaim. Generally, filing a counterclaim is a voluntary act by the counterclaimant, who willingly submits to the jurisdiction of the court of origin for purposes of adjudication of the counterclaim. However, the voluntary quality of the act is diminished greatly if the legal system fundamentally coerces it, as is the situation in which a person haled into court proceedings is presented with the Hobson's choice of pressing a counterclaim or losing the ability to pursue their underlying claim in that legal system. The Convention does not penalize such a counterclaimant in this latter circumstance by making a failed counterclaim eligible for recognition or enforcement against them. Both this sub-paragraph and its limiting condition fit well with the international judicial assistance model that, in a globally interdependent world, suggests the existence of identifiable circumstances in which a requested court should contribute to the operation of justice in another Contracting State, but with appropriate limitations.

13. Article 5(1)(m)—Designated Court

Article 5

Bases for recognition and enforcement

1. A judgment is eligible for recognition and enforcement if one of the following requirements is met—

...

(m) the judgment was given by a court designated in an agreement concluded or documented in writing or by any other means of communication which renders information accessible so as to be usable for subsequent reference, other than an exclusive choice of court agreement.

For the purposes of this sub-paragraph, an 'exclusive choice of court agreement' means an agreement concluded by two or more parties that designates, for the purpose of deciding disputes which have arisen or may arise in connection with a particular legal relationship, the courts of one State or one or more specific courts of one State to the exclusion of the jurisdiction of any other courts.

6.158 Article 5(1)(m) provides criteria of eligibility for recognition or enforcement of judgments given by a particular court designated in a choice of court agreement, while excluding such judgments if they were given by a court designated in an exclusive choice of court agreement. It both gives effect to the will of the parties in this regard, while coordinating this Convention with COCA, which primarily deals with exclusive choice of court agreements.[39] Because this Convention is complementary to COCA, the interpretation and application of terms and concepts in Article 5(1)(m) should hew as closely as possible to those accorded to the same terms or concepts used in COCA.[40] However, even if a judgment fails to be eligible for recognition or enforcement under Article 5(1)(m), it may still meet eligibility criteria of other paragraphs within Article 5(1).

The effective active subject of Article 5(1)(m) is a person who enters into an agreement designating a court to resolve a dispute, provided that the agreement meets certain formal requirements and does not designate that court to the exclusion of any other courts. A 'designation' of a court in an agreement requires both an agreement and some sort of affirmative identification of the court or courts intended to resolve a dispute. Neither this Convention nor COCA stipulates a particular form of words required either to constitute an agreement or the designation of a court. **6.159**

Article 5(1)(m) requires an *agreement*. There must be a meeting of the minds concluded or documented in a way that meets certain formal requirements, and that does certain things (ie designates courts to resolve disputes). Absent the consent of the parties, there simply can be no choice of court agreement. **6.160**

The issue of the existence of an agreement, vel non is different from the substantive validity of that agreement.[41] Depending on the applicable law, the latter inquiry may encompass such matters as fraud in the inducement, misrepresentation, mistake, duress, or capacity issues. Article 5(1)(m) puts no limit on the number of parties to the agreement, or to the identity of such parties (eg natural or legal persons).[42] **6.161**

The designation in the agreement must be explicit;[43] when this Convention contemplates the possibility of a designation by implication, the text is plain and direct in that regard.[44] While Article 5(1)(m) does not explicitly require that the designation be to a court of a Contracting State, the obligation to recognize or enforce in Article 4(1) runs only between Contracting States. (Issuance of a judgment by a court of a non-Contracting State would not be eligible for recognition or enforcement pursuant to this Convention.) The agreement must be concluded or documented in writing or by any other means of communication that renders information accessible so as to be usable for subsequent reference.[45] Consequently, oral agreements or 'hand-shake' deals are not eligible for recognition or enforcement under this paragraph. **6.162**

[39] This aspect of art 5(1)(m) should be read as an explicit reinforcement of COCA with respect to exclusive choice of court agreements covered in COCA, a separation further bolstered by the preservation of previous international agreements provided in art 23(2) (relationship with other international instruments).

[40] Accordingly, our treatment leans heavily on relevant sections of Brand and Herrup (n 8).

[41] See Ronald A Brand, 'Consent, Validity, and Choice of Forum Agreements in International Contracts' in I Boone, L Claeys, and L Lavrysen (eds), *Liber Amicorum Hubert Bocken* (Die Keure 2009) 541–53, <https://papers.ssrn.com/sol3/papers.cfm?abstract_id=1517810>.

[42] However, the Convention may not apply to certain issues that might be presented in this regard, such as legal capacity of natural persons. See, eg, art 2(1)(a).

[43] The designation of a chosen court in one party's general terms and conditions, which are explicitly incorporated by reference in the text of a main contract, is an explicit designation.

[44] See art 5(1)(k)(ii) (designation of principal place of administration of a trust in a trust instrument 'expressly or impliedly').

[45] This formulation follows art 3(c) of COCA and should be given a like interpretation and application. The formal requirement of a writing or any other means of communication in art 5(1)(m) of this Convention should be contrasted with the requirement in art 5(1)(k) that requires that a trust be evidenced in writing. When the Convention requires a writing to the exclusion of other means of communication, it says so.

6.163 Article 5(1)(m) states both minimum and maximum requirements of form for a choice of court agreement for eligibility for recognition or enforcement. Put simply, if an agreement does not comply with the requirements of form in this paragraph, it fails on grounds of lack of formal validity for the resulting judgment to be eligible for recognition or enforcement. If an agreement does comply with the formal requirements, the resulting judgment will be eligible for recognition or enforcement unless the choice of court is exclusive. National law cannot add further requirements of form for an agreement to qualify for Article 5(1)(m) treatment. Thus, a requirement of national law of the requested State that a choice of court agreement is not valid unless it is notarized, or unless it has a red ribbon and seal affixed, cannot be interposed to bar recognition or enforcement of a judgment if the underlying agreement meets the requirements of Article 5(1)(m).

6.164 Article 5(1)(m) presents a low threshold for bringing an agreement within its scope as a matter of form. It is sufficient for an agreement to satisfy the requirements of form if it is 'concluded' in writing, or if it is 'documented' (undefined) in writing—but a writing (also undefined) in and of itself is not necessary to meet the formal requirements of Article 5(1)(m). Even in the absence of a writing, an agreement may meet the formal requirement of this paragraph if it is 'concluded' or is 'documented' by any other means of communication that renders information accessible so as to be usable for subsequent reference. This threshold accommodates emerging forms of contract concluded by electronic means. While certain formal requirements are not necessary to create an agreement for purposes of Article 5(1)(m) (eg a single document with original signatures of all parties), it is difficult to predict in light of changing media and practice the precise forms of agreement that ultimately will be found sufficient or insufficient as a matter of form.

6.165 Because the formal threshold of Article 5(1)(m) is set quite low, the paragraph is likely to make a very large number of judgments resulting from non-exclusive choice of court agreements eligible for recognition or enforcement. A high threshold requirement in terms of form would have been likely to reduce disputes on a number of issues (eg if there was even a meeting of the minds). The price of a low threshold—and resulting wide scope of application—is likely to be an increase in litigation on issues such as consent and substantive validity.

6.166 Article 5(1)(m) has a limiting condition: it does not apply to an exclusive choice of court agreement. An 'exclusive choice of court agreement' is defined in Article 5(1)(m) as an 'agreement concluded by two or more parties that designates, for the purpose of deciding disputes which have arisen or may arise in connection with a particular legal relationship, the courts of one State or one or more specific courts of one State *to the exclusion of the jurisdiction of any other courts*' (emphasis added).[46] An exclusive choice of court agreement is a kind of choice of court agreement; for purposes of this paragraph: its only distinguishing characteristic is that it is exclusive. Likewise, the general characteristic listed for exclusive choice of court agreements (a designation 'for the purpose of deciding disputes which have arisen or may arise in connection with a particular legal relationship') applies to non-exclusive choice of court agreements.

6.167 Article 5(1)(m) places no restrictions on the types of claims that may be adjudicated pursuant to an agreement. The operative limitation is that the matter resolved

[46] This language is taken from art 3(a) of COCA and should be interpreted and applied in like fashion.

pursuant to the choice of court agreement must be a civil or commercial matter within Articles 1 and 2. Of course, it is possible for the parties to agree that only certain types of claims (eg those sounding in contract but not those sounding in tort) are subject to their agreement.

The purpose of the choice of court agreement must be to decide some or all disputes between some or more of the persons bound by the agreement, which disputes have arisen (ie the agreement can operate retrospectively), or may arise (ie the agreement can operate prospectively) in connection with a particular legal relationship. Whether the agreement operates retrospectively or prospectively, it must meet the requirements of form contained in Article 5(1)(m).[47] **6.168**

Article 5(2)(b) disables Article 5(1)(m) if recognition or enforcement is sought against a consumer in matters relating to a consumer contract or against an employee in matters relating to the employee's contract of employment. **6.169**

B. Article 5(2)—Consumers and Individual Contracts of Employment

Article 5

Bases for recognition and enforcement

2. **If recognition or enforcement is sought against a natural person acting primarily for personal, family or household purposes (a consumer) in matters relating to a consumer contract, or against an employee in matters relating to the employee's contact of employment—**
   (a) **paragraph 1(e) applies only if the consent was addressed to the court, orally or in writing;**
   (b) **paragraph 1(f), (g), (m) do not apply.**

Article 5(2) limits or eliminates the operation of four paragraphs of Article 5(1) in cases involving recognition or enforcement of judgments against natural persons acting in consumer contract matters or against employees in employment contract matters. The persons to whom Article 5(2) applies are identical or nearly identical to those subject to the exclusion from scope of Article 2(1) of COCA, and the terms should be accorded similar interpretation and application. **6.170**

Article 5(2) embodies the view that certain classes of persons (or persons acting in a certain capacity) deserve and require 'protection' from the full rigours of the mechanical application of generally-phrased law, often because these persons are viewed as intrinsically vulnerable in civil or commercial transactions ('weaker parties'), and that such protection should be provided through rules of private international law rather than through substantive law protections. There are frequently mandatory rules of national law that apply in these situations and express strong local public policy,[48] and it may be viewed as inappropriate to displace them by treaty. **6.171**

[47] Examples of choice of court agreements, both exclusive and non-exclusive, are provided in Brand and Herrup (n 8) 43–44, and Hague Conference on Private International Law, Convention of 30 June 2005 on Choice of Court Agreements, Explanatory Report by Trevor Hartley and Masato Dogauchi (2007) 108–09.

[48] For a discussion of the differences in legal systems concerning the use of private international law rules for purposes of protecting 'weaker' parties, see Ronald A Brand, 'Transaction Planning Using Rules on Jurisdiction

6.172 However, Article 5(2) in this Convention provides more precise and modulated protections than its COCA counterpart. Article 5(2) protects persons generally viewed as constituting a class of weaker parties: natural persons and employees, and only when recognition or enforcement is sought against them. In situations outside consumer and employment contracts and when these persons seek to have a judgment recognized or enforced, the natural person is within the Convention, entitled to the full benefits, and subject to its obligations. In contrast, Article 2(1) of COCA is an exclusion from the scope of COCA: if a choice of court agreement is one to which a consumer is a party or relates to a contract of employment, COCA does not apply to it, either in its jurisdictional or its recognition and enforcement aspects.

6.173 To qualify for the protections of Article 5(2), a natural person must be acting primarily for personal, family, or household purposes in matters relating to a consumer contract. The three purposes (personal, family, or household) essentially provide an Article 5(2) definition of a consumer. If a natural person is one or other of these, they are a consumer for purposes of the Convention. The three listed purposes are a disjunct: fulfilment of any one of them satisfies Article 5(2), and they are not mutually exclusive. However, the list is exhaustive. The action of the natural person must be for at least one of these purposes.

6.174 The action of the natural person need not be solely for these purposes, but must be primarily for one of them. '[P]rimarily' is not quantified, it can mean either more than any other single purpose, or more than the other purposes combined. Here, reference to the origin of the term in COCA may be helpful in ultimate interpretation. The COCA definition aligns with the definition of consumer found in the United Nations Convention on Contracts for the International Sale of Goods (art 2(a)); and the Hague Convention of 22 December 1986 on the Law Applicable to Contracts for the International Sale of Goods (art 2(c)). In accordance with Article 20, the sense of both 'consumer' and 'consumer contract' used in Article 5(2) should maintain consistency with the evolving body of international law and standards in this area, while remaining faithful to the words of the text.

6.175 Even if a person satisfies the definition of a consumer, they do not qualify for the protections of Article 5(2) unless the person's actions are in 'matters relating to a consumer contract'. We have identified the lack of specificity of the phrase 'matters' in our discussion of Article 2(1), and the general inclusion of the term sheds no further enlightenment. The term excludes little: if the action relates to a consumer contract and is primarily for a listed purpose, the protections of Article 5(2) should apply.

6.176 '[R]elating to' has been discussed in reference to Article 5(1)(i) (a claim relating to a right *in rem*), where it was pointed out that it should be interpreted in the sense of 'ruled on'. This is inapposite in the very different situation posed by Article 5(2), which deals not with the characterization of a claim but an activity of a person that has some sort of connection with a contract, whether it is a consumer or employment contract. While the English-language text gives no guidance, the French-language text is most helpful: it has no phrase equivalent to 'relating to' but simply references activity '*en judgmen de contrat de consummation*'. The term should be given a broad interpretation, consistent with the protective function performed by Article 5(2). Any action by a consumer involving a consumer contract that was primarily for a personal, family, or household purpose should qualify for protection if it

and the Recognition and Enforcement of Judgments' (2013) 358 Hague Academy of Private International Law *Recueil des cours* 191–217.

becomes the subject of a judgment for which recognition or enforcement is sought against the consumer, including activity prior to signing a consumer contract, or in preparation for or contemplation of entering into a contract that was not ultimately signed.

Article 5(2) also provides protection if recognition or enforcement of a judgment is sought against 'an employee in matters relating to the employee's contract of employment'.[49] As with consumers, the scope of this provision should be interpreted broadly in view of its protective function. Courts should strive to create an autonomous Convention sense of the terms 'employee' and 'contract of employment' with regard to Article 20 and international laws and standards that employ these terms. However, independent professionals offering services pursuant to individual personal service contracts are not likely to be 'employees' within the Article 5(2) sense of the term, and thus will not qualify for the protections of this paragraph. **6.177**

Article 5(2) provides no limitation on the contracts of employment that fall within it. The employment can be for any trade or activity. The contract can be individual, standard for multiple employees, or collective. The only requirement is that it be the contract of employment of the specific employee against whom recognition or enforcement of a judgment is sought. **6.178**

The contract of employment must be that of the employee against whom recognition or enforcement is sought. A contract of employment of a different employee provides no shield under Article 5(2). Nor do contracts of a person who happens to be an employee unless the contract is for their employment. There must be a contract of employment of the individual employee upon which the judgment ruled. If there is no contract—even if one was expected but never materialized, or if the dispute occurs after termination or lapse of a contract and does not refer back to it, the judgment falls outside the protections of Article 5(2). A dispute between an employer and a non-natural person, such as a trade union, regarding collective bargaining agreements or other general framework agreements, will fall outside Article 5(2). The provision applies to individual contracts of employment. **6.179**

The phrase 'relating to' (French '*relativement au*') should be interpreted to give effect to the policies underlying protective jurisdiction.[50] For example, it should include not simply cases involving termination, benefits, or conditions of employment governed by local employment law, but also cases arising out of a person's employment as well. **6.180**

Article 5(2) either limits or eliminates four of the criteria in Article 5(1) of eligibility for recognition or enforcement against a consumer or an employee. Article 5(1)(e), express consent to the jurisdiction of the court of origin, is limited by requiring that the consent of a consumer or employee be addressed to the court, orally or in writing. In contrast to the criterion in Article 5(1)(e), that creates eligibility for recognition or enforcement if express consent to the jurisdiction of the court of origin is given to another person, whether in court or out of court, and in any medium, so long as consent was given in the course of the proceedings, Article 5(2) requires that the consent must be addressed to the court. Addressed to the court should be interpreted literally as consent addressed to the bench: for example, a remark in passing in a courtroom corridor, no matter how **6.181**

[49] The parallel COCA text is phrased somewhat differently, and more broadly, excluding from scope choice of court agreements 'relating to contracts of employment, including collective agreements'. Art 2(1)(b).

[50] The French-language text does not reference 'relating to' with respect to consumer contracts, and does not indicate a need for 'matters' with respect to employment contracts. Interpretation of the English-language text should touch lightly on terms that the French-language text could do without.

explicit the consent given, does not satisfy the requirement. Consent given in the course of an exchange of emails with the vendor of consumer goods likewise does not qualify. Furthermore, Article 5(2) requires that consent be given orally or in writing, whereas Article 5(1)(e) makes no reference to the mode of the consent. All other requirements of Article 5(1)(e) obtain with respect to Article 5(2); for example, Article 5(2) does not affect what constitutes consent and when it is made 'expressly'. The reader should consult the treatment of Article 5(1)(e) for further discussion. Suffice it to say that the basic effect of the relationship of these two provisions is that a valid consent to jurisdiction by a consumer must be made in court—after the dispute has arisen.

6.182 Article 5(2) eliminates the operation of three paragraphs of Article 5(1) if recognition or enforcement is sought of a judgment against a consumer or employee. Article 5(1)(f), argument on the merits; Article 5(1)(g), contractual obligations; and Article 5(1)(m), choice of court agreements, do not provide criteria of eligibility for recognition or enforcement of a judgment against a person who falls within Article 5(2). However, all other paragraphs of Article 5(1) operate unimpaired by Article 5(2), as does the possibility of recognition or enforcement under national law pursuant to Article 15.

C. Article 5(3)—Leases of Immovable Property

Article 5

Bases for recognition and enforcement

3. Paragraph 1 does not apply to a judgment that ruled on a residential lease of immovable property (tenancy) or ruled on the registration of immovable property. Such a judgment is eligible for recognition and enforcement only if it was given by a court of the State where the property is situated.

6.183 Similar to the disabling function of Article 5(2), Article 5(3) disables the operation of Article 5(1) in two situations—tenancies and registration of immovable property, and instead provides specific criteria of eligibility for recognition or enforcement in those circumstances. If a judgment ruled on a tenancy or on the registration of immovable property, it is only eligible for recognition or enforcement if it falls within the criterion of Article 5(3), namely, it was given by a court of the State where the property is situated. Other criteria of eligibility in Article 5(1) simply do not apply.

6.184 '[R]uled on' appears twice in Article 5(3), once for each of the situations in which the paragraph operates. It should be given a Convention sense. '[R]uled on' is an expansive and expandable term. It has no Convention definition, nor an international law referent. The meaning of the phrase may vary significantly from State to State and circumstance to circumstance, from inclusion of dicta to a glancing reference to squarely resolving all issues in a dispute. For reasons that have been identified generally and in other contexts,[51] it is important that courts create a sense of the term for purposes of the Convention rather than acquiesce in the development of asymmetries of application and an increase of litigation

[51] See Chapter 4 for a discussion on issues of interpretation.

costs. A pragmatic approach to the sense of 'ruled on' would include judgments, with respect to tenancies, determining (1) whether the relevant relationship is or is not a 'lease'; (2) whether, if it is a lease, it is or is not a residential lease; (3) whether it is a residential lease (or not) of property; (4) that property is or is not immovable; (5) the rights or obligations under the lease; and (6) to whom rights under the lease run and from whom, and who is burdened by obligations under the lease, and to whom. A pragmatic approach to the sense of 'ruled on' would involve the judgment's determining, with respect to registration, whether (1) the relevant relationship is found in a 'registration' (as classified in the law of the State of origin); (2) that registration is a registration (or not) of property; and (3) that property is or is not immovable.

Neither 'immovable' nor 'property' is defined in the Convention, and may be subject to some variation State to State. The term appears in Article 5(1)(h), 5(1)(i), 5(3) and in Article 6, and should be given as consistent an interpretation as possible in each instance. The law of the requested State, including its private international law rules, will provide the classification of whether a thing is 'property' and, if so, whether it is 'immovable'. 'Tenancy' is used in Article 5(3) not as a term of art or gateway term, but as a familiar signpost because a residential lease of 'immovable property' is labelled a tenancy in some national legal systems. The controlling term is 'residential lease of immovable property'. Whether a legal arrangement constitutes a lease, and its classification as residential or not, will be determined by the requested court under its own law, including its rules of private international law, but giving due weight to findings of fact made by the court of origin. In contrast, registration involves a person taking a step in the legal system of a State to secure a legal right. Its interpretation should come from the law of the State of origin. **6.185**

If a judgment rules on a tenancy or on the registration of immovable property, it is eligible for recognition or enforcement under the Convention only if it was given by a court of the State where the property is situated. However, under Article 15, such a judgment may be recognized or enforced in the requested State pursuant to its national law, in contrast to judgments ruling on rights *in rem* in immovable property in Article 6, to which Article 15 does not apply. **6.186**

IV. Article 6—Exclusive Mechanism for Rights In Rem

Article 6

Exclusive basis for recognition and enforcement

Notwithstanding Article 5, a judgment that ruled on rights in rem in immovable property shall be recognised and enforced if and only if the property is situated in the State of origin.

Article 6 provides the exclusive mechanism available to a Contracting State for recognition or enforcement of a judgment that ruled on rights *in rem* in immovable property. If the property is situated in the State of origin, and that State is a Contracting State, a judgment ruling on rights *in rem* in that property must be recognized or enforced (subject to art 7 discretionary grounds for refusal and any applicable declaration). If the judgment comes from a court in a Contracting State other than the State where the property is situated, recognition or enforcement is barred, regardless of any other criterion of eligibility under the **6.187**

Convention, and that judgment may not separately be recognized or enforced pursuant to national law.

6.188 Article 6 consists of an implied active subject (a court) with a specific geographic attribute (in the State in which the property is situated) that acted (issued a judgment) with a characteristic (it ruled) with a specific feature (the ruling was on rights *in rem* in immovable property).

6.189 The concepts of 'court' and 'judgment' have been discussed above in relation to the scope of the Convention and the definition of 'judgment' in Article 3(1)(b). The reader is referred to the relevant sections above.

6.190 As in Article 5, 'ruled on' should be given an autonomous Convention sense; in general, this should encompass the sense that the judgment determined a specific right or obligation for which recognition or enforcement is sought. In Article 6, this requires that the judgment (1) determined the existence or not of a right 'in immovable property;' (2) fixed the content of any such right; and (3) specified the property to which the right attached.

6.191 Consistent with the general obligation in the Convention for the requested court to determine whether a judgment qualifies for recognition or enforcement (or denial thereof) under the Convention, it is our view that whether or not a right is 'in rem' should be determined by the requested court under the law of the requested State, including its private international law rules. Otherwise, a significant imbalance would arise in the international law obligations created by the Convention in the required exercise of the coercive powers of the requested State in favour of Contracting States that bestow a wide ambit to the concept of 'rights in rem' or to the kinds of immovable property to which they can apply, and could create a temptation to further unilateral expansion.[52] However, the Convention text provides some constraints on permissible national law interpretations, and helps identify the ground on which national law should operate. The Convention refers to immovable property in four places: Article 5(1)(h), Article 5(1)(i), Article 5(3), and Article 6. In Article 5(1)(i) and Article 6, the reference is to a right *in rem*, and such a right is referred to as 'in immovable property'. In Article 5(1)(h) and Article 5(3), the references are to leases or registration 'of immovable property'. The French-language text is helpful. The equivalent usage for 'rights in rem' in French is '*droits reels*'. The sense appears to be that a 'right in rem' somehow is *in* the property itself, it attaches to the property, and, from the French '*droit reel*' the core of which is ownership or possession of immovable property. In these situations, the Convention calls for application of mixed sources of law: the Convention requires, eg, that a right of ownership in immovable property be considered a right *in rem*, but the precise attributes of 'ownership' will be provided by the law of the requested State.

6.192 Article 6 is the overriding provision of this Convention. At its core is a prohibition: a prohibition on recognition and enforcement, even when recognition or enforcement is permitted under the Convention or otherwise required by national law. The presence of

[52] Of course, if as an empirical matter of comparative law, there is uniformity or near uniformity in national law conceptions of immovable property and rights in rem, there should be no difference in result between the application of the law of the State of origin, the law of the requested State, or an autonomous Convention sense. Indeed, this purported uniformity was one of the points made in support of inclusion of art 6. However, even if there is current uniformity, there is the possibility of temptations to future unilateral expansions of these categories in national law. As noted, if States succumb to such a temptation, recourse to the law of the State of origin effectively allows a unilateral expansion of international legal obligations of other Contracting States.

Article 6 defies any attempt to assert that the object and purpose of this Convention is to maximize recognition or enforcement of judgments, and that the terms of the Convention and its application must follow suit. The accurate characterization of the object and purpose of the Convention is to regulate and to provide conditions for recognition and enforcement, rather than to promote a general result of some ideal maximum of recognition or enforcement.

7
Additional Provisions Relating to the Recognition and Enforcement Obligation (Articles 7–15)

I. Introduction

Chapter II, 'Recognition and Enforcement', contains the operational core of the Convention. Chapter II regulates recognition and enforcement of judgments within the scope of the Convention; its rules are mandatory, but their operation does not necessarily mandate actual recognition or enforcement of judgments within scope. Articles 4–6 provide the basic framework for judgment recognition and enforcement under the Convention and are discussed in Chapter 6 of this book. Articles 7–15 then add additional rules layered on top of that framework and are discussed in this chapter. **7.01**

As an overview, Chapter II begins with Article 4, the first paragraph of which provides that a judgment given by a court of a Contracting State shall be recognized and enforced in other Contracting States in accordance with the provisions of Chapter II. Article 5 then provides criteria of eligibility for recognition and enforcement of judgments with certain features, but these criteria of eligibility are specific and often narrow. Article 6 then creates an obligation, that overrides other provisions of the Convention, both requiring, on the one hand, and prohibiting on the other, recognition or enforcement of certain judgments. **7.02**

Article 7 provides discretionary grounds for refusal of recognition or enforcement of judgments that are both within scope and meet the Article 5(1) eligibility criteria; these **7.03** grounds in some respects are broader than the grounds in the similar list in the 2005 Convention on Choice of Court Agreements (COCA). As a consequence, the Convention regulates the recognition and enforcement of judgments within its scope, rather than controlling or purporting to establish policy to control all recognition and enforcement of judgments.

7.04 Article 8 addresses the status of certain judgments that may contain content outside of the scope of the Convention, including 'preliminary questions'. Article 9 provides a severability rule. Article 10 addresses the handling of damage awards. Article 11 brings 'judicial settlements' (*transactions judiciaries*) into the Convention for purposes of enforcement. Article 12 describes documents to be produced when recognition or enforcement is sought, while Article 13 addresses other points of procedure. Article 14 addresses costs of proceedings. Article 15 preserves the ability of Contracting States to recognize or enforce judgments under their national law, including their conflict of laws rules, but then bars doing so with respect to judgments ruling on rights *in rem* in immovable property that are subject to Article 6.

II. Article 7—Grounds for Non-Recognition of a Judgment

A. The Article 7(1) Chapeau—Discretionary Non-Recognition or Enforcement

Article 7

Refusal of recognition and enforcement

1. Recognition or enforcement may be refused if—

7.05 Article 7 provides a list of grounds that permit the requested court to refuse either recognition or enforcement (or both). Article 7 contains a number of critical features. The first is that the grounds for refusal of recognition or enforcement are permissive. There is nothing mandatory about them. A judgment may meet a criterion listed in Article 7, and the requested court may still order recognition or enforcement under the Convention.[1] Second, Article 7 consists of a list. The list is exhaustive: no other grounds for refusal are to be found (except where identified explicitly in the Convention, such as in art 4(4) or art 10(1)). If a judgment is within the scope of the Convention and satisfies at least one criterion of eligibility for recognition or enforcement under Article 5, it must be recognized or enforced unless a specific ground of refusal is identified in Article 7 (unless recognition and enforcement is prohibited by art 6). However, the grounds listed in Article 7 are not exclusive: more than one ground may apply to deny recognition or enforcement. Nor is there a hierarchy; a given ground of refusal listed in Article 7 is not subordinate to or precluded by any other ground. Finally, Article 7 is a disjunct: it permits refusal of either recognition or enforcement. Accordingly, a requested court may use Article 7 to deny both recognition

[1] Because art 7 is permissive, a Contracting State in implementing legislation or other statute may provide that only some of the listed grounds shall apply in its courts, or even that none shall apply. The legislation may also define, or provide examples or guidelines, for the interpretation of the grounds of refusal that will operate in the Contracting State, such as illustrations of situations that the State views as manifestly incompatible with its public policy.

and enforcement of a judgment, or it may recognize a judgment—notwithstanding the existence of an Article 7 ground of refusal of recognition—but could deny enforcement of that judgment under Article 7.

Article 7(1) permits the court to examine and ground refusal of recognition or enforcement on specified aspects of the proceedings in the court of origin that produced the judgment presented for recognition or enforcement. Articles 7(1)(a)(ii), 7(1)(c), and 7(2) permit the requested court to examine and ground refusal of recognition or enforcement on interests of the requested State. Article 7 largely is cognate to similar COCA provisions, but there are significant and revealing differences at some points. **7.06**

B. Article 7(1)(a)—Lack of Proper Notice

Article 7

Refusal of recognition and enforcement

1. **Recognition or enforcement may be refused if—**
   (a) **the document which instituted the proceedings or an equivalent document, including the essential elements of the claim—**
      (i) **was not notified to the defendant in sufficient time and in such a way as to enable them to arrange for their defense, unless the defendant entered an appearance and presented their case without contesting notification in the court of origin, provided that the law of the State of origin permitted notification to be contested; or**
      (ii) **was notified to the defendant in the requested State in a manner that is incompatible with fundamental principles of the requested State concerning service of documents;**

Article 7(1)(a) of this Convention is virtually identical to Article 9(c) of COCA.[2] The effect of the time, place, and manner of notification of proceedings in the court of origin on the Convention obligation of the court addressed to recognize and enforce a resulting judgment was among the most difficult matters encountered by the negotiators of COCA. Some States view the regulation of local service of process for foreign judicial proceedings as an integral element of sovereignty. Others allow service to be made by private persons, so long as proper notice is satisfied. The Convention would lose predictability if the Convention allowed obstruction of recognition or enforcement based on the failure of proceedings in one State to comply with every detail of the formal requirements for service in the State where the defendant may have been served. This would be a substantial deterrent to wide ratification. **7.07**

The provisions in Article 7(1)(a) represent a very careful and delicate balance of these concerns and interests. Article 7(1)(a) permits refusal of recognition or enforcement in two circumstances related to service. The first, which is phrased in the negative, provides a minimum floor of fairness to a defendant in the court of origin. It is largely (but not purely) a **7.08**

[2] The only difference is the use of the more gender-neutral 'them' and 'their' for 'his' and 'him' in COCA. This discussion leans heavily on Ronald A Brand and Paul M Herrup, *The 2005 Hague Convention on Choice of Agreements* (CUP 2008) 113–16.

matter of fact. The second, which is phrased in an affirmative fashion followed by a negative, Article 7(2)(b) provides some protection to the sovereignty interests of the State of the court of the requested State. It requires two initial factual findings, then legal conclusions.

7.09 It must be stressed that Article 7(1)(a) addresses only the *effect* of methods of 'notification' in the court of origin on the Convention obligation to recognize and enforce. Nothing in Article 7(1)(a) mandates particular rules or *methods* of service, notice, or notification. These are matters for the national law of the State of origin, as determined by the court of origin. The requested court may not examine compliance of the court of origin with its own law, with the law of third countries in which notification might have occurred, or with international conventions.

7.10 A deliberate choice was made to use the term 'notified' rather than terms such as 'notice' or 'service', which may have specific and technical meaning and requirements in the national law of various States. The text carefully avoids embroiling this provision, especially Article 7(1)(a)(i), in the specifics of national law. ('Service' is used once in art 7(1)(a)(ii), but the reference is carefully restricted: it does not affirmatively require compliance of service of documents with the general procedural law of the State of the requested court, but refers to a permissive grounds of refusal of recognition or enforcement if notification was affirmatively 'incompatible' with 'fundamental principles of the requested State concerning service of documents'.)

7.11 As with all grounds for refusal of recognition or enforcement under Article 7, this ground of refusal is permissive ('may be refused') rather than mandatory.

7.12 The document to be 'notified to the defendant' is either the document that instituted the proceedings in the court chosen, or an equivalent document. In some systems, the document that institutes proceedings in the court may not be identical to the document presented to a defendant to satisfy requirements of notification. Article 7(1)(a) does not discriminate between legal systems on this basis. However, Article 7(1)(a) specifically permits a court to refuse to recognize or enforce a judgment if the document providing notification of the underlying proceeding does not include the essential elements of the claim, whether review in the requested court proceeds under Article 7(1)(a)(i) or under Article 7(1)(a)(ii).

7.13 Article 7(1)(a) refers only to documents that instituted the proceedings in the court of origin. Once initial notification is effected by proper delivery of such documents, service of all other documents in the proceeding follow the applicable rules of that court. The Convention has nothing to say regarding the movement of papers once the threshold requirement is met for notification that there is a proceeding, and of the essential elements of the claim.

7.14 While subparagraph (a)(i) of Article 7(1) comprises three clauses, the rule is found in the independent clause and allows for the refusal of recognition or enforcement if the threshold document was not notified to the defendant in sufficient time and in such a way as to enable him to arrange for his defence. The key element in this general rule is that the circumstances of notification allow the defendant to arrange for the defence. Consistent with the basic consideration underlying this particular provision—to protect fairness to defendants—'defence' must be read as 'effective defence'.

7.15 This ground for refusal of recognition or enforcement under the Convention is not triggered by a failure of the defendant to arrange for an effective defence. It is triggered by either (1) absence of notification, or (2) notification that does not either provide sufficient time or occur in a proper manner for the defendant to arrange for an effective defence. Consequently, the court addressed may inquire into:

(1) the existence of a document providing notification of institution of proceedings;
(2) the occurrence of notification to the defendant of the document;
(3) the time provided between notification and the date on which the defendant was required to take a step in the proceedings;
(4) whether any lack of sufficiency of the time provided in (3) prevented the defendant from arranging an effective defence (because the clause is phrased in the negative, it would appear that lack of sufficiency rather than sufficiency is the appropriate inquiry);
(5) the way in which notification was effected; and
(6) whether inadequacies in the manner of notification prevented the defendant from arranging an effective defence.

While the thrust of these inquiries is generally factual, there are issues of causation and characterization (eg what is an 'effective' defence) that may constitute mixed questions of fact and law. 7.16

It should be noted in particular that the standard for determining whether notice is received in 'sufficient time' under this provision is not necessarily the time provided in the relevant rules of the State of origin. A requested court has discretion to conclude under this provision that, due to matters such as the nature of the claims, the distance of the forum, or problems of language and translation, notification did not meet a Convention threshold of fairness, even if the requirements of the court of origin's national law were met. Obviously, this discretion should be exercised cautiously. Otherwise, this limited ground for refusal of recognition or enforcement under the Convention has the capacity to swell to an unacceptable size. 7.17

The basic requirement of sufficient notice found in Article 7(1)(a)(i) is immediately qualified by the phrase 'unless the defendant entered an appearance and presented their case without contesting notification in the court of origin'. This clause effectively prohibits a defendant from raising issues of notification in proceedings for recognition or enforcement that could and should have been raised in the proceedings at first instance. Article 7(1)(a)(i) does not provide an opportunity to relitigate the point after presentation of a full defence in the court of origin. 7.18

The failure to contest qualification applies only if the defendant appeared in the original proceeding and failed to raise issues of notification, even though notification occurred at a time or in a manner that prevented preparation of an adequate defence. If the defendant was prejudiced in the original proceeding by the time or manner of notification, many systems of law will allow the defendant to raise the issue and to seek an adjournment, continuance, or postponement. If the law of the State of origin permits such an application by a defendant, and the defendant fails to protect their interests in this regard, while entering an appearance and presenting their case, the Convention will not allow re-examination of notification at the stage of recognition or enforcement. 7.19

This qualification does not operate if the defendant contested notification and failed—or if the law of the originating court did not allow notification to be contested. In such an event, the defendant may raise the point again before the requested court. 7.20

The 'unless' clause in Article 7(1)(a)(i) is modified in turn by the phrase 'provided that the law of the State of origin permitted notification to be contested'. This clause preserves 7.21

the ability of a defendant to raise the issue of insufficient notification in recognition or enforcement proceedings, even if the defendant appeared and did not contest the point in the court of origin, *if* the law of the State of the court of origin does not permit notification to be contested. In such conditions, there is little point in the Convention requiring a futile motion that will be a waste of resources. Examination of this point will require determination by the requested court of a matter of foreign law (ie whether notification may be contested).

7.22 With respect to governmental litigation, Article 2(5) is unaffected by Article 7(1)(a)(i). Nothing in Article 7(1)(a)(i) affects the requirement in public international law that a foreign State defendant receive service by diplomatic or other specified channels, which allows at least a sixty-day response time between the date of service and the date that the foreign State must take a step in the proceedings.[3]

7.23 Article 7(1)(a)(ii) protects the sovereign interests of States. This provision requires an initial factual finding that notification of the defendant occurred *in the requested State*. This provision allows a court in the requested State to vindicate its own interests, not those of some other State. The requested State should have no sovereign interest in the manner of notification of a defendant in any other State. This bar to recognition and enforcement will apply even if notification occurred in several States, so long as the manner of notification in the requested State was incompatible with fundamental principles of that State concerning service of documents.

7.24 In order for recognition or enforcement to be refused under Article 7(1)(a)(ii), the method of giving notice in the requested State must be incompatible with fundamental principles of that State concerning service of documents. This requires that the requested court first make a finding of the manner of notification. This should be a matter of fact. Once this finding is made, the exception only applies if there is an 'incompatibility' between the manner of notification and 'fundamental principles' of the requested State concerning service of documents. This requires two determinations:

(1) The court must first identify 'fundamental principles' concerning service of documents. This in turn requires a court to distinguish between fundamental principles and mere rules and regulations applicable to service of documents.
(2) The court must then determine whether there exists an 'incompatibility' between the manner of notification and the fundamental principles concerning service of documents. While 'incompatibility' is not defined in the Convention, nor, probably, in anyone's national law, it would appear to require far more than mere technical non-compliance.

7.25 It is only in this clause of Article 7(1)(a)(ii) that the term 'service' is used. 'Service' here is used to refer to the principles underlying the national law of the requested State regarding legal requirements. This is something different from the use of 'notified' in Article 7(1)(a)(i) and the accompanying factual inquiry that is required for that provision.[4]

[3] See, eg, European Convention on State Immunity, art 16(5), May 16, 1972, CETS No 074 <https://www.coe.int/en/web/conventions/full-list?module=treaty-detail&treatynum=074> (accessed 1 July 2023).

[4] Art 7(1)(c) permits refusal of recognition or enforcement if doing so would be manifestly incompatible with the public policy of the requested State, including situations involving infringements of its sovereignty. Some States may view methods of service as matters of sovereignty. However, art 7(1)(a)(ii) is a form of narrow *lex specialis*

C. Article 7(1)(b)—Fraud

Article 7
Refusal of recognition and enforcement

1. **Recognition or enforcement may be refused if—**

...

(b) the judgment was obtained by fraud;

Article 7(1)(b) provides that the requested court may refuse recognition or enforcement of an otherwise eligible judgment if the judgment was obtained by fraud. '[F]raud' is not defined in the Convention, and, as a practical matter, it will be difficult to fashion an autonomous definition. The meaning of the term will lean heavily on the law of the requested State, bearing in mind the injunction of Article 20 that regard shall be had to the international character of the Convention and the need to promote uniformity in application. **7.26**

COCA has a similar fraud ground of refusal of recognition or enforcement in Article 9(1)(d). Article 7(1)(b) deliberately is more expansive than its COCA cognate, and comparison of the two provides parameters for the interpretation of the term in this Convention: the ground for refusal here contains everything encompassed in the COCA provision and more. Accordingly, we will begin with an examination of Article 9(1)(d) of COCA. **7.27**

Article 9(1)(d) of COCA provides that 'recognition or enforcement may be refused if the judgment was obtained by fraud in connection with a matter of procedure'. This ground of refusal is consistent with (and originated in) the extrinsic fraud rule applied in US courts, as distinguished from intrinsic fraud. It is impossible to provide an exhaustive catalogue of the types of conduct that constitute extrinsic, as opposed to intrinsic, fraud. The classic statement of the extrinsic fraud rule in the United States may be found in *Allegheny Corporation v Kirby*: **7.28**

> In cases seeking to set aside the judgment of another Court, or to prevent a party from pleading that judgment as res judicata, the Courts have drawn a distinction between extrinsic fraud and intrinsic fraud. The distinguishing between extrinsic and intrinsic fraud is an attempt by the Courts to reconcile two competing considerations—justice to the parties and a finality of litigation. *See United States v. Throckmorton*, 98 U.S. 61, at pp.68–69. The distinction between extrinsic and intrinsic fraud was well express by Judge Phillips in *Chisholm v. House*, 160 F.2d 632, at p.643 (10th Cir. 1947). He said:
>
>> Fraud is regarded as extrinsic or collateral where it prevents a party from having a trial or from presenting his cause of action or his defense, or induces him to withdraw a defense, or operates upon matters pertaining not to the judgment itself, but to the manner in which it was procured. Where, however, the judgment was founded on a

pertaining to service within the requested State, and, as such, cannot be expanded to fit the more general ground of public policy in art 7(1)(c).

fraudulent instrument or perjured evidence, or the fraudulent acts pertained to an issue involved in the original action and litigated therein, the fraud is regarded as intrinsic.[5]

Fraud in connection with a matter of procedure does *not* extend to issues of disputed evidence actually let into the record during proceedings in the court of origin. This would constitute a review of the merits of the judgment not contemplated in Article 4(2) of this Convention.

7.29 Accordingly, the grounds of refusal for fraud in this Convention include the kinds of conduct identified in *Allegheny Corporation*, and more. The 'more' must be construed in light of a central limiting factor contained in the text: the thing to which the fraud pertains. '*[T]he judgment*' must be '*obtained*' by fraud (emphasis added). It is not a ground of refusal that some aspect of the underlying conduct from which the claim arose was fraudulent or allegedly was tainted by fraud. A fraud must have procured the judgment. This would add to the list of examples of extrinsic fraud in *Allegheny Corporation* the use of perjury in the proceedings to obtain the judgment (although the meaning of the term 'perjury' will be provided by the law of the requested State). Furthermore, it is not sufficient to trigger this ground of refusal that perjured testimony has been presented in the proceedings in the court of origin; the requested court must determine that the perjury was an essential factor in obtaining the judgment presented to it for recognition or enforcement.

7.30 There may be additional limiting factors in constraining this ground of refusal of recognition or enforcement. The general presumption of regularity of judicial proceedings should place the burden of proof, production, and persuasion on the person resisting recognition or enforcement. Insofar as there may be pleading rules requiring fraud to be pleaded with particularity, they will add to the burden. Given that refusal of recognition or enforcement under all paragraphs of Article 7 is permissive rather than mandatory, a requested court presented with an application to refuse for fraud may well take into account whether the legal system of the State of origin provided meaningful opportunities within its own institutions to rectify allegations of perjury or the like and, if so, whether the person resisting recognition or enforcement exhausted local remedies. Insofar as a part of a judgment that is tainted may be severable from the remainder, Article 9 of this Convention provides that the untainted remainder shall be recognized or enforced. Nonetheless, particularly in legal systems that provide for broad discovery, Article 7(1)(b) has the potential to increase significantly litigation costs.

D. Article 7(1)(c)—Public Policy

Article 7

Refusal of recognition and enforcement

1. **Recognition or enforcement may be refused if—**

…

(c) recognition or enforcement would be manifestly incompatible with the public policy of the requested State, including situations where the specific proceedings

[5] *Allegheny Corporation v Kirby*, 218 F Supp 164, 183 (SDNY 1963).

leading to the judgment were incompatible with fundamental principles of procedural fairness of that State and situations involving infringements of security or sovereignty of that State;

Article 7(1)(c) provides a ground for refusal of recognition or enforcement of a judgment based upon considerations of public policy. It is identical to Article 9(c) of COCA, but the paragraph in this Convention adds a final clause that clarifies that situations involving infringements of the security or the sovereignty of the requested State are encompassed by this ground of refusal. **7.31**

The ground for refusal in Article 7(1)(c) requires that the requested court determine that recognition or enforcement would be not simply 'incompatible' but 'manifestly incompatible' with the public policy of its State. This conveys—and was intended to convey—a very high bar. Furthermore, the phrase 'manifestly incompatible' is used in COCA, and should be interpreted in parallel in this Convention. Refusal requires not simply a showing of a possible inconsistency with some narrow or technical rule, but that using State coercive power to recognize or enforce the particular judgment unavoidably will lead to a violation of a fundamental tenet of the moral, political, or social organization of the requested State, or of its ability to defend itself and to organize the way it attends to its vital interests. **7.32**

'[P]ublic policy' is unmodified; it can include any aspect of public policy, whether classified as procedural, substantive, or something else. There is a tinge of absurdity to the proposition that a court, knowing that recognition or enforcement of a foreign judgment would be manifestly incompatible with the public policy of the sovereign which created that court, could refuse to give effect to a judgment if the offended policy was procedural but not substantive. The Convention does not require that public policy be found in any particular form, such as a constitutional provision, statute, regulation, or other law. Within these constraints, the requested court will apply its own law to this ground of refusal. **7.33**

It must be stressed that this ground of refusal requires a set of concrete determinations in the particular case. Article 7(1)(c) refusal of recognition or enforcement occurs when the requested court is asked to give effect to a specific act of a foreign public body (here, a court). The requested court is in the position to examine and compare the definite features of a foreign judgment already rendered with the dictates of the public policy of the State in which recognition or enforcement is sought. Incompatibility between giving recognition or enforcement to an actual judgment and the imperatives of public policy can be known, not projected or merely predicted. **7.34**

The operation of the public policy ground of refusal is further constrained by the existence of more specific provisions in the Convention that might implicate matters viewed in some States as public policy, such as service requirements addressed in Article 7(1)(a) and damages in Article 10. The public policy exception should not be used to expand any grounds of refusal or other constraints on recognition or enforcement contained in more specialized provisions of the Convention. **7.35**

The general ground for refusal of recognition or enforcement contained in the first clause of Article 7(1)(c) is further elaborated in the clause immediately following. The first part of the elaborating clause clarifies and makes explicit that public policy includes situations where the specific proceedings leading to the judgment were incompatible with fundamental principles of procedural fairness of the requested State. This part of the clause refers to 'situations' where 'specific proceedings leading to the judgment' were incompatible **7.36** with fundamental principles of procedural fairness of the requested State. In accord with the general tenor of Article 7, it focuses the requested court on the examination of specific situations and what happened in specific proceedings leading to the judgment. These words were chosen with care. Examination may be undertaken in the requested court of something identified with specificity that may have occurred in the particular case leading to the particular judgment for which recognition or enforcement is sought. Article 7(1)(c) is not an invitation to a broad scale attack on the nature, character, or alleged conduct of the foreign judicial or legal system as a whole.

7.37 The language of Article 7(1)(c) establishes proceedings that are 'incompatible with fundamental principles of procedural fairness' as a sub-class of the realm of conditions that can render a judgment 'manifestly incompatible with the public policy of the requested State'. This language was carefully crafted. The phrase 'fundamental principles of procedural fairness' is intended to capture an aspect (albeit not an identical one) of many legal systems, identified as constitutional due process, or natural justice, or a right to a fair trial.[6] This realm implicates basic values of the society involved. A court addressed should not be expected to exercise the power of the State that created it to give effect to a judgment resulting from a specific proceeding that was incompatible with bedrock principles of procedural justice operating in the requested court's legal system.

7.38 The second elaborating clause in Article 7(1)(c) contains additional language that runs parallel to the procedural fairness clause that precedes it, to clarify and make explicit that incompatibility with public policy may include situations involving infringements of 'security or sovereignty' of the requested State. However, it is worded in a much broader fashion than its immediate predecessor. While both clauses arise in 'situations', the security clause does not further specify and restrict aspects of the judgment or the type of infringements that justify refusal. Furthermore, this clause makes no reference to the infringement as somehow involving an analogue to 'fundamental principles' or the like, although interpretation of the phrase should be constrained by the general approach to public policy for which this is an example, namely that it involves critical aspects of the ability of the requested State to defend itself, maintain internal order, or to attend to the fundamental tasks that it has set for itself. It is worth repeating here that any infringement of security or sovereignty must still be viewed in the context of 'manifestly incompatible with public policy', which is the foundation of the provision.

7.39 '[S]ecurity or sovereignty' is a disjunct; recognition or enforcement may be refused if either is infringed, and infringement of sovereignty need not infringe security, and vice versa. (Of course, recognition or enforcement can infringe both as well.) As with all questions of interpretation and application of the public policy exception, this is determination for the requested court applying its own law, subject to constraints found in the Convention text.

7.40 The final two clauses of Article 7(1(c) are clarifications and examples, not limitations on what may constitute public policy under this paragraph. The security clarification in Article 7(1)(c) also establishes that 'public policy' refers to both procedural public policy and substantive public policy. Even if one aspect of a judgment may fall within this ground

[6] Examples include the European Convention on Human Rights (ECHR), art 6, as well as the Due Process Clauses of the Fifth and Fourteenth Amendments of the United States Constitution.

of refusal, the remainder of the judgment may still be recognized or enforced if severable under Article 9.[7]

E. Article 7(1)(d)—Contrary to Designation of Another Court

Article 7

Refusal of recognition and enforcement

1. **Recognition or enforcement may be refused if—**

...

(d) the proceedings in the court of origin were contrary to an agreement, or a designation in a trust instrument, under which the dispute in question was to be determined in a court of a State other than the State of origin;

Article 7(1)(d) provides that recognition or enforcement may be refused if the judgment is issued by a court other than one designated to determine the dispute in an agreement or a designation in a trust instrument. Article 7(1)(d) dovetails with and buttresses the criteria of eligibility for recognition and enforcement for such clauses in Articles 5(1)(k) and (m). Effectively, Articles 5(1)(k)(i) and (m) make judgments issued by courts agreed upon or designated as eligible for recognition or enforcement under the Convention, while Article 7(1)(d) allows a requested court to refuse recognition or enforcement of a judgment from any court other than the court agreed upon or designated in these circumstances. The terms of Article 7(1)(d) should be interpreted in the same manner as in clauses it is intended to reinforce, subject to the observations that follow. For additional information, the reader generally is referred to the discussions of those provisions in Article 5(1).[8] **7.41**

While Article 5(1)(m) follows COCA to distinguish between exclusive and non-exclusive choice of court agreements in its criterion for eligibility of the resulting judgment for recognition or enforcement, Article 7(1)(d) operates regardless of the exclusivity or not of the choice of court agreement. It only requires that the agreement provide that the dispute was to be determined by a court in a State other than the State of origin. Furthermore, the operation of Article 7(1)(d) does not pivot on whether the court chosen by the parties or designated in the trust instrument was the court of a Contracting State: Article 7(1)(d) operates on the basis of any deviation from a court chosen or designated, whether that court is in a Contracting State or not. As with Articles 5(1)(k) and 5(1)(m), the requested court will apply the law of its own State, including its private international law rules, to determine the question of consent vel non to the agreement. **7.42**

Because Article 7 only applies as a general matter to judgments within the scope of the Convention and that satisfy a criterion of eligibility for recognition or enforcement under Article 5(1), this ground of refusal will only catch judgments that satisfy a criterion of eligibility separate from those in Article 5(1)(k) or (m). As with the other grounds in Article 7, **7.43**

[7] The Convention text does not resolve the question in non-unified legal systems, the subject of art 22, of whether 'public policy' as it is used in art 7(1)(c) is restricted to that of the Contracting State only, or may include the public policy of a relevant territorial sub-unit.

[8] Art 7(1)(d) has no direct parallel in COCA.

it is permissive, and does not block recognition or enforcement under national law, as provided in Article 15.

F. Article 7(1)(e)—Inconsistent Domestic Judgment

Article 7

Refusal of recognition and enforcement

1. **Recognition or enforcement may be refused if—**

...

(e) **the judgment is inconsistent with a judgment given by a court of the requested State in a dispute between the same parties; or**

7.44 Article 7(1)(e) allows the requested court to accord priority to a judgment from a court within its own State rather than recognizing or enforcing the judgment of a court in another Contracting State, if the two judgments are between the same parties and are 'inconsistent'.

7.45 Articles 7(1)(e) and (f) recognize the realities of parallel proceedings and litigation in multiple courts in a number of countries that could generate inconsistent judgments, to which Article 5(1) or Article 6 may apply. Article 7(1)(e) addresses the situation in which a judgment comes from a court in the requested State. Article 7(1)(f) addresses the situation in which a judgment comes from a court given by another Contracting State. Articles 7(1)(e) and (f) are identical to Articles 9(f) and (g) of COCA, and should be given a parallel interpretation and application.[9]

7.46 In order for a requested court to deploy this ground of refusal, there must first be a judgment from a court in the requested State. It may be a judgment from the requested court or not; the determining factor is that it come from a court in the requested State. It does not matter if judgment in the requested State was given by default.

7.47 It also does not matter for purposes of this ground of refusal in which forum proceedings were started first, or even in which forum judgment was reached first. If judgment was reached in the requested State after judgment was reached in the other court, but proceedings for recognition or enforcement were not started until after the judgment was rendered in the requested State, this ground of refusal may still block recognition or enforcement. It might be suggested that the text of Article 7(1)(e) ('given by a court of the requested State') means that the inconsistent judgment from a court in the requested State must be rendered prior to institution of the recognition or enforcement proceedings and cannot be rendered at any time during the pendency of the recognition and enforcement proceedings for the judgment from the other court. However, the parallel provision in Article 7(1)(f) specifies that the judgment be inconsistent with an 'earlier judgment' given by a court in another State. When the Convention requires a time sequence in this regard, the text provides it, and did not do so here. It should be noted that there is nothing in the Convention that would seem to allow a court in the requested State to stay or suspend proceedings for recognition or enforcement under the Convention to allow another court in the requested State to come

[9] Accordingly, our treatment leans heavily Brand and Herrup (n 2) 119–22.

to judgment in a dispute between the same parties (although the requested court might do so if permitted by its national law).

The local inconsistent judgment must be rendered in a dispute between the same parties. It need not be in precisely the same dispute, or involving the same cause or causes of action, so long as the judgment is inconsistent. Whether various parties are 'the same' will be determined by the law of the requested court. Especially in insurance and reinsurance litigation, there may be issues of substitution or subrogation.[10] The reference to 'parties' is to parties to the judgment, not necessarily to the 'defendant' as defined in Article 3(1)(a) of this Convention. It should be noted that, in this respect, Article 7(1)(e) occupies a broader field than does Article 7(1)(f) or Article 7(2), which require for their operation that the dispute be 'between the same parties on the same subject matter'. **7.48**

The Convention does not define 'inconsistent' for the purposes of Article 7(1)(e). While the term could be given an autonomous but as yet undefined meaning for this Convention, it would appear that the test of inconsistency will be found in the national law of the requested State. Possible tests that focus on the content of the two judgments at play are inconsistent relief, inconsistent holdings, inconsistent *ratio decidendi*. Taking this approach is likely to lead to some variation of application. In contrast, consistent with the general approach of this book, the critical point should be functional: the requested court is being asked to recognize or enforce a judgment from another Contracting State, and is permitted to refuse if recognition or enforcement of that judgment will yield results inconsistent with those of a domestic judgment. **7.49**

The Convention does not disturb the operation of the law of preclusion or estoppel within a State. A determination by a court in the requested State that a party lacked capacity to conclude an agreement, or that giving effect to the agreement would be incompatible with the public policy of the requested State, may well have preclusive effect under the national law of the requested State. As with all the grounds for refusal of recognition or enforcement in Article 7(1), this paragraph is discretionary rather than mandatory. **7.50**

G. Article 7(1)(f)—Inconsistent Foreign Judgment

Article 7
Refusal of recognition and enforcement

1. **Recognition or enforcement may be refused if—**

...

(f) **the judgment is inconsistent with an earlier judgment given by a court of another State between the same parties on the same subject matter, provided that the earlier judgment fulfils the conditions necessary for its recognition in the requested State.**

Article 7(1)(f) regulates the situation in which the requested court is presented with judgments from two or more foreign courts. In this situation, the requested court may refuse recognition or enforcement of a later judgment, but only if conditions are met that are more stringent than those in Article 7(1)(e). **7.51**

[10] See the discussion of art 17 in Chapter 8.

7.52 As noted in the discussion of paragraph (e) of Article 7(1) above, there is no Convention definition for the term 'inconsistent' as applied to judgments, or parts of judgment. There is no apparent change of meaning of the term from section to section in this article.

7.53 Article 7(1)(f) contains several requirements that must be met before a judgment from a foreign court may prevent recognition or enforcement of a judgment from another foreign court, when the second judgment is otherwise eligible for recognition or enforcement under the Convention. First, the judgment that can block recognition or enforcement of another must be 'earlier' than the judgment from the second court. Unlike the provision in Article 7(1)(e), application of Article 7(1)(f) involves a race to judgment. Application of this paragraph does not depend on the date of institution of proceedings in the underlying case, nor on the date of presentation of judgments for recognition or enforcement, but on their date of issue from the court of origin.

7.54 Second, the parties to the judgments must be the same. This element parallels the requirement discussed under Article 7(1)(e) above. Again, the reference is to the 'parties' to the judgment, not necessarily the 'defendant' as defined in Article 3(1)(a) of this Convention.

7.55 Third, the two judgments must be 'on' the same 'subject matter'. This is an additional and more stringent requirement than is found in Article 7(1)(e). It comes with some unresolved issues. The reference is specifically to the content of the two judgments: they must have the 'same subject matter'—and there is no Convention sense of commensurability, what constitutes a matter, or how one determines the 'subject' of this rather inchoate entity. We can say that Article 7(1)(f), as phrased, provides broader grounds for refusal than if it were phrased as 'the same cause of action' or the like. The reference is to the subject matter of the judgments, which may be a narrower field than the subject matter of the claims that gave rise to the judgments. This is, after all, a convention on recognition and enforcement of judgments, and judgments are the proper focus of the analysis. Thus, the Convention does not require that the requested court be bound by the language of the pleadings in each case in making the determination that the subject matter of the judgments are the 'same'.

7.56 A fourth general requirement for the Article 7(1)(f) ground of refusal is that the earlier judgment must fulfil the conditions necessary for its recognition in the requested State. It would make little sense if a judgment otherwise eligible for recognition or enforcement under the Convention was denied recognition or enforcement on the basis of the existence of another judgment which, itself, would not be eligible for recognition in the requested State.

H. Article 7(2)—Parallel Proceedings in the Requested State

Article 7

Refusal of recognition and enforcement

2. Recognition or enforcement may be postponed or refused if proceedings between the same parties on the same subject matter are pending before a court of the requested State, where—

(a) the court of the requested State was seized before the court of origin; and

(b) there is a close connection between the dispute and the requested State.

A refusal under this paragraph does not prevent a subsequent application for recognition or enforcement of the judgment.

Article 7(2) permits postponement or refusal of recognition or enforcement of a judgment from another Contracting State if proceedings are pending in the requested State and certain other conditions are met. Article 7(2) addresses the situation in which, during the pendency of original proceedings in the requested State, a judgment from a foreign court is presented for recognition or enforcement, as opposed to the two situations addressed in Articles 7(1)(e) and (f), which involve competing judgments rather than a judgment and a pending proceeding. The proceedings may be pending in any court ('a court') in the requested State: it need not be in the same court presented with the request for recognition or enforcement. 7.57

Article 7(2) permits postponement or refusal of recognition or enforcement of a judgment from another Contracting State only if the parties to the judgment and the parties to the pending proceeding are the 'same' and the subject matter is the 'same'. These terms have been discussed under Article 7(1)(f), and the reader is referred to that discussion. 7.58

In addition, Article 7(2) presents additional hurdles to non-recognition of the foreign judgment. First, the court of the requested State must have been 'seized' before the court of origin. The Convention provides neither definition nor sense of the term 'seized', which is a technical term of art in many legal systems. The requested court will apply its own law to make this determination, particularly as the operation of Article 7(2) depends in large part on a procedural step taken by a party in the courts of its own State. Second, there must be a 'close connection' between the dispute and the requested State. Neither the notion of 'connection' nor of 'close connection' can be given a Convention sense: this will be an issue determined by the law of the requested State and the judgment of its court. However, this language may play an important blocking function: it might prevent suits with little connection to the requested State from being filed in that State in an effort to use Article 7(2) to block recognition or enforcement of a judgment from another Contracting State. 7.59

If the criteria for refusal of recognition or enforcement in Article 7(2) are satisfied, the requested court may either postpone or refuse recognition or enforcement. Postponement will involve the mechanisms available to the requested court under its national law, if provision is made for such a step. The choice to postpone or to refuse is entirely that of the requested court, pursuant to its national law. Article 7(2) potentially does intrude on national law of preclusion with respect to timing: it creates a Convention rule that postponement or refusal of recognition or enforcement under it does not prevent a subsequent application for recognition or enforcement of the foreign judgment. However, if a judgment on the merits within the Convention does issue from the court of the requested State, Article 7(1)(e) may come into play to provide a discretionary ground for refusal at that time. 7.60

III. Article 8—Preliminary Questions

Article 8

Preliminary questions

1. **A ruling on a preliminary question shall not be recognized or enforced under this Convention if the ruling is on a matter to which this Convention does not apply or on a matter referred to in Article 6 on which a court of a State other than the State referred to in that Article ruled.**

2. **Recognition or enforcement of a judgment may be refused if, and to the extent that, the judgment was based on a ruling on a matter to which this Convention does not apply, or on a matter referred to in Article 6 on which a court of a State other than the State referred to in that Article ruled.**

7.61 Article 8 provides for the treatment of 'preliminary questions'. Article 8 consists of two paragraphs: the first regulates the treatment of 'rulings' and the second regulates treatment of judgments that fall within the scope of Article 8. The first is mandatory ('shall not be recognized or enforced'), the second is permissive (recognition or enforcement 'may be refused').[11] Each paragraph in turn consists of a disjunct: the first branch addresses matters to which the Convention does not apply, the second branch addresses matters that fall within the Article 6 treatment of rights *in rem* in immovable property.

7.62 The concept of a 'preliminary question' first appears in, and has been discussed with reference to, Article 2(2). The reader is referred to that discussion.

7.63 Article 8(1) bars recognition or enforcement under the Convention of a *ruling* on a preliminary question. In its first branch, Article 8(1) applies this bar to matters to which the Convention does not apply, notably items found in Article 1 (matters other than civil or commercial matters) and Article 2, or in the declarations in Articles 17–20.

7.64 The first branch of Article 8(1) does not bar a court from giving some effect to a ruling on a preliminary question on a matter to which the Convention does not apply. It only bars recognition or enforcement under the Convention of that ruling. Insofar as national law may allow preclusive effects or the equivalent to such a ruling in a manner that does not constitute recognition or enforcement, the first branch of Article 8(1) does not disable national law from doing so.

7.65 The second branch of Article 8(1) bars recognition or enforcement of a ruling on a preliminary question on rights *in rem* in immovable property if the ruling was made by a court of a State other than the State in which the property was situated. While it appears as an equal disjunct with the first branch, given the prohibitions in Article 6, it is an open question whether the second branch of Article 8(1) should be interpreted to allow or prevent preclusive effects short of recognition or enforcement under national law to a judgment ruling on rights *in rem* in immovable property when the judgment was issued by a court in a State other than the State in which the property was situated.

7.66 Article 8(2) regulates the recognition and enforcement of judgments, as opposed to rulings. It provides a limited ground for refusal of recognition or enforcement of a judgment in addition to the grounds specified in Article 7. However, it applies to judgments that are 'based on' rulings with certain features: the ruling was on a matter to which the Convention does not apply, or on a right *in rem* in immovable property referred to in Article 6 and issued by a court in a State other than the State in which the property is situated.

7.67 Because Article 8(2) is permissive rather than mandatory, it does not bar recognition or enforcement of judgments within its scope, nor prohibit preclusive effects that might be accorded such judgments under national law. Furthermore, the permission for refusal is given only to the extent that the judgment was 'based on' a ruling that falls within the scope

[11] Art 10 of COCA addresses similar topics, but consists of four paragraphs rather than two, and is somewhat more complicated due to the jurisdictional aspects of COCA and its partial inclusion of intellectual property, features not found in this Convention. On the other hand, COCA contains nothing similar to the overriding prohibition on recognition and enforcement found in art 6 of this Convention.

of Article 8(2). Any part of the judgment not tainted by association with the ruling on the preliminary question must be recognized and enforced in accordance with the other provisions of the Convention.

The word 'based' is used in the Convention at several points with variant referents. Here, it is used with respect to the relationship between a ruling and a judgment. In Article 2(1)(p) (anti-trust), it refers to a relationship between conduct and a judgment, while in Article 5(1)(c) (claimants), which uses the formulation 'is based', it refers to a relationship between a claim and a judgment. It is not clear that 'based' deserves the same interpretation in each of these different contexts, or that its interpretation necessarily should be drawn from the same sources of law (an autonomous Convention sense, the law of the State of origin, or the law of the requested State). The French text deploys '*porte sur*' for anti-trust (usually rendered in the English text as 'ruled on'), and a variant of '*fonder*' with respect to the relationships in Article 5(1)(c) and this article. The possibilities of interpretation range from a strict test of logical entailment with the burden of proof on the party resisting recognition or enforcement (ie the judgment will be enforced except to the extent that, as a matter of logic, there was no conceivable route to the judgment or a part thereof that did not pass through the preliminary question) to a test that requires a showing that the ruling on the preliminary question played no part in the actual process of decision-making of the court of origin. Either of these extremes would be difficult to apply in practice: the French text would seem to import something less than logical entailment.[12] This is an issue on which requested courts will have to use good judgement, and give due regard to the international character of the Convention in approaching its interpretation. 7.68

Article 8(2) also is a disjunct, with two branches similar to those in Article 8(1). In its first branch, Article 8(2) deploys this bar to matters to which the Convention does not apply, notably items found in Article 1 (matters other than civil or commercial matters) and Article 2, or in the declarations in Articles 17–20. The second branch of Article 8(2) applies the same rules to judgments based on rulings on rights in rem in immovable property issued by a court of a State other than the State in which the property is situated. 7.69

IV. Article 9—Severability

Article 9

Severability

Recognition or enforcement of a severable part of a judgment shall be granted where recognition or enforcement of that part is applied for, or only part of the judgment is capable of being recognized or enforced under this Convention.

Article 9 requires that recognition or enforcement 'shall be granted' even to a part of a judgment if severable from a tainted part. Even if another part of a judgment may be refused recognition or enforcement, the remainder must thus be recognized or enforced under the Convention unless that remainder is so entangled with the part refused as not to be able to 7.70

[12] COCA does not provide a reliable guide on this issue; it can be said without contradiction that the purpose and object of COCA was to require recognition and enforcement of judgments from courts chosen in exclusive choice of court clauses. Such a proposition is impossible to sustain with respect to this Convention, and more so with respect to art 8, which revolves around the restrictions in art 6.

stand on its own. The Convention is not restricted to operating on an all-or-nothing basis. The obligation to recognize or enforce severable parts of a judgment is mandatory (recognition or enforcement 'shall be granted'). Article 9 is identical to Article 15 of COCA, and should be interpreted in the same fashion.[13]

7.71 There is no Convention definition of 'severable part' of a judgment. Any dispute over the concept of 'severability' or its application to the judgment in hand will thus be resolved by recourse to the national law of the requested State.

7.72 The obligation to recognize or enforce exists even though the judgment holder has asked for recognition and enforcement only of a severable part of a judgment. The Convention imposes no obligation on the judgment holder to present the entire judgment for recognition or enforcement, and no adverse inference should be drawn from a failure to request recognition or enforcement of part of a judgment. Nor does the Convention impose a penalty if recognition or enforcement is sought at a given time only for a severable part of a judgment, although local rules on splitting of claims may become relevant in such a situation.

7.73 The obligation to recognize or enforce a severable part of a judgment also exists where the judgment holder has applied for recognition or enforcement of the entire judgment, and the court concludes that part of the application may or must be refused under the Convention. There is no obligation on the part of the judgment holder to make a preliminary determination as to the parts of a judgment a foreign court is likely not to recognize or enforce, and to abstain from seeking recognition or enforcement of those parts. Similarly, there is no penalty if the judgment holder seeks recognition and enforcement of the entire judgment, and the court addressed concludes that recognition or enforcement of some elements or aspects of the judgment will be refused

V. Article 10—Damages

Article 10
Damages

1. **Recognition or enforcement of a judgment may be refused if, and to the extent that, the judgment awards damages, including exemplary or punitive damages, that do not compensate a party for actual loss or harm suffered.**
2. **The court addressed shall take into account whether and to what extent the damages awarded by the court of origin serve to cover costs and expenses relating to the proceedings.**

7.74 Article 10 regulates the recognition or enforcement under the Convention of damages that are not purely compensatory. It allows, but does not require, the court addressed to refuse recognition or enforcement to portions of a judgment that are given for non-compensatory damages. It does not allow refusal to recognize damages awarded that are for compensatory purposes. Article 10(2) then provides additional guidance for courts in assessing whether certain components of a damages award may be classified as compensatory or not.

7.75 Article 10 of this Convention is identical to Article 11 in COCA. The COCA provision was one of the key—and most difficult—compromises in the formulation of that treaty.

[13] Accordingly, our discussion leans heavily on Brand and Herrup (n 2) 137–38.

Article 10 in this Convention should be treated identically, including with reference to the travaux generated in the Diplomatic Session for Article 11 of COCA.[14]

The damages provision is the result of a long debate on differences in the ways in which legal systems award damages in civil litigation. The language represents a difficult balancing of the interests of legal systems. On the one hand, a party is generally entitled to the amount determined by the court of origin under its law. On the other hand, courts do deny recognition of non-compensatory (usually punitive or multiple) damages on the basis of public policy,[15] and the Convention is not considered a tool to change that practice. At the same time, the public policy ground for denial of recognition and enforcement was considered insufficient in some States to deal with this issue. The final language of Article 10 is considered a workable compromise intended to clarify the obligation of recognition and enforcement of compensatory elements of civil judgments, allow for the refusal to recognize or enforce non-compensatory damages, and prevent the back-door review of the judgment 'on the merits'—the requested court may only consider the question of damages awarded by the court of origin. **7.76**

This compromise was considered important enough in COCA that delegations determined it critical not only to conclude the language of the article itself, but to agree on specific language to be included in the Explanatory Report on that Convention regarding Article 11.[16] The following is the language agreed upon to describe the purpose and effect of Article 11 of COCA (adjusted to conform to the article numbering adopted in the final COCA text), which carries over into this Convention: **7.77**

(a) Let us start *with a basic and never disputed principle*: judgments awarding damages are within the scope of the Convention. So a judgment given by a court designated in an exclusive choice of court agreement which, in whole or in part, awards damages to the plaintiff, will be recognized and enforced in all Contracting States under the Convention. As such judgments are not different from other decisions falling within the scope of the Convention, Article 8 applies without restriction. This means *both* the obligation to recognize and enforce *and* all the grounds for refusal.

(b) During the negotiations, it has become obvious that some delegations have problems with judgments awarding *damages that go far beyond the actual loss of the plaintiff*. Punitive or exemplary damages are an important example. Some delegations thought that the public policy exception in Article 9(e) could solve those problems, but others made it clear that this was not possible under their limited concept of public policy. Therefore it was agreed that there should be an *additional ground for*

[14] Accordingly, our treatment follows Brand and Herrup (n 2) 126–29. Evidence that the damages provisions of each treaty are to be treated identically is provided by the wording of art 10 of this Convention. Art 10(2) is the only place in this Convention in which the language of COCA, 'the court addressed' is used rather than the formulation adopted generally in this Convention, 'the requested court'. Our references generally will be to art 10 in this Convention, even though the material was generated largely as part of the formulation of art 11 of COCA, unless context requires reference to COCA.

[15] See, eg, *Entscheidungen des Bundesgerichtshofes (Zivilsachen) BGHZ* 118, 312 (1993) (IX ZR 149/91 Civil Division), English translation at 32 ILM 1320 (1993) (recognizing compensatory aspects of California judgment (including amounts for pain and suffering in excess of what a German court would have awarded) but refusing recognition of accompanying punitive damages). For a thorough discussion of the case, see Volker Behr, 'Enforcement of United States Money Judgments in Germany' (1994) 13 JL & Com 211.

[16] See Minutes No 19 of the Diplomatic Session, Commission II, Twentieth Session, Hague Conference on Private International Law, 13 and 14.

refusal for judgments on damages. This is the new Article 11. As in the case of all other grounds for refusal, this provision should be interpreted and applied in as restrictive a way as possible.

(c) Article 11 is based on the *undisputed primary function of damages*; they should compensate for the actual loss. Therefore the new Article 11(1) says that recognition and enforcement of a judgment may be refused if, and to the extent that, *the damages do not compensate a party for actual loss or harm suffered*. It should be mentioned that the English word 'actual' has a different meaning from the French 'actuel' (which is not used in the French text); so future losses are covered as well.

(d) This does not mean that the court addressed is allowed to examine whether it could have awarded the same amount of damages or not. *The threshold is much higher*. Article 11 only operates when it is *obvious* from the judgment that the award appears to go beyond the actual loss or harm suffered. In particular, this applies to punitive or exemplary damages. These types of damages are therefore explicitly mentioned. But in exceptional cases, damages which are characterized as compensatory by the court of origin could also fall under this provision.

(e) This provision also treats as compensation for actual loss or harm damages that are awarded on the basis of a party agreement (liquidated damages) or of a statute (statutory damages). With regard to such damages, the court addressed could refuse recognition and enforcement only if and to the extent that those damages are intended to punish the defendant rather than to provide for a fair estimate of an appropriate level of compensation.

(f) It would be wrong to ask whether the requested court has to apply the law of the State of origin or the law of the State addressed. Article 11 contains an autonomous concept. It is of course the *requested* court which *applies* this provision, but this application does *not* lead to a simple application of the law of the requested State concerning damages.

(g) Recognition and enforcement may only be refused *to the extent that* the judgment goes beyond the actual loss or harm suffered. For most delegations, this might already be a logical consequence of the limited purpose of this provision. However, it is useful to state this expressly. This avoids a possible 'all or nothing approach' some legal systems apply to the public policy exception.

(h) Both paragraph 1 and paragraph 2 of the old Article 15 contained very *sophisticated rules* on how much of the damages awarded by the court of origin had to be recognized and enforced *in any case*. The Working Group felt that this might be understood as giving the wrong message. Article 11 only provides for a review whether the judgment awards damages not compensating for actual loss; it does not allow any other review as to the merits of the case. Like all other grounds of refusal, it will only apply in exceptional cases. Any over-drafting with respect to those cases would have given them too much political weight.

(i) Article 11 does not *oblige* the court to refuse recognition and enforcement. This is obvious from its wording—the court *may refuse—and* it is consistent with the general approach in Article 9. So the provision in no way limits recognition and enforcement of damages under national law or other international instruments, and it allows (but does not require) recognition and enforcement under the Convention.

Once again, the Working Group felt that an express provision would have been an over-drafting giving too much weight to the issue of damages.

(j) Article 11(2) is the old Article 15(3). Under Article 11(1), it could be argued that damages intended to cover the costs of proceedings were not compensating for an actual loss. This would of course be wrong from a comparative perspective. But it is nevertheless reasonable to have an express reference to this problem within the provision. This reference does not contain a hard rule; the fact that damages are intended to cover costs and expenses is only to be taken into account.

(k) To sum up: the new Article 11 is shorter than the old Article 15, it is more in line with the general drafting of the Convention, and it addresses the real issues without adding complex and sophisticated rules which might be understood in the wrong way. Therefore the Working Group proposes that this provision be adopted.

Refusal of recognition or enforcement under Article 10(1) is limited to damages that go beyond compensation of a party for actual loss or harm suffered. This provision does not limit damages to one or the other if both actual loss and harm are present. Recognition or enforcement may be refused only when damages awarded exceed the sum of actual loss or harm suffered, and only to the extent of the excess. The disjunct 'actual loss or harm suffered' is not exclusive. Both 'actual loss' and 'harm suffered' are compensable, even if they occur in the same case. **7.78**

Recognition or enforcement of a judgment may be refused if and to the extent that, for any reason, the damages awarded go beyond compensation for actual loss or harm suffered. However, the language of Article 10 offers no clear threshold for determining how to measure what is compensatory and what is not. The COCA Working Group statement, at paragraph (f), indicates that the concepts to be applied for this purpose are not the unalloyed law of the requested State. The requested State is not to apply its own concepts of compensation without regard to what would be considered appropriate compensation in the court of origin. This caveat recognizes that different social and legal systems may find different amounts appropriate in order to compensate for the same loss, and the requested court must take that into account. **7.79**

Article 10(2) qualifies and narrows the discretion of a court to refuse recognition or enforcement of damages under Article 10(1). Even if a portion of the judgment awards damages that do not compensate for actual loss or harm suffered, Article 10(2) mandates that the court addressed *shall* take into account 'whether and to what extent the damages awarded by the court of origin serve to cover costs and expenses related to the proceedings'. Paragraph (j) of the COCA Working Group statement explicitly states that damages awarded to cover costs and expenses related to the proceeding should be viewed as compensatory under the Convention.[17] In such a case, recognition and enforcement of the judgment will proceed **7.80**

[17] An example of such a situation could arise in a case like the *Bundesgerichtshof* decision cited in n 15, where that court refused recognition and enforcement of the punitive damages portion of the California judgment, but indicated that (1) punitive damages may in some cases compensate the plaintiff for the fact that the US legal system requires each party to pay its own attorney fees, and (2) if the Bundesgerichtshof could have determined that portion of the punitive award that actually served this purpose it might have recognized and enforced the judgment to that extent.

under the Convention, and will include both the 'compensatory' component of damages *and* such additional amounts as cover costs and expenses related to the proceedings.[18]

VI. Article 11—Judicial Settlements (*transactions judiciaries*)

Article 11
Judicial settlements (transactions judiciaries)

Judicial settlements (transactions judiciaries) which a court of a Contracting State has approved, or which have been concluded in the course of proceedings before a court of a Contracting State, and which are enforceable in the same manner as a judgment in the State of origin, shall be enforced under this Convention in the same manner as a judgment.

7.81 Article 11 provides for enforcement under the Convention of 'judicial settlements'. The Convention obligation is enforcement: Article 11 does not require recognition, for reasons to be explained below. Article 11 is virtually identical to Article 12 of COCA, and should be interpreted in like fashion.[19]

7.82 Many States employing civil code systems of law have an institution, most commonly given the French label *transaction judiciaire*, and rendered for purposes of this Convention in English as a 'judicial settlement'.[20] The *transaction judiciaire*, in its fundamental features, is

(1) a contract between parties to a dispute;
(2) to resolve all or parts of the dispute;
(3) concluded before a judge (who usually must be present with the parties when they assent to the *transaction judiciaire*); and
(4) usually enforceable in the same manner as a judgment.

The parties, by means of this contract, agree to the resolution of a dispute, or part of a dispute. Regardless of the details of the system of national law, there must be a dispute. Depending on the State involved, the ability to conclude a *transaction judiciaire* may or may not require that an actual judicial proceeding has been instituted, or instituted in that State. The *transaction judiciaire* usually (but not necessarily) involves mutual concessions by the parties to avoid the institution or continuance of litigation.

[18] Art 10(2) appears to open review in the requested court of what constitutes a cost or expense 'relating to' the proceedings. It may also open review of the reasonableness of amounts asserted as costs or expenses in the proceedings before the court of origin. It is unclear from the face of the text whether such review would proceed under the rules and standards applicable in the court of origin, or those applicable in the requested court. However, since the issue regards costs and expenses relating to the proceedings resulting in a judgment from the court of origin, the rules and standards applicable in that court should apply. Issues regarding interest components of judgments may also arise.

[19] Accordingly, our discussion leans heavily on Brand and Herrup (n 2) 130–32. The difference in content in the respective articles is that art 12 of COCA hinges on a reference to choice of court agreements.

[20] The use of the French '*transactions judiciaries*' is as a further descriptive label for convenience. The usage does not mean that the Convention treatment of these instruments is restricted to the rules specific to them in French law. Where applicable, the requested court should consult the law of the State of origin.

7.83 The force and effect of the *transaction judiciaire* is, first and foremost, a consequence of the agreement of the parties rather than of the authority of the court before which the agreement is concluded. The presence of the judge at the conclusion of the *transaction judiciaire* does not, in itself, transform the agreement into a judgment of the court. The court usually does not issue any determinations, either of law or of fact. Indeed, in some systems the *transaction judiciaire* need not contain any recitation of predicate points of law or fact. It may simply state the dispute or part of the dispute that it intends to resolve, and a particular act that constitutes the resolution by way of *transaction judiciaire* (eg 'Party A shall give to Party B three peppercorns. Party B will go away'). The *transaction judiciaire* may or may not have *res judicata* effect in its State of origin, as a matter of the law of that State. However, insofar as the *transaction judiciaire* requires subsequent enforcement, usually that enforcement will be effected in the same manner as a judgment.

7.84 Although there might be *transactions judiciaires* without an enforceable content (eg the parties agree that a contract is [null and] void, or that the defendant owes nothing), in most instances there will be enforceable obligations arising from the *transaction* (eg paying the peppercorns, refraining from certain actions).

7.85 The nature of the *transaction judiciaire* means that it occupies an intermediate position between two instruments well-known in common law systems: (1) a consent judgment issued by a court, and (2) an out-of-court settlement between the parties. A consent judgment is a judgment within the meaning of Article 3(1)(b) of the Convention. It has the full authority of the court of origin—even if the judgment simply embodies terms of an agreement made by the parties (and even if, as a matter of fact, the judgment was drafted by one of the parties for the court).

7.86 A *transaction judiciaire*, on the other hand, while not a judgment under Article 3(1)(b), is more than an out-of-court settlement between the parties. A court neither participates in, nor scrutinizes a common law, out-of-court settlement between parties to a dispute. A court in a common law settlement may or may not be informed of the existence of a settlement or of the terms of a settlement, even if the settlement purports to resolve a pending case. If there is no pending case, there is no court to inform of the settlement. At least in a formal sense, the court before which a *transaction judicaire* is concluded has the opportunity to scrutinize the *transaction judiciaire*, and to decline to participate in the process. For example, if the proffered *transaction judiciaire* does not satisfy requirements of formal validity imposed by national law, or if it violates mandatory rules or principles of public policy, a court might decline to provide its imprimatur.

7.87 Article 11 requires only enforcement of a *transaction judicaire*. Matters of recognition of a *transaction judiciaire* are not governed by the Convention, but may be permitted by national law. Article 11 provides for enforcement of a *transaction judiciaire* in the same manner as a judgment if certain conditions are satisfied:

(1) The *transaction judiciaire* must be approved by a court. (The form of this approval varies from national legal system to national legal system. Some systems require a separate order (eg France), while others may simply include the *transaction* in the minutes of the proceedings (eg Germany).)
(2) The approving court must be a court of a Contracting State. While the effect of Article 11 is inherently asymmetric in some senses (common law systems do not issue *transactions judiciaires* that might be enforced, while civil code jurisdictions

normally do not provide for consent judgments), it is not non-reciprocal as to all the world. The benefit is restricted to those Contracting States that have accepted the Convention regime.

(3) The enforceability under the Convention of a *transaction judiciaire* does not depend on the actual institution of proceedings on the merits, whether before the court of origin or some other court. Enforceability follows from approval of a *transaction judiciaire* by a court in the State of origin. On the face of the text, such approval may occur even if no proceedings on the merits have been instituted.

(4) To be eligible for enforcement under the Convention, the *transaction judiciaire* must be 'enforceable in the same manner as a judgment in the State of origin'. Because the *transaction judiciaire* as an instrument is not known in common law systems, and because enforceability in the State of origin may vary from State to State, the Convention provides mechanisms by which the requested court can satisfy itself that this condition has been met.

(5) Article 12(1)(d) requires the party applying for enforcement of a *transaction judiciaire* to produce ('shall produce') a certificate of a court of the State of origin that the *transaction judiciaire* or a part of it is enforceable in the same manner as a judgment in the State of origin.

(6) Under Article 12(2), a common law court that remains in a state of perplexity is permitted to require ('may require') the party applying for enforcement to provide any other documents necessary (as judged by the requested court) to verify compliance with the conditions imposed on enforcement by Chapter II of the Convention.

7.88 As noted above, the Convention requires only enforcement of a *transaction judiciaire*, not its recognition. While probably infrequent, there are conceivable situations in which a requested court will be presented with an issue of the recognition of a *transaction judiciaire* approved by a court in another State. For example, a party may institute an action seeking sums of money in excess of what it had agreed to accept in a *transaction judiciaire*. The defendant may interpose the terms of the *transaction judiciaire*, fixing the amount to be paid, as a defence. Issues involving recognition will be resolved under the law of the State of the court addressed.

VII. Article 12—Documents To Be Produced

Article 12

Documents to be produced

1. The party seeking recognition or applying for enforcement shall produce—

(a) a complete and certified copy of the judgment;

(b) if the judgment was given by default, the original or a certified copy of a document establishing that the document which instituted the proceedings or an equivalent document was notified to the defaulting party;

(c) any documents necessary to establish that the judgment has effect or, where applicable, is enforceable in the State of origin;

(d) in the case referred to in Article 11, a certificate of a court including an officer of the court) of the State of origin stating that the judicial settlement or a part of it is enforceable in the same manner as a judgment in the State of origin.

2. If the terms of the judgment do not permit the court addressed to verify whether the conditions of this Chapter have been complied with, that court may require any necessary documents.

3. An application for recognition or enforcement may be accompanied by a document relating to the judgment, issued by a court (including an officer of the court) of the State of origin, in the form recommended and published by the Hague Conference on Private International Law.

4. If the documents referred to in this Article are not in an official language of the requested State, they shall be accompanied by a certified translation into an official language, unless the law of the requested State provides otherwise.

Article 12 sets forth the documents that must be produced to the requested court by the party seeking recognition or enforcement, permits that court to require production of other documents that may be necessary to apply the Convention, references a form that might be used to facilitate the proceeding, and addresses translation requirements. It is similar in most respects to Article 13 of COCA, and should be interpreted accordingly.[21] **7.89**

Recognition or enforcement requires the exercise of public authority by a court in the requested State in regard to a prior exercise of public authority by a court of a foreign sovereign. The requested court must have a solid basis for providing domestic effects to a foreign public act. This basis is provided by documents establishing that there was an act of a foreign public authority, and providing the content and result of that act. Article 12 requires, as a prerequisite to recognition or enforcement, production of specific documents by the party seeking recognition or applying for enforcement. It seeks to meet the need for a secure documentary foundation as a condition of recognition or enforcement without creating requirements that would sharply increase costs of recognition or enforcement. The documents listed in Article 12 as those to be produced were viewed as the minimum essential universe of documents to undergird a request for recognition or enforcement.[22] Article 12(1) mandates that certain documents be produced to the requested court ('shall produce'). It also limits the documents that national law otherwise might require as a condition of recognition or enforcement. Article 13 provides that procedure is governed by the law of the requested State—unless the Convention provides otherwise. With respect to documents to be produced, Article 12 is a provision 'otherwise' that overrides the operation of Article 13 in this regard. **7.90**

While Article 12(1) lists the documents that 'shall' be produced when seeking recognition or applying for enforcement under the Convention, Article 12(2) permits the requested court to require production of additional documents, but as a matter of Convention rule rather than national law, and solely to allow the court addressed to verify compliance of the judgment with Chapter II of the Convention. **7.91**

[21] Thus, this treatment will follow Brand and Herrup (n 2) 132–36. The substantive variation between the two articles is a sub-paragraph in art 13(1) of COCA requiring production of the choice of court agreement or evidence thereof.

[22] It is unclear from the text, however, whether the requested court is prevented from moving forward to consider recognition or enforcement, or barred from recognizing or enforcing a judgment, if a document specified in art 12(1) is not produced and the person resisting fails to demand its production. This may devolve to national law of the requested court.

7.92 While the Convention generally does not intrude on the local law of evidence (which may or may not be classified as part of local procedural law, depending on the national legal system), Article 12(1) specifies that the burden of production of the listed documents is upon the party seeking recognition or applying for enforcement.

7.93 Article 12(1)(a) requires production of a complete and certified copy of the judgment. The term 'judgment' here must be taken as defined in Article 3(1)(b) to be a 'decision on the merits ... including a decree or order'. Thus, the document required is more than simply a final order directing a party to do something or to refrain from doing something. It includes both the operative final order or decree, and any memorandum opinion (or equivalent) containing the court's discussion of the basis for its action.

7.94 Article 12(1)(b) applies in the special case of default. It places the burden of production as to notification on the party seeking recognition or applying for enforcement of the judgment when the judgment issued by default. Article 7(1)(a), which deals with notification as a ground for refusal of recognition or enforcement, is silent as to burden of production on the issue. As noted in the introductory discussion to Article 7, some legal systems may view the grounds of potential refusal contained in Article 7 as affirmative defences, with either burden of production, or burden of persuasion, or both on the party resisting recognition or enforcement. This remains a matter of national law in Article 7, whereas Article 12(1)(b) specifies the burden as a matter of Convention rule. Article 12(1)(b) is without prejudice to the ability of a person opposing recognition or enforcement to find shelter within the ground for refusal of Article 7(1)(a), whether the judgment issued by default or not.

7.95 Article 12(1)(c) requires production of documents 'necessary' to establish that the judgment has effect or is enforceable in the State of origin. The use of the phrase 'any documents' and the logical term 'necessary' in Article 12(1)(c) is somewhat awkward, and perhaps unfortunate. The provision is best read as requiring production by the party seeking recognition or applying for enforcement of a document or set of documents sufficient to establish that the judgment has effect or is enforceable in the State of origin. '[A]ny documents' should not be construed as 'each and every existing document' or 'all possible documents' and the entire phrase does not imply that there might be some specific document present and identical in every national legal system that is somehow viewed as 'necessary' either in the State of the court of origin or in the requested State to establish effect or enforceability. Production requirements should not be invoked as unwarranted obstacles to recognition or enforcement.

7.96 Article 12(1)(d) specifies production requirements for *transactions judiciaires*, which were discussed under Article 11 above.

7.97 Article 12(2) permits the requested court to require production of additional documents over and above those specified in Article 12(1) if they are necessary to allow the court addressed to verify compliance of the judgment or judicial settlement with the recognition and enforcement criteria in Chapter II of the Convention. The court may make the request if the terms of the judgment, or other documents provided, do not, in themselves, allow the court to verify whether the criteria have been satisfied.

7.98 In an effort to expedite proceedings under the Convention, a form was developed by the Hague Conference on Private International Law to provide useful information to the requested court about the judgment (or judicial settlement) and its contents. The form is to emanate from the court of origin. Use of the form is not obligatory. (Art 12(3) uses 'may be accompanied by'.) A party may seek recognition or apply for enforcement without it.

If the standard form is used, its submission does not dispense with other obligations to produce documents under Article 12(1). The form is informational. It has neither privileged nor preclusive effect under the Convention. The information provided is not conclusive by being contained in the form. The requested court must make its own determination regarding application of the Convention criteria to the judgment, and may make such inquiries necessary to that determination, including weighing the value and utility of information presented to it from whatever source not barred to it by the Convention itself. Article 12(3) does not state that the form may only be issued by the court of origin to the person seeking recognition or enforcement in the court addressed. Nor does it state that the only mechanism by which the form may be presented to the requested court is in the application for recognition or enforcement. Thus, nothing in Article 12(3) should prevent a party opposing recognition or enforcement from requesting and receiving the form from the court of origin, and presenting it to the requested court as evidence to refute statements made in an application for recognition or enforcement. **7.99**

Article 12(4) creates a translation requirement. It provides that, where the documents required under paragraphs (1)–(3) of Article 12 are not in an official language of the requested State, they 'shall be accompanied by a certified translation into an official language, unless the law of the requested State provides otherwise'. While some requirement of this sort is necessary, there is a practical concern that translation may add substantially to the expense of recognition or enforcement in international cases. Article 12(4) applies only if documents referred to in Article 12(1)–(3) are not in an official language of the requested State. In the event that the State of the requested court has no official language, the phrase 'official language' is best read as including any language in which submissions may be made to, and will be considered by, the requested court.[23] **7.100**

If Article 12(4) applies, the documents 'shall be accompanied' by a 'certified translation' into an official language. The language employed is phrased in mandatory terms, even if, as will be discussed below, national procedural law would not require either a translation or a certified translation. The 'certified translation' must be of 'the documents referred to in this Article' and not simply of the critical parts of those documents. **7.101**

The Convention does not determine when a translation is 'certified' or specify modes of certification. It is not clear in the Convention text whether the applicable criteria are to come from the standards of the court of origin or those of the requested court. There is a distinct possibility that applications for recognition or enforcement may be refused—and refused multiple times—because of a perceived failure to comply with all the requirements of 'certification' of translation of documents. As with all potential procedural barriers to the efficient conduct of proceedings to resolve issues of recognition and enforcement of judgments under the Convention, this requirement should be administered by the court addressed in a common-sense fashion to reduce transaction costs. **7.102**

Even if Article 12(4) applies, requirements of 'certified translation' of all the documents into an official language of the requested State should give way if the law of the requested State provides otherwise, as permitted by Article 13. While this qualification may ameliorate **7.103**

[23] If the Hague Conference prepares a country profile for this Convention, it could invite Contracting States to identify any official language(s).

some of the potentially harsh effects of Article 12(4), it appears to operate only if there is a countervailing provision in the law of the requested State. If there is no such countervailing provision in national law, or a qualification included in the relevant State's instrument of ratification, acceptance, approval, or accession, the Convention rule (phrased in mandatory terms) will apply. It is not stated in the text whether the reference to the 'law of the requested State' includes only (a) statute law, (b) statute law and case law in place prior to the application for recognition or enforcement, or (c) might include a determination by the court addressed in the particular case to dispense with the full rigors of the requirements under the Convention.[24]

VIII. Article 13—Procedure

Article 13
Procedure

1. **The procedure for recognition, declaration of enforceability or registration for enforcement, and the enforcement of the judgment, are governed by the law of the requested State unless this Convention provides otherwise. The court of the requested State shall act expeditiously.**
2. **The court of the requested State shall not refuse the recognition or enforcement of a judgment under this Convention on the ground that recognition or enforcement should be sought in another State.**

7.104 Article 13 subjects procedures connected with recognition and enforcement in national courts to national procedural law, except in the instances in which the Convention prescribes a different rule of procedure. Having stated that procedure is governed by the law of the requested State in Article 13(1), it then invades the law of the requested State in certain situations in which *forum non conveniens* or related doctrines might otherwise be available. Article 13(1) is identical to Article 14 of COCA, and should be interpreted as such.[25] Article 13(2) has no COCA analogue.

7.105 Article 13 applies to all types of proceedings whose object is recognition or enforcement. It applies when recognition or enforcement may be effected only by means of mandatory procedure in a court. It also applies in States where there is no special procedure, or only summary procedures, to obtain recognition.[26] It applies in States where there are expedited procedures to obtain declarations of enforceability, or where there is a registration system that allows expedited enforcement.

7.106 In some respects, the first sentence of Article 13 constitutes a rule of national procedural treatment for recognition and enforcement of foreign judgments under the Convention.

[24] With respect to formalities, it should be noted that this Convention contains no analogue to art 18 of COCA (no legalization), 'All documents forwarded or delivered under this Convention shall be exempt from legalization or any analogous formality, including an Apostille'. In this Convention, the resolution of this issue will be according to the laws of the requested State, including any obligations from other international instruments that might apply. See also art 23, Relationship with Other International Instruments.

[25] Accordingly, our treatment of art 13(1) leans heavily on Brand and Herrup (n 2) 136–37.

[26] See, eg, Reform of the Italian System of Private International Law, Law No 218, art 64, 31 May 1995, Gazz Uff No 128, Supp Ord 7.68, 3 June 1995, translated in 35 ILM 760, 779–80 (1996).

This rule of national procedural treatment, however, gives way whenever the Convention specifies a different rule as a matter of international obligation.[27]

The reference to procedure in Article 13(1) should be read as procedure specific to one of the four court processes listed in the paragraph, and only those processes, namely, recognition, declaration of enforceability, registration for enforcement, and enforcement of the judgment. However, each term should be read to encompass its negative: for example, 'recognition' can include an application for non-recognition of the foreign judgment, a declaration of enforceability can include a declaration of non-enforceability, and so on. **7.107**

'Procedure' here refers to the mechanics of getting one or another of these four things done in connection with a court or legal process. It does not apply to anything whatsoever that might be labelled as 'procedural' in a given national legal system. While the legal mechanics of the requested State are deployed to implement recognition or enforcement (or not), the requested court should be wary lest rules of mechanics be used to stymie a result otherwise dictated by the Convention. For example, a judgment must be recognized and enforced by the court addressed if it meets the criteria of Article 5(1), unless there is a ground for refusal specified in the Convention. Recognition or enforcement must be denied if a judgment fails to meet the criterion set in Article 6. These results should occur regardless of a local procedural law which, if applied, might yield a different result in a given case.[28] **7.108**

The second sentence of Article 13(1) requires that the court 'shall act expeditiously'. While this may appear to be purely hortatory, and while there is no explicit sanction for failure by the requested court to comply, it directs the requested court to use the most rapid procedure available under its national law for determining to recognize or enforce a foreign judgment. If the rule in the first sentence of Article 13(1) requires national procedural treatment, the rule in the second sentence requires 'most favoured' national procedural treatment. **7.109**

Article 13(2) prevents a court in a requested State from refusing recognition or enforcement under the Convention on the ground that these should be sought in another State. It purports to disable certain doctrines of declination of jurisdiction, such as *forum non conveniens*, in favour of a State foreign to the requested State. Article 13(2) is likely to have little real-world impact. **7.110**

Article 13(2) does not require a requested court to make a decision on the merits of an application for recognition or enforcement if it would have no jurisdiction over the parties under its national law. For example, this would be the case if none of the parties is resident or has significant connections with the forum, or there are no assets within that State. It does not require a requested court to make a decision on the merits if the matter is not justiciable (eg it might require ordering performance in another jurisdiction), or the judgment **7.111**

[27] It may also give way to legal obligations from other sources, such as rules against discrimination or unequal treatment of domestic and foreign persons, etc.

[28] Limitations and prescription periods may be classified as 'substantive' or 'procedural' in various legal systems—and the meanings of the terms 'substantive' and 'procedural' are, themselves, various. It is our view that the reference to the procedure with respect to specific legal processes in art 13(1) does not reach limitation or prescription periods, and certainly not when they are of a general nature. This leaves the question of the situation in which the limitations period for recognition or enforcement in the law of the requested State is shorter than the period in which the judgment has effect in the State of origin or is enforceable in that State under art 4(3). This may be a particular issue in States with non-unified legal systems. Given that this Convention is a lock and key model that opens the door to the legal system of the requested State and assimilates the foreign judgment into that legal system, the Convention does not require that a foreign judgment be treated better than a domestic judgment.

would constitute little more than an advisory opinion. It does not override venue rules; if the application belongs in a different court in the requested State, the requested court is not, nevertheless, required to decide the application on the merits. Article 13(2) does not prevent use of the doctrine of *forum non conveniens* among courts within a Contracting State; it only prevents declination on the grounds that recognition or enforcement should be sought in another Contracting State (or another State that is not a Contracting State).

7.112 A requested court may still deny recognition or enforcement on grounds of public policy in Article 7(1)(c) if the judgment has so little connection with the forum that the imposition of litigation on it constitutes an unjustifiable abuse and burden on the courts and taxpayers of the requested State. The presence of Article 13(2) is yet another testimonial to the inclusion of provisions based upon dogmatic preconceptions rather than a proper evaluation of real-world significance.[29]

IX. Article 14—Costs of Proceedings

Article 14
Costs of proceedings

1. **No security, bond or deposit, however described, shall be required from a party who in one Contracting State applies for enforcement of a judgment given by a court of another Contracting State on the sole ground that such party is a foreign national or is not domiciled or resident in the State in which enforcement is sought.**
2. **An order for payment of costs or expenses of proceedings, made in a Contracting State against any person exempt from requirements as to security, bond, or deposit by virtue of paragraph 1 or of the law of the State where proceedings have been instituted, shall, on the application of the person entitled to the benefit of the order, be rendered enforceable in any other Contracting State.**
3. **A State may declare that it shall not apply paragraph 1 or designate by a declaration which of its courts shall not apply paragraph 1.**

7.113 Article 14 regulates certain aspects of the costs of proceedings under the Convention. It consists of three paragraphs: Article 14(1) protects foreign nationals, residents, or domiciliaries who have applied for enforcement of a judgment from imposition of security, bond, or deposit requirements solely on the basis of their being foreign. Article 14(2) makes enforceable in any Contracting State an order for payment of costs or expenses against a person exempt from the requirements listed in paragraph 1. Article 14(3) provides for a declaration that a State will not apply paragraph 1, or designate by declaration specific courts that will not apply it.[30] The effect of Article 14(1) is that a local rule on security cannot operate to put a foreigner seeking enforcement under the Convention in a worse position

[29] In a small number of situations, art 13(2) provides the one potential exception in which the Convention may invade and annul a rule of direct jurisdiction of the requested State. In States in which *forum conveniens* and *forum non conveniens* are elements of the direct jurisdiction inquiry, *forum non conveniens* is disabled and, accordingly, the Convention affects direct jurisdiction. This invasion of direct jurisdiction rules will not be the case in States such as the United States, in which the application of *forum non conveniens* assumes the existence of jurisdiction, and the inquiry is whether an existing jurisdiction may be declined.

[30] COCA has no correlate to art 14.

than a domestic litigant solely on the basis of national affiliations, while Article 14(2) then deprives the foreigner of potential advantages that might flow from that status.

Article 14(1) bars requiring security, bond, or deposit in certain circumstances for applications for enforcement under the Convention. The paragraph sweeps broadly: it prohibits 'security, bond or deposit, however described'. Regardless of the label, certain costs should not be imposed on litigants who have recourse to the Convention. Article 14(1) applies to 'a party' without restriction to whether the party is a natural or non-natural person, so long as that party is not a national or domiciled or 'resident' in the requested State.[31] The critical focus is that the application be under the Convention; there is no requirement that the party sheltered by this paragraph be a national, or domiciled, or resident in a Contracting State. There are two limitations to the 'no security' rule: first, it only attaches to applications for enforcement of a judgment and does not mention applications for recognition. Second, it attaches only if the 'sole ground' for requiring security is that the applicant is an alien. Article 14(1) does not bar imposition of security on a foreigner if there are independent grounds for doing so with respect to all persons under local law. **7.114**

Article 14(2) adjusts for a potential imbalance in favour of foreign parties and unfairness to persons who successfully resist an application for enforcement under the Convention. It provides that an order issued in a Contracting State to the benefit of a successful judgment debtor for payment of their costs or expenses of the proceedings will be enforceable in other Contracting States. This provision fills a gap resulting from the definition of 'judgment' in Article 3(1)(b). The order in Article 14(2), which is geared to costs of successfully resisting an application for enforcement of a judgment on the merits, may not be considered a 'decision on the merits' under the Convention definition. Article 14(2) effectively brings such orders within the scope of the Convention and creates a criterion for their enforceability outside of Article 5. Because they are treated as judgments under the Convention, the grounds for refusal in Article 7 may operate as to them. However, the operation of Article 14(2) is subject to and limited by a disjunct. It only operates if the person against whom the order for costs or expenses was made was exempt from the requirements of security by virtue of Article 14(1) (ie the security was imposed solely by virtue of foreign status), or if the person against whom the order issued was exempt from security requirements under some other provision of law of the requested State. In other words, Article 14(2) provides some protection for costs and expenses to a person who successfully resists an application for enforcement in situations in which the applicant may have few or no assets in the requested State. Finally, Article 14(2) requires that the order for costs in this situation be made on the application of the person entitled to the benefit of the order. This encompasses any person who is entitled to the benefit of the order, not simply a party to the original application for enforcement of the judgment. **7.115**

Article 14(3) permits a State to declare that it shall not apply Article 14(1), either in the courts of the State generally or in specific courts, designated in the declaration. The declaration only disables the 'no security' rule in Article 14(1). It does not apply to the 'cost order' rule in Article 14(2). It effectively permits a declaring State, or courts it specifically designates, to require security for proceedings brought under the Convention solely on the basis **7.116**

[31] Art 14(1) refers to 'resident' rather than to 'habitual resident'. 'Resident' would appear to be a broader term than 'habitual resident' and thus gives protections to, eg, transitory natural persons or entities or non-natural persons that do not qualify as 'habitual residents' of a State under art 3(2).

of the foreign affiliation of the party bringing the proceeding. Article 14(3) does not address the effect of the declaration on other Contracting States.

X. Article 15—Recognition and Enforcement under National Law

Article 15

Recognition and enforcement under national law

Subject to Article 6, this Convention does not prevent the recognition or enforcement of judgments under national law.

7.117 Article 15 explicitly preserves the ability of Contracting States to recognize or enforce judgments under their national law. However, Article 15 explicitly is subject to Article 6, which prevents recognition and enforcement under national law of a judgment that ruled on rights *in rem* in immovable property unless the property is situated in the State of origin. Accordingly, it reinforces the prohibition on recognition and enforcement of judgments in Article 6 as the paramount obligation of the Convention.[32] The Convention sets a floor for recognition and enforcement of judgments required under it. For recognition and enforcement, Contracting States cannot sink below that floor except to the extent that the Article 7 grounds for refusal come into play. However, Article 15 allows recognition and enforcement under national law that may exceed that floor. At the same time, Article 6 in its sphere of operation sets both a floor and a ceiling: a judgment ruling on a right *in rem* of immovable property either must be recognized or enforced pursuant to Article 6, or recognition or enforcement must be denied pursuant to that article.

[32] Art 15 is introduced by the clause 'Subject to Article 6 . . . '. This placement punctuates the importance of art 6 in the Convention scheme. Art 8(1) of COCA was re-written in part due to objections to its similar structure ('Without prejudice to such review as is necessary for the application of the provisions of this Chapter') on the grounds, correct or not, that it placed too much emphasis on the qualification to the general rule. Here, the preservation of art 6 stands on an equal footing with the general rule regarding national law.

8
General Clauses (Articles 16–23)

I. Introduction

The 'General Clauses' chapter of the Convention contains eight articles that have potential for major impact on the outcome of specific requests for recognition or enforcement. These include transitional rules determining when Convention provisions will apply to recognition and enforcement of judgments based on the date when the Convention has effect between the State of origin and the requested State (art 16). In Articles 17–19, the Convention authorizes certain declarations by States that will tailor the application of specific Convention rules under specific circumstances. Article 20 provides a statement regarding the desire to promote uniformity in the interpretation and application of the Convention, and Article 21 authorizes review of the operation of the Convention. Article 22 specifies rules for application of the Convention in 'non-unified legal systems', and Article 23 addresses the issue of the relationship between the Convention and other international instruments. **8.01**

II. Article 16—Transitional Provision

Article 16
Transitional provision

This Convention shall apply to the recognition and enforcement of judgments if, at the time the proceedings were instituted in the State of origin, the Convention had effect between that State and the requested State

8.02 Article 16 establishes the temporal rule concerning the application of the Convention to judgments presented under it. It sets a point in time from which the Convention shall apply to a judgment—the time the proceedings were instituted in the State of origin—and then makes application of the Convention pivot on whether the Convention 'had effect' at that point in time between the State of origin and the requested State. Thus, at the time of institution of proceedings in the State of origin, the parties should be able to ascertain whether a resulting judgment will satisfy this temporal requirement with respect to the State of origin, and, if so, with respect to other identified States.

8.03 The Convention does not define either what is a 'proceeding[]' under it or when such a proceeding is 'instituted'.[1] In the vein of our pragmatic approach to definitions, 'proceedings' should be treated as any court process that might issue a judgment within the meaning of that term in the Convention. 'Institut[ion]' of proceedings is a reference to a specific step (institution) in a legal proceeding taken in the State of origin, and the term should be interpreted with reference to the law of the State of origin. Once the point in time is identified at which the proceedings were instituted in the State of origin, the requested court must determine whether the Convention had effect between that State and the requested State. The term 'effect' is drawn from Article 29 of this Convention (Establishment of relations pursuant to the Convention), and its meaning should be drawn operationally from the provisions of that article and from the international law of treaties. Functionally, this criterion requires that the Convention has entered into force for both the State of origin and the requested State pursuant to Article 28, and that neither State has notified the depositary in a timely fashion that the ratification, acceptance, approval, or accession by the other State shall not have the effect of establishing Convention relations between the two States (art 29).

III. Articles 17–19—Declarations

A. General Concerns

8.04 Our discussion of the substantive scope provisions of the Convention in Chapter 5 of this book indicates that the Convention will often have a wide scope of application. During the negotiations, this expansive scope resulted in concern on the part of some delegations that the Convention might be over-inclusive in some areas. Others would have preferred to see the Convention encompass an even broader field of application. Taking these concerns together, the Convention could be viewed as simultaneously over-inclusive and under-inclusive.

8.05 Three concerns regarding over-inclusiveness are addressed in the declarations provisions found in Articles 17–19. The first concern was that a State might find itself obligated to recognize or enforce a judgment from a foreign court, even though from the vantage point of the requested State the matter is wholly domestic to it (art 17). A second concern stems from the inescapable fact that different States have different values and policies, and litigation arrangements, which reflect and implement those differences. A matter that might be caught in the Convention net might also be of such importance to a particular State as to impede ultimate acceptance of the Convention in that State (art 18). Third, and to some extent related to the second point, was the concern of some States that the scope provisions in,

[1] For the same, see art 5(1)(k) (trusts) which also pivots on the concept of the time proceedings were instituted.

inter alia, Articles 2(1)(q), 2(4), and 2(5) were not sufficiently protective of the interests of sovereign States in litigation (art 19).

The declaration system introduces flexibility designed to make the Convention more palatable to those concerned about over-inclusiveness, and more desirable to those concerned about under-inclusiveness. In doing so, there is a danger of creating an extensive and confusing series of available derogations from the rules of the Convention. Broad derogations from the Convention in terms of the content of the declarations could diminish the effectiveness of the Convention in reaching its goals, while the prospect of numerous States carving out specific niches could diminish the intelligibility of the Convention, as parties would have to examine *ex ante* and *ex post* precisely what each State connected to a transaction (either as a State of origin or a requested State) might have undertaken as Convention obligations.[2] **8.06**

The Convention also addresses declarations in the context of Hague Conference review under Article 21, to considerations of application in States with non-unified legal systems in Article 22, and to the requirements of Articles 30 and 32. The reader should consult our discussions with respect to those articles. **8.07**

B. Article 17—Declarations Limiting Recognition and Enforcement

Article 17

Declarations limiting recognition and enforcement

A State may declare that its courts may refuse to recognise or enforce a judgment given by a court of another Contracting State if the parties were resident in the requested State, and the relationship of the parties and all other elements relevant to the dispute, other than the location of the court of origin, were connected only with the requested State.

Article 17 provides an optional solution to a potential consequence of Article 1(2) (the Convention applies to judgments given by a court of another Contracting State) in conjunction with Article 4(1) (providing the principal obligation to recognize and enforce a judgment), namely that a requested court might find itself obligated under the Convention to recognize and enforce a judgment from a foreign court when the requested court views the original case as wholly domestic.[3] **8.08**

Article 17 essentially allows a State to permit its courts to refuse recognition or enforcement of a judgment under the Convention if the underlying case was completely domestic to the requested State. Recognition or enforcement may not be refused if the case is wholly domestic to some State other than the requested State. Article 17 does not authorize a free-wheeling and open-ended review of the scope or jurisdictional determinations of the court of origin, but only allows a requested court to refuse recognition and enforcement in the event that the case is wholly domestic to the requested State. Recognition or enforcement may be refused only if a court of the requested State determines that there is no connection to a State other than the requested State. **8.09**

[2] Provision for a declaration is also found in art 14(3) (costs of proceedings).

[3] Art 17 is virtually identical to the Convention on Choice of Court Agreements, done at The Hague 30 June 2005 (COCA), art 20, although the latter refers to the location of the chosen court rather than the court of origin. Accordingly, this section leans heavily on Ronald A Brand and Paul M Herrup, *The 2005 Hague Convention on Choice of Court Agreements* (CUP 2008) 149–50.

8.10 Article 17 is phrased in the past tense. The examination contemplated by Article 17 is of the residence of the parties and the relationship of the parties and all other elements of the case at some point in time. However, Article 17 does not specify whether that point in time is at the initiation of proceedings, at the point of judgment, or during the entire interval occupied by the proceedings. The preferable reading is that the operative point in time is that of institution of the proceedings in the court of origin: otherwise, the application of the Convention might pivot on moves, deliberate or by chance, during the course of the proceedings. What is clear is that the operation of the Convention cannot be frustrated by a move in residence after conclusion of the proceedings in the court of origin.

8.11 Article 17 provides for a declaration that courts 'may refuse to recognize or enforce a judgment' in certain conditions. While somewhat opaque, the use of the term 'may' provides some flexibility for Contracting States in crafting their declarations. Article 17 does not use the mandatory term 'shall' in this context. It is conceivable that a declaration under Article 17, or implementing legislation (provided it is consistent with the declaration), could provide discretion in national courts or guidance to them concerning refusal to recognize or enforce a relevant judgment under Article 17. Doing so would limit the derogation from the basic Article 4(1) obligation of recognition and enforcement, but would also introduce uncertainty regarding the fate of some judgments. Equally available is a mandate that requires the refusal to recognize or enforce judgments that meet the criteria of the declaration.

8.12 It is not clear that an Article 17 declaration will apply to all courts within the declaring State, or, whether for States with multiple court systems it might apply only to courts in some of those systems. This is an issue to which Article 22 (non-unified legal systems) may also apply.

8.13 The meaning of the term 'connected only with' in Article 17 will be determined by the requested court under forum law.

8.14 As with declarations under Articles 18 and 19, the Convention addresses Article 17 declarations in the context of Hague Conference review under Article 21, to considerations of application in States with non-unified legal systems in Article 22, and to the requirements of Articles 30 and 32. The reader should consult our discussions with respect to those articles.

8.15 Unlike the language of Articles 18 and 19, nothing in Article 17 provides for reciprocal effect of the declaration that limits recognition and enforcement. Thus, an Article 17 declaration does not affect the Convention obligations of other Contracting States—including their obligation to recognize and enforce the judgment affected by the Article 17 declaration.

C. Article 18—Declarations with Respect to Specific Matters

Article 18

Declarations with respect to specific matters

1. **Where a State has a strong interest in not applying this Convention to a specific matter, that State may declare that it will not apply the Convention to that matter. The State making such a declaration shall ensure that the declaration is no broader than necessary and that the specific matter excluded is clearly and precisely defined.**

2. **With regard to that matter, the Convention shall not apply—**
   (a) **in the Contracting State that made the declaration;**
   (b) **in other Contracting States, where recognition or enforcement of a judgment given by a court of a Contracting State that made the declaration is sought.**

Article 18 allows a State by declaration to extend the list of exclusions from scope in Article 2. An article performing the function of Article 18 was essential to maintaining the potentially broad appeal of the Convention, by allowing a State to insulate specific matters of great policy concern from the sweep of the Convention. However, Article 18 does open the possibility of numerous parochial declarations that would both blunt the force of the Convention and make it extremely confusing to use. Consequently, while permitting additional exceptions to scope, Article 18 does include safeguards designed to limit its own operation.[4] The effectiveness of those safeguards will have to be assessed in its application. For example, as has been extensively discussed with respect to scope, the term 'matter' as used in the Convention has little coherence and provides little by way of practical limitation on what might be included in an Article 18 declaration. **8.16**

A precondition of an Article 18 declaration is that the State 'has a strong interest' in not applying the Convention to that matter. The Convention makes no effort to provide a gauge of intensity of interest that justifies recourse to Article 18. However, an Article 18 declaration represents a unilateral derogation from the Convention regime and should not be made lightly. **8.17**

The strong interest which may justify an Article 18 declaration must be with respect to a 'specific matter'. Unlike the phraseology in Articles 1 and 2, whose matters are unadorned, the use of 'specific' in Article 18 implies that the substance of exclusions under an Article 18(1) declaration properly is more narrowly focused than is the substance of exclusions under the Article 1 and 2 provisions. **8.18**

As with the other declarations available under the Convention, a declaration under Article 18 is a voluntary modification of the Convention. A State 'may' declare that its courts will not apply the Convention to a specific subject matter. Unlike Article 17 however, which appears to provide some discretion to the declaring State in terms of the locus, force, and effect of a declaration on its courts ('State may declare that its courts may refuse'), the focus of Article 18 is on the declaring State, and results in a general rule of non-application of the Convention within that State ('State may declare that it will not apply this Convention'). In effect, the 'will not apply' language in Article 18(1) (and the 'shall not apply' language in Article 19(1)) create smaller rules of scope expressed in the same language as Article 2(1), unlike the declaration in Article 17, which goes to recognition and enforcement of judgments that are within scope. **8.19**

Article 18(1) creates two obligations of declaring States as a matter of Convention rule. The State 'shall ensure' both 'that the declaration is no broader than necessary', and 'that the specific matter excluded is clearly and precisely defined'. **8.20**

While the Convention contains no criteria for determining what makes a declaration 'necessary', the phrase 'no broader than necessary', when combined with the restriction of the declaration to 'a specific matter' which must be 'clearly and precisely defined', implies that a State making a declaration must 'ensure' that no more may be excluded in an Article **8.21**

[4] Art 18 is similar to art 21 of COCA. Accordingly, this discussion leans heavily on Brand and Herrup (n 3) 150–53.

18 declaration than what is absolutely required to protect the 'strong interest' of the State. The State has the obligation to adopt a minimalist approach to declarations under Article 18—the declaration should exclude only what will significantly and demonstrably damage the strong State interest that is a precondition of the declaration, and no more.

8.22 The declaring State must also ensure that the specific matter excluded is 'clearly and precisely defined'. Again, the Convention contains no criteria for determining what constitutes a clear and precise definition. At the least, however, this requirement, when combined with the requirement that the exclusion be of a specific matter, should lead to an interpretive rule that something can come within the exclusion under Article 18 only if it is clearly and precisely stated in the declaration. Because the burden of providing a clear and precisely drafted exclusion is on the declaring State, any doubt over the field of application of an Article 18 declaration should be resolved in favour of a matter remaining included within the scope of the Convention for the declaring Contracting State. The Convention does not prevent a Contracting State from elaborating on its declaration where other Contracting States question whether it is clearly and precisely defined.

8.23 In an effort to provide incentives for self-discipline in declarations under Article 18(1), Article 18(2) provides for reciprocity in the application of the declaration. When a declaring State takes the specific matter out of the Convention for itself under Article 18(1), this paragraph provides that the same matter is also taken out of the Convention in every other Contracting State in which a judgment from a court of the declaring State is presented for recognition or enforcement. A Contracting State cannot deprive its treaty partners of the benefits of the Convention through an Article 18 declaration, then claim those benefits for itself. However, nothing in the Convention prevents a requested court under Article 15 from using its national law to recognize or enforce a judgment from a declaring State that is within the scope of a declaration.

8.24 Article 18(2) implies that a court of another Contracting State may determine for itself the proper field of application of the Article 18 declaration of a foreign State.

8.25 As a practical matter, the reciprocity provision in Article 18(2) may not have much bite. Article 18 declarations are most likely to occur when the declaring State does not wish to undertake a treaty obligation to recognize and enforce foreign judgments on a given matter, especially against a local party haled into a foreign court.

8.26 As with declarations under Articles 17 and 19, the Convention addresses Article 18 declarations in the context of Hague Conference review under Article 21, in the context of considerations of application in States with non-unified legal systems in Article 22, and in the context of the requirements of Articles 30 and 32. The reader should consult our discussions with respect to those articles.

D. Article 19—Declarations with Respect to Judgments Pertaining to a State

Article 19

Declarations with respect to judgments pertaining to a State

1. **A State may declare that it shall not apply this Convention to judgments arising from proceedings to which any of the following is a party—**
   (a) that State, or a natural person acting for that State; or

(b) a government agency of that State, or a natural person acting for such a government agency.

The State making such a declaration shall ensure that the declaration is no broader than necessary and that the exclusion from scope is clearly and precisely defined. The declaration shall not distinguish between judgments where the State, a government agency of that State or a natural person acting for either of them is a defendant or claimant in the proceedings before the court of origin.

2. Recognition or enforcement of a judgment given by a court of a State that made a declaration pursuant to paragraph 1 may be refused if the judgment arose from proceedings to which either the State that made the declaration or the requested State, one of their government agencies or a natural person acting for either of them is a party, to the same extent as specified in the declaration.

Article 19 makes available to a Contracting State a declaration that it shall not apply the Convention to judgments arising from proceedings with specified parties. Unlike Article 18, for which the declaration hinges on the content of the judgment, Article 19 hinges its operation on the identity of one party to a proceeding—the State making the declaration or a person or agency with a specified connection to that State. **8.27**

As with Article 18, and unlike Article 17, the declaration in Article 19 goes to the scope of application of the Convention rather than to the 'international' character of the case. However, the declaration in Article 19 differs from the declaration in Article 18 because it focuses on the identity of a party to a judgment rather than to the content ('a specific matter') of the judgment as in Article 18.[5] A judgment subject to an Article 19 declaration must arise from 'proceedings' to which the State making the declaration or a natural person acting for that State, or a government agency of that State, or a natural person acting for such a government agency, is a party. The reference is to the State making the declaration: declarations from other States do not count for Article 19 purposes (except in the context of reciprocity as addressed in art 19(2)). If a listed entity intervenes in a proceeding in a way that it does not become a party to them for litigation purposes, Article 19 declarations cannot bar recognition or enforcement of the judgment in the declaring State as between the parties to the litigation. **8.28**

An Article 19 declaration may operate with respect to judgments to which one of three kinds of entities is a party: a State, a natural person, or a governmental agency. These are independent disjuncts: any one will do. Nor is the declaring State required to extend its declaration to all three. 'State' inescapably will mean Contracting State, which pragmatically makes unnecessary any speculation as to what a State is for purposes of the Convention. Government 'agency' is undefined; insofar as the purpose of the declaration is to provide added protection for a State that might be called upon to recognize or enforce a judgment against itself or one of its entities, and in light of the pragmatic motivation to minimize disincentives to ratification, this determination should be left to the law of the declaring State. However, that determination should be constrained, consistent with the Article 20 obligation to give regard to the international character of the Convention. An intuitive Convention sense of 'government agency' might begin with the proposition that a government agency is anything created by or directed by the State, including political sub-divisions. Several **8.29**

[5] Art 18 is phrased as a declaration that 'will not apply' while art 19 uses 'shall not apply'. No difference in sense should be assigned to the difference in usage. The French text is uniform, '*ne l'appiquera pas*'.

limitations may then be applied to this starting point. First, a governmental agency is not a natural person (else the inclusion of natural persons acting for the agency would be largely surplusage). Second, the mere chartering of a non-natural person, or requirements for its registration, or its regulation, do not transform that non-natural person into a governmental agency. More is required for purposes of an Article 19 declaration.

8.30 Article 19 also permits a State to make a declaration when a natural person 'acting for that State' or 'acting' for a government agency is a party. This criterion only applies to natural persons. Non-natural persons do not fall within an Article 19 declaration except if the State itself is so classified under the law of the declaring State, or an agency of that State is classified as a non-natural person. The natural person who attracts the declaration only needs to be 'acting for the State' or a governmental agency. Article 19 sets no further requirements as to the nature, purpose, qualities, or State or governmental oversight of that action, such that it involve discharge of a nebulous and undefined sense of sovereign function, which, thus far, has escaped consensus in international law.

8.31 The declaration only applies if a person designated in Article 19 is a 'party'. Any person not a party, such as someone having an 'interest' in or being affected by the judgment, may not benefit from an Article 19 declaration.[6]

8.32 Within these parameters, Article 19(1) contains two additional limitations on the content of the declaration. The first is that the State making the declaration 'shall ensure that the declaration is no broader than necessary' and that the exclusion from scope is clearly and precisely defined. This language is almost identical to the limitation contained in Article 18, and the reader is referred to our treatment of it in the context of that article. The second limitation is that the declaration shall not distinguish between judgments where the listed entity is a defendant or claimant in the proceedings before the court of origin. This bars the declaring State from reserving to itself the benefits of recognition or enforcement of successful affirmative claims while preventing others from reaping the benefits of successful claims against that State.

8.33 The language of Article 19(1) ('shall not apply this Convention to judgments') specifically acknowledges that the declaration effectively works an exclusion from scope. Article 19(2) spells out the consequences of that exclusion in other Contracting States. Recognition or enforcement of a judgment given by a court of a declaring State may be refused if the judgment arose from proceedings to which a listed entity either of the declaring State or the requested State is a party. While this provision enables a court of a declaring State to refuse to recognize or enforce a judgment against the declaring State, it also removes any obligation of another Contracting State to recognize or enforce a judgment in favour of the declaring State, even where the judgment is made by a court of the declaring State. Article 19(2) uses the permissive 'may be refused'. The contours of the refusal, if exercised at all, are left to the law and institutions of the requested State, whether by court decision or legislation. Of course, recognition or enforcement may proceed under national law as well, pursuant to Article 15.

8.34 As with declarations under Articles 17 and 18, the Convention addresses Article 19 declarations in the context of Hague Conference review under Article 21, in the context of application

[6] There is a touch of vagueness in the text of art 19 with respect to whether the person who triggers its operation is a party to the initial proceedings or to the judgment presented for recognition or enforcement. On the basis of the content and the grammatical structure of both the English- and French-language texts, we believe that the former is the better reading.

in States with non-unified legal systems in Article 22, and in the context of the requirements of Articles 30 and 32. The reader should consult our discussions with respect to those articles.

IV. Article 20—Uniform Interpretation

Article 20
Uniform interpretation

In the interpretation of this Convention, regard shall be had to its international character and to the need to promote uniformity in its application.

There is no international court to determine the 'correct' interpretation and application of Convention provisions. The Convention will be interpreted and applied by domestic courts in requested States in the context of particular cases. If those domestic courts take a parochial approach to the Convention, the benefits of the Convention in terms of uniformity, certainty, and efficiency will be lost. Loss of these benefits, in turn, would encourage parties not to use the Convention, but rather to find other mechanisms to deal with the additional risks and costs of trans-border commerce.[7] **8.35**

Article 20 is a response to these concerns. It reminds Contracting States and their courts that they will be interpreting and applying an international convention governing the movement of judgments across borders ('regard shall be had to its international character'). They should consider the interpretation given to Convention text by other Contracting States, but are not bound to apply the same interpretation in their own courts. **8.36**

While the Article 20 reference to regard for the need to promote uniformity in application gives some advantage to early ratifiers and courts that are early in addressing issues of interpretation, the requirement is of 'regard' to the need to 'promote' uniformity. This regard for the need to promote uniformity in application is limited by the requirements of the text itself: it provides no warrant for misapplication in the pursuit of uniformity. While interpretation should take into account the case law on point, the best reading of the text still controls, including the need to interpret that text in light of its international character. Early interpretations carry no force simply by virtue of being early. **8.37**

Nonetheless, there are limitations to the force and impact of Article 20. By its terms, it is addressed to 'the interpretation' of the Convention. However, use and application of the Convention may entail operations other than what might traditionally be considered to constitute 'interpretation'. Thus, it is appropriate to give a broad interpretation to the word 'interpretation'. Any matter touching upon or touched by the Convention should be treated with due regard to the international context, insofar as possible. **8.38**

It is useful at this point to provide a closer examination of the sources of law embedded in the Convention, and the limitations these may place on the quest for uniformity. First, domestic law remains important to the interpretation and application of the Convention. Domestic law will govern the operation of the Convention at numerous points. This was a deliberate choice. Where domestic law remains applicable, the Convention cannot **8.39**

[7] Art 20 is identical to art 23 of COCA, and should be interpreted in like manner. Accordingly, this discussion leans heavily on Brand and Herrup (n 3) 159–61. Similar language appears in other instruments adopted by the Hague Conference on Private International Law as well as other private international law organizations.

force dual interpretations of domestic law—one interpretation for proceedings under the Convention and another interpretation for everything else. Obviously, in implementing the Convention, it would be desirable for Contracting States to examine their laws to determine if specific modifications to accommodate the Convention are appropriate. However, there is no obligation under the Convention that they do so.

8.40 Second, the Convention contains autonomous terms and rules. Most of the terms and rules within the Convention that are not governed by domestic law may be autonomous to this Convention. They must be built up over time through national practice. The call for international consideration in Article 20 applies with full vigour to these terms and rules.

8.41 Third, the Convention incorporates certain terms and rules common to other Conventions adopted by the Hague Conference on Private International Law, such as the use of the term 'manifest' to qualify public policy, and some of the Final Clauses in Chapter IV. Such terms and rules should be interpreted and applied in light of the collective body of rules and practices which have grown up around these other Conventions.

8.42 Fourth, the Convention contains terms and provisions from other private international law treaties. Article 20 is itself an example of this type of provision. Its language is taken largely from Article 7(1) of the United Nations Convention on Contracts for the International Sale of Goods (CISG), which reads, '[i]n the interpretation of this Convention, regard is to be had to its international character and to the need to promote uniformity in its application and the observance of good faith in international trade'.[8] Thus, the cases interpreting Article 7(1) of the CISG, as well as other conventions that contain similar language, may be instructive in the interpretation and application of Article 20 of this Convention as well. A number of Convention provisions, such as the provisions applicable to non-unified legal systems, are also similar to provisions often found in private international law conventions. Insofar as understandings have developed about such provisions in the other conventions, those understandings should not be disturbed without good reason in the interpretation and application of this Convention. Domestic case law construing such provisions in the context of other private international law treaties should be consulted but is not binding.

8.43 Finally, rules of public international law applicable to the interpretation of treaties apply as well to this Convention. Matters of Convention interpretation that are generally regulated by general treaty law will be subject to those rules of public international law.

V. Article 21—Review of Operation of the Convention

Article 21

Review of operation of the Convention

The Secretary General of the Hague Conference on Private International Law shall at regular intervals make arrangements for review of the operation of this Convention, including any declarations, and shall report to the Council on General Affairs and Policy.

[8] United Nations Convention on Contracts for the International Sale of Goods, Art 7(1), UN Doc A/CONF.97/18, Annex I, English version reprinted in 52 Fed Reg 6264 (1987) and in 19 ILM 668 (1980).

Article 21 is similar to language found in conventions adopted by the Hague Conference on Private International Law beginning in 1993 with the Convention on Protection of Children and Co-operation in Respect of Intercountry Adoption. Unlike the provision on the review of the operation of the convention contained in the Convention on Choice of Court Agreements, Article 21 of this Convention does not authorize the Secretary General to make arrangements for consideration of whether any amendments to this Convention are desirable.[9] Particularly as Article 20 of the Judgments Convention highlights the need to promote uniformity in the application of the Convention, periodic meetings convened to review the operation of the Convention can allow for discussion of the manner in which the Convention is being applied in different countries. In addition, Article 21 envisages the review of declarations made pursuant to the Convention. The Convention includes provisions addressing declarations in Article 14(3) (permitting a State to declare that all or certain of its courts may require security, bond, or deposit from a person applying for the enforcement of a judgment given by a court of another State on the sole ground that such person is a foreign national or is not domiciled in the State in which enforcement is sought); Article 17 (permitting a State to declare that its courts may refuse to recognize or enforce a judgment given by a court of another State if the parties were resident in the requested State, and the relationship between the parties and all other elements relevant to the dispute, other than the location of the court giving the judgment, were connected only with the requested State); Article 18 (permitting a State to declare that it will not apply the Convention to a specific matter, where the State has a strong interest in not applying the Convention to that matter); Article 19 (permitting a State to declare that it will not apply the Convention to which that State, a natural person acting for that State, a government agency of that State, or a natural person acting for such a government agency is a party to the litigation resulting in the judgment sought to be enforced); Article 25 (permitting a State having two or more territorial units in which different systems of law apply in relation to matters dealt with in the Convention to declare that the Convention may apply to all or only identified territorial units); and Article 27 (permitting a Regional Economic Integration Organization (REIO) to declare that it exercises competence over all the matters governed by the Convention and that its Member States will not be Parties to the Convention but shall be bound by virtue of the signature, acceptance, approval, or accession of the REIO). **8.44**

When the Hague Conference on Private International Law has convened meetings to review the operation of other conventions, it has invited as participants representatives of States Parties to the relevant conventions, Member States of the Hague Conference on Private International Law regardless of whether they are party to the relevant conventions or taken any step to become party, and representatives of international organizations, non-governmental organizations (NGOs), and other entities deemed to have expertise to add to the discussions. While the discussions at these meetings may be helpful in the implementation of the Convention, given the traditional makeup of the participants in these meetings, any interpretation resulting from the meetings should not be considered to constitute **8.45**

[9] Pursuant to art 24 of COCA, 'The Secretary General of the Hague Conference on Private International Law shall at regular intervals make arrangements for—

a) review of the operation of this Convention, including any declarations; and

b) consideration of whether any amendments to this Convention are desirable'.

a subsequent agreement between the parties regarding the interpretation of the treaty or the application of its provisions.

8.46 While this article obligates the Secretary General 'to make arrangements' for the review of the Convention, it does not grant any other authority to the Secretary General.[10] In particular, Article 21 of this Convention does not authorize the Secretary General to depart from the obligations contained in the Statute of the Hague Conference on Private International Law. The Council on General Affairs and Policy would be expected to continue to direct the Permanent Bureau, which includes the Secretary General, of the Hague Conference pursuant to Article 6 of the Statute. In addition, the costs for the review of the Convention would need to be included in the organization's budget, which would need to be approved by the organization's Council of Diplomatic Representatives of Member States at The Hague pursuant to Article 10(1) of the Statute.

8.47 Article 21 imposes an obligation on the Secretary General and does not constitute the exclusive method for the review of the operation of the Convention. The States Parties may, on their own initiative, meet, bilaterally or multilaterally, to discuss the Convention.

8.48 Article 21 does not authorize the convening of any meeting to discuss amendments to the Convention. The Convention does not address the possibility of its amendment. The rules and procedures to be applied for the amendment of the Convention would be based on practice, the Statute of the Hague Conference on Private International Law, and otherwise applicable international law, as is reflected in Article 40 of the Vienna Convention on the Law of Treaties (VCLT), done at Vienna 23 May 1969.

VI. Article 22—Non-Unified Legal Systems

Article 22
Non-unified legal systems

1. In relation to a Contracting State in which two or more systems of law apply in different territorial units with regard to any matter dealt with in this Convention—
   (a) any reference to the law or procedure of a State shall be construed as referring, where appropriate, to the law or procedure in force in the relevant territorial unit;
   (b) any reference to the court or courts of a State shall be construed as referring, where appropriate, to the court or courts in the relevant territorial unit;
   (c) any reference to a connection with a State shall be construed as referring, where appropriate, to a connection with the relevant territorial unit;
   (d) any reference to a connecting factor in relation to a State shall be construed as referring, where appropriate, to that connecting factor in relation to the relevant territorial unit.

2. Notwithstanding paragraph 1, a Contracting State with two or more territorial units in which different systems of law apply shall not be bound to apply this Convention to situations which involve solely such different territorial units.

[10] By comparison, the Convention on Jurisdiction, Applicable Law, Recognition, Enforcement and Co-operation in Respect of Parental Responsibility and Measures for the Protection of Children, done at The Hague, 19 October 1996, art 56 states that 'The Secretary General of the Hague Conference on Private International Law shall at regular intervals convoke a Special Commission in order to review the practical operation of the Convention'.

3. **A court in a territorial unit of a Contracting State with two or more territorial units in which different systems of law apply shall not be bound to recognise or enforce a judgment from another Contracting State solely because the judgment has been recognised or enforced in another territorial unit of the same Contracting State under this Convention.**
4. **This Article shall not apply to Regional Economic Integration Organisations.**

The Hague Conference on Private International Law incorporated provisions addressing what the Judgments Convention refers to as 'non-unified legal systems' beginning with the Twelfth Diplomatic Session in 1973. Article 22 applies to States that are divided into sub-units, as well as States that are responsible for the administration of law over foreign territories. Thus, the use of 'territorial units' includes both the domestic sub-units as well as the territories for which the country is responsible. Application of the article requires more than the existence of territorial units, however. As suggested by the title of the article ('Non-unified legal systems'), the relevant law applicable in at least two of a Contracting State's territorial units must differ. Beyond this, however, the Convention does not identify, for example, whether the 'systems of law' must relate to substantive or procedural matters, or both, to trigger the application of this article; the extent to which the 'systems of law' would need to have 'regard to any matter dealt with in this Convention' to trigger the application of this article; whether the existence of identical provisions in separate legislative instruments in different territorial units would trigger the application of this article; or the relevance of common law to the application of this article. **8.49**

Article 22 contains multiple rules. Paragraph 1 establishes a rule of construction as it provides guidance in interpreting the references to the law of, procedure of, a court of, courts of, connection with, and a connecting factor in relation to a State. Paragraph 2 establishes a rule of internationality that clarifies that the Convention does not establish an obligation in one territorial unit of a State to recognize or enforce a judgment from another territorial unit of that State. Finally, paragraphs 3 and 4 contain rules that limit the mandatory operation of the Convention. Paragraph 3 does so by providing discretion. Paragraph 4 does so by limiting the scope of the Convention. **8.50**

Article 22 serves multiple purposes with respect to any Contracting State comprised of multiple territorial units in which different systems of law are applied concerning the subject matter of the Convention. First, this article identifies, for the benefit of other Contracting States, the manner in which the Convention applies to judgments originating in this Contracting State. Second, Article 22 identifies the manner in which a Contracting State is obliged to implement the Convention in its territorial units with respect to judgments originating in other Contracting States. **8.51**

This article does not apply to REIOs. The application of the Convention to such Organizations is addressed in Articles 27 and 28. **8.52**

A. Covered Contracting States

Article 22 raises several fundamental questions, such as: (1) who determines whether a Contracting State is one in which two or more systems of law apply in different territorial units with regard to any matter dealt with in the Convention; (2) what constitutes a system **8.53** of law; (3) must the content of the systems of law differ; and (4) when does a system of law apply to any matter dealt with in the Convention. Each of these questions is addressed below.

1. Who determines whether a Contracting State is one in which two or more systems of law apply in different territorial units with regard to any matter dealt with in the Convention?

8.54 A Contracting State that has two or more territorial units in which different systems of law apply in relation to matters dealt with in the Convention may avail itself of a declaration authorized by Article 25 (discussed in detail paras 9.05–9.08). However, as an Article 25 declaration is discretionary, a Contracting State may decide not to make this declaration even where that the State has determined that it is comprised of multiple territorial units and that two or more systems of law apply in different territorial units with regard to any matter dealt with in the Convention. Thus, it may often be necessary for the requested court to determine whether two or more systems of law apply in different territorial units of the State of the court of origin with regard to any matter dealt with in the Convention. The Hague Conference should consider the creation of a country profile in which each Contracting State would be invited to identify whether it is a Contracting State in which two or more systems of law apply in different territorial units with regard to any matter dealt with in the Convention. In contrast, a requested court in a Contracting State comprised of multiple territorial units, that is requested to recognize or enforce a foreign judgment, will be better situated to determine the manner in which Article 22 applies to that Contracting State.

2. What is a system of law?

8.55 The Convention neither defines 'systems of law' nor provides a test for determining what constitutes 'systems of law'. Since 1973, conventions adopted by the Hague Conference that have included non-unified legal systems provisions have referred to 'systems of law',[11] 'rules of law',[12] both 'rules of law' and 'systems of law',[13] as well as both 'systems of law' and 'sets of rules of law'.[14]

[11] See Convention Concerning the International Administration of the Estates of Deceased Persons, done at The Hague, 2 October 1973, Arts 35, 36; Convention on the Recognition and Enforcement of Decisions Relating to Maintenance Obligations, done at The Hague, 2 October 1973, Arts 28, 33; Convention on the Law Applicable to Maintenance Obligations, done at The Hague, 2 October 1973, Arts 17, 23; Convention on the Law Applicable to Matrimonial Property Regimes, done at The Hague, 14 March 1978, Arts 16, 17, 18, 25; Convention on Celebration and Recognition of the Validity of Marriages, done at The Hague, 14 March 1978, Arts 17, 18, 19, 27; Convention on International Access to Justice, done at The Hague, 25 October 1980, Art 26; Convention on Choice of Court Agreements, done at The Hague, 30 June 2005, Arts 25, 28.

[12] See Convention on the Law Applicable to Products Liability, done at The Hague, 2 October 1973, Art 12; Convention on the Law Applicable to Agency, done at The Hague, 14 March 1978, Arts 19, 20, 21; Convention on the Law Applicable to Certain Rights in Respect of Securities Held with an Intermediary, done at The Hague, 5 July 2006, Art 1 (defining 'Multi-unit State').

[13] See Convention on the Law Applicable to Maintenance Obligations, done at The Hague, 2 October 1973, Arts 17, 23; Convention on the Civil Aspects of International Child Abduction, done at The Hague, 25 October 1980, Arts 31, 33, 40; Convention on the Law Applicable to Trusts and on Their Recognition, done at The Hague, 1 July 1985, Arts 23, 24, 29; Convention on the Law Applicable to Contracts for the International Sale of Goods, done at The Hague, 22 December 1986, Arts 19, 20, 26; Convention on the Law Applicable to Succession to the Estates of Deceased Persons, done at The Hague, 1 August 1989, Arts 19, 27; Convention on Protection of Children and Co-operation in Respect of Intercountry Adoption, done at The Hague, 29 May 1993, Arts 36, 38, 45.

[14] Convention on Jurisdiction, Applicable Law, Recognition, Enforcement and Co-operation in Respect of Parental Responsibility and Measures for the Protection of Children, done at The Hague, 19 October 1996, Arts 29,

The Judgments Convention does not state whether a system of law must be substantive in nature, may be entirely procedural, or may be a combination of both. As Article 22(1)(a) refers to law and procedure, thus a system of law might include a combination of substantive and procedural law.[15] It should be recalled that these systems of law 'apply ... with regard to any matter dealt with in this Convention'. As discussed in para 8.58 and 8.59, in response to the fourth question, the Convention deals with many 'matter[s]'. Many of these matters are indeed substantive. Thus 'systems of law' should be understood to extend to substantive law, regardless of whether they apply to procedural rules. **8.56**

3. Must the content of the systems of law differ?

The chapeau of Article 22(1) refers to 'a Contracting State in which two or more systems of law apply in different territorial units'. The text requires that two or more systems of law apply. However, it does not address whether the substance of these systems of law must differ. A State comprised of multiple territorial units, where each unit has its own body of substantive law, would seem to fall within this provision.[16] The Convention does not address, however, whether it would be necessary for the substantive law that applies in each territorial unit to differ. Thus, it is important to address the question of whether a 'system of law' is defined by its content or by the form it takes, whether by codification, judge-made law, or otherwise. If the former, attorneys and courts would be required to compare the law applicable within each territorial unit of a Contracting State. In so doing, they would need to understand what degree of difference between systems of law would cause them to be considered to be different. If the latter, the evaluation would be simplified; however, this might be arbitrary as the only difference might be the name of a legislative act. **8.57**

4. When does a system of law apply to a matter dealt with in the Convention?

The final issue to be addressed to determine whether Article 22 is relevant to a particular Contracting State that is comprised of multiple territorial units in which different systems of law apply is whether those differing systems of law apply with regard to a matter addressed in the Convention. The text of the Convention does not address the extent to which the system of law would need to apply with regard to the matter. **8.58**

A literal reading of the word 'any' in 'any matter dealt with in this Convention' provides for a broad application of this provision. Article 1(1) of the Convention provides that the 'Convention shall apply to the recognition and enforcement of judgments in civil or commercial matters'. Article 2(1) identifies those 'matters' to which the Convention does not apply. As a result, the Convention applies to any civil or commercial matter that is not identified in Article 2(1). Any system of law that applies to a matter that is not identified in Article **8.59**

47, 48, 59; Convention on the International Protection of Adults, done at The Hague, 13 January 2000, Arts 28, 45, 46, 55; Convention on the International Recovery of Child Support and Other Forms of Family Maintenance, done at The Hague, 23 November 2007, Arts 46, 47, 61; Protocol on the Law Applicable to Maintenance Obligations, done at The Hague, 23 November 2007, Arts 16, 26.

[15] The Convention does not define 'law' or 'procedure', or provide guidance as to the difference between the two.

[16] The drafters of the Explanatory Report refer to such a State as a 'non-unified legal system'. See Convention of 2 July 2019 on the Recognition and Enforcement of Foreign Judgments in Civil or Commercial Matters, Text adopted by the Twenty-Second Session, Explanatory Report by Francisco Garcimartín & Geneviève Saumier (Explanatory Report), para 355 <https://assets.hcch.net/docs/a1b0b0fc-95b1-4544-935b-b842534a120f.pdf>.

2(1) would be relevant to the consideration of Article 22(1). For example, a Contracting State that has two or more territorial units in which different systems of law apply in relation to marine pollution in areas within national jurisdiction[17] would fall within the category of States to which Article 22(1) applies.

B. Application to a Contracting State from which the Judgment Originated

8.60 Pursuant to Article 22(1)(a):

> **In relation to a Contracting State in which two or more systems of law apply in different territorial units with regard to any matter dealt with in this Convention— any reference to the law or procedure of a State shall be construed as referring, where appropriate, to the law or procedure in force in the relevant territorial unit.**

A literal reading of this provision would result in the application of this provision only in situations in which the Convention uses the precise words 'law' or 'procedure'. It can be questioned whether such a literal reading is required. By comparison, Article 22(1)(d) refers to 'any reference to a connecting factor'. As the Convention does not otherwise use the term 'connecting factor', a literal reading is inappropriate in that context. If a similar approach is to be used to interpret Article 22(1)(a), it might be appropriate to consider when the Convention focuses on law or procedure without using those exact terms. At a minimum, this provision should provide guidance when the terms 'law' and 'policy' are used in the Convention. When looking at the Contracting State in which the judgment originated, the references to 'law' in Articles 5(1)(f),[18] 5(1)(l)(ii),[19] and 7(1)(a)(i)[20] would be affected by this provision. The reference to 'law' in Article 5(1)(g)[21] may invoke the law of any State

[17] See Art 2(1)(g).

[18] Pursuant to art 5(1)(f):

> A judgment is eligible for recognition and enforcement if one of the following requirements is met—the defendant argued on the merits before the court of origin without contesting jurisdiction within the timeframe provided in the law of the State of origin, unless it is evident that an objection to jurisdiction or to the exercise of jurisdiction would not have succeeded under that *law*. (Emphasis added.)

[19] Pursuant to art 5(1)(l)(ii):

> A judgment is eligible for recognition and enforcement if one of the following requirements is met—to the extent that it was against the counterclaimant, unless the *law* of the State of origin required the counterclaim to be filed in order to avoid preclusion. (Emphasis added.)

[20] Pursuant to art 7(1)(a)(i):

> Recognition or enforcement may be refused if... the document which instituted the proceedings or an equivalent document, including a statement of the essential elements of the claim... was not notified to the defendant in sufficient time and in such a way as to enable them to arrange for their defence, unless the defendant entered an appearance and presented their case without contesting notification in the court of origin, provided that the *law* of the State of origin permitted notification to be contested. (Emphasis added.)

[21] Pursuant to art 5(1)(g):

> A judgment is eligible for recognition and enforcement if one of the following requirements is met—the judgment ruled on a contractual obligation and it was given by a court of the State in which performance of that obligation took place, or should have taken place, in accordance with (i) the agreement of the parties, or (ii) the *law* applicable to the contract, in the absence of an agreed place of performance, unless the activities of the defendant in relation to the transaction clearly did not constitute a purposeful and substantial connection to that State. (Emphasis added.)

as it focuses on the law applicable to a contract; however, if that law is of a Contracting State in which two or more systems of law apply in different territorial units with regard to any matter dealt with in the Convention, the reference in Article 5(1)(g) would be to the law of the relevant territorial unit of that Contracting State.

Pursuant to Article 22(1)(b): 8.61

> **In relation to a Contracting State in which two or more systems of law apply in different territorial units with regard to any matter dealt with in this Convention— any reference to the court or courts of a State shall be construed as referring, where appropriate, to the court or courts in the relevant territorial unit.**

As the Convention requires the recognition and enforcement of an existing judgment, which is a decision on the merits given by a court,[22] in order for the Convention's obligations concerning recognition and enforcement to apply, a court in the State of Origin will have been identified at the time that the initial judgment is issued. For a Contracting State in which individual courts have jurisdiction within particular territorial units, identification of the judgment and the court that issued it might help to identify the relevant territorial unit of that Contracting State. Generally, where the Convention refers to a court in the State of Origin, it is referring to the court that issued the relevant judgment. This would render Article 22(1)(b) largely meaningless as the definition of 'judgment' and the obligation in Article 4(1) would already achieve this result. There are, however, two sets of provisions in which Article 22(1)(b) might have independent meaning with regard to the State of Origin.

First, Article 5(1)(g) provides that: 8.62

> A judgment is eligible for recognition and enforcement if one of the following requirements is met—the judgment ruled on a contractual obligation and it was given by a *court* of the State in which performance of that obligation took place, or should have taken place, in accordance with (i) the agreement of the parties, or (ii) the law applicable to the contract, in the absence of an agreed place of performance, unless the activities of the defendant in relation to the transaction clearly did not constitute a purposeful and substantial connection to that State. (Emphasis added.)

This provision would appear to require that, for a Contracting State in which two or more systems of law apply in different territorial units with regard to any matter dealt with in the Convention, the court issuing the judgment sought to be recognized or enforced must be in the territorial unit in which performance of the contractual obligation took place or should have taken place. A judgment from a court of that Contracting State that is applying the law of another territorial unit of that Contracting State would not be eligible for recognition and enforcement pursuant to Article 5(1)(g).

Second, Article 5(1)(h) provides that 'A judgment is eligible for recognition and enforcement if one of the following requirements is met—the judgment ruled on a lease of immovable property (tenancy) and it was given by a court of the State in which the property is situated'. 8.63
Similarly, Article 5(3) states that Article 5(1) 'does not apply to a judgment that ruled on a

[22] See the definition of 'judgment' in art 3(1)(b). See also art 4(1) ('A judgment given by a court of a Contracting State (State of origin) shall be recognised and enforced in another Contracting State (requested State) in accordance with the provisions of this Chapter').

residential lease of immovable property (tenancy) or ruled on the registration of immovable property. Such a judgment is eligible for recognition and enforcement only if it was given by a court of the State where the property is situated.' These provisions would appear to require that, for a Contracting State in which two or more systems of law apply in different territorial units with regard to any matter dealt with in the Convention, the court issuing the judgment ruling on a lease of immovable property is sought to be recognized or enforced must be in the territorial unit in which property is situated. A judgment from a court of that Contracting State that is applying the law or another territorial unit of that Contracting State would not be eligible for recognition and enforcement pursuant to Article 5(1)(h) or 5(3).

8.64 Pursuant to Article 22(1)I:

> **In relation to a Contracting State in which two or more systems of law apply in different territorial units with regard to any matter dealt with in this Convention—any reference to a connection with a State shall be construed as referring, where appropriate, to a connection with the relevant territorial unit.**

The only relevant provision addressing a connection to a State from which a judgment originated is found in Article 5(1)(g).[23]

8.65 Pursuant to Article 22(1)(d):

> **In relation to a Contracting State in which two or more systems of law apply in different territorial units with regard to any matter dealt with in this Convention—any reference to a connecting factor in relation to a State shall be construed as referring, where appropriate, to that connecting factor in relation to the relevant territorial unit.**

If a literal reading were applied such that this provision would apply only where the Convention uses the term 'connecting factor', it would be superfluous as there are no references to 'connecting factor[s]' in the Convention outside of Article 22(1)(d). For this provision to have meaning and effect, it would need to apply to Convention provisions involving connecting factors, even where the words 'connecting factor[s]' do not appear.

C. Application to Contracted State Requested to Recognize or Enforce a Judgment

8.66 As stated in Section B immediately above, Article 22(1)(a) provides that:

> **In relation to a Contracting State in which two or more systems of law apply in different territorial units with regard to any matter dealt with in this Convention—any reference to the law or**

[23] Pursuant to art 5(1)(g):

> A judgment is eligible for recognition and enforcement if one of the following requirements is met—the judgment ruled on a contractual obligation and it was given by a court of the State in which performance of that obligation took place, or should have taken place, in accordance with (i) the agreement of the parties, or (ii) the law applicable to the contract, in the absence of an agreed place of performance, unless the activities of the defendant in relation to the transaction clearly did not constitute a purposeful and substantial *connection to that State*. (Emphasis added.)

procedure of a State shall be construed as referring, where appropriate, to the law or procedure in force in the relevant territorial unit.

Article 12(4),[24] Article 13(1)[25] (which also contains a reference to 'procedure'), and Article 14(2)[26] refer to the 'law' of the Contracted State requested to recognize or enforce a judgment. Article 22(1)(a) does not apply to the reference to 'law' in Article 15,[27] because that article makes reference to 'national law' rather than the 'law of a State'. Moreover, it does not make sense for the Convention to limit the application of Article 15, beyond the limitation related to Article 6, as the decision to recognize or enforce a foreign judgment would already find its basis outside of the Convention and the Convention should not limit the identification of applicable law in such situations. When a provision contains an explicit limitation or exception, care should be taken in finding additional implicit limitations.

As is stated in Section B immediately above, Article 22(1)(b) provides that: **8.67**

In relation to a Contracting State in which two or more systems of law apply in different territorial units with regard to any matter dealt with in this Convention—any reference to the court or courts of a State shall be construed as referring, where appropriate, to the court or courts in the relevant territorial unit.

This provision is expected to have limited effect as each reference to a 'court' in the context of a court in the requested Contracting State will apply to the court that has before it a request for the recognition or enforcement of a foreign judgment without the need to distinguish between that court and other courts of that Contracting State. There are, however, several references to courts in the requested Contracting State, including in Article 7(1)(e),[28] Article 7(2),[29] Article 13(1),[30] and Article 13(2).[31]

[24] Pursuant to art 12(4), 'If the documents referred to in this Article are not in an official language of the requested State, they shall be accompanied by a certified translation into an official language, unless the law of the requested State provides otherwise'.

[25] Art 13(1) states, in part, 'The procedure for recognition, declaration of enforceability or registration for enforcement, and the enforcement of the judgment, are governed by the law of the requested State unless this Convention provides otherwise'.

[26] Pursuant to art 14(2):

> An order for payment of costs or expenses of proceedings, made in a Contracting State against any person exempt from requirements as to security, bond, or deposit by virtue of paragraph 1 [of Article 14] or of the law of the State where proceedings have been instituted, shall, on the application of the person entitled to the benefit of the order, be rendered enforceable in any other Contracting State.

[27] Pursuant to art 15, 'Subject to Article 6, this Convention does not prevent the recognition or enforcement of judgments under national law'.

[28] Pursuant to art 7(1)(e), '[r]ecognition or enforcement may be refused if—the judgment is inconsistent with a judgment given by a court of the requested State in a dispute between the same parties'.

[29] Art 7(2) provides, in part:

> Recognition or enforcement may be postponed or refused if proceedings between the same parties on the same subject matter are pending before a court of the requested State, where—(a) the court of the requested State was seised before the court of origin; and (b) there is a close connection between the dispute and the requested State.

[30] Art 13(1) provides, in part, 'The court of the requested State shall act expeditiously'.

[31] Pursuant to art 13(2), 'The court of the requested State shall not refuse the recognition or enforcement of a judgment under this Convention on the ground that recognition or enforcement should be sought in another State'.

8.68 As stated in Section B immediately above, Article 22(1)(c) provides that:

In relation to a Contracting State in which two or more systems of law apply in different territorial units with regard to any matter dealt with in this Convention—any reference to a connection with a State shall be construed as referring, where appropriate, to a connection with the relevant territorial unit.

This provision relates to Article 7(2), which allows a Contracting State to postpone or refuse to recognize or enforce a judgment if several factors are satisfied including 'a close connection between the dispute and the requested State'.

8.69 As stated in Section B immediately above, Article 22(1)(d) would not have any effect were it to apply only where the words 'connecting factor' are used in the Convention.

D. International Effect of Convention

8.70 Article 22(2) provides that the Convention only applies when a judgment from one Contracting State is requested to be recognized or enforced in another Contracting State. The Convention would not apply to a domestic situation in which a judgment of a court of one territorial unit of a Contracting State is sought to be recognized or enforced in another territorial unit of that Contracting State.

E. Precedential Effect of Recognition and Enforcement by a Domestic Court

8.71 Article 22(3) clarifies that, in a Contracting State with two or more territorial units in which different systems of law apply with regard to any matter dealt with in the Convention, a decision by a court in one territorial unit to recognize or enforce a foreign judgment pursuant to the Convention does not bind a court of another territorial unit of that Contracting State to do the same. What this provision does not state, but which should be equally true, is that a decision of a court in one territorial unit to recognize or enforce a foreign judgment pursuant to the Convention should not bind, pursuant to the treaty, a second court in that territorial unit to do the same. The Convention has no rule on this matter, and leaves it to the internal law of each Contracting State.

VII. Article 23—Relationship with Other International Instruments

Article 23
Relationship with other international instruments

1. **This Convention shall be interpreted so far as possible to be compatible with other treaties in force for Contracting States, whether concluded before or after this Convention.**
2. **This Convention shall not affect the application by a Contracting State of a treaty that was concluded before this Convention.**

3. This Convention shall not affect the application by a Contracting State of a treaty concluded after this Convention as concerns the recognition or enforcement of a judgment given by a court of a Contracting State that is also a Party to that treaty. Nothing in the other treaty shall affect the obligations under Article 6 towards Contracting States that are not Parties to that treaty.

4. This Convention shall not affect the application of the rules of a Regional Economic Integration Organisation that is a Party to this Convention as concerns the recognition or enforcement of a judgment given by a court of a Contracting State that is also a Member State of the Regional Economic Integration Organisation where—

(a) the rules were adopted before this Convention was concluded; or

(b) the rules were adopted after this Convention was concluded, to the extent that they do not affect the obligations under Article 6 towards Contracting States that are not Member States of the Regional Economic Integration Organisation.

Article 23 establishes rules for the interpretation and application of the Convention by Contracting States that are party to other treaties where those other treaties might conflict with the Convention. Article 23(1) states the basic rule that the two instruments should 'so far as possible' be interpreted in a compatible manner. The remainder of the article is intended to address the situation in which the Convention cannot be interpreted in a manner compatible with another treaty. **8.72**

Article 23(2) establishes that the Convention, which was concluded on 2 July 2019, shall not affect the application of any treaty that was concluded before that date. Should a Contracting State be unable to apply the Judgments Convention in a manner compatible with its implementation of a treaty concluded after 2 July 2019, subject to Article 23(3), the Contracting State may apply the provisions of the Judgments Convention notwithstanding the other treaty. **8.73**

Article 23(3) contains a rule concerning the implementation of a treaty concluded after 2 July 2019. According to Article 23(3), the Judgments Convention shall not affect the implementation of that other treaty 'as concerns the recognition or enforcement of a judgment given by a court of a Contracting State [to the Judgments Convention] that is also a Party to that treaty'.[32] **8.74**

[32] Art 23(3) applies only in the circumstance involving the following: (a) two or more Contracting States to the Judgments Convention enter into an agreement, to which other States might or might not be party, that is concluded after 2 July 2019, the date of conclusion of the Judgments Convention; and (b) the other agreement concerns the recognition or enforcement of a judgment given by a court of a Contracting State to the Judgments Convention that is also a party to the other agreement. According to art 23(3), the Judgment Convention shall not affect the application of that other agreement, except to the extent that the other agreement affects obligations pursuant to art 6 owed to a Contracting State that is not also a party to the other agreement. The likelihood of any such occurrence where a State undertakes two conflicting treaty obligations regarding the recognition or enforcement of foreign judgments is far from clear. The justification for this provision shifted during the course of the negotiations, but the original rationale was that it would prevent two or more States from acting jointly in bad faith to deny a third State a benefit of this Convention. To prevent this unlikely problem, the Convention resorts to a solution that is phrased in a way that generalist judges and lawyers might find confusing. Furthermore, art 23(3) embodies the wrong policy: given the problems with the Convention described previously, there will be a need for empirical experimentation to find better solutions to some of the less functional aspects of the text, rather than a provision that discourages such experimentation. If, in the unlikely event that experimentation results in an obligation that conflicts with the Judgments Convention, a Contracting State to the Judgments Convention with a grievance has adequate alternative remedies in the law of treaties through complaint, assertion of responsibility of the infringing State, and countermeasures. In addition, the Convention itself provides for periodic review of its operation and, ultimately the possibility of denunciation.

8.75 Article 23(3) also includes a statement that '[n]othing in the [subsequently concluded] treaty shall affect the obligations under Article 6 towards Contracting States that are not Parties to that treaty'. As this Convention cannot serve to limit the discretion of a State in concluding a future treaty addressing immovable property, notwithstanding its wording, this provision should serve to address conflicts between the Judgments Convention and the subsequently concluded treaty. Article 6 provides that 'a judgment that ruled on rights in rem in immovable property shall be recognised and enforced if and only if the property is situated in the State of origin'. As we state in Chapter 6 of this book, Article 6 creates an obligation, that overrides other provisions of the Convention, both requiring, on the one hand, and prohibiting on the other, recognition or enforcement of certain judgments.

8.76 Article 23(4) contains special rules applicable to an REIO that is Party to the Judgments Convention. Pursuant to this paragraph, the Convention shall not affect the rules of that Organization concerning the recognition and enforcement of a judgment given by a Contracting State to the Convention that is also a member of the Organization where the rules of the Organization were adopted before 2 July 2019 or, if the rules were adopted after 2 July 2019, they do not affect obligations under Article 6 towards Contracting States that are not members of the Organization. This paragraph is intended to allow for the application of special rules concerning recognition and enforcement of judgments amongst members of an REIO that is a party to the Convention. The Convention does not contain a definition of the term 'Regional Economic Integration Organization', which is discussed in greater detail in Chapter 9 of this book.

9

Final Clauses (Articles 24–32)

I. General

Chapter IV of the Judgments Convention contains what are referred to as 'Final Clauses'. These provisions establish rules applicable to the Convention as a treaty. Article 24 addresses how States may sign, ratify, accept, approve, or accede to the Convention. Article 25 allows States with two or more territorial units, in which different systems of law apply in relation to matters addressed by the Convention, to tailor the application of the Convention with respect to those units. Articles 26 and 27 contain rules applicable to any Regional Economic Integration Organization (REIO). Article 28 addresses the entry into force of the Convention. Article 29 contains rules applicable to the effect of the Convention between Contracting States. Article 31 identifies how a Contracting State may denounce the Convention. Article 32 provides rules regarding depositary notifications. **9.01**

II. Article 24—Signature, Ratification, Acceptance, Approval, and Accession

Article 24

Signature, ratification, acceptance, approval or accession

1. **This Convention shall be open for signature by all States.**
2. **This Convention is subject to ratification, acceptance or approval by the signatory States.**
3. **This Convention shall be open for accession by all States.**
4. **Instruments of ratification, acceptance, approval or accession shall be deposited with the Ministry of Foreign Affairs of the Kingdom of the Netherlands, depositary of the Convention.**

9.02 This Convention is open to any State that wishes to become a Contracting State. Any State may sign the Convention. A State may express its consent to be bound by the Convention by ratification, acceptance, or approval. For purposes of the Convention, it is irrelevant whether a State becomes a Contracting State through ratification, acceptance, or approval. These are domestic processes that achieve the same result—they allow a State to express its consent to be bound by a treaty.[1] In lieu of signature and subsequent action, a State may instead become a Contracting State by accession to the Convention. Unlike other conventions of the Hague Conference, the Judgements Convention does not distinguish States that have become party to this Convention by accession from those that become party by the other means.[2]

9.03 The Depositary of the Convention is the Ministry of Foreign Affairs of the Kingdom of the Netherlands. As is recognized by Article 77 of the Vienna Convention on the Law of Treaties (VCLT), a depositary performs numerous functions that may include keeping custody of the original text of the treaty; receiving signatures to the treaty; keeping custody of instruments, notifications, and communications relating to the treaty; and informing State of acts, notifications, and communications relating to the treaty.[3] Upon ratification, acceptance, approval, or accession, Contracting States shall deposit the relevant instrument with the Depositary.

9.04 Pursuant to Article 32(a), the depositary shall notify Members of the Hague Conference and other States and REIOs that have signed, ratified, accepted, approved, or acceded to the Convention, of such a signature or the deposit of an instrument of ratification, acceptance, approval, or accession.

III. Article 25—Declarations with Respect to Non-Unified Legal Systems

Article 25
Declarations with respect to non-unified legal systems

1. **If a State has two or more territorial units in which different systems of law apply in relation to matters dealt with in this Convention, it may declare that the Convention shall extend to all its territorial units or only to one or more of them. Such a declaration shall state expressly the territorial units to which the Convention applies.**
2. **If a State makes no declaration under this Article, the Convention shall extend to all territorial units of that State.**
3. **This Article shall not apply to Regional Economic Integration Organisations.**

9.05 This article applies to any Contracting State that 'has two or more territorial units in which different systems of law apply in relation to matters dealt with in the Convention'. See the discussion of Article 22 in Chapter 8 of this book for a detailed analysis of this language.

9.06 A covered Contracting State may declare that the Convention shall apply only to identified territorial units or to all of its territorial units. As is discussed in the context of Article

[1] See the Vienna Convention on the Law of Treaties (VCLT), arts 2(1)(b) and 14, done at Vienna, 23 May 1969, United Nations Treaty Series, vol 1155, p 331. See also Draft Articles on the Law of Treaties with commentaries, Yearbook of the International Law Commission, 1966, vol II, p 189.

[2] For information on how other conventions distinguish these States, see discussion of art 29 in paras 9.21 and 9.22.

[3] See art 77 of the VCLT for a more detailed list of depositary functions.

22, a covered Contracting State is not required to make a declaration pursuant to this article. If a covered Contracting State does not make a declaration, the Convention shall apply to all of its territorial units.

Pursuant to Article 30(1), there is no time limit with respect to this declaration. A State may make this declaration upon signature; upon deposit of its instrument of ratification, acceptance, approval, or accession; or any time thereafter. Moreover, a State may modify or withdraw this declaration at any time. **9.07**

This article does not apply to REIOs. **9.08**

IV. Articles 26 and 27—REIOs

A. Article 26—An REIO as a Contracting State

Article 26

Regional Economic Integration Organisations

1. **A Regional Economic Integration Organisation which is constituted solely by sovereign States and has competence over some or all of the matters governed by this Convention may sign, accept, approve or accede to this Convention. The Regional Economic Integration Organisation shall in that case have the rights and obligations of a Contracting State, to the extent that the Organisation has competence over matters governed by this Convention.**
2. **The Regional Economic Integration Organisation shall, at the time of signature, acceptance, approval or accession, notify the depositary in writing of the matters governed by this Convention in respect of which competence has been transferred to that Organisation by its Member States. The Organisation shall promptly notify the depositary in writing of any changes to its competence as specified in the most recent notice given under this paragraph.**
3. **For the purposes of the entry into force of this Convention, any instrument deposited by a Regional Economic Integration Organisation shall not be counted unless the Regional Economic Integration Organisation declares in accordance with Article 27(1) that its Member States will not be Parties to this Convention.**
4. **Any reference to a 'Contracting State' or 'State' in this Convention shall apply equally, where appropriate, to a Regional Economic Integration Organisation.**

An REIO is an entity that is created by sovereign States, to which these Member States have transferred competence in respect of, *inter alia*, economic matters. An example of such an REIO is the European Union (EU). **9.09**

To the extent that an REIO has been granted competence over any of the matters addressed in the Judgments Convention,[4] the REIO may become a party to the Convention. When it signs, accepts, approves, or accedes to the Convention, the REIO shall inform the depositary of those matters to which the Judgments Convention applies that have been transferred to the REIO by its Member States. In addition, the REIO is obliged to inform the depositary of any changes to the REIO's authority that are relevant to the implementation of the Judgments Convention. **9.10**

Pursuant to Article 28(1), the entry into force of the Judgments Convention is triggered by the deposit of the second instrument of ratification, acceptance, approval, or accession. The deposit of such an instrument by an REIO will not count as one of the first two instruments **9.11**

[4] See Chapter 4 for a discussion of these 'matters'.

deposited, unless the REIO declares, pursuant to Article 27(1), that it exercises competence over all matters governed by the Judgments Convention and that the Member States of the REIO will not be Parties to the Judgments Convention but will instead be obliged to comply with the Convention as a result of the signature, acceptance, approval, or accession of that REIO.

9.12 Article 26(4) establishes a general rule that an REIO shall be considered to be a 'State' and, where appropriate, a 'Contracting State' for the purposes of the Judgments Convention. This provision does not apply to all references to a 'State' as is evidenced by the inclusion of 'where appropriate'. For example, the references to a 'State' and a 'Contracting State' in Article 22 shall not be considered to be a reference to an REIO.[5]

B. Article 27—An REIO as a Contracting Party Without its Member States

Article 27

Regional Economic Integration Organisation as a Contracting Party without its Member States

1. **At the time of signature, acceptance, approval or accession, a Regional Economic Integration Organisation may declare that it exercises competence over all the matters governed by this Convention and that its Member States will not be Parties to this Convention but shall be bound by virtue of the signature, acceptance, approval or accession of the Organisation.**
2. **In the event that a declaration is made by a Regional Economic Integration Organisation in accordance with paragraph 1, any reference to a 'Contracting State' or 'State' in this Convention shall apply equally, where appropriate, to the Member States of the Organisation.**

9.13 Article 27 applies to any REIO to which its Member States have transferred competence over all matters governed by the Judgments Convention.[6] At the time of its signature, acceptance, approval, or accession, such an REIO may declare that it exercises competence over all matters governed by the Judgments Convention and that the Member States of the REIO will not be Parties to the Judgments Convention but will instead be obliged to comply with the Convention as a result of the signature, acceptance, approval, or accession of that REIO.

9.14 If an REIO makes a declaration pursuant to Article 27(1), Article 27(2) establishes a general rule that references in the Judgments Convention to a 'State' or a 'Contracting State' shall extend to Member States of that REIO. As with Article 26(4), this provision does not apply to all references to a 'State' or a 'Contracting State' as is evidenced by the inclusion of 'where appropriate'. For example, the references to 'Contracting States' in Article 29 would not extend to the Member States of an REIO that made the Article 27(1) declaration. In the latter scenario, only the REIO would be considered to be a 'Contracting State' to the Judgments Convention.

9.15 The Convention does not address whether the Member States of an REIO may be subject to Article 22. While Article 22(4) excludes REIOs from the application of that article,

[5] See art 22(4), which states that art 22 'shall not apply to Regional Economic Integration Organisations'.
[6] See n 4.

unless the words 'where appropriate' have the effect of achieving a different result, individual Member States may be considered to be non-unified legal systems for purposes of Article 22.

V. Article 28—Entry into Force

Article 28
Entry into force

1. **This Convention shall enter into force on the first day of the month following the expiration of the period during which a notification may be made in accordance with Article 29(2) with respect to the second State that has deposited its instrument of ratification, acceptance, approval or accession referred to in Article 24.**
2. **Thereafter this Convention shall enter into force—**
   (a) **for each State subsequently ratifying, accepting, approving or acceding to it, on the first day of the month following the expiration of the period during which notifications may be made in accordance with Article 29(2) with respect to that State;**
   (b) **for a territorial unit to which this Convention has been extended in accordance with Article 25 after the Convention has entered into force for the State making the declaration, on the first day of the month following the expiration of three months after the notification of the declaration referred to in that Article.**

Article 28 establishes the rules pursuant to which the Convention will enter into force generally and will enter into force for individual States or REIOs. In doing so, Article 28 looks to the deposit of instruments of ratification, acceptance, approval, and accession with the Convention's depositary, the Ministry of Foreign Affairs of the Kingdom of the Netherlands, pursuant to Article 24(4). 9.16

Pursuant to Article 28(1), the deposit of the second instrument of ratification, acceptance, approval, or accession will trigger the entry into force of the Convention. In particular, the Convention will enter into force on the first day of the month commencing after the completion of a twelve-month period following the notification by the depositary of that second deposit. On 29 August 2022, the EU deposited an instrument of accession and Ukraine deposited an instrument of ratification. As a result of these first two deposits, the Judgments Convention entered into force on 1 September 2023. 9.17

The Convention contains a separate rule for a State or REIO that deposits its instrument of ratification, acceptance, approval, or accession after the deposit of the second instrument. Pursuant to Article 28(2)(a), the Convention shall enter into force with respect to such a State or REIO on the first day of the month commencing after the completion of a twelve-month period following the notification by the depositary of that deposit.[7] 9.18

[7] The possibility exists that the Convention might enter into force with respect to the third depositing State on the same day that it enters into force for the first two depositing States. If, eg, the third deposit occurs the day following the deposit of the second instrument but before the depositary notification pursuant to art 32(a), if the subsequent depositary notification makes reference to the deposits of instruments by the second and third depositing States, the Convention would enter into force on the same day with respect to each State.

9.19 Although the Convention will enter into force for each State pursuant to Article 28, it will not necessarily affect relations between these Contracting States. Whether the Convention applies to relations between specific Contracting States is governed by Article 29.

9.20 Article 28(2)(b) contains a special entry into force rule where a Contracting State declares, in accordance with Article 25, that the Convention shall extend to a territorial unit after the Convention has entered into force for that Contracting State. The Convention shall enter into force with respect to that territorial unit on the first day of the month commencing after the completion of a three-month period following the receipt of the notification of the declaration by the depositary.

VI. Article 29—Establishment of Relations Pursuant to the Convention

Article 29

Establishment of relations pursuant to the Convention

1. **This Convention shall have effect between two Contracting States only if neither of them has notified the depositary regarding the other in accordance with paragraph 2 or 3. In the absence of such a notification, the Convention has effect between two Contracting States from the first day of the month following the expiration of the period during which notifications may be made.**
2. **A Contracting State may notify the depositary, within 12 months after the date of the notification by the depositary referred to in Article 32(a), that the ratification, acceptance, approval or accession of another State shall not have the effect of establishing relations between the two States pursuant to this Convention.**
3. **A State may notify the depositary, upon the deposit of its instrument pursuant to Article 24(4), that its ratification, acceptance, approval or accession shall not have the effect of establishing relations with a Contracting State pursuant to this Convention.**
4. **A Contracting State may at any time withdraw a notification that it has made under paragraph 2 or 3. Such a withdrawal shall take effect on the first day of the month following the expiration of three months following the date of notification.**

9.21 Prior to the adoption of the Judgments Convention, several of the other conventions of the Hague Conference on Private International Law afforded a Contracting State a relatively limited opportunity to object to convention relationships between that Contracting State and another Contracting State. Several other conventions identify which States may become party to that convention as a result of signature and subsequent ratification, acceptance, or approval of that convention. Those conventions allow States not identified to become party through the act of accession.

9.22 Existing conventions of the Hague Conference contain various provisions regarding the manner in which each such convention might affect relations between a State that acceded to the convention and another Contracting State. Several conventions will only affect relations between an acceding State and another Contracting State if the latter does not object to the accession. For example, the Convention Abolishing the Requirement of Legalisation for Foreign Public Documents and the Convention on the Protection of Children and Co-operation in Respect of Intercountry Adoption each provide that an accession affects relations between States if the non-acceding State has not objected to the accession within six months of receipt of notification of the accession from the depositary.[8] The Convention on the International Recovery of Child Support and Other Forms of Family Maintenance contains a similar provision, but provides Contracting States with twelve months to object to an accession.[9] Other conventions will only affect relations between an acceding State and another Contracting State if the latter accepts the accession. For example, the Convention on the Taking of Evidence Abroad in Civil or Commercial Matters and the Convention on the Civil Aspects of International Child Abduction each only affect relations between an acceding State and another Contracting State after the latter accepts the accession.[10] By comparison, the Convention on the Service Abroad of Judicial and Extrajudicial Documents in Civil or Commercial Matters will not enter into force for an acceding State should any Contracting State that ratified that Convention prior to the deposit of the instrument of ratification object to the accession within six months of the notification from the depositary of the deposit of the instrument of accession.[11]

The Judgments Convention is unlike many of the earlier conventions adopted by the Hague Conference. This Convention would require Contracting States, with very limited exceptions, to recognize and enforce foreign judgments in civil or commercial matters. Where other Conventions of the Hague Conference have required recognition or enforcement of foreign judgments, they have been rather narrow in scope.[12] Some delegations to the Diplomatic Session that adopted the Convention expressed concern about the potential for support amongst national legislatures for a convention that would require one Contracting State to recognize and enforce all judgments within the scope of the Convention, albeit with some bases for refusal,[13] from all other Contracting States.[14] As a result of these concerns, an article addressing the establishment of relations pursuant to the Convention was included. This article permits a Contracting State to limit its obligations pursuant to the Convention to a subset of the other Contracting States. 9.23

Pursuant to Article 29(1), the Convention shall have effect between two Contracting States if neither has notified the depositary, in accordance with either Article 29(2) or Article 29(3), that the Convention shall not have effect between it and the other Contracting State. 9.24

[8] Convention Abolishing the Requirement of Legalisation for Foreign Public Documents, done at The Hague, 5 October 1961, art 12; Convention on the Protection of Children and Co-operation in Respect of Intercountry Adoption, done at The Hague, 29 May 1993, art 44(3).

[9] Convention on the International Recovery of Child Support and Other Forms of Family Maintenance, done at The Hague, 23 November 2007, art 58(5).

[10] Convention on the Taking of Evidence Abroad in Civil or Commercial Matters, done at The Hague, 18 March 1970, art 39; Convention on the Civil Aspects of International Child Abduction, done at The Hague, 25 October 1980, art 38.

[11] Convention on the Service Abroad of Judicial and Extrajudicial Documents in Civil or Commercial Matters, done at The Hague, 15 November 1965, art 28.

[12] See, eg, the Convention on Jurisdiction, Applicable Law, Recognition, Enforcement and Co-operation in Respect of Parental Responsibility and Measures for the Protection of Children, done at The Hague, 19 October 1996; the Convention on Choice of Court Agreements, done at The Hague, 30 June 2005; and the Convention on the International Recovery of Child Support and Other Forms of Family Maintenance, done at The Hague, 23 November 2007.

[13] Where a judgment comes from a court of a problematic State from the perspective of the Contracting State being asked to recognize or enforce the judgment, the latter Contracting State may refuse to recognize or enforce the judgment for any of the reasons identified in art 7(1). Art 7(1)(c) ('Recognition or enforcement may be refused if—recognition or enforcement would be manifestly incompatible with the public policy of the requested State, including situations where the specific proceedings leading to the judgment were incompatible with fundamental principles of procedural fairness of that State and situations involving infringements of security or sovereignty of that State') might be the most relevant basis in such a situation.

[14] See, eg, opening statement of the head of the US delegation to the Diplomatic Conference. Office of the Legal Adviser, United States Department of State, *Digest of United States Practice in International Law 2019*, at 481, <https://2017-2021.state.gov/digest-of-united-states-practice-in-international-law-2019/index.html>.

Pursuant to Article 32(c), the depositary shall notify Members of the Hague Conference and other States and REIOs that have signed, ratified, accepted, approved, or acceded to the Convention, of such a notification.

9.25 For any two Contracting States for which neither Contracting State notifies the depositary about the other, the Convention shall have effect once it is in force for both Contracting States.

9.26 Article 29(2) applies when a Contracting State is notified by the depositary that another State has ratified, accepted, approved, or acceded to the Convention. If the Contracting State does not want the Convention to have effect between it and the other State, the Contracting State may so notify the depositary within twelve months after the depositary's notification pursuant to Article 32(a) of the ratification, acceptance, approval, or accession.

9.27 Article 29(3) applies when a second Contracting State does not want the Convention to have effect between it and an existing Contracting State. In such a situation, the second Contracting State may so notify the depositary when the second Contracting State deposits with the depositary pursuant to Article 24(4) its instrument of ratification, acceptance, approval, or accession.

9.28 A Contracting State that has notified the depositary that the Convention shall not have effect between it and another Contracting State may withdraw that notification at any time. Pursuant to Article 29(4), such a withdrawal shall take effect on the first day of the month following the expiration of three months after the date on which the Contracting State notified the depositary of the withdrawal of the notification. Once the withdrawal takes effect, the Convention shall have effect between the Contracting State that had originally notified the depositary and the Contracting State with respect to which the original notification had been made. Pursuant to Article 16, the Convention applies to judgments for which proceedings were instituted in the State of origin after the Convention has effect between the State of origin and the requested State.

VII. Article 30—Declarations

Article 30
Declarations

1. **Declarations referred to in Articles 14, 17, 18, 19 and 25 may be made upon signature, ratification, acceptance, approval or accession or at any time thereafter, and may be modified or withdrawn at any time.**
2. **Declarations, modifications and withdrawals shall be notified to the depositary.**
3. **A declaration made at the time of signature, ratification, acceptance, approval or accession shall take effect simultaneously with the entry into force of this Convention for the State concerned.**
4. **A declaration made at a subsequent time, and any modification or withdrawal of a declaration, shall take effect on the first day of the month following the expiration of three months following the date on which the notification is received by the depositary.**
5. **A declaration made at a subsequent time, and any modification or withdrawal of a declaration, shall not apply to judgments resulting from proceedings that have already been instituted before the court of origin when the declaration takes effect.**

The Judgments Convention contains elections for each Contracting State to make to tailor the application of the Convention to that State. In particular: 9.29

(1) Article 14(3) permits a Contracting State to declare that all or a subset of its courts shall not apply Article 14(1);[15]
(2) Article 17 permits a Contracting State to declare that its courts may refuse to recognize or enforce a judgment given by a court of another Contracting State if the parties were resident in the requested State, and the relationship of the parties and all other elements relevant to the dispute, other than the location of the court of origin, were connected only with the requested State;
(3) Article 18 permits a Contracting State to declare that it will not apply the Convention to a particular matter;[16]
(4) Article 19(1) permits a Contracting State to declare that it shall not apply the Convention to judgments arising from proceedings to which that State or a government agency of that State, or a natural person acting for that State or a government agency, is a party;[17] and
(5) Article 25(1) permits a Contracting State that has two or more territorial units in which different systems of law apply in relation to matters dealt with in the Convention to declare that the Convention shall extend to all or only some of these territorial units.

A Contracting State may make any of these declarations at any time, including at the time of signature, ratification, acceptance, approval, or accession. Similarly, a Contracting State may modify or withdraw a declaration at any time.

A Contracting State must notify the depositary of any declaration or any modification or withdrawal thereof. Pursuant to Article 32(c), the depositary shall notify Members of the Hague Conference and other States and REIOs that have signed, ratified, accepted, approved, or acceded to the Convention, of such a declaration, modification or withdrawal. 9.30

If a Contracting State notifies the depositary of a declaration at the time it signs the Convention or deposits its instrument of ratification, acceptance, approval, or accession with the depositary pursuant to Article 24(4), such declaration takes effect when the Convention enters into force for that Contracting State. 9.31

If a Contracting State makes, modifies, or withdraws a declaration after it signs the Convention or after it deposits its instrument of ratification, acceptance, approval, or accession with the depositary pursuant to Article 24(4), such declaration, modification, or withdrawal takes effect on the first day of the month following the expiration of three 9.32

[15] Pursuant to art 14(1), 'No security, bond or deposit, however described, shall be required from a party who in one Contracting State applies for enforcement of a judgment given by a court of another Contracting State on the sole ground that such party is a foreign national or is not domiciled or resident in the State in which enforcement is sought'.

[16] Pursuant to art 18(1), a Contracting State may make this declaration '[w]here [it] has a strong interest in not applying this Convention to a specific matter'.

[17] Art 19(1) clarifies that '[t]he State making such a declaration shall ensure that the declaration is no broader than necessary and that the exclusion from scope is clearly and precisely defined. The declaration shall not distinguish between judgments where the State, a government agency of that State or a natural person acting for either of them is a defendant or claimant in the proceedings before the court of origin.'

months from the date on which the notification of the declaration, or its modification or withdrawal, is received by the depositary. However, pursuant to Article 30(5), such a declaration, including a modification or withdrawal of a declaration, made by a Contracting State after it deposits its instrument of ratification, acceptance, approval, or accession shall not apply to any judgment that results from proceedings that were instituted before the court of origin before the declaration takes effect.

VIII. Article 31—Denunciation

Article 31
Denunciation

1. **A Contracting State to this Convention may denounce it by a notification in writing addressed to the depositary. The denunciation may be limited to certain territorial units of a non-unified legal system to which this Convention applies.**
2. **The denunciation shall take effect on the first day of the month following the expiration of 12 months after the date on which the notification is received by the depositary. Where a longer period for the denunciation to take effect is specified in the notification, the denunciation shall take effect upon the expiration of such longer period after the date on which the notification is received by the depositary.**

9.33 Article 31 provides a mechanism by which a Contracting State may withdraw from (or denounce) the Convention. The Contracting State may denounce the Convention for the entire State or, if the State has two or more territorial units in which different systems of law apply in relation to matters dealt with in the Convention, for certain territorial units of that State.

9.34 A Contracting State denouncing the Convention must provide written notification to the depositary of the denunciation. Pursuant to Article 32(d), the depositary shall notify Members of the Hague Conference and other States and REIOs that have signed, ratified, accepted, approved, or acceded to the Convention, of such denunciation.

9.35 Any denunciation takes effect on the first day of the month following the expiration of twelve months from the date on which the depositary receives notification of the denunciation. A Contracting State may undertake a longer period for the denunciation to become effective by identifying the longer period in the notification of the denunciation.

9.36 As a result of a denunciation, a State will no longer have any obligations pursuant to the Convention.

IX. Article 32—Notifications by the Depositary

Article 32
Notifications by the depositary

The depositary shall notify the Members of the Hague Conference on Private International Law, and other States and Regional Economic Integration Organisations which have signed,

ratified, accepted, approved or acceded to this Convention in accordance with Articles 24, 26 and 27 of the following—

(a) the signatures, ratifications, acceptances, approvals and accessions referred to in Articles 24, 26 and 27;

(b) the date on which this Convention enters into force in accordance with Article 28;

(c) the notifications, declarations, modifications and withdrawals referred to in Articles 26, 27, 29 and 30; and

(d) the denunciations referred to in Article 31.

Consistent with general treaty practice, the depositary (the Ministry of Foreign Affairs of the Kingdom of the Netherlands) is responsible for notifying States of certain treaty-related actions. These notifications are particularly relevant for the Judgments Convention, which allows each Contracting State to make declarations regarding the manner in which it will implement the Convention and to decide that the Convention shall not have effect between that State and another Contracting State. **9.37**

In particular, the Depositary shall notify the Members of the Hague Conference and other States and REIOs that have signed, ratified, accepted, approved, or acceded to the Convention of the following: **9.38**

(1) Signatures of the Convention by States or REIOs;
(2) Deposit of instruments of ratification, acceptance, approval, or accession by States or REIOs;
(3) Dates of entry into force of the Convention;
(4) Notifications, declarations, modifications, and withdrawals by States and REIOs; and
(5) Notifications of denunciation from States and REIOs.

10

The Place of the Convention in Current Practice in the United States

I. Introduction

As is discussed in Chapter 2 of this book, courts in the United States have been receptive to the recognition and enforcement of foreign judgments for over a century. The basis for, and contours of, this practice has evolved since the US Supreme Court decided *Hilton v Guyot*[1] in 1895. However, litigants in the United States have not had a reliable expectation that the judgments they obtain in a court in the United States will be recognized or enforced by a foreign court. The Convention on the Recognition and Enforcement of Foreign Judgments in Civil or Commercial Matters might finally result in such an expectation. **10.01**

In *Hilton v Guyot*, the US Supreme Court concluded that: **10.02**

> where there has been opportunity for a full and fair trial abroad before a court of competent jurisdiction, conducting the trial upon regular proceedings, after due citation or voluntary appearance of the defendant, and under a system of jurisprudence likely to secure an impartial administration of justice between the citizens of its own country and those of other countries, and there is nothing to show either prejudice in the court, or in the system of laws under which it was sitting, or fraud in procuring the judgment, or any other special reason why the comity of this nation should not allow it full effect, the merits of the case should not, in an action brought in this country upon the judgment, be tried afresh, as on a new trial or an appeal, upon the mere assertion of the party that the judgment was erroneous in law or in fact.[2]

In 1938, the US Supreme Court decided *Erie Railroad v Tompkins*, in which it determined that where federal courts are exercising diversity jurisdiction,[3] they are to apply the substantive **10.03**

[1] 159 US 113 (1895).

[2] 159 US 202–03.

[3] See 28 USC § 1332. In particular, § 1332(a) provides:

law of the relevant US state, including the common law of that state.[4] Both state and federal courts have subsequently looked to the applicable state law concerning the recognition and enforcement of judgments rather than relying on the entirety of the Supreme Court decision in *Hilton v Guyot*.[5] However, the US Supreme Court has not decided whether federal or state law governs the recognition or enforcement of foreign judgments. Nonetheless, '[t]he consensus among the state courts and lower federal courts that have passed upon the question is that, apart from federal question cases, such recognition is governed by [s]tate law and that the federal courts will apply the law of the state in which they sit'.[6]

II. The Existing Uniform Acts

10.04 The Uniform Law Commission of the United States recognized that, prior to 1962, most states in the United States had not codified a law on the recognition of foreign judgments.[7] On the assumption that the enactment of state law on the topic might serve to encourage foreign courts to recognize judgments from courts in the United States as a matter of reciprocity, the Uniform Law Commission embarked on the drafting of a uniform act to be enacted by US states.[8] In 1962, the Uniform Law Commission approved, and recommended for US state enactment, the Uniform Foreign Money-Judgments Recognition Act (the '1962 Recognition Act'). The 1962 Recognition Act has been enacted, at some point, in thirty-two states.[9]

10.05 Over time, as case law developed regarding the application of the 1962 Recognition Act, the Uniform Law Commission decided to draft a new uniform act that clarified the provisions of the 1962 Recognition Act and corrected interpretive problems.[10] As a result, in 2005, the Uniform Law Commission approved, and recommended for US state adoption, the Uniform Foreign-Country Money Judgments Recognition Act ('the 2005 Recognition Act'). The 2005 Recognition Act has been enacted by thirty US states.[11]

The district courts shall have original jurisdiction of all civil actions where the matter in controversy exceeds the sum or value of $75,000, exclusive of interest and costs, and is between—(1) citizens of different [s]tates; (2) citizens of a [S]tate and citizens or subjects of a foreign [S]tate, except that the district courts shall not have original jurisdiction under this subsection of an action between citizens of a [s]tate and citizens or subjects of a foreign [S]tate who are lawfully admitted for permanent residence in the United States and are domiciled in the same [s]tate; (3) citizens of different [s]tates and in which citizens or subjects of a foreign [S]tate are additional parties; and (4) a foreign [S]tate, defined in section 1603(a) of this title, as plaintiff and citizens of a [s]tate or of different [s]tates.

[4] *Erie R.R. v Tompkins*, 304 US 64 (1938).

[5] See, eg, Ronald A Brand, 'New Challenges in the Recognition and Enforcement of Judgments' in Franco Ferrari and Diego P Fernandez Arroyo (eds), *The Continuing Relevance of Private International Law and Its Challenges* (Edward Elgar Publishing 2019) 360–89, <https://papers.ssrn.com/sol3/papers.cfm?abstract_id=3246053>.

[6] Restatement, Second, Conflict of Laws, Revised, § 98, cmt. c. Federal question jurisdiction is established by 28 USC § 1331 ('The district courts shall have original jurisdiction of all civil actions arising under the Constitution, laws, or treaties of the United States').

[7] See 1962 Uniform Foreign Money-Judgments Recognition Act, Prefatory Note.

[8] ibid.

[9] Uniform Law Commission, The Uniform Foreign-Country Money Judgments Recognition Act, A Summary, <https://higherlogicdownload.s3-external-1.amazonaws.com/UNIFORMLAWS/Eh7AmUDZSPanFqdvrTey_UFCMJRA_Summary.pdf?AWSAccessKeyId = AKIAVRDO7IEREB57R7MT&Expires = 1670886133&Signature = Lhmfzx02 IuJ8hAMb3Pn5z%2FvQNVA%3D>.

[10] See 2005 Uniform Foreign-Country Money Judgments Recognition Act, Prefatory Note.

[11] Uniform Law Commission, <https://www.uniformlaws.org/committees/ community-home?communitykey = ae280c30–094a-4d8f-b722–8dcd614a8f3e&tab = groupdetails> accessed 12 December 2022. Some of the US states that had enacted the 1962 Recognition Act also enacted the 2005 Recognition Act and repealed, or amended, the former act.

The Judgments Convention provides a significant point of departure from the 1962 and 2005 uniform acts and existing common law in US states. Were the United States to become a party to the Convention, it would create an international obligation on courts in the United States to recognize and enforce certain foreign judgments. While doing so, it will also impose an international obligation on other Contracting States to recognize and enforce judgments issued by courts in the United States. This result is intended to promote global commerce and facilitate the cross-border movement of persons and goods.[12] **10.06**

III. Looking Ahead—US Options Upon Ratification

In its considerations of whether to sign and ratify the Convention, the US government will need to decide how to properly implement the Convention domestically. Options available to the United States include implementation through federal law, state law, or a combination thereof. **10.07**

A. A Self-Executing Treaty Approach

Should the United States decide to implement the Convention exclusively through federal law, it may decide to authorize courts to rely on the text of the Convention itself or it may decide to enact federal legislation. Pursuant to the US Constitution, 'all Treaties made, or which shall be made, under the Authority of the United States, shall be the supreme Law of the Land; and the Judges in every [s]tate shall be bound thereby, any Thing in the Constitution or Laws of any [s]tate to the Contrary notwithstanding'.[13] **10.08**

The United States may decide to treat the Convention as a self-executing treaty, with the result that courts would look directly to the provisions of the Convention as the source of the applicable law.[14] In considering whether the Convention should be self-executing, matters such as the following will need to be considered: (1) whether the Convention should be implemented at the federal level; (2) whether there is sufficient constitutional authority to implement the Convention at the federal level; (3) whether the Convention language contains rules capable of providing rights in US courts without further legislation; (4) whether courts might benefit from additional detail to be found in implementing legislation; (5) what domestic law already exists that might facilitate the implementation of the Convention; (6) whether there might be confusion between the Convention and the 1962 Recognition Act and the 2005 Recognition Act such that additional federal legislation might be helpful; and (7) whether changes to state law, to include the 1962 Recognition Act and the 2005 Recognition Act, might be appropriate. **10.09**

[12] See 18 June 2019 statement of Michael Coffee to the Twenty-Second Diplomatic Session. Digest of United States Practice in International Law 2019, Chapter 15, 482–83, <https://www.state.gov/digest-of-united-states-practice-in-international-law/> ('Coffee Statement').

[13] US Constitution, art VI.

[14] For a discussion of self-execution of treaties, see Duncan B Hollis and Carlos Manuel Vazquez, 'Treaty Self-Execution as "Foreign" Foreign Relations Law' in Curtis A Bradley (ed), *The Oxford Handbook of Comparative Foreign Relations Law* (online edn, OUP 2019).

10.10 If the United States decides that the Convention should be treated as a self-executing treaty, the President and the Senate may agree to this when the Senate considers whether to provide its advice and consent to US ratification of the Convention.

B. Federal Statutory Implementation

10.11 Alternatively, in considering factors such as those identified above, the United States might decide that it is appropriate that a federal statute be enacted to address the implementation of the Convention. Should the United States decide to implement the Convention exclusively through a federal statute, and not by the direct application of the Convention, both the Senate and the House of Representatives would need to agree to the content of that statute.[15] The President may propose the content of such legislation.[16]

C. Coordination with State Law

10.12 Given the years of practice in the United States in which state law has been relied upon for the recognition and enforcement of foreign judgments, it is likely that attorneys and judges have become accustomed to looking to state law on this topic. That law is likely to continue to apply to matters falling outside the scope of the Judgments Convention and for judgments from States that are not Contracting States to the Convention. US state law might also have some impact through Article 15 of the Convention.

10.13 US implementation of a treaty through coordination with state law can be a complicated matter, however. As the United States, and not the individual states, would be party to the treaty with the obligations that flow from the treaty, the federal government would be responsible for US compliance with its treaty obligations. Were the Convention to be implemented entirely or in part by state law, that law would need to properly implement the Convention to ensure that the United States complies with its international obligations. The US Constitution does not authorize the federal government to require that the states enact particular legislation in support of treaty ratification and implementation. However, the Constitution does allow the federal government to preempt state legislation contrary to federal interests. In addition, the Constitution permits the federal government to use incentives to encourage the states to enact legislation.[17]

10.14 Against this constitutional construct, the federal government may rely on what is referred to as 'cooperative federalism' for the implementation of the Convention at the federal

[15] Even with federal legislation, the Senate would need to separately provide its advice and consent to US ratification of the Convention before the United States may deposit its instrument of ratification of the Convention.

[16] See, eg, Letter of Transmittal from the President to the Senate for the Hague Convention on the International Recovery of Child Support and Other Forms of Family Maintenance, adopted at The Hague on 23 November 2007, Treaty Doc 110–21 ('The Departments of State and Health and Human Services have been working on preparation of the necessary amendments to Federal law to ensure compliance with the Convention, and that legislation will soon be ready for submission to the Congress for its consideration').

[17] See *New York v United States*, 505 US 144, 188 (1992), although that case focused on state regulations rather than legislation.

and state levels.[18] There are two available options within cooperative federalism: (1) conditional preemption and (2) conditional spending.

Pursuant to conditional preemption, a federal statute may be enacted on a particular topic with the result that federal law will apply to that topic. However, the federal statute will allow for a state statute to apply instead if the state statute meets conditions identified in the federal statute.[19] Ultimately, a court presented with a particular matter would need to decide whether it would apply the federal statute or a relevant state statute, if that state statute satisfies the conditions identified in the federal law. This methodology can be expected to present significant issues in determining which courts will provide the ultimate authority on interpretation, which could complicate the interpretation of both the statute and the treaty. Of course, final authority for treaty interpretation within the US legal system would lie with the US Supreme Court. **10.15**

Pursuant to conditional spending, the federal government might subject the provision of federal funding to a particular state to certain conditions. One such condition might include state enactment of particular legislation.[20] Unlike with conditional preemption, there might not be a fallback federal statute that would address the substance that would be contained in the state statute. Therefore, it would be necessary that all states enact statutes that would enable the United States to comply with its treaty obligations. As a result, should conditional spending be relied upon, it would be important to identify a significant amount of money of sufficient importance to states to entice them to enact, without substantial modification, particular legislation. The requirement of a funding source in the federal government reduces the likelihood that this option will be selected. **10.16**

Should the United States decide to utilize cooperative federalism in the implementation of the Convention, it is likely that the federal government would work with the Uniform Law Commission.[21] As indicated above, the Uniform Law Commission drafted and approved the 1962 Recognition Act and the 2005 Recognition Act. It is, therefore, reasonable to expect that this body would want to review these acts to determine what, if any, changes would be needed for purposes of giving effect to the Convention.[22] **10.17**

[18] For a description of cooperative federalism and its history, see Eric M Fish, 'The Uniform Interstate Support Act (UIFSA) 2008: Enforcing International Obligations Through Cooperative Federalism' (2011) 24 J Am Acad Matrimonial Law 33.

[19] See, eg, Electronic Signatures in Global and National Commerce Act, Pub L No 106–229, § 102 (codified at 15 USC 7002).

[20] In the United States, the Hague Convention on the International Recovery of Child Support and Other Forms of Family Maintenance is implemented through a combination of federal and state statutes involving conditional spending. The federal implementing legislation can be found in Title III of the Preventing Sex Trafficking and Strengthening Families Act Pub L No 113–83, which amended 42 USC Chapter 7, Subchapter IV, Part D (§§ 651–669b) to encourage US states, the District of Columbia, and several territories to enact a revised version of the Uniform Law Commission's Uniform Interstate Family Support Act.

[21] Since 1892, the Uniform Law Commission (also known as the National Conference of Commissioners on Uniform State Laws) has promoted the principle of uniformity by drafting and proposing specific statutes in areas of the law where uniformity between the States is desirable.

[22] The federal government has worked with the Uniform Law Commission on actual or potential implementation of multiple private international law treaties. The Uniform Law Commission adopted changes to its Uniform Interstate Family Support Act to give effect to the provisions of the Hague Child Support Convention. Similarly, the Uniform Law Commission has adopted changes to its Uniform Child Custody Jurisdiction and Enforcement Act (UCCJEA) to give effect to the provisions of the Hague Convention on Jurisdiction, Applicable Law, Recognition, Enforcement and Co-operation in Respect of Parental Responsibility and Measures for the Protection of Children ('the Child Protection Convention'), should the United States become party to that treaty.

D. Article 15 and Convention Implementation

10.18 Independent of the manner in which the Convention is to be implemented in the United States, it would be appropriate for the federal government and state governments to conduct a more holistic review of the manner in which foreign judgments are, and should be, recognized and enforced in the United States. According to Article 15 of the Convention, the Convention 'does not prevent the recognition or enforcement of judgments under national law'.[23] Therefore, legislatures may be afforded the opportunity to consider how to recognize and enforce all foreign judgments, or, at a minimum, those foreign judgments for which recognition or enforcement is not required by the Convention. A potential benefit of such an exercise is the creation of a regime whereby a party might seek to have a foreign judgment recognized or enforced pursuant to the principal mechanism included in the Convention (with a resulting focus on the connecting factors found in art 5(1)) or instead pursuant to otherwise-applicable domestic law (through the application of art 15), provided that such otherwise-applicable domestic law is consistent with the Convention.

IV. External Issues of Implementation

10.19 Regardless of the method of implementation, parties and courts in the United States should be cognizant of the effect of the Convention and the resulting implementation process when recognition or enforcement of a judgment might be sought in a foreign court. This will additionally require consideration of whether any change in judicial practice should be reflected in statute, court rules, or merely left to develop through practice. The primary issue to be considered is whether judgments, to include any accompanying opinions, address matters that might assist a foreign court in deciding whether to recognize or enforce the judgment pursuant to the Convention. For example, Article 5(1) identifies requirements that make a judgment eligible for recognition and enforcement pursuant to the Convention. Were a court in the United States to include in its opinion whether the facts when it exercised jurisdiction would satisfy one of the connecting factors in Article 5(1) in the particular case, this might facilitate recognition and enforcement. Similarly, Article 7 provides the grounds for refusal of recognition or enforcement. A court issuing a judgment might want to include in the judgment, or accompanying opinion, information that might be relevant to a foreign court's consideration of Article 7. However, it might not be clear at the time that the judgment is issued that recognition or enforcement will be sought pursuant to the Convention. As a result, should courts in the United States decide that they should include connecting factor information in their opinions for purposes of the Convention, they might need to decide whether to do so for all or only a subset of judgments.[24]

[23] The role of art 15 in implementation of the treaty generally is discussed in Chapter 2.

[24] The Child Protection Convention (n 22) provides for recognition and enforcement of certain foreign judgments. The Child Protection Convention, art 23, allows a Contracting State to recognize a foreign judgment in certain situations. The Uniform Law Commission drafted and adopted revisions to the UCCJEA (n 22) to facilitate the implementation of the Child Protection Convention. The revised UCCJEA authorizes a litigating party to

Another issue that the United States will need to address, should it become party to the Convention, is the process the US government will follow in applying Article 29 (Establishment of relations pursuant to the Convention).[25] This mechanism was important to the United States during the negotiation of the Convention.[26] Article 29(2) gives a Contracting State twelve months after the date of notification of a ratification, acceptance, approval, or accession of another State to notify the depositary that such action shall not have the effect of establishing relations between the two States pursuant to the Convention. This is a somewhat novel provision and will require that the United States identify a process by which it will consider the possibility of the establishment of relations with other States pursuant to the Convention. In addition to a process, the United States will need to identify the types of information that it will want to consider in making any decision regarding Article 29. **10.20**

V. Conclusion

No matter how the Convention is implemented in the United States, it should provide significant benefits to persons who have litigated in courts in the United States. **10.21**

request that the court include relevant information in its determination or findings. In particular, the revised s 211 UCCJEA would provide that:

(a) If requested by a party, a court of this state that makes or modifies a child-custody determination or orders or modifies a decision with regard to a child to which [Article] 4 applies shall include in the determination or decision the court's findings and conclusions on the following:
   (1) the basis for the assumption of jurisdiction by the court;
   (2) the manner in which notice and opportunity to be heard was given to each person entitled to notice of the proceeding;
   (3) the opportunity for the child to be heard or the reasons why the child was not heard; and
   (4) the country of the habitual residence of the child.
(b) A child-custody determination or a decision with regard to a child to which [Article] 4 applies may be supplemented at any time to include the findings and conclusions described in subsection (a) without the supplement being construed as a modification.

Uniform Child-Custody Jurisdiction and Enforcement Act (with 2013 Amendments Pertaining to International Proceedings), s 211. The comment accompanying s 211 observes that '[i]t is meant to help those parents who contemplate possible foreign enforcement of a child custody determination, or measure of protection, under Article 4, that, when entered, is a solely domestic United States proceeding'.

[25] See paras 9.21–9.28 for analysis of art 29.
[26] See Coffee Statement (n 12).

11

Final Comments and Thoughts About the Future

I. Introduction

We conclude this book with three general points. First, taken in its entirety and on balance, the 2019 Hague Judgments Convention is an important positive development for transnational litigation in that it provides a framework in one document for the recognition and enforcement of a significant number of foreign country judgments. Second, however, we believe that some of its central provisions will prove to be flawed and anachronistic. Third, there are measures available that should be explored and utilized to limit these problems. **11.01**

II. The Convention Is an Improvement Over the Status Quo

The Convention potentially improves recognition and enforcement practice in transnational litigation, both from the perspective of litigants and States generally, and from the perspective of those holding judgments from courts in the United States in particular. It represents a general improvement by replacing the current patchwork of confusing and often conflicting local, bilateral, and regional mechanisms with a global instrument for the regulation of judgments that fall within its scope. The Convention rules may assist in reducing transaction costs in transnational litigation by providing in one document a set of rules addressing the recognition and enforcement of civil or commercial judgments that meet certain descriptions or requirements identified in the Convention. This will be particularly useful to holders of US judgments, who have had to navigate a maze of requirements imposed by foreign States, often to find themselves frustrated by parochial provisions in those States. Anecdotally, these requirements may serve to discourage holders of judgments from the United States from attempting to seek recognition or enforcement of those judgments. **11.02**

III. The Convention Contains Significant Flaws

11.03 While the Convention offers significant benefits over the existing global framework for judgments recognition, it brings with it significant flaws in architecture and in substance that appear to make it already anachronistic and inadequate in some respects and will make it increasingly and predictably less adaptable to future developments, including being far more likely to yield results that bear little resemblance to the underlying realities of modern global mobility. As we have noted, the choice to structure the text of Articles 5 and 6, so that the criteria of eligibility for recognition or enforcement are derived largely from the pre-existing Brussels regime of the European Union (EU), results in a framework that is logically complex and cumbersome, and not particularly amenable to uniform interpretation and application of the Convention. By tying the core criteria of eligibility for recognition and enforcement to twentieth-century terminology and concepts that rely heavily on the physical location of persons or on formal aspects of transactions, events, and activities, rather than taking account of developments in technology and the non-tangible (and thus difficult to restrict to one particular geographic location) nature of many twenty-first-century relationships, the criteria of eligibility for judgment circulation are already outdated and incapable of dealing with many significant real-world developments—often the same developments that must establish the need for a global instrument of this type.

11.04 While we have provided extensive analysis of the linguistic and logical structure of the provisions of the Convention, with careful attention to Article 5 in particular, it is also worth taking some time in this conclusion to make the point here that the provisions in Article 5 have been and are being field tested—and have shown themselves not to be well-suited for a convention of global applicability. The Brussels regime experience has demonstrated that, even on a regional basis with a single court in control of interpretation of similar rules, it has been difficult to achieve clear interpretation and application of those rules.[1] Even a small sample of recent cases from the Court of Justice of the European Union (CJEU) in 2020 and 2021 demonstrates this problem. These rules and approaches are likely to fare no better on a global scale of diverse legal views and practices.

11.05 The CJEU cases involve a sample of issues routinely presented in current and future recognition and enforcement practice, such as what is civil or commercial, what is a sovereign and when is its immunity implicated, what is the place of occurrence of a harm, what is a 'centre of interest',[2] and what is the extent of jurisdiction that a 'centre of interest' brings in its train. The cases involve relatively simple facts and issues compared to the increasing complexity of transnational litigation: parking fees, tampering with a product, and related issues such as infringement of privacy by publication, and interlocutory proceedings against a foreign State corporation.[3] The results exhibit a variety of critical flaws.

[1] This section of this chapter borrows heavily from Paul Herrup and Ronald A Brand, 'A Hague Convention on Parallel Proceedings' (2022) 63 Harv Int'l LJ Online 1, <https://harvardilj.org/2022/02/a-hague-convention-on-parallel-proceedings/> and <https://papers.ssrn .com/sol3/papers.cfm?abstract_id = 3894502>.

[2] Although the Judgments Convention does not include the term 'centre of interest', it is included in the EU Regulations and relates to analysis that will likely be undertaken with respect to some of the factors identified in art 5(1).

[3] While some of these issues are formally outside of the scope of the Judgments Convention, they are likely to exist in recognition and enforcement practice.

Verein fur Konsumenteninformation v Volkswagen AG[4] involved construing the 'place where the harmful event occurred' test of Article 7(2) of the Brussels I (Recast) Regulation,[5] in the context of the 'Dieselgate' affair and the resulting products liability actions brought on behalf of automobile purchasers in a number of countries. The CJEU held that 'where a manufacturer in a Member State has unlawfully equipped its vehicles with software that manipulates data relating to exhaust gas emissions before those vehicles are purchased from a third party in another Member State, the place where the damage occurs is in that latter Member State'.[6] The CJEU opted for a test that avoided any requirement of foreseeability and instead relied on factors unique to the action by the particular defendant in the 'Dieselgate' affair. Such a simple and mechanistic legal test ignores the underlying realities of harm and injury—particularly when dealing with an inherently mobile object (a car), which can be subject to frequent re-sale in a string of purchases.[7] Right or wrong, however, the case and the test indicate the difficulties that come with the use of a rule such as that found in Article 7(2) of the Brussels I (Recast) Regulation. 11.06

The *Obala* case, decided by the CJEU on 25 March 2021, provides a more telling indication of potential problems of a global system of connecting factors based on the Brussels regime.[8] There the Court determined that: (1) an action for recovery of a parking fee is a 'civil and commercial matter' within Article 1(1) of the Brussels I (Recast) Regulation; (2) a ticket issued when a person parks an automobile is not a 'tenancy of immovable property' within Article 24(1) of the Brussels I (Recast) Regulation; and (3) a ticket issued when a person parks an automobile is a contract for the provision of services within Article 7(1)(b) of the Brussels I (Recast) Regulation.[9] These results are counter-intuitive in many legal systems, to say the least. The myriad of potential problems for predictability and uniformity of interpretation of the global Judgments Convention with similar connecting factors in Article 5(1) are almost unlimited. 11.07

Other Brussels regime cases before the CJEU during this period demonstrate similar problems and similar issues even though the specific provisions do not have literal counterparts in the Judgments Convention.[10] 11.08

[4] Case C-343/19 (2 April 2020) ('AG Dieselgate Opinion').

[5] Regulation (EU) No 1215/2012 of the European Parliament and of the Council of 12 December 2012 on Jurisdiction and the Recognition and Enforcement of Judgments in Civil and Commercial Matters (Brussels I Recast Regulation) [2012] OJ L351/1, 20 December 2012 <https://eur-lex.europa.eu/legal-content/EN/ALL/?uri=celex%3A32012R1215>.

[6] AG Dieselgate Opinion (n 4) para 41.

[7] This recourse to a simple, mechanistic test should be contrasted with the complexities of the test to which the CJEU was driven in *Mittelbayerischer Verlag KG v SM*, Case C800/19 (17 June 2021), which again raised interpretation problems with the Brussels I (Recast) Regulation, art 7(2). In this case, the CJEU wrestled with the location of a claim that an individual's personality rights have been infringed by content published on a website. The Court ruled that 'the courts of the place in which the centre of interests' of that person bringing the claim could exercise jurisdiction under art 7(2) 'in respect of the entirety of the alleged damage, … only if that content contains objective and verifiable elements which make it possible to identify, directly or indirectly, that person as an individual' (para 47). Although the subject matter of this case would appear to fall outside of the scope of the Convention, the judgment illustrates potential difficulties of uniform interpretation and application on a global scale of such an analysis when multiple courts in Contracting States have final interpretive authority of the provisions of art 5(1) of the Convention.

[8] Case C-307/19 *Obala I lucice d.o.o. v NLB Leasing d.o.o.* (25 March 2021).

[9] ibid para 99.

[10] In Case C-641/18 *LJ and Others v Rina SpA* (7 May 2020) (First Chamber), the CJEU considered the difficult concerns raised by the Brussels regime when sovereign immunity is asserted on behalf of a State-owned entity. The Court concluded that '[t]he principle of customary international law concerning immunity from jurisdiction does not preclude the national court seised from exercising the jurisdiction provided for by [the Brussels I (Recast) Regulation] in a dispute relating to such an action, where that court finds that such corporations have not had recourse to public powers within the meaning of international law' (para 61). The case foreshadows the great

11.09 These cases arose in a period of only two years resulting from relatively simple situations, demonstrating problems of interpretation and technical evolution that will face the global Judgments Convention built upon tests requiring mechanical connecting factors. One of the principal goals of any Convention of the Hague Conference on Private International Law should be to improve the world of transnational litigation by reducing the time and expense involved. The litigant loss of time demonstrated in the two years of CJEU cases discussed foreshadow some of the difficulties that lie ahead for the Judgments Convention as the courts of each Contracting State undertake to interpret Article 5(1).

11.10 It is apparent from the record of the recent CJEU cases that applying the connecting factors used for direct jurisdiction purposes in the Brussels I (Recast) Regulation will not eliminate uncertainty, reduce litigation, or make resolution of real-world disputes easier or less expensive. Seemingly, the frequency of these challenges is on the increase: hardly a surprise given the complexities of global mobility, which simply cannot be accommodated by approaches such as Brussels Boxes, rooted as they are in nineteenth-century concepts of physical presence. And the Judgments Convention will not have the benefits of an apex tribunal to resolve issues of interpretation.

11.11 In addition to being increasingly anachronistic, the provisions in Articles 5 and 6 of the Judgments Convention demonstrate the logical and semantic complexity of their criteria of eligibility for recognition and enforcement. Those criteria create a dual challenge for judicial interpretation. First, in many States they will have to be applied without previous foundation in courts not familiar with this approach. On the other hand, those States that deploy words similar to those used in the Convention face a perhaps even more difficult challenge if they wish to honour the Convention's goal of uniformity in application.[11] In a global convention bedecked with terms that demand an autonomous Convention meaning rather than being captive to parochial national or regional usage, courts cannot operate properly on the basis of meanings and understandings that may have accumulated over time in the practice of specific States or regions based on their experience with instruments other than the Judgments Convention. These courts, if they are conscientious in giving autonomous meanings to Convention terms, will have to 'unlearn' past local interpretive practices.

11.12 Indeed, Articles 5 and 6 may create a perverse channelling effect away from use of the Convention. Insofar as local law on recognition and enforcement is simpler and more readily understood than the complexities of the Convention criteria of eligibility, local practitioners and judges may choose to seek recognition and enforcement under that local law, provided that the results of the application of such local law is consistent with the obligations contained in the Convention.[12]

difficulty in expanding the analysis to a global treaty context. Similar issues of sovereignty and jurisdiction were raised in Case C-73/19 *Belgische Staat v Movic BV* (16 July 2020), where the question involved whether Belgian authorities, which had brought interlocutory proceedings against a foreign corporation, were acting in a public or private (commercial) manner and thus governed by the jurisdictional rules of the Brussels I (Recast) Regulation. See ibid paras 23–24. We note that art 2(5) of the Convention states that 'Nothing in this Convention shall affect privileges and immunities of States or of international organisations, in respect of themselves and of their property'.

[11] Judgments Convention, art 20 ('In the interpretation of this Convention, regard shall be had to its international character and to the need to promote uniformity in its application').

[12] Where the local law does more than implement the Judgments Convention, recognition and enforcement of judgments pursuant to this law is permitted by art 15 of the Convention.

IV. Potential for Post-Implementation Improvements

A. Bilateral and Regional Legal Laboratories

Regardless of the problems created by the structure found in Articles 5 and 6 of the Judgments Convention, the Convention is an improvement in the transnational litigation landscape. Nonetheless, its provisions will have to be interpreted and applied in ways that make sense in the context of dynamic global mobility, and that minimize any damage flowing from their potential inadequacies. We hope that our discussion of these articles in earlier chapters might contribute to this objective by illuminating the complexities and difficulties that we now describe. But this is simply a starting point. Serious thought informed by due attention to the shape of the real world must be given to preparation for the replacement provisions that can be substituted for many of the gateway rules found in Articles 5 and 6 if, and when, the opportunity presents itself for such replacement. Should the Contracting States decide later that the regime needs to be updated for the reasons we describe, they may negotiate a new treaty to replace the Judgments Convention. Alternatively, should the Contracting States seek to amend the existing Convention, the architecture of the Convention is such that Articles 5 and 6 may be replaced without too much damage to the remainder—if, and when, States again find the time and energy to address the task. Either approach, a new convention or an amendment of the existing convention, would involve complicated international and domestic procedures. 11.13

However, the Hague Conference has a serious challenge with overcoming parochial dogmatism. For understandable reasons, its solutions tend to mirror the domestic regimes of its most active, or largest grouping of, members, trying to create a bridge between those current regimes while preserving as much as possible of the current practices of the Member States. The problem is that, if current legal rules are not well-suited to current and predictable future realities, a bridge between these systems creates a not particularly good long-term instrument. 11.14

There is an opportunity for useful experimentation to see what actually works. One avenue to be followed will be developments in both direct and indirect jurisdiction in States. Jurisdiction rules represent value judgments by each sovereign as to the situations in which certain forms of State power should be exercised. As the world changes, and perhaps as values shift as well, these rules will and should be adapted to the changes. Article 15 of the Convention then permits Contracting States to recognize and enforce foreign judgments where the Convention does not require them to do so, subject to the restrictions of Article 6 on judgments relating to real property. 11.15

Another avenue for dealing with the problems created by the current structure may be through a series of bilateral, regional, or specialized agreements involving States with different legal systems, that can provide a laboratory for what works in a world in which many relationships do not involve the physical geographic presence required by the provisions of Articles 5 and 6 of the Judgments Convention. This, of course, may be combined with national experimentation. 11.16

As we discussed in Chapter 1, the Brussels regime model was not the only approach available for the architecture of the Judgments Convention.[13] A more flexible model was available that would have allowed evolution consistent with technical developments in methods 11.17

[13] See Chapter 1.

of trade as well as the concerns of uniformity of interpretation in multiple national courts. The bottom-up approach we suggest in Chapter 1 would have developed the text of the Convention by focusing on the problems of judgments recognition and then determining a solution that focuses on the needs of the international legal system rather than on existing rules in some legal systems that have been developed to deal with problems of a past age of commerce and human interaction. It is not necessary to restate that alternative model here. The decision on structure of the Convention was an early one in the negotiation of the Convention. With the Convention in place the more appropriate concern is with how it can and will be used going forward. However, it is our view that the alternative approach we explored in Chapter 1 warrants further, serious experimentation.

11.18 In addition, yet another model was available to the framers, and might be worth considering in other agreements. This model builds on a feature of international trade conventions—and one of the goals of this Convention, as stated in the Preamble, is to facilitate the development of international trade.

11.19 The Preamble of the Convention states that the Contracting Parties 'desir[e] ... to facilitate rule-based multilateral trade and investment'. This suggests that a desirable framework for recognition and enforcement of judgments across borders—the movement of a thing with potential value—should also consider the proven features of trade agreements. A fundamental rule found in just about every trade treaty is a rule of non-discrimination.[14] Contracting States to trade treaties take on reciprocal obligations in order to create an international system that is fair and balanced. Article 5(1) does not necessarily result in balance. Rather, through the choice of a specific set of connecting factors, it allows for the possibility that some States will have broader rules relating to the exercise of jurisdiction for their courts than those rules applied to determine whether the basis upon which a foreign court exercised jurisdiction will warrant the recognition or enforcement of a judgment from that foreign court.

11.20 This possibility arises because some States have a gap between those bases of jurisdiction a State allows for purposes of direct jurisdiction to bring an action in its own courts and those bases of jurisdiction that same State considers to be sufficient when relied upon by the courts of other States resulting in judgments that are subsequently submitted to that State for recognition and enforcement. This gap reflects the discriminatory nature of these legal systems. This latter jurisdictional list is sometimes referred to as 'rules of indirect jurisdiction' as the court addressed for purposes of recognition and enforcement indirectly reviews the bases for the jurisdiction of the court of origin.[15] Many States have an identical set of bases of direct and indirect jurisdiction. Other States allow a broader reach in the bases of direct jurisdiction but apply narrower bases of indirect jurisdiction. If one believes that recognition and enforcement of foreign judgments serve to facilitate international trade, then

[14] See, eg, General Agreement on Tariffs and Trade, art III, opened for signature on 30 October 1947, 61 Stat pts 5 & 6, TIAS No 1700, 55 UNTS 187, reprinted in IV GATT, *Basic Instruments and Selected Documents* (1969) 1–78, as amended by the Final Act Embodying the Results of the Uruguay Round of Multilateral Trade Negotiations, opened for signature on 15 April 1994. See also Ronald A Brand, 'New Challenges in the Recognition and Enforcement of Judgments' in Franco Ferrari and Diego P Fernández Arroyo (eds), *Private International Law: Contemporary Challenges and Continuing Relevance* (Elgar 2019).

[15] See the discussion of direct and indirect jurisdiction rules in Chapter 1.

this latter group of States create a discriminatory system that effectively denies national treatment to foreign judgments on this basis.[16]

It would have been possible to draft a Judgments Convention without the complexity of Article 5(1).[17] Like the law in many States prior to the Convention, the gateway rule in the Convention could have been that a court addressed would recognize or enforce a judgment whenever the judgment was based on a rule of direct jurisdiction in the State of origin that also is an acceptable rule of direct jurisdiction in the State of the court addressed, subject to rules and discretion of the court addressed allowing non-recognition in specific circumstances. This would have brought a requirement of non-discrimination into the Convention. This is an option that remains available for subsequent bilateral, regional, or specialized agreements. 11.21

Unfortunately, Article 23(3) of the Convention might limit the willingness of States to consider such bilateral or regional experimentation. Article 23(3) is directed at the narrow possibility that two Contracting States to the Convention will enter into a subsequent agreement that might affect the treatment of a judgment issued in the courts of a third Contracting State. See note 32 in Chapter 8 for our thoughts on this provision. Given the deficiencies in this text and the need to gauge empirically how possible rules might work in the modern world, it is inadvisable to inhibit countries from trying small-scale experiments over time that might make sense, provided that the results are otherwise consistent with the Judgments Convention, even if there is an occasional over-extension which may be remedied in other fashions. 11.22

B. National Legal Laboratories

For Contracting States whose judgments recognition law does not contain a jurisdiction gap between direct and indirect jurisdiction rules, it is possible to implement the Convention in a way that both continues that positive element of non-discriminatory effect and complies with Convention rules. Under Article 15, Contracting States are not prohibited from recognizing and enforcing judgments beyond the requirements found in the Convention. Thus, the complexity and potential for non-uniform interpretation presented by the list of criteria of eligibility for recognition and enforcement found in Article 5(1) may be avoided by applying existing domestic law in order to recognize and enforce a judgment. Given the desirability of broader recognition and enforcement of judgments, it would be odd if a Contracting State used the Convention to restrict recognition and enforcement that would occur absent the Convention rules (other than as a result of the mandatory rule of art 6). This will allow States to continue to develop the law of judgments recognition beyond both the substantive and structural limitations of the Convention provided that Contracting States comply with their obligations undertaken when they became party to the Judgments Convention. The use of an Article 15 route to judgments recognition and enforcement may also offer courts the familiarity of domestic law as an alternative to the complexity and 11.23

[16] For a more complete discussion of this discriminatory jurisdiction gap, see Ronald A Brand, 'The Hague Judgments Convention in the United States: A "Game Changer" or a New Path to the Old Game?' (2021) 82 U Pitt L Rev 847, <https://papers.ssrn.com/sol3/papers.cfm?abstract_id = 3747078>.

[17] See Chapter 1.

difficulty that might result through the application of the criteria for eligibility for recognition and enforcement found in Article 5(1).[18]

V. Final Comments

11.24 The 2019 Judgments Convention represents a step forward by providing more uniform rules on the recognition and enforcement of foreign judgments. The Convention framework that resulted from years of negotiation represents a good deal of compromise, and compromise comes with limitations. The decision to follow the Brussels regime format in Articles 5 and 6 provides consistency with the practice of many European States as well as some sense of appealing familiarity for those from other civil law legal systems. At the same time, however, it brings with it the problems demonstrated within the Brussels regime, along with the difficulties inherent in a fixed and anachronistic exclusive list of criteria for eligibility for recognition and enforcement in an age of rapid change, and the additional problem of achieving global uniformity of interpretation when every Contracting State's courts will have independent interpretive authority. The application of tests tied to nineteenth-century concepts of physical presence within given geographic boundaries in a future of international commercial activity destined to be carried out in a virtual environment that does not recognize physical geographic boundaries points to potential limitations on the Convention's present and future effectiveness.

11.25 The Convention structure creates the risk of an exhaustive list that locks in what may become outdated tests that can be changed only by a difficult treaty amendment process; the risk of diminishing predictability through national court interpretation and the attendant 'homeward trend' that has been evident in similar conventions that provide 'uniform' rules; and the risk of assuming that national or regional legal frameworks can automatically be transplanted to a global scale, even when those frameworks have demonstrated significant problems within a much more homogenous legal system.

11.26 Accordingly, there is a strong case to be made for further experimentation through both domestic practice and new treaties designed to be more forward-looking in approach and architecture. Such developments, and the lessons learned, can be valuable to the international community in planning both cross-border transactions and transnational litigation.

[18] For further discussion of this possibility, see Brand (n 16).

APPENDIX

Judgments Convention Explanatory Report

THE HAGUE CONVENTION OF 2 JULY 2019 ON THE RECOGNITION AND ENFORCEMENT OF FOREIGN JUDGEMENTS IN CIVIL OR COMMERCIAL MATTERS

Convention Text

Convention on the Recognition and Enforcement of Foreign Judgments in Civil and Commercial Matters

The Contracting Parties to the present Convention,
Desiring to promote effective access to justice for all and to facilitate rule-based multilateral trade and investment, and mobility, through judicial co-operation,
Believing that such co-operation can be enhanced through the creation of a uniform set of core rules on recognition and enforcement of foreign judgments in civil or commercial matters, to facilitate the effective recognition and enforcement of such judgments, Convinced that such enhanced judicial co-operation requires, in particular, an international legal regime that provides greater predictability and certainty in relation to the global circulation of foreign judgments, and that is complementary to the *Convention of 30 June 2005 on Choice of Court Agreements*,
Have resolved to conclude this Convention to this effect and have agreed upon the following provisions –

CHAPTER I—SCOPE AND DEFINITIONS

Article 1
Scope

1. This Convention shall apply to the recognition and enforcement of judgments in civil or commercial matters. It shall not extend in particular to revenue, customs or administrative matters.
2. This Convention shall apply to the recognition and enforcement in one Contracting State of a judgment given by a court of another Contracting State.

Article 2
Exclusions from scope

1. This Convention shall not apply to the following matters –
   (a) the status and legal capacity of natural persons;
   (b) maintenance obligations;
   (c) other family law matters, including matrimonial property regimes and other rights or obligations arising out of marriage or similar relationships;
   (d) wills and succession;
   (e) insolvency, composition, resolution of financial institutions, and analogous matters;
   (f) the carriage of passengers and goods;
   (g) transboundary marine pollution, marine pollution in areas beyond national jurisdiction, ship-source marine pollution, limitation of liability for maritime claims, and general average;
   (h) liability for nuclear damage;
   (i) the validity, nullity, or dissolution of legal persons or associations of natural or legal persons, and the validity of decisions of their organs;
   (j) the validity of entries in public registers;
   (k) defamation;

(a) privacy;
(b) intellectual property;
(c) activities of armed forces, including the activities of their personnel in the exercise of their official duties;
(d) law enforcement activities, including the activities of law enforcement personnel in the exercise of their official duties;
(e) anti-trust (competition) matters, except where the judgment is based on conduct that constitutes an anti-competitive agreement or concerted practice among actual or potential competitors to fix prices, make rigged bids, establish output restrictions or quotas, or divide markets by allocating customers, suppliers, territories or lines of commerce, and where such conduct and its effect both occurred in the State of origin;
(f) sovereign debt restructuring through unilateral State measures.

2. A judgment is not excluded from the scope of this Convention where a matter to which this Convention does not apply arose merely as a preliminary question in the proceedings in which the judgment was given, and not as an object of the proceedings. In particular, the mere fact that such a matter arose by way of defence does not exclude a judgment from the Convention, if that matter was not an object of the proceedings.
3. This Convention shall not apply to arbitration and related proceedings.
4. A judgment is not excluded from the scope of this Convention by the mere fact that a State, including a government, a governmental agency or any person acting for a State, was a party to the proceedings.
5. Nothing in this Convention shall affect privileges and immunities of States or of international organisations, in respect of themselves and of their property.

Article 3
Definitions

1. In this Convention –
   (a) "defendant" means a person against whom the claim or counterclaim was brought in the State of origin;
   (b) "judgment" means any decision on the merits given by a court, whatever that decision may be called, including a decree or order, and a determination of costs or expenses of the proceedings by the court (including an officer of the court), provided that the determination relates to a decision on the merits which may be recognised or enforced under this Convention. An interim measure of protection is not a judgment.
2. An entity or person other than a natural person shall be considered to be habitually resident in the State –
   (a) where it has its statutory seat;
   (b) under the law of which it was incorporated or formed;
   (c) where it has its central administration; or
   (d) where it has its principal place of business.

CHAPTER II—RECOGNITION AND ENFORCEMENT

Article 4
General provisions

1. A judgment given by a court of a Contracting State (State of origin) shall be recognised and enforced in another Contracting State (requested State) in accordance with the provisions of this Chapter. Recognition or enforcement may be refused only on the grounds specified in this Convention.
2. There shall be no review of the merits of the judgment in the requested State. There may only be such consideration as is necessary for the application of this Convention.
3. A judgment shall be recognised only if it has effect in the State of origin, and shall be enforced only if it is enforceable in the State of origin.
4. Recognition or enforcement may be postponed or refused if the judgment referred to under paragraph 3 is the subject of review in the State of origin or if the time limit for seeking ordinary review has not expired. A refusal does not prevent a subsequent application for recognition or enforcement of the judgment.

Article 5
Bases for recognition and enforcement

1. A judgment is eligible for recognition and enforcement if one of the following requirements is met –
   (a) the person against whom recognition or enforcement is sought was habitually resident in the State of origin at the time that person became a party to the proceedings in the court of origin;
   (b) the natural person against whom recognition or enforcement is sought had their principal place of business in the State of origin at the time that person became a party to the proceedings in the court of origin and the claim on which the judgment is based arose out of the activities of that business;
   (c) the person against whom recognition or enforcement is sought is the person that brought the claim, other than a counterclaim, on which the judgment is based;
   (d) the defendant maintained a branch, agency, or other establishment without separate legal personality in the State of origin at the time that person became a party to the proceedings in the court of origin, and the claim on which the judgment is based arose out of the activities of that branch, agency, or es–tablishment;
   (e) the defendant expressly consented to the jurisdiction of the court of origin in the course of the proceedings in which the judgment was given;
   (f) the defendant argued on the merits before the court of origin without contesting jurisdiction within the timeframe provided in the law of the State of origin, unless it is evident that an objection to jurisdiction or to the exercise of jurisdiction would not have succeeded under that law;
   (g) the judgment ruled on a contractual obligation and it was given by a court of the State in which performance of that obligation took place, or should have taken place, in accordance with
      (i) the agreement of the parties, or

(i) the law applicable to the contract, in the absence of an agreed place of performance, unless the activities of the defendant in relation to the transaction clearly did not constitute a purposeful and substantial connection to that State;

(b) the judgment ruled on a lease of immovable property (tenancy) and it was given by a court of the State in which the property is situated;

(c) the judgment ruled against the defendant on a contractual obligation secured by a right *in rem* in immovable property located in the State of origin, if the contractual claim was brought together with a claim against the same defendant relating to that right *in rem*;

(d) the judgment ruled on a non-contractual obligation arising from death, physical injury, damage to or loss of tangible property, and the act or omission directly causing such harm occurred in the State of origin, irrespective of where that harm occurred;

(e) the judgment concerns the validity, construction, effects, administration or variation of a trust created voluntarily and evidenced in writing, and –

(i) at the time the proceedings were instituted, the State of origin was designated in the trust instrument as a State in the courts of which disputes about such matters are to be determined; or

(ii) at the time the proceedings were instituted, the State of origin was expressly or impliedly designated in the trust instrument as the State in which the principal place of administration of the trust is situated.

This sub-paragraph only applies to judgments regarding internal aspects of a trust between persons who are or were within the trust relationship;

(f) the judgment ruled on a counterclaim –

(i) to the extent that it was in favour of the counterclaimant, provided that the counterclaim arose out of the same transaction or occurrence as the claim; or

(ii) to the extent that it was against the counterclaimant, unless the law of the State of origin required the counterclaim to be filed in order to avoid preclusion;

(g) the judgment was given by a court designated in an agreement concluded or documented in writing or by any other means of communication which renders information accessible so as to be usable for subsequent reference, other than an exclusive choice of court agreement.

For the purposes of this sub-paragraph, an "exclusive choice of court agreement" means an agreement concluded by two or more parties that designates, for the purpose of deciding disputes which have arisen or may arise in connection with a particular legal relationship, the courts of one State or one or more specific courts of one State to the exclusion of the jurisdiction of any other courts.

2. If recognition or enforcement is sought against a natural person acting primarily for personal, family or household purposes (a consumer) in matters relating to a consumer contract, or against an employee in matters relating to the employee's contract of employment –

(a) paragraph 1(e) applies only if the consent was addressed to the court, orally or in writing;

(b) paragraph 1(f), (g) and (m) do not apply.

3. Paragraph 1 does not apply to a judgment that ruled on a residential lease of immovable property (tenancy) or ruled on the registration of immovable property. Such a judgment is eligible for recognition and enforcement only if it was given by a court of the State where the property is situated.

Article 6

Exclusive basis for recognition and enforcement

Notwithstanding Article 5, a judgment that ruled on rights *in rem* in immovable property shall be recognised and enforced if and only if the property is situated in the State of origin.

Article 7

Refusal of recognition and enforcement

1. Recognition or enforcement may be refused if –
   (a) the document which instituted the proceedings or an equivalent document, including a statement of the essential elements of the claim –
      (i) was not notified to the defendant in sufficient time and in such a way as to enable them to arrange for their defence, unless the defendant entered an appearance and presented their case without contesting notification in the court of origin, provided that the law of the State of origin permitted notification to be contested; or
      (ii) was notified to the defendant in the requested State in a manner that is incompatible with fundamental principles of the requested State concerning service of documents;
   (b) the judgment was obtained by fraud;
   (c) recognition or enforcement would be manifestly incompatible with the public policy of the requested State, including situations where the specific proceedings leading to the judgment were incompatible with fundamental principles of procedural fairness of that State and situations involving infringements of security or sovereignty of that State;
   (d) the proceedings in the court of origin were contrary to an agreement, or a designation in a trust instrument, under which the dispute in question was to be determined in a court of a State other than the State of origin;
   (e) the judgment is inconsistent with a judgment given by a court of the requested State in a dispute between the same parties; or
   (f) the judgment is inconsistent with an earlier judgment given by a court of another State between the same parties on the same subject matter, provided that the earlier judgment fulfils the conditions necessary for its recognition in the requested State.
2. Recognition or enforcement may be postponed or refused if proceedings between the same parties on the same subject matter are pending before a court of the requested State, where–
   (a) the court of the requested State was seised before the court of origin; and
   (b) there is a close connection between the dispute and the requested State.

   A refusal under this paragraph does not prevent a subsequent application for recognition or enforcement of the judgment.

Article 8

Preliminary questions

1. A ruling on a preliminary question shall not be recognised or enforced under this Convention if the ruling is on a matter to which this Convention does not apply or on a matter referred to in Article 6 on which a court of a State other than the State referred to in that Article ruled.

2. Recognition or enforcement of a judgment may be refused if, and to the extent that, the judgment was based on a ruling on a matter to which this Convention does not apply, or on a matter referred to in Article 6 on which a court of a State other than the State referred to in that Article ruled.

Article 9

Severability

Recognition or enforcement of a severable part of a judgment shall be granted where recognition or enforcement of that part is applied for, or only part of the judgment is capable of being recognised or enforced under this Convention.

Article 10

Damages

1. Recognition or enforcement of a judgment may be refused if, and to the extent that, the judgment awards damages, including exemplary or punitive damages, that do not compensate a party for actual loss or harm suffered.
2. The court addressed shall take into account whether and to what extent the damages awarded by the court of origin serve to cover costs and expenses relating to the proceedings.

Article 11

Judicial settlements (transactions judiciaires)

Judicial settlements (*transactions judiciaires*) which a court of a Contracting State has approved, or which have been concluded in the course of proceedings before a court of a Contracting State, and which are enforceable in the same manner as a judgment in the State of origin, shall be enforced under this Convention in the same manner as a judgment.

Article 12

Documents to be produced

1. The party seeking recognition or applying for enforcement shall produce –
   (a) a complete and certified copy of the judgment;
   (b) if the judgment was given by default, the original or a certified copy of a document establishing that the document which instituted the proceedings or an equivalent document was notified to the defaulting party;
   (c) any documents necessary to establish that the judgment has effect or, where applicable, is enforceable in the State of origin;
   (d) in the case referred to in Article 11, a certificate of a court (including an officer of the court) of the State of origin stating that the judicial settlement or a part of it is enforceable in the same manner as a judgment in the State of origin.
2. If the terms of the judgment do not permit the court addressed to verify whether the conditions of this Chapter have been complied with, that court may require any necessary documents.

3. An application for recognition or enforcement may be accompanied by a document relating to the judgment, issued by a court (including an officer of the court) of the State of origin, in the form recommended and published by the Hague Conference on Private International Law.
4. If the documents referred to in this Article are not in an official language of the requested State, they shall be accompanied by a certified translation into an official language, unless the law of the requested State provides otherwise.

Article 13

Procedure

1. The procedure for recognition, declaration of enforceability or registration for enforcement, and the enforcement of the judgment, are governed by the law of the requested State unless this Convention provides otherwise. The court of the requested State shall act expeditiously.
2. The court of the requested State shall not refuse the recognition or enforcement of a judgment under this Convention on the ground that recognition or enforcement should be sought in another State.

Article 14

Costs of proceedings

1. No security, bond or deposit, however described, shall be required from a party who in one Contracting State applies for enforcement of a judgment given by a court of another Contracting State on the sole ground that such party is a foreign national or is not domiciled or resident in the State in which enforcement is sought.
2. An order for payment of costs or expenses of proceedings, made in a Contracting State against any person exempt from requirements as to security, bond, or deposit by virtue of paragraph 1 or of the law of the State where proceedings have been instituted, shall, on the application of the person entitled to the benefit of the order, be rendered enforceable in any other Contracting State.
3. A State may declare that it shall not apply paragraph 1 or designate by a declaration which of its courts shall not apply paragraph 1.

Article 15

Recognition and enforcement under national law

Subject to Article 6, this Convention does not prevent the recognition or enforcement of judgments under national law.

CHAPTER III—GENERAL CLAUSES

Article 16

Transitional provision

This Convention shall apply to the recognition and enforcement of judgments if, at the time the proceedings were instituted in the State of origin, the Convention had effect between that State and the requested State.

Article 17

Declarations limiting recognition and enforcement

A State may declare that its courts may refuse to recognise or enforce a judgment given by a court of another Contracting State if the parties were resident in the requested State, and the relationship of the parties and all other elements relevant to the dispute, other than the location of the court of origin, were connected only with the requested State.

Article 18

Declarations with respect to specific matters

1. Where a State has a strong interest in not applying this Convention to a specific matter, that State may declare that it will not apply the Convention to that matter. The State making such a declaration shall ensure that the declaration is no broader than necessary and that the specific matter excluded is clearly and precisely defined.
2. With regard to that matter, the Convention shall not apply –
   (a) in the Contracting State that made the declaration;
   (b) in other Contracting States, where recognition or enforcement of a judgment given by a court of a Contracting State that made the declaration is sought.

Article 19

Declarations with respect to judgments pertaining to a State

1. A State may declare that it shall not apply this Convention to judgments arising from proceedings to which any of the following is a party –
   (a) that State, or a natural person acting for that State; or
   (b) a government agency of that State, or a natural person acting for such a government agency.

The State making such a declaration shall ensure that the declaration is no broader than necessary and that the exclusion from scope is clearly and precisely defined. The declaration shall not distinguish between judgments where the State, a government agency of that State or a natural person acting for either of them is a defendant or claimant in the proceedings before the court of origin.

2. Recognition or enforcement of a judgment given by a court of a State that made a declaration pursuant to paragraph 1 may be refused if the judgment arose from proceedings to which either the State that made the declaration or the requested State, one of their government agencies or a natural person acting for either of them is a party, to the same extent as specified in the declaration.

Article 20
Uniform interpretation

In the interpretation of this Convention, regard shall be had to its international character and to the need to promote uniformity in its application.

Article 21
Review of operation of the Convention

The Secretary General of the Hague Conference on Private International Law shall at regular intervals make arrangements for review of the operation of this Convention, including any declarations, and shall report to the Council on General Affairs and Policy.

Article 22
Non-unified legal systems

1. In relation to a Contracting State in which two or more systems of law apply in different territorial units with regard to any matter dealt with in this Convention –
   (a) any reference to the law or procedure of a State shall be construed as referring, where appropriate, to the law or procedure in force in the relevant territorial unit;
   (b) any reference to the court or courts of a State shall be construed as referring, where appropriate, to the court or courts in the relevant territorial unit;
   (c) any reference to a connection with a State shall be construed as referring, where appropriate, to a connection with the relevant territorial unit;
   (d) any reference to a connecting factor in relation to a State shall be construed as referring, where appropriate, to that connecting factor in relation to the relevant territorial unit.
2. Notwithstanding paragraph 1, a Contracting State with two or more territorial units in which different systems of law apply shall not be bound to apply this Convention to situations which involve solely such different territorial units.
3. A court in a territorial unit of a Contracting State with two or more territorial units in which different systems of law apply shall not be bound to recognise or enforce a judgment from another Contracting State solely because the judgment has been recognised or enforced in another territorial unit of the same Contracting State under this Convention.
4. This Article shall not apply to Regional Economic Integration Organisations.

Article 23

Relationship with other international instruments

1. This Convention shall be interpreted so far as possible to be compatible with other treaties in force for Contracting States, whether concluded before or after this Convention.
2. This Convention shall not affect the application by a Contracting State of a treaty that was concluded before this Convention.
3. This Convention shall not affect the application by a Contracting State of a treaty concluded after this Convention as concerns the recognition or enforcement of a judgment given by a court of a Contracting State that is also a Party to that treaty. Nothing in the other treaty shall affect the obligations under Article 6 towards Contracting States that are not Parties to that treaty.
4. This Convention shall not affect the application of the rules of a Regional Economic Integration Organisation that is a Party to this Convention as concerns the recognition or enforcement of a judgment given by a court of a Contracting State that is also a Member State of the Regional Economic Integration Organisation where –
   (a) the rules were adopted before this Convention was concluded; or
   (b) the rules were adopted after this Convention was concluded, to the extent that they do not affect the obligations under Article 6 towards Contracting States that are not Member States of the Regional Economic Integration Organisation.

CHAPTER IV—FINAL CLAUSES

Article 24

Signature, ratification, acceptance, approval or accession

1. This Convention shall be open for signature by all States.
2. This Convention is subject to ratification, acceptance or approval by the signatory States.
3. This Convention shall be open for accession by all States.
4. Instruments of ratification, acceptance, approval or accession shall be deposited with the Ministry of Foreign Affairs of the Kingdom of the Netherlands, depositary of the Convention.

Article 25

Declarations with respect to non-unified legal systems

1. If a State has two or more territorial units in which different systems of law apply in relation to matters dealt with in this Convention, it may declare that the Convention shall extend to all its territorial units or only to one or more of them. Such a declaration shall state expressly the territorial units to which the Convention applies.

2. If a State makes no declaration under this Article, the Convention shall extend to all territorial units of that State.
3. This Article shall not apply to Regional Economic Integration Organisations.

Article 26

Regional Economic Integration Organisations

1. A Regional Economic Integration Organisation which is constituted solely by sovereign States and has competence over some or all of the matters governed by this Convention may sign, accept, approve or accede to this Convention. The Regional Economic Integration Organisation shall in that case have the rights and obligations of a Contracting State, to the extent that the Organisation has competence over matters governed by this Convention.
2. The Regional Economic Integration Organisation shall, at the time of signature, acceptance, approval or accession, notify the depositary in writing of the matters governed by this Convention in respect of which competence has been transferred to that Organisation by its Member States. The Organisation shall promptly notify the depositary in writing of any changes to its competence as specified in the most recent notice given under this paragraph.
3. For the purposes of the entry into force of this Convention, any instrument deposited by a Regional Economic Integration Organisation shall not be counted unless the Regional Economic Integration Organisation declares in accordance with Article 27(1) that its Member States will not be Parties to this Convention.
4. Any reference to a "Contracting State" or "State" in this Convention shall apply equally, where appropriate, to a Regional Economic Integration Organisation.

Article 27

Regional Economic Integration Organisation as a Contracting Party without its Member States

1. At the time of signature, acceptance, approval or accession, a Regional Economic Integration Organisation may declare that it exercises competence over all the matters governed by this Convention and that its Member States will not be Parties to this Convention but shall be bound by virtue of the signature, acceptance, approval or accession of the Organisation.
2. In the event that a declaration is made by a Regional Economic Integration Organisation in accordance with paragraph 1, any reference to a "Contracting State" or "State" in this Convention shall apply equally, where appropriate, to the Member States of the Organisation.

Article 28

Entry into force

1. This Convention shall enter into force on the first day of the month following the expiration of the period during which a notification may be made in accordance with Article 29(2) with respect to the second State that has deposited its instrument of ratification, acceptance, approval or accession referred to in Article 24.
2. Thereafter this Convention shall enter into force –

   (a) for each State subsequently ratifying, accepting, approving or acceding to it, on the first day of the month following the expiration of the period during which notifications may be made in accordance with Article 29(2) with respect to that State;
   (b) for a territorial unit to which this Convention has been extended in accordance with Article 25 after the Convention has entered into force for the State making the declaration, on the first day of the month following the expiration of three months after the notification of the declaration referred to in that Article.

Article 29

Establishment of relations pursuant to the Convention

1. This Convention shall have effect between two Contracting States only if neither of them has notified the depositary regarding the other in accordance with paragraph 2 or 3. In the absence of such a notification, the Convention has effect between two Contracting States from the first day of the month following the expiration of the period during which notifications may be made.
2. A Contracting State may notify the depositary, within 12 months after the date of the notification by the depositary referred to in Article 32(a), that the ratification, acceptance, approval or accession of another State shall not have the effect of establishing relations between the two States pursuant to this Convention.
3. A State may notify the depositary, upon the deposit of its instrument pursuant to Article 24(4), that its ratification, acceptance, approval or accession shall not have the effect of establishing relations with a Contracting State pursuant to this Convention.
4. A Contracting State may at any time withdraw a notification that it has made under paragraph 2 or 3. Such a withdrawal shall take effect on the first day of the month following the expiration of three months following the date of notification.

Article 30

Declarations

1. Declarations referred to in Articles 14, 17, 18, 19 and 25 may be made upon signature, ratification, acceptance, approval or accession or at any time thereafter, and may be modified or withdrawn at any time.
2. Declarations, modifications and withdrawals shall be notified to the depositary.
3. A declaration made at the time of signature, ratification, acceptance, approval or accession shall take effect simultaneously with the entry into force of this Convention for the State concerned.

1. A declaration made at a subsequent time, and any modification or withdrawal of a declaration, shall take effect on the first day of the month following the expiration of three months following the date on which the notification is received by the depositary.
2. A declaration made at a subsequent time, and any modification or withdrawal of a declaration, shall not apply to judgments resulting from proceedings that have already been instituted before the court of origin when the declaration takes effect.

Article 31

Denunciation

1. A Contracting State to this Convention may denounce it by a notification in writing addressed to the depositary. The denunciation may be limited to certain territorial units of a non-unified legal system to which this Convention applies.
2. The denunciation shall take effect on the first day of the month following the expiration of 12 months after the date on which the notification is received by the depositary. Where a longer period for the denunciation to take effect is specified in the notification, the denunciation shall take effect upon the expiration of such longer period after the date on which the notification is received by the depositary.

Article 32

Notifications by the depositary

The depositary shall notify the Members of the Hague Conference on Private International Law, and other States and Regional Economic Integration Organisations which have signed, ratified, accepted, approved or acceded to this Convention in accordance with Articles 24, 26 and 27 of the following –

(a) the signatures, ratifications, acceptances, approvals and accessions referred to in Articles 24, 26 and 27;
(b) the date on which this Convention enters into force in accordance with Article 28;
(c) the notifications, declarations, modifications and withdrawals referred to in Articles 26, 27, 29 and 30; and
(d) the denunciations referred to in Article 31.

In witness whereof the undersigned, being duly authorised thereto, have signed this Convention.

Done at The Hague, on the 2nd day of July 2019, in the English and French languages, both texts being equally authentic, in a single copy which shall be deposited in the archives of the Government of the Kingdom of the Netherlands, and of which a certified copy shall be sent, through diplomatic channels, to each of the Members of the Hague Conference on Private International Law at the time of its Twenty-Second Session and to each of the other States which have participated in that Session.

Recommended Form

RECOMMENDED FORM
UNDER THE CONVENTION OF 2 JULY 2019 ON THE RECOGNITION AND ENFORCEMENT OF FOREIGN JUDGMENTS IN CIVIL OR COMMERCIAL MATTERS ("THE CONVENTION")

Recommended form containing information about the existence, issuance and content of a judgment given by the court of origin for the purposes of recognition and enforcement in another Contracting State under the Convention*

1. DETAILS OF THE COURT OF ORIGIN

Name of Court...
City (and state—province, if applicable) ....
Country...

2. COURT OF ORIGIN CASE REFERENCE—DOCKET NUMBER ....

3. PARTIES

3.1 Contact information of the claimant(s)

Claimant(s): ....
Address: ....
Telephone: ....
Fax (if applicable): ....
E-mail (if applicable): ....

3.2 Contact information of the defendant(s)
Defendant(s): ....
Address:..
Telephone: ....
Fax (if applicable): ....
E-mail (if applicable): ....

4. JUDGMENT

4.1 The proceedings were instituted (Art. 16) on...
(dd/mm/yyyy)

4.2 The judgment (Art. 3(1)(b)) was given on...
(dd/mm/yyyy)

4.3 The judgment was given by default (Art. 12(1)(b)):
☐ YES
☐ NO

* A final determination regarding whether there is an obligation under the Convention should be made based on the provisions of the Convention.

5. **THE EFFECT OF THE JUDGMENT**

5.1 This judgment has effect in the State of origin (Art. 12(1)(c)):
☐ YES (Art. 4(3)) ☐ NO
☐ YES, but only the following part: ....
☐ Unable to confirm

5.2 This judgment is enforceable in the State of origin (Art. 12(1)(c)):
☐ YES (Art. 4(3)) ☐ NO
☐ YES, but only the following part: ....
☐ Unable to confirm

5.3 If there is more than one person who is held liable, this judgment is enforceable against:
☐ All of them
☐ The following person(s): ....

5.4 This judgment (or a part thereof) is currently the subject of review in the State of origin:
☐ YES (please specify the nature and status of such review) (Art. 4(4)):..........
☐ NO
☐ Unable to confirm

5.5 The time limit for seeking ordinary review of this judgment has expired:
☐ YES (Art. 4(4)) ☐ NO
☐ Unable to confirm

6. **JUDICIAL SETTLEMENT (transaction judiciaire) AND THE EFFECT OF THE JUDICIAL SETTLEMENT, WHERE APPLICABLE**

6.1 The judicial settlement (Art. 11) was approved by the court, or was concluded in the course of proceedings before the court on.......... *(dd/mm/yyyy)*

6.2 This judicial settlement is enforceable in the same manner as a judgment in the State of origin (Art. 11)
☐ YES
☐ YES, but only the following part: ....
☐ NO
☐ Unable to confirm

7. **OBLIGATIONS IMPOSED BY THE JUDGMENT (OR THE JUDICIAL SETTLEMENT, WHERE APPLICABLE)**

According to the judgment given by the Court (Art. 3(1)(b)) (or where applicable, the judicial settlement approved by the court or concluded in the course of proceedings before the court (Art. 11)),

7.1 the following amount of money has to be paid: ....
to be paid by: ....
to be paid to: ....
Where applicable, please indicate any relevant categories of damages, including which are exemplary or punitive damages; the currency of the award; and any prescribed terms of payment of the monetary award such as the date and amount of any instalments:
....

7.2 the following non-monetary relief has to be performed: ....

7.3 the following costs and expenses relating to the proceedings (Art. 3(1)(b)) have to be paid: ....

Please specify, where applicable, any amount(s) included within a monetary award but not mentioned explicitly which is—are intended to cover costs and expenses relating to the proceedings: ....
to be paid by: ....
to be paid to: ....

7.4 the following interest has to be paid: ....
to be paid by: ....
to be paid to: ....

Please specify the rate(s) of interest; the portion(s) of the award, including the part awarding cost and expenses, if applicable, to which interest applies; the date from and until which interest is computed; and any further information regarding interest that would assist the court addressed.

7.5 If more than one person has been held liable for one and the same claim, the whole amount may be collected from any one of them.

☐ YES (please specify to which (part of the) claim this applies to money award, interest, costs and expenses, as applicable, and the corresponding amount):

....

☐ NO

8. **ANY OTHER RELEVANT INFORMATION**

9. Dated this.................................. day of....................., 20............. at..

10. Signature and—or stamp by the Court or officer of the Court: ....

11. **CONTACT DETAILS**

CONTACT PERSON IN THE COURT OF ORIGIN: ....
TEL.: ....
FAX: ....
E-MAIL: ....
CONTACT PERSON COMMUNICATION LANGUAGE(S): ....

*****

Note that: in accordance with Article 12 of the Convention, parties seeking recognition or applying for enforcement under the Convention shall produce:

- a complete and certified copy of the judgment (Art. 12(1)(a));
- if the judgment was given by default, the original or a certified copy of a document establishing that the document which instituted the proceedings or an equivalent document was notified to the defaulting party (Art. 12(1)(b));
- any documents necessary to establish that the judgment has effect or, where applicable, is enforceable in the State of origin (Art. 12(1)(c));
- in the case referred to in Article 11 of the Convention, a certificate of a court (including an officer of the court) of the State of origin stating that the judicial settlement or a part of it is enforceable in the same manner as a judgment in the State of origin (Art. 12(1)(d));
- if the above attached documents are not in an official language of the requested State, the party seeking recognition or applying for enforcement of the judgment shall provide a certified translation into an official language of the requested State, unless the law of the requested State provides otherwise (Art. 12(4)).

Garcimartín—Saumier Report

PART I. PREFACE

Adoption of the Convention

1. The text of the Convention was drawn up at the Twenty-Second Session of the Hague Conference on Private International Law (hereinafter, "HCCH") by its Commission I on Judgments from 18 June to 2 July 2019. The Final Act was adopted by the Plenary Session on 2 July 2019 and the Convention was opened for signature on that date.[1]

Officers at the Twenty-Second Session

2. Officers at the Twenty-Second Session consisted of: the Chairperson Mr Paul Vlas (the Netherlands); vice-Chairpersons Mr Pieter André Stemmet (South Africa), Mr Hong Xu (People's Republic of China), Mr Andreas Stein (European Union), Mr Mikhail L. Galperin (Russian Federation), Mr Paul Herrup (United States of America) and Mr Marcos Dotta Salgueiro (Uruguay); Chairperson of Commission I on Judgments Mr David Goddard (New Zealand); vice-Chairpersons of Commission I on Judgments Mr Boni de M. Soares (Brazil), Ms Kathryn Sabo (Canada), Ms Tonje Meinich (Norway) and Ms Elizabeth Pangalangan (the Philippines); *co-Rapporteurs* Ms Geneviève Saumier (Canada) and Mr Francisco Garcimartín (Spain); and Chairperson of the Drafting Committee Mr Fausto Pocar (Italy). The Permanent Bureau, led by Mr Christophe Bernasconi, Secretary General, provided assistance throughout the Session.

Origins of the Convention

3. The origins of the Convention date back to 1992 when a proposal was made for work on uniform rules on both the jurisdiction of courts and the recognition and enforcement of judgments in cross-border cases in civil and commercial matters. Progress between 1992 and 2001 resulted in a draft Convention on those two areas.[2] However, at the conclusion of the First part of the Nineteenth Session in 2001, consensus had not been reached on a number of important issues.[3]
4. The HCCH then decided to separately consider areas for which a consensus-based instrument could be achieved. This led to the development of a narrower instrument, limited to exclusive choice of court agreements, including jurisdictional rules and a regime for the recognition and enforcement of judgments. This work, which took

[1] Uruguay is the first signatory, having signed the Convention on the date of its adoption. At the time of writing, Ukraine had also signed the Convention on 4 March 2020. The status table of the Convention is available on the HCCH website at <www.hcch.net> under "Judgments".

[2] "Preliminary draft Convention on Jurisdiction and Foreign Judgments in Civil and Commercial Matters, adopted by the Special Commission and Report by Peter Nygh & Fausto Pocar", Prel. Doc. No 11 of August 2000 drawn up for the attention of the Nineteenth Session of June 2001, in *Proceedings of the Twentieth Session*, Tome II, *Judgments*, Cambridge—Antwerp—Portland, Intersentia, 2013, pp. 191–313 (hereinafter, "Nygh/Pocar Report"). The Nygh/Pocar Report is available on the HCCH website at <www.hcch.net> under "Judgments".

[3] See "Some Reflections on the Present State of Negotiations on the Judgments Project in the Context of the Future Work Programme of the Conference", Prel. Doc. No 16 of February 2002, in *Proceedings of the Nineteenth Session*, Tome I, *Miscellaneous Matters*, Koninklijke Brill NV, 2008, pp. 429 and 431, para. 5.

place between 2002 and 2005, concluded with the adoption of the HCCH *Convention of 30 June 2005 on Choice of Court Agreements* (hereinafter, "HCCH 2005 Choice of Court Convention"),[4] which aimed to ensure the effectiveness of choice of court agreements in civil and commercial matters. It entered into force on 1 October 2015.[5]

5. In 2011, the HCCH agreed to reconsider the feasibility of a global instrument on matters relating to jurisdiction and the recognition and enforcement of judgments in civil and commercial matters. In April 2012, an Experts' Group concluded that further work on cross-border litigation was desirable, provided that it met real, practical needs not met by existing instruments and institutional frameworks. The Experts' Group also determined that further work was essential to identify gaps in the existing framework for resolving cross-border disputes of particular practical significance. The HCCH then agreed that work should proceed and established a Working Group to prepare proposals on the recognition and enforcement of judgments in civil and commercial matters.[6] From 2013, the Working Group met on five occasions to develop a draft text of core provisions aimed at facilitating the global circulation of judgments.
6. The Working Group completed its work on a Proposed draft Text for a Convention on the recognition and enforcement of judgments in civil and commercial matters at its fifth meeting in October 2015. The HCCH then convened four Special Commission meetings to advance work on this draft Convention. The First Meeting was convened in June 2016 and produced a 2016 preliminary draft Convention, which was published as Working Document No 76 Revised.[7] At the Second Meeting in February 2017, the Special Commission reconsidered all provisions in the 2016 preliminary draft Convention and discussed general and final clauses, producing a revised draft of the Convention (hereinafter, "the February 2017 draft Convention"), published as Working Document No 170 Revised. [8]At its Third Meeting in November 2017, the Special Commission reviewed and discussed the square-bracketed matters reflected in Chapters I and II of the February 2017 draft Convention, including a detailed discussion on matters related to intellectual property and general and final clauses. This meeting produced a further revised draft of the Convention (hereinafter,

[4] More information about the origins of the HCCH 2005 Choice of Court Convention is available in the "Explanatory Report by Trevor Hartley and Masato Dogauchi" (hereinafter, "Hartley/Dogauchi Report"). See the *Proceedings of the Twentieth Session*, Tome III, *Choice of Court Agreements*, Antwerp—Oxford—Portland, Intersentia, 2010, pp. 785 and 787. The Hartley/Dogauchi Report is available on the HCCH website at <www.hcch.net> under "Choice of Court".

[5] At the time of writing, Mexico, the European Union, Singapore and Montenegro are Contracting Parties to the Convention. The Convention was also signed by the United States of America on 19 January 2009, by Ukraine on 21 March 2016, by the People's Republic of China on 12 September 2017, and by the Republic of North Macedonia on 9 December 2019. The status table of the Convention is available on the HCCH website at <www.hcch.net> under "Choice of Court Section".

[6] The HCCH also established an Experts' Group to further study and discuss the desirability and feasibility of making provisions in relation to jurisdiction. In February 2013, the Working Group and the Experts' Group each met in The Hague, where they decided to consider whether work for the Experts' Group on jurisdiction and the Working Group on recognition and enforcement could progress simultaneously. Following extensive consultations, it was recommended that the Working Group's activity should advance first and that the discussions of the Experts' Group should be resumed at a later stage. The Experts' Group met for a third time between 18 and 21 February 2020 and recommended to the Council on General Affairs and Policy of the HCCH (hereinafter, "CGAP") that work should continue. At its 2020 meeting, CGAP mandated two further meetings of the Experts' Group to be held before the 2021 CGAP meeting.

[7] Work. Doc. No 76 REV of June 2016, "2016 preliminary draft Convention" (Special Commission on the Recognition and Enforcement of Foreign Judgments (1–9 June 2016)).

[8] Work. Doc. No 170 REV of February 2017, "February 2017 draft Convention" (Special Commission on the Recognition and Enforcement of Foreign Judgments (16–24 February 2017)).

"the November 2017 draft Convention"), published as Working Document No 236 Revised.[9] In May 2018, the Special Commission met for a fourth time to discuss issues arising from the Third Meeting, producing the 2018 draft Convention (hereinafter, "the 2018 draft Convention"), which was published as Working Document No 262 Revised.[10] The 2018 draft Convention formed the basis of the text considered at the Twenty-Second Session in June and July 2019, where the final text of the Convention was adopted on 2 July 2019.[11]

Acknowledgments

7. This Explanatory Report (hereinafter, "the Report") was prepared by Francisco Garcimartín [12] and Geneviève Saumier,[13] the *co-Rapporteurs* appointed by the First Meeting of the Special Commission. The purpose of the Report is to assist in the interpretation of the Convention, in light of its international character and the need to promote uniformity in its practical operation, by providing an explanation of each provision and examples where appropriate.[14] The *co-Rapporteurs* have endeavoured to reflect the discussion and, where appropriate, consensus reached during Commission I on Judgments of the Twenty-Second Session in 2019. Where provisions were not expressly discussed during that Commission, the Report endeavours to reflect the discussion and, where appropriate, consensus reached during previous meetings of the Special Commission.[15] Drafting of the Report started following the conclusion of the First Meeting of the Special Commission. It was then revised and updated following each subsequent meeting of the Special Commission. Delegations were invited to review the report at various stages of its drafting. The *co—Rapporteurs* endeavoured to take delegations' views into account before finalising the Report and before its submission to delegations for a silent approval procedure. Unlike the text of the Convention, the Report is not binding in nature.
8. The *co-Rapporteurs* wish to extend their sincere thanks to Ms Ning Zhao, Senior Legal Officer at the Permanent Bureau of the HCCH, for her indispensable contribution to their work. They also wish to express their gratitude for the support provided by Ms Marta Pertegás (former member of the Permanent Bureau; First Secretary during the First and Second Meetings of the Special Commission) and Mr João Ribeiro—Bidaoui (First Secretary as of the Twenty-Second Session). A special word of thanks is also extended to Ms Lydie de Loof, Graphic Designer—Publications Officer at the Permanent Bureau of the HCCH, for her exceptional contribution to the French version of this Report. Finally, they would like to thank the delegations who commented on earlier drafts of the Report. Those comments were of great assistance and have contributed significantly to the final version.

[9] Work. Doc. No 236 REV of November 2017, "November 2017 draft Convention" (Special Commission on the Recognition and Enforcement of Foreign Judgments (13–17 November 2017)).

[10] Work. Doc. No 262 REV of May 2018, "2018 draft Convention" (Special Commission on the Recognition and Enforcement of Foreign Judgments (24–29 May 2018)).

[11] All documents relating to the Convention are available on the HCCH website at <www.hcch.net> under "Judgments".

[12] Professor, Universidad Autónoma de Madrid (Spain).

[13] Professor and Peter M. Laing Chair, Faculty of Law, McGill University (Canada).

[14] See Art. 32 of the *Vienna Convention of 23 May 1969 on the Law of Treaties* (hereinafter, "Vienna Convention of 1969").

[15] In the very few instances where interpretive issues were not expressly addressed either in the Special Commission or in Commission I on Judgments of the Twenty-Second Session, the *co-Rapporteurs* have so indicated.

Terminology

The following terminology is used in the Convention:

"**court of origin**": the court which granted the judgment;

"**State of origin**": the State in which the court of origin is situated;

"**court addressed**": the court which is asked to recognise or enforce the judgment;

"**requested State**": the State in which the court addressed is situated.

Structure of the Report

9. There are three parts to the Report, including the present part (Part I). Part II ("Overview") explains the aim, architecture and structure of the Convention, emphasising the function of the different provisions and how they relate to one another. Part III ("Article-by-Article Commentary") analyses each individual Article to clarify its meaning.

Examples

10. In the examples provided, it is assumed (unless the contrary is stated) that the Convention is in force and that the States mentioned are Parties to it.

PART II. OVERVIEW—Objective, Architecture and Outline of the Convention

11. The Convention is a private international law instrument in civil or commercial matters. It deals with one of the three classical areas of private international law, namely the recognition and enforcement of foreign judgments. In so doing, it furthers one of the main goals of private international law: international judicial co-operation, with a view to enhancing predictability and justice in cross-border legal relations in civil or commercial matters. The Convention does not deal with the other two traditional areas of private international law, relating to court jurisdiction to adjudicate disputes in cross-border cases and rules determining the law applicable to such cases. Those matters are not affected by the Convention.
12. **Objective.** This Convention seeks to promote access to justice globally through enhanced judicial cooperation, which will reduce risks and costs associated with cross-border legal relations and dispute resolution. As a result, implementation of the Convention should facilitate rule-based multilateral trade and investment, and mobility.
13. These goals will be advanced in a number of ways.
14. First and most importantly, the Convention provides a framework for the recognition and enforcement of foreign judgments in all Contracting States ("States"),[16] thereby enhancing the practical effectiveness of those judgments. Access to justice is frustrated if a wronged party obtains a judgment that cannot be enforced in practice because the other party or the other party's assets are in a State where the judgment is not readily enforceable.
15. Second, the Convention will reduce the need for duplicative proceedings in two or more States; a judgment determining the claim in one State will be effective in other States, without the need to re-litigate the merits of the claim.
16. Third, the Convention will reduce the cost and timeframe of obtaining recognition and enforcement of judgments; access to practical justice will be faster and at lower cost.
17. Fourth, the Convention will improve the predictability of the law; individuals and businesses[17] will be able to more readily ascertain the circumstances in which judgments will circulate among States.
18. Fifth, it will enable claimants to make informed choices about where to bring proceedings, taking into account the ability to enforce the resulting judgment in other States and the need to ensure fairness to defendants.
19. In a globalised and interconnected world, with ever-increasing movement of people, information and assets across borders, the practical importance of achieving these goals is self-evident. The Convention's potential to reach these goals is significant.

[16] For simplicity, the term "States" is used in this Report to refer to "Contracting States". The distinction between Contracting and non-Contracting States is drawn only where relevant.

[17] The English version uses "business" and the French version uses "professionnel" as a noun and an adjective.

20. **Relationship with the HCCH 2005 Choice of Court Convention.** The HCCH 2005 Choice of Court Convention pursues the same objectives by enabling parties to agree on the court that will hear a claim and providing for the recognition and enforcement of a judgment given by the chosen court.[18] But in many cases there is no exclusive choice of court agreement between the parties to a dispute. This Convention seeks to extend the benefits of enhanced access to justice and reduced costs and risks of cross-border dealings to a broader range of cases. It is intended to complement the HCCH 2005 Choice of Court Convention.
21. **Outline.** The Convention is designed to provide an efficient and effective system for recognising and enforcing foreign judgments in civil or commercial matters in largely uncontroversial circumstances. The Convention provides for the recognition and enforcement of judgments that meet certain requirements (Arts 5 and 6) and sets out the grounds on which recognition or enforcement of such judgments may be refused (Art. 7).[19] To facilitate the circulation of judgments, the text does not prevent States from recognising or enforcing judgments under national law or under other treaties (Arts 15, 23), subject to one exclusive basis for recognition and enforcement (Art. 6).
22. **Architecture.** The Convention is divided into four chapters. Chapter I deals with scope and definitions. The scope of the Convention extends to judgments in civil or commercial matters (Art. 1), but excludes certain matters from scope (Art. 2), either because they are covered by other instruments or because multilateral consensus cannot readily be achieved on them. Article 3 defines "judgment" and "defendant", and specifies when a legal person will be considered to be habitually resident in a State.
23. Chapter II is the core of the Convention. Its first article establishes the general principle of circulation of judgments among the States (Art. 4). A judgment given by a court of a State shall be recognised and enforced in another State in accordance with the provisions of Chapter II. The main criterion for circulation is provided in Article 5, which sets out the bases for recognition and enforcement of a judgment in the form of jurisdictional filters against which the judgment from the State of origin is to be assessed by the State where recognition or enforcement is sought. These grounds are limited by one exclusive filter in Article 6. Where a judgment meets the requirements of Articles 4, 5 and 6, the grounds for refusal to recognise or enforce it are provided in Article 7.[20] This Article establishes an exhaustive list of grounds for refusal that allow, but do not require, the requested State to refuse recognition or enforcement. It is useful to point immediately to Article 15, which reserves the right of a requested State to recognise or enforce foreign judgments based on national law (subject to Art. 6).
24. Chapter II also deals with specific issues of interpretation and application: preliminary questions (Art. 8), severability (Art. 9), damages including punitive damages (Art. 10), and judicial settlements (Art. 11). Finally, Chapter II addresses procedural matters to facilitate access to the mechanism of the Convention: documents to be produced (Art. 12), procedure (Art. 13) and costs of proceedings (Art. 14).

[18] More information on the HCCH 2005 Choice of Court Convention is available on the HCCH website at <www.hcch.net> under "Choice of Court".

[19] It should be noted that the text of the Convention usually employs the expression "recognition and enforcement" when referring to the positive obligation laid down by Art. 4, and the expression "recognition or enforcement" when referring to the possibility of refusing the fulfilment of this obligation, *e.g.*, under Art. 7. The Explanatory Report follows that formulation where appropriate.

[20] It should be noted that Arts 8(2) and 10 also provide grounds for refusal in specific circumstances.

25. Chapter III deals with general clauses: transitional provision (Art. 16), allowable declarations (Arts 17–19), uniform interpretation (Art. 20), non-unified legal systems (Art. 22) and relationship with other instruments (Art. 23).
26. Chapter IV provides final clauses on the process for becoming a Party to the Convention (Arts 24–27), entry into force (Art. 28), establishment of treaty relations (Art. 29), procedure for declarations (Art. 30), denunciation (Art. 31) and notifications (Art. 32).

PART III. ARTICLE-BY-ARTICLE COMMENTARY

Chapter I—Scope and definitions

Article 1

Scope

1. **This Convention shall apply to the recognition and enforcement of judgments in civil or commercial matters. It shall not extend in particular to revenue, customs or administrative matters.**
2. **This Convention shall apply to the recognition and enforcement in one Contracting State of a judgment given by a court of another Contracting State.**

27. Article 1 addresses the scope of the Convention, defining it in substantive and geographic terms. Paragraph 1 defines the substantive scope, providing that the Convention applies to the recognition and enforcement of judgments in civil or commercial matters. This provision must be read in conjunction with Article 2(1), which excludes certain matters. (See also Articles 18 and 19, which allow States to make declarations restricting the scope of application of the Convention.) Paragraph 2 addresses the geographical or territorial application of the Convention, providing that it applies to the recognition and enforcement in one State of a judgment given by the court of another State.

Paragraph 1—This Convention shall apply to the recognition and enforcement of judgments in civil or commercial matters. It shall not extend in particular to revenue, customs or administrative matters.

28. The Convention applies to judgments in civil or commercial matters. It does not extend, in particular, to revenue, customs or administrative matters. Whether a judgment relates to civil or commercial matters is determined by the nature of the claim or action that is the subject of the judgment. The nature of the court of the State of origin or the mere fact that a State was a party to the proceedings are not determinative factors.
29. The Convention applies whatever the nature of the court, *i.e.*, irrespective of whether the civil or commercial action was brought before a civil, criminal, administrative or labour court.[21] Thus, for example, the Convention applies to a judgment on civil

[21] See "Note on Article 1(1) of the 2016 preliminary draft Convention and the term 'civil or commercial matters'", drawn up by the *co-Rapporteurs* of the draft Convention and the Permanent Bureau, Prel. Doc. No 4 of December 2016 for the attention of the Special Commission of February 2017 on the Recognition and Enforcement of Foreign Judgments (hereinafter, "Prel. Doc. No 4 of December 2016"), para. 6.

claims brought before a criminal court where that court had jurisdiction to hear the matter under its procedural law.

30. The application of the Convention is not affected by the nature of the parties, *i.e.*, legal or natural persons, private or public. As indicated in Article 2(4), a judgment is not excluded from the scope of the Convention by the mere fact that a State—including a government, a governmental agency or any person acting for a State—was a party to the proceedings in the State of origin (see *infra,* commentary on Art. 2(4)).
31. Furthermore, the characterisation of an action is not affected by the mere fact that the claim is transferred to another person, such as by assignment, succession or assumption of the obligation by another person. Transfer of a claim from a private body to a State does not preclude the claim being characterised as civil or commercial. The same holds in cases of subrogation, *i.e.*, when a governmental agency is subrogated to the rights of a private party.
32. **Autonomous meaning.** The Convention requires that the courts of the requested State decide whether a judgment relates to civil or commercial matters. In making this determination, courts should consider the need to promote uniformity in the application of the Convention. Accordingly, the concept of "civil or commercial matters", like other legal concepts used in the Convention, must be defined autonomously, *i.e.*, by reference to the objectives of the Convention and its international character, and not by reference to national law. [22]This requirement supports a uniform interpretation and application of the Convention (see *infra,* Art. 20). Furthermore, the interpretation of those terms should be applied consistently across other HCCH instruments, in particular the HCCH 2005 Choice of Court Convention.
33. The use of the terms "civil" and "commercial" matters is mostly relevant for legal systems where "civil" and "commercial" are regarded as separate and mutually exclusive categories, although the use of both terms is not incompatible with legal systems in which commercial proceedings are a sub-category of civil proceedings.[23] While other international instruments have used the terms "civil *and* commercial matters",[24] the Convention follows the HCCH 2005 Choice of Court Convention and refers to "civil *or* commercial matters". Both alternatives must be considered interchangeable.
34. The concept of "civil or commercial matters" is used to differentiate situations where the State acts in its sovereign capacity. [25]Unlike the HCCH 2005 Choice of Court Convention, Article 1(1) clarifies that the Convention does not apply, "[...] in particular, to revenue, customs or administrative matters". This enumeration is not exhaustive and other matters of public law, *e.g.*, constitutional and criminal matters, are obviously also excluded from the scope of the Convention. The enumeration is intended to facilitate the application of the Convention in States where there is no

[22] Hartley/Dogauchi Report, para. 49; Prel. Doc. No 4 of December 2016, para. 5.

[23] Hartley/Dogauchi Report, para. 49.

[24] See Regulation (EU) No 1215/2012 of the European Parliament and of the Council of 12 December 2012 on jurisdiction and the recognition and enforcement of judgments in civil and commercial matters (hereinafter, "Brussels Ia Regulation"), Art. 1.

[25] Hartley/Dogauchi Report, para. 49; Prel. Doc. No 4 of December 2016, para. 40.

established distinction between private and public law.[26] The new terms included in this Convention are not intended as departures from the HCCH 2005 Choice of Court Convention; both instruments must be interpreted in the same way.

35. A key element distinguishing public law matters from "civil or commercial" matters is whether one of the parties is exercising governmental or sovereign powers that are not enjoyed by ordinary persons. [27]It is therefore necessary to identify the legal relationship between the parties to the dispute and to examine the legal basis of the action brought before the court of origin to establish whether the judgment relates to civil or commercial matters. If the action derives from the exercise of public powers (including regulatory powers or duties), the Convention does not apply. A typical example of public power is the capacity to enforce a claim by way of administrative proceedings without requiring court action. Thus, for example, the Convention does not apply to orders by governments or governmental agencies such as health and safety authorities or financial supervisors, which seek to ensure compliance or to prevent non-compliance with regulatory requirements. [28]Nor does it apply to judgments on judicial actions brought either to enforce or appeal such orders. The Convention does not apply to claims against officials[29] who act on behalf of the State or to liability for the acts of public authorities, including the acts of publicly appointed officeholders acting in that capacity.
36. Criminal or penal matters are typical examples involving the exercise of public powers, which are therefore excluded from the scope of the Convention. This exclusion covers actions in which a State or public authority seeks to punish a person for conduct proscribed by criminal law, including by pecuniary sanctions (but see *supra*, para. 29).
37. Conversely, if neither party is exercising public powers, the Convention applies. For example, it applies to private claims for harm caused by non-excluded anti—competitive conduct (see *infra*, para. 69).[30] By the same token, when a governmental agency is acting on behalf of private parties, such as consumers or investors, and is not exercising governmental or sovereign powers, the Convention applies (see *infra*, commentary on Art. 2(4)).
38. **Joining of actions.** The principle of severability applies where a judgment involves more than one action, one of which is "civil or commercial" and another which is not (see *infra*, Art. 9). The Convention only applies to the civil or commercial action and not to the others.

[26] See Nygh/Pocar Report, para. 23: "[. . .] the expressions 'civil matters' or 'civil law' are not technical terms in common law countries such as England and the Republic of Ireland and can have more than one meaning. In the widest sense they exclude only criminal law. On that basis, constitutional law, administrative law and tax law are included in the description of 'civil matters'. This is clearly not the intention of the preliminary draft Convention, which in the second sentence of paragraph 1 explains that matters of a revenue, customs or administrative nature are not to be regarded as falling within the scope of 'civil and commercial matters'" (notes omitted). This clarification was considered unnecessary in the HCCH 2005 Choice of Court Convention: see Hartley/Dogauchi Report, para. 49, note 73.

[27] Hartley/Dogauchi Report, para. 85; Prel. Doc. No 4 of December 2016, para. 40. The terms "sovereign powers", "governmental powers" and "public powers" are to be considered equivalent for the purposes of this Report (see also *infra*, para. 83 for a further elaboration of these terms).

[28] Prel. Doc. No 4 of December 2016, para. 41.

[29] References to "officials" in this Report refer both to current and former officials.

[30] Prel. Doc. No 4 of December 2016, para. 41.

Paragraph 2—This Convention shall apply to the recognition and enforcement in one Contracting State of a judgment given by a court of another Contracting State.

39. Paragraph 2 defines the geographical or territorial application of the Convention: it applies to the recognition and enforcement in one State of a judgment given by a court of another State. Both the State of origin, being the State in which the court granting the judgment is situated, and the requested State, being the State where recognition and enforcement of that judgment is sought, must be parties to the Convention (Art. 4(1)). This provision must be read with Article 22 ("Non-unified legal systems"), and in particular with Article 29 ("Establishment of relations pursuant to the Convention"): the Convention shall only apply if both the State of origin and the requested State are parties to the Convention, and if neither has objected to the establishment of relations with the other under this provision, *i.e.*, if the Convention has effect between them.
40. **Relevant time.** The relevant time is the date proceedings are instituted in the State of origin. The Convention must have effect between the requested State and the State of origin at that moment for it to apply (see *infra,* Art. 16).
41. **Definition of the time proceedings are instituted.** Although the Convention refers to "the time the proceedings were instituted" in some provisions (*e.g.*, Art. 5(1)(k) or 16), it does not define this concept. The institution of proceedings should focus on the completion of the first procedural act that gives rise to the commencement of the proceedings in the State of origin, *e.g.*, the filing of the document instituting the proceedings with the court, or if that document has to be served before filing, the reception by the authority responsible for service.[31]

[31] This is consistent with the principle of predictability stated in paras 17, 18 and 328.

Article 2

Exclusions from scope

1. This Convention shall not apply to the following matters –
   (a) the status and legal capacity of natural persons;
   (b) maintenance obligations;
   (c) other family law matters, including matrimonial property regimes and other rights or obligations arising out of marriage or similar relationships;
   (d) wills and succession;
   (e) insolvency, composition, resolution of financial institutions, and analogous matters;
   (f) the carriage of passengers and goods;
   (g) transboundary marine pollution, marine pollution in areas beyond national jurisdiction, ship-source marine pollution, limitation of liability for maritime claims, and general average;
   (h) liability for nuclear damage;
   (i) the validity, nullity, or dissolution of legal persons or associations of natural or legal persons, and the validity of decisions of their organs;
   (j) the validity of entries in public registers;
   (k) defamation;
   (l) privacy;
   (m) intellectual property;
   (n) activities of armed forces, including the activities of their personnel in the exercise of their official duties;
   (o) law enforcement activities, including the activities of law enforcement personnel in the exercise of their official duties;
   (p) anti-trust (competition) matters, except where the judgment is based on conduct that constitutes an anti—competitive agreement or concerted practice among actual or potential competitors to fix prices, make rigged bids, establish output restrictions or quotas, or divide markets by allocating customers, suppliers, territories or lines of commerce, and where such conduct and its effect both occurred in the State of origin;
   (q) sovereign debt restructuring through unilateral State measures.
2. A judgment is not excluded from the scope of this Convention where a matter to which this Convention does not apply arose merely as a preliminary question in the proceedings in which the judgment was given, and not as an object of the proceedings. In particular, the mere fact that such a matter arose by way of defence does not exclude a judgment from the Convention, if that matter was not an object of the proceedings.
3. This Convention shall not apply to arbitration and related proceedings.

4. **A judgment is not excluded from the scope of this Convention by the mere fact that a State, including a government, a governmental agency or any person acting for a State, was a party to the proceedings.**
5. **Nothing in this Convention shall affect privileges and immunities of States or of international organisations, in respect of themselves and of their property.**

42. Article 2 refines the scope of the Convention set out in Article 1(1). First, it excludes certain matters (para. 1). Second, it provides that the Convention applies even if a matter excluded from its scope arose as a preliminary question in proceedings in the State of origin (para. 2). Third, it contains a specific provision excluding arbitration and related proceedings (para. 3). Finally, it provides that the mere fact that a State or government body was a party to the proceedings does not exclude a judgment from the scope of the Convention, and the Convention does not affect the privileges and immunities enjoyed by States or international organisations (paras 4 and 5). In applying these provisions, courts of the requested State are not bound by the decision of courts of the State of origin regarding whether the judgment relates to an excluded matter.

Paragraph 1—This Convention shall not apply to the following matters –

43. Paragraph 1 of Article 2 lists specific matters excluded from the scope of the Convention. However, paragraph 2 explains that these exclusions only apply where a listed matter was the "object" of the proceedings, and not where it arose as a preliminary question, in particular by way of defence (see *infra*, para. 76).
44. **Rationale.** In general terms, the rationale for the exclusions is that (i) the listed matter is already governed by other international instruments, in particular other HCCH Conventions, and it was deemed preferable that these instruments operate without any interference by the Convention,[32] (ii) the listed matter is of particular sensitivity for many States and it would be difficult to reach broad acceptance on how the Convention should deal with it, or (iii) it is preferable to expressly list the matter as excluded to avoid any uncertainty based on diverging interpretations under national law. Most matters mentioned in the list are similar to those contained in the parallel provision of the HCCH 2005 Choice of Court Convention but there are significant differences. The scope of the Convention is broader than the scope of the HCCH 2005 Choice of Court Convention. For example, unlike the HCCH 2005 Choice of Court Convention, which is limited to commercial transactions, the Convention applies to employment and consumer contracts, physical injuries, damage to tangible property, rights *in rem* and leases of immovable property, and some anti—trust (competition) matters.

[32] Hartley/Dogauchi Report, para. 53.

Sub-paragrap h (a)—the status and legal capacity of natural persons;

45. Sub-paragraph (a) excludes the status and legal capacity of natural persons from the scope of the Convention. This exclusion encompasses judgments on divorce, legal separation, annulment of marriage, establishment or contestation of parent-child relationships, adoption, emancipation, and the status and capacity of minors or persons with disabilities. The exclusion also covers judgments on guardianship, curatorship or equivalent measures, as well as measures for the protection of children or the administration, conservation or disposal of children's property (see also *infra*, para. 47).[33] Judgments ruling on the name or nationality of natural persons are also captured under this exclusion. Maintenance obligations and other family matters are excluded under sub-paragraphs (b) and (c).

Sub-paragraph (b)—maintenance obligations;

46. Sub-paragraph (b) excludes maintenance obligations, which encompasses any maintenance obligation deriving from family relationships, parentage, marriage or affinity. [34]As both maintenance obligations and matrimonial property regimes are excluded, there is no need to draw an exact definitional boundary between them.

Sub-paragraph (c)—other family law matters, including matrimonial property regimes and other rights or obligations arising out of marriage or similar relationships;

47. Sub-paragraph (c) excludes matrimonial property regimes and other rights or obligations arising out of marriage or similar relationships. [35]As in the HCCH 2005 Choice of Court Convention, "matrimonial property" includes the special rights that a spouse has to the matrimonial home in some jurisdictions.[36] In general terms, this exclusion covers judgments on claims between spouses—and exceptionally with third parties—during or after dissolution of the marriage, and which affect rights in property arising out of the matrimonial relationship. The exclusion encompasses rights of administration and disposal of property belonging to the spouses, and matrimonial property agreements by which spouses organise their matrimonial property regime. Conversely, claims between spouses arising under the general law of property, contracts or torts are not excluded from the scope of the Convention.[37] The term "similar relationships" covers relationships between unmarried couples, *e.g.*, registered partnerships, to the extent that they are given legal recognition.[38] One may have different views on whether issues such as parental responsibility, custody or right of access, or measures for the protection of children are covered by sub-

[33] Nygh/Pocar Report, para. 30, note 16. The exclusion of matters under sub-para. (a) must be consistent with other HCCH instruments, in particular, as regards: (i) parental responsibility and measures for the protection of children, with Art. 3 of the HCCH *Convention of 19 October 1996 on Jurisdiction, Applicable Law, Recognition, Enforcement and Co-operation in respect of Parental Responsibility and Measures for the Protection of Children* (hereinafter, "HCCH 1996 Child Protection Convention"); and (ii) the protection of adults, with Art. 3 of the HCCH *Convention of 13 January 2000 on the International Protection of Adults* (hereinafter, "HCCH 2000 Protection of Adults Convention").

[34] See, on maintenance obligations, the HCCH *Convention of 15 April 1958 concerning the Recognition and Enforcement of Decisions Relating to Maintenance Obligations toward Children*; the HCCH *Convention of 2 October 1973 on the Recognition and Enforcement of Decisions Relating to Maintenance Obligations*; and the HCCH *Convention of 23 November 2007 on the International Recovery of Child Support and Other Forms of Family Maintenance* (hereinafter, "HCCH 2007 Child Support Convention").

[35] See the HCCH *Convention of 14 March 1978 on the Law Applicable to Matrimonial Property Regimes*.

[36] Hartley/Dogauchi Report, para. 55.

[37] Nygh/Pocar Report, para. 35.

[38] Ibid.; Hartley/Dogauchi Report, para. 55.

paragraph (a) ("status and legal capacity of natural persons") or by sub-paragraph (c) ("other family matters").[39] However, as with sub-paragraph (b), there is no need to draw an exact definitional boundary between the categories as both are excluded from the scope of the Convention.73

Sub-paragraph (d)—wills and succession;

48. Sub-paragraph (d) excludes wills and succession from the scope of the Convention.[40] The exclusion refers to succession to the estate of a deceased person and covers all forms of transfer of assets, rights and obligations by reason of death, whether by way of voluntary transfer under a disposition of property on death or a transfer through intestate succession. The use of the word "wills" simply indicates that matters concerning the form and material validity of dispositions on death are excluded.[41] In relation to trusts created by testamentary disposition, judgments on the validity and interpretation of the will creating the trust are excluded. But judgments on the effects, administration or variation of the trust between persons who are or were within the trust relationships are included.[42]

Sub-paragraph (e)—insolvency, composition, resolution of financial institutions, and analogous matters;

49. Sub-paragraph (e) excludes insolvency, composition, resolution of financial institutions, and analogous matters. The term "insolvency" covers bankruptcy of both individuals and legal persons. It includes the winding-up or liquidation of corporations in insolvency proceedings, while the winding-up or liquidation of corporations for reasons other than insolvency is dealt with by sub-paragraph (i).[43] The term "composition" refers to proceedings where the debtor enters into an agreement with their creditors to restructure or reorganise a company to prevent its liquidation. These agreements usually imply a moratorium on the payment of debts and a discharge.[44] Purely contractual arrangements—*i.e.*, voluntary out-of-court agreements—are, however, not covered by the exclusion. The term "analogous matters" is used to cover a wide range of other methods whereby insolvent or financially distressed persons are assisted to regain solvency while continuing to trade.[45]
50. The term "resolution of financial institutions" is not included in the parallel provision of the HCCH 2005 Choice of Court Convention. This is a relatively new concept that refers to the legal framework enacted in many jurisdictions to address the risk of

[39] See Work. Doc. No 242 of May 2018, "Proposal of the delegation of Uruguay" (Special Commission on the Recognition and Enforcement of Foreign Judgments (24–29 May 2018)).

[40] See the HCCH *Convention of 5 October 1961 on the Conflicts of Laws Relating to the Form of Testamentary Disposition*; the HCCH *Convention of 2 October 1973 Concerning the International Administration of the Estates of Deceased Persons*; the HCCH *Convention of 1 August 1989 on the Law Applicable to Succession to the Estates of Deceased Persons* (not yet in force).

[41] Nygh/Pocar Report, para. 36.

[42] Ibid.

[43] Ibid.; Hartley/Dogauchi Report, para. 56.

[44] Ibid. Note that there is a separate provision on sovereign debt in Art. 2(1)(q).

[45] Such as Chapter 11 of the United States Bankruptcy Code. See Hartley/Dogauchi Report, para. 56. Some national proceedings may be subsumed under the concept of "composition" or under "analogous matters", but since both are excluded from the scope of the Convention, the distinction is not relevant here.

failure of financial institutions.[46] A resolution may include liquidation and depositor reimbursement, transfer or sale of assets and liabilities, establishment of a temporary bridge institution, and write-down or conversion of debt to equity.[47] Most of these measures fall outside the scope of application of the Convention as administrative rather than civil or commercial matters, but many delegations at the Second Meeting of the Special Commission considered an explicit reference to this new framework appropriate to avoid ambiguity.[48]

51. **Insolvency-related judgments.** Sub-paragraph (e) excludes judgments directly concerning insolvency.[49] This exclusion applies if the right or the obligation that was the legal basis of the action in the State of origin was based on rules pertaining specifically to insolvency proceedings, rather than general rules of civil or commercial law. If the action derives from insolvency rules, the exclusion precludes the circulation of the judgment under the Convention. But if the action derives from civil or commercial law, the judgment may circulate (see, however, *infra*, para. 53). Courts of the requested State may consider the following criteria when deciding whether the judgment was based on insolvency rules: whether the judgment was given on or after the commencement of the insolvency proceedings, whether the proceedings from which the judgment derived served the interest of the general body of creditors, and whether the proceedings from which the judgment derived could not have been brought but for the debtor's insolvency.[50] Thus, the Convention does not apply, for example, to judgments opening insolvency proceedings, concerning their conduct and closure, approving a restructuring plan, or setting aside transactions detrimental to the general body of creditors or on the ranking of claims.[51]
52. The Convention does, however, apply to judgments on actions based on general rules of civil or commercial law, even if the action is brought by or against a person acting as insolvency administrator in one party's insolvency proceedings. Thus, the Convention applies to judgments on actions for the performance of obligations under a contract concluded by the debtor, or actions on non-contractual damages.[52] For example, where X enters into a sale contract with Y, and X is then declared bankrupt in State A, the Convention will apply to any judgment against Y to perform the contract even if the action was brought by the person appointed as insolvency administrator in X's bankruptcy. By the same token, the Convention will apply if such action was brought by Y against X acting through the person appointed as insolvency administrator in X's bankruptcy.
53. The application of the Convention will, however, be of limited effect in cases where the judgment debtor is in insolvency proceedings. These are collective proceedings that usually prevent individual creditors from enforcing their claims by means of separate enforcement actions (otherwise, the orderly administration and liquidation

46 Such national frameworks have been established following guidance provided by the Financial Stability Board, an international body set up after the G20 London summit in April 2009, that monitors and makes recommendations about the global financial system.

47 See Financial Stability Board, *Key Attributes of Effective Resolution Regimes for Financial Institutions,* 15 October 2014.

48 Minutes of the Special Commission on the Recognition and Enforcement of Foreign Judgments (16–24 February 2017), Minutes No 2, paras 30–50.

49 Hartley/Dogauchi Report, para. 57.

50 See Work. Doc. No 104 of February 2017, "Proposal of the delegation of the European Union" (Special Commission on the Recognition and Enforcement of Foreign Judgments (16–24 February 2017)).

51 Ibid.

52 Ibid.; Hartley/Dogauchi Report, para. 57.

of the estate or the reorganisation of the debtor would not be feasible), and the effect of commencing insolvency proceedings on individual enforcement actions is not governed by the Convention. Accordingly, if the judgment is favourable to the insolvent debtor's counterparty—Y in the above example—the enforcement of such judgment may be affected by the insolvency proceedings. The judgment creditor (Y) may seek recognition and enforcement of the judgment under the Convention in the jurisdiction where insolvency proceedings are commenced—State A in the example—but will only receive payment through the insolvency process or reorganisation plan. In this sense, the foreign judgment must be treated the same as a domestic judgment, but no better. Likewise, the judgment creditor (Y) may seek recognition and enforcement of the judgment in States other than where insolvency proceedings are commenced, but the enforcement of the judgment may be affected by the commencement of the insolvency proceedings if those proceedings are recognised in the requested State (under the UNCITRAL Model Law or otherwise).

Sub-paragraph (f)—the carriage of passengers and goods;

54. Sub-paragraph (f) excludes contracts for the national or international carriage of passengers or goods, regardless of the means of transport. The exclusion extends to carriage by sea, land and air, or any combination of the three.[53] The international carriage of persons or goods is subject to a number of other important conventions, and this exclusion prevents conflicts arising with those instruments. In any event, the exclusion is not limited to commercial contracts for carriage and, therefore, it also covers consumer contracts and contracts between non-professionals, *e.g.*, the Convention does not apply to a judgment for personal injury to a passenger injured in an accident as a result of the driver's negligence. Conversely, this exclusion does not cover damages to third parties, *e.g.*, a victim in an accident who was not a passenger. Nor does it cover complex contracts that combine tourist services, such as transport, accommodation and other services, where the transport alone is not the main object of the contract.

Sub-paragraph (g)—transboundary marine pollution, marine pollution in areas beyond national jurisdiction, ship-source marine pollution, limitation of liability for maritime claims, and general average;

55. Sub-paragraph (g) excludes three maritime matters: marine pollution in three circumstances (transboundary, beyond areas of national jurisdiction and ship—source), limitation of liability for maritime claims, and general average. The maritime matters exclusion was introduced by the HCCH 2005 Choice of Court Convention.[54] With regard to marine pollution in particular, there are several international marine pollution-related instruments dealing with the recognition and enforcement of foreign judgments; the application of the Convention in this matter might have given rise to problems in terms of the relationships between international instruments.[55] There was consensus at the Twenty-Second Session to limit this exclusion to the three specific contexts listed in sub-paragraph (g): transboundary (i.e., cross-border) marine pollution, marine pollution in areas beyond national jurisdiction, and ship-

53 Hartley/Dogauchi Report, para. 58.

54 See "Note on reconsidering 'marine pollution and emergency towage and salvage' within the scope of the draft Convention on the recognition and enforcement of foreign judgments in civil or commercial matters", Prel. Doc. No 12 of June 2019 for the attention of the Twenty-Second Session on the Recognition and Enforcement of Foreign Judgments (18 June—2 July 2019) (available on the HCCH website at <www.hcch.net>, under the "Judgments Section" then "Preparatory Work" and "22nd Diplomatic Session") (hereinafter, "Prel. Doc. No 12 of June 2019"), para. 10.

55 Ibid., para. 77.

source marine pollution.[56] Other judgments involving marine pollution fall within the scope of the Convention. Unlike the HCCH 2005 Choice of Court Convention, the Convention does not exclude emergency towage and emergency salvage, as these matters are not covered by other instruments, and there are strong reasons to encourage the provision of these services, while failure to effectively compensate providers can lead to a diminution in the willingness to take the risks and bear the costs for providing them.[57] Moreover, subject to the limitation of liability exclusion, other maritime matters, such as marine insurance, shipbuilding or ship mortgages and liens, are also included in the scope of the Convention.[58]

Sub-paragraph (h)—liability for nuclear damage;

56. Sub-paragraph (h) excludes liability for nuclear damage. The explanation for this exclusion in the Hartley/Dogauchi Report is that nuclear damage is the subject of various international conventions providing that the State where the nuclear accident takes place has exclusive jurisdiction over actions for damages for liability resulting from the accident.[59] In some cases, Article 23 of the Convention might give those instruments priority over this Convention. There are, however, some States with nuclear power plants that are not parties to any of the nuclear liability conventions. Such States might be reluctant to recognise judgments given in another State by virtue of one of the filters laid down by Article 5 of the Convention. Where the operators of the nuclear power plants benefit from limited liability under the law of the State in question, or where compensation for damage is paid out of public funds, a single collective procedure in that State under its internal law would be necessary for a uniform resolution of liability and an equitable distribution of a limited fund among the victims. This exclusion addresses nuclear accidents and therefore does not cover tortious medical claims regarding nuclear medicine (including radiation therapy, for example).

Sub-paragraph (i)—the validity, nullity, or dissolution of legal persons or associations of natural or legal persons, and the validity of decisions of their organs;

57. Sub-paragraph (i) excludes the validity, nullity or dissolution of legal persons, and the validity of decisions of their organs. The exclusion also encompasses "associations of natural or legal persons", *i.e.*, entities without legal personality. These matters are often subject to the exclusive jurisdiction of the State whose law applies to those entities in order to avoid a plurality of fora in this field and to ensure legal certainty.[60] Judgments on these matters are excluded from the scope of the Convention

[56] These terms, and specifically "areas of national jurisdiction", are used in international instruments and other documents dealing with maritime matters and are used here to assist with the uniform interpretation of this exclusion from scope. Therefore, a necessary reference for interpreting those terms is international law, in particular the *United Nations Convention on the Law of the Sea* (UNCLOS).

[57] However, since some emergency towage and salvage are mandatory operations regulated by or conducted under States' authorities, certain judgments will not qualify as civil or commercial matters under Art. 1(1) of the Convention; see Prel. Doc. No 12 of June 2019, para. 76.

[58] Hartley/Dogauchi Report, para. 59. For an explanation of the scope of the terms "limitation of liability for maritime claims", see P. Schlosser, "Report on the Convention of 9 October 1978 on the Association of the Kingdom of Denmark, Ireland and the United Kingdom of Great Britain and Northern Ireland to the Convention on jurisdiction and the enforcement of judgments in civil and commercial matters and to the Protocol on its interpretation by the Court of Justice", *Official Journal of the European Communities*, 5.3.1979, No C 59/71, Luxembourg, 1979 (hereinafter, "Schlosser Report"), paras 124–130.

[59] Hartley/Dogauchi Report, para. 64 (notes omitted).

[60] Nygh/Pocar Report, para. 170.

because they are not usually recognised and enforced in other States.[61] The exclusion only covers the validity, nullity or dissolution of legal persons and associations, or the validity or nullity of decisions of their organs, *e.g.*, the shareholders' meeting or the board of directors. But the exclusion does not cover other judgments related to company law issues, such as judgments on directors' liability, claims for dividend payments or for payments of members' contributions. Naturally, any contract or tortious matter relating to the activities of a legal person or association remains within the scope of the Convention.

Sub-paragraph (j)—the validity of entries in public registers;

58. Sub-paragraph (j) excludes the validity or nullity of entries in public registers, including land registers, land charges registers and commercial registers.[62] Public registers are kept by public authorities and imply the exercise of a sovereign power, and actions on validity of entries must usually be brought against the public authority keeping the register.[63] This includes, for example, cases where registration is refused or amended by the Registrar and the applicant appeals against the decision. This litigation often takes place between the applicant and the Registrar. Accordingly, in principle, entries in public registers are administrative matters outside the scope of the Convention. Article 2(1)(j) prevents doubt.
59. The exclusion does not extend, however, to the legal effects of the entries. Thus, for example, an action against a third-party purchaser of immovable property based on a right of pre-emption registered in the land register is not excluded. By the same token, an action against a private person based on the invalidity of the conveyance of ownership over an immovable property is not excluded either, even if the defendant's ownership is registered in the land register. This judgment is not on the "validity of the entry" as such, but on the validity of the title (*i.e.*, the contract) that gave rise to that entry.

Sub-paragraph (k)—defamation;

60. Sub-paragraph (k) excludes defamation from the scope of the Convention. Defamation is a sensitive matter for many States, since it touches on freedom of expression and therefore may have constitutional implications. The exclusion covers defamation of both natural and legal persons, and includes statements made by any means of public communication, such as press, radio, television or the internet. This exclusion also covers cases of libel and slander (*i.e.*, news or opinions affecting the honour or reputation of a person).

[61] Hartley/Dogauchi Report, para. 70.

[62] The Hartley/Dogauchi Report explains that "some people may not regard this as civil or commercial matters. However, as some international instruments (for instance, Art. 22(3) of the Brussels I Regulation) provide for the exclusive jurisdiction over proceedings that have the validity of such entries as their object, it was thought better to exclude them explicitly in order to avoid any doubts." Ibid., para. 82.

[63] These registers may also be established by international treaties and are also covered by this exclusion, e.g., the registries established under the *UNIDROIT Cape Town Convention on International Interests in Mobile Equipment* and its Protocols (these instruments are available at <www.unidroit.org>).

Sub-paragraph (l)—privacy;

61. **Introduction.** Sub-paragraph (l) excludes privacy. As with defamation, privacy involves a delicate balance between fundamental or constitutional rights, in particular freedom of expression, and is a sensitive matter for many States. While this issue could be addressed on a case-by-case basis by way of the public policy exception under Article 7, it was thought preferable to exclude privacy from the scope of the Convention. Privacy law is currently in great flux in many States, and the scope and definition of privacy varies greatly. [64]The text of the Convention thus avoids defining privacy.
62. **Scope of application.** This exclusion applies to the disclosure of information in any form, including, *e.g.*, text, pictures, audio or video recordings. The core definition of privacy for the purposes of this exclusion refers to situations involving an unauthorised public disclosure of information relating to private life. [65]Such a definition limits the exclusion to natural persons since legal persons do not have a "private life". It entails the exclusion of any judgment ruling on a privacy-based claim by a natural person for compensation due to public disclosure of private information or to prevent such disclosure. While there was consensus that privacy includes such cases, the privacy exclusion is not limited to these situations. In considering whether to apply the exclusion to other situations involving privacy, courts should consider the purpose of the exclusion, having regard also to the international character of the Convention and the need to promote uniformity in its application, as provided by Article 20.
63. **Data protection.** There was agreement that the exclusion does not extend to judgments ruling on contracts involving or requiring the protection of personal data in the business-to-business context, for example, a contract between the holder of personal data and a provider of services in relation to the use of that data.[66]

Sub-paragraph (m)—intellectual property;

64. Sub-paragraph (m) excludes intellectual property. The concept of intellectual property is used in a broad sense, covering matters that are internationally recognised as intellectual property,[67] and other matters that are not internationally recognised as intellectual property but benefit from equivalent protection under certain national laws, such as is currently the case with traditional knowledge or cultural expressions and genetic resources. In the draft Convention prepared by the Special Commission of May 2018, the expression "analogous matters" was used to

[64] See C. North, "Note on the possible exclusion of privacy matters from the Convention as reflected in Article 2(1)(k) of the February 2017 draft Convention", drawn up with the assistance of the Permanent Bureau, Prel. Doc. No 8 of November 2017 for the attention of the Third Meeting of the Special Commission on the Recognition and Enforcement of Foreign Judgments (13–17 November 2017) (available on the HCCH website at <www.hcch.net>, under the "Judgments Section" then "Preparatory Work" and "Meetings of the Special Commission"), para. 51.

[65] See Minutes of the Twenty-Second Session on the Recognition and Enforcement of Foreign Judgments (18 June—2 July 2019), Minutes No 5, paras 39–41 and 43.

[66] Ibid., Minutes No 8, paras 116–119.

[67] See e.g., the *Paris Convention for the Protection of Industrial Property*, as revised at Stockholm in 1967 (the "Paris Convention"), the *Convention establishing the World Intellectual Property Organization* ("WIPO") (as amended 28 September 1979), the *Agreement on Trade related Aspects of Intellectual Property Rights* ("TRIPS"), the *Berne Convention for the Protection of Literary and Artistic Works* (the Berne Convention), or the WIPO Copyright Treaty. As regards the rights and matters covered by those instruments, see in particular the references in Arts 1 and 2 of TRIPS. Of course, this list is not exhaustive.

capture this latter category, to ensure equal treatment of judgements on intellectual property, whether internationally recognised as such or not. However, it was decided during the Twenty-Second Session not to include "analogous matters" in the text of the Convention as this expression is not found in the HCCH 2005 Choice of Court Convention, and in light of concerns expressed by some delegations about the ambiguity of the phrase. The decision to exclude the phrase "analogous matters" has no implications on the scope of the intellectual property exclusion, which is broadly defined as indicated above.

65. The exclusion of intellectual property covers, for example, judgments on validity and registration of intellectual property rights, subsistence of copyright or related rights, and infringement of these rights. However, as regards contracts relating to intellectual property rights, the exclusion is more nuanced, and will depend on whether the dispute is better characterised as contractual. The relevant criterion to define the scope of the exclusion is thus whether the judgment to be recognised or enforced was mainly based on general contract law or on intellectual property law.[68] On the one hand, there are judgments clearly included within the scope of the Convention, e.g., a judgment on a trademark license agreement that rules on the determination of royalties due or a judgment on a distribution contract, which includes a license of intellectual property right, that rules on the under-reporting of sales. In such cases, the judgment is based on general contract law and only indirectly concerns intellectual property matters. On the other hand, there are judgments clearly excluded from the scope of the Convention, e.g., a judgment on a standard essential patent (SEP) involving a fair, reasonable and non-discriminatory (FRAND) licensing obligation, or a judgment determining the patent ownership of an invention made in the course of an employment relationship. In such cases, where the judgment is directly based on the substantive rules governing intellectual property law as opposed to general contract law, the Convention does not apply. Between these two groups, there are difficult or borderline cases, *e.g.*, when the action is based on general contract law but the intellectual property matter arises as a defence. In principle, these judgments must be addressed case by case under the general criterion; if the defence was ruled out as meritless or frivolous, and therefore the judgment is based on general contract law, the Convention will apply. On the other hand, when the contractual aspect was secondary and the judgment was mainly based on intellectual property matters, the Convention does not apply.

Sub-paragraph (n)—activities of armed forces, including the activities of their personnel in the exercise of their official duties;

66. Sub-paragraph (n) excludes judgments related to the activities of armed forces, including the activities of their personnel in the exercise of their official duties. In principle, these judgments will be excluded under Article 1(1) because they are not judgments on civil or commercial matters. The persons who carry out such activities may also benefit from jurisdictional immunity under international law, which is unaffected by the Convention (Art. 2(5); see *infra*, paras 85–89). However, there are no uniform or standard definitions for *acta iure imperii* and *acta iure gestionis*, so States may have different views on this issue. This exclusion is accordingly included to provide greater certainty. It clarifies that activities of armed forces are in any event outside the scope of the Convention and that States are not obliged to recognise or

[68] The three Work. Docs presented in the Twenty-Second Session on this issue used the same sentence to define the scope of this exclusion in contractual disputes: "a judgment is excluded if the dispute is better characterized as an intellectual property matter instead of as a contractual matter" (see Work. Docs Nos 75, 80 and 84).

enforce judgments on these matters, irrespective of whether those activities qualify as *acta iure imperii* in the State of origin or in the requested State. This exclusion also ensures consistency with other bilateral or multilateral treaties that provide for exclusive dispute resolution mechanisms for certain private law claims against armed forces (including both contractual and tort claims).[69] Naturally, this provision must not be interpreted *a contrario*, i.e., it does not imply that the activities of other State authorities are included within the scope of the Convention; insofar as those activities do not qualify as civil or commercial matters, they will be excluded under Article 1(1).

67. Sub-paragraph (n) covers judgments related to the activities of armed forces as such, but it specifically mentions that it includes the activities of their personnel "in the exercise of their official duties". Thus, any judgment against (or in favour of) the armed forces is excluded, whereas a judgment concerning their personnel is only excluded if it rules on a dispute arising from the exercise of their official duties. Thus, for example, a judgment on a civil claim against a soldier deriving from their personal activities, such as a purchase of a private vehicle or a car accident during a holiday trip, is covered by the Convention. Conversely, if the accident occurs in the context of a military exercise, any judgment against the individual soldier will be excluded. The term "personnel" may also include civilians enrolled or employed by the armed forces, *i.e.*, the relevant element is the activities they are carrying out, not their employment status.

Sub-paragraph (o)—law enforcement activities, including the activities of law enforcement personnel in the exercise of their official duties;

68. Sub-paragraph (o) excludes judgments related to law enforcement activities, including the activities of law enforcement personnel in the exercise of their official duties. This exclusion is closely linked to the exclusion of the activities of armed forces in sub-paragraph (n) and follows the same formulation—but with an important difference. To avoid definitional disputes about whether an agency is a law enforcement entity, the exclusion refers to "law enforcement activities" rather than a person or entity, such as the armed forces. The exclusion therefore typically covers bodies that carry out law enforcement activities, such as the police force or border control officers, extending not only to investigations, arrests, etc., but also to subsequent prosecutions. It also includes any activities undertaken pursuant to mutual legal assistance treaties or extradition treaties. This difference aside, both the law enforcement and armed forces provisions have many elements in common. As with the activities of armed forces, most judgments regarding law enforcement activities would not fall within the "civil or commercial" scope of the Convention but were specified in Article 2(1) to address potential divergences in interpretation of *acta iure imperii* under national law. The term "personnel" includes any person carrying out official law enforcement activities irrespective of their employment status. And as with the exclusion of the activity of armed forces under sub-paragraph (n), this exclusion has no implications for the rules on privileges and immunities, which are entirely preserved under Article 2(5).

[69] If a court in one State ignored these mechanisms and gave a judgment, this might give rise to a request under the Convention to recognise and enforce such a judgment, which would undercut the integrity of those bilateral or multilateral treaties.

Sub-paragraph (p)—anti-trust (competition) matters, except where the judgment is based on conduct that constitutes an anti-competitive agreement or concerted practice among actual or potential competitors to fix prices, make rigged bids, establish output restrictions or quotas, or divide markets by allocating customers, suppliers, territories or lines of commerce, and where such conduct and its effect both occurred in the State of origin;

69. Sub-paragraph (p) excludes judgments on anti-trust (competition) matters but only partially. The boundary of this exclusion is determined by: (i) a material element (the scope of the Convention only includes certain categories of anti-trust conduct expressly); and (ii) a connecting factor (the Convention only applies to these categories of anti-trust conduct where there is a particular connection with the State of origin). The formulation of this exclusion in this way is a compromise between conflicting approaches.[70] On the one hand, some delegations favoured including this matter without restrictions, arguing that contemporary anti-trust laws largely share the same objectives and have largely common characteristics at a global level, and that the Convention would only cover private enforcement actions, which would promote those objectives, and not public enforcement actions or orders by anti-trust authorities. On the other hand, another group of delegations favoured a complete exclusion of this matter. These delegations argued that there is a strong element of public interest involved in this field—even with regard to private claims—and it might be difficult (or even inappropriate) to distinguish between public and private enforcement, especially but not only with regard to cases brought by public authorities. This group was also concerned about the potential extra-territorial effect: anti-trust (competition) rules are jurisdiction-specific and allowing judgments in such matters to circulate under the Convention might lead to a "spill-over" effect. This sub—paragraph is formulated as a balanced compromise between these two approaches.
70. The exclusion is phrased "anti-trust (competition) matters", as in the HCCH 2005 Choice of Court Convention (see Art. 2(1)(h)), because different terms are used in different legal systems for rules of similar substantive content. In the United States, for example, the standard term is "anti-trust law", while in Europe "competition law" is used. Therefore, both terms are used in the English version of the Convention.
71. In relation to its material scope, sub-paragraph (p) excludes anti-trust (competition) matters, "except where the judgment is based on conduct that constitutes an anti- competitive agreement or concerted practice among actual or potential competitors to fix prices, make rigged bids, establish output restrictions or quotas, or divide markets by allocating customers, suppliers, territories or lines of commerce". This formulation seeks to include within the scope of the Convention a violation of anti—trust (competition) law on which there appears to be global consensus, i.e., the so—called "hard-core cartels". The wording is inspired by the 1998 OECD Recommendation, [71]and clarifies that anti-competitive agreements or concerted practices among "potential competitors" (*e.g.*, an agreement not to compete or not to enter the market) are also included.[72] The term "concerted practice" or "concerted actions" is commonly used in anti-trust (competition) law and refers to cooperative

[70] For a further analysis of the different views on this matter, see "Report of informal working group V—possible exclusions of anti-trust (competition) matters", Prel. Doc. No 6 of April 2019 for the attention of the Twenty-Second Session on the Recognition and Enforcement of Foreign Judgments (18 June—2 July 2019).

[71] Recommendation of the OECD Council Concerning Effective Action against Hard Core Cartels, adopted on 25 March 1998; now replaced by Recommendation of the OECD Council concerning Effective Action against Hard Core Cartels, adopted on 2 July 2019 (hereinafter "2019 OECD Recommendation").

[72] The words "actual or potential" have also been added in the 2019 OECD Recommendation.

actions among undertakings that do not reach the stage of a formal agreement. The OECD Recommendation is a helpful source of guidance when interpreting this provision, indicating, for example, that the limitation on the exclusion in sub—paragraph (p) does not cover agreements, concerted practices, or arrangements that are reasonably related to the lawful realisation of cost-reducing or output-enhancing efficiencies.[73] Conversely, the Convention does not apply to other categories of anti—trust (competition) law, in particular, prohibitions or restrictions on the unilateral conduct of market operators (*e.g.* abuse of dominance) or prohibitions on mergers and acquisitions that restrict competition.

72. In order to address concerns about extraterritoriality, the inclusion of the listed anti—competitive conduct within the scope of the Convention is restricted to cases with a significant link to the State of origin. Per the last sentence of sub-paragraph (p), the Convention applies in cases of listed anti-competitive conduct but only "[. . .] where such conduct and its effect both occurred in the State of origin". In principle, the term "conduct" refers to the anti-competitive agreement or concerted practice, which must have taken place in the State of origin. The term "effect" refers to the effect in a market of the State of origin. The conduct must have taken place in the State of origin and must have affected the market of this State, irrespective of whether it may have also affected other markets.[74] This requirement for a connection with the State of origin only pertains to the scope of the Convention. Even within scope, to circulate, a judgment must also meet one of the jurisdictional filters laid down by Article 5 (note however that the filter for non-contractual actions in Art. 5(1)(j) does not cover mere financial or economic injury).
73. In any event, since the Convention only applies in civil or commercial matters, any judgment resulting from anti-trust (competition) authorities exercising governmental or sovereign powers is excluded (see *supra*, para. 35). On the other hand, judgments on contractual or non-contractual claims are included, regardless of the nature of the parties (see *supra*, para 30 and 37, and *infra*, para. 82). The contractual context includes, for example, when a person who is a party to an anti-competitive agreement invokes the nullity of this agreement, or when a buyer seeks repayment of excessively high prices paid to the seller as a result of the latter having engaged in a price-fixing arrangement. A non-contractual example would be a claim by a third party for compensation as a result of price fixing or exclusionary conduct. Such actions are included irrespective of whether or not they are based on a prior decision concerning a violation of competition laws by an anti-trust (competition) authority or by a court on application by the authority, *i.e.*, whether they are brought as stand—alone or as follow-on actions.

Sub-paragraph (q)—sovereign debt restructuring through unilateral State measures.

74. Sub-paragraph (q) excludes sovereign debt restructuring through unilateral State measures. The concept of "sovereign debt restructuring" is taken from the resolutions of the United Nations on this matter, which recognise the right of a sovereign State, in the exercise of its discretion, to design its macroeconomic policy, including

[73] See Art. 2(b) of the 1998 OECD Recommendation.

[74] If the judgment covers anti-competitive effects in States other than the State of origin, the application of the Convention will be limited to the part of the judgment ruling on the effects in the State of origin, if it is severable (see Art. 9).

restructuring its sovereign debt.[75] The word "unilateral" is included, however, to reduce the scope of the exclusion. It covers compulsory debt restructuring measures adopted by a State, i.e. measures that were not provided for in the initial borrowing terms and are adopted without or against the consent of the investors. Conversely, the Convention does not exclude debt restructuring measures adopted in accordance with the borrowing terms or that were freely negotiated with the investors. To a large extent, unilateral measures of sovereign debt restructuring fall outside the scope of the Convention under Article 1(1). But the Twenty-Second Session considered it appropriate to add an express exclusion of those matters to prevent any misinterpretation.[76]

Paragraph 2—A judgment is not excluded from the scope of this Convention where a matter to which this Convention does not apply arose merely as a preliminary question in the proceedings in which the judgment was given, and not as an object of the proceedings. In particular, the mere fact that such a matter arose by way of defence does not exclude a judgment from the Convention, if that matter was not an object of the proceedings.

75. Preliminary questions are legal issues that must be addressed before the plaintiff's claim can be decided but which are not the main object or principal issue of the proceedings.[77] This paragraph recognises that legal issues within a judgment may be separate from one another but considered sequentially, with a decision on the principal issue predicated on a decision on another, preliminary question. For example, in an action for damages for breach of a sales contract (main object), the court might first have to decide on the capacity of a party to enter into such a contract (preliminary question), or in an action seeking the payment of corporate dividends (as the main object), the court might have to rule on the decision of the shareholders' meeting approving such payment (as a preliminary question). Preliminary questions are usually, but not always, introduced by the defendant by way of defence. Of course, whether the final judgment can be understood to depend on the answer to the preliminary question can arise irrespective of whether the decision on such a preliminary question is formally part of the final judgment.
76. Paragraph 2 provides that a judgment is not excluded from the scope of the Convention where one of the excluded matters is involved merely as a preliminary question, and in particular where it arises by way of defence. Thus, the application of the Convention is determined by the object of the proceedings. If the object of the proceedings in the court of origin falls within the scope of the Convention, as is the case in the examples mentioned above, this instrument applies. This provision should be read in conjunction with Article 8, which deals with the consequences of a ruling on a preliminary question, including whether a judgment that rules on such matters may circulate under the Convention (see *infra*, paras 277–287).

[75] See Resolution adopted by the General Assembly on 9 September 2014, 68/304, Towards the establishment of a multilateral legal framework for sovereign debt restructuring processes; Resolution adopted by the General Assembly on 29 December 2014, 69/247, Modalities for the implementation of resolution 68/304; and Resolution adopted by the General Assembly on 10 September 2015, 69/319, Basic Principles on Sovereign Debt Restructuring Processes.

[76] In fact, the characterisation of sovereign debt restructuring measures as "civil or commercial matters" has been discussed in preliminary rulings by the Court of Justice of the European Union (CJEU). See, in particular, Judgment of 15 November 2018, *Hellenische Republik v. Leo Kuhn*, C-308/17, EU:C:2018:911.

[77] "Object" is intended to mean the matter with which the proceedings are directly concerned, and which is mainly determined by the plaintiff's claim. See Hartley/Dogauchi Report, paras 77 and 194. The terms "incidental questions" and "principal issue" are used in the Nygh/Pocar Report, para. 177.

77. Article 2(2) of the Convention refers to any matter "to which this Convention does not apply", which captures matters excluded under Article 1(1), Article 2(1) or Article 18. Thus, for example, a judgment on contractual damages based on a finding that the defendant had the necessary capacity to contract—that finding being a matter that would otherwise be excluded under Article 2(1)(a)—is not excluded from the scope of the Convention, although its recognition or enforcement may be refused under Article 8 (see *infra,* paras 285–286).

Paragraph 3—This Convention shall not apply to arbitration and related proceedings.

78. Paragraph 3 excludes arbitration and related proceedings. This exclusion should be interpreted widely to prevent the Convention from interfering with arbitration and international conventions on this subject, particularly the 1958 New York Convention.[78] The exclusion covers both arbitral awards and court decisions relating to arbitration. For example, the Convention does not apply to the recognition and enforcement of arbitral awards, or to the recognition and enforcement of court decisions giving assistance to the arbitral process, *e.g.*, declaring whether the arbitration clause is valid, inoperative or incapable of being performed; ordering parties to proceed to arbitration or to discontinue arbitration proceedings; appointing or dismissing arbitrators; fixing the place of arbitration; or extending the time-limit for making awards.[79] The exclusion also covers judgments declaring whether an arbitral award should be recognised or enforced, as well as judgments setting aside, annulling or amending an arbitral award.

79. Where the judgment concerns civil or commercial matters, the exclusion of arbitration and related proceedings may affect the application of other Articles in the Convention, such as Article 4(1), which concerns the obligation to recognise and enforce judgments given in another State. Thus, pursuant to the paragraph 3 exclusion of arbitration and related proceedings, the requested State may refuse, under its national law or other international instruments, to recognise or enforce a judgment given in another State if the proceedings in the State of origin were contrary to an arbitration agreement, even if the court of origin ruled on the validity of the arbitration agreement.[80] Since the purpose of this exclusion is to ensure that the Convention does not interfere with arbitration, it entails that the court of the requested State can also refuse to recognise or enforce a judgment given despite an arbitration agreement even if the validity of this agreement was not addressed by the court of origin, *e.g.*, if it is a default judgment. However, if the defendant appeared before the court of origin and argued on the merits without invoking the arbitration agreement, the judgment would not, in principle, be contrary to the arbitration agreement and should therefore not be excluded from the scope of the Convention under this provision.

80. By the same token, the requested State may refuse, under its national law or other international instruments, to recognise or enforce a judgment given in another State if the judgment is irreconcilable with an arbitral award.

[78] The *Convention on the Recognition and Enforcement of Foreign Arbitral Awards*, New York, 1958 (hereinafter, "1958 New York Convention"). See also Hartley/Dogauchi Report, para. 84.

[79] Hartley/Dogauchi Report, para. 84.

[80] It should be noted that neither Art. 2(2) nor 8(2) are relevant to this issue. Those provisions refer to "matters" in the sense of subject matters, while the exclusion of arbitration is of a different nature and is included in a separate provision.

81. **Alternative dispute resolution.** Paragraph 3 does not, however, cover other forms of alternative dispute resolution (ADR), *e.g.*, conciliation or mediation. Accordingly, the fact that the proceedings in the court of origin were contrary to an agreement on an ADR mechanism (as an alternative to or prior to the court proceedings) is not a basis to refuse recognition or enforcement. Naturally, the Convention does not apply to the recognition and enforcement of ADR settlements since they do not qualify as "judgments" according to Article 3(1)(b) of the Convention, *i.e.*, they are not "decisions on the merits given by a court" (for their possible qualification as "judicial settlements", see *infra*, paras 295–296).

Paragraph 4—A judgment is not excluded from the scope of this Convention by the mere fact that a State, including a government, a governmental agency or any person acting for a State, was a party to the proceedings.

82. Paragraphs 4 and 5 deal with the application of the Convention to disputes involving States and other governmental bodies. Paragraph 4 provides that the mere fact that a State, including a government, a governmental agency or any person acting for a State, was a party to the proceedings in the State of origin does not exclude a judgment from the scope of the Convention. This paragraph confirms that it is the nature of the dispute that is determinative, rather than the nature of the parties or the courts (Art. 1(1): see *supra*, paras 28–30). Paragraph 4 is thus merely clarificatory. It should, however, be read in conjunction with Article 19, which permits States to declare that they will not apply the Convention to judgments from proceedings where they were a party (see *infra*, paras 343–351), and with Article 2(5), which safeguards the applicable rules on privileges and immunities (see *infra*, para. 86).

83. Declarations under Article 19 aside, the Convention applies when a State or a governmental agency is acting as a private person, *i.e.*, without exercising sovereign powers, and regardless of whether the public entity is the judgment creditor or the judgment debtor. Three core criteria are relevant in determining whether the Convention applies to disputes involving State parties:
"(i) the conduct upon which the claim is based is conduct in which a private person can engage;
(ii) the injury alleged is an injury which can be sustained by a private person;
(iii) the relief requested is of a type available to private persons seeking a remedy for the same injury as the result of the same conduct."[81]

84. Unlike paragraph 5, which concerns privileges and immunities, this provision does not explicitly refer to "international organisations". Nevertheless, a judgment is not excluded by the mere fact that an international organisation was a party to the proceedings insofar as it was acting as a private person.

Paragraph 5—Nothing in this Convention shall affect privileges and immunities of States or of international organisations, in respect of themselves and of their property.

85. Paragraph 5 provides that nothing in the Convention shall affect privileges and immunities of States or international organisations, in respect of themselves and of their property. It also covers State officials, other persons entitled to diplomatic and

[81] Prel. Doc. No 4 of December 2016, para. 40.

consular immunity, and public bodies, such as central banks, to the extent that they have the privileges and immunities to which Article 2(5) refers.[82]

86. This paragraph is a "nil-effect clause", intended only to prevent the misinterpretation of paragraph 4.[83] It does not affect the meaning or scope of privileges or immunities under international law. There are no implications for State claims to jurisdictional immunity before the court of origin, or claims to jurisdictional immunity or immunity from execution before the court of the requested State.[84]
87. In principle, there is no conflict between the scope of the Convention as set down in Article 1(1) and the privileges and immunities of States. As these privileges and immunities are usually linked to the exercise of State authority (*acta iure imperii*), situations involving privileges and immunities will not give rise to judgments in civil or commercial matters. Accordingly, where a judgment is outside the scope of the Convention under Article 1(1), even if a State waives its immunity and submits itself to the jurisdiction of the court of a foreign State, the Convention will not apply to the recognition and enforcement of that judgment.[85]
88. The immunities of States and governmental bodies may be relevant in civil or commercial matters, e.g., if the immunity covers a tort claim against a diplomatic agent deriving from *acta iure gestionis* (see Art. 31 of the *Vienna Convention of 18 April 1961 on Diplomatic Relations*). In such a case, the effect of paragraph 5 will be that the Convention does not apply unless the State waives its immunity and submits itself to the jurisdiction of the court of the State of origin.[86] Even in such a case, nothing in the Convention itself affects immunity from execution in the requested State.
89. Although the scope of privileges and immunities of States or governmental agencies is determined by public international law, this may be specified in domestic legislation in some States. In such cases, courts will refer to the relevant legislation when applying paragraph 5.

[82] Nygh/Pocar Report, para. 46.

[83] Hartley/Dogauchi Report, para. 87.

[84] Accordingly, the Convention does not interfere with the right of a State to invoke its privileges and immunities before the court of the requested State as a defence to refuse recognition or enforcement. In such a case, since Art. 2(5) is a "nil-effect clause", there is no need to resort to Art. 7.

[85] See Minutes of the Special Commission on the Recognition and Enforcement of Foreign Judgments (1–9 June 2016), Minutes No 8, para. 59.

[86] Prel. Doc. No 4 of December 2016, para. 42.

Article 3
Definitions

1. In this Convention –
(a) "defendant" means a person against whom the claim or counterclaim was brought in the State of origin;
(b) "judgment" means any decision on the merits given by a court, whatever that decision may be called, including a decree or order, and a determination of costs or expenses of the proceedings by the court (including an officer of the court), provided that the determination relates to a decision on the merits which may be recognised or enforced under this Convention. An interim measure of protection is not a judgment.
2. An entity or person other than a natural person shall be considered to be habitually resident in the State –
(a) where it has its statutory seat;
(b) under the law of which it was incorporated or formed;
(c) where it has its central administration; or
(d) where it has its principal place of business.

90. Article 3 defines "defendant" and "judgment" (para. 1) and specifies how to determine the habitual residence of legal persons (para. 2), supporting a uniform interpretation and application of the Convention (see Art. 20).

Paragraph 1—In this Convention – Sub-paragraph (a)—"defendant" means a person against whom the claim or counterclaim was brought in the State of origin;

91. The term "defendant" is used in several provisions of the Convention (Art. 5(1)(d), (e), (f), (g), (i), Art. 7(1)(a) and Art. 19(1)). Article 3(1)(a) defines "defendant" as the person against whom the claim or counterclaim was brought in the State of origin. In the context of a counterclaim, the term refers to the initial claimant or any other counterclaim defendant.[87] In the context of a third-party claim, *i.e.*, an action brought by the defendant to force a third party to join the proceedings, "defendant" must be interpreted as referring to the third party against whom this claim was made.

92. Because sub-paragraph (a) focuses on a person against whom the claim or the counterclaim was *brought*, the "defendant" may be different from the person against whom the judgment was given. Further, a "defendant" may even be different from the person against whom recognition and enforcement is sought in the requested State (for particular cases of subrogation, assignment or succession, see *infra*, paras 144–146).

[87] The terms "plaintiff" and "claimant" are used interchangeably in this Report.

Sub-paragraph (b)—"judgment" means any decision on the merits given by a court, whatever that decision may be called, including a decree or order, and a determination of costs or expenses of the proceedings by the court (including an officer of the court), provided that the determination relates to a decision on the merits which may be recognised or enforced under this Convention. An interim measure of protection is not a judgment.

93. Following the HCCH 2005 Choice of Court Convention, sub-paragraph (b) defines "judgment" as any decision on the merits given by a court, including a default judgment, regardless of what that decision is called, such as a decree, order, etc. A "judgment" includes a determination of costs or expenses by the court (including an officer of the court), provided that the determination relates to a decision on the merits that may be recognised or enforced under the Convention. An interim measure of protection, however, is not a judgment for the purpose of the Convention.
94. This definition contains two main elements: the judgment must be (i) "a decision on the merits" and (ii) given by a "court".
95. **A decision on the merits.** "A decision on the merits" implies some kind of contentious judicial proceedings in which a court disposes of the claim (for judicial settlements, see *infra,* Art. 11). Insofar as it involves a disposition of a claim, it includes money and non-money judgments, judgments given by default (see, however, Arts 7(1) and 12(1)(b)),[88] and judgments in collective actions. Conversely, procedural rulings (different from orders determining costs or expenses) are excluded from the definition of judgments. [89]Thus, for example, decisions ordering the disclosure of documents or the hearing of a witness are not judgments. Similarly, ex parte orders for payment concerning uncontested pecuniary claims, which may be issued by a court in some jurisdictions, do not qualify as a judgment. [90]Finally, decisions on recognition and enforcement of foreign judgments or arbitral awards given by the court of a State cannot be recognised or enforced in another State under the Convention (*exequatur sur exequatur ne vaut*). Likewise, enforcement orders, such as garnishee orders or orders for seizure of property, do not qualify as judgments.
96. **Non-monetary judgments.** Judgments that order the debtor to perform or refrain from performing a specific act, such as an injunction or an order for specific performance of a contract (final non-monetary or non-money judgments) fall within the scope of the Convention. In some legal systems, non-monetary judgments sometimes include pecuniary penalties (in French, *astreintes*) to "reinforce" the main part of the judgment. Such judgments contain a non-monetary primary obligation—to perform or not to perform an act—and a monetary "penalty" as a conditional

[88] Judgments by default are within the scope of the Convention irrespective of the process giving rise to the judgment under the law of the State of origin, including whether the judgment is entered or recorded by an officer of the court or by a judge.

[89] Hartley/Dogauchi Report, para. 116.

[90] Some States have established a simplified procedure for uncontested pecuniary claims. This procedure is based on an initial order for payment issued by the court on the basis of the information provided by the claimant, which gives the defendant the option of paying the amount awarded to the claimant or lodging a statement of opposition. If within a certain time limit no statement of opposition is lodged, the court will then confirm or declare the order for payment enforceable. This latter judgment will fall within the scope of the Convention.

secondary obligation in anticipation of non-compliance and to encourage compliance. The legal regimes governing these pecuniary penalties vary significantly.[91]

97. Inclusion of these pecuniary "penalties" was discussed during the Fourth Meeting of the Special Commission but no definitive conclusion was reached.[92] Three factors may be relevant to the application of the Convention to these pecuniary "penalties". In relation to the process, in some jurisdictions these penalties are ordered by the court that gives the non-monetary judgment, but in others they are ordered by a different authority in a separate enforcement procedure. In relation to their content, in some cases these pecuniary penalties may be for a fixed sum or a periodic penalty, *e.g.*, a sum of money for each day of delay.[93] Finally, in relation to the beneficiary of the order, in some jurisdictions these pecuniary penalties are payable to the courts or State authorities (civil fines), but in others they are payable to the judgment creditor even though they are not truly compensatory.[94] The Twenty-Second Session did not discuss this issue and therefore it is a question that remains open for future development by courts and legal scholars.
98. **Decision on costs.** The definition of judgment in sub-paragraph (b) includes two additional elements. First, a determination of costs or expenses of proceedings by a court,[95] including an officer of the court,[96] is also a judgment for the purposes of the Convention, provided it relates to a decision on the merits which may be recognised and enforced under the Convention (see also *infra*, Art. 14(2)). Second, the determination of costs may be included in the same judgment as the decision on the merits or in a separate judgment. In both cases, recognition and enforcement under the Convention is linked to the decision on the merits. If the decision on the merits may not be recognised or enforced under the Convention (for example, because it is outside its scope, it is not eligible for recognition, or a ground for refusal is applicable), then the decision on costs will also not be recognised or enforced. For a costs determination to be recognised and enforced, it is sufficient that the decision on the

[91] For a discussion, see "Treatment of penalty orders that are imposed on the non-compliance with non-monetary judgments under the 2018 draft Convention", Prel. Doc. No. 3 of February 2019 for the attention of the Twenty-Second Session on the Recognition and Enforcement of Foreign Judgments (18 June—2 July 2019) (see path indicated in note 54).

[92] See Minutes of the Special Commission on the Recognition and Enforcement of Foreign Judgments (24–29 May 2018), Minutes No 6, paras 42–51.

[93] Under the Brussels Ia Regulation, for example, judgments that order a payment by way of a penalty shall be enforceable "only if the amount of the payment has been finally determined by the court of origin" (see Art. 55). A similar rule is contained in the *Convention of 30 October 2007 on jurisdiction and the recognition and enforcement of judgments in civil and commercial matters* (hereinafter, the "2007 Lugano Convention") (see Art. 49).

[94] The CJEU has concluded that the Brussels I Regulation applies to a pecuniary penalty that must be paid to the State insofar as it is related to a dispute between two private persons (see CJEU, Judgment of 18 October 2011, *Realchemie Nederland vs Bayer*, C-406/09, EU:C:2011:668).

[95] The words "of the proceedings" were added to "costs or expenses" in the English version only to be in line with the French version of this Convention and of the equivalent provision in the HCCH 2005 Choice of Court Convention. This does not affect the interpretation of "judgment" under either convention.

[96] The French text uses the expression "une personne autorisée par le tribunal". Unlike the HCCH 2005 Choice of Court Convention, which refers to "le greffier du tribunal", the Convention uses a different term to include whichever court official is authorised in the State of origin to determine the cost of the proceedings.

merits "may be" recognised and enforced in the requested State, and not that it already has been. Even if, under such a condition, the decision on costs should be recognised and enforced under the Convention, Article 7 also applies. Thus, in exceptional cases, the decision on the merits may be recognised and enforced but the determination of costs may not, for example, because it was obtained by fraud (see Art. 7(1)(b)).

99. **Interim measures of protection.** Sub-paragraph (b) provides that an interim measure of protection is not a judgment for the purposes of the Convention. "Interim measure of protection" covers measures that serve two main purposes: providing a preliminary means of securing assets out of which a final judgment may be satisfied, or maintaining the *status quo* pending determination of an issue at trial. [97]Thus, for example, an order freezing the defendant's assets, an interim injunction or an interim order for payment cannot be recognised or enforced under the Convention. Naturally, they may still be recognised and enforced under national law.

100. It follows that any costs order relating to interim measures of protection cannot be recognised or enforced because interim measures of protection are not eligible for recognition and enforcement.

101. **Court.** For a decision on the merits to qualify as a judgment under sub-paragraph (b), it must have been given by a "court". The Convention does not define "court". A definition was proposed at the Second Meeting of the Special Commission in the following terms:
"'court' means: (i) a tribunal belonging to the Judiciary of a Contracting State at any level, and (ii) any other permanent tribunal that, according to the law of a Contracting State, exercises jurisdictional functions on a particular subject matter, according to pre-established procedural rules, being independent and autonomous."[98]

102. The proposal was not adopted because it was difficult to articulate a precise definition. [99]In principle, the term "court" must be interpreted autonomously and refers to authorities or bodies that are part of the judicial branch or system of a State and which exercise judicial functions. It does not include administrative authorities, notaries public or non-State authorities.

103. The Convention is also silent on so-called "common courts" although there was sustained discussion on the topic until the Twenty-Second Session. A common court refers to a court to which a group of States have transferred or delegated their judicial power in one or several matters. For example, common courts have been established

[97] On the definition of interim measures, see Nygh/Pocar Report, paras 178–180.

[98] Work. Doc. No 166 of February 2017, "Proposal of the delegations of Ecuador and Uruguay" (Special Commission on the Recognition and Enforcement of Foreign Judgments (16–24 February 2017)). See also Work. Doc. No 235 of November 2017, "Proposal of the delegations of Ecuador and Uruguay" (Special Commission on the Recognition and Enforcement of Foreign Judgments (13–17 November 2017)).

[99] See *Aide memoire* of the Chair of the Special Commission (Special Commission on the Recognition and Enforcement of Foreign Judgments (16–24 February 2017)), para. 21. This definitional difficulty has been encountered in other international conventions and has resulted in the general absence of a comprehensive definition of the term "court" from instruments such as the HCCH 2005 Choice of Court Convention. It is also worth noting that at the Second Meeting of the Special Commission, experts considered that a court may have further characteristics; see Minutes of the Special Commission on the Recognition and Enforcement of Foreign Judgments (16–24 February 2017), Minutes No 11, paras 48–56.

for intellectual property matters.[100] The exclusion of intellectual property from the scope of the Convention under Article 2(1)(m) removed the main impetus for including special rules on these courts. This does not mean that judgments given by a common court that is exercising jurisdiction on matters covered by the Convention are not eligible for recognition and enforcement. Such judgments will circulate if the conditions under the Convention are met, including the definition of judgment in Article 3 and the indicia of "court" indicated in the previous paragraph. In the event that a judgment of a common court were to be brought for recognition and enforcement, it will be for the court of the requested State to determine whether this court can properly be considered a court of a Contracting State and, if so, how the filters laid down by Articles 5 and 6 should be applied.[101]

Paragraph 2—An entity or person other than a natural person shall be considered to be habitually resident in the State –

104. Paragraph 2 deals with the "habitual residence" of entities or persons other than natural persons. These entities are considered to be habitually resident in the State
   (i) where they have their statutory seat, (ii) under whose law they were incorporated or formed, (iii) where they have their central administration, or (iv) where they have their principal place of business.[102] The term "habitually resident" is used in Article 5(1)(a).[103]

105. This provision will typically apply to corporations but it also covers legal persons and associations or unincorporated entities, *i.e.*, associations of natural or legal persons that lack legal personality but are capable, under the law that governs them, of being a party to proceedings.

[100] See e.g., Unified Patent Court, Court of Justice of the Andean Community.

[101] One issue to consider is whether the common court in question is common exclusively to a group of Contracting States. The application of the filters does not give rise to difficulties when all of the States the common court exercises jurisdiction on behalf of are Contracting States. If this is not the case, the free-rider problem may arise whereby a non-Contracting State could unilaterally benefit from the Convention through its membership in the common court. However, where the applicable filter under Art. 5 points to an objective territorial connection with the State of origin, this risk can be avoided even where the common court membership includes non-Contracting States by accepting only those judgments where the connection is established with a Contracting State. The same approach may be applied if all are Contracting States but with regard to one or more of them a third Contracting State has made a declaration under Art. 29. As part of the extensive discussions on common courts it was accepted that where a court serves more than one State but only has appellate functions, e.g., the Judicial Committee of the Privy Council, it is a court of a Contracting State in relation to any judgment it gives on appeal from a court of a Contracting State.

[102] The Hartley/Dogauchi Report (paras 120–123) explains the rationale underpinning these alternative criteria. Note also that the Hartley/Dogauchi Report explains that "A State or a public authority of a State would be resident only in the territory of that State", see note 148 of Hartley/Dogauchi Report. The same should hold for the purposes of the Convention.

[103] Arts 14 and 17 only use the term "resident" (without any qualification) to increase flexibility for those two rules.

Sub-paragraph (a)—where it has its statutory seat;

Sub-paragraph (b)—under the law of which it was incorporated or formed;

106. The terms "statutory seat" and the law under which "the entity is incorporated or formed" refer to two different legal circumstances. The former is the "domicile" of the entity as determined by its bylaws or other constituent documents. The nearest equivalent term in English law is "registered office". The latter refers to the law of the State under which the entity was created, *i.e.*, that gave birth to it and endowed it with legal personality or procedural capacity.[104] In practice, the statutory seat and the place of incorporation will usually coincide in the same State.

Sub-paragraph (c)—where it has its central administration; or Sub-paragraph (d)—where it has its principal place of business.

107. The terms "central administration" and "principal place of business" refer to two different factual circumstances. The former refers to the place where the head office functions are located, *i.e.*, where the most important decisions about the running of the entity are made. The term concerns the "brain" of the entity. The latter refers to the principal centre of the entity's economic activities.[105] It concerns the "muscles" of the entity. For example, a mining company may have its headquarters in London but carry out its mining activity in Namibia.[106]
108. Both sub-paragraphs use the possessive pronoun "its" and therefore refer to the central administration or the principal place of business of the entity or person referred to in the chapeau of paragraph 2, and not to its subsidiary or another entity with legal personality.
109. The four criteria in paragraph 2 are alternatives and there is no hierarchy among them. They are also not mutually exclusive. If the defendant is habitually resident in two or more different States concurrently, the defendant may be considered to be habitually resident in any one of them. For example, if Company X is incorporated in State A, has its central administration in State B, and has its principal place of business in State C, a judgment against Company X given by a court of any of those three States will be eligible for recognition and enforcement under Article 5(1)(a).

[104] Hartley/Dogauchi Report, para. 120.
[105] Ibid.
[106] Ibid.

Chapter II—Recognition and enforcement

Article 4

General provisions

1. A judgment given by a court of a Contracting State (State of origin) shall be recognised and enforced in another Contracting State (requested State) in accordance with the provisions of this Chapter. Recognition or enforcement may be refused only on the grounds specified in this Convention.

2. There shall be no review of the merits of the judgment in the requested State. There may only be such consideration as is necessary for the application of this Convention.

3. A judgment shall be recognised only if it has effect in the State of origin, and shall be enforced only if it is enforceable in the State of origin.

4. Recognition or enforcement may be postponed or refused if the judgment referred to under paragraph 3 is the subject of review in the State of origin or if the time limit for seeking ordinary review has not expired. A refusal does not prevent a subsequent application for recognition or enforcement of the judgment.

110. Article 4 establishes the obligation of mutual recognition and enforcement of judgments among States (para. 1), and sets forth the general conditions and consequences of that obligation. A judgment given in another State shall be recognised and enforced in the requested State without reviewing the merits of the decision (para. 2), but only insofar as it has effect and is enforceable in the State of origin (para. 3). Finally, paragraph 4 deals with cases where the judgment is the subject of review in the State of origin or where the time limit for seeking such review has not expired.

Paragraph 1—**A judgment given by a court of a Contracting State (State of origin) shall be recognised and enforced in another Contracting State (requested State) in accordance with the provisions of this Chapter. Recognition or enforcement may be refused only on the grounds specified in this Convention.**

111. Paragraph 1 establishes the central obligation imposed on States by the Convention: the mutual recognition and enforcement of judgments. Under this provision, a judgment given by a court of a State (the State of origin) shall be recognised and enforced in another State (the requested State) in accordance with the provisions of Chapter II. This obligation presupposes three positive conditions: (i) that the judgment falls within the scope of application of the Convention (see Arts 1 and 2); (ii) that it has effect and is enforceable in the State of origin (Art. 4(3)); and (iii) that it is eligible for recognition and enforcement under Article 5 or 6.

112. The second sentence of paragraph 1 provides that, if the Convention applies, recognition or enforcement may be refused only on the grounds specified in the Convention. Thus, if a judgment is eligible for recognition and enforcement within the scope of the Convention, and the criteria laid down in the following provisions of Chapter II are met, it is not open to a State to refuse recognition or enforcement on other grounds under national law.

113. **Recognition.** Recognition usually implies that the court addressed gives effect to the determination of the legal rights and obligations made by the court of origin. For example, if the court of origin held that a plaintiff had (or did not have) a given right, the court of the requested State would accept that this is the case, *i.e.*, it would treat that right as existing (or not existing). Or, if the court of origin gives a declaratory judgment on the existence of a legal relationship between the parties, the court of the requested State accepts that judgment as determining the issue. [107]Such determination of legal rights is binding on the parties in subsequent litigation. Thus, if the foreign judgment is recognised, it could be invoked, for example, to prevent proceedings between the same parties with the same subject matter (*res judicata* or issue preclusion defence) in the requested State and the judgment creditor would not be burdened with arguing the same claim twice.

114. **Res judicata.** Earlier drafts of the Convention provided that recognition of a judgment would require the court of the requested State to give it "the same effects" it had in the State of origin.[108] This wording entailed that the scope of the *res judicata* effect was determined by the law of the State of origin rather than the law of the requested State. The same applied to similar effects of the judgment, such as issue preclusion or collateral estoppel. This approach was based on the so-called "doctrine of extension of effects": *i.e.*, that recognising a foreign judgment implies *extending* the effects that such judgment has under the law of the State of origin, and not equating it to a domestic judgment of the requested State.

115. The Third Meeting of the Special Commission deleted this provision on the basis that the HCCH 2005 Choice of Court Convention was silent on the issue and several delegations were concerned about its practical consequences, in particular, when the law of the State of origin has a broad approach to the extension of effects based on issue preclusion or collateral estoppel doctrines.[109] But the Convention does not require applying the law of the requested State to determine the effects of a foreign judgment either. The silence of the Convention on this issue must be interpreted consistently with its objectives. The obligation to recognise a foreign judgment under the Convention implies that the same claim or cause of action cannot be re-litigated in another State. Thus, if the foreign judgment determines rights or obligations asserted in a claim, those rights or obligations shall not be subject to further litigation in the courts of the requested State.[110]

[107] Hartley/Dogauchi Report, para. 170.

[108] According to Art. 9 (first sentence) of the draft Convention of February 2017, "[a] judgment recognised or enforceable under this Convention shall be given *the same effect* it has in the State of origin".

[109] See *Aide memoire* of the Chair of the Special Commission (Special Commission on the Recognition and Enforcement of Foreign Judgments (13–17 November 2017)), para. 33.

[110] See Minutes of the Special Commission on the Recognition and Enforcement of Foreign Judgments (13–17 November 2017), Minutes No 9, para. 28; and Work. Doc. No 195 of October 2017, "Proposal of the delegation of the United States of America" (Special Commission on the Recognition and Enforcement of Foreign Judgments (13–17 November 2017)). The Hartley/Dogauchi Report makes it clear that the recognition of rulings on preliminary questions on the basis of doctrines such as issue estoppel, collateral estoppel or issue preclusion is not required by the Convention, but may be granted under national law, see para. 195.

116. **Enforcement.** Enforcement means the application of legal procedures by the courts (or any other competent authority) of the requested State to ensure that the judgment debtor obeys the judgment given by the court of origin. Enforcement is usually needed when the foreign judgment rules that the defendant must pay a sum of money (monetary judgment) or must do or refrain from doing something (injunctive relief), and implies the exercise of the State's coercive power to ensure compliance. Thus, if the court of origin rules that the defendant must pay the plaintiff USD 10,000, the court addressed would enable the judgment creditor to obtain the money owed by the judgment debtor through an enforcement procedure and measures of execution. Because this would be legally indefensible if the defendant did not owe USD 10,000 to the plaintiff, a decision to enforce the judgment typically presupposes recognition of the judgment. [111]Enforcement may also be needed in cases of injunctive relief through the court of the requested State requiring the defendant to meet the obligations to do or refrain from doing something deriving from the judgment (see *supra*, paras 96–97).

117. In contrast, recognition need not be accompanied or followed by enforcement.[112] For example, if the court of origin held that the defendant did not owe any money to the plaintiff, the court of the requested State may simply recognise this finding by dismissing a subsequent claim on the same issue.

118. **Adaptation of remedies.** Former drafts of the Convention contained a rule on adaptation of remedies.[113] The Third Meeting of the Special Commission decided to delete this provision since the HCCH 2005 Choice of Court Convention was silent on this issue. This silence should, therefore, be interpreted in the same manner as in the HCCH 2005 Choice of Court Convention. According to the Hartley/Dogauchi Report (para. 89):

"The Convention does not require a Contracting State to grant a remedy that is not available under its law, even when called upon to enforce a foreign judgment in which such a remedy was granted. Contracting States do not have to create new kinds of remedies for the purpose of the Convention. However, they should apply the enforcement measures available under their internal law in order to give as much effect as possible to the foreign judgment."

Paragraph 2—There shall be no review of the merits of the judgment in the requested State. There may only be such consideration as is necessary for the application of this Convention.

119. A court deciding on recognition and enforcement of a judgment is not entitled to review the merits of the judgment given by the court of origin. That is, if a judgment meets the criteria set out by the Convention for recognition and enforcement, the judgment will not be revisited in the requested State. This rule is a necessary corollary of the principle of mutual recognition of judgments; there would be little purpose to the Convention if the court of the requested State could review the

[111] Because the Convention does not apply to interim measures of protection or to maintenance obligations (and other family matters), any challenge related to the absence of *res judicata* effect of an otherwise enforceable judgment does not arise. See the discussion on this issue in the Nygh/Pocar Report, paras 302–315.

[112] Ibid.

[113] According to Art. 9 (second sentence) of the draft Convention of February 2017, "If the judgment provides for relief that is not available under the law of the requested State, that relief shall, to the extent possible, be adapted to relief with effects equivalent to, but not going beyond, its effects under the law of the State of origin."

underlying factual or legal basis upon which the court of origin reached its decision. Such a circumstance would imply that the parties may be forced to re-litigate the same case in the requested State.[114] Accordingly, as a general matter, the court addressed is not to examine the substantive correctness of that judgment: it may not refuse recognition or enforcement if it considers that a point of fact or law has been wrongly decided. Furthermore, the court addressed cannot refuse recognition or enforcement on the ground that there is a discrepancy between the law applied by the court of origin and the law which would have been applied by the court addressed.

120. **Differences with the wording of the HCCH 2005 Choice of Court Convention.** There are several differences between the wording of Article 4(2) of the Convention and the parallel provision in the HCCH 2005 Choice of Court Convention (Art. 8(2)).[115] The first difference is simply a change in the structure of the first sentence, with no intention to change its substance, that emphasises the primacy of the "no review of the merits" principle. The second difference is the use of two distinct terms in the Convention—"consideration" and "review"—to add precision and avoid misinterpretation. Also, the reference to the "Convention" instead of "this Chapter" clarifies that any consideration of the scope of the Convention according to Article 1 or 2 is covered by Article 4(2).
121. The final difference is substantive. Article 8(2) of the HCCH 2005 Choice of Court Convention provides that the court of the requested State is bound by findings of fact on which the court of origin has based its jurisdiction, unless the judgment has been given by default. That provision only applies to "jurisdiction" under the HCCH 2005 Choice of Court Convention, *i.e.*, when the court of origin bases its jurisdiction on a choice of court agreement. Such a provision makes sense when the instrument establishes harmonised rules on *direct* jurisdiction. This Convention, however, only contains rules on recognition and enforcement of foreign judgments, and not direct rules on jurisdiction. The First Meeting of the Special Commission therefore concluded that it was preferable not to include such a proviso in the Article dealing with review of the merits.[116]
122. **Consideration strictly limited.** Paragraph 2 recognises that, while the primary principle is that no review of the merits of the foreign judgment is permitted, applying the Convention may require consideration of legal or factual issues connected to the foreign proceedings or the foreign judgment. This paragraph is worded to strictly constrain such consideration, ensuring respect of the primary obligation not to review the merits of the foreign judgment.
123. Under Article 5, for example, the court addressed must determine that the judgment is eligible for recognition and enforcement on the basis of the connection between the action giving rise to the judgment and the State of origin. That determination may require identifying the legal or factual bases of connection to the State of origin. For example, the application of Article 5(1)(a) may require that the court addressed consider facts relevant for determining where a legal person had its habitual residence (Art. 3(2)) at the time that person became a party to the proceedings in the State of origin. Regardless of what the court of origin may have stated in relation to

[114] Nygh/Pocar Report, para. 347.

[115] That provision reads: "Without prejudice to such review as is necessary for the application of the provisions of this Chapter, there shall be no review of the merits of the judgment given by the court of origin. The court addressed shall be bound by the findings of fact on which the court of origin based its jurisdiction, unless the judgment was given by default."

[116] Minutes of the Special Commission on the Recognition and Enforcement of Foreign Judgments (1–9 June 2016), Minutes No 3, paras 4–16, and Minutes No 13, paras 3 and 4.

that issue, if it was relevant at all, the court in the requested State makes its own determination for the purpose of applying the Convention. While this should not be understood as a review of the merits,[117] Article 4(2) nevertheless implicitly cautions that such an exercise may give the appearance of impugning the foreign judgment and should therefore be limited to what is strictly necessary for the proper application of the Convention. The same holds for consideration of other paragraphs of Article 5 and other provisions of Chapter II, in particular Article 7 ("refusal of recognition and enforcement") or Article 10 ("damages") as well as provisions in Chapter I, in particular Article 1 ("civil or commercial") and Article 2 ("exclusions from scope").

Paragraph 3—A judgment shall be recognised only if it has effect in the State of origin, and shall be enforced only if it is enforceable in the State of origin.

124. The obligation to recognise and enforce entails conferring on the foreign judgment the authority and effectiveness accorded to it in the State of origin within the judicial and execution system of the requested State. Paragraph 3 contains a corollary to this principle: a judgment shall be recognised only if it has effect in the State of origin, and shall be enforced only if it is enforceable in the State of origin.

125. Paragraph 3 affirms that a judgment will be recognised only if it has effect in the State of origin. [118]Having effect means that the judgment is legally valid and operative. Thus, if the judgment does not have effect in the State of origin, it should not be recognised under the Convention in any other State. Moreover, if the judgment ceases to have effect in the State of origin, it should not thereafter be recognised under the Convention in other States.

126. Likewise, if the judgment is not enforceable in the State of origin, it should not be enforced elsewhere under the Convention. It is possible that a judgment will be effective in the State of origin without being enforceable there, for example, because enforceability has been suspended pending an appeal (either automatically or by an order of the court). Moreover, a judgment that is no longer enforceable in the State of origin—because, for example, it has been overturned on appeal or the limitation period for its enforcement in the State of origin has expired (see *infra*, para. 310)—should not thereafter be enforceable in another State under the Convention.[119]

[117] This is the case whether or not the court addressed comes to a conclusion different from one expressly made in the foreign judgment. Indeed, the court addressed might come to a different conclusion but this relates only to its application of the Convention for the sole purpose of recognition and enforcement of the judgment and is not to be construed as a review of the reasoning or conclusion arrived at by the foreign court in its decision on the merits.

[118] Nygh/Pocar Report, paras 302–315.

[119] Ibid.

Paragraph 4—Recognition or enforcement may be postponed or refused if the judgment referred to under paragraph 3 is the subject of review in the State of origin or if the time limit for seeking ordinary review has not expired. A refusal does not prevent a subsequent application for recognition or enforcement of the judgment.

127. Paragraph 4 deals with judgments subject to review (such as by appeal) in the State of origin or where the time limit for seeking ordinary review has not expired. In these specific situations, the court is not obliged to recognise or enforce the judgment. Instead, paragraph 4 allows for the possibility that the court addressed postpone its decision or refuse recognition or enforcement. Paragraph 4 applies to judgments "referred to in paragraph 3".

128. **Rationale.** The impact of review or appeal mechanisms on the effectiveness or enforceability of judgments varies across legal systems and there is no uniform position on when a decision acquires the effect of *res judicata* or "autorité de chose jugée". In the common law, *res judicata* typically arises when a final judgment is given on issues between the parties which cannot be reconsidered by the same court in ordinary proceedings, even though the decision may potentially or actually be the subject of appeal to a higher court. In contrast, many, if not most, civil law systems take the view that a judgment does not have the status of *res judicata* or "autorité de chose jugée" until the decision is no longer subject to ordinary forms of review.[120] The same holds with regard to enforcement. In some jurisdictions, a judgment is enforceable even if it is the subject of appeal to a higher court. In other jurisdictions, a judgment only becomes enforceable if the time limit for seeking ordinary review has expired.

129. Accordingly, the Convention does not require that the judgment be "final and conclusive", as there is no uniform definition of this status. Instead, according to paragraph 3, it is sufficient that the judgment has effect or is enforceable under the law of the State of origin. This implies that a judgment may be recognised and enforced under the Convention even though it may not be considered to be final either in the State of origin or under the law of the requested State. This solution protects the interest of the judgment creditor and simplifies the application of the Convention insofar as the concepts of "final and conclusive judgment" or "*res judicata* effect" have no uniform meaning.[121] But the lack of a requirement that a judgment be final and conclusive could result in a judgment already recognised or enforced in the requested State subsequently being reversed or set aside in the State of origin.[122] Paragraph 4 addresses this problem by providing an exception to the obligation to recognise and enforce a judgment, applicable where there is a pending appeal or where the time for seeking ordinary review has not expired.

[120] *Ibid.* para. 304.

[121] Ibid., paras 306–311.

[122] Hartley/Dogauchi Report, para. 174. The Convention does not deal with the issue of how to rescind a foreign judgment that has already been enforced in the requested State but is subsequently annulled or amended in the State of origin. This issue was thoroughly discussed in the First and Second Meetings of the Special Commission, and different solutions were considered. See Minutes of the Special Commission on the Recognition and Enforcement of Foreign Judgments (1–9 June 2016), Minutes No 2, para. 48, Minutes No 3, paras 51–66, Minutes No 6, paras 41–49; Minutes of the Special Commission on the Recognition and Enforcement of Foreign Judgments (16–24 February 2017), Minutes No 4, paras 76–82, Minutes No 10, paras 6–8. Finally, the Second Meeting of the Special Commission considered it preferable to leave this issue to the procedural law of the requested State.

130. **Review in the State of origin and unexpired time limit for review.** The court of the requested State is not obliged to grant recognition and enforcement if the judgment is the subject of review in the State of origin or the time limit for seeking ordinary review has not expired. Being "the subject of review" implies that proceedings for the review of the judgment are already pending in the State of origin. Non-expiry of the time limit for seeking ordinary review implies that review of the judgment has not been sought but could still be requested. This phrase only applies to *ordinary* review.[123] The Convention does not define "ordinary review". In principle, it includes any review that: (i) may result in change to the judgment; (ii) is part of the normal course of an action and therefore a step any party must reasonably expect; and (iii) under the law of the State of origin, can only happen before the expiry of a period of time, which typically runs from either the date of the judgment or the date of notification of the judgment to the judgment debtor.

131. **Postponing the decision.** Where the conditions set out in paragraph 4 are met, the Convention provides that the decision on recognition and enforcement may be postponed. In this case, the procedure on recognition and enforcement is stayed or suspended until the review is decided or the time limit for seeking it has expired. This provision does not prevent the court addressed from granting protective measures pursuant to its national law while the procedure is suspended, to ensure future enforcement of the judgment.

132. **Refusing recognition or enforcement.** Paragraph 4 also allows for the refusal to recognise or enforce until the review is decided or the time limit for seeking it has expired. In principle, this provision envisages a refusal of recognition or enforcement based merely on the fact that a review is ongoing in the State of origin, or the time limit for seeking ordinary review has not expired. For this reason, the paragraph clarifies that a refusal does not prevent a subsequent application for recognition or enforcement. Here, refusal means dismissal without prejudice.[124] This provision does not prevent the court addressed from granting protective measures pursuant to its national law while the judgment remains subject to review in the State of origin or while the time for filing such review is yet to expire, to ensure future enforcement of the judgment. Once the judgment becomes final, the judgment creditor may again seek its recognition and enforcement. Naturally, recognition or enforcement might still be denied on other grounds, *e.g.*, that the judgment is not eligible for recognition or enforcement under Article 5 or 6 of the Convention. A decision by the court addressed to deny recognition or enforcement on such other grounds will prevent a subsequent application for recognition and enforcement in the requested State.

[123] On the differentiation between "ordinary" and "extraordinary" review, see Hartley/Dogauchi Report, para. 173, note 209.

[124] Hartley/Dogauchi Report, para. 174.

133. **Granting recognition or enforcement.** Nothing in Article 4(4) prohibits the recognition or enforcement of the foreign judgment in the requested State.[125] This possibility is indicated by the use of "may" instead of "shall" in Article 4(4). In some legal systems, this language will be sufficient to enable courts to exercise their discretion whether or not to postpone or refuse recognition. In legal systems where this is not the case, national rules on treaty implementation may already provide, or national legislation could be adopted to determine, whether granting recognition or enforcement is still possible and, if not, which of the two options in Article 4(4) is available.[126] Recognition or enforcement could also be made subject to the provision of security, where appropriate and available under national law, to compensate the judgment debtor if the judgment is eventually annulled or amended following the review process in the State of origin.

[125] Ibid., para. 173.

[126] This reflects a general principle of the law of treaties, which is also relevant in Arts 7 (see *infra*,para. 245), 8(2) and 10.

Article 5
Bases for recognition and enforcement

1. A judgment is eligible for recognition and enforcement if one of the following requirements is met –
   (a) the person against whom recognition or enforcement is sought was habitually resident in the State of origin at the time that person became a party to the proceedings in the court of origin;
   (b) the natural person against whom recognition or enforcement is sought had their principal place of business in the State of origin at the time that person became a party to the proceedings in the court of origin and the claim on which the judgment is based arose out of the activities of that business;
   (c) the person against whom recognition or enforcement is sought is the person that brought the claim, other than a counterclaim, on which the judgment is based;
   (d) the defendant maintained a branch, agency, or other establishment without separate legal personality in the State of origin at the time that person became a party to the proceedings in the court of origin, and the claim on which the judgment is based arose out of the activities of that branch, agency, or establishment;
   (e) the defendant expressly consented to the jurisdiction of the court of origin in the course of the proceedings in which the judgment was given;
   (f) the defendant argued on the merits before the court of origin without contesting jurisdiction within the timeframe provided in the law of the State of origin, unless it is evident that an objection to jurisdiction or to the exercise of jurisdiction would not have succeeded under that law;
   (g) the judgment ruled on a contractual obligation and it was given by a court of the State in which performance of that obligation took place, or should have taken place, in accordance with
      (i) the agreement of the parties, or
      (ii) the law applicable to the contract, in the absence of an agreed place of performance,
   unless the activities of the defendant in relation to the transaction clearly did not constitute a purposeful and substantial connection to that State;
   (h) the judgment ruled on a lease of immovable property (tenancy) and it was given by a court of the State in which the property is situated;
   (i) the judgment ruled against the defendant on a contractual obligation secured by a right in rem in immovable property located in the State of origin, if the contractual claim was brought together with a claim against the same defendant relating to that right in rem;
   (j) the judgment ruled on a non-contractual obligation arising from death, physical injury, damage to or loss of tangible property, and the act or omission directly causing such harm occurred in the State of origin, irrespective of where that harm occurred;

(k) the judgment concerns the validity, construction, effects, administration or variation of a trust created voluntarily and evidenced in writing, and –
   (i) at the time the proceedings were instituted, the State of origin was designated in the trust instrument as a State in the courts of which disputes about such matters are to be determined; or
   (ii) at the time the proceedings were instituted, the State of origin was expressly or impliedly designated in the trust instrument as the State in which the principal place of administration of the trust is situated.

This sub-paragraph only applies to judgments regarding internal aspects of a trust between persons who are or were within the trust relationship;

(l) the judgment ruled on a counterclaim –
   (i) to the extent that it was in favour of the counterclaimant, provided that the counterclaim arose out of the same transaction or occurrence as the claim; or
   (ii) to the extent that it was against the counterclaimant, unless the law of the State of origin required the counterclaim to be filed in order to avoid preclusion;

(m) the judgment was given by a court designated in an agreement concluded or documented in writing or by any other means of communication which renders information accessible so as to be usable for subsequent reference, other than an exclusive choice of court agreement.

For the purposes of this sub-paragraph, an "exclusive choice of court agreement" means an agreement concluded by two or more parties that designates, for the purpose of deciding disputes which have arisen or may arise in connection with a particular legal relationship, the courts of one State or one or more specific courts of one State to the exclusion of the jurisdiction of any other courts.

2. If recognition or enforcement is sought against a natural person acting primarily for personal, family or household purposes (a consumer) in matters relating to a consumer contract, or against an employee in matters relating to the employee's contract of employment –
   (a) paragraph 1(e) applies only if the consent was addressed to the court, orally or in writing;
   (b) paragraph 1(f), (g) and (m) do not apply.
3. Paragraph 1 does not apply to a judgment that ruled on a residential lease of immovable property (tenancy) or ruled on the registration of immovable property. Such a judgment is eligible for recognition and enforcement only if it was given by a court of the State where the property is situated.

134. Article 5 is a central provision of the Convention. It identifies the connections with the State of origin that are considered sufficient ("jurisdictional filters") for the judgment to be recognised and enforced under the Convention, as provided for in Article 4. In addition to the exclusive filter in Article 6, Article 5 provides an exhaustive list of jurisdictional filters that trigger the mutual recognition principle embodied in the Convention. States can still recognise foreign judgments on the basis of other filters under national law, as per Article 15, but only those filters listed in Articles 5 and 6 create obligations under the Convention. As such, Article 5 defines the perimeter of "eligible judgments", *i.e.*, judgments that circulate under the Convention.

135. **Direct versus indirect jurisdiction.** In some States, the filters listed in Article 5 are described as *indirect* jurisdictional bases, distinguishing them from the rules determining the jurisdiction of the court of the State of origin under its own law—the so-called *direct* jurisdictional bases. The Convention is not concerned with issues of "direct jurisdiction" which remain to be determined by national law. The jurisdictional filters listed in Article 5 are those that a court of a requested State will apply to determine whether a judgment is entitled to recognition or enforcement. In considering whether a foreign judgment meets the threshold conditions of Article 5 or 6, the court addressed does not evaluate the court of origin's application of that State's own jurisdictional rules. While the Convention does not purport to affect existing national laws on jurisdiction in international cases, judgments from States with direct jurisdictional rules similar to the filters in Articles 5 and 6 will be more likely to circulate under the Convention.

136. Article 5 is divided into three paragraphs. The first paragraph lists the connections with the State of origin that are accepted under the Convention for recognition and enforcement of the judgment in the requested State. The second paragraph deals with judgments given against consumers or employees and modifies or excludes the application of certain connections listed in the first paragraph. The third paragraph establishes the jurisdictional filter applicable to judgment on a residential lease of immovable property (tenancy) or registration of immovable property and excludes the application of all filters listed in the first paragraph.

137. **Plurality of parties.** When a judgment is given against more than one party, the filters laid down by Article 5 must be assessed individually for each party. Thus, if the judgment is given against three jointly and severally liable defendants, the connection with the State of origin required by Article 5 must be verified individually for each of them. The mere fact that only one of them has, for example, their habitual residence in the State of origin (Art. 5(1)(a)) is not sufficient for the other co-defendants to be considered to be habitually resident in that State. In such a case, the judgment will not be eligible for recognition and enforcement against the other two co—defendants unless another Article 5 filter is satisfied.

Paragraph 1—A judgment is eligible for recognition and enforcement if one of the following requirements is met –

138. This paragraph contains 13 jurisdictional filters belonging to three traditional categories of connections to the State of origin: connections between the State of origin and the defendant, connections established by consent, and connections between the claim and the State of origin. Many of the connections listed in paragraph 1 are found in national laws but may be formulated more precisely or narrowly in the Convention. There is no hierarchy among the filters in paragraph 1; none are more legitimate than any other for the purpose of recognition and enforcement under the Convention. Moreover, satisfaction of a single filter is sufficient, as expressly stated in paragraph 1.

Sub-paragraph (a)—the person against whom recognition or enforcement is sought was habitually resident in the State of origin at the time that person became a party to the proceedings in the court of origi

139. This sub-paragraph sets out a general rule based on the idea of the "natural" or "home State" forum. Living or being established in the State of origin—i.e., being habitually resident there—is a reasonable connection to the State of origin. This principle holds irrespective of the procedural position of that person in the State of origin. Although this sub-paragraph will typically apply to the defendant, it is not limited to the defendant and can include any other person, natural or legal, against whom recognition or enforcement is sought. Recognition or enforcement may be granted against the defendant, the claimant or a third party that was habitually resident in the State of origin at the time that person became a party to the proceedings.

140. Sub-paragraph (a) is the only filter in Article 5 that concerns links solely with the person against whom recognition or enforcement is sought. All the other filters in paragraph 1 relate either to consent or to connections with the dispute giving rise to the judgment.

141. **"Person against whom recognition or enforcement is sought".** The Convention focuses on the relationship between the State of origin and the person against whom the judgment was given. Because that person may not have been the defendant in the court of origin, it would be too narrow to limit sub-paragraph (a) to that one party. It may be that the claimant lost the case and the defendant seeks recognition and enforcement of the cost order against that person in the requested State. To capture this, sub-paragraphs (a), (b) and (c) use the expression "person against whom recognition or enforcement is sought". Throughout paragraph 1, the terms "person against whom recognition or enforcement is sought" and "defendant" are used, depending on whether the filter could apply to anyone other than a defendant. When that issue does not arise, "defendant" suffices. While this approach causes some overlap between sub-paragraphs (a) and (c), it captures some situations that would not be caught by sub-paragraph (c) alone.[127]

142. **"Habitual residence" as a connecting factor.** The Convention uses "habitual residence" as a connecting factor, as opposed to other approaches found in national law or uniform law instruments, such as domicile or nationality. This approach is consistent with modern instruments from the HCCH, which have preferred habitual residence. Habitual residence is also a more fact-based connecting factor than either domicile or nationality and expresses a close connection between a person and their socio-economic environment. Admittedly, the absence of a definition of habitual residence for natural persons in the Convention may give rise to divergent national interpretations, although this should be discouraged by Article 20 ("uniform interpretation"). With regard to a person or entity other than a natural person, it should be recalled that the definition of habitual residence in Article 3(2) includes four alternatives. As a result, under sub-paragraph (a), the requested State must consider that the State of origin was connected with an entity or person other than a natural person if any one of the four connecting factors listed in Article 3(2) is satisfied.

[127] Thus, if costs were awarded to the claimant against a third party, this filter would apply if that third party was habitually resident in the State of origin when it became party to the proceedings.

143. **"At the time" of the proceedings in the court of origin.** The location of a person's habitual residence may change over time, possibly over the course of litigation before the judgment is eventually given or even after the judgment but before recognition or enforcement is sought. For the purposes of sub-paragraph (a), habitual residence is to be assessed at the time the person against whom recognition or enforcement is sought became a party to the proceedings in the court of origin.[128] It is not necessary that this person still be habitually resident in the State of origin at the moment that the requested State is assessing the connection, so long as the connection at the time the person became a party to the original proceedings is established.

144. **Subrogation, assignment or succession.** The wording of sub-paragraph (a) assumes that the person against whom recognition or enforcement is sought is the same person who was a party to the proceedings in the State of origin. But this provision does not preclude recognition or enforcement against a person other than the person who was a party to the proceedings in the State of origin, provided the person against whom recognition or enforcement is sought has "assumed" the obligations of the person who was a party to the proceedings in the State of origin. Obligations could be assumed by transfer, succession or any other equivalent means, either by consent or by operation of the law. This would be the case, for example, if the party to the proceedings in the State of origin has died and their heirs have assumed their obligations before recognition or enforcement is sought, or if the party to the proceedings in the State of origin was a company that has merged with another company (which has absorbed it) before recognition or enforcement is sought. In these situations, recognition and enforcement may be granted against a person different from that who was a party to the proceedings in the State of origin, *insofar as the former has validly succeeded to the obligations of the latter.* Whether there has been a "valid succession" is governed by the law of the requested State, including its private international law rules.

145. **Example 1.** X brings a claim against Y in State A, where Y is habitually resident. A judgment is given against Y. But during the proceedings in State A or after the judgment is given but before recognition and enforcement is sought, Y dies and her obligations are transferred to her heir. In this case, the judgment is eligible for recognition and enforcement under sub-paragraph (a) since Y had her habitual residence in the State of origin when she became a party to the proceedings in the court of origin and the person against whom recognition or enforcement is sought has validly succeeded to Y's obligations. Naturally, the habitual residence of the heir is irrelevant in this case.

146. **Example 2.** Company X brings a claim against Company Y in State A, where Company Y has its statutory seat. In the course of the proceedings, Company Y merges with Company Z (the acquiring company) and, as a consequence, the former transfers all its assets and liabilities to the latter. In this case, the judgment is given against a person (Company Z) different from the defendant as defined in Article 3(1)(a). Likewise, the merger may take place after the judgment was given in the State of origin but before its recognition and enforcement is sought in the requested State. In this second case, the person against whom recognition or

[128] As explained, this person may be the plaintiff initiating the proceedings against a single defendant, but this "person" could also be a person added in accordance with the procedural rules of the State of origin subsequent to the initiation of proceedings, such as an additional plaintiff or defendant added through a forced or voluntary joinder mechanism, an intervenor, a third-party, etc. It is therefore more precise to refer to the time a person became a party to the proceedings rather than to the time the proceedings were originally instituted.

enforcement is sought (Company Z) is also different from the person against whom the proceedings were instituted in the State of origin (Company Y). In both cases, the judgment is, however, eligible for recognition and enforcement under sub—paragraph (a) since the defendant had its habitual residence in the State of origin at the time it became a party to the proceedings in the court of origin and the person against whom recognition or enforcement is sought has validly succeeded to such defendant.

Sub-paragraph (b)—the natural person against whom recognition or enforcement is sought had their principal place of business in the State of origin at the time that person became a party to the proceedings in the court of origin and the claim on which the judgment is based arose out of the activities of that business;

147. This sub-paragraph is targeted at natural persons engaged in business or in the exercise of a profession and is based on the same principle as sub-paragraph (a). Natural persons may carry on business or professional activities through establishments located in States other than the State of their habitual residence. This is particularly likely in border towns, but with the ease of personal travel it may also occur beyond this context. The Convention provides that there will be sufficient connection with a State of origin for the purposes of recognition and enforcement if a natural person's principal place of business[129] was in that State at the time that person became a party to the proceedings in the court of origin, but only where the claim on which the judgment is based arose from the activities of that business.

148. **Rationale.** Natural persons carrying on business activities are analogous to legal persons with respect to connections to a State. A business that is a legal person will be considered to be habitually resident, *inter alia*, at its principal place of business under Article 3(2). If the business is not a legal person separate from the natural person who provides the goods or services, the connection to the State of the principal place of business under sub-paragraph (a) is not established. Nevertheless, from the perspective of a plaintiff, the two situations are analogous but for the legal status of the business. To reflect this equivalence, sub-paragraph (b) establishes that the location of the principal place of business of a natural person is a sufficient connection for the purpose of recognition and enforcement of a judgment on a claim made against that natural person arising from their business activity.

149. **Conditions.** Sub-paragraph (b) includes two conditions. First, the claim on which the judgment is based must have arisen from the activities of the natural person's business. This is a more limited filter than the general filter of habitual residence under sub-paragraph (a). The wording of sub-paragraph (b) indicates that the judgment must be on a claim that arose from "business activities" but does not require that the activities in question were connected specifically to the principal place of business. The very fact that sub-paragraph (b) refers to the "principal" place of business implies that a natural person may carry on business in more than one place, but only one of them will qualify as a "principal" place of business. Of course, these distinctions are more likely to be present in face-to-face rather than online situations.

[129] The French version refers to "établissement professionnel principal" in Art. 5(1)(b) and "principal établissement" in Art. 3(2)(d), whereas the English version refers to "principal place of business" in both sub-paras. The distinction in the French version was not intentional and therefore should not lead to any differences in interpretation between the two texts.

150. **Example.** X is an accountant who is habitually resident in State A, in a town on the border of States B and C. X's main office is located in a town in State B, where she does most of her business and works on a regular basis. However, she also travels to State C once a week to provide services to her smaller clientele there. Because the price of copier paper is lower in State C, X purchases her weekly supply of copier paper for both offices on Fridays from Y Paper Inc when she is in State C. Should a dispute arise regarding this paper supply, a judgment given against X on such a claim by a court of origin in State B would satisfy sub-paragraph (b) because State B is the State of the principal place of business of X (even though the claim arises out of a transaction that took place in State C), and the claim arises out of the "business activities" of the natural person engaged in those activities. Conversely, when the judgment is on a claim deriving from the personal or family activities of X, sub—paragraph (b) will not apply.

151. The second condition relates to the timing of the claim and the establishment of the principal place of business. Sub-paragraph (b) requires that the natural person's principal place of business be situated in the State of origin at the time that person became a party to the proceedings brought before the court of origin. This requirement of contemporaneity is the same as that in sub-paragraph (a) for habitual residence.

Sub-paragraph (c)—the person against whom recognition or enforcement is sought is the person that brought the claim, other than a counterclaim, on which the judgment is based;

152. Bringing a civil or commercial claim to a court typically indicates acceptance of the jurisdiction of that court, even though a claimant may have limited or no choice about where proceedings can be initiated, which will be determined by the direct jurisdiction rules of each State. This reasoning does not apply to people other than the claimant, such as the defendant, who may have no choice but to respond to the proceedings or risk a default judgment. Sub-paragraph (c) states that the very fact of bringing a claim in the court of origin makes any judgment on that claim enforceable in the requested State against the person who brought the claim in the court of origin.

153. **Example.** X, habitually resident in State A, travels to State B for a camping holiday, where he encounters Y, habitually resident in State C. Damage is caused to X's camping equipment, which X claims is due to Y's negligence. X decides to bring proceedings before the courts of State C, seeking compensation for the loss allegedly caused by Y's fault. Y successfully defends the claim, and the court declares that Y is not liable for any of X's loss and grants Y an award of costs. If X attempts to start new proceedings on the negligence claim in State B, Y could request recognition of the judgment from State C, referring to Article 5(1)(c). As X initiated the claim in State C, the judgment given by the court in State C is eligible for recognition against X in any other Contracting State. Furthermore, if Y wants to enforce the cost award against X in State A, [130]a court in State A may rely on Article 5(1)(c) to enforce the judgment.

[130] This cost award is considered to be a judgment under the Convention as per Art. 3(1)(b).

154. **Relationship with other provisions.** If the claimant was habitually resident in the State of origin when the claim was brought, recognition or enforcement of a judgment against the claimant may also be sought pursuant to sub-paragraph (a). Note also that sub-paragraph (c) does not apply to counterclaims, which are dealt with specifically in sub-paragraph (l).

Sub-paragraph (d)—the defendant maintained a branch, agency, or other establishment without separate legal personality in the State of origin at the time that person became a party to the proceedings in the court of origin, and the claim on which the judgment is based arose out of the activities of that branch, agency, or establishment;

155. Where a branch of the defendant is located in the State of origin, a judgment on a claim arising from the activities of that branch will satisfy the filter in sub—paragraph (d), even if the defendant's habitual residence is in another State. The Convention takes a narrow approach by requiring that the judgment against the defendant involve a claim that arose directly from the activities of the branch located in the State of origin, and not from the general activities of the defendant.
156. **Rationale.** A person who sets up an establishment in another State intentionally creates connections with that State. Judgments from that State's courts on claims arising from the activities of that establishment are thus equally connected to the State of origin.
157. **Branch, agency or other establishment.** The provision refers to "branch, agency or other establishment without separate legal personality". The Convention does not define this concept. In principle, an establishment implies a stable physical presence of the defendant in the State of origin where the defendant carries out an activity. The provision is expressly limited to establishments without legal personality separate from the defendant. This criterion excludes subsidiaries and any other part of a commercial organisation that is constituted as a separate legal entity. [131]This terminology does not exclude natural persons, and therefore may coexist with Article 5(1)(b) when a natural person is, for example, a professional who has a principal place of business in one State and a secondary establishment in another State.
158. **Scope.** For sub-paragraph (d) to apply, there must be a link between the claim on which the judgment is based and the activities of the branch, agency or establishment in the State of origin. In other words, it is not sufficient that the claim arises from the general activities of the defendant; it must arise out of the activities of the branch or establishment in the State of origin. Thus, for example, in a judgment on a contractual dispute, the contract must have been concluded through the establishment in the State of origin or the establishment must be responsible for its performance. A mere remote or incidental connection is not sufficient.

[131] In applying Art. 7(5) of the Brussels Ia Regulation that deals with this type of connection, the CJEU has also included subsidiaries, *i.e.*, establishments with legal personality, under the doctrine of appearance, that is, when they appear vis à vis third parties as a mere branch of the foreign defendant. See Judgment of 9 December 1987, *SAR Schotte GmbH v. Parfums Rothschild SARL*, C-218/86, EU:C:1987:536.

159. This activity-based connection is, however, not limited according to the nature of the claim. The judgment may be on a dispute that arises out of the internal management of the branch or from conduct in the course of its operations, and it may relate to any type of action whether in contract or tort. It might therefore partially overlap with other sub-paragraphs dealing with contractual (sub-para. (g)) and non-contractual obligations (sub-para. (j)).

Sub-paragraphs (e) and (f)—consent

160. These two sub-paragraphs deal with connections to the court of origin established by consent. Article 5(1) envisages three forms of consent: unilateral express consent during proceedings (sub-para. (e)), implied consent (sub-para. (f)) and agreement of the parties (sub-para. (m)). Any one of these forms of consent meets the jurisdictional filter under Article 5(1), regardless of the absence of any other connections with the State of origin.

161. As will be seen below, specific limitations apply to the consent-based filters where judgments are given against defendants who are consumers or employees, as per paragraph 2.

Sub-paragraph (e)—the defendant expressly consented to the jurisdiction of the court of origin in the course of the proceedings in which the judgment was given;

162. The filter in Article 5(1)(e) applies where a defendant expressly consented to the jurisdiction of the court of origin during the course of proceedings in which the judgment is given. The existence of express consent, and whether it was given "in the course of proceedings", is a question of fact to be determined by the court of the requested State. Sub-paragraph (e) does not prescribe the form or substance of this express consent, *i.e.*, it could be oral or in writing. However, other provisions of the Convention should be considered when interpreting the concept of "express consent". First, a separate provision deals with implied consent (sub-para. (f)). The scope for express consent is therefore narrowed and should require a positive act (orally or in writing), as opposed to a failure to raise an objection, for example, or the mere withdrawal of a challenge to jurisdiction of the court of origin. Second, unlike in Article 5(2)(a), this sub-paragraph does not require that the consent be addressed to the court; it may be addressed to the court or to the other party, as long as it is in the course of the proceedings.

163. This manner of consenting may not be known or recognised in all procedural systems. This possibility is not, however, an impediment to the assessment of such consent by the requested State. Indeed, under paragraph 1, the requested State is not assessing whether the court of origin was properly seised under its own rules of *direct* jurisdiction. Rather, the requested State is verifying whether one of the filters in Article 5 is satisfied, regardless of the basis for jurisdiction in the court of origin.

164. **Examples.** The following scenarios illustrate how express consent in the sense of sub-paragraph (e) might present itself:

(i) X initiates proceedings against Y in State A. Under the procedural law of State A, the court is obligated to verify its jurisdiction *ex officio* in claims against foreign defendants. Noting that there is no connection between the claim and State A, the court asks Y, habitually resident in State B, if she wishes to raise any objections to jurisdiction. Y answers that she accepts the jurisdiction of the court in State A and is prepared to proceed before it.

(ii) X initiates proceedings against Y in State A. Y reacts by inviting negotiations to resolve the dispute. The parties successfully resolve part of the dispute but are unable to agree on other aspects. As part of the settlement agreement, X expressly agrees to amend the claim brought before the court in State A and Y expressly accepts that this amended claim will be decided by the court in State A.[132]

(iii) X initiates proceedings against Y in State A and Y is properly notified. In its email response, Y reminds X that their contract includes an arbitration clause but that the cost of arbitration would be prohibitive given the value of the claim. Y expressly agrees that it will defend in State A in this case but reserves its right to raise the arbitration clause in any future disputes under the parties' contract.

Sub-paragraph (f)—the defendant argued on the merits before the court of origin without contesting jurisdiction within the timeframe provided in the law of the State of origin, unless it is evident that an objection to jurisdiction or to the exercise of jurisdiction would not have succeeded under that law;

165. Unlike the express consent contemplated in sub-paragraph (e), the consent in sub—paragraph (f) is implied, typically from the defendant arguing on the merits and failing to contest the jurisdiction of the court of origin. By failing to object to the jurisdiction of the court of origin, the defendant is taken to have accepted that the claim brought against it will be decided by that court.

166. **Rationale.** Consent, either express or implied, is considered to establish a legitimate connection between a court and a defendant. A defendant may accept that the dispute will be adjudicated by the court where the claim was brought, even though there may have been some basis for an objection to that court's jurisdiction. The defendant might wish to avoid the cost and delay of a jurisdictional challenge, or sees no significant advantage in being sued elsewhere, or is unaware that a challenge to jurisdiction is available. Whatever the reason for individual defendants, many States consider that a defendant can implicitly consent to the jurisdiction of their courts.[133]

167. **Conditions.** The application of sub-paragraph (f) is subject to two conditions. First, the defendant must have argued on the merits before the court of origin. Second, the defendant must have failed to contest jurisdiction, except where it is evident that an objection to jurisdiction would have been unsuccessful.

168. **The defendant argued on the merits.** The first condition for the application of sub—paragraph (f) is that the defendant must have argued on the merits before the court of origin. The Convention does not define the precise contours of arguing on the merits. In certain States, any act by a defendant that goes beyond mere contestation of jurisdiction, such as a request to change counsel, will be considered to fall within "arguing on the merits". Of course, the assessment of "arguing on the merits" under sub-paragraph (f) is not dependant on the way it would be determined under the law of the State of origin. The court addressed must make its own evaluation of whether the defendant took any steps in the proceedings before the court of origin that involved contestation of the merits of the dispute.

[132] This scenario might also be considered to fall within sub-para. (m) if the clause within the settlement agreement is interpreted as the "designation of a court".

[133] This is a very general statement, which is obviously subject to numerous limitations.

169. The defendant did not contest the jurisdiction of the court of origin. This is the second condition under sub-paragraph (f). If the defendant is considered to have argued on the merits and did so without having contested the jurisdiction of the court of origin, the filter in sub-paragraph (f) will be satisfied and the resulting judgment will be eligible for recognition and enforcement under the Convention. On the other hand, if a defendant responded to a claim for the sole purpose of objecting to jurisdiction, and the objection was rejected, any ensuing judgment will not satisfy the filter.[134] Moreover, even if a defendant argues on the merits following an unsuccessful challenge to the jurisdiction of the court of origin, the ensuing judgment will not satisfy the filter. In either case, of course, the judgment may circulate if another filter in Article 5 is satisfied.

170. **Contesting jurisdiction "within the timeframe provided in the law of the State of origin".** Procedural rules in the law of the State of origin may set a specific timeframe for a defendant to object to jurisdiction. This might be in terms of days from a certain point, such as notice of the claim, or in terms of sequence, such as prior to engaging in any other procedure. Some legal systems may also envisage the inclusion of all defences, procedural and substantive, in the same procedural document. Under sub-paragraph (f), untimely objections will not avoid a conclusion that the filter is satisfied. If the defendant does not abide by the procedural rules of the State of origin to contest jurisdiction, and argues on the merits, the judgment will circulate under sub-paragraph (f).

171. **Objection to jurisdiction would not have succeeded.** The filter in sub-paragraph (f) is based on the premise that the defendant has implicitly agreed that the dispute will be adjudicated by the court where the claim was brought, even though there may have been some basis for an objection to that jurisdiction. It is the failure to raise the objection that grounds the implied consent of the defendant. A major assumption of this filter is that the procedural law in the court of origin allows the defendant to challenge jurisdiction. It is only in such a case that the failure to contest can be interpreted as implied consent. Sub-paragraph (f) reflects this assumption by framing the rule in terms of a challenge to jurisdiction.

172. Sub-paragraph (f) also takes into account whether such a challenge would have had any chance of success given that it would otherwise be unreasonable to require that the defendant have undertaken such a challenge. In other words, the Convention does not impose an unconditional obligation on the defendant to have contested jurisdiction in the court of origin. If the defendant can show, in the requested State, that any attempt to contest the jurisdiction of the court of origin would not have succeeded, the defendant's failure to raise such a challenge before the court of origin will not satisfy the filter.

173. However, to prevent strategic or opportunistic behaviour by the defendant, the Convention sets out a relatively high standard of proof. It must be *evident* that the objection to jurisdiction would not have succeeded under the law of the State of origin.

[134] This follows whether or not a challenge to jurisdiction is considered to be an argument on the merits. Indeed, the filter makes that issue irrelevant since objecting to jurisdiction is a way to avoid the application of sub-para. (f).

174. **Example.** The court of origin takes jurisdiction on the sole basis that the foreign defendant has property in the jurisdiction even though there is no relation between the claim and that property. Prior decisions in the court of origin indicate that challenges to such jurisdiction are always denied and, as a result, the defendant does not contest jurisdiction in the court of origin. In such a case, the eventual judgment of the court of origin will not be considered to satisfy the filter in sub-paragraph (f) despite the fact that the defendant did not contest jurisdiction before that court and argued on the merits.

175. **Objection to the exercise of jurisdiction.** The wording of sub-paragraph (f) includes not only objections to the jurisdiction of the court of origin but also objections to the exercise of that jurisdiction. This will be relevant where the law in the State of origin includes the doctrine of *forum non conveniens,* which allows a defendant to request that a court decline to exercise its jurisdiction.

176. In most States where *forum non conveniens* is available, it is distinguished from jurisdiction per se. The doctrine allows a court to *decline to exercise jurisdiction*, and thus does not involve any admission by the court that it is *without jurisdiction*. Where this doctrine applies, it is not uncommon for the defendant to first contest jurisdiction and then, in the event the court rejects that challenge, to request that the court decline to exercise its jurisdiction. Defendants may even *concede* jurisdiction and only request that the court decline to exercise it.

177. The language used in sub-paragraph (f) requires that a defendant raise all possible challenges to the jurisdiction of the court of origin or to its exercise of jurisdiction in order to avoid the filter applying in the requested State. If a defendant who had the opportunity to challenge the jurisdiction of a court chose not to do so, or had the opportunity to request that a court decline to exercise its jurisdiction and failed to do so, or fails to show that such requests would have had no chance of success, the filter will be satisfied. In such circumstances, if the defendant argued on the merits, the judgment would be eligible for recognition and enforcement under sub—paragraph (f).

178. **Examples.** Suppose that in the State of origin where the doctrine of *forum non conveniens* is available, a defendant only invoked *forum non conveniens* without also contesting jurisdiction per se. Unless the defendant can show, before the requested State, that jurisdiction per se was not challenged because it had no chance of success, the judgment will be considered to satisfy the filter, even though the defendant asked the court to decline jurisdiction. Similarly, if a defendant did contest jurisdiction but, after this objection was dismissed, did not request that the court decline to exercise its jurisdiction, the defendant must prove that this request had no chance of success. Finally, if the defendant neither contested jurisdiction nor requested that the court of origin decline to exercise its jurisdiction, the defendant will need to show that neither option had a chance of success to avoid a finding that sub-paragraph (f) was satisfied.

179. In all of these scenarios, it does not matter whether the failure to contest jurisdiction or to request that the court decline to exercise jurisdiction amounts to implied consent under the law of the court of origin. The Convention only contains jurisdictional filters for the purpose of determining the eligibility of judgments to circulate. Accordingly, the court in the requested State is not concerned with how the court of origin assesses jurisdiction, but only with whether any one of the filters in Article 5 is satisfied. To avoid the filter in sub-paragraph (f), the defendant must have resisted being subjected to the jurisdiction of the court of origin in every manner available before the court of origin, either explicitly before that court or later before the court addressed by showing that it did not do so in the court of origin because it

had no chance of success in that court. Such actions or arguments by a defendant will, of course, not bar circulation of the judgment if there is another applicable filter under Article 5 or 6. In other words, a defendant cannot simply raise a jurisdictional objection or request that the court of origin decline to exercise its jurisdiction and expect that this will prevent circulation of the judgment under the Convention.

Sub-paragraph (g)—the judgment ruled on a contractual obligation and it was given by a court of the State in which performance of that obligation took place, or should have taken place, in accordance with

(i) the agreement of the parties, or
(ii) the law applicable to the contract, in the absence of an agreed place of performance,
unless the activities of the defendant in relation to the transaction clearly did not constitute a purposeful and substantial connection to that State;

180. This sub-paragraph provides a filter for judgments on contractual obligations. The rule is the result of a compromise between two approaches. On the one hand, some States consider that the place of performance is a sufficient connection to the State of origin, without further qualifications. On the other hand, some States require a more factual appraisal based on the activities of the defendant in the State of origin. It is worth noting that, because parties to international contracts often include choice of court agreements or arbitration clauses in their contracts, this sub-paragraph may not be invoked frequently at the enforcement stage.[135]

181. **Place of performance as a starting point.** Sub-paragraph (g) represents the first approach where the place of performance of a contractual obligation is a basis for recognition and enforcement of a judgment. This formulation means that the connection may vary according to the source of the dispute between the parties that is the object of the judgment. For example, in a contract for the sale of goods, if the vendor files a claim for payment and the judgment is based on that claim, sub—paragraph (g) will recognise the connection to a court at the place where the payment was due. But if the purchaser files a claim for delayed delivery, sub—paragraph (g) will refer instead to the courts in the place of delivery. This approach differs from that in other instruments, such as the Brussels Ia Regulation, which for certain types of contracts posit a single contractual forum that does not vary depending on the obligation forming the basis of the claim.[136]

182. **The place of performance of the contractual obligation: parties' agreement.** The Convention envisages two sources to identify the place of performance of contractual obligations: the contract itself, or the law governing the contract. If the contract specifies the place of performance of the obligation, a judgment given by a court at that place will satisfy the filter in sub-paragraph (g)(i), irrespective of whether performance actually took place in that location. In other words, the parties' agreement as to the place of performance is determinative. In practice, it is very common that the place of performance is included among the general contractual conditions of one or both parties. The validity of such contractual conditions will be determined by the law of the requested State, including its private international law rules.

[135] For judgments given by the court designated in an agreement, see sub-para. (m) below. For a discussion on the exclusion of arbitration from the Convention, see Art. 2(3) above.

[136] See Art. 7(1) of the Brussels Ia Regulation.

183. Where the terms of the contract do not specify the place of performance but the parties have included a choice of law clause in the contract, either sub-paragraph (i) or (ii) may be relevant. Arguably, "the agreement of the parties" could include an agreement on the applicable law, which will then identify the place of performance of the relevant obligation. But the Convention does not establish choice of law rules for contracts. It may be that in a given requested State, no effect or a limited effect would be given to the parties' choice of law clause under sub-paragraph (g)(ii). Thus, to be consistent with the scope of the Convention, which does not intend to set down choice of law rules, it would be preferable to limit sub-paragraph (g)(i) to cases where the terms of the contract specify the place of performance directly.

184. **Applicable law.** The second situation arises where there is no agreement on the place of performance or where the agreement on the place of performance is not valid. In such a case, the place of performance will have to be identified pursuant to the law governing the contract. The Convention does not specify how that law is to be identified and therefore this determination is left to the law of the requested State, including its rules of private international law.

185. **Example.** X brings a claim against Y in State A. The basis of the claim is Y's failure to pay for certain goods delivered to Y in State B. The contract was concluded by telephone and the parties did not designate the place of payment. In this case, if X obtains a favourable judgment based on that claim, it will be recognised and enforced under sub-paragraph (g) if, in accordance with the law governing the contract, the place of payment was State A. The law of the requested State, including its private international law rules, will determine what law governs that contract.

186. **Several places of performance.** Sub-paragraph (g) refers to the place of performance of the contractual obligation on which the judgment ruled. This will usually be the obligation forming the basis of the plaintiff's action. If the same contract contains different and severable obligations for one party, the rule must be applied separately for each of them. For example, if the seller has the obligation to deliver goods in two States, A and B, a judgment given in State A will only circulate under this filter as regards the obligation to deliver goods in this State (Art. 9 on severability may however apply, see *infra*). The application of this rule to negative obligations, *i.e.*, obligations not to do something, was briefly discussed during the Twenty-Second Session but left open for further analysis by courts and legal scholars.

187. **Safeguard: "purposeful and substantial connection to the State of origin".** The place of performance may point to a place that is arbitrary, random or insufficiently related to the transaction between the parties. Recognising the connection to such a place as satisfying the filter might be considered unfair to the defendant. For example, in the case of contracts performed online, the connection with the State of origin may be merely virtual and therefore insufficient to justify circulation of the judgment under the Convention. Accordingly, the Convention provides for recognition or enforcement of a judgment given in the State of the place of performance unless the defendant's activities in relation to the transaction clearly did not constitute a purposeful and substantial connection to that State.

188. This clause has no counterpart in other instruments or national laws, although it reflects concerns in some systems about the fairness afforded to non-resident defendants or to their due process rights. The terms "purposeful and substantial" are used to ensure that the sub-paragraph (g) filter is not satisfied by geographical links that are arbitrary, random or insufficiently related to the transaction between the

parties.[137] Thus, following the example in paragraph 185, Y could raise the safeguard and argue that they clearly did not intend to engage in activities that constitute a purposeful and substantial connection to State A.

Sub-paragraph (h)—the judgment ruled on a lease of immovable property (tenancy) and it was given by a court of the State in which the property is situated;

189. Sub-paragraph (h) is a compromise between two conflicting views in relation to leases over immovable property, called tenancies in many States. Leases of immovable property refer to a legal relationship arising from an agreement where one party undertakes to provide the other party with a temporary right of use of an immovable property, or part of it, in exchange for rent. In some States, such leases are treated in the same way as rights *in rem* and claims regarding them are subject to the exclusive jurisdiction of the State where the property is situated. In other States, such leases are treated as contracts (*i.e.*, rights *in personam*) without the accompanying exclusivity accorded to the courts of the State where the immovable property is located for claims related to the lease.

190. In accordance with sub-paragraph (h), a judgment that rules on a lease of immovable property (tenancy) is eligible for recognition and enforcement if it was given in the State in which the property is situated. It includes any tenancy irrespective of its nature, *i.e.*, for a professional, commercial or personal purpose (except a residential lease subject to the special rule in para. 3). Furthermore, the provision covers disputes between landlord and tenant including, for example, on the existence or interpretation of the tenancy agreement, eviction, compensation for damages caused by the tenant, or the recovery of rent.

191. This provision does not exclude the application of other filters, such as sub—paragraph (a) (the habitual residence of the defendant). Thus, a judgment given by the courts of the State where the defendant was habitually resident will circulate under the Convention even if it ruled on a tenancy over an immovable property located in another State. In relation to sub-paragraph (g) (contractual obligations), the special rule for tenancies may become relevant when, for example, the payment of the rent by the tenant is to be performed in a State different from the State where the property is located. Paragraph 3 provides a distinct rule for residential leases.

Sub-paragraph (i)—the judgment ruled against the defendant on a contractual obligation secured by a right in rem in immovable property located in the State of origin, if the contractual claim was brought together with a claim against the same defendant relating to that right in rem;

192. This provision recognises that it is efficient to allow a claim on a contractual obligation secured by a right *in rem* to be joined with a claim relating to that right *in rem* in the same proceeding.[138] Under Article 6, only the State where the immoveable property is located is considered to fit within the filter with respect to *in rem* claims. Without sub-paragraph (i), it might not be possible to recognise a judgment on the related

[137] See *Burger King Corp. v. Rudzewicz*, 471 U.S. 462 (1985), especially Brennan J. at pp. 478–479 (the United States of America).

[138] Combining these two claims in a single proceeding is to be expected in jurisdictions where the realisation of a security on an immoveable property is judicially administered. Where realisation can be unilaterally effected by the creditor—that is, where extrajudicial enforcement is permitted—only the claim on the possible deficiency will need to be brought, reducing the relevance of this sub—paragraph for those legal systems.

contractual claim brought in that State where, for example, the debtor was not habitually resident in that State (sub-para. (a)) or if payments were not due in that State (sub-para. (g)).

193. **Example.** Z, habitually resident in State A, purchases an immovable property in State B. The purchase price is financed by a mortgage loan granted by a bank in State C. The mortgage agreement provides that payments are due in State C. Z defaults on the mortgage and the bank takes proceedings in State B to obtain a judicial sale of the property and a judgment against Z for any deficiency resulting from the judicial sale. The property sells for less than the amount remaining on the mortgage. The judgment from the court in State B declaring Z liable for the deficiency will be enforceable in State A under sub-paragraph (i).[139]

Sub-paragraph (j)—the judgment ruled on a non-contractual obligation arising from death, physical injury, damage to or loss of tangible property, and the act or omission directly causing such harm occurred in the State of origin, irrespective of where that harm occurred;

194. This sub-paragraph establishes a filter for recognition and enforcement of judgments in matters concerning non-contractual obligations. Again, this connection is not necessary if the person against whom enforcement is sought was habitually resident in the State of origin at the relevant time (sub-para. (a)). With respect to the defendant in the court of origin, this provision would thus be limited to judgments on claims against foreign defendants in the court of origin.[140] Such cases are, admittedly, the situations where enforcement outside the State of origin is more likely to occur, assuming the defendant is found liable and ordered to pay compensation.

195. The Convention does not define non-contractual obligations, just as it does not define contractual obligations in sub-paragraph (g). In principle, these concepts must be defined by national courts in an autonomous manner, taking into account the international character of the Convention and the need to promote uniformity in its application (see Art. 20). The application of this sub-paragraph is, however, limited to certain types of harm suffered.

196. **Non-contractual obligations arising from death, physical injury, damage to or loss of tangible property.** Not all claims involving non-contractual obligations are covered by this provision. It is limited in scope to judgments on obligations arising from two types of injuries: to persons and to property. Even within these categories, the provision is limited to physical injury (including death) for individuals, and to tangible property (damage or loss). This provision will not apply where the judgment is given on a claim based on losses that are not connected to a physical injury or to damage to tangible property.

[139] For another example in the context of a similar provision laid down by the Brussels Ia Regulation, see CJEU, Judgment of 14 February 2019, *Anica Milivojević v. Raiffeisenbank St. Stefan-Jagerberg—Wolfsberg eGen*, C-630/17, EU:C:2019:123 (an action for a declaration of the invalidity of a credit agreement and of the notarised deed relating to the creation of a mortgage taken out as a guarantee for the debt arising from that agreement).

[140] Where judgments are given against multiple defendants or declare such defendants to be jointly liable, the filters under Art. 5, including sub-para. (j), must be satisfied on an individual basis for the judgment against a particular defendant to circulate under the Convention (see also *supra*, para. 137).

197. **The place where the act or omission causing the harm occurred.** The Convention has adopted a narrow basis for non-contractual obligations: it is limited to the place of the act (or omission) directly causing the harm. This approach differs from some national and regional legal systems that also recognise jurisdiction exercised by the court in the State where the harm occurred.[141] This restriction to a single connection, and the limitation on the types of harm noted above, may reduce interpretive difficulties that have arisen in other systems. For example, arguments that some types of injuries are merely "indirect" often arise with respect to non-physical injuries suffered by so-called secondary victims, whose losses arise as a consequence of a physical injury or death suffered by another person. An obvious example is that of a spouse or child claiming for moral or economic loss subsequent to the wrongful death of a spouse or parent. It is possible that judgments on claims by dependents pursuant to wrongful death will not be covered by sub-paragraph (j) because that provision excludes non-physical injuries and deals only with harm directly caused. Alternatively, as sub-paragraph (j) deals with non-contractual obligations *arising* from death, such judgments on claims for dependents may well be included within this filter. This will need to be determined by courts applying the Convention, guided by the Convention's objective of uniform application expressed in Article 20.

198. On the other hand, the wording of sub-paragraph (j) eliminates any question as to whether continuing pain and suffering in the State of origin consequent to a physical injury suffered in another State is sufficient to satisfy the filter. By restricting sub—paragraph (j) to the place where the act or omission causing the harm occurred, there is no room for an alternative connection at the place of the "continuing injury". Other interpretive difficulties relating to the exclusion of the place of injury in sub—paragraph (j) may still arise. For example, a judgment on a claim brought against a foreign manufacturer in the State where a physical injury allegedly occurred may not satisfy the requirements under sub-paragraph (j) if the place of the act (defective design or production) is understood to be in the State where the manufacturer is located. However, if the judgment is on a claim based on an alleged failure to warn, it might be argued that this omission occurred at the place of injury, being where the product was sold or used. If the location of the omission is considered to be a question of law rather than fact in the requested State, the scope of sub-paragraph (j) may vary according to the way in which this question is resolved in the requested State. [142]As in the previous paragraph, this matter will need to be determined by courts applying the Convention, guided by the Convention's objective of uniform application as expressed in Article 20.

Sub-paragraph (k)—the judgment concerns the validity, construction, effects, administration or variation of a trust created voluntarily and evidenced in writing, and –

- (i) **at the time the proceedings were instituted, the State of origin was designated in the trust instrument as a State in the courts of which disputes about such matters are to be determined; or**
- (ii) **at the time the proceedings were instituted, the State of origin was expressly or impliedly designated in the trust instrument as the State in which the principal place of administration of the trust is situated.**

[141] Of course, this is only relevant if this place is different from the place of the act or omission. See Brussels Ia Regulation, Art. 7(2) as interpreted by the CJEU, Judgment of 30 November 1976, Handelskwekerij G. J. Bier BV v. Mines de potasse d'Alsace, C-21/76, EU:C:1976:166.

[142] In other words, the court addressed may look to its domestic law or to the law applicable to the issue according to its choice of law rules.

This sub-paragraph only applies to judgments regarding internal aspects of a trust between persons who are or were within the trust relationship;

199. This sub-paragraph applies to judgments concerning the validity, construction, effects, administration or variation of a trust.[143] As specified in the final part of sub—paragraph (k), only judgments dealing with disputes internal to the trust are included. Judgments dealing with disputes between the parties to the trust and third parties must be considered under other provisions of Article 5(1).
200. **Trusts.** The term "trust" is not defined in the Convention. It is essentially a common law concept and may not be known in other legal systems. It is, however, defined in Article 2 of the HCCH 1985 Trusts Convention for the purposes of that Convention.[144] That definition will be instructive if any question of definition arises because it recites the attributes of a trust according to existing common law concepts.[145]
201. This sub-paragraph applies to a trust created voluntarily and evidenced in writing.[146] It does not include situations under common law where a resulting or constructive trust is imposed by law. Although the trust must be created voluntarily it need not be the product of an agreement; it can be created unilaterally by a trust deed or in a testamentary instrument. The exclusion of wills and succession from the substantive scope of the Convention (Art. 2(1)(d)) does not conflict with the inclusion of testamentary trusts within sub-paragraph (k). Article 2(1)(d) excludes preliminary questions, such as questions as to the validity or interpretation of the will even in so far as they relate to the validity and meaning of the trust. But judgments on other issues arising in the course of the administration of a testamentary trust that has been validly created are covered by sub-paragraph (k) (see also Art. 8(2)).[147]
202. **Designation of a State for determination of listed issues.** Sub-paragraph (k) envisages two alternate connections depending on the instrument creating the trust. The first option is where the trust instrument designates the courts of a State for the determination of the validity, construction, effects, administration or variation of the trust. If that State is the State of origin, the filter is met. Sub-paragraph (k)(i) does not require that the designation in the instrument be exclusive. Moreover, the designation must be included in the instrument at the time the proceedings were instituted. If that is the case, any later modification of the designation will not bar recognition of the eventual judgment at a later date.
203. **Designation of the place of administration of the trust.** The second option is where the trust instrument contains an express or implied designation of the State in which the principal place of administration of the trust is situated. If that State is the State of origin, the filter is met. As with the first option above, the designation must exist at the time the proceedings are instituted. A later variation of the designation will not retroactively extinguish the connection at the moment of recognition or enforcement of the judgment.

[143] According to Art. 8 of the HCCH *Convention of 1 July 1985 on the Law Applicable to Trusts and on their Recognition* (hereinafter, the "HCCH 1985 Trusts Convention"), which on this point reflects established common law doctrine, these matters are determined by the law governing the trust.

[144] At the time of writing, this Convention is in force in 14 Contracting States: Australia, Canada, People's Republic of China (Hong Kong SAR), Cyprus, Italy, Liechtenstein, Luxembourg, Malta, Monaco, the Netherlands, Paraguay, San Marino, Switzerland and the United Kingdom.

[145] Nygh/Pocar Report, para. 150.

[146] This is also the limit of application of the HCCH 1985 Trusts Convention (see Art. 3).

[147] See, for a similar exclusion, the HCCH 1985 Trusts Convention (Art. 4).

204. **Implied designation.** Sub-paragraph (k)(ii) refers to designation of the trust's principal place of administration in the trust instrument itself. In the absence of an express designation, the task of the court addressed is to identify whether there is an implied designation in the trust instrument by interpreting the terms of that instrument, taken as a whole. The court may consider other circumstances of the case only as an aid to interpreting whether the terms of the trust instrument disclose an implied designation. In each case, the court should determine whether the intentions of the settlor are apparent from the terms of the trust instrument in question, without applying any specific presumptions as to those intentions.

205. To assist with this determination, the following are non-exhaustive examples of terms that might provide evidence as to the implied intentions of the settlor: (i) the trustee or trustees are resident in one State, and their identity was stipulated in the trust instrument itself; (ii) a trustee is a company established in a particular jurisdiction specifically to hold the trust assets; (iii) a trust is established for a particular purpose stipulated in the trust instrument (for instance, to benefit a charity in a particular State); (iv) a clause in the trust instrument stipulates that the trust assets are to be retained or invested in a particular jurisdiction.

206. The options in sub-paragraph (k)(i) and (ii) are alternatives and a judgment given by a State that is designated in either manner will satisfy the filter in sub-paragraph (k). In the case of sub-paragraph (k)(ii), recognition or enforcement of such a judgment may nevertheless be refused under Article 7(1)(d).

207. **Internal aspects.** The final sentence of sub-paragraph (k) limits the filter to judgments on disputes that are internal to the trust, *i.e.*, disputes between persons within the trust relationship (such as the settlor, the trustees and the beneficiaries) and not persons external to the trust. The use of "*are or were* within the trust relationship" ensures that a person who was within the trust relationship but was no longer in such a position at the time of recognition or enforcement remains covered by the filter. Judgments dealing with disputes between the parties to the trust and third parties must be considered under other provisions of paragraph 1.

Sub-paragraph (l)—the judgment ruled on a counterclaim –

(i) to the extent that it was in favour of the counterclaimant, provided that the counterclaim arose out of the same transaction or occurrence as the claim; or

(ii) to the extent that it was against the counterclaimant, unless the law of the State of origin required the counterclaim to be filed in order to avoid preclusion;

208. This sub-paragraph establishes filters for counterclaims. In many legal systems, a defendant may respond to a claim not only by a direct defence against that claim, which would have the effect of wholly or partially extinguishing the plaintiff's claim, but also by making an independent claim of its own that seeks a judgment against the original claimant, called a counterclaim. For example, in a contract for the sale of goods on instalment, if the vendor sues for payment of the remaining part of the price, the purchaser can defend against that claim on the basis that this amount is not due and add a counterclaim for damages on the basis that the goods were delivered late. The counterclaim does not need to arise from the same contract but typically has to be connected to the relationship between the parties. While the counterclaim could have been brought separately in another proceeding, it is considered more efficient to allow it to be advanced within the initial proceeding.

In some jurisdictions and in certain circumstances, it may even be compulsory for the defendant to bring its own claim as a counterclaim; failure to do so entails that the claim is considered waived and cannot be brought later in a separate proceeding.[148]

209. Sub-paragraph (l) contains two filters depending on whether the judgment on the counterclaim was for or against the counterclaimant. The differential treatment of successful and unsuccessful counterclaims is included to balance the interests of the parties with regard to the counterclaim and to account for the possibility of compulsory counterclaims under the procedural law in the court of origin.

210. **Judgments in favour of the counterclaimant.** There is no reason to limit circulation where the counterclaim is successful. Indeed, in such a case, any possible prejudice flowing from being forced to bring the counterclaim is balanced by the favourable outcome to the counterclaimant. However, to ensure fairness to the original claimant (the defendant in the counterclaim), the counterclaim must arise out of the transaction or occurrence on which the original claim is based. The original claimant consented to the jurisdiction of the court of origin by voluntarily bringing a claim before that court. It is therefore legitimate that this court may also rule on a counterclaim but only insofar as it derives from the same transaction or occurrence.

211. The word "transaction" is intended to have a wide scope, referring to the parties' relationship. In other words, the counterclaim need not arise out of the actual contract on which the original claim is based; it may arise out of another collateral contract which is part of the wider transaction between the parties. Otherwise, the English word "same occurrence" has been used to represent the French "des mêmes faits" to emphasise that the facts on which the counterclaim is based need not be identical and may arise out of a broader, but still related, set of circumstances.[149]

212. **Judgments against the counterclaimant.** Where the counterclaim fails, there is no need to protect the original claimant by imposing a close connection requirement. The interest of the original claimant is precisely to benefit from the Convention, and the counterclaimant implicitly consented to the jurisdiction of the court of origin by bringing the counterclaim. Since the defendant is essentially a claimant with respect to the counterclaim, this filter may replicate sub-paragraph (c). But the above rationale presupposes that the counterclaimant voluntarily brought the counterclaim. Therefore, to account for the possibility that the counterclaim was compulsory under the law of the State of origin, sub-paragraph (l)(ii) protects the counterclaimant in the event the counterclaim fails by not preventing the losing counterclaimant from instituting the same claim elsewhere.

213. Importantly, this provision will not prevent circulation of the judgment on the counterclaim if another filter in paragraph 1 applies. For example, if the counterclaimant is habitually resident in the State of origin, the judgment against that counterclaimant will satisfy sub-paragraph (a) and the exception for compulsory counterclaims in sub-paragraph (l)(ii) will not protect that unsuccessful counterclaimant. Similarly, if the original claimant is habitually resident in the State of origin, the judgment on the successful counterclaim will also satisfy the filter in sub—paragraph (a) even if the counterclaim did not arise out of the same transaction.

[148] E.g., under Rule 13 of the US Federal Rules of Civil Procedure.

[149] Nygh/Pocar Report, para. 200. Contrast the narrower formulation of Art. 8(3) of the Brussels Ia Regulation, which contains the phrase "the same contract or facts on which the original claim was based".

Sub-paragraph (m)—the judgment was given by a court designated in an agreement concluded or documented in writing or by any other means of communication which renders information accessible so as to be usable for subsequent reference, other than an exclusive choice of court agreement.

For the purposes of this sub-paragraph, an "exclusive choice of court agreement" means an agreement concluded by two or more parties that designates, for the purpose of deciding disputes which have arisen or may arise in connection with a particular legal relationship, the courts of one State or one or more specific courts of one State to the exclusion of the jurisdiction of any other courts.

214. This sub-paragraph provides a filter based on express consent. Where parties have agreed in advance on the forum to resolve their disputes, adjudication in that forum is considered fair to both parties and will usually satisfy jurisdictional requirements for recognition and enforcement purposes in the requested State. The HCCH 2005 Choice of Court Convention provides for the recognition and enforcement of such agreements and the resulting judgments with respect to exclusive choice of court agreements. The definition of a choice of court agreement in sub-paragraph (m) is drawn from the HCCH 2005 Choice of Court Convention, both with respect to the form of the agreement and to its nature as exclusive or non-exclusive, which should ensure consistency in interpretation across the two instruments.

215. **Relationship with the HCCH 2005 Choice of Court Convention.** The Convention seeks to avoid overlap with the HCCH 2005 Choice of Court Convention. To that end, the Convention only deals with non-exclusive choice of court agreements in sub—paragraph (m). This allows the court in the requested State to consider that the filter is met where the parties' agreement designated the court of origin as one before which disputes could be brought but not where that designation excludes all other courts. In the latter case, i.e., when the choice of court agreement is exclusive, the judgment may be recognised and enforced under the HCCH 2005 Choice of Court Convention or, when it is not applicable, under national law.[150]

216. **Non-exclusive agreements.** The Convention defines non-exclusive agreements in the negative. It includes a definition of an "exclusive choice of court agreement" taken from Article 3(a) of the HCCH 2005 Choice of Court Convention and declares that the Convention applies to any agreement "other than an exclusive choice of court agreement". Furthermore, the HCCH 2005 Choice of Court Convention contains a presumption that a choice of court agreement that designates the courts of one State, or one or more specific courts of one State, is deemed to be exclusive unless the parties expressly provided otherwise (Art. 3(b)). In principle, the approach followed by the Convention seeks to avoid gaps between the two instruments.

217. Non-exclusive agreements can take various forms. The agreement may provide for a list of courts in different States among which the claimant is invited (or required) to choose. It may merely indicate that the parties agree not to object to jurisdiction if the claim is brought before a designated court. The agreement may instead be "asymmetrical" (or "hybrid"), meaning that it is exclusive for one party but non—exclusive for another. Asymmetrical clauses are not considered exclusive under the

[150] For more details on the relationship between the HCCH 2005 Choice of Court Convention and the Convention, see *infra*, paras 375–378.

HCCH 2005 Choice of Court Convention and therefore fall within the scope of the Convention.[151] The Hartley/Dogauchi Report includes the following concrete examples of non-exclusive choice of court agreements:

> "– The courts of State A shall have non-exclusive jurisdiction to hear proceedings under this contract."
>
> "– Proceedings under this contract may be brought before the courts of State A, but this shall not preclude proceedings before the courts of any other State having jurisdiction under its law."
>
> "– Proceedings under this contract may be brought before court X in State A or court Y in State B, to the exclusion of all other courts."
>
> "– Proceedings against X may be brought exclusively at X's residence in State A; proceedings against Y may be brought exclusively at Y's residence in State B."

218. The Convention, like the HCCH 2005 Choice of Court Convention, limits this filter to agreements concluded or documented in writing or by any other means of communication that render information accessible so as to be usable for subsequent reference.[152] Oral agreements, therefore, do not benefit from this sub-paragraph.

219. **Examples.** The written agreement between X (habitually resident in State A) and Y (habitually resident in State B) contains the following clause: "For any disputes arising from this distribution agreement, the parties agree to the jurisdiction of the courts of State C." Following a dispute that the parties are unable to resolve amicably, Y brings a claim against X before the courts of State C. Judgment is granted in Y's favour and enforcement is sought in State A where X has assets. In such a case, sub—paragraph (m) will apply only if the court in State A finds that the clause is a non—exclusive choice of court agreement. If not, then sub-paragraph (m) does not apply and the judgment will not be eligible to circulate under the Convention unless there is some other applicable filter under paragraph 1. If State A and State C are both party to the HCCH 2005 Choice of Court Convention, such a clause will be presumed to be exclusive, and the judgment would be eligible to circulate under that instrument.

220. The written agreement between X (habitually resident in State A) and Y (habitually resident in State B) contains the following clause: "For any disputes arising from this agreement, the parties resolve to bring claims exclusively to the commercial courts of Capital City, State C." Following a dispute that the parties are unable to resolve amicably, Y brings a claim against X in State C. Judgment is granted in Y's favour and enforcement is sought in State A where X has assets. Sub-paragraph (m) is not applicable to this case since the clause designating the courts of State C is an exclusive choice of court agreement. Moreover, if no other ground listed in paragraph 1 is applicable, the requested State is not obliged to recognise the judgment under Article 4 of the Convention, although it may recognise it under its national law, as allowed by Article 15. If States C and A are both party to the HCCH 2005 Choice of Court Convention, then the judgment is eligible to circulate under that instrument. That is the intended result as a matter of policy, as the two Conventions are complementary.

[151] Hartley/Dogauchi Report, paras 32, 106 and 249.

[152] On this formal requirement, see Hartley/Dogauchi Report, paras 110–114.

Paragraph 2—If recognition or enforcement is sought against a natural person acting primarily for personal, family or household purposes (a consumer) in matters relating to a consumer contract, or against an employee in matters relating to the employee's contract of employment –

Sub-paragraph (a)—paragraph 1(e) applies only if the consent was addressed to the court, orally or in writing;

Sub-paragraph (b)—paragraph 1(f), (g) and (m) do not apply.

221. **Consumer and employment contracts.** Paragraph 2 provides exceptions to the general rules in paragraph 1 for consumer and employment contracts.[153] These exceptions only apply to recognition and enforcement against a consumer or employee, and not to recognition and enforcement sought by a consumer or employee. These exceptions are consistent with the protection accorded to consumers or employees within the contractual sphere by many legal systems, whether in domestic or private international law. Paragraph 2 does not create special filters for these two types of contracts, which remain subject to the rules set down in paragraph 1. Instead, paragraph 2 limits or excludes, in favour of the weaker party, reference to the three sub-paragraphs in paragraph 1 that deal with filters based on consent (sub-paras (e), (f) and (m)), and to sub-paragraph (g), which deals with the filter on contractual obligations. In practice, these exceptions are likely to restrict the circulation of judgments against a consumer or employee to those given in the State of that person's habitual residence, absent express consent to the jurisdiction of another court by the consumer or employee directed at that court.
222. **Definition of consumer.** The Convention defines a consumer as "a natural person acting primarily for personal, family or household purposes". This is the same definition found in the HCCH 2005 Choice of Court Convention, which excludes consumer contracts from its scope in Article 2(1)(a). It is also consistent with the definition of consumer found in the *Vienna Convention of 11 April 1980 on Contracts for the International Sale of Goods* (Art. 2(a)), and the HCCH *Convention of 22 December 1986 on the Law Applicable to Contracts for the International Sale of Goods* (Art. 2(c)). The other option would have been the negative formulation found in the Brussels Ia Regulation (Art. 17(1)) and Rome I Regulation[154] (Art. 6(1)): "for a purpose […] outside his trade or profession […]". Unlike the European Regulations, the Convention does not specify that the other contracting party must be acting in its trade or professional capacity. This raises the question whether consumer to consumer contracts are included under paragraph 2. As the Twenty-Second Session did not discuss this issue, it will need to be determined by courts applying the Convention, guided by the Convention's objective of uniform application as expressed in Article 20.
223. **Employment contracts.** Employment contracts are not defined under the Convention but it is clear from the phrase "contract of employment" that paragraph 2 is intended to cover salaried workers at any level and not people carrying on independent professional activity.[155]

[153] The HCCH 2005 Choice of Court Convention excludes from its scope choice of court agreements in consumer and employment contracts: Art. 2(1)(a) and (b).

[154] Regulation (EC) No 593/2008 of the European Parliament and of the Council of 17 June 2008 on the law applicable to contractual obligations (Rome I), *Official Journal of the European Union*, 4.7.2008, No L 177, pp. 6–16.

[155] Nygh/Pocar Report, para. 117.

224. **Collective bargaining agreements.** The reference to "matters relating to the employee's contract of employment" indicates paragraph 2 is intended to apply to judgments related to individual employment contracts, *i.e.*, to disputes between employee and employer arising from their labour relationship. This includes any claim between employer and employee based on the legal framework applicable to that relationship, including labour law or collective bargaining agreements.[156] Conversely, disputes arising from a collective bargaining agreement between the parties to this agreement—typically a trade union or a body representative of the employees, on the one hand, and an employer or an association of employers, on the other—are not covered by this paragraph.

225. **Exception to paragraph 1 regarding consent.** Paragraph 2(a) limits the effect of paragraph 1(e), concerning express consent given in the course of proceedings. Where employees and consumers are concerned, the consent must have been "addressed to the court, orally or in writing". In other words, the second and third examples provided above for paragraph 1(e) (see *supra*, para. 164) would not satisfy paragraph 2(a) but the first would, it being the only situation where the expression of consent was directed at the court and not at the other party. The other modes of consenting recognised in paragraph 1 are implied consent (para. 1(f)) and consent by advance agreement between the parties (para. 1(m)). With respect to consumers and employees, neither form of consent is treated as sufficient. In other words, a judgment against a consumer or an employee will not circulate under the Convention if the connection to the State of origin was based solely on consent of either type. Of course, paragraph 1(a) will be satisfied where the employee or consumer was habitually resident in the State of origin.[157]

226. **Exclusion of the filter based on the place of performance of a contractual obligation.** Similar to the above, paragraph 2 excludes recourse to paragraph 1(g), which concerns the place of performance of contractual obligations. A judgment will not be recognised or enforced against a consumer or employee if the only connection to the State of origin was the place of performance of the relevant contractual obligation.

Paragraph 3—Paragraph 1 does not apply to a judgment that ruled on a residential lease of immovable property (tenancy) or ruled on the registration of immovable property. Such a judgment is eligible for recognition and enforcement only if it was given by a court of the State where the property is situated.

227. Paragraph 3 establishes an exception to the filters in paragraph 1 for residential leases and registration of immovable property. The specific filter in paragraph 3 excludes any other filter in paragraph 1, and accordingly any other filter in paragraph 2.

228. **Residential leases.** A residential lease refers to a contract for the use of living accommodation for personal, family or household purposes in exchange for rent. Sub-paragraph (h) already provides a specific filter for a judgment ruling on a lease of immovable property (tenancy), but such a judgment could also circulate under any other relevant filter in paragraph 1. Many States treat residential leases as a special category of leases and seek to protect the residential lessee—considered vulnerable

[156] In the HCCH 2005 Choice of Court Convention, Art. 2(1)(b) excludes choice of court agreements "relating to contracts of employment, including collective agreements".

[157] Other filters under Art. 5(1) could also be satisfied.

in the same manner as a consumer or employee—or to facilitate access to housing through exclusive jurisdiction at the place where the immovable property is situated, ensuring that any mandatory regime governing residential leases under the law of that State applies.[158] Paragraph 3 covers judgments on disputes between landlord and tenant, including, *e.g.*, judgments on the existence or interpretation of the tenancy agreement, eviction, compensation for damages caused by the tenant, or the recovery of rent.

229. **Registration of immovable property.** Paragraph 3 also applies to judgments ruling on the registration of immovable property. This provision covers judgments that rule on the act of registration of immovable property and derive from a dispute between two private parties, typically a judgment ordering the registration of a transfer of immovable property in the context of a dispute between the buyer of the property and the seller (*i.e.*, an action *in personam*). Conversely, other contractual disputes based on contracts for the transfer of immovable property are not covered by this provision, *e.g.*, payment of the price or liability of the seller. In turn, judgments on the registration of immovable property based on rights *in rem* fall within the scope of Article 6. And finally, judgments ruling on the validity of entries in public registers are excluded under Article 2(1)(j) (for the meaning of this exclusion, see *supra*, para. 58).

230. Under paragraph 3, a judgment ruling on a residential lease of immovable property or on the registration of immovable property can only be recognised and enforced under the Convention if it was given by a court of the State where the property is situated. No other filter under paragraph 1 will apply. Thus, for example, a judgment given in State A, where the defendant is habitually resident, relating to a residential lease over an immovable property located in State B, will not circulate under the Convention.[159] However, unlike Article 6, Article 5(3) does not prevent recognition or enforcement under national law (Art. 15).

[158] In most States that provide protective regimes for residential leases, these do not extend to temporary vacation rentals for which contracts often include other services in addition to use of living accommodation. Those States will usually not consider that their courts have exclusive jurisdiction over such contracts. While a uniform interpretation of the term "residential lease" should be pursued (under Art. 20), the exceptional nature of para. 3 and its protective purpose should be considered in determining its scope of application in the court of the requested State.

[159] It is debatable whether the first sentence of Art. 5(3), which excludes the application of para. 1, also applies when the immovable property is situated in a non-Contracting State. The rule is formulated in absolute terms and thus, in principle, it covers any judgment ruling on residential leases or registration of immovable property without any territorial limitation. In the 2018 draft Convention prepared by the Special Commission of May 2018 (see *supra*, note 10), Art. 6(c) contained an exclusive basis for recognition and enforcement with regard to tenancies of immovable property, the application of which was limited to cases where the property was located in a Contracting State. As a result of the compromise reached in the Twenty-Second Session, this provision was amended and moved to Art. 5(3), but this particular issue was not discussed (see also *infra* paras 237–243).

Article 6
Exclusive basis for recognition and enforcement

Notwithstanding Article 5, a judgment that ruled on rights in rem in immovable property shall be recognised and enforced if and only if the property is situated in the State of origin.

231. Article 6 provides a single exclusive basis for the recognition and enforcement of judgments that rule on rights *in rem* in immovable property. This provision has both a positive and negative effect. Judgments that meet the filter in Article 6 are eligible for recognition and enforcement. Judgments that do not meet the filter must neither be recognised nor enforced, either under the Convention or under national law. Article 6 applies, therefore, "[n]otwithstanding Article 5", and provides that such judgments will be enforced "only if" the prescribed connection is present. It lays down an "absolute" exclusive filter for judgments on rights *in rem* over immovable property. Thus, for example, if X brings a claim against Y in State A on a right *in rem* over an immovable property situated in State B, the ensuing judgment shall not be recognised or enforced in any other State. That is why Article 15, which provides that the Convention does not prevent recognition or enforcement under national law, is expressed to be subject to Article 6.
232. Article 6, however, only applies to judgments where a ruling on rights *in rem* over immovable property is the main object of the proceedings. The Convention contains special rules where such a matter arose merely as a preliminary question (see Arts 2(2) and 8).
233. **Rationale.** It is common and largely uncontroversial that a State will consider itself to have exclusive jurisdiction on claims relating to rights *in rem* over immovable property located in that State. The courts of the State where the immovable property is situated are the best placed, for reasons of proximity, to ascertain the facts and apply the rules and practices governing rights *in rem,* which are generally those of the State in which the property is situated. Such proceedings also usually involve public registers or other public documents.[160]
234. **Scope: rights in rem.** Article 6 applies to judgments in proceedings that had as their object rights *in rem*, *i.e.*, rights that directly concern an immovable property and are enforceable "against everybody (*erga omnes*)".[161] The notion of a right *in rem* under the Convention should be given an autonomous meaning, focusing on the effects of the right under the law of the State where the immovable property is situated. Any right over an immovable property that has *erga omnes* effect under that law should be considered to fall within the category of rights *in rem* for the purposes of Article 6. In most States this will include, for example, ownership, mortgages, usufructs or servitudes; other States may grant *erga omnes* effect to certain rights of possession or use, or to some types of long-term leases. Judgments on such rights fall under the exclusive rule of Article 6.

[160] For the arguments in favour of this filter, see Nygh/Pocar Report, para. 164.
[161] Ibid.

235. Article 6 covers judgments on actions that seek to determine the existence of those rights, their extent and content, and to provide the holders with the protection of the powers attached to their entitlements. Conversely, actions based on rights connected with immovable property that do not have *erga omnes* effect are not included within the scope of this provision. For example, an action for the delivery of an immovable property based on a contract for sale (*i.e.*, where the issue is the defendant's obligation to carry out all acts necessary to transfer and hand over the property) or an action in tort for damages to immovable property are not covered by this provision. Rights *in rem* over movable property also do not fall within the scope of this Article.

236. **Immovable property.** The term "immovable property" is not defined under the Convention, but it should be taken to include land, benefits or improvements to land, and fixtures (as opposed to chattels), including things embedded, attached, or affixed to the earth, or permanently fastened to anything embedded, attached, or affixed to the earth. This guidance in relation to immovable property is not exhaustive.

237. **Application vis à vis non-Contracting States.** To understand the application of this provision vis à vis non-Contracting States it is helpful to distinguish three scenarios that vary depending on the location of the immovable property and the State of origin of the judgment.

238. *First scenario: the immovable property is situated in a Contracting State and the State of origin is also a Contracting State.* There is no doubt that Article 6 applies when the immovable property is situated in a Contracting State. In such a case, the judgment will be recognised and enforced *if and only if* the property is situated in the State of origin. Otherwise, the judgment shall neither be recognised nor enforced under the Convention or under national law (see Art. 15). Furthermore, any treaty concluded after this Convention shall not affect this result if the Contracting State where the property is situated is not a party to this later treaty (see Art. 23(3) and (4)).

239. *Second scenario: the immovable property is situated in a non-Contracting State but the State of origin is a Contracting State and one of the filters set out in Article 5 is met.* This scenario requires a more nuanced interpretation.

240. Article 6 begins with "Notwithstanding Article 5 [...]". Thus, it constitutes an exception to the rule that judgments given in a Contracting State are eligible for recognition and enforcement if any of the filters laid down by Article 5 are met. In that sense, therefore, where rights *in rem* over immovable property are concerned, Article 5 is not applicable. Furthermore, Article 6 does not expressly exclude judgments on rights *in rem* over immovable property situated in non-Contracting States.[162] This

[162] To understand this statement, it is important to briefly recall the precedents of this provision. As referred to in note 159, in the 2018 draft Convention (see *supra*, note 10) Art. 6 contained three exclusive bases for recognition and enforcement: (i) one for judgments on validity of registered intellectual property rights; (ii) another for judgments on rights *in rem* in immovable property; and (iii) a third for tenancies of immovable property. As explained in the corresponding version of the revised draft Explanatory Report (Prel. Doc. No 1 of December 2018, "Judgments Convention: revised draft Explanatory Report", para. 271), the first two bases were formulated in absolute terms, whereas the third was limited to cases where the exclusive basis pointed to a Contracting State. As a consequence, Art. 5 did not cover judgments ruling on the validity of an intellectual property right, irrespective of whether this right was registered in a Contracting or non-Contracting State, or on rights *in rem* in immovable property, irrespective of whether the immovable was situated in a Contracting or non-Contracting State (see ibid., para. 263, with an example). Conversely, Art. 5 did cover judgments on tenancies of immovable property when the immovable was situated in a non—Contracting State.

reading of Article 6 would deny circulation of the judgment in the scenario described. This approach would be consistent with national law in many States that deny recognition or enforcement of a foreign judgment given, for example, in the State where the defendant has their habitual residence if it rules on a right *in rem* over immovable property situated in a different State. Following this interpretation, a judgment given in State A, which is a party to the Convention, that rules on a right *in rem* over an immovable property situated in State B, which is not a party, does not circulate under the Convention. The other Contracting States would therefore not be obliged to recognise or enforce that judgment under the Convention, even if a filter in Article 5(1) is met and there is no ground for refusal under Article 7 or 8.

241. However, Article 6 does not create an obligation toward non-Contracting States. It does not seem reasonable to hold that Contracting States have voluntarily restrained their sovereignty in this way. As a result, there is no reason to understand that, in the example above, the other Contracting States are prevented from recognising or enforcing the judgment given in State A over an immovable property situated in a non-Contracting State, either under their national law (notwithstanding Art. 15) or under another international instrument. This conclusion may be drawn from the wording of Article 23(3) and (4), which refer to "[…] the obligations under Article 6 *towards Contracting States* […]" (emphasis added).

242. Thus, the preferable interpretation appears to be that Contracting States are not obliged to recognise or enforce a judgment given in another Contracting State on immovable property situated in a non-Contracting State. Under this view, the Convention does not prevent such recognition or enforcement either under national law or under another international instrument.

243. *Third scenario: the immovable property is situated in a Contracting State and the State of origin is a non-Contracting State.* The Convention does not apply to the recognition and enforcement of judgments given in non-Contracting States and therefore does not address this scenario. National law will govern and, as mentioned above, most national laws would deny recognition in such cases anyway. But if national law did not do so, it may not be coherent for a Contracting State to recognise and enforce such a judgment, given the policy and objectives of the Convention.

Article 7

Refusal of recognition and enforcement

1. Recognition or enforcement may be refused if –
   (a) the document which instituted the proceedings or an equivalent document, including a statement of the essential elements of the claim –
      (i) was not notified to the defendant in sufficient time and in such a way as to enable them to arrange for their defence, unless the defendant entered an appearance and presented their case without contesting notification in the court of origin, provided that the law of the State of origin permitted notification to be contested; or
      (ii) was notified to the defendant in the requested State in a manner that is incompatible with fundamental principles of the requested State concerning service of documents;
   (b) the judgment was obtained by fraud;
   (c) recognition or enforcement would be manifestly incompatible with the public policy of the requested State, including situations where the specific proceedings leading to the judgment were incompatible with fundamental principles of procedural fairness of that State and situations involving infringements of security or sovereignty of that State;
   (d) the proceedings in the court of origin were contrary to an agreement, or a designation in a trust instrument, under which the dispute in question was to be determined in a court of a State other than the State of origin;
   (e) the judgment is inconsistent with a judgment given by a court of the requested State in a dispute between the same parties; or
   (f) the judgment is inconsistent with an earlier judgment given by a court of another State between the same parties on the same subject matter, provided that the earlier judgment fulfils the conditions necessary for its recognition in the requested State.
2. Recognition or enforcement may be postponed or refused if proceedings between the same parties on the same subject matter are pending before a court of the requested State, where –
   (a) the court of the requested State was seised before the court of origin; and
   (b) there is a close connection between the dispute and the requested State.

   A refusal under this paragraph does not prevent a subsequent application for recognition or enforcement of the judgment.

244. The Convention provides a framework for the recognition and enforcement of judgments. To that end, Article 4 sets forth the general obligation with respect to recognition and enforcement of judgments, with filter requirements set out in Articles 5 and 6, and specific defences in Article 7. These defences are grouped into two categories. The first, in paragraph 1, lists grounds that *allow*, but do not require, the requested State to refuse recognition or enforcement based either on the way the proceedings took place in the State of origin or on the nature or content of the judgment itself. As confirmed in Article 4(1), this is an exhaustive list, which limits the grounds a judgment debtor can invoke to avoid recognition or enforcement in the requested State and what a court in the requested State can do. The second category deals with the particular situation of international *lis pendens* and is covered by paragraph 2.

Paragraph 1—Recognition or enforcement may be refused if –

245. This paragraph includes seven grounds that can lead to the refusal to recognise or enforce a judgment in the requested State. They largely replicate the equivalent provision in the HCCH 2005 Choice of Court Convention.[163] The grounds in sub—paragraphs (a), (b) and (d) relate to the way in which proceedings were instituted and conducted in the State of origin. Grounds in sub-paragraphs (c) and (e) concern the effect that recognition or enforcement would have in the requested State. Finally, sub-paragraph (f) takes account of earlier judgments given in a third State.

246. Article 7 establishes that States "*may*" refuse recognition or enforcement if one or more grounds are met. This provision is addressed to States. States can (i) adopt domestic legislation that does not provide for refusal in some of these circumstances or provide for refusal in all these circumstances, (ii) require recognition and enforcement in some of these circumstances, (iii) specify additional criteria that are relevant to the exercise of the discretion, or (iv) leave everything to the discretion of the court.

Sub-paragraph (a)—the document which instituted the proceedings or an equivalent document, including a statement of the essential elements of the claim –

(i) was not notified to the defendant in sufficient time and in such a way as to enable them to arrange for their defence, unless the defendant entered an appearance and presented their case without contesting notification in the court of origin, provided that the law of the State of origin permitted notification to be contested; or

(ii) was notified to the defendant in the requested State in a manner that is incompatible with fundamental principles of the requested State concerning service of documents;

247. The first defence to recognition or enforcement refers to the manner in which the defendant was notified of the claim brought in the State of origin. Essentially, it provides that a lack of proper notification to the defendant will justify non-recognition or non-enforcement.

[163] Art. 9 of the HCCH 2005 Choice of Court Convention.

248. **Document instituting the proceedings.** The document that must be notified to the defendant is the document which instituted the proceedings or an equivalent document, including a statement of the essential elements of the claim. This provision aims to ensure that the defendant was notified of the elements of the claim and had the opportunity to arrange for their defence. Thus, the concept of the document instituting the proceedings includes any document that, under the law of the State of origin, initiates proceedings in a manner that enables the plaintiff to obtain a judgment that may circulate under the Convention. [164]Moreover, the document must contain the "essential elements of the claim" to allow the defendant to make a reasonable decision on a procedural response.

249. Sub-paragraph (a) defines two circumstances in which the notification process may justify a refusal to recognise or enforce a judgment. The first concerns the interests of the defendant while the second concerns the interests of the requested State when notification occurred in that State.[165]

250. **Protection of the defendant.** The ground for refusing recognition or enforcement under sub-paragraph (a)(i) is when the defendant was not made aware in a timely manner of the claim brought in the State of origin. This ground ensures the most basic principle of procedural justice: the right to be heard.[166] The test for appropriate notification is factual rather than technical.[167] Whether a defendant can rely on sub—paragraph (a)(i) depends on that defendant's behaviour in the State of origin. If the defendant did not enter an appearance in the court of origin and the judgment was given by default, the defence based on improper notification could be invoked to refuse recognition or enforcement. If the defendant "entered an appearance and presented their case" in the court of origin without contesting notification, the defence based on improper notification will not be available in the requested State.[168] This condition ensures that notification is contested at the first opportunity and before the court best capable of addressing any deficiencies in notification, such as by granting an adjournment. Where the law in the State of origin does not permit objections to notification, the condition does not apply.

251. **Notification.** Sub-paragraph (a)(i) does not specify the means of the notification. In particular, it does not require personal service on the defendant and other methods of service may suffice, such as, notification on certain persons other than the defendant, *e.g.*, an employee of, or a relative living with, the defendant, or even by public notice. The Convention only requires that notification be sufficient to enable

[164] This recognises the variety of means by which procedural law determines how claims are started.

[165] Hartley/Dogauchi Report, para. 185.

[166] As such, this overlaps with sub-para. (c), which specifically refers to fundamental principles of procedural fairness. Sub-para. (a) can thus be understood as a specific application of sub-para. (c) in relation to notification, with its own conditions that should, arguably, exclude recourse to sub-para. (c) on questions falling within sub-para. (a).

[167] Hartley/Dogauchi Report, para. 186, esp. note 225.

[168] This recalls the filter in Art. 5(1)(f). The different expressions used ("argued on the merits" and "entered an appearance and presented their case") indicate that the possible actions by the defendant under Art. 7(1)(a)(i) are conceived more broadly. An appearance coupled with an objection to jurisdiction, for example, will suffice to exclude an objection based on insufficient notification at the stage of recognition and enforcement under the Convention, even though the defendant is not considered to have argued on the merits.

the defendant to arrange their defence. As to the adequacy of public notice, some courts have concluded that the right to be heard is not violated if the court addressed is satisfied that all investigations required by the principles of diligence and good faith have been undertaken to trace the defendant albeit without success.[169]

252. **Protection of the requested State.** Under sub-paragraph (a)(ii), the issue is whether the defendant was notified in a manner incompatible with fundamental principles of the requested State concerning service of documents. This sub-paragraph only applies where notification of the defendant took place in the requested State. It is thus of very limited application and does not allow the requested State to assess notification in another State according to the law of the requested State or even under the law of the State where service was effected. [170]Nor does it allow the requested State to assess notification in the requested State according merely to the general law of that State, *i.e.*, the *lex fori*; sub-paragraph (a)(ii) restricts the reference to the "fundamental principles [. . .] concerning service of documents" in the requested State.[171]
253. **Rationale.** Many States do not object to service of a foreign document instituting proceedings on their territory without participation of their authorities, and would recognise such service as effective.[172] Other States consider service of documents instituting proceedings to be a sovereign act and unauthorised service of foreign documents an infringement of their sovereignty and ineffective service unless permission has been given through an international agreement.[173] Sub—paragraph (a)(ii) accounts for this latter point of view by providing that the court addressed may refuse recognition or enforcement if the defendant was served in the requested State in a manner that was incompatible with fundamental principles of that State concerning service of documents.
254. The Convention does not define "fundamental principles concerning service of documents". The reference in sub-paragraph (a)(ii) to the principles *of the requested State*, suggests that no uniform or autonomous meaning is required (nevertheless, interpretation must always take into account the call for uniform interpretation in Art. 20). The HCCH 1965 Service Convention, in force in 78 Contracting States at the time of writing of this Report, provides that notification under that instrument can only be refused if compliance would infringe the sovereignty or security of the requested

[169] CJEU, Judgment of 15 March 2012, *G v. Cornelius de Visser*, C-292/10, EU:C:2012:142.

[170] Sub-para. (a) is concerned solely with whether or not the court addressed may refuse to recognise or enforce the judgment. The court of origin will have applied its own procedural law, including international conventions on the service of documents that are in force for the State in question and applicable on the facts of the case. These rules, which might require service to be effected in conformity with the law of the State in which it takes place, are not affected by sub-para. (a). However, except to the limited extent provided in sub-para. (a)(ii), the court addressed may not refuse to recognise or enforce the judgment merely on the ground that service did not comply with the law of the State in which it took place, with the law of the State of origin, or with international conventions on the service of documents. Hartley/Dogauchi Report, note 224.

[171] This provision also overlaps with sub-para. (c), which specifically refers to fundamental principles of procedural fairness (see *supra*, note 166).

[172] Hartley/Dogauchi Report, para. 187.

[173] The HCCH *Convention of 15 November 1965 on the Service Abroad of Judicial and Extrajudicial Documents in Civil or Commercial Matters* (hereinafter, "HCCH 1965 Service Convention") is the most important example. See also Regulation (EC) No 1393/2007 of the European Parliament and of the Council of 13 November 2007 on the service in the Member States of judicial and extrajudicial documents in civil or commercial matters (service of documents).

State.[174] While the two instruments apply in different contexts, the protection resulting from their respective grounds for refusal is similar, i.e., of fundamental principles of the requested State with regard to notification of foreign proceedings in that State.

Sub-paragraph (b)—the judgment was obtained by fraud;

255. Sub-paragraph (b) provides that fraud in obtaining the judgment is a ground for refusing recognition or enforcement. Fraud refers to behaviour that deliberately seeks to deceive in order to secure an unfair or unlawful gain or to deprive another of a right. While some states subsume a defence based on fraud within the public policy defence, others treat fraud as a self-standing defence to recognition and enforcement.[175]
256. The equivalent provision in the HCCH 2005 Choice of Court Convention specifies that it applies to fraud "in connection with a matter of procedure". [176]The Hartley/Dogauchi Report states that the additional specificity in the HCCH 2005 Choice of Court Convention is because "there may be some legal systems in which public policy cannot be used with regard to procedural fraud".[177] That report provides the following examples for the application of the defence: where a party deliberately "serves the writ […] on the wrong address", "gives the wrong information as to the time and place of the hearing", "seeks to corrupt a judge or witness" or "conceals key evidence". [178]These examples relate to the fundamental principles of procedural fairness, including the right to be heard by an impartial and independent tribunal.[179] They concern fraud perpetrated by one party to the proceedings to the detriment of the other party.
257. Unlike the HCCH 2005 Choice of Court Convention, this Convention does not include the limitation that fraud be "in connection with a matter of procedure". This presupposes that substantive fraud may also justify a refusal to enforce. While sub—paragraph (b) is not drafted as narrowly as the corresponding provision in the HCCH 2005 Choice of Court Convention, the Hartley/Dogauchi Report indicates that "fraud as to the substance could fall under the public policy exception".[180] As a result, the difference between these two Conventions is unlikely to have an impact in practice.

[174] Art. 13(1). This assumes that the request for notification otherwise complies with the other requirements of the Convention. For a discussion of the very sparse jurisprudence on this provision, see Permanent Bureau of the HCCH, *Practical Handbook on the Operation of the Service Convention*, 4th ed., The Hague, 2016, paras 220–224. The limitation based on "sovereignty or security" is also included in the HCCH *Convention of 18 March 1970 on the Taking of Evidence Abroad in Civil and Commercial Matters* (Art. 12(1)(b)). See Permanent Bureau of the HCCH, *Practical Handbook on the Operation of the Evidence Convention*, 3rd ed., The Hague, 2016, para. 310.

[175] These are mainly States in the common law tradition. For a discussion on the fraud defence in negotiations for the 1999 preliminary draft Convention, see C. Kessedjian, "Synthesis of the Work of the Special Commission of March 1998 on International Jurisdiction and the Effects of Foreign Judgments in Civil and Commercial Matters", Prel. Doc. No 9 of July 1998, in *Proceedings of the Twentieth Session (2005)*, Tome II, *Judgments*, Cambridge—Antwerp—Portland, Intersentia, 2013, pp. 109–143, paras 40–45.

[176] Art. 9(d) of the HCCH 2005 Choice of Court Convention.

[177] Hartley/Dogauchi Report, note 228.

[178] Ibid., para. 188.

[179] See, *e.g.*, the 1966 *United Nations International Covenant on Civil and Political Rights* (Art. 14) and the *European Convention on Human Rights* (Art. 6(1)).

[180] Hartley/Dogauchi Report, note 228.

Sub-paragraph (c)—recognition or enforcement would be manifestly incompatible with the public policy of the requested State, including situations where the specific proceedings leading to the judgment were incompatible with fundamental principles of procedural fairness of that State and situations involving infringements of security or sovereignty of that State;

258. The public policy defence to recognition or enforcement of foreign judgments is widely admitted across legal systems. Internationally, it has been included in relevant HCCH Conventions for decades[181] and is found in the 1958 New York Convention. The text in the Convention largely follows the formulation used in the HCCH 2005 Choice of Court Convention.[182]
259. **Manifestly incompatible with public policy.** The public policy defence is a final safeguard against recognition or enforcement of a foreign judgment that is considered to be "manifestly incompatible with the public policy of the requested State". It is widely accepted that the concept of public policy must be "interpreted strictly" and recourse thereto "is to be had only in exceptional cases".[183] Recognition or enforcement of the judgment in question "would have to constitute a manifest breach of a rule of law regarded as essential in the legal order of the State in which enforcement is sought or of a right recognised as being fundamental within that legal order".[184]
260. "Manifestly" is a high threshold, intended to ensure that judgments of States are recognised and enforced by other States unless there is a compelling public policy reason not to do so in a particular case. The word "manifestly" has been used in previous cases to discourage the overuse of the public policy exception and to limit its use to situations where recognition or enforcement would lead to an "intolerable result".[185]
261. **Principles of procedural fairness.** The formulation of the defence in sub—paragraph (c) is more specific than the one found in previous HCCH instruments, save for the HCCH 2005 Choice of Court Convention. Under sub-paragraph (c), public policy expressly includes "situations where the specific proceedings leading to the judgment were incompatible with fundamental principles of procedural fairness" of

[181] See, *e.g.*, the *Convention of 15 April 1958 concerning the recognition and enforcement of decisions relating to maintenance obligations towards children*, at Art. 2; the *Convention of 5 October 1961 concerning the powers of authorities and the law applicable in respect of the protection of infants*, at Art. 16; the *Convention of 1 June 1970 on the Recognition of Divorces and Legal Separations*, at Art. 10; the *Convention of 14 March 1978 on Celebration and Recognition of the Validity of Marriages*, at Arts 5 and 14; the HCCH 1985 Trusts Convention, at Art. 18; the *Convention of 29 May 1993 on Protection of Children and Co-operation in Respect of Intercountry Adoption*, at Art. 24; the HCCH 1996 Child Protection Convention, at Arts 22 and 23; the HCCH 2000 Protection of Adults Convention, at Arts 21 and 22; the HCCH 2005 Choice of Court Convention, at Arts 6 and 9; and the HCCH 2007 Child Support Convention, at Art. 22. It is noted that some of these conventions refer to the public policy exception in the context of determining the applicable law to the dispute.

[182] Art. 9(e) of the HCCH 2005 Choice of Court Convention. See also Hartley/Dogauchi Report, paras 189–190.

[183] See "Note on Article 7(1)(c) of the 2016 Preliminary Draft Convention", drawn up by the *co-Rapporteurs* of the draft Convention and the Permanent Bureau, Prel. Doc. No 5 of December 2016 for the attention of the Special Commission of February 2017 on the Recognition and Enforcement of Foreign Judgments (hereinafter, "Prel. Doc. No 5 of December 2016"), para. 28.

[184] See the *Explanatory Report by Professor Fausto Pocar to the Convention on jurisdiction and the recognition and enforcement of judgments in civil and commercial matters*, (hereinafter, "Pocar Report to the 2007 Lugano Convention"), *Official Journal of the European Union*, 23.12.2009, No C 319/01.

[185] See Prel. Doc. No 5 of December 2016, para. 29.

the requested State. The Hartley/Dogauchi Report[186] explains that in some States, fundamental principles of procedural fairness (also known as due process of law, natural justice or the right to a fair trial) are constitutionally mandated. [187]In such States, it might be unconstitutional to recognise a foreign judgment obtained in proceedings where a fundamental breach of these principles occurred. The reference in sub-paragraph (c) overlaps with the procedural safeguards and fundamental principles regarding notification in sub-paragraph (a), and with the concerns regarding procedural fairness in the face of fraud in sub-paragraph (b). This overlap should ensure that adequate procedural protection is provided to parties facing recognition and enforcement proceedings regardless of the particular way in which those issues are dealt with in the requested State.[188]

262. **Content of public policy.** The content of the public policy defence is notoriously difficult to define. Its scope in the Convention should, however, be understood in relation to other provisions in the text. As mentioned above, other defences under paragraph 1 overlap with the public policy defence, which should be interpreted accordingly, extending beyond the specifics of the particular defences only where doing otherwise would be a "manifest" contradiction with essential policies of the requested State.

263. The exceptional character of the public policy defence means that it is not sufficient for the party opposing recognition or enforcement to point to a mandatory rule of the law of the requested State that the foreign judgment fails to uphold. Indeed, this mandatory rule may be considered imperative for domestic cases but not for international situations. The public policy defence of sub-paragraph (c) should be triggered only where such a mandatory rule reflects a fundamental value, the violation of which would be manifest if enforcement of the foreign judgment was permitted. In some jurisdictions, this is referred to as "international public policy" as distinguished from "internal public policy".[189]

264. Sub-paragraph (c) does specify that it refers to the public policy *of the requested State*, indicating that there is no expectation of uniformity as to the content of public policy in each State. While the general purpose of the Convention to facilitate the circulation of judgments should limit recourse to this defence, as should the narrow scope of its application described in the previous paragraphs, it remains up to each State to define the public policy defence. The provision refers to infringements of the sovereignty or security of the State as situations where recognition and enforcement

[186] Hartley/Dogauchi Report, para. 190.

[187] For some States in Europe, see Art. 6 of the *European Convention on Human Rights*; for the United States of America, see the Fifth and Fourteenth Amendments to the United States Constitution. Many other States have similar provisions.

[188] See, for example, Hartley/Dogauchi Report, para. 153, on the exclusion of procedural fraud from the public policy defence in some States.

[189] A proposal to include the term "international public policy" in the text of Art. 7(1)(c) was discussed during the negotiations of the Convention. See Work. Doc. No 136 of February 2017, "Proposal of the delegation of Uruguay" and the related discussion in the Minutes of the Special Commission on the Recognition and Enforcement of Foreign Judgments (16–24 February 2017), Minutes No 7, paras 91-105. During the discussions, while the proposal received some support, some delegations noted that they were unfamiliar with the term "international public policy" and expressed concerns in respect of its inclusion in the text of the Convention.

may be manifestly incompatible with public policy. Despite this addition, the scope of this provision is no different from the scope of the equivalent provision in the HCCH 2005 Choice of Court Convention. The addition simply reflects the greater potential for issues involving infringements of security or sovereignty to arise in the context of this Convention than under the HCCH 2005 Choice of Court Convention.

265. **Damages.** The Convention includes damages awards within its scope but allows a requested State to refuse to enforce a judgment to the extent that it involves an award of punitive or exemplary damages (Art. 10). In some States, where punitive or exemplary damages are not typically allowed, refusals to enforce such awards have been assessed under the public policy defence. However, because Article 10 addresses punitive or exemplary damages, the public policy defence in sub—paragraph (c) should not be used to address challenges to the recognition or enforcement of judgments on that basis.[190] This further narrows the scope of the public policy defence under the Convention.

266. Although the availability of the public policy defence is widely accepted, it is rarely successful as a means of denying recognition or enforcement of a foreign judgment, particularly in civil or commercial matters. [191]Examples where it has succeeded include: where the foreign court enforced a contract to commit an illegal act (smuggling),[192] where the foreign judgment impinged on constitutionally guaranteed fundamental rights (freedom of speech),[193] and where the foreign judgment enforced a gambling debt.[194]

Sub-paragraph (d)—the proceedings in the court of origin were contrary to an agreement, or a designation in a trust instrument, under which the dispute in question was to be determined in a court of a State other than the State of origin;

267. This sub-paragraph allows the court addressed to refuse to give effect to a judgment given by a court when the proceedings in the State of origin were contrary to a choice of court agreement or a designation in a trust instrument. Its rationale is to uphold the agreement or the designation, and therefore to respect party autonomy. Recourse to

[190] The possibility of severing the punitive damages component from the compensatory component, and only enforcing the latter, is further supported by Art. 9 of the Convention.

[191] In a 1998 decision of the England and Wales Court of Appeal, only three refusals to enforce on public policy grounds were noted, two of which were in family law matters, excluded under the Convention (see *Soleimany v. Soleimany*, [1998] EWCA Civ 285). In the most recent edition of the *Jurisclasseur de droit international*, almost all of the examples of refusal by French courts arise in family law matters (divorce, filiation and adoption)—see Fascicule 584–40.

[192] See *Soleimany v. Soleimany* (*id.*). Although this case involved an arbitration award rather than a foreign judgment, the court asserted that it would clearly have refused to enforce the award had it been a judgment given by a foreign court.

[193] See *Bachchan v. India Abroad Publ'n Inc.*, 154 Misc. 2d 228, 235 (N.Y. sup. Ct. 1992) (the United States of America), where an English libel judgment was refused recognition in New York. See, however, the discussion on public policy and freedom of speech in *Yahoo! v. LICRA*, 433 F.3d 1199 (9th Cir. 2006) (the United States of America).

[194] See *Sporting Index Limited v. John O'Shea* [2015] IEHC 407 (Irish High Court); *The Ritz Hotel Casino Ltd v. Datuk Seri Osu Haji Sukam*, [2005] 6 *Malayan Law Journal* 760 (High Court of Malaysia). But other courts have rejected this use of public policy if gambling was legal where the debt was incurred: see for example *Boardwalk Regency Corp. v. Maalouf* (1992), 6 O.R. (3d) 737 (Ontario C.A.); *G.N.L.V. Corp. v. Wan*, [1991] B.C.J. No 3725 (British Columbia S.C.); *Liao Eng Kiat v. Burswood Nominees Ltd*, [2004] 4 S.L.R. 690 (Singapore C.A.).

this sub-paragraph would only be necessary where the judgment satisfied a filter under Article 5. Indeed, if the judgment did not satisfy one of the filters, the judgment could not be considered for recognition and enforcement under the Convention (save under national law as permitted under Art. 15).

268. **Examples.** X brings a contractual claim against Y in State A, where the contractual obligation on which the judgment was based had to be performed. The parties, however, had agreed to submit such a claim to the exclusive jurisdiction of the courts of State B. Y appears before the court of origin and contests jurisdiction on the basis of the choice of court agreement, but this defence is dismissed. The judgment on the merits is favourable to X. Recognition or enforcement of this judgment may, however, be refused under sub-paragraph (d) since the proceedings in State A were contrary to the choice of court agreement. Note that if Y appeared before the courts of State A and argued on the merits without contesting jurisdiction, sub-paragraph (d), in principle, will not apply.[195]

269. This sub-paragraph applies wherever the choice of court agreement validly excluded the jurisdiction of the court of origin, irrespective of whether the agreement is exclusive or non-exclusive. It also applies irrespective of whether the court chosen by the parties or designated in the trust instrument was the court of a Contracting State or a third State. The validity and effectiveness of the agreement or the designation is governed by the law of the requested State, including its private international law rules.

Sub-paragraphs (e) and (f)—inconsistent judgments

270. These two sub-paragraphs reflect the fact that in international situations, more than one court may have jurisdiction over a dispute and parallel or multiple proceedings may be brought in these courts, leading to more than one judgment. When conflicting judgments exist, a question of hierarchy arises: which judgment should be given precedence? Article 7(1) distinguishes two situations: first, where the competing judgment was given by a court in the requested State and, second, where the competing judgment was given in another State (other than the State of origin). These provisions are identical to the ones found in the HCCH 2005 Choice of Court Convention (Art. 9(f) and (g)). Article 7(2), in turn, deals with cases where proceedings in the requested State are still pending when recognition or enforcement is sought.

Sub-paragraph (e)—the judgment is inconsistent with a judgment given by a court of the requested State in a dispute between the same parties; or

271. In the first case, sub-paragraph (e) specifies that the judgment from the State of origin can be refused recognition or enforcement where that judgment is inconsistent with a judgment from the requested State. There are two conditions: the judgments must be "inconsistent" and the judgment from the requested State must be "in a dispute between the same parties".[196] The judgment does not need to have been given prior

[195] Such conduct may be considered as implicitly derogating from the choice of court agreement and therefore the judgment would not be contrary to it.

[196] Hartley/Dogauchi Report, note 231, states: "The requirement regarding the parties will be satisfied if the parties bound by the judgments are the same even if the parties to the proceedings are different, for example where one judgment is against a particular person and the other judgment is against the successor to that person." (see *supra*, para. 92).

to the competing judgment, nor does it need to be based on the same cause of action. Sub-paragraph (e) is therefore wider than sub-paragraph (f) and paragraph 2 of Article 7 because it does not require that the two judgments involve the same subject matter.[197] The two judgments will be "inconsistent" when it is not possible to act in accordance with one without violating the other in whole or in part.

Sub-paragraph (f)—the judgment is inconsistent with an earlier judgment given by a court of another State between the same parties on the same subject matter, provided that the earlier judgment fulfils the conditions necessary for its recognition in the requested State.

272. In the second case, sub-paragraph (f) applies where the conflicting judgments are both from foreign States. It specifies that a judgment from the State of origin can be refused recognition or enforcement where it is inconsistent with an earlier judgment given in another State, irrespective of whether it is a Contracting State or not. Three further conditions must be met for sub-paragraph (f) to apply. First, the judgment from the third State must have been given *prior to* the judgment from the State of origin, irrespective of which court was first seised. The first judgment in time has priority. Second, both judgments must concern the same parties and the same subject matter. This is narrower than the condition under sub-paragraph (e) but parallel to the *lis pendens* ground formulated in paragraph 2.[198] The French version uses the expression *ayant le même objet* to refer to the "same subject matter". These expressions are considered equivalent under the Convention and are meant to exclude the requirement that the two judgments involve exactly the same "cause of action", as is required in the HCCH 2005 Choice of Choice Convention. That approach was considered too restrictive in this Convention given the variety of causes of action in different States. The key element is that the "central or essential issue" must be the same in both judgments. Third, the earlier judgment must be eligible for recognition and enforcement in the requested State, whether or not recognition or enforcement has been sought yet.[199]

[197] In the context of the Brussels I*a* Regulation, this difference has been illustrated in the Judgment of 4 February 1988, *Hoffmann v. Krieg*, C-145/86, EU:C:1988:61, where the CJEU decided that a foreign judgment ordering a person to make maintenance payments to his spouse arising from his obligation under a marriage that had not been terminated was irreconcilable with a national judgment pronouncing the divorce of the spouses. Note, however, that the Convention does not apply to maintenance obligations. In any event, the application of this provision should not encourage strategic or opportunistic behaviour by the judgment debtor, as might be the case when the proceedings in the requested State are instituted while the declaration of enforceability (*exequatur*) is already pending. Thus, a reasonable rule may be to suspend those proceedings until the decision on the *exequatur* is made. The Convention, however, does not impose such a rule.

[198] See the Pocar Report to the 2007 Lugano Convention, para. 139: "In cases of this kind the fact that the judgments are irreconcilable prevents recognition of the later one, but only if the judgments were delivered in disputes between the same parties and have the same subject-matter and the same cause of action, always provided of course that they satisfy the tests for recognition in the State addressed. If the subject-matter or the cause of action are not the same, the judgments are both recognised, even if they are irreconcilable with one another. The irreconcilability will then have to be resolved by the national court before which enforcement is sought, which may apply the rules of its own system for the purpose, and may indeed give weight to factors other than the order in time of the judgments, such as the order in which the proceedings were instituted or the order in which they became *res judicata*, which is not a requirement for recognition under the Convention."

[199] Obviously, if the earlier judgment comes from a non-Contracting State, the question of whether the judgment is eligible for recognition and enforcement will be determined under the national law of the requested State.

Paragraph 2—Recognition or enforcement may be postponed or refused if proceedings between the same parties on the same subject matter are pending before a court of the requested State, where –

273. It may occur that parallel proceedings, between the same parties on the same subject matter, take place in different States. Article 7 establishes three rules to address how judgments are dealt with in these situations. Paragraphs 1(e) and (f), discussed above, deal with cases where the parallel proceedings have concluded and the resulting judgments are inconsistent. Paragraph 2 deals with cases where proceedings are still pending in the requested State when recognition or enforcement of a judgment given in another State is sought.[200] *Lis pendens* in another State cannot be invoked to refuse recognition or enforcement. Furthermore, the proceedings pending in the requested State must be "between the same parties on the same subject matter". In these cases, recognition or enforcement may be postponed or refused if two cumulative conditions are met.

Sub-paragraph (a)—the court of the requested State was seised before the court of origin; and

274. **First condition.** According to paragraph 2(a), the court of the requested State must have been the court first seised. This ground for refusal may therefore only be invoked if the proceedings in the requested State commenced before the proceedings in the State of origin. The rationale for this condition is that the requested State should be allowed to proceed on the basis that the court of origin should have yielded to the priority of the court first seised and suspended or refused the commencement of the proceedings since the same dispute was already pending in another State (with regard to the moment when a court is seised, see *supra*, para. 41).

Sub-paragraph (b)—there is a close connection between the dispute and the requested State.

275. **Second condition.** Mere priority is, however, not sufficient. According to paragraph 2(b), there must also be a close connection between the dispute and the requested State. This condition is to prevent strategic or opportunistic behaviour. For example, without the condition, a potential defendant in one State could move to another State and sue the other party there, seeking a so-called "negative declaration" just to prevent the future recognition or enforcement of the foreign judgment and on the basis of an exorbitant jurisdictional ground. The Convention does not determine which bases of jurisdiction meet the "close connection" condition. In principle, any of the filters listed in Article 5 satisfy this condition, but there may be others that do so as well, *e.g.*, the place where the harm was directly suffered in non-contractual disputes. Conversely, the mere nationality of the claimant or their domicile in the requested State would not be sufficient.

200 The 1999 preliminary draft Convention contained a parallel provision (see Art. 28(1)(a)).

A refusal under this paragraph does not prevent a subsequent application for recognition or enforcement of the judgment.

276. **Consequences.** If the proceedings are pending between the same parties on the same subject matter in the requested State and the above two conditions are met, recognition or enforcement of the judgment may be postponed or refused. Paragraph 2 clarifies that a refusal under this paragraph does not prevent a subsequent application for recognition and enforcement. This provision addresses situations where proceedings on the same subject matter in the requested State conclude without a judgment on the merits (*e.g.*, for procedural reasons) or with a decision on the merits that is consistent with the foreign judgment.

Article 8

Preliminary questions

1. A ruling on a preliminary question shall not be recognised or enforced under this Convention if the ruling is on a matter to which this Convention does not apply or on a matter referred to in Article 6 on which a court of a State other than the State referred to in that Article ruled.
2. Recognition or enforcement of a judgment may be refused if, and to the extent that, the judgment was based on a ruling on a matter to which this Convention does not apply, or on a matter referred to in Article 6 on which a court of a State other than the State referred to in that Article ruled.

277. Article 8 deals with preliminary questions, which are legal issues that must be addressed before the plaintiff's claim can be decided but are not the main object or principal issue of the proceedings.[201] Article 8 recognises that, conceptually, legal issues within a judgment may be separate from one another but considered sequentially, *i.e.*, that a decision on the principal issue is predicated on a decision on another, preliminary question. For example, in an action for damages for breach of a sale contract (main object), the court might first have to decide on the capacity of a party to enter into such a contract (preliminary question). These preliminary questions are usually, but not always, introduced by the defendant by way of defence.

278. Under Article 2(2), judgments that include preliminary rulings on excluded matters are not, for that reason alone, excluded from the scope of the Convention (see *supra*, paras 75–77). Article 8 deals with a separate issue, which is the recognition and enforcement of judgments that rule on preliminary questions dealing with excluded matters. Article 8 also addresses judgments that rule on a preliminary question referred to in Article 6: where the court of origin is not a court of the State where the immovable property is situated.

279. **Structure of Article 8.** This provision contains two rules concerning rulings on preliminary questions. Paragraph 1 excludes rulings on certain preliminary questions from recognition or enforcement under the Convention. Paragraph 2 allows the court addressed to refuse to recognise or enforce judgments that are based on rulings on certain preliminary questions.

[201] As pointed out in *supra*, note 77, "object" is intended to mean the matter with which the proceedings are directly concerned, and which is mainly determined by the plaintiff's claim; see Hartley/Dogauchi Report, paras 77 and 149. The terms "incidental questions" and "principal issue" are used in the Nygh/Pocar Report, para. 177.

Paragraph 1—A ruling on a preliminary question shall not be recognised or enforced under this Convention if the ruling is on a matter to which this Convention does not apply or on a matter referred to in Article 6 on which a court of a State other than the State referred to in that Article ruled.

280. Paragraph 1 provides that where a matter to which the Convention does not apply arose as a preliminary question, the ruling on the preliminary question shall not be recognised or enforced under the Convention. The same result follows where a preliminary question arose with regard to a matter referred to in Article 6 in a court other than a court of the State where the immovable property is situated.

281. The general principle is that the application of the Convention is determined by the object of the proceedings, and not by the preliminary question (see *supra,* Art. 2(2)). Therefore, a judgment is eligible for recognition and enforcement if it meets any of the filters laid down in Article 5 or 6 as regards the *main object* of the proceedings. If the court of origin has also ruled on a preliminary question, that ruling may have effects in future proceedings according to the law of that State. For example, under the doctrine of issue estoppel, collateral estoppel or issue preclusion, rulings on preliminary questions must be recognised in future proceedings.[202] The purpose of paragraph 1 is to clarify that the recognition of these effects is not provided for under the Convention.[203]

282. **Matters excluded from the scope of the Convention.** Paragraph 1 refers to those rulings on matters to which the Convention "does not apply". This covers matters that do not qualify as civil or commercial under Article 1(1), matters expressly excluded under Article 2(1), and matters excluded by a declaration made by the requested State under Article 18. Rulings on matters to which the Convention does not apply should not benefit from its application, whether they arise as preliminary questions or as principal issues. States are not precluded from recognising and enforcing those rulings under national law.

283. **Examples.** If a judgment on a breach of contract ruled, as a preliminary question, on the legal capacity of one of the parties (a natural person) to enter into such a contract, the ruling on this preliminary question would not be recognised under the Convention because such a matter is beyond the scope of the Convention under Article 2(1)(a). Or, if a judgment on directors' liability ruled, as a preliminary question, on the validity of a decision of the shareholders' meeting, this ruling would not be recognised under the Convention because such a matter is beyond its scope under Article 2(1)(i). However, the judgment on the main object would benefit from recognition and enforcement under the Convention, subject to paragraph 2, discussed below. Thus, for example, where a judgment ruled that a party is entitled to receive compensation for breach of contract, but contained a ruling on a preliminary question of legal capacity of the co-contracting natural person to enter

[202] See Hartley/Dogauchi Report, paras 195–196.

[203] Since the Convention does not require the recognition of rulings on preliminary questions, Art. 8(1) may be unnecessary, (as stated in the Hartley/Dogauchi Report, *id.*, "[. . .] the Convention never requires the recognition or enforcement of such rulings, though it does not preclude Contracting States from recognising them under their national law", para. 195). This explains why the Convention is silent on those cases where the preliminary question does not fall under either of the two categories referred to in Art. 8. For example, in an action for damages to a movable asset (main object), the court might have to decide on the ownership of that asset (preliminary question). In principle, the part of the judgment ruling on a preliminary question will not circulate under the Convention and, therefore, Art. 8(1) should not be interpreted *a contrario*. However, "in the case of rulings on matters outside the scope of the Convention [. . .] the question is so important that it was thought desirable to have an express provision", Hartley/Dogauchi Report, para. 196.

into the contract, the ruling on the judgment's main object—the order for damages—could be recognised and enforced under the Convention (subject to Art. 8(2)). The Convention, however, does not require recognition of the ruling on the preliminary question in subsequent proceedings in the requested State concerning or involving that question. It follows, for example, that the judgment on damages may not prevent proceedings being commenced in the requested State on the legal capacity of the natural person (or, in the second example, on the validity of a decision of the shareholders meeting).[204]

284. **Matters falling under Article 6.** Paragraph 1 also refers to rulings on preliminary questions concerning a matter referred to in Article 6 from a court of a State other than the State referred to in this provision, i.e., the State where the immovable property is situated. For example, if a judgment on damages given in State A, on the basis of the defendant's residence, ruled as a preliminary question on the ownership of an immovable property situated in State B, the ruling on this preliminary question would not be recognised under the Convention because courts of the State where immoveable property is located have exclusive jurisdiction to rule on ownership (Art. 6). The judgment from State A may not prevent new proceedings in State B to rule on the right *in rem* over the immovable property, as explained in the preceding paragraph referring to proceedings in the requested State about the legal capacity of a natural person or the validity of the decision of the shareholders' meeting.

Paragraph 2—Recognition or enforcement of a judgment may be refused if, and to the extent that, the judgment was based on a ruling on a matter to which this Convention does not apply, or on a matter referred to in Article 6 on which a court of a State other than the State referred to in that Article ruled.

285. Paragraph 2 allows a court to refuse recognition or enforcement of a judgment if it is based on rulings on preliminary questions on the same matters dealt with by paragraph 1. This provision adds an additional ground for non-recognition to those contained in Article 7. Recognition or enforcement of a judgment may be refused *if, and to the extent that*, the judgment was based on a ruling on a matter (i) to which the Convention does not apply, or (ii) referred to in Article 6 on which a State other than the State where the immovable property is situated ruled. Thus, for example, under paragraph 2, the court of the requested State may refuse recognition of a judgment on the nullity of a contract (main object), or a judgment awarding damages for breach of contract (main object), if and to the extent that, it was based on a ruling on the lack of capacity of a natural person to enter into such a contract (preliminary question).

286. The practical application of this provision requires the court of the requested State to examine the content of the foreign judgment and verify if, and to what extent, the decision on the main object of the proceedings is based on the ruling on the preliminary question. The question is whether a different ruling on the preliminary question would have led to a different judgment on the main object of the proceedings. In other words, the court of the requested State must verify whether the ruling on the preliminary question provides a necessary premise on which the judgment is based.[205] For example, if the court of origin declares the nullity of a contract because of the absence of legal capacity and the existence of fraud, the

[204] If the rulings are incompatible, it would be for the law of the requested State to determine the consequences. It may be that the effects of the foreign judgment are revised when a new judgment on the "preliminary question" is given in the requested State but this time as the main object.

[205] Hartley/Dogauchi Report, para. 200.

ruling of legal capacity is not necessary to the judgment since fraud would have been sufficient on its own to nullify the contract. The Hartley/Dogauchi Report clarifies that this exception should be used only where the court of the requested State would have decided the preliminary question differently,[206] such that the decision on the main object would also have been different. The Twenty-Second Session confirmed that this condition is also required when applying Article 8(2) of Convention. This could arise with a judgment that orders the payment of damages for breach of contract, as the main object, but on the basis of a preliminary decision on the capacity of a natural person to enter into that contract. In such a case, the court addressed may only refuse recognition or enforcement if that court would have decided the question of capacity in a different way,[207] and this would also have led to a different judgment on the obligation to pay damages.

287. **Difference with the HCCH 2005 Choice of Court Convention.** The parallel provision in the HCCH 2005 Choice of Court Convention contains a third paragraph dealing with judgments ruling on the validity of an intellectual property right other than copyright or a related right as a preliminary question (Art. 10(3)). According to this provision, recognition or enforcement of the judgment may only be refused if, and to the extent that, the ruling on the validity of the intellectual property right is inconsistent with a judgment, or a decision of a competent authority, given in the State under the law of which the intellectual property right arose, or if proceedings concerning the validity of the intellectual property right are pending in that State. The main purpose of this rule is to limit the strategic use of the invalidity of a registered intellectual property right by way of defence.

288. This provision has not been included in the Convention. The Twenty-Second Session decided to depart from the solution of the HCCH 2005 Choice of Court Convention for two main reasons. First, when the jurisdiction of the court of origin is based on the agreement of the parties, it may be reasonable to limit the defendant's option to invoke the invalidity of a registered intellectual property right by way of defence. The defendant voluntarily assumed this risk. But this is not the case in relation to most of the filters laid down by Article 5 of the Convention. And second, the scope of the exclusion of intellectual property matters in the Convention requires a granular analysis that may vary depending on the circumstances of the case, especially in the context of contracts relating to those matters (see *supra*, para. 65). The inclusion of a parallel provision may have prejudiced the interpretation of that exclusion; in particular, it may have invited an interpretation according to which all contractual disputes relating to intellectual property rights would fall within the scope of the Convention.[208] Because of this deletion, and assuming that the Convention applies to the main object of the judgment, Article 8 will apply to intellectual property matters in the same way as it applies to any other excluded matter.

[206] Ibid., para. 197.

[207] This is to be determined under the law of the requested State, including its private international law rules.

[208] See, Hartley/Dogauchi Report, paras 199–200.

Article 9

Severability

Recognition or enforcement of a severable part of a judgment shall be granted where recognition or enforcement of that part is applied for, or only part of the judgment is capable of being recognised or enforced under this Convention.

289. Article 9 provides for the recognition and enforcement of a severable part of a judgment where this is applied for, or where only part of the judgment is capable of being recognised or enforced under the Convention.[209] Examples include situations where parts of the judgment would not be subject to recognition or enforcement because they involve matters that fall outside the scope of the Convention, are contrary to public policy, or are not as yet enforceable in the State of origin. A further example is a judgment on several contractual obligations where the criterion of Article 5(1)(g) is only satisfied in relation to one of them.[210]

290. In order to be severable, the part of a judgment must be capable of standing alone. This would normally depend on whether enforcing only that part of the judgment would significantly change the obligations of the parties. If severability raises issues of law, they will have to be determined according to the law of the requested State.[211]

[209] This Art. replicates Art. 15 of the HCCH 2005 Choice of Court Convention. See also Hartley/Dogauchi Report, para. 217.

[210] This example assumes that there is no other filter available under Art. 5(1).

[211] Nygh/Pocar Report, para. 374.

Article 10
Damages

1. Recognition or enforcement of a judgment may be refused if, and to the extent that, the judgment awards damages, including exemplary or punitive damages, that do not compensate a party for actual loss or harm suffered.
2. The court addressed shall take into account whether and to what extent the damages awarded by the court of origin serve to cover costs and expenses relating to the proceedings.

291. Article 10 allows a court to refuse recognition or enforcement of a judgment if, and to the extent that, the award of damages does not compensate the plaintiff for actual loss or harm suffered. The compensatory portion of the judgment remains enforceable.
292. "Exemplary" and "punitive" damages mean the same thing and reflect the fact that these damages have an expressly punitive, as opposed to a primarily compensatory objective. While it is generally accepted that compensatory damages can have a deterrent effect, their primary objective is to repair the actual loss suffered. Punitive or exemplary damages, on the other hand, are typically awarded to express condemnation of particularly egregious behaviour on the part of the person who caused harm.
293. The text of Article 10 replicates the equivalent provision in the HCCH 2005 Choice of Court Convention.[212] To clarify the source and scope of the rule, the Explanatory Report on that Convention included the following detailed statement that had been adopted at the Twentieth Session:[213]

> "(a) Let us start with a basic and never disputed principle: judgments awarding damages are within the scope of the Convention. So a judgment given by a court designated in an exclusive choice of court agreement which, in whole or in part, awards damages to the plaintiff, will be recognised and enforced in all Contracting States under the Convention. As such judgments are not different from other decisions falling within the scope of the Convention, Article 8 applies without restriction. This means both the obligation to recognise and enforce and all the grounds for refusal.

[212] Art. 11 of the HCCH 2005 Choice of Court Convention.

[213] Only those parts of the statement that are relevant to the Convention are included. Portions of the statement that refer to previous versions of the Article on damages in the HCCH 2005 Choice of Court Convention have been omitted. The omissions have been indicated by [. . .]. For the full statement as it appears in the Explanatory Report of the HCCH 2005 Choice of Court Convention, see Hartley/Dogauchi Report, paras 203–205.

(b) During the negotiations, it has become obvious that some delegations have problems with judgments awarding damages that go far beyond the actual loss of the plaintiff. Punitive or exemplary damages are an important example. Some delegations thought that the public policy exception in Article 9 e) could solve those problems, but others made it clear that this was not possible under their limited concept of public policy. Therefore it was agreed that there should be an additional ground for refusal for judgments on damages. This is the new Article 11. As in the case of all other grounds for refusal, this provision should be interpreted and applied in restrictive a way as possible.

(c) Article 11 is based on the undisputed primary function of damages: they should compensate for the actual loss. Therefore the new Article 11(1) says that recognition and enforcement of a judgment may be refused if, and to the extent that, the damages do not compensate a party for actual loss or harm suffered. It should be mentioned that the English word 'actual' has a different meaning from the French 'actuel' (which is not used in the French text); so future losses are covered as well.

(d) This does not mean that the court addressed is allowed to examine whether it could have awarded the same amount of damages or not. The threshold is much higher. Article 11 only operates when it is obvious from the judgment that the award appears to go beyond the actual loss or harm suffered. In particular, this applies to punitive or exemplary damages. These types of damages are therefore explicitly mentioned. But in exceptional cases, damages which are characterised as compensatory by the court of origin could also fall under this provision.

(e) This provision also treats as compensation for actual loss or harm damages that are awarded on the basis of a party agreement (liquidated damages) or of a statute (statutory damages). With regard to such damages, the court addressed could refuse recognition and enforcement only if and to the extent that those damages are intended to punish the defendant rather than to provide for a fair estimate of an appropriate level of compensation.

(f) It would be wrong to ask whether the court addressed has to apply the law of the State of origin or the law of the requested State. Article 11 contains an autonomous concept. It is of course the court addressed which applies this provision, but this application does not lead to a simple application of the law of the requested State concerning damages.

(g) Recognition and enforcement may only be refused to the extent that the judgment goes beyond the actual loss or harm suffered. For most delegations, this might already be a logical consequence of the limited purpose of this provision. However, it is useful to state this expressly. This avoids a possible 'all or nothing approach' some legal systems apply to the public policy exception.

(h) [...] Article 11 only provides for a review whether the judgment awards damages not compensating for actual loss; it does not allow any other review as to the merits of the case. Like all other grounds of refusal, it will only apply in exceptional cases. Any over—drafting with respect to those cases would have given them too much political weight.

(i) Article 11 does not oblige the court to refuse recognition and enforcement. This is obvious from its wording—the court may refuse—and it is consistent with the general approach in Article 9 [on refusal to recognise or enforce]. So the provision in no way limits recognition and enforcement of damages under national law or other international instruments, and it allows (but does not require) recognition and enforcement under the Convention. Once again, the Working Group felt that an express provision would have been an over-drafting giving too much weight to the issue of damages.

(j) [. . .] Under Article 11(1), it could be argued that damages intended to cover the costs of proceedings were not compensating for an actual loss. This would of course be wrong from a comparative perspective. But it is nevertheless reasonable to have an express reference to this problem within the provision. This reference does not contain a hard rule; the fact that damages are intended to cover costs and expenses is only to be taken into account."

294. This statement is equally applicable to the Convention.

Article 11

Judicial settlements (transactions judiciaires)

Judicial settlements (transactions judiciaires) which a court of a Contracting State has approved, or which have been concluded in the course of proceedings before a court of a Contracting State, and which are enforceable in the same manner as a judgment in the State of origin, shall be enforced under this Convention in the same manner as a judgment.

295. The Convention applies to judicial settlements (*transactions judiciaires*). According to Article 11, settlements which a court of a State has approved, or which have been concluded in the course of the proceedings before a court of a State, and which are enforceable in the State of origin, are to be enforced under the Convention in the same manner as a judgment.

296. **Judicial settlements.** The English term "judicial settlements" is used in this Article as equivalent to the French term *transaction judiciaire*. Judicial settlements, a common institution in civil law jurisdictions, are an agreement concluded before, or approved by, the court in which the parties settled their dispute, usually by making mutual concessions.[214] Such agreements have some, or even all, of the effects of a final judgment. A judicial settlement is typically distinguished from a "consent order" or "consent judgment" ("*jugement d'accord*") granted by the court with the consent of both parties. Such consent orders or consent judgments are dealt with under Article 4 and not Article 11.[215]

297. Article 11 covers both "in-court" settlements, *i.e.*, settlements approved or concluded before a court in the course of the proceedings (as is usually the case in most civil law jurisdictions), and "out-of-court" settlements, *i.e.*, agreements concluded by the parties outside judicial proceedings, which are subsequently approved or confirmed by a court.[216] Thus, for example, settlements concluded as a result of mediation are covered by Article 11 if they are subsequently approved by a court.[217] This possibility arises from the distinction drawn in the text between settlements "approved by a court" and settlements "concluded in the course of the proceedings before a court".

[214] See Hartley/Dogauchi Report, para. 207. The Brussels Ia Regulation defines a court settlement as "a settlement which has been approved by a court of a Member State or concluded before a court of a Member State in the course of the proceedings".

[215] Nygh/Pocar Report, para. 379; Hartey/Dogauchi Report, para. 207.

[216] The HCCH 2005 Choice of Court Convention contains an equivalent provision on judicial settlements (Art. 12). The Hartley/Dogauchi Report does not expressly address the treatment of out of court agreements subsequently approved by a court (see, para. 207). Interpretation provided in this Explanatory Report is consistent with the language of the provision in both instruments.

[217] This interpretation does not overlap with the *UNICTRAL Convention on International Settlement Agreements Resulting from Mediation* or the Model Law of the same name. Both instruments expressly exclude mediated settlements that are either approved by courts or concluded in the course of court proceedings.

In both cases, the judicial settlement must be enforceable, in the same manner as a judgment, in the State of origin. To prove this, the party seeking enforcement must produce the certificate referred to in Article 12(1)(d), *i.e.*, a certificate of a court of the State of origin stating that the judicial settlement or a part of it is enforceable in the same manner as a judgment in the State of origin.

298. Enforcement versus recognition. Article 11 provides for the enforcement of judicial settlements, but not their recognition.[218] Therefore, under the Convention, a judicial settlement from another State may not be invoked in the requested State as, for example, a procedural defence to a new claim.219[219] The Nygh/Pocar Report explains that in some jurisdictions, judicial settlements do not have the force of res judicata and therefore cannot be recognised in another State.[220] The Hartley/Dogauchi Report adds that the HCCH 2005 Choice of Court Convention does not provide for the recognition of judicial settlements "mainly because the effects of settlements are so different in different legal systems",[221] but "the Convention does not preclude a court from treating the settlement as a contractual defence to the claim on the merits" to prove that the matter has already been resolved.[222] Likewise, the Convention does not preclude a court from granting *res judicata* effect to a foreign judicial settlement under national law.

299. The grounds for refusing enforcement of judicial settlements are the same as those applicable to judgments. But issues of jurisdiction will not arise because settlements are essentially consensual; the same holds for other grounds for refusal set out in Article 7, *e.g.*, defective notification. In practice, the most relevant ground for refusing enforcement will be public policy.

[218] See supra, paras 113–117.

[219] Hartley/Dogauchi Report, paras 208–209 (with an example).

[220] Nygh/Pocar Report, para. 123. Note, however, that under the 1999 preliminary draft Convention, in order to be recognised, judgments must have the effect of res judicata in the State of origin (Art. 25(2)). This condition is not contained in the Convention.

[221] Hartey/Dogauchi Report, para. 209.

[222] Ibid.

Article 12

Documents to be produced

1. The party seeking recognition or applying for enforcement shall produce
   (a) a complete and certified copy of the judgment;
   (b) if the judgment was given by default, the original or a certified copy of a document establishing that the document which instituted the proceedings or an equivalent document was notified to the defaulting party;
   (c) any documents necessary to establish that the judgment has effect or, where applicable, is enforceable in the State of origin;
   (d) in the case referred to in Article 11, a certificate of a court (including an officer of the court) of the State of origin stating that the judicial settlement or a part of it is enforceable in the same manner as a judgment in the State of origin
2. If the terms of the judgment do not permit the court addressed to verify whether the conditions of this Chapter have been complied with, that court may require any necessary documents.
3. An application for recognition or enforcement may be accompanied by a document relating to the judgment, issued by a court (including an officer of the court) of the State of origin, in the form recommended and published by the Hague Conference on Private International Law.
4. If the documents referred to in this Article are not in an official language of the requested State, they shall be accompanied by a certified translation into an official language, unless the law of the requested State provides otherwise.

300. Article 12 lists the documents to be produced by the party applying for recognition or enforcement of a judgment under the Convention.[223] In legal systems without a special procedure for recognition (see *infra*, para. 308), the party requesting recognition may have to produce those documents when they seek to rely on the foreign judgment, *e.g.*, by way of defence.[224]

[223] This provision is essentially similar to Art. 13 of the HCCH 2005 Choice of Court Convention and to Art. 29(1) of the 1999 preliminary draft Convention.

[224] Hartley/Dogauchi Report, para. 210, limits this requirement to circumstances where "the other party disputes the recognition of the judgment". This, however, does not preclude third parties or local authorities (for example, a Registrar) from requesting those documents.

Paragraph 1—The party seeking recognition or applying for enforcement shall produce

Sub-paragraph (a)—a complete and certified copy of the judgment;

Sub-paragraph (b)—if the judgment was given by default, the original or a certified copy of a document establishing that the document which instituted the proceedings or an equivalent document was notified to the defaulting party;

Sub-paragraph (c)—any documents necessary to establish that the judgment has effect or, where applicable, is enforceable in the State of origin;

Sub-paragraph (d)—in the case referred to in Article 11, a certificate of a court (including an officer of the court) of the State of origin stating that the judicial settlement or a part of it is enforceable in the same manner as a judgment in the State of origin.

301. Paragraph 1(a) requires production of a complete and certified copy of the judgment. A "judgment" includes, where applicable, the court reasoning and not only the final order (dispositif).[225] If the judgment was given by default, paragraph 1(b) requires the production of the original or a certified copy of a document establishing that the document that instituted the proceedings or an equivalent document was notified to the defaulting party. Conversely, if the judgment was not given by default, it is assumed that the defendant was notified unless they produce evidence to the contrary (see Art. 7(1)(a)). Paragraph 1(c) requires the production of any document necessary to prove that the judgment has effect or, where applicable, is enforceable in the State of origin. In principle, this will be stated by the court of origin in the Recommended Form prepared by the Permanent Bureau of the HCCH (see para. 3). Other means of proof may also be used in accordance with the procedural rules of the requested State, *e.g.*, official statements or legal opinions. [226]For judicial settlements, paragraph 1(d) requires the production of a certificate from a court of the State of origin, including an officer of the court,[227] stating that the settlement or a part of it is enforceable in the same manner as a judgment in the State of origin (see *supra*, paras 295–296). This certificate may be issued by a court other than the court involved in the settlement.
302. The Hartley/Dogauchi Report clarifies two issues with regard to paragraph 1. First, the law of the requested State determines the consequences of the failure to produce the required documents. Second, excessive formalism should be avoided. If the judgment debtor was not prejudiced by the absence of documents, the judgment creditor should be allowed to rectify omissions.[228]

[225] Hartley/Dogauchi Report, para. 211.

[226] To ensure the effectiveness of the Convention, Contracting States must provide for some means of satisfying this requirement.

[227] The reference to an officer of the court in Art. 12(1)(d) is not contained in the parallel provision of the HCCH 2005 Choice of Court Convention (see Art. 13(1)(e)). The Twenty-Second Session did not find a particular reason to exclude this possibility, which is provided in Art. 12(3) and in the parallel provision of the HCCH 2005 Choice of Court Convention (see Art. 13(3)). As a result, the reference to an officer of the court in Art. 12(1)(d) was included but with no intention to depart from the HCCH 2005 Choice of Court Convention.

[228] Hartley/Dogauchi Report, para. 211.

Paragraph 2—If the terms of the judgment do not permit the court addressed to verify whether the conditions of this Chapter have been complied with, that court may require any necessary documents.

303. Paragraph 2 provides that the court addressed may require the production of additional documents to verify whether the conditions of Chapter II of the Convention have been satisfied. This indicates that the list of documents contained in paragraph 1 is not exhaustive. Unnecessary burdens on the parties should, however, be avoided.

Paragraph 3—An application for recognition or enforcement may be accompanied by a document relating to the judgment, issued by a court (including an officer of the court) of the State of origin, in the form recommended and published by the Hague Conference on Private International Law.

304. Paragraph 3 provides that an application for recognition or enforcement can be accompanied by the Form recommended and published by the HCCH.[229] This Form is issued by a court (including by an officer of that court) of the State of origin. The Convention does not require that the court issuing the Form be the court that gave the judgment. Although States are not required to adopt the Form, its use may facilitate the process of recognition or enforcement. If the Form is used, the court addressed may rely on information contained in it in the absence of challenge. But even if there is no challenge, the information is not conclusive; the court addressed can decide the matter based on all the evidence before it.[230]

305. The Form includes a section on judicial settlements. Where the Form is used in relation to a judicial settlement, it satisfies the requirement for a certificate under paragraph 1(d).

Paragraph 4—If the documents referred to in this Article are not in an official language of the requested State, they shall be accompanied by a certified translation into an official language, unless the law of the requested State provides otherwise.

306. Paragraph 4 deals with the language of the documents listed in Article 12. If the documents are not in an official language of the requested State, they must be accompanied by a certified translation into an official language, unless the requested State provides otherwise. This State may, therefore, provide that a translation is not necessary at all or that a non-certified translation is sufficient.

307. Unlike the HCCH 2005 Choice of Court Convention (see Art. 18), this Convention does not include a provision on the exemption from legalisation. As a consequence, the certification of foreign legal documents (i.e., legalisation or apostille) is governed by the rules of the requested State, including the international conventions ratified by that State.

[229] For ease of reference, the Form is presented on pages 35–40 of this publication. It is also available on the HCCH website at <www.hcch.net> under "Judgments".

[230] Hartley/Dogauchi Report, para. 213.

Article 13
Procedure

1. The procedure for recognition, declaration of enforceability or registration for enforcement, and the enforcement of the judgment, are governed by the law of the requested State unless this Convention provides otherwise. The court of the requested State shall act expeditiously.
2. The court of the requested State shall not refuse the recognition or enforcement of a judgment under this Convention on the ground that recognition or enforcement should be sought in another State.

Paragraph 1—The procedure for recognition, declaration of enforceability or registration for enforcement, and the enforcement of the judgment, are governed by the law of the requested State unless this Convention provides otherwise. The court of the requested State shall act expeditiously.

308. Paragraph 1 provides that the procedure for recognition, declaration of enforceability or registration for enforcement, and the enforcement of the judgment, are governed by the law of the requested State unless the Convention provides otherwise. Thus, the law of the requested State determines whether recognition is automatic or requires a special procedure. Where the law of the requested State does not require a special procedure for the recognition of a foreign judgment, a judgment will be recognised automatically, *i.e.*, by operation of law, based on Article 4 of the Convention.[231]
309. **Enforcement process.** Article 13 refers to distinct phases of the enforcement process in the requested State.[232] In many States, enforcement will proceed in two phases: first, proceedings will be instituted by the judgment creditor to obtain from the competent authority of the requested State a confirmation or declaration that the foreign judgment is enforceable in that State. Such a declaration of enforceability is called "*exequatur*" in many States. In other States a registration procedure may be provided. The second phase of enforcement refers to the legal procedure by which the courts (or competent authorities) of the requested State ensure that the judgment debtor obeys the foreign judgment. It includes measures such as seizure, confiscation, attachment, or judicial sale. This second phase—often referred to as "execution" of the judgment—presupposes a declaration of enforceability or a registration for enforcement. Typically, once the first phase has been completed, the foreign origin of the judgment is no longer relevant, and the judgment creditor will have access to the same measures of execution (the second phase of enforcement) in the requested State that would be available for a domestic judgment. In other States, these two phases can be combined into a single proceeding, where the court

[231] Ibid., para. 215.

[232] Note, however, that in other provisions of the Convention, the term "enforcement" is used with the meaning of "declaration of enforceability or registration for enforcement" (see, *e.g.*, Art. 5 or 7).

may grant a declaration of enforceability of the foreign judgment and also order measures of execution. Regardless of the precise process in a given State, paragraph 1 subjects both phases of the enforcement process to the law of the requested State.

310. Limitation periods. In referring to the procedure for enforcement, Article 13 is intended to include the rules of the law of the requested State that provide a limitation period for enforcement of a judgment.[233] Such rules are applicable, unless, as expressly stated in Article 13, the "Convention provides otherwise". The Convention does provide, in Article 4(3), that enforcement in the requested State depends on the judgment being enforceable in the State of origin. As a consequence, a longer period of limitation for enforcement in the requested State will not extend the enforceability of a foreign judgment that is no longer enforceable in the State of origin.[234]

311. However, this does not address the situation where a shorter limitation period is applicable to the enforcement of judgments in the requested State. A judgment creditor might seek to bring enforcement proceedings in the requested State during the period of enforceability of the judgment under the law of the State of origin but after the limitation period for enforcement under the law of the requested State has expired. Even if the foreign judgment remains enforceable under the law of the State of origin, Article 13 does not prevent the application of a shorter limitation period for enforcement of a judgment under the law of the requested State. For example, if according to the law of the State of origin (State A) the judgment remains enforceable for 15 years but the law of the requested State (State B) establishes a 5-year period, the latter is entitled to prevail. That is, once this latter period has expired, the judgment given in State A will no longer be enforceable in State B.

312. The reference to the law of the requested State in Article 13 is not necessarily to be understood as a direct reference to its internal law. Indeed, the law of the requested State may instead identify the relevant limitation period by reference back to the law of the State of origin or even apply the limitation period governing the substantive right on which the judgment rules. The approaches to this issue vary significantly among jurisdictions and the Convention takes no position on the way the applicable limitation period is determined under the law of the requested State. This interpretation is necessary to ensure the equal treatment of States in relation to the limitation period issue.

313. **General principle under the law of treaties.** Notwithstanding the preceding paragraphs, the reference to the law of the requested State is not a blanket reference. In accordance with Article 31(1) of the Vienna Convention of 1969, a treaty

[233] The limitation period referred to here only relates to the enforcement of a foreign judgment and should not be conceptually confused with the limitation period governing the original substantive right or claim at stake, *i.e.*, the limitation period to bring a legal action on the merits before a court. This matter relates to the merits of the judgment given by the court of origin and may not be reviewed by the requested State in accordance with Art. 4(2).

[234] Distinct limitation periods may apply under national law to the two phases of enforcement. An initial limitation period may apply to the time limit for instituting proceedings to seek a declaration or confirmation of enforceability (this may apply equally in those States where the two phases are combined in a single proceeding). Once that judgment is obtained, its concrete execution may become subject to a different limitation period. In such a case, the eventual execution of the judgment in the requested State may be possible beyond the limitation period in the State of origin. This may be explained by the fact that once a judgment is declared enforceable under the Convention in the requested State, the judgment becomes equivalent to a domestic judgment and the Convention no longer has any application to its treatment in the requested State.

must be interpreted "in good faith in accordance with the ordinary meaning to be given to the terms of the treaty in their context and in the light of its object and purpose". An essential element to ensure the effectiveness of the Convention (see para. 2 of the Preamble) is the principle of non-discrimination: judgments given in other States, once they have been determined to be enforceable under the Convention, are to be treated in the same manner as domestic judgments. This principle has implications for limitation periods. In particular, a national law that provides for shorter limitation periods for enforcement of foreign judgments than for domestic judgments would not be compatible with this principle. Similarly, when the law of the requested State establishes a special rule on the limitation period for the declaration of enforceability of foreign judgments, an unreasonably short period may be incompatible with the principle of effectiveness of the Convention.

314. Paragraph 1 also provides that in proceedings covered by this provision, the courts (or the competent authorities) of the requested State must act expeditiously. States should consider provisions to avoid unnecessary delays.[235]

315. **Application for refusal.** Article 13 only refers to a procedure for recognition, declaration of enforceability or registration for enforcement. But it does not preclude States from providing for applications to *refuse* recognition or enforcement. Thus, States may provide for a judgment debtor to request a declaration of non-recognition (or non-enforceability) of a judgment given in another State on the basis that the judgment is not eligible for recognition under Article 5 or 6, or on one of the grounds referred to in Article 7.

Paragraph 2—The court of the requested State shall not refuse the recognition or enforcement of a judgment under this Convention on the ground that recognition or enforcement should be sought in another State.

316. Paragraph 2 provides that the court of the requested State shall not refuse the recognition or enforcement of a judgment under the Convention on the ground that recognition and enforcement should be sought in another State. This prevents a court refusing on the basis that, for example, there is an alternative forum where recognition or enforcement of the judgment is more appropriate and convenient.

317. Under the Convention, the judgment creditor may seek recognition and enforcement of the judgment in any State. Even if it entails more costs, a judgment creditor may have a legitimate interest in seeking the enforcement of a judgment in more than one State, such as in cases of worldwide injunctions or in cases of monetary judgments against a party with assets in different States but which are each alone insufficient to satisfy the judgment.

318. The existence of different approaches to the issue addressed in this paragraph explains the need for this provision. In many legal systems, enforcement does not require a basis of jurisdiction, i.e., a special connection between the judgment debtor and the requested State, such as the presence of the debtor's assets in that State. The mere interest of the judgment creditor is sufficient.

[235] Hartley/Dogauchi Report, para. 216.

319. Conversely, in other legal systems, enforcement of a foreign judgment does require a basis of jurisdiction, such as the domicile of the judgment debtor or the presence of the judgment debtor's assets in the requested State. In some of these legal systems, the judgment debtor may even oppose the *exequatur* on the basis of the *forum non conveniens* doctrine, *i.e.*, arguing that the enforcement should be sought in another, more appropriate and convenient State. Such disputes may delay the proceedings and become cumbersome for the judgment creditor. Paragraph 2 is addressed to this group of legal systems and establishes an exception to paragraph 1. Although the procedure for recognition, declaration of enforceability or registration for enforcement, and the enforcement of the judgment, are governed by the law of the requested State, the courts of the requested State cannot refuse the recognition or enforcement of a judgment under the Convention on the ground that they should be sought in another State. In practice, this prevents reliance on the doctrine of *forum non conveniens* as a ground to refuse recognition or enforcement.

Article 14

Costs of proceedings

1. No security, bond or deposit, however described, shall be required from a party who in one Contracting State applies for enforcement of a judgment given by a court of another Contracting State on the sole ground that such party is a foreign national or is not domiciled or resident in the State in which enforcement is sought.
2. An order for payment of costs or expenses of proceedings, made in a Contracting State against any person exempt from requirements as to security, bond, or deposit by virtue of paragraph 1 or of the law of the State where proceedings have been instituted, shall, on the application of the person entitled to the benefit of the order, be rendered enforceable in any other Contracting State.
3. A State may declare that it shall not apply paragraph 1 or designate by a declaration which of its courts shall not apply paragraph 1.

320. Article 14 deals with security that may be required to guarantee payment of the costs of proceedings, including declaration of enforceability or registration for enforcement, and the enforcement of the judgment. [236]The provision reflects a compromise. Some States supported a "no-security rule". Others preferred to leave this question to national law. The first approach is reflected in the first and second paragraphs, while the second approach is reflected in the third paragraph by means of an opt-out mechanism.

Paragraph 1—No security, bond or deposit, however described, shall be required from a party who in one Contracting State applies for enforcement of a judgment given by a court of another Contracting State on the sole ground that such party is a foreign national or is not domiciled or resident in the State in which enforcement is sought.

321. The first paragraph of Article 14 mirrors a traditional view that no security, bond or deposit may be required from the applicant for the sole reason that they are a national of another State or their residence or domicile is in another State.[237] Paragraph 1 only prohibits requirements for security based exclusively on such grounds. A requirement for security is therefore permissible on other grounds,

[236] There is no equivalent provision in the HCCH 2005 Choice of Court Convention.
[237] Nygh/Pocar Report, para. 356.

e.g., that the judgment creditor has no assets in the requested State. The clause applies to both natural and legal persons, irrespective of whether they are a national of another Contracting State or of a third State (or whether they have their residence or domicile in another Contracting State or in a third State).[238]

Paragraph 2—An order for payment of costs or expenses of proceedings, made in a Contracting State against any person exempt from requirements as to security, bond, or deposit by virtue of paragraph 1 or of the law of the State where proceedings have been instituted, shall, on the application of the person entitled to the benefit of the order, be rendered enforceable in any other Contracting State.

322. The second paragraph of Article 14 is a corollary to the "no-security rule". It protects the judgment debtor when enforcement of the judgment is refused and an order for payment of costs or expenses is issued against the judgment creditor. According to paragraph 2, such an order falls within the scope of the Convention and is enforceable in any other State. This exceptional provision is required because such a cost order would not otherwise be considered to be a judgment for the purposes of the Convention. Under Article 3(1)(b), only orders for payment of costs or expenses that relate to a "decision on the merits which may be recognised or enforced under the Convention" are entitled to enforcement under the Convention. A decision on enforcement of a foreign judgment is not a "decision on the merits" in the sense of Article 3(1)(b). Although the enforcement of an order for payment of costs or expenses is authorised under Article 14(2), it may be refused on the grounds contained in Article 7 of the Convention.

323. This paragraph applies in two situations. First, it applies when an exemption from security for costs has been granted in accordance with paragraph 1. This presupposes that the law of the requested State requires, in general, security for costs for the enforcement of foreign judgments on the sole ground of the nationality, domicile or residency of the judgment creditor, but that an exemption has been granted by virtue of paragraph 1, *i.e.*, for judgments given in another Contracting State. This exemption may arise automatically by operation of law or on a case by case basis by a decision of the court addressed. Second, this paragraph applies when such security does not even exist under the law of the requested State, *i.e.*, when the law of the requested State does not require security for costs solely based on the foreign nationality, domicile or residency of the judgment creditor. Naturally, these States must also receive the full benefit of this provision in the sense that their courts' orders for costs will also circulate under the Convention. The words "or the law of the State where proceedings have been commenced" reflect this second situation.[239]

[238] Note that in this provision, the term "resident" is not qualified by the adjective "habitual". This may be explained by the fact that this Article reproduces the first sentence of Art. 14 of the HCCH *Convention of 25 October 1980 on International Access to Justice* (hereinafter "HCCH 1980 Access to Justice Convention"), which uses the same wording.

[239] See Art. 15 of the HCCH 1980 Access to Justice Convention

Paragraph 3—A State may declare that it shall not apply paragraph 1 or designate by a declaration which of its courts shall not apply paragraph 1.

324. Finally, the third paragraph sets out a declaration mechanism to opt-out from the no—security rule. A State may declare that it shall not apply paragraph 1 in some or all of its courts. Thus, it is possible to exclude the application of paragraph 1 to certain courts, e.g., to federal courts but not state courts.

325. Article 14 does not clarify how the reciprocity principle would apply when a State makes a declaration under paragraph 3. If the origin of the judgment is taken as a reference, where that judgment is given by the courts of a State that made the declaration, the judgment creditor should not benefit from the no-security rule in paragraph 1. The second paragraph should not apply to cost orders given by a court of the State that made the declaration, where that court imposed security for costs.[240]

[240] Naturally, this is only likely to occur where the security for costs was insufficient to cover the entirety of the costs order.

Article 15

Recognition and enforcement under national law

Subject to Article 6, this Convention does not prevent the recognition or enforcement of judgments under national law.

326. Article 15 deals with how the Convention relates to national law, providing that, subject to Article 6, the Convention does not prevent the recognition or enforcement of judgments under national law. This provision is based on a favor recognitionis principle. If a judgment cannot be recognised or enforced under the Convention, because, e.g., it is not eligible according to Article 5, a party may still seek recognition and enforcement under national law. In other words, the Convention sets a minimum standard for mutual recognition and enforcement of judgments but States may go further. If a judgment is not eligible for recognition or enforcement under the Convention, the national law of the requested State determines whether a party may resort to national law "as a whole" or may combine provisions from both systems.
327. However, Article 6 prevents national law being invoked to grant recognition or enforcement to a judgment that infringes the exclusive basis of jurisdiction in that provision (see *supra*, para. 231).

Chapter III—General clauses

Article 16

Transitional provision

This Convention shall apply to the recognition and enforcement of judgments if, at the time the proceedings were instituted in the State of origin, the Convention had effect between that State and the requested State.

328. Article 16 deals with the temporal application of the Convention. The Convention shall apply if, at the time the proceedings were instituted in the State of origin, it already had effect between that State and the requested State. The court addressed must verify (i) the date when the proceedings were instituted in the State of origin (see *supra,* para. 41) and (ii) whether at that time the Convention was effective between the State of origin *and* the requested State. Article 16 is thus based on a non—retroactivity principle. This solution provides legal certainty. All parties will be able to determine, prior to the initiation of the proceedings, whether the future judgment will circulate under the Convention and prepare their procedural strategies accordingly.
329. The determination of the temporal application of the Convention is distinct from the issue of its entry into force (see *infra,* Art. 28) and the establishment of relations between two Contracting States (see *infra,* Art. 29). Since the Convention only operates between two Contracting States (see *supra,* Art. 1(2)), Article 16 presupposes that (i) the Convention has entered into force (Art. 28) and (ii) that neither the State of origin nor the requested State has objected to the establishment of relations with the other under Article 29, *i.e.*, it presupposes that the Convention "has effect" between the State of origin and the requested State.
330. **Example.** State A ratifies the Convention in April 2020 and State B in May 2020. According to Articles 28 and 29(1), if neither of them makes a declaration under Article 29(2) or 29(3), the Convention shall enter into force and have effect between those two States on 1 June 2021 (see *infra,* para. 401). Pursuant to Article 16, it will apply to the recognition and enforcement of judgments deriving from proceedings that are instituted on or after that date.

Article 17

Declarations limiting recognition and enforcement

A State may declare that its courts may refuse to recognise or enforce a judgment given by a court of another Contracting State if the parties were resident in the requested State, and the relationship of the parties and all other elements relevant to the dispute, other than the location of the court of origin, were connected only with the requested State.

331. Article 17 provides that a State may declare that its courts may refuse to recognise or enforce a judgment given by a court of another State if the parties were resident in the requested State and the relationship of the parties and all other elements relevant to the dispute (other than the location of the court of origin) were connected only with the requested State. This provision is from the HCCH 2005 Choice of Court Convention (see Art. 20).

332. **Rationale.** Article 17 deals with situations that are, from the point of view of the requested State, wholly domestic. It allows a State to relieve itself from the obligation to recognise and enforce a judgment under the Convention in these cases. Typically, HCCH instruments only apply to international cases. However, for the purposes of recognition and enforcement, a case is always international if the judgment was given by a court in a State other than that in which recognition or enforcement is sought. Yet there may be scenarios where the internationality of the case has been engineered by the parties. Some of the filters laid down by Article 5 may be met in a wholly domestic situation, in particular those based on implied or express consent (see Art. 5(1)(c), (e), (f), (k), (l), or (m)). A judgment given in such cases would ordinarily circulate under the Convention even if the dispute had no additional connections with the State of origin. Article 17 recognises that such a case may not be a true international case, and that, on a proper analysis of the connecting elements of the dispute, the dispute ought to have been heard in the requested State. States may make a declaration to address such scenarios.

333. **Relevant time.** The relevant time to determine whether a situation is wholly domestic is the time when the proceedings were instituted in the State of origin. Thus, if the requested State has made the declaration envisaged by Article 17, the court addressed must verify if, at the time when the proceedings were instituted in the State of origin, the parties were resident in the requested State and their relationships and all other relevant elements were also connected only with the requested State.[241] Only in such a case may the court addressed refuse to recognise or enforce the judgment under Article 17.

[241] Note that this provision, like Art. 20 in the HCCH 2005 Choice of Court Convention, does not use the term "habitual residence" but simply "residence". In practice, this is not relevant since, if the residence is not habitual, the conditions for the application of this provision will not be met.

334. **Example.** The parties are resident in State A and all other relevant elements are connected only with that State. One of the parties brings proceedings before a court in State B, and the defendant argues on the merits without contesting jurisdiction. If the court of State B gives a judgment on the merits, that judgment will circulate under the Convention (see Art. 5(1)(f)). However, if State A has made the declaration envisaged by Article 17, it will not be required to recognise or enforce that judgment. Other States, however, may not invoke the declaration made by State A to refuse recognition or enforcement of the judgment.

Article 18

Declarations with respect to specific matters

1. Where a State has a strong interest in not applying this Convention to a specific matter, that State may declare that it will not apply the Convention to that matter. The State making such a declaration shall ensure that the declaration is no broader than necessary and that the specific matter excluded is clearly and precisely defined.
2. With regard to that matter, the Convention shall not apply –
   (a) in the Contracting State that made the declaration;
   (b) in other Contracting States, where recognition or enforcement of a judgment given by a court of a Contracting State that made the declaration is sought.

335. Article 18 permits States to extend the list of matters excluded from the scope of the Convention beyond those enumerated in Article 2(1) through a declaration. It provides that, where a State has a strong interest in not applying the Convention to a specific matter, it may declare that it will not do so.

336. **Rationale.** This provision facilitates the ratification of the Convention by "relaxing" its scope of application. If such opt-outs were not possible, some States might not become Parties to the Convention.[242] However, this policy must be balanced against the interests of the other States and the fundamental objectives of the Convention itself, *i.e.*, to enhance the cross-border effectiveness of judgments in civil and commercial matters. To achieve this balance, Article 18 contains certain safeguards.

Paragraph 1—Where a State has a strong interest in not applying this Convention to a specific matter, that State may declare that it will not apply the Convention to that matter. The State making such a declaration shall ensure that the declaration is no broader than necessary and that the specific matter excluded is clearly and precisely defined.

337. **Safeguards.** First, a State should only make a declaration where it has a strong interest to do so and the declaration should meet the proportionality principle, *i.e.*, the scope of the declaration should not be broader than necessary. In accordance with this principle, the exclusion may be defined by a reference to a specific subject matter, *e.g.*, "contracts over immovable property", "consumer contracts", "labour contracts", "environmental damage" or "anti-trust". Such a reference may be narrowed down, *e.g.*, by: (i) a particular link between the subject matter and the

[242] See also Hartley/Dogauchi Report, para. 236.

requested State, *e.g.*, "contracts over immovable property situated in the requested State"; or (ii) a particular type of remedy in that subject matter, *e.g.*, "injunctions in anti- trust matters". This approach is consistent with the policy underpinning the provision since it ensures that the declaration "is no broader than necessary".[243]

338. Secondly, the specific matter excluded must be clearly and precisely defined. This ensures that the parties and other States are able to easily identify the scope and reach of the declaration.[244] Under Article 30, any declaration under Article 18 must be notified to the depositary, which will inform the other States (Art. 32 (c)). The declarations will also be posted on the website of the HCCH to ensure transparency.

339. The Convention does not require any particular form for the declarations. However, where a State makes a declaration stating that the Convention does not apply to matters within its exclusive jurisdiction, for example, it should include a clear and precise list of such matters.[245]

340. **Non-retroactivity.** A declaration under Article 18 made at the time the Convention comes into force in the requested State will take effect simultaneously. But a declaration made *after* the Convention comes into force for the requested State will take effect on the first day of the month following the expiration of three months following the date on which the notification is received by the depositary (see Art. 30(4)). Such a declaration will not apply to judgments resulting from proceedings that have already been instituted before the court of origin when the declaration takes effect (see Art. 30(5)). This ensures that the parties will be able to determine, when the proceedings are instituted, whether or not the future judgment will be affected by this declaration.

Paragraph 2—With regard to that matter, the Convention shall not apply—Sub-paragraph (a)—in the Contracting State that made the declaration;
Sub-paragraph (b)—in other Contracting States, where recognition or enforcement of a judgment given by a court of a Contracting State that made the declaration is sought.

341. **Reciprocity.** Paragraph 2 establishes reciprocity for declarations made under Article 18(1). With regard to matters excluded by a declaration, the Convention shall not apply (i) in the State that made the declaration and (ii) in other States where recognition or enforcement of a judgment given in a State that made the declaration is sought. In this latter case, however, the reciprocity principle does not prevent the recognition or enforcement of the judgment under national law.

342. **Review of declarations.** Article 21 envisages that the operation of declarations under Article 18 may be considered from time to time (see *infra*, para. 354).

[243] Note that the Hartley/Dogauchi Report, at para. 235, may be read to suggest a stricter interpretation of the parallel provision in the HCCH 2005 Choice of Court Convention. The only declaration made under Art. 21 of the HCCH 2005 Choice of Court Convention at this point is consistent with the interpretation put forward in this Report (see Declaration of the European Union, under Art. 21 of the HCCH 2005 Choice of Court Convention, of 11 June 2015, available on the HCCH website at <www.hcch.net> under "Choice of Court Section" then "Status table").

[244] The Hartley/Dogauchi Report, at note 274, points out that where the State making the declaration so wished, the declaration could first be sent in draft to the Secretary General of the HCCH for circulation to the other States for their comments.

[245] See *Aide memoire* of the Chair of the Special Commission (Special Commission on the Recognition and Enforcement of Foreign Judgments (13–17 November 2017)), para. 23.

Article 19

Declarations with respect to judgments pertaining to a State

1. A State may declare that it shall not apply this Convention to judgments arising from proceedings to which any of the following is a party –
   (a) that State, or a natural person acting for that State; or
   (b) a government agency of that State, or a natural person acting for such a government agency.

   The State making such a declaration shall ensure that the declaration is no broader than necessary and that the exclusion from scope is clearly and precisely defined. The declaration shall not distinguish between judgments where the State, a government agency of that State or a natural person acting for either of them is a defendant or claimant in the proceedings before the court of origin.
2. Recognition or enforcement of a judgment given by a court of a State that made a declaration pursuant to paragraph 1 may be refused if the judgment arose from proceedings to which either the State that made the declaration or the requested State, one of their government agencies or a natural person acting for either of them is a party, to the same extent as specified in the declaration.

343. This provision permits a State to make a declaration that it shall not apply the Convention to judgments which arose from proceedings to which that State, a government agency of that State, or a natural person acting for either of them, was a party, even though the judgment relates to civil or commercial matters.

344. **Rationale.** The Convention does not exclude judgments from its scope merely because a State was a party to the proceedings (Art. 2(4)). While the Convention expressly applies only to civil or commercial matters (Art. 1(1)), some delegations maintained that this limitation could be challenging to apply with regard to a State party, in particular with respect to whether a State party was exercising sovereign powers. A further concern was that the preservation of immunities in Article 2(5) might be insufficient to protect State interests. Article 19 responds to these concerns by allowing States to make a declaration excluding the application of the Convention to judgments that arose from proceedings to which such a State was a party.

Paragraph 1—A State may declare that it shall not apply this Convention to judgments arising from proceedings to which any of the following is a party –

Sub-paragraph (a)—that State, or a natural person acting for that State; or

Sub-paragraph (b)—a government agency of that State, or a natural person acting for such a government agency.

The State making such a declaration shall ensure that the declaration is no broader than necessary and that the exclusion from scope is clearly and precisely defined. The declaration shall not distinguish between judgments where the State, a government agency of that State or a natural person acting for either of them is a defendant or claimant in the proceedings before the court of origin.

345. Paragraph 1 identifies the parties who can be included in the declaration. According to paragraph 1(a) and (b), these include the State itself and a government agency of that State. It also includes a natural person acting for either of them,[246] but it does not include legal persons acting for the State, unless they qualify as government agencies.[247] In all cases, paragraph 1 identifies parties who have the authority to exercise sovereign power, whether directly or in a delegated manner, generally or in a specific field, and natural persons acting for them, regardless of their employment status. For example, an entity charged with the enforcement of competition or consumer law would fall within paragraph 1, regardless of whether it is integrated within the government structure or established as an autonomous and independent entity. Political sub-divisions of a State (including regional or local government) can also be included in a declaration under this provision. In essence, an Article 19 declaration can only be made in relation to a party who has the capacity to exercise sovereign power, even though it may also engage in commercial activities. The terms are broad to capture the diversity of government structures and procedural definitions of juridical personality or capacity among States. Paragraph 1 also requires that the declaration be no broader than necessary and that the exclusion from scope be clearly and precisely defined. As a result, a State making a declaration under Article 19 should identify which government agencies are covered by its declaration and the circumstances under which they would be included.

346. **Safeguards.** The structure and content of Article 19 is largely parallel to Article 18. As in Article 18, the State making such declaration shall ensure that the declaration is no broader than necessary (see *supra,* para. 337) and that the exclusion from scope is clearly and precisely defined (see *supra,* para. 338). For example, the declaration may refer to any proceedings, in civil or commercial matters, or to only certain categories of proceedings. The declaration may be limited to certain subject matters and additional criteria may be specified to narrow down its scope, *e.g.*, to certain government agencies, a particular link between the subject matter and the requested State or certain types of remedies (see *supra,* para. 337). Additionally, paragraph 1 clarifies that the declaration shall not distinguish between judgments where the State, a government agency or a natural person acting for either of them,

[246] The expression "acting for" is also used in Art. 2(4). It covers cases where the natural person is acting "in the name of" the State or a government agency; typically, the person is acting as an "agent" of the State. Conversely it does not cover those cases where the natural person is acting in their own name, *e.g.*, entering into a contract with a third party in their own name and capacity, even if the contract is in the interest of the State.

[247] For background on this part of Art. 19(1), see Minutes of the Twenty-Second Session on the Recognition and Enforcement of Foreign Judgments (18 June—2 July 2019), Minutes No 6, paras 36–43, and Minutes No 15, paras 155–162, in particular the consensus that this provision does not cover legal persons, irrespective of their ownership, be they commercial enterprises owned by the State or privately owned, except where they are governmental agencies.

is a defendant or claimant in the proceedings before the court of origin. Moreover, it should not distinguish between judgments depending on whether they are the judgment creditor or the judgment debtor.[248] When the declaring State merely intervenes in the proceedings in the State of origin as a third party, the judgment may circulate as between the claimant and the defendant, who are not affected by the declaration.

347. **Non-retroactivity.** As in Article 18, a declaration made *after* the Convention enters into force for the State making it will take effect on the first day of the month following the expiration of three months following the date on which the notification is received by the depositary (see *infra*, Art. 30(4)). Such a declaration will not apply to judgments resulting from proceedings that have already been instituted by or against the State party, or to which the State party has already been added, before the court of origin when the declaration takes effect (see *infra*, Art. 30(5)).

Paragraph 2—Recognition or enforcement of a judgment given by a court of a State that made a declaration pursuant to paragraph 1 may be refused if the judgment arose from proceedings to which either the State that made the declaration or the requested State, one of their government agencies or a natural person acting for either of them is a party, to the same extent as specified in the declaration.

348. As in Article 18, paragraph 2 establishes reciprocity for declarations made under Article 19(1).[249] When a declaration is made under Article 19(1), another State may refuse to recognise or enforce a judgment given by a court of the State that made the declaration and arising from proceedings to which one or more of the following is a party: (i) the declaring State, (ii) the requested State, (iii) a government agency of the declaring State or the requested State, (iv) a natural person acting for the declaring State or the requested State, or (v) a natural person acting for a government agency of the declaring State or the requested State.[250] The scope of the refusal to recognise or enforce based on reciprocity should reflect the extent of the declaration.

349. **Example 1.** State A has made a declaration under Article 19(1), which covers any judgment arising out of proceedings to which that State is a party. A judgment given in State B against State A will not be recognised or enforced in State A under the Convention. Such a judgment will however circulate under the Convention in other States (assuming, naturally, that the conditions for such circulation are met, in particular the filters laid down by Art. 5, and subject to Art. 2(5), which confirms that nothing in the Convention affects the immunities of State A).

[248] The safeguard seeks to prevent strategic or opportunistic declarations. However, in practice, it cannot prevent the declaring State from recognising or enforcing the favourable judgment under its own national law. This would occur outside the scope of the Convention, *i.e.*, not under Art. 15.

[249] Unlike Art. 18(2), the reciprocity principle in Art. 19(2) does not operate to exclude the application of the Convention.

[250] The wording of para. 2 confirms that recognition or enforcement may make sense when the declaring State is the judgment debtor.

350. **Example 2 (reciprocity).** If a judgment is given in State A (declaring State) against State B (requested State), the latter State may invoke Article 19(2) to refuse to recognise or enforce such a judgment. State B however may not invoke the reciprocity clause if recognition or enforcement of that judgment is sought in another State, *e.g.*, State C. Likewise, if the judgment had been given in State C (State of origin) and State A (declaring State) is the judgment creditor, State B (requested State) may not refuse to recognise or enforce such a judgment under Article 19(2).

351. **Review of declarations.** Article 21 envisages that the operation of declarations under Article 19 may be considered from time to time (see *infra*, para. 354).

Article 20

Uniform interpretation

In the interpretation of this Convention, regard shall be had to its international character and to the need to promote uniformity in its application.

352. Article 20 states that in interpreting the Convention regard must be had to its international character and the need to promote uniformity in its application. Courts applying the Convention must interpret it in an international spirit to promote uniformity of application. Where reasonably possible, foreign decisions and commentary should be taken into account, keeping in mind that concepts and principles axiomatic in one legal system may be unknown or rejected in another. The objectives of the Convention can be attained only if all courts apply it in an open—minded way.[251]
353. This Article must be read jointly with Article 21 below (Review of operation of the Convention) because both Articles share the objective of a proper and uniform application of the Convention.

[251] This clause is also present in the HCCH 2005 Choice of Court Convention (Art. 23). See Hartley/Dogauchi Report, para. 256; the HCCH *Convention of 5 July 2006 on the Law Applicable to Certain Rights in Respect of Securities held with an Intermediary* (Art. 13); and the HCCH 2007 Child Support Convention (Art. 53).

Article 21

Review of operation of the Convention

The Secretary General of the Hague Conference on Private International Law shall at regular intervals make arrangements for review of the operation of this Convention, including any declarations, and shall report to the Council on General Affairs and Policy.

354. Article 21 requires the Secretary General of the HCCH to make arrangements at regular intervals for the review of the operation of the Convention, including any declarations made under it, and to report to the Council on General Affairs and Policy. One major purpose of these reviews is to examine the operation of declarations under Article 14, 17, 18 or 19. The Council on General Affairs and Policy will determine whether there is a need to begin the process to consider possible amendments to the Convention.

Article 22

Non-unified legal systems

1. In relation to a Contracting State in which two or more systems of law apply in different territorial units with regard to any matter dealt with in this Convention –
   (a) any reference to the law or procedure of a State shall be construed as referring, where appropriate, to the law or procedure in force in the relevant territorial unit;
   (b) any reference to the court or courts of a State shall be construed as referring, where appropriate, to the court or courts in the relevant territorial unit;
   (c) any reference to a connection with a State shall be construed as referring, where appropriate, to a connection with the relevant territorial unit;
   (d) any reference to a connecting factor in relation to a State shall be construed as referring, where appropriate, to that connecting factor in relation to the relevant territorial unit.
2. Notwithstanding paragraph 1, a Contracting State with two or more territorial units in which different systems of law apply shall not be bound to apply this Convention to situations which involve solely such different territorial units.
3. A court in a territorial unit of a Contracting State with two or more territorial units in which different systems of law apply shall not be bound to recognise or enforce a judgment from another Contracting State solely because the judgment has been recognised or enforced in another territorial unit of the same Contracting State under this Convention.
4. This Article shall not apply to Regional Economic Integration Organisations.

355. Article 22 is concerned with potential difficulties resulting from non-unified legal systems, i.e., States composed of two or more territorial units, each with its own judicial or legal system. The individual territorial units of such States may have separate courts and civil procedure (non-unified judicial system) or distinct substantive law rules (non-unified legal system) such that references to "courts of State A" or the "law of State A" are either meaningless or insufficiently precise. Some States may exhibit both of these "non-unified" characteristics. In principle, since the Convention deals with procedural matters (recognition and enforcement of judgments), this Article will typically be relevant only for States that are composed of two or more territorial units, each with its own judicial system.[252]

[252] See also Hartley/Dogauchi Report, para. 258.

356. This situation occurs most often in the case of federations, such as Canada or the United States of America, but can also occur in other States as well, such as the People's Republic of China or the United Kingdom. In these cases, the question may arise whether a reference to a State in the Convention is to the State as a whole ("State" in the international sense) or whether it is to a particular territorial unit within that State.

Paragraph 1—In relation to a Contracting State in which two or more systems of law apply in different territorial units with regard to any matter dealt with in this Convention –

Sub-paragraph (a)—any reference to the law or procedure of a State shall be construed as referring, where appropriate, to the law or procedure in force in the relevant territorial unit;

Sub-paragraph (b)—any reference to the court or courts of a State shall be construed as referring, where appropriate, to the court or courts in the relevant territorial unit;

Sub-paragraph (c)—any reference to a connection with a State shall be construed as referring, where appropriate, to a connection with the relevant territorial unit;

Sub-paragraph (d)—any reference to a connecting factor in relation to a State shall be construed as referring, where appropriate, to that connecting factor in relation to the relevant territorial unit.

357. Interpretive rule. Article 22(1) provides that where different systems of law apply in the territorial units with regard to any matter dealt with in the Convention, the Convention is to be construed as applying either to the State in the international sense or to the relevant territorial unit, whichever is appropriate. Article 22(1) serves as an interpretive guide to those provisions of the Convention that require the identification of a geographical or territorial location. It has no implications on the scope of the Convention.

358. The words "where appropriate" in the four sub-paragraphs of Article 22(1) do not provide the court in the requested State with discretion on the issue. Rather, this refers to the fact that the reference to the territorial unit rather than the State will only occur where such reference is appropriate because of the relevant non-unified characteristic of the State.

359. The point of departure for this analysis is that the Convention applies to a judgment if it has effect or is enforceable in the State of origin (Art. 4(3)). Where the judgment in question comes from a State with a non-unified judicial system, it may be the case that a judgment from a court in a territorial unit has effect or is enforceable as a domestic judgment only in the territorial unit whose court issued the judgment and not throughout the State as a whole. In other words, while the judgment from the territorial unit may become effective or enforceable in other territorial units within the State, it is not regarded as a domestic judgment in those other territorial units. Depending on the particular configuration or nature of the State's judicial system, judgments from its courts may instead be considered as domestic judgments throughout the State.[253] Where judgments of courts are considered to be domestic only within a particular territorial unit, it may be "appropriate" to refer to that territorial unit whenever the Convention refers to the "State".

[253] Art. 22(2) specifies that the Convention does not apply to situations involving recognition and enforcement between territorial units of non-unified States (see *infra*, para. 365).

360. Filters. The application of filters in Articles 5 and 6 may involve recourse to the interpretive rules provided in Article 22. The words "where appropriate" in Article 22 indicate that reliance on the interpretive rule is restricted to situations where the non—unified characteristic of the State of origin is relevant. In cases where the filter refers to a connecting factor with the territory of a State (e.g., in Art. 5(1)(a), (b), (d) or (g)), the analysis provided in the previous paragraph will be relevant to the interpretation of that filter. That is, where the judgment from the territorial unit is a domestic judgment only for that territorial unit and not for the State as a whole, it would be appropriate to treat the reference to "State" in the filter as a reference to the territorial unit. Thus, for example, the condition of Article 5(1)(a) will only be met if the habitual residence of the party against whom recognition or enforcement is sought is within the territorial unit over which the court of origin exercises its jurisdiction. Conversely, if the judgment is one that is effective and enforceable as a domestic judgment throughout the State, then it would be appropriate to treat the reference to "State" in the filter as a reference to the State as a whole.

361. Not all filters include connecting factors. Some only refer to the law of the State. For example, Article 5(1)(f) refers to contesting jurisdiction within the timeframe provided by the "law of the State of origin". In such a case, it would be appropriate to refer to the procedural law of the territorial unit in the non-unified judicial system of that State, since the law applicable to the issue varies from one territorial unit to the other. Indeed, a reference to the law of the State as a whole would be ineffectual to determine if the filter is met.

362. **Other provisions in the Convention.** The issue of interpretation may also arise when the *requested* State is a non-unified State. For example, under Article 13, the rule that the procedure for recognition or enforcement is governed by the law of the requested State may appropriately be a reference to the law of the territorial unit in a State with a non-unified judicial system.

363. Under Article 7(2), recognition or enforcement may be postponed or refused if proceedings between the parties on the same subject matter are pending before a court of the requested State. The interpretive rule in Article 22(1)(c) justifies a restrictive reading of this provision by limiting its application to parallel proceedings before a court of the territorial unit, if this is the appropriate consequence of the non—unified judicial system of the State. Without Article 22(1)(c), it might be open to the court of a territorial unit to refuse to enforce a judgment because of parallel proceedings before the courts of a different territorial unit within the State, even though this would not normally be an option available within its domestic law. This in turn reinforces the general principle of the Convention that foreign judgments be treated in the same manner as domestic judgments when the relevant criteria for recognition and enforcement are met.

364. **Difference with the HCCH 2005 Choice of Court Convention.** The structure of Article 22 differs slightly from its parallel provision in the HCCH 2005 Choice of Court Convention (Art. 25). These differences arise from the need to adapt this provision to the particularities of the Convention, not from an intention to change its meaning. In Article 25 of the HCCH 2005 Choice of Court Convention, the reference to the term "residence" is expressly mentioned in an independent limb. Conversely, Article 22 of this Convention includes all connecting factors, including "residence", in one limb (Art. 22(1)(d)) and keeps the reference to "a connection" with a State in a different one (Art. 22(1)(c)). The former encompasses all connecting factors in relation to a State mentioned in the Convention, in particular in Articles 5 and 6 (filters). The latter covers the reference to the term "connection" with a State used in Articles 5(1)(g) and 7(2) of the Convention.

Paragraph 2—Notwithstanding paragraph 1, a Contracting State with two or more territorial units in which different systems of law apply shall not be bound to apply this Convention to situations which involve solely such different territorial units.

365. Article 22(2) specifies that a State with two or more territorial units in which different systems of law are applied is not bound to apply the Convention to situations involving solely such different territorial units. This is consistent with Article 1(2) of the Convention that defines the scope of the Convention in terms of recognition and enforcement in one State of judgments given in another State. The recognition and enforcement obligations under the Convention only arise with respect to foreign judgments, understood in the international sense.

Paragraph 3—A court in a territorial unit of a Contracting State with two or more territorial units in which different systems of law apply shall not be bound to recognise or enforce a judgment from another Contracting State solely because the judgment has been recognised or enforced in another territorial unit of the same Contracting State under this Convention.

366. Article 22(3) states that there is no obligation of recognition or enforcement in one territorial unit flowing from the recognition or enforcement of a foreign judgment in another territorial unit of the same State. Thus, for example, a French judgment enforced under the Convention in Quebec, Canada need not be automatically enforced in Ontario, Canada. This is a natural consequence of the scope of the Convention, as defined in Article 1(2), but it is explicitly addressed in Article 22(3) to avoid confusion.

Paragraph 4—This Article shall not apply to Regional Economic Integration Organisations.

367. Finally, Article 22(4) indicates that these special rules applying to non-unified legal systems do not apply to an REIO, which is instead governed by its own rules in Articles 26 and 27 (see below).

Article 23

Relationship with other international instruments

1. This Convention shall be interpreted so far as possible to be compatible with other treaties in force for Contracting States, whether concluded before or after this Convention.
2. This Convention shall not affect the application by a Contracting State of a treaty that was concluded before this Convention.
3. This Convention shall not affect the application by a Contracting State of a treaty concluded after this Convention as concerns the recognition or enforcement of a judgment given by a court of a Contracting State that is also a Party to that treaty. Nothing in the other treaty shall affect the obligations under Article 6 towards Contracting States that are not Parties to that treaty.
4. This Convention shall not affect the application of the rules of a Regional Economic Integration Organisation that is a Party to this Convention as concerns the recognition or enforcement of a judgment given by a court of a Contracting State that is also a Member State of the Regional Economic Integration Organisation where –
   (a) the rules were adopted before this Convention was concluded; or
   (b) the rules were adopted after this Convention was concluded, to the extent that they do not affect the obligations under Article 6 towards Contracting States that are not Member States of the Regional Economic Integration Organisation.

368. Article 23 deals with the relationship between the Convention and other international instruments.[254] The starting point is Article 30 of the Vienna Convention of 1969, Article 30(2) of which provides that, where a treaty states that it is subject to another treaty (whether earlier or later), the other treaty will prevail. Article 23 of this Convention specifies three cases (Art. 23(2)-(4)) in which another treaty will prevail over it, including where there is a conflict between the Convention and the rules of an REIO that is a Party to the Convention. Outside of these three cases, the Convention has effect to the fullest extent permitted by international law.

[254] For a background discussion, see A. Schulz, "The Relationship between the Judgments Project and other International Instruments", Prel. Doc. No 24 of December 2003 for the attention of the Special Commission of December 2003. See also the discussion of customary international law for Contracting States to the Convention which are not party to the Vienna Convention of 1969 (at paras 36 *et seq.*)

369. The problem of conflicting instruments arises only if two conditions are fulfilled. First, the State of the court addressed must be a Party to both instruments. If that State is a Party to only one, its courts will simply apply that one. Article 23 is, therefore, addressed to States that are parties to both the Convention and to another legally binding international instrument that conflicts with it.

370. Second, there must be an actual incompatibility between the two instruments. In other words, the application of the two instruments must lead to incompatible results in a concrete situation. Where this is not the case, both instruments can be applied. In some cases, an apparent incompatibility may be eliminated through interpretation. Where this is possible, the problem is solved. Article 23(1) reflects this approach.

Paragraph 1—This Convention shall be interpreted so far as possible to be compatible with other treaties in force for Contracting States, whether concluded before or after this Convention.

371. The first paragraph of Article 23 contains a rule of interpretation. It provides that the Convention must be interpreted, as far as possible, to be compatible with other instruments in force for Contracting States. This applies irrespective of whether the other instrument was concluded before or after the Convention. Thus, where a provision in the Convention is reasonably capable of two meanings, the meaning that is most compatible with the other instrument should be preferred. This does not, however, mean that a strained interpretation should be adopted in order to achieve compatibility.

Paragraph 2—This Convention shall not affect the application by a Contracting State of a treaty that was concluded before this Convention.

372. Where two instruments are not compatible in their application to a concrete situation, Article 23(2) allows for the earlier instrument to prevail. Article 23(2) does not require the earlier instrument to have been in force prior to the entry into force of this Convention, but merely to have been concluded prior to the conclusion of the Convention, *i.e.*, prior to 2 July 2019. Of course, if the earlier treaty is not yet in force, no possible incompatibility can arise. This specificity avoids any uncertainty in the timing element.[255] Furthermore, unlike paragraphs 3 and 4, paragraph 2 does not require that the State of origin also be a party to the earlier treaty.

373. **Example 1 (treaty between Contracting States).**[256] State A (State of origin) and State B (requested State) are parties to the 2007 Lugano Convention and Contracting States of this Convention. In relation to an insurance judgment, under the 2007 Lugano Convention, the beneficiary of the insurance (i.e., the injured person or the policy holder) may only be sued before the courts of their domicile. If they are sued

[255] Note that Art. 23 takes the time of the Convention's conclusion as the relevant element for distinguishing between *earlier* and *later* treaties, and not the date it entered into force. The date of conclusion is an objective element (determined by public international law) common to all States, whereas the date of entry into force may vary among States. Therefore, the reference to the date of entry into force might have implied that, with regard to the same treaty, some States would have applied Art. 23(2) and others Art. 23(3). See "Report of the informal working group III—Relationship with other international instruments", Prel. Doc. No 9 Rev Rev of June 2019 for the attention of the Twenty-Second Session on the Recognition and Enforcement of Foreign Judgments (18 June—2 July 2019) (hereinafter, "Prel. Doc. No 9 of June 2019"), para. 4

[256] The example is taken from Prel. Doc. No 9 of June 2019, paras 11 and 14 of the Annex.

elsewhere, recognition or enforcement of the judgment shall be refused (Art. 35). This Convention, however, does not include a special rule for insurance contracts to protect beneficiaries, policyholders or injured parties (unless they qualify as consumers). If a judgment satisfies the filter laid down, e.g., in Article 5(1)(g), then State B will be obliged to recognise and enforce the judgment under the Convention, though the 2007 Lugano Convention forbids it. In such a case, Article 23(2) gives priority to the application of the 2007 Lugano Convention and thus allows State B to refuse to recognise or enforce the judgment without breaching its obligation under the Convention.[257]

374. **Example 2 (treaty with third States).** State A (State of origin) and State B (requested State) are both Contracting States of the Convention. State B is also a party to an earlier treaty on international settlement agreements.[258] Assume that a judgment given by a court of State A is presented for recognition and enforcement under the Convention in State B, and the judgment debtor objects on the grounds that it conflicts with a settlement agreement between the same parties. In such a case, the court of State B may give priority to the treaty on international settlement agreements and refuse to recognise or enforce the judgment, even if State A is not a party to that treaty and even if that treaty entered into force in State B after the Convention. It is sufficient that it was concluded before the Convention. The rationale is that when State A adhered to the Convention, the other treaty had already been concluded and therefore State A somehow assumed the risk that other Contracting States might ratify it.

375. **Relationship with the HCCH 2005 Choice of Court Convention.** Since the HCCH 2005 Choice of Court Convention was concluded in 2005, and involves recognition and enforcement of foreign judgments, it is useful to mention it specifically in relation to Article 23(2). In general, there are no tensions or inconsistencies between the HCCH 2005 Choice of Court Convention and the Convention, as neither instrument restricts or limits recognition and enforcement of judgments under national law,[259] including under other treaties.

376. **Example 1.** Where the two States (the State of origin and the requested State) are Contracting States of the Convention and parties to the HCCH 2005 Choice of Court Convention, and, for example, the judgment was given by the chosen court under an exclusive choice of court agreement and the State of origin was also the habitual residence of the person against whom recognition and enforcement is sought, there should be no tension in principle between the two instruments. In most systems, the party seeking recognition and enforcement can rely on either instrument, or on both instruments, in the alternative. There may be a ground for refusal under one instrument that does not exist under the other. This would be the case if the grounds for refusal under the Convention diverged significantly from the grounds for refusal under Article 9 of the HCCH 2005 Choice of Court Convention. The result would be that the State addressed must still recognise and enforce the judgment under the instrument that does not permit refusal. This is because the grounds for refusal under

257 Note, however, that this example is unlikely to occur when the other treaty also establishes rules on direct jurisdiction, as is the case with the 2007 Lugano Convention.

258 The *co-Rapporteurs* note that any similarity between this hypothetical example and the 2018 Convention on International Settlement Agreements resulting from Mediation is purely coincidental.

259 The only limitation to enforcement under national law in the Convention refers to Art. 6, but rights *in rem* over immovable property are excluded from the scope of the HCCH 2005 Choice of Court Convention (see Art. 2(2)(l)), thereby avoiding any risk of inconsistencies on that point.

both instruments are permitted grounds for refusal, not mandated grounds for refusal. There is therefore no requirement to refuse recognition or enforcement under the instrument that permits refusal. If there is an obligation to recognise and enforce under the HCCH 2005 Choice of Court Convention—or national law—then they will apply and there will be no inconsistency with the Convention.

377. **Example 2.** State A (State of origin) and State B (requested State) are both Contracting States of the Convention, while State B and State C are parties to the HCCH 2005 Choice of Court Convention. A judgment is given in State A, where the defendant is habitually resident, but in spite of an exclusive choice of court agreement designating the courts of State C. In such a case, State B may refuse to recognise and enforce that judgment under Article 7(1)(d) of the Convention. It is therefore not even necessary to refer to Article 23 as there is no inconsistency between the two instruments.

378. **Example 3.** A further example might involve two judgments. State A (State of origin) and State B (requested State) are both Contracting States of the Convention, while State B and State C are parties to the HCCH 2005 Choice of Court Convention. State A gives a judgment falling within one of the bases for recognition and enforcement under Article 5 of the Convention and afterwards State C gives another judgment on the basis of an exclusive choice of court agreement. The judgments are inconsistent. In principle, both judgments might have a claim for recognition and enforcement in State B. In such circumstances, Article 7(1)(d) of the Convention would allow giving priority to the judgment of the chosen court (State C). The court addressed is then required to recognise and enforce the judgment of the chosen court unless the other judgment was given first, in which case recognition or enforcement could be refused under Article 9(g) of the HCCH 2005 Choice of Court Convention. In this paradoxical situation, where the judgment of the non-chosen court was the earlier judgment, the court addressed is not compelled to enforce either judgment. In principle, it should be left to the discretion of the requested State whether the ground for refusal will actually lead to the refusal to recognise or enforce a judgment as both Conventions provide that the requested State "may refuse". However, in light of both Conventions' purpose to promote the recognition or enforcement of judgments, the requested State should not refuse the recognition or enforcement of both judgments.[260]

Paragraph 3—This Convention shall not affect the application by a Contracting State of a treaty concluded after this Convention as concerns the recognition or enforcement of a judgment given by a court of a Contracting State that is also a Party to that treaty. Nothing in the other treaty shall affect the obligations under Article 6 towards Contracting States that are not Parties to that treaty.

379. Article 23(3) provides for the situation where a Contracting State enters into a treaty dealing with the recognition and enforcement of judgments with another Contracting State, and the other treaty has been concluded *after* this Convention. Unlike Article 23(2), this paragraph requires that the State of origin and the requested States are both Contracting States of the Convention and parties to the later instrument. Furthermore, Article 23(3) uses the expression "as concerns the recognition or enforcement of a judgment" to allow Contracting States to apply a later instrument for the purpose of granting or refusing recognition or enforcement of judgments

[260] See Prel. Doc. No 9 of June 2019, para. 4 of the Annex.

given by a court of a Contracting State that is also a party to that instrument, *i.e.*, the prevalence of the later instrument is not limited by a *favor recognitionis* principle.[261] The general requirement of incompatibility between the two instruments continues to apply.

380. The second difference between earlier and later treaties relates to Article 6 of the Convention. This rule of priority for later instruments does not affect the obligations under Article 6 of the Convention owed to Contracting States that are not parties to the later instrument. This ensures the protection of the exclusive filter contained in Article 6 for Contracting States that are not parties to the later instrument. It does not apply, however, with respect to immovable property in non-Contracting States (see *supra,* paras 237–243).

381. **Example 1.** States A and B are both Contracting States of the Convention. They later conclude a bilateral treaty on enforcement of judgments. This treaty provides that neither of those States will enforce non-monetary judgments in certain matters. According to Article 23(3), this treaty prevails over the Convention and therefore State B may refuse the enforcement of a non-monetary judgment given in State A even if one or more of the filters laid down by Article 5 of the Convention is met. Obviously, this later treaty cannot be invoked against other Contracting States of the Convention to refuse recognition or enforcement of non-monetary judgments given in these States.

382. **Example 2.** States A and B are both Contracting States of the Convention. They later conclude a bilateral treaty on enforcement of judgments. This treaty provides for, among other things, recognition and enforcement of judgments on claims involving rights *in rem* related to immovable property situated in either State. The treaty provides that such judgments can originate either from courts in the State where the immoveable property is situated or in the State of the defendant's habitual residence. Under the Convention, the latter judgment could *not* be recognised, even under national law, due to Article 6. This would produce a conflict with the later bilateral treaty. In such a case, the later treaty may prevail under Article 23(3), and justify the recognition and enforcement of the judgment under that treaty.

383. **Example 3.** States A, B and C are all Contracting States to the Convention. States A and B subsequently conclude a bilateral treaty according to which judgments on claims relating to rights *in rem* over immovable property are mutually recognised and enforced even if the immovable property is situated in a third State, as long as the claimant and the defendant are habitually resident in either State A or State B. A court in State A gives such a judgment relating to a right *in rem* over immovable property in State C. The judgment is brought for enforcement in State B. Under the Convention, this judgment cannot be enforced because it does not satisfy the rule in Article 6. In such a case, Article 23(3) cannot be invoked to justify recognition and enforcement since the property is located in a Contracting State that is not a party to the other treaty.

[261] Ibid., para. 3

Paragraph 4—This Convention shall not affect the application of the rules of a Regional Economic Integration Organisation that is a Party to this Convention as concerns the recognition or enforcement of a judgment given by a court of a Contracting State that is also a Member State of the Regional Economic Integration Organisation where –

Sub-paragraph (a)—the rules were adopted before this Convention was concluded; or

Sub-paragraph (b)—the rules were adopted after this Convention was concluded, to the extent that they do not affect the obligations under Article 6 towards Contracting States that are not Member States of the Regional Economic Integration Organisation.

384. Article 23(4) deals with the situation where a Regional Economic Integration Organisation becomes a Contracting Party to the Convention and relates to the circulation of judgments within the REIO. In this context, it is possible that rules (legislation) adopted by the REIO conflict with the Convention. Article 23(4) contains two priority rules. First, the Convention does not affect the application of rules adopted by the REIO before the conclusion of the Convention. Second, the Convention does not prejudice the application of rules adopted by the REIO after the Convention was concluded, to the extent they do not affect the obligations under Article 6 towards Contracting States that are not Member States of the REIO. In practice, this implies that the REIO cannot adopt a rule, after the Convention is concluded, allowing for the circulation among its Member States of judgments on a right *in rem* over immovable property situated in another Contracting State.

Chapter IV—Final clauses

Article 24

Signature, ratification, acceptance, approval or accession

1. This Convention shall be open for signature by all States.
2. This Convention is subject to ratification, acceptance or approval by the signatory States.
3. This Convention shall be open for accession by all States.
4. Instruments of ratification, acceptance, approval or accession shall be deposited with the Ministry of Foreign Affairs of the Kingdom of the Netherlands, depositary of the Convention.

385. This provision is concerned with the ways in which a State may become a Party to the Convention. It provides two methods, either (i) by signature followed by ratification, acceptance or approval (paras 1 and 2), or (ii) by accession (para. 3). The mere signing of the Convention obliges the State to refrain from acts that defeat the object and purpose of the Convention (see Art. 18 of the Vienna Convention of 1969). The deposit of the instrument of ratification, acceptance, approval or accession constitutes, in each case, an international act whereby a State expresses its consent to be bound by the Convention (see Art. 2(1)(b) of the Vienna Convention of 1969).

386. Whatever method is adopted by a State, the result is the same.[262] Both methods are equally available to Member States and non-Member States of the HCCH. Article 24 also makes no distinction between States that participated at the Twenty-Second Session at which the text was adopted and those that did not. States are free to choose through which method it is most convenient for them to become a Party, which facilitates widespread adherence to the Convention.

387. The relevant instruments are deposited with the Ministry of Foreign Affairs of the Kingdom of the Netherlands. The depositary then notifies those indicated in Article 32 of any signature, ratification, acceptance, approval or accession under this Article. The entry into force of the Convention, both on an international level and for a specific Contracting State, is governed by Article 28, and the establishment of treaty relations between Contracting States is governed by Article 29.

[262] The Hartley/Dogauchi Report points out that in other HCCH Conventions, an acceding State is in a less favourable position than a ratifying State, since accession to those Conventions is subject to the agreement of the States that are already Parties (para. 311). This is not the case with either the HCCH 2005 Choice of Court Convention or with this Convention (see para. 407).

Article 25

Declarations with respect to non-unified legal systems

1. If a State has two or more territorial units in which different systems of law apply in relation to matters dealt with in this Convention, it may declare that the Convention shall extend to all its territorial units or only to one or more of them. Such a declaration shall state expressly the territorial units to which the Convention applies.
2. If a State makes no declaration under this Article, the Convention shall extend to all territorial units of that State.
3. This Article shall not apply to Regional Economic Integration Organisations.

388. The Convention deals with "non-unified legal systems" in two different provisions, Articles 22 and 25. The former determines how the Convention must be construed and interpreted in those cases (see supra, paras 355–359). The latter envisages a declaration mechanism to extend the application of the Convention to all the territorial units or only one or more of them.

389. **Non-unified legal systems.** Article 25, like Article 22, refers to States that have two or more territorial units in which different systems of law apply in relation to matters dealt with in this Convention. Since the Convention deals with procedural matters (recognition and enforcement of judgments), such a definition really refers to States composed of two or more territorial units, each with its own judicial system (see *supra*, paras 355–356). This is the case for federal States, *e.g.*, Canada or the United States of America, but it may occur in other States as well, *e.g.*, the People's Republic of China or the United Kingdom. REIOs, however, are not covered by this Article (see para. (3)).

390. **Declaration.** Article 25(1) permits States to declare that the Convention shall extend to all their territorial units or only to one or more of them. This declaration may be made at the time of signature, ratification, acceptance, approval or accession or any time thereafter. It may also be modified by submitting another declaration at any time afterwards. These declarations shall be notified to the depositary and shall state expressly the territorial unit or units to which the Convention applies. The entry into force and the application in time of the Convention in these cases are addressed by Article 28 (see *infra*, paras 405–406).

391. If a State to which this Article applies makes no declaration, the Convention shall extend to all territorial units of that State.

392. Finally, paragraph 3 establishes that this provision does not apply to an REIO. Article 25 only applies to States (in the international sense) and territorial units *within a State* in which different systems of law apply. Conversely, REIOs are constituted by two or more sovereign States and are dealt with in the next two Articles.

Article 26

Regional Economic Integration Organisations

1. A Regional Economic Integration Organisation which is constituted solely by sovereign States and has competence over some or all of the matters governed by this Convention may sign, accept, approve or accede to this Convention. The Regional Economic Integration Organisation shall in that case have the rights and obligations of a Contracting State, to the extent that the Organisation has competence over matters governed by this Convention.
2. The Regional Economic Integration Organisation shall, at the time of signature, acceptance, approval or accession, notify the depositary in writing of the matters governed by this Convention in respect of which competence has been transferred to that Organisation by its Member States. The Organisation shall promptly notify the depositary in writing of any changes to its competence as specified in the most recent notice given under this paragraph.
3. For the purposes of the entry into force of this Convention, any instrument deposited by a Regional Economic Integration Organisation shall not be counted unless the Regional Economic Integration Organisation declares in accordance with Article 27(1) that its Member States will not be Parties to this Convention.
4. Any reference to a "Contracting State" or "State" in this Convention shall apply equally, where appropriate, to a Regional Economic Integration Organisation.

393. Articles 26 and 27 enable REIOs to become a Contracting Party to the Convention. An REIO constituted solely by sovereign States may sign, accept, approve or accede to the Convention (the absence of the term ratify is intentional, as only States ratify conventions), but only to the extent that it has competence over matters covered by the Convention.[263] REIOs are not considered to be non-unified legal systems within the meaning of the Convention and therefore it is necessary to include a provision permitting them to become a Contracting Party.

394. The Convention contemplates the REIO and its Member States becoming Parties (Art. 26) or the REIO alone becoming a Party (Art. 27).

[263] The Hartley/Dogauchi Report, at note 351, explains that REIOs should have an autonomous meaning (not depending on the law of any State) and that it should be interpreted flexibly to include sub—regional and trans-regional organisations as well as organisations whose mandate extends beyond economic matters.

395. Article 26 is concerned with the first possibility, *i.e.*, where both the REIO and its Member States become Parties to the Convention. This may occur if they enjoy concurrent external competence over the subject matter of the Convention (joint competence), or if some matters fall within the external competence of the REIO and others within that of the Member States (which would result in shared or mixed competence for the Convention as a whole).

396. In view of the importance of this matter, REIOs are to notify the depositary in writing of the matters covered by this Convention in respect of which competence has been transferred to that organisation by its Member States. The notification has to be made at the time of signature, acceptance, approval or accession. Furthermore, REIOs must *promptly* notify the depositary in writing of any changes to their competence as specified in the most recent notice (Art. 26(2)).

397. Where the number of States is relevant for the purposes of the entry into force of the Convention, paragraph 3 provides that any instrument deposited by an REIO shall not be counted unless it declares, in accordance with Article 27(1), that its Member States will not be Parties to it.

398. **Meaning of "State".** A Contracting REIO has, within the limits of its competence, the same rights and duties as a Contracting State. Thus, paragraph 4 provides that where an REIO becomes a Party to the Convention, whether under Article 26 or under Article 27, any reference in the Convention to "Contracting State" or to "State" applies equally, where appropriate, to the REIO. In the case of the European Union, this means that "State" could mean either the European Union or one of its Member States, depending on what is appropriate. It follows that, since the European Union as an REIO may become a party to the Convention and qualify as a Contracting State, its judicial arm, the Court of Justice of the European Union, should be considered as the court of a Contracting State for the purposes of this Convention.[264]

[264] See also Hartley/Dogauchi Report, para. 17: "It follows from this that a choice of court agreement designating 'the courts of the European Community' or referring specifically to 'the Court of Justice of the European Communities (Court of First Instance)' would be covered by the Convention."

Article 27

Regional Economic Integration Organisation as a Contracting Party without its Member States

1. At the time of signature, acceptance, approval or accession, a Regional Economic Integration Organisation may declare that it exercises competence over all the matters governed by this Convention and that its Member States will not be Parties to this Convention but shall be bound by virtue of the signature, acceptance, approval or accession of the Organisation.
2. In the event that a declaration is made by a Regional Economic Integration Organisation in accordance with paragraph 1, any reference to a "Contracting State" or "State" in this Convention shall apply equally, where appropriate, to the Member States of the Organisation.

399. Article 27 deals with the second possibility mentioned above, *i.e.*, where the REIO alone becomes a Party. This may occur where it has exclusive external competence over the subject matter of the Convention. In such a case, the REIO may declare its Member States bound by the Convention by virtue of the agreement of the REIO. As in the former case, any reference to "Contracting State" or "State" under the Convention shall apply equally, where appropriate, to the Member States of the REIO.

Article 28

Entry into force

1. This Convention shall enter into force on the first day of the month following the expiration of the period during which a notification may be made in accordance with Article 29(2) with respect to the second State that has deposited its instrument of ratification, acceptance, approval or accession referred to in Article 24.
2. Thereafter this Convention shall enter into force –
   (a) for each State subsequently ratifying, accepting, approving or acceding to it, on the first day of the month following the expiration of the period during which notifications may be made in accordance with Article 29(2) with respect to that State;
   (b) for a territorial unit to which this Convention has been extended in accordance with Article 25 after the Convention has entered into force for the State making the declaration, on the first day of the month following the expiration of three months after the notification of the declaration referred to in that Article.

400. Article 28 specifies when the Convention enters into force. It distinguishes between the entry into force of the Convention as such, *i.e.*, as an international instrument (para. 1), and the entry into force thereafter for each subsequent adhering State (para. 2).[265] In both cases, the date of entry into force is determined by reference to the period laid down by Article 29(2), during which Contracting States may refuse the establishment of relations pursuant to the Convention as regards a new adhering State, in order to keep the parallelism between the entry into force of the Convention and its effectiveness between two Contracting States. Paragraph 2(b) contains a special rule for non-unified States.

Paragraph 1—This Convention shall enter into force on the first day of the month following the expiration of the period during which a notification may be made in accordance with Article 29(2) with respect to the second State that has deposited its instrument of ratification, acceptance, approval or accession referred to in Article 24.

401. Paragraph 1 establishes that the Convention shall enter into force on the first day of the month following the expiration of the period during which a notification may be made in accordance with Article 29(2) with respect to the second State that has deposited its instrument of adherence to the Convention. Article 28(1) must be read together with Article 29, which allows Contracting States to refuse the establishment

[265] To facilitate the reading of this part of the Report, the generic terms "adherence" or "adhering State" are used to mean the act by which a State expresses its consent to be bound by the Convention, and include "ratification", "acceptance", "approval" or "accession" (see Art. 24).

of relations pursuant to the Convention. This possibility of opt-out may be exercised by (i) those States that are Contracting States as regards new States adhering to the Convention, and (ii) by the adhering States in relation to those States that are already Contracting States. The period to exercise the opt-out is 12 months from the date of the notification of adherence of a new State. By the reference to the period laid down in Article 29(2), Article 28(1) entails that the Convention shall enter into force after 12 months from the date when the adherence of the second State has been notified to the first Contracting State. At such a date, the Convention shall enter into force simultaneously for both States.

402. **Example.** State A ratifies the Convention on 14 April 2020, while State B ratifies it one month later on 14 May 2020. State B does not notify that its ratification shall not have the effect of establishing relations with State A (see Art. 29(3)). The ratification by State B is notified by the depositary to State A on 16 May 2020. In accordance with Article 29(2), State A may still make a notification under this provision, and thus opt for not establishing relations pursuant to the Convention with State B, up to and including 16 May 2021. Two situations are then imaginable. If State A does not make such a notification, the Convention will enter into force, and shall have effect between State A and B, on 1 June 2021. If, however, State A makes such a notification, the Convention will enter into force on 1 June 2021, but will not have effect between State A and State B.[266]

Paragraph 2—Thereafter this Convention shall enter into force –

Sub-paragraph (a)—for each State subsequently ratifying, accepting, approving or acceding to it, on the first day of the month following the expiration of the period during which notifications may be made in accordance with Article 29(2) with respect to that State;

Sub-paragraph (b)—for a territorial unit to which this Convention has been extended in accordance with Article 25 after the Convention has entered into force for the State making the declaration, on the first day of the month following the expiration of three months after the notification of the declaration referred to in that Article.

403. **Subsequent adherences.** Paragraph 2 specifies when the Convention enters into force for subsequent adhering States. To preserve the parallelism between the entry into force and the date of effectiveness, it also includes a reference to the 12-month period laid down by Article 29(2), as in paragraph 1. According to paragraph 2, for each State subsequently adhering to the Convention, it shall enter into force on the first day of the month following the expiration of the period during which notifications may be made in accordance with Article 29(2) with respect to that State. Thus, taking the example above, where State A does not make a notification regarding State B, if State C ratifies the Convention on 15 June 2021, and this ratification is notified by the depositary to States A and B on 17 June 2021, the Convention shall enter into force with regard to State C on 1 July 2022. If, for example, before 18 June 2022, State A has notified that the adherence to the Convention of State C does not have the effect of establishing relations between the two States (see Art. 29(2)), the Convention shall enter into force for State C on 1 July 2022, but will only have effect as regards State B. Thus, at this date, the Convention will be in force in the three States, but will only have effect between States A and B, and between States B and C.

[266] In theory, when adhering to the Convention, State B may have also notified that its adherence will not have the effect of establishing relations with State A, but this improbable circumstance would not affect the conclusion; the Convention will enter into force on 1 June 2021, but will have no effect.

404. The rule established by Article 28(2) starts with the adverb "thereafter" and thus applies after the Convention is already in force. However, it does cover cases where a third State adheres before the Convention enters into force, provided that two States have already adhered to it. If a third State adheres to the Convention before its entry into force, the relevant date to start counting the 12-month period as regards this third State is the date of its adherence, not the date of entry into force of the Convention. Thus, for example, State A adheres to the Convention on 14 April 2020, State B on 14 May 2020 and State C on 14 September 2020. The notification of the adherence of State C to States A and B takes place on 16 September 2020. In such a case, the Convention shall enter into force for State C on 1 October 2021.

405. **Special rule for non-unified States.** Paragraph 2(b) establishes a special rule for non—unified States (see *supra,* paras 390–391). In accordance with Article 25, a non-unified State, when adhering to the Convention, may declare that the Convention shall apply to all its territorial units. In such a case, the entry into force is governed by Article 28(2)(a). Article 25 also allows a non-unified State to declare that the Convention shall only apply to one or more of its territorial units. In this case, the State may subsequently extend the Convention to other territorial units. Article 28(2)(b) establishes a special rule for the entry into force of the Convention in these situations, i.e., when a non-unified State that is already a party to the Convention extends its application to a territorial unit that was not initially covered by its adherence. In such a case, the Convention shall enter into force for this territorial unit on the first day of the month following the expiration of three months after the notification of the declaration of that extension. Since Article 29(2) does not apply to individual territorial units, but to the Contracting State as a whole (see *infra,* para. 411), the longer 12-month period is not needed.

406. **Example.** Let us imagine that State A has three territorial units with different judicial systems: A1, A2 and A3. The Convention is in force from May 2022. State A ratifies the Convention in May 2024 and declares, in accordance with Article 25, that the Convention shall only extend to the territorial unit A1. The entry into force of the Convention for State A with respect to territorial unit A1 is governed by the general rule explained above, *i.e.,* Article 28(2)(a). Two years later, on 14 May 2026, State A makes a declaration extending the Convention to territorial unit A2. As regards this declaration, Article 29 does not apply: State A cannot notify that it will not establish treaty relations between A2 and other Contracting States; likewise Contracting States may not notify that the Convention shall not have effect in relation to A2. Thus, in accordance with Article 28(2)(b), the Convention shall enter into force and have effect in relation to territorial unit A2 on 1 September 2026.

Article 29

Establishment of relations pursuant to the Convention

1. This Convention shall have effect between two Contracting States only if neither of them has notified the depositary regarding the other in accordance with paragraph 2 or 3. In the absence of such a notification, the Convention has effect between two Contracting States from the first day of the month following the expiration of the period during which notifications may be made.
2. A Contracting State may notify the depositary, within 12 months after the date of the notification by the depositary referred to in Article 32(a), that the ratification, acceptance, approval or accession of another State shall not have the effect of establishing relations between the two States pursuant to this Convention.
3. A State may notify the depositary, upon the deposit of its instrument pursuant to Article 24(4), that its ratification, acceptance, approval or accession shall not have the effect of establishing relations with a Contracting State pursuant to this Convention.
4. A Contracting State may at any time withdraw a notification that it has made under paragraph 2 or 3. Such a withdrawal shall take effect on the first day of the month following the expiration of three months following the date of notification.

407. Article 29 fulfils two functions: it defines when the Convention becomes effective between two Contracting States and it allows for a limited opt-out option to avoid the establishment of treaty relations with other Contracting States. Such an option was considered fundamental for some States and consensus to include it was reached with a view to facilitating adherence by individual States and to maximise the reach of the Convention. Opt-out mechanisms are included in other HCCH instruments[267] but not in the HCCH 2005 Choice of Court Convention. Because the latter instrument applies only to exclusive choice of court agreements, such a mechanism would have been inconsistent with the goal of securing the effect of party autonomy. The present Convention is much broader in scope and therefore a departure from the HCCH 2005 Choice of Court Convention can be justified.

[267] See for example the HCCH *Convention of 25 October 1980 on the Civil Aspects of International Child Abduction* (Art. 38); the HCCH *Convention of 5 October 1961 Abolishing the Requirement of Legalisation for Foreign Public Documents* (Apostille Convention) (Art. 12). See also *supra*, note 262.

Paragraph 1—This Convention shall have effect between two Contracting States only if neither of them has notified the depositary regarding the other in accordance with paragraph 2 or 3. In the absence of such a notification, the Convention has effect between two Contracting States from the first day of the month following the expiration of the period during which notifications may be made.

408. The principal result of Article 29 is that the Convention has effect between two Contracting States only if neither has deposited a notification in respect of the other in accordance with paragraph 2 or 3. Paragraph 1 specifies that in the absence of any such notification, the Convention has effect between the two States from the first day of the month following expiration of the period during which notifications may be made.
409. As explained above (see *supra,* paras 401–402), there is a close link between the Convention's entry into force under Article 28 and the effectiveness condition in Article 29. Effectiveness is also the operative condition under Article 16: the Convention will apply to any given judgment only where the Convention had effect between two Contracting States at the moment proceedings were instituted in the State of origin (see *supra,* paras 328–330).
410. The opt-out mechanism is limited in that it is only available once for bilateral relations between each pair of States. Paragraph 3 provides for the withdrawal of this notification to allow for the establishment of treaty relations and the effectiveness of the Convention between two States.
411. **Non-unified legal systems and REIOs.** Notifications under Article 29 can only be made by one Contracting State in respect of another Contracting State. The opt-out option is not available to, or applicable in relation to, individual territorial units of non—unified States or the individual Member States of REIOs (where the REIO is a Contracting Party), *i.e.*, it applies to the non-unified State or to the REIO as a whole.

Paragraph 2—A Contracting State may notify the depositary, within 12 months after the date of the notification by the depositary referred to in Article 32(a), that the ratification, acceptance, approval or accession of another State shall not have the effect of establishing relations between the two States pursuant to this Convention.

412. Paragraph 2 deals with notification by Contracting States with respect to adhering States.[268] It grants a 12-month period for notifying the depositary that treaty relations will not be established with an adhering State. The 12-month period starts to run from the moment the depositary has notified Contracting States of the adhesion. If a Contracting State does not act within the 12-month period, the Convention will have effect between that State and the adhering State, unless the adhering State has made the notification in respect of the Contracting State as permitted under paragraph 3.

[268] As indicated in note 265, to facilitate the reading of this part of the Report, the generic terms "adherence" or "adhering State" are used to mean the act by which a State expresses its consent to be bound by the Convention and include "ratification", "acceptance", "approval" or "accession" (see Art. 24).

Paragraph 3—A State may notify the depositary, upon the deposit of its instrument pursuant to Article 24(4), that its ratification, acceptance, approval or accession shall not have the effect of establishing relations with a Contracting State pursuant to this Convention.

413. Paragraph 3 deals with notification by adhering States with respect to Contracting States. It provides that adhering States may notify the depositary that such adherence shall not establish treaty relations with one or more specified Contracting States. This notification is only possible at the time of deposit of the instrument of adherence under Article 24(4). This distinction is explained by the fact that the identity of existing Contracting States is known to adhering States, requiring that the latter make their decision regarding the opt-out prior to depositing their instrument of adherence.

414. **Example.** The Convention has entered into force on 1 May 2022 following the adherence of States A and B, neither of whom has made a notification in relation to the other. State C then adheres to the Convention on 14 May 2022. It is only at that moment that State C is allowed to notify the depositary that its adherence will not have the effect of establishing treaty relations with State A or State B or both (para. 3). States A and B, on the other hand, have 12 months from the moment the depositary notifies them of State C's adherence (say on 16 May 2022) to make the notification regarding treaty relations with State C (para. 2). States A and B will have up to and including 16 May 2023 to do so and therefore the Convention cannot become effective between these three States before 1 June 2023 (para. 1). If State A does make a notification under Article 29(2) but State B does not, the Convention will be effective between States B and C but not States A and C, as of 1 June 2023. It will not be open for either State B or State C to opt-out of treaty relations with the other State at any later point.

Paragraph 4—A Contracting State may at any time withdraw a notification that it has made under paragraph 2 or 3. Such a withdrawal shall take effect on the first day of the month following the expiration of three months following the date of notification.

415. If a State has exercised its opt-out option, whether under paragraph 2 or 3, it can withdraw it at any time. This withdrawal will take effect on the first day of the month following the expiration of three months following the date of notification. Of course, this will not affect the treaty relations with the designated State if that State had also made a notification under paragraph 2 or 3 and has not withdrawn it.

416. **Example.** Continued from the previous example, if State A decides to withdraw its notification regarding State C and does so on 15 September 2024, it will become effective on 1 January 2025 and therefore the Convention will be effective between States A and C as of that date. Judgments given from proceedings instituted in either State from 1 January 2025 will therefore be eligible for recognition or enforcement in either State. It will not be open for either State to opt-out of relations pursuant to the Convention with the other State at any later point.

Article 30

Declarations

1. Declarations referred to in Articles 14, 17, 18, 19 and 25 may be made upon signature, ratification, acceptance, approval or accession or at any time thereafter, and may be modified or withdrawn at any time.
2. Declarations, modifications and withdrawals shall be notified to the depositary.
3. A declaration made at the time of signature, ratification, acceptance, approval or accession shall take effect simultaneously with the entry into force of this Convention for the State concerned.
4. A declaration made at a subsequent time, and any modification or withdrawal of a declaration, shall take effect on the first day of the month following the expiration of three months following the date on which the notification is received by the depositary.
5. A declaration made at a subsequent time, and any modification or withdrawal of a declaration, shall not apply to judgments resulting from proceedings that have already been instituted before the court of origin when the declaration takes effect.

417. **Timing of declarations.** The declarations referred to in Articles 14, 17, 18, 19 and 25 may be made upon signature, ratification, acceptance, approval or accession or at any time thereafter, and may be modified or withdrawn at any time. They are made to the depositary (the Ministry of Foreign Affairs of the Netherlands).

418. **Entry into effect of declarations at the time of signature or adherence.** A declaration made at the time of signature, ratification, acceptance, approval or accession takes effect simultaneously with the entry into force of the Convention for the State concerned.

419. **Entry into effect of declarations made at a subsequent time.** A declaration made at a subsequent time, and any modification or withdrawal of a declaration, takes effect on the first day of the month following the expiration of three months following the date on which the notification is received by the depositary. However, such a declaration shall not apply to judgments resulting from proceedings that have already been instituted before the court of origin when the declaration takes effect. As a result, declarations will not have any retroactive effect in terms of their application to proceedings that have been instituted prior to the coming into effect of the declaration. The same applies to any modification or withdrawal of a declaration. This ensures greater predictability in the operation of the Convention for all parties to the proceedings.

420. **Reservations.** The Convention does not contain any provision prohibiting reservations. This means that reservations are permitted, subject to the normal rules of customary international law (as reflected in Art. 2(1)(d) and Arts 19–23 of the Vienna Convention of 1969).

Article 31
Denunciation

1. A Contracting State to this Convention may denounce it by a notification in writing addressed to the depositary. The denunciation may be limited to certain territorial units of a non—unified legal system to which this Convention applies.
2. The denunciation shall take effect on the first day of the month following the expiration of 12 months after the date on which the notification is received by the depositary. Where a longer period for the denunciation to take effect is specified in the notification, the denunciation shall take effect upon the expiration of such longer period after the date on which the notification is received by the depositary.

421. Article 31 provides that a State may denounce the Convention by a notification in writing to the depositary. The denunciation may be limited to certain territorial units of a non-unified legal system to which the Convention applies. The denunciation takes effect on the first day of the month following the expiration of 12 months after the date on which the notification is received by the depositary. Where a longer period for the denunciation to take effect is specified in the notification, the denunciation shall take effect on the expiration of the longer specified period, after the date on which the notification is received by the depositary.

Article 32

Notifications by the depositary

The depositary shall notify the Members of the Hague Conference on Private International Law, and other States and Regional Economic Integration Organisations which have signed, ratified, accepted, approved or acceded to this Convention in accordance with Articles 24, 26 and 27 of the following –

(a) the signatures, ratifications, acceptances, approvals and accessions referred to in Articles 24, 26 and 27;
(b) the date on which this Convention enters into force in accordance with Article 28;
(c) the notifications, declarations, modifications and withdrawals referred to in Articles 26, 27, 29 and 30; and
(d) the denunciations referred to in Article 31.

422. Article 32 requires the depositary to notify the Members of the HCCH, and other States and REIOs that have signed, ratified, accepted, approved or acceded to the Convention, of various matters relevant to the Convention, such as signatures, ratifications, entry into force, declarations and denunciations.

Index

The manufacturer's authorised representative in the EU for product safety is Oxford University Press España S.A. of el Parque Empresarial San Fernando de Henares, Avenida de Castilla, 2 – 28830 Madrid (www.oup.es/en or product.safety@oup.com). OUP España S.A. also acts as importer into Spain of products made by the manufacturer.

www.ingramcontent.com/pod-product-compliance
Lightning Source LLC
LaVergne TN
LVHW062205200926
848484LV00006B/1319
* 9 7 8 0 1 9 2 8 8 9 8 3 6 *